THE OPTICS PROBLEM SOLVER®

REGISTERED TRADEMARK

Staff of Research and Education Association,
Dr. M. Fogiel, Director

 Research and Education Association
505 Eighth Avenue
New York, N. Y. 10018

THE OPTICS PROBLEM SOLVER ®

Printed in the United States of America

Library of Congress Catalog Card Number 82- 50899

International Standard Book Number 0- 87891- 526- 5

Revised Printing, 1983

PROBLEM SOLVER is a registered trademark of
Research and Education Association, New York, N. Y. 10018

WHAT THIS BOOK IS FOR

Students have generally found optics a difficult subject to understand and learn. Despite the publication of hundreds of textbooks in this field, each one intended to provide an improvement over previous textbooks, students continue to remain perplexed as a result of the numerous conditions that must often be remembered and correlated in solving a problem. Various possible interpretations of terms used in optics have also contributed to much of the difficulties experienced by students.

In a study of the problem, REA found the following basic reasons underlying students' difficulties with optics taught in schools:

(a) No systematic rules of analysis have been developed which students may follow in a step-by-step manner to solve the usual problems encountered. This results from the fact that the numerous different conditions and priciples which may be involved in a problem, lead to many possible different methods of solution. To prescribe a set of rules to be followed for each of the possible variations, would involve an enormous number of rules and steps to be searched through by students, and this task would perhaps be more burdensome than solving the problem directly with some accompanying trial and error to find the correct solution route.

(b) Textbooks currently available will usually explain a given principle in a few pages written by a professional who has an insight in the subject matter that is not shared by students. The explanations are often written in an abstract manner which leaves the students confused as to the application of the principle. The explanations given are not sufficiently detailed and extensive to make the student aware of the wide range of applications and different aspects of the principle being studied. The numerous possible variations of principles and their applications are usually not discussed, and it is left for the students to discover these for themselves while doing exercises. Accordingly, the average student is expected to rediscover that which has been long known and practiced, but not published or explained extensively.

(c) The examples usually following the explanation of a topic are too few in number and too simple to enable the student to obtain a thorough grasp of the principles involved. The explanations do not provide sufficient basis to enable a student to solve problems that may be subsequently assigned for homework or given on examinations.

The examples are presented in abbreviated form which leaves out much material between steps, and requires that students derive the omitted material themselves. As a result, students find the examples difficult to understand--contrary to the purpose of the examples.

Examples are, furthermore, often worded in a confusing manner. They do not state the problem and then present the solution. Instead, they pass through a general discussion, never revealing what is to be solved for.

Examples, also, do not always include diagrams/graphs, wherever appropriate, and students do not obtain the training to draw diagrams or graphs to simplify and organize their thinking.

(d) Students can learn the subject only by doing the exercises themselves and reviewing them in class, to obtain experience in applying the principles with their different ramifications.

In doing the exercises by themselves, students find that they are required to devote considerably more time to optics than to other subjects of comparable credits, because they are uncertain with regard to the selection and application of the theorems and principles involved. It is also often necessary for students to discover those "tricks" not revealed in their texts (or review books), that make it possible to solve problems easily. Students must usually resort to methods of trial-and-error to discover these "tricks," and as a result they find that they may sometimes spend several hours to solve a single problem.

(e) When reviewing the exercises in classrooms, instructors usually request students to take turns in writing solutions on the boards and explaining them to the class. Students often find it difficult to explain in a manner that holds the interest of the class, and enables the remaining students to follow the material written on the boards. The remaining students seated in the class are, furthermore, too occupied with copying the material from the boards, to listen to the oral explanations and concentrate on the methods of solution.

This book is intended to aid students in optics to overcome the difficulties described, by supplying detailed illustrations of the solution methods which are usually not apparent to students. The solution methods are illustrated by problems selected from those that are most often assigned for class work and given on examinations. The problems are arranged in order of complexity to enable students to learn and understand a particular topic by reviewing the problems in sequence. The problems are illustrated with detailed step-by-step explanations, to save the students the large amount of time that is often needed to fill in the gaps that are usually found between steps of illustrations in textbooks or review/outline books.

The staff of REA considers optics a subject that is best learned by allowing students to view the methods of analysis and solution techniques themselves. This approach to learning the subject matter is similar to that practiced in various scientific laboratories, particularly in the medical fields.

In using this book, students may review and study the illustrated problems at their own pace; they are not limited to the time allowed for explaining problems on the board in class.

When students want to look up a particular type of problem and solution, they can readily locate it in the book by referring to the index which has been extensively prepared. It is also possible to locate a particular type of problem by glancing at just the material within the boxed portions. To facilitate rapid scanning of the problems, each problem has a heavy border around it. Furthermore, each problem is identified with a number immediately above the problem at the right-hand margin.

To obtain maximum benefit from the book, students should familiarize themselves with the section, "How To Use This Book," located in the front pages.

To meet the objectives of this book, staff members of REA have selected problems usually encountered in assignments and examinations, and have solved each problem meticulously to illustrate the steps which are usually difficult for students to comprehend. Special gratitude, for added outstanding support in this area, is due to:

Prof. Paul R. Byerly Jr.
University of Nebraska

Prof. Peter J. Riley
University of Texas

Prof. William R. Cochran
Youngstown State University

Prof. Om P. Rutgi
S. U. N. Y. College at Buffalo

Gratitude is also expressed to the many participants in this program including Thom Bessoir, David Chin, W. Foulkes, J. Goldstein, Simon Halapir, Craig Jay, Leonard Lubarsky, Arthur McCombs, R. Rao, Lisa Schurberg, Joel Stern.

The manuscript that was evolved with its endless inserts, changes, modifications to the changes, and editorial remarks, must have been an arduous typing task for Agnes Czirjak, Louise Dennis, Yvette Fuchs, Sophie Gerber and Sara Nicoll. These ladies typed the manuscript expertly with almost no complaints about the handwritten material and the numerous symbols that require much patience and special skill.

For their efforts in the graphic-arts required in the layout arrangement, and completion of the physical features of the book, gratitude is expressed to Bruce Arendash, Alex Bentsman, John Chamberlain, Berit Koenigswarter, Carolyn Oscar, and Robert Puig.

The difficult task of coordinating the efforts of all persons was carried out by Carl Fuchs. His conscientious work deserves much appreciation. He also trained and supervised art and production personnel in the preparation of the book for printing.

Finally, special thanks are due to Helen Kaufmann for her unique talents to render those difficult border-line decisions and constructive suggestions related to the design and organization of the book.

Max Fogiel, Ph.D.
Program Director

HOW TO USE THIS BOOK

This book can be an invaluable aid to students in optics as a supplement to their textbooks. The book is subdivided into 27 chapters, each dealing with a separate topic. The subject matter is developed beginning with wave theory and extending through properties of light, refraction, reflection, opthalmic optics, interferometry, diffraction, absorption and scattering, polarization, and ray tracing. Sections have also been included on lenses, optical instruments, aberration, prisms, dispersion, color, lasers and holography. An extensive number of applications have been included, since these appear to be most troublesome to students.

TO LEARN AND UNDERSTAND
A TOPIC THOROUGHLY

1. Refer to your class text and read there the section pertaining to the topic. You should become acquainted with the principles discussed there. These principles, however, may not be clear to you at that time.

2. Then locate the topic you are looking for by referring to the "Table of Contents" in front of this book, "The Optics Problem Solver."

3. Turn to the page where the topic begins and review the problems under each topic, in the order given. For each topic, the problems are arranged in order of complexity, from the simplest to the more difficult. Some problems may appear similar to others, but each problem has been selected to illustrate a different point or solution method.

To learn and understand a topic thoroughly and retain its contents, it will be generally necessary for students to review the problems several times. Repeated review is essential in order to gain experience in recognizing the principles that should be applied, and to select the best solution technique.

TO FIND A PARTICULAR PROBLEM

To locate one or more problems related to a particular subject matter, refer to the index. In using the index, be certain to note that the numbers given there refer to problem numbers, not to page numbers. This arrangement of the index is intended to facilitate finding a problem more rapidly, since two or more problems may appear on a page.

If a particular type of problem cannot be found readily, it is recommended that the student refer to the "Table of Contents" in the front pages, and then turn to the chapter which is applicable to the problem being sought. By scanning or glancing at the material that is boxed, it will generally be possible to find problems related to the one being sought, without consuming considerable time. After the problems have been located, the solutions can be reviewed and studied in detail. For this purpose of locating problems rapidly, students should acquaint themselves with the organization of the books as found in the "Table of Contents."

In preparing for an exam, it is useful to find the topics to be covered in the exam from the Table of Contents, and then review the problems under those topics several times. This should equip the student with what might be needed for the exam.

CONTENTS

CHAPTER 1

WAVES

WAVE ANALYSIS

If the frequency of an oscillating source on the surface of a pool of water is 3 Hz, what is the speed of the wave if the wavelength is observed to be 0.5 m?

Solution: Three important characteristics of an oscillating wave are its velocity of propagation, its frequency, and its wavelength. The frequency f is defined to be the number of cycles per unit time at which any point oscillates or, expressed another way, the number of waves that pass a given point per unit time. The wavelength λ is the distance between two adjacent crests of the wave. To find a relation between these quantities, note that the time t required for the wave to make one oscillation (called the period of the wave) is equal to 1/f. During this time, the wave moves a distance d = λ. From the relation

$$d = vt ,$$

it follows that

$$\lambda = v \cdot \frac{1}{f} = \frac{v}{f}$$

or

$$v = f\lambda .$$

Substituting the known values for f and λ into this equation gives

$$v = (3 \text{ Hz})(5 \times 10^{-1} \text{m}) = 1.5 \text{ m/sec}$$

(Note: 1 Hz = 1 sec^{-1}).

1

A source particle executing a periodic motion defined by
y = 6 sin πt sends out waves which travel through a
homogeneous medium at the rate of 6 cm per second.   Find
the displacement of a second particle 80 cm from the source
one minute after the source began to vibrate.   (Assume the
medium to be of one dimension, like a stretched cord.)

Solution: Since the wave disturbance travels at the rate
of 6 cm per sec, the second particle will not begin to
vibrate until 80/6 or 13.3 sec after the source begins to
vibrate.

   Therefore, since y = 6 sin πt defines the motion of
the source, and since in simple wave motion each particle
executes the same to and fro motion,

$$y = 6 \sin \pi\left(t - \frac{80}{6}\right)$$

defines the motion of the second particle.

   Hence, when t = 60 sec, the displacement of the second
particle will be given by

$$y = 6 \sin \pi\left(60 - \frac{80}{6}\right)$$

$$= 5.2 \text{ cm.}$$

A traveling wave is described by the equation

$$y = \exp(-az^2 - bt^2 - 2\sqrt{ab}\ zt) \ .$$

1) In what direction is the wave traveling?
2) What is the wave speed?
3) Sketch this wave for time t = 0 and for time t = 3 sec,
   using a = 144/cm², b = 9/sec².

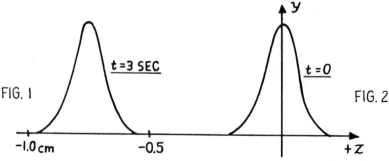

FIG. 1   t = 3 SEC   t = 0   FIG. 2

y

-1.0 cm   -0.5   +z

Solution: Factoring out -a, the expression $-az^2 - bt^2 - 2\sqrt{ab}\ zt$

becomes $-a(z^2 + \frac{b}{a} t^2 + 2\sqrt{(b/a)} zt) = -a(z + \sqrt{(b/a)} t)^2$. Thus, $y(z,t) = \exp[-a(z + \sqrt{(b/a)} t)^2]$.

    1)   The wave is traveling toward the left, or toward negative values of z, since as t increases, z must get smaller in order to keep the exponent the same.

    2)   The wave speed is

$$c = -\sqrt{(b/a)} = -\tfrac{1}{4} \text{ cm/sec.}$$

    3)   The following tables of values can be constructed:

For $t = 0$, $y(z,t) = \exp(-az^2) = \exp\left(-\frac{144}{cm^2} z^2\right)$

z (cm)	y (z,t)
-.4	9.86×10^{-11}
-.2	.003
0	1
.2	.003
.4	9.86×10^{-11}

For $t = 3$ sec, $y(z,t) = \exp\left[-a(z + \sqrt{(b/a)} (3 \text{ sec}))^2\right] =$

$= \exp\left[-\frac{144}{cm^2} (z + \sqrt{(9 \text{ cm}^2/144 \text{ sec}^2)} (3 \text{ sec}))^2\right] =$

$= \exp\left[-\frac{144}{cm^2} (z + .75 \text{ cm})^2\right]$

z (cm)	y (z,t)
-1.0	0.0001
-0.9	0.0392
-0.8	0.6977
-0.75	1.0000
-0.7	0.6977
-0.6	0.0392
-0.5	0.0001

From these tables, Figures 1 and 2 can be drawn as shown.

● **PROBLEM 1-4**

The equation of a transverse wave is given by $y = 6.0 \sin(.020\pi x + 4.0\pi t)$ where x and y are expressed in cm and t is expressed in seconds. calculate the following:

(a)   the amplitude of the wave;

(b)   the wavelength of the wave;

(c)   the frequency of the wave;

(d)   the speed of the wave;

(e)   the direction of propagation of the wave; and

(f)   the maximum transverse speed of a particle of the
      wave.

Solution: The general expression for a sinusoidal wavetrain traveling to the left is

$$y = y_m \sin(Kx + \omega t - \phi) ; \qquad\qquad (1)$$

K is the angular wave number given by $K = \frac{2\pi}{\lambda}$ where λ is
the wavelength of the wave, ω is the angular frequency
given by $\omega = \frac{2\pi}{T}$ where T is the period of the wave, y_m is
the amplitude of the wave, and ϕ is the phase constant.
The phase velocity v is found from the equation $\lambda = vT$ or
$v = \frac{\lambda}{T}$, where the period T is the time required for the
wave to travel a distance of one wavelength λ. λ and T
may be expressed as $\lambda = \frac{2\pi}{K}$ and $T = \frac{2\pi}{\omega}$.   Thus,
$v = (2\pi/K)/(2\pi/\omega) = \omega/K$.

    Comparing equation (1) with the given wave, it is
seen that $y_m = 6$ cm, $K = .020\pi$ cm^{-1}, $\omega = 4\pi$ sec^{-1},
and $\phi = 0$.   Then,

(a)   the amplitude is 6 cm.

(b) $\lambda = \frac{2\pi}{K} = \frac{2\pi}{.020\pi} = 100$ cm; the wavelength is 100 cm.

(c) $f = \frac{1}{T} = \frac{1}{2\pi/\omega} = \frac{\sec^{-1}}{2\pi/4\pi} = 2$ sec^{-1} = 2 cycles/sec; the
      frequency is 2 cycles/sec or 2 Hz.

(d) $v = \frac{\omega}{K} = \frac{4\pi \text{ cm}}{.020\pi \text{ sec}} = 200$ cm/sec; the velocity is
      200 cm/sec.

(e)   A wave moving in the positive x direction has the
      form $y = y_m \sin(Kx - \omega t)$ while one moving in the
      negative x direction has the form $y = y_m \sin(Kx + \omega t)$.
      Thus since the wave given in this problem has the
      latter form, it is moving to the left.

(f)   To determine the particle velocity which shall be
      designated by the symbol u, let us fix our attention
      on a particle at a particular position x (that is, x
      is now a constant in this equation) and find how the
      particle displacement y changes with time (transverse
      displacement refers to displacement in the vertical
      direction).   In general, $y = y_m \sin(Kx + \omega t)$.   u is
      equal to the derivative of y with respect to t.

4

Differentiating y with respect to t gives

$$u = \frac{\partial y}{\partial t} = y_m \omega \cos(Kx + \omega t)$$

To find the maximum transverse speed, let
$\cos(Kx + \omega t) = 1$, since this is the maximum value the
cosine function can assume. Then $u_{max} = y_m \omega$.

$$u_{max} = (6 \text{ cm})(4\pi) \sec^{-1} \cong 75 \text{ cm/sec}$$

The maximum transverse speed is thus about 75 cm/sec.

● **PROBLEM** 1-5

A particle executing simple harmonic motion given by
$y = 4 \sin(\frac{2\pi t}{6} + \alpha)$ is displaced +1 unit when t = 0. Find:

(a) the phase angle when t = 0;
(b) the difference in phase between any two positions of
the particle 2 seconds apart;
(c) the phase angle corresponding to a displacement of +2;
(d) the time necessary to reach a displacement of +3 from
the initial position.

Solution:

(a) We are given an equation for simple harmonic motion
in the form $y = y_m \sin(\omega t + \phi)$ where y_m is the amplitude,
ω is the angular frequency, and ϕ is the phase constant.
In this problem, $y_m = 4$, $\omega = \frac{2\pi}{6}$, and $\phi = \alpha$. We are also
given an initial condition; that is, y = 1 when t = 0.
Using this condition, it is possible to solve for α as
follows:

$$y = 4 \sin\left(\frac{2\pi t}{6} + \alpha\right)$$

$$1 = 4 \sin(0 + \alpha)$$

$$\sin\alpha = \frac{1}{4}$$

$$\alpha = \sin^{-1}\left(\frac{1}{4}\right) = 14°30' = \pi/12.4 .$$

The equation now reads

$$y = 4 \sin\left(\frac{2\pi t}{6} + \frac{\pi}{12.4}\right)$$

and the phase angle corresponding to t = 0 is

$$\left(\frac{2\pi(0)}{6} + \frac{\pi}{12.4}\right)$$

5

or $\frac{\pi}{12.4}$ radians.

(b) Let t_1 and t_2 be any two times such that $t_2 - t_1 = 2$ sec. Then since

$$Y_1 = 4 \sin\left(\frac{2\pi t_1}{6} + \frac{\pi}{12.4}\right)$$

and

$$Y_2 = 4 \sin\left(\frac{2\pi t_2}{6} + \frac{\pi}{12.4}\right)$$

the required phase difference is

$$\left(\frac{2\pi t_2}{6} + \frac{\pi}{12.4}\right) - \left(\frac{2\pi t_1}{6} + \frac{\pi}{12.4}\right) = \frac{2\pi}{6}(t_2 - t_1)$$

$$= \frac{2\pi}{6} \cdot 2 = 120°$$

(c) When y = 2, the initial equation becomes

$$2 = 4 \sin\left(\frac{2\pi t}{6} + \frac{\pi}{12.4}\right) = 4 \sin(\text{phase angle})$$

then $\sin(\text{phase angle}) = \frac{2}{4} = \frac{1}{2}$

$$\text{phase angle} = \sin^{-1}\left(\frac{1}{2}\right) = 30°.$$

(d) When y = 3 the initial equation becomes

$$3 = 4 \sin\left(\frac{2\pi t}{6} + \frac{\pi}{12.4}\right)$$

$$\sin\left(\frac{2\pi t}{6} + \frac{\pi}{12.4}\right) = \frac{3}{4}$$

$$\frac{2\pi t}{6} + \frac{\pi}{12.4} = \sin^{-1}\frac{3}{4} = 48°40'.$$

Solving for t gives the result t = .57 sec.

Note that in problems where periodic functions are involved, more than one numerical answer is possible. In part (a) the principal value of arcsin 1/4 was taken to get $\alpha = 14°30'$, but since $\sin(\pi - \alpha) = \sin\pi \cos\alpha - \cos\pi \sin\alpha = \sin\alpha$, α may also have the value $(180° - 14°30')$. α may also take on the values $(14°30' + 360°)$, etc., since $\sin(\alpha + 2\pi) = \sin\alpha$.

THE RESULTANT OF TWO OR MORE WAVES

Devise a method to determine the resultant amplitude of
any number of simple harmonic motions of the same period.

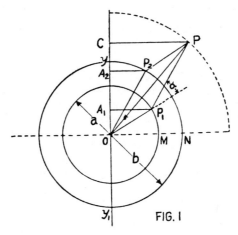

FIG. I

Solution: Consider the combination of two such simple
harmonic motions given by

$$y = a \sin \frac{2\pi t}{T} , \quad \text{and} \quad y = b \sin \left(\frac{2\pi t}{T} + \alpha\right) ,$$

which represent two simple harmonic motions of the same
period, of unequal amplitude, differing in phase by α, and
in the same straight line.

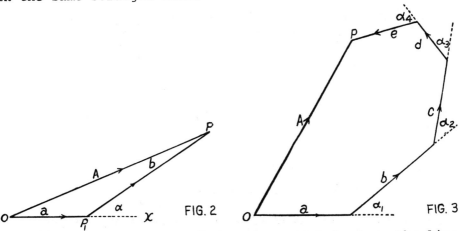

FIG. 2   FIG. 3

Suppose these two motions are executed along the line
YOY_1, as shown in Figure 1, and that, at any time t, the
displacement due to the first alone is OA_1, and that due
to the second alone is OA_2. P_1 and P_2 will then represent
the corresponding positions of the particles in the circles
of reference, the angle P_1OM being equal to $\frac{2\pi t}{T}$, the angle

7

$$P_2ON = \left(\frac{2\pi t}{T} + \alpha\right).$$

Now complete the parallelogram, P_1OP_2P by drawing P_1P through P_1 parallel to the radius OP_2 and P_2P through P_2 parallel to the radius OP_1. Drop a perpendicular PC to the YOY_1 line.

Applying the principle of superposition, we have the resultant displacement at time t = $OA_2 + OA_1 = OA_2 + A_2C$, since $OA_1 = A_2C$ (because OP_1 and P_2P are equal and parallel), or resultant displacement = OC.

But if the point P revolves in a circle of radius OP with the same period as the two simple harmonic motions, then OC represents the displacement of a simple harmonic motion of amplitude OP, the radius of this circle, at the time P is in the position shown in the figure. Since the foregoing construction is perfectly general, one may conclude that the resultant of two simple harmonic motions of the same period is also a simple harmonic motion of amplitude given by OP and differing in phase from the one of amplitude OP_1 by the angle POP_1.

Therefore, the resultant amplitude can be found easily, since it is represented by the side OP of the triangle OP_1P, the other two sides of which represent the two individual amplitudes. In the problem which has been discussed, for example, all that is necessary is to draw a diagram like Figure 2, in which the angle $PP_1X = \alpha$. By the law of cosines,

$$OP^2 = OP_1{}^2 + PP_1{}^2 - 2OP_1 \cdot P_1P \cos(180° - \alpha) \qquad (1)$$

By the double angle formula for the cosine function, $\cos(180° - \alpha) = \cos 180° \cos \alpha + \sin 180° \sin \alpha = -\cos \alpha$. Hence, equation (1) becomes

$$OP^2 = OP_1{}^2 + PP_1{}^2 + 2OP_1 \cdot P_1P \cos \alpha . \qquad (2)$$

Thus, the resultant amplitude A may be calculated from the relation

$$A^2 = a^2 + b^2 + 2ab \cos \alpha , \qquad (3)$$

where a,b and A are as shown in Figure 2.

This method may readily be extended to any number of simple harmonic motions in the same straight line. For, having taken two of them, and having found the resultant OP in the manner just described, this resultant may be combined with the third, and so on. Thus, OP in Figure 3 represents the resultant of 5 simple harmonic motions of the same period, with individual amplitudes a, b, c, d, e, with phase difference between first and second = α_1, between second and third = α_2, etc.

A wave vibrates according to the equation
$y = .5 \sin \frac{\pi x}{3} \cos 40\pi t$, where x and y are expressed in
centimeters and t is expressed in seconds. (a) What are
the amplitudes and velocities of the component waves whose
superposition can give rise to this vibration? (b) What
is the distance between nodes? (c) What is the velocity
of a particle at the position x = 1.5 cm when t = 9/8
seconds?

Solution:

(a) The given wave is of the form

$$y = A \sin(\alpha x) \cos(\beta t).$$

Comparing this with the trigonometric identity

$$\frac{1}{2} [\sin A + \sin B] = \sin \frac{1}{2} (A + B) \cos \frac{1}{2} (A - B)$$

gives

$$y = \frac{A}{2} [\sin A + \sin B]$$

where

$$\frac{1}{2} (A + B) = \alpha x$$

and

$$\frac{1}{2} (A - B) = \beta t$$

Solving for A and B in terms of x and t,

$$A + B = 2\alpha x$$
$$\underline{A - B = 2\beta t}$$
$$2A = 2\alpha x + 2\beta t$$

so

$$A = \alpha x + \beta t$$

and

$$B = 2\alpha x - A = 2\alpha x - (\alpha x + \beta t) = \alpha x - \beta t$$

Then

$$y = \frac{A}{2} [\sin(\alpha x + \beta t) + \sin(\alpha x - \beta t)]$$

$$y = \frac{A}{2} \sin(\alpha x + \beta t) + \frac{A}{2} \sin(\alpha x - \beta t).$$

9

For the given wave,

$$A = .5, \quad \alpha = \frac{\pi}{3}, \quad \text{and} \quad \beta = 40\pi.$$

Then the component waves whose superposition gives rise to this vibration are

$$y_1 = .25 \sin\left(\frac{\pi}{3}x + 40\pi t\right)$$

$$y_2 = .25 \sin\left(\frac{\pi}{3}x - 40\pi t\right)$$

Comparing y_1 and y_2 with the general expression for a wavetrain traveling to the left, namely $y = y_m \sin(Kx + \omega t)$, where K denotes the angular wavenumber, ω is the angular frequency and y_m is the amplitude of the wave, it can be seen that the amplitude of the waves is .25 cm. The velocity is given by

$$v = \frac{\omega}{K}$$

and since $\omega = 40\pi \text{ sec}^{-1}$, and $K = \frac{\pi}{3} \text{ cm}^{-1}$,

$$v = \frac{40\pi \text{ sec}^{-1}}{\pi/3 \text{ cm}^{-1}} = 120 \text{ cm/sec}$$

(b) The distance between nodes is half the wavelength, $\frac{\lambda}{2}$.

$$\lambda = \frac{2\pi}{K} = \frac{2\pi \text{ cm}}{\pi/3} = 6 \text{ cm}.$$

Then the distance between nodes is 3 cm.

(c) To find the (transverse) velocity of a particle of the wave, we look at the wave at a particular value of x (i.e., x is constant) and find how y changes with time. Let u = particle velocity. Then, differentiating y with respect to t gives

$$u = \frac{\partial y}{\partial t} = \frac{\partial}{\partial t}\left[.5 \sin\left(\frac{\pi}{3}x\right)\cos(40\pi t)\right]$$

$$= -.5(40\pi) \sin\left(\frac{\pi}{3}x\right)\sin(40\pi t).$$

At x = 1.5 cm, t = 9/8 sec, we have

$$u = -.5(40\pi) \sin\left(\frac{1.5}{3}\pi\right)\sin 40\pi(9/8)$$

$$= -5.(40\pi)(1)(0).$$

Thus, the particle velocity = 0.

Two waves are described by $f_1(x,t) = 3 \exp\left[-\dfrac{(x+ct)^2}{25 \text{ cm}^2}\right]$

and $f_2(x,t) = \begin{cases} 2 \sin\left[\dfrac{2\pi}{4 \text{ cm}} (x-ct)\right], & (ct-8) < x < (ct+8) \\ \\ 0 & \text{elsewhere} \end{cases}$

$c = 6$ cm/sec. Graph the sum of these functions:

$f_T = f_1 + f_2$, at $t = -2$ sec, $t = -\dfrac{1}{2}$ sec, and $t = 0$.

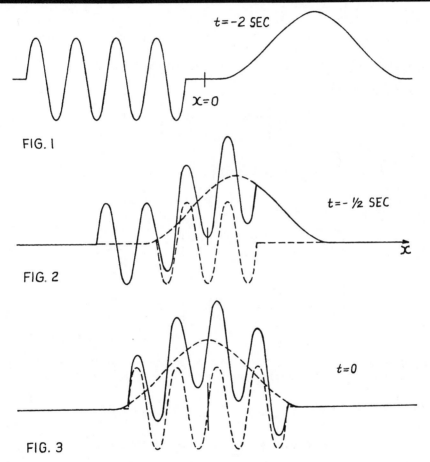

$t = -2$ SEC

$X = 0$

FIG. 1

$t = -\frac{1}{2}$ SEC

FIG. 2

$t = 0$

FIG. 3

Solution: Since $c = 6$ cm/sec, the given expressions for

$f_1(x,t)$ and $f_2(x,t)$ become $f_1(x,t) = 3 \exp\left[\dfrac{-[x+(6 \text{ cm/sec})t]^2}{25 \text{ cm}^2}\right]$

and $f_2(x,t) = \begin{cases} 2 \sin\left[\dfrac{2\pi}{4 \text{ cm}} (x-(6 \text{ cm/sec})t)\right], & (6 \text{ cm/sec})t - 8 \\ & < x < (6 \text{ cm/sec})t + 8 \\ \\ 0, & \text{elsewhere} \end{cases}$

At t = -2 sec, $f_1(x, -2\text{ sec}) = 3 \exp\left[\dfrac{-(x - 12 \text{ cm})^2}{25 \text{ cm}^2}\right]$ and

$$f_2(x, -2\text{ sec}) = \begin{cases} 2 \sin\left[\dfrac{2\pi}{4 \text{ cm}} (x + 12 \text{ cm})\right], & -20 \text{ cm} < x < -4 \text{ cm} \\[4mm] 0, & \text{elsewhere} \end{cases}$$

Hence, $f_T = \begin{cases} 3 \exp\left[\dfrac{-(x - 12 \text{ cm})^2}{25 \text{ cm}^2}\right], & x \leq -20 \text{ cm and } x \geq -4 \text{ cm} \\[5mm] 3 \exp\left[\dfrac{-(x - 12 \text{ cm})^2}{25 \text{ cm}^2}\right] + 2 \sin\left[\dfrac{2\pi}{4 \text{ cm}} (x + 12 \text{ cm})\right], \\[3mm] \qquad\qquad\qquad\qquad -20 \text{ cm} < x < -4 \text{ cm} \end{cases}$

The graph of this function is shown in Figure 1.

At $t = -\dfrac{1}{2}$ sec,

$f_1(x, -\dfrac{1}{2}\text{ sec}) = 3 \exp\left[\dfrac{-(x - 3 \text{ cm})^2}{25 \text{ cm}^2}\right]$ and

$$f_2 = \begin{cases} 2 \sin\left[\dfrac{2\pi}{4 \text{ cm}} (x + 3 \text{ cm})\right], & -11 \text{ cm} < x < 5 \text{ cm} \\[4mm] 0, & \text{elsewhere} \end{cases}$$

Hence, $f_T = \begin{cases} 3 \exp\left[\dfrac{-(x - 3 \text{ cm})^2}{25 \text{ cm}^2}\right], & x \leq -11 \text{ cm and } x \geq 5 \text{ cm} \\[5mm] 3 \exp\left[\dfrac{-(x - 3 \text{ cm})^2}{25 \text{ cm}^2}\right] + 2 \sin\left[\dfrac{2\pi}{4 \text{ cm}} (x + 3 \text{ cm})\right], \\[3mm] \qquad\qquad\qquad\qquad -11 \text{ cm} < x < 5 \text{ cm} \end{cases}$

The graph of this function is indicated in Figure 2, where the dotted graphs correspond to f_1 and f_2, and the solid graph corresponds to f_T. At t = 0, $f_1(x,0) = 3 \exp\left[\dfrac{-x^2}{25 \text{ cm}^2}\right]$

and $f_2(x,0) = \begin{cases} 2 \sin\left(\dfrac{2\pi x}{4 \text{ cm}}\right), & -8 \text{ cm} < x < 8 \text{ cm} \\[4mm] 0, & \text{elsewhere} \end{cases}$

Hence, $f_T = \begin{cases} 3 \exp\left[\dfrac{-x^2}{25 \text{ cm}^2}\right], & x \leq -8 \text{ cm and } x \geq 8 \text{ cm} \\[5mm] 3 \exp\left[\dfrac{-x^2}{25 \text{ cm}^2}\right] + 2 \sin\left(\dfrac{2\pi x}{4 \text{ cm}}\right), & -8 \text{ cm} < x < 8 \text{ cm} \end{cases}$

12

The solid line graph indicated in Figure 3 is the graph of f_T while the dotted lines represent the graphs of f_1 and f_2.

Find the resultant motion when a single particle is acted on simultaneously by three waves obeying simple harmonic motion, their motions being given by the relations,

$$y_1 = a \sin \frac{2\pi t}{T} \;;\quad y_2 = a \sin \frac{2\pi}{T}\left(t - \frac{T}{12}\right);$$

$$y_3 = a \sin \frac{2\pi}{T}\left(t - \frac{T}{6}\right).$$

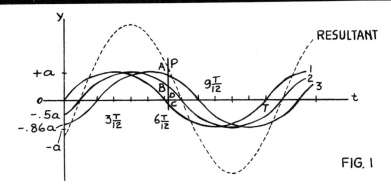

FIG. 1

Solution: Method I. Give t successive values; calculate for each the corresponding displacement due to each simple harmonic motion; find the resultant displacement by algebraic summation; and finally plot resultant values of the displacement against corresponding values of t. A few such values are given in Table 1.

Table 1

t	y_1	y_2	y_3	Resultant y
0	0	−0.5a	−0.86a	−1.36a
1 T/12	+0.5a	0	−0.5a	0
2 T/12	+0.86a	+0.5a	0	+1.36a
3 T/12	+1.0a	+0.86a	+0.5a	+2.36a

By obtaining in this manner a large number of corresponding values of y and t, and plotting, a curve is obtained similar to the broken one in Figure 1. This curve then represents the required resultant motion of the particle.

The method involves an important principle, called the Principle of Superposition, according to which the resultant displacement at any instant is equal to the algebraic sum of the individual displacements at that instant. This holds, provided the displacements are small, its justification being found in the fact that it leads to correct results.

13

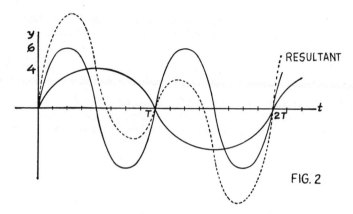

FIG. 2

Method II. The method just outlined involves a good deal of calculation, and for that reason the following more graphical method is recommended. In this method, the graph of each simple harmonic motion is plotted separately to the same scale and with the same set of coordinates. Points on the resultant graph are then obtained by applying the principle of superposition. For example, at the time represented by OD (Fig. 1), the displacement due to the first simple harmonic motion is DC(-), due to the second DB(+), due to the third DA(+), from which the resultant displacement at this instant = DA + DB - DC = DP. Similarly, other points are obtained in sufficient number to enable a smooth graph to be drawn. The curve obtained, of course, will be exactly the same as by Method I.

By inspection it is seen that the resultant motion (a) is periodic; (b) because of its shape, probably is simple harmonic; (c) by actual measurement has an amplitude = 2.7a.

Both of these methods are perfectly general and may be applied whether the individual simple harmonic motions are of the same period, as in this problem, or of different periods, as in Figure 2, where two waves obeying simple harmonic motion are superimposed, with periods in the ratio of 1 to 2. The essential condition is that they all represent motion in the same straight line.

● **PROBLEM 1-10**

Add the functions $E_1 = E_0 \cos \omega t$ and $E_2 = E_0 \cos(\omega t + \phi)$ and plot a graph showing the amplitude of the resulting sinusoidal function, as a function of the phase angle ϕ. What is the amplitude when $\phi = 0$, $\pi/4$, $\pi/2$, $3\pi/4$, π?

Solution: Let E represent the sum of the functions E_1 and E_2.

$$E = E_1 + E_2$$

$$= E_0 \cos \omega t + E_0 \cos(\omega t + \phi)$$

$$= E_0 [\cos \omega t + \cos(\omega t + \phi)] \qquad (1)$$

14

Now, using the trigonometric identity for the sum of two cosines,

$$\cos x + \cos y = 2 \cos \tfrac{1}{2} (x + y) \cos \tfrac{1}{2} (x - y)$$

equation (1) becomes

$$E = E_0 \left[2 \cos \tfrac{1}{2} (\omega t + \omega t + \phi) \cos \tfrac{1}{2} (\omega t - (\omega t + \phi)) \right]$$

$$E = 2E_0 \cos(\omega t + \phi/2) \cos(- \phi/2)$$

Note that the amplitude of the function E is given by $2E_0 \cos(- \phi/2)$, since $\cos(\omega t + \phi/2)$ represents the same wave with different phase shifts corresponding to different values of ϕ. Also note that $\cos(- \phi/2) = \cos(\phi/2)$, so that the amplitude as a function of ϕ is given by

$$A(\phi) = 2E_0 \cos \phi/2$$

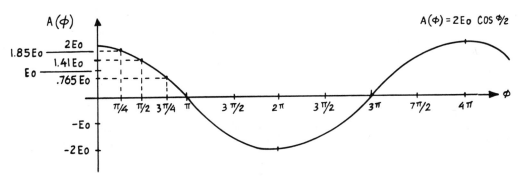

Graphing this function, we obtain the figure shown in this problem.

When $\phi = 0$ $A(\phi) = (2E_0)(\cos 0/2) = 2E_0$

$\phi = \pi/4$ $A(\phi) = (\cos \pi/8)(2E_0) = 1.85E_0$

$\phi = \pi/2$ $A(\phi) = (\cos \pi/4)(2E_0) = 1.41E_0$

$\phi = 3\pi/4$ $A(\phi) = (\cos 3\pi/8)(2E_0) = .765E_0$

$\phi = \pi$ $A(\phi) = (\cos \pi/2)(2E_0) = 0$

● **PROBLEM 1-11**

Two harmonic wave motions, $y_1 = \sin x$ and $y_2 = 1/2 \sin 2x$, are added together.

(1) Write the equation of the resultant wave motion.

(2) What is the period of the resultant wave?

15

(3)   Draw a graph of the two initial wave motions and of
      the resultant wave.

(4)   Find the maxima by differentiating the resultant wave
      with respect to x.

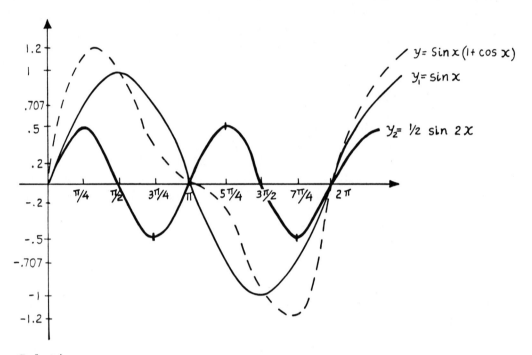

Solution:

(1)   The principle of superposition says that the resultant
wave can be found by summing the given individual waves.
Thus,

$$y = y_1 + y_2$$

$$y = \sin x + \frac{1}{2} \sin 2x$$

$$= \sin x + \frac{1}{2} (2 \sin x \cos x)$$

$$y = \sin x (1 + \cos x).$$

(2)   The period of the resultant wave is 2π, since the
wave equation is a function of $\sin x$ and $\cos x$ (each of
which has a period of 2π).

(3)   First make a table of values as follows:

y	$\pi/4$	$\pi/2$	$3\pi/4$	π	$5\pi/4$	$3\pi/2$	$7\pi/4$	2π
$\sin x$	.707	1	.707	0	-.707	-1	-.707	0
$\frac{1}{2} \sin 2x$	.5	0	-.5	0	.5	0	-.5	0
$\sin x (1 + \cos x)$	1.2	1	.2	0	-.2	-1	-1.2	0

16

Now plotting these values yields the figure.

(4)   Differentiating the equation

$$y = \sin x \, (1 + \cos x)$$

with respect to x gives

$$\frac{dy}{dx} = \sin x \, (-\sin x) + (1 + \cos x)\cos x \, .$$

Then,

$$\frac{dy}{dx} = \cos^2 x - \sin^2 x + \cos x \, .$$

To find the maxima, set $\frac{dy}{dx}$ equal to zero.

$$\cos^2 x - \sin^2 x + \cos x = 0 \, .$$

By the trigonometric identity $\cos^2 x + \sin^2 x = 1$, $\sin^2 x = 1 - \cos^2 x$ and so, the above equation becomes

$$\cos^2 x - (1 - \cos^2 x) + \cos x = 0$$

or

$$2 \cos^2 x + \cos x - 1 = 0 \, .$$

By the quadratic equation,

$$\cos x = \left[-1 \pm \sqrt{1^2 - 4(2)(-1)} \right] \Big/ 2(2)$$

$$\cos x = \frac{-1 \pm 3}{4}$$

and thus, the two solutions are

$$\cos x = \frac{1}{2} \, , \text{ and } \cos x = -1 \, .$$

$\cos x = \frac{1}{2}$ gives maxima and/or minima, at $x = \cos^{-1}\left(\frac{1}{2}\right) =$ $x = \pi/3$, $x = -\pi/3$ and $5\pi/3$.

From the graph, it is apparent that $x = 5\pi/3$ is a minimum.   Hence, maxima occur at $x = \pi/3$ and $x = -\pi/3$. From the graph, it can be seen that $\cos x = -1$, which gives $x = \pi$, is a point of inflection.   This can be proven by taking the second derivative of y with respect to x and setting it equal to zero.

17

Six simple harmonic motions, each of the same amplitude and period, acting along the same straight line, are superimposed. If the phase difference between each successive pair is the same, find one value of this phase difference for which the resultant amplitude is zero.

Solution: Call the amplitude of the waves A and the period T. Since the angular frequency, ω, is given by $\omega = \frac{2\pi}{T}$, then ω is the same for each wave. The phase difference between each successive pair can be represented by ϕ. Using this information the six waves can now be represented in the following way:

$$y_1 = A \sin \omega t$$

$$y_2 = A \sin (\omega t + \phi)$$

$$y_3 = A \sin (\omega t + 2\phi)$$

$$y_4 = A \sin (\omega t + 3\phi)$$

$$y_5 = A \sin (\omega t + 4\phi)$$

$$y_6 = A \sin (\omega t + 5\phi) .$$

By the principle of superposition, these motions can be added in order to obtain the resultant motion. In addition, since it is desired to find the value of the phase difference required for the resultant amplitude to equal zero, the following must hold true:

$$y_1 + y_2 + y_3 + y_4 + y_5 + y_6 = 0$$

or

$$A \sin \omega t + A \sin(\omega t + \phi) + A \sin(\omega t + 2\phi)$$

$$+ A \sin(\omega t + 3\phi) + A \sin(\omega t + 4\phi) + A \sin(\omega t + 5\phi) = 0.$$

Since $A \neq 0$, both sides of the equation may be divided by A. Then,

$$\sin \omega t + \sin(\omega t + \phi) + \sin(\omega t + 2\phi) + \sin(\omega t + 3\phi)$$

$$+ \sin(\omega t + 4\phi) + \sin(\omega t + 5\phi) = 0.$$

Now, using the following formula for the sum of two sine functions,

$$\sin x + \sin y = 2 \sin \frac{1}{2} (x + y) \cos \frac{1}{2} (x - y) \qquad (1)$$

and applying it three times, it is found that

$$2 \sin \frac{1}{2} (\omega t + \omega t + \phi) \cos \frac{1}{2} [\omega t - (\omega t + \phi)]$$

$$+ 2 \sin \frac{1}{2} (\omega t + 2\phi + \omega t + 3\phi) \cos \frac{1}{2} [\omega t + 2\phi - (\omega t + 3\phi)]$$

$$+ 2 \sin \frac{1}{2} (\omega t + 4\phi + \omega t + 5\phi) \cos \frac{1}{2} [\omega t + 4\phi - (\omega t + 5\phi)] = 0.$$

Dividing by 2 and gathering terms, the above equation becomes

$$\sin (\omega t + \phi/2) \cos (-\phi/2) + \sin (\omega t + 5\phi/2) \cos (-\phi/2)$$

$$+ \sin (\omega t + 9\phi/2) \cos (-\phi/2) = 0.$$

Factoring out $\cos (-\phi/2)$ gives

$$\cos (-\phi/2) \Big[\sin (\omega t + \phi/2) + \sin (\omega t + 5\phi/2)$$

$$+ \sin (\omega t + 9\phi/2) \Big] = 0. \tag{2}$$

Note that one solution is already apparent; that is, $\cos (-\phi/2) = 0$, or $\phi = \pi$. This result is easy to interpret physically; any two waves of equal frequency and amplitude will interfere destructively (that is, cancel each other with a resultant amplitude = 0) when their phase difference is 180° (the crest of one wave corresponds exactly to the trough of the other). Thus, any even number of waves with equal amplitude and frequency will have a resultant amplitude of zero. Since this is a very general solution that holds for any even number of waves, let us proceed to try to find a more specific solution which holds for the given case; that is, for six waves.

From equation (2), another solution is

$$\sin (\omega t + \phi/2) + \sin (\omega t + 5\phi/2) + \sin (\omega t + 9\phi/2) = 0.$$

Using the double angle formula

$$\sin (x + y) = \sin x \cos y + \cos x \sin y, \tag{3}$$

the above equation becomes

$$\sin \omega t \cos \phi/2 + \cos \omega t \sin \phi/2 + \sin \omega t \cos 5\phi/2$$

$$+ \cos \omega t \sin 5\phi/2 + \sin \omega t \cos 9\phi/2$$

$$+ \cos \omega t \sin 9\phi/2 = 0.$$

Factoring out $\sin \omega t$ and $\cos \omega t$ gives

$$\sin \omega t (\cos \phi/2 + \cos 5\phi/2 + \cos 9\phi/2)$$

$$+ \cos \omega t (\sin \phi/2 + \sin 5\phi/2 + \sin 9\phi/2) = 0. \tag{4}$$

Now, look at one particular value of t, so that the factor ωt can be eliminated. (Note that if the resultant wave amplitude is zero, it is zero everywhere; that is, for every value of t; thus, this is perfectly valid.) Let $t = T$. Since $\omega = \dfrac{2\pi}{T}$, $\omega t = \left(\dfrac{2\pi}{T}\right)(T) = 2\pi$ and so,

$$\sin \omega t = \sin 2\pi = 0 \text{ and } \cos \omega t = \cos 2\pi = 1 \ .$$

Then equation (4) becomes

$$\sin \phi/2 + \sin 5\phi/2 + \sin 9\phi/2 = 0 \ .$$

From equation (1),

$$2 \sin \tfrac{1}{2} (\phi/2 + 5\phi/2) \cos \tfrac{1}{2} (\phi/2 - 5\phi/2) + \sin 9\phi/2 = 0$$

or

$$2 \sin(3\phi/2) \cos(-\phi) + \sin 9\phi/2 = 0 \ .$$

Since $\cos \phi$ is symmetric around the point $\phi = 0$, $\cos(-\phi) = \cos \phi$. Thus,

$$2 \sin(3\phi/2) \cos \phi + \sin(9\phi/2) = 0 . \tag{5}$$

By the double angle formula for the sine function,

$$\sin(9\phi/2) = \sin(3\phi/2 + 3\phi)$$

$$= \sin(3\phi/2)\cos(3\phi) + \cos(3\phi/2)\sin(3\phi). \tag{6}$$

$$\cos(3\phi) = \cos(3\phi/2 + 3\phi/2) .$$

By the double angle formula for the cosine function,

$$\cos(3\phi) = \cos(3\phi/2 + 3\phi/2)$$

$$= \cos^2(3\phi/2) - \sin^2(3\phi/2). \tag{7}$$

In addition, reapplying the double angle formula for the sine function gives

$$\sin(3\phi) = \sin(3\phi/2 + 3\phi/2) = 2 \sin(3\phi/2)\cos(3\phi/2). \tag{8}$$

Substituting the expressions for $\cos(3\phi)$ and $\sin(3\phi)$ given in equations (7) and (8), respectively, into equation (6) gives

$$\sin(9\phi/2) = \sin(3\phi/2)\left[\cos^2(3\phi/2) - \sin^2(3\phi/2)\right]$$

$$+ \cos(3\phi/2)\left[2 \sin(3\phi/2)\cos(3\phi/2)\right]$$

$$= \sin(3\phi/2)\cos^2(3\phi/2) - \sin^3(3\phi/2)$$

$$+ 2 \sin(3\phi/2)\cos^2(3\phi/2)$$

$$= \sin(3\phi/2)\left[3 \cos^2(3\phi/2) - \sin^2(3\phi/2)\right] \ .$$

Substituting this expression for sin(9φ/2) into equation (5) gives

$$\sin(3\phi/2)\left[2\cos\phi + 3\cos^2(3\phi/2) - \sin^2(3\phi/2)\right] = 0.$$

One solution to this equation is $\sin(3\phi/2) = 0$, which is satisfied if $3\phi/2 = m\pi$, where m is an integer. Choose m = 1. Then

$$\phi = \frac{2\pi}{3} = \frac{2}{3}(180°) = 120°,$$

and this is a particular value of φ for which the resultant amplitude is zero.

THE HALF-WAVE PLATE

● **PROBLEM** 1-13

Show that a particle subjected to two simple harmonic vibrations of the same frequency, at right angles and out of phase, traces an elliptical path which degenerates to two coincident straight lines if the phase difference is π. Indicate the relevance of this to a half-wave plate.

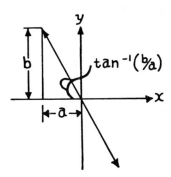

Solution: Let the vibrations be taking place along the x- and y-axes with a phase difference of φ between them. Then if x = a sin ωt, y = b sin(ωt + φ). Since sin(α + β) = sin α cos β + cos α sin β,

$$\frac{y}{b} = \sin\omega t \cos\phi + \cos\omega t \sin\phi.$$

$\frac{x}{a}$ can be substituted for sin ωt and from the trigonometric identity $\sin^2\omega t + \cos^2\omega t = 1$, $\cos\omega t = \sqrt{1 - \sin^2\omega t} = \sqrt{1 - x^2/a^2}$. Thus, the above equation becomes

$$\frac{y}{b} = \frac{x}{a}\cos\phi + \sqrt{1 - x^2/a^2} \cdot \sin\phi.$$

This equation can be rearranged to the following:

$$\frac{y}{b} - \frac{x}{a} \cos \phi = \sqrt{1 - x^2/a^2} \cdot \sin \phi .$$

Squaring this equation gives

$$\frac{y^2}{b^2} + \frac{x^2}{a^2} \cos^2\phi - \frac{2xy}{ab} \cos \phi = \left(1 - \frac{x^2}{a^2}\right) \sin^2\phi$$

or grouping the terms involving $\frac{x^2}{a^2}$ together,

$$\frac{x^2}{a^2}(\cos^2 \phi + \sin^2 \phi) + \frac{y^2}{b^2} - \frac{2xy}{ab} \cos \phi = \sin^2 \phi.$$

Since $\cos^2 \phi + \sin^2 \phi = 1$, this equation becomes

$$\frac{x^2}{a^2} + \frac{y^2}{b^2} - \frac{2xy}{ab} \cos \phi = \sin^2\phi .$$

This is the general equation of an ellipse where the major and minor axes do not coincide with the x- and y- axes. Thus, the particle always has x- and y-coordinates such that the point they define lies on an ellipse. The particle thus follows an elliptical path.

If $\phi = \pi/2, 3\pi/2, 5\pi/2,\ldots$, the equation of the path reduces to $(x^2/a^2) + (y^2/b^2) = 1$, which is an ellipse with the major and minor axes coincident with the coordinate axes.

When $\phi = \pi$, the equation of the path becomes

$$\frac{x^2}{a^2} + \frac{y^2}{b^2} + \frac{2xy}{ab} = 0 ,$$

or

$$\left(\frac{x}{a} + \frac{y}{b}\right)^2 = 0 .$$

This is the equation of two coincident straight lines $x/a = -y/b$, inclined to the negative x-axis at an angle $\tan^{-1}(b/a)$. (See figure.)

In the case of a half-wave plate, plane-polarized light striking the plate is split up into two components, O and E, plane-polarized at right angles to one another and initially in phase. These pass through the plate at different speeds and the thickness is such that on emergence the two beams are out of phase by π. Any particle affected by the two components will thus be

22

affected by two simple harmonic vibrations at right angles, out of phase by π. As can be seen from the above analysis, the particle would trace a straight-line path. This means that the two components are equivalent to a single vibration at an angle $\tan^{-1}(b/a)$ to the slower component, b/a being the ratio of the amplitudes of the components of the incident light on entering the plate. If the plane-polarized light is striking the plate at an angle of 45° to the two transmission directions, then it is resolved into two equal components so that b = a. The emerging light is thus plane-polarized in a direction making an angle of -45° with each of the principal directions in the plate.

BEATS

● PROBLEM 1-14

A familiar (and useful) system of beats is a moiré pattern. Consider two picket fences, one with boards (and spaces) 50 mm wide, and another with boards and spaces 51 mm wide placed next to it. As you drive past at a speed of 20 km/hr, how frequently can you not see through the two fences?

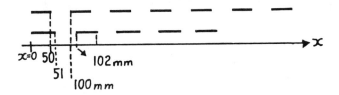

Solution: For waves in general, the frequency ν is given by $\nu = \frac{v}{\lambda}$ where v is the speed of the wave and λ its wavelength. Looking first at fence 1, the positions of the boards can be written as $x_1 = m_1 \cdot 100$ mm, where $m_1 = 0,1,2,3,\ldots$. Similarly, for fence 2, the boards can be seen at distances of $x_2 = m_2 \cdot 102$ mm, $m_2 = 0,1,2,3,\ldots$. When $x_1 = x_2$ the boards are coincident (as is the case at x = 0), and we cannot see through the two fences. At such points,

$$x_1 = x_2 ,$$

and so,

$$m_1 \cdot 100 = m_2 \cdot 102$$

$$m_1 = \frac{102}{100} m_2 = 1.02 \; m_2 .$$

23

Since both m_1 and m_2 are integers, the situation first occurs when $m_2 = 50$ and $m_1 = 51$, again when $m_2 = 100$, $m_1 = 102$, etc. Since this occurs every 51 times for the first fence (in effect, after 51 "wavelengths"), the distance between beats is

$$x_1 = m_1 \cdot 100 \text{ mm}$$

$$= (51)(100) \text{ mm}$$

$$= 5.1 \text{ m} .$$

Now, the wave is stationary but the observer is moving with a velocity $v = 20$ km/hr with respect to the wave. So

$$\nu_{\text{beat}} = \frac{v}{\lambda} = \frac{2 \times 10^4 \text{ m/hr}}{(3.6 \times 10^3 \text{ sec/hr})(5.1 \text{ m})}$$

$$\nu_{\text{beat}} = 1.09 \text{ sec}^{-1}$$

Therefore, you can not see through the fences 1.09 times per second.

CHAPTER 2

VELOCITY OF LIGHT

THE SPEED OF LIGHT IN EMPTY SPACE

What is the speed of an electromagnetic wave in empty space?

Solution: The speed of an electromagnetic wave in a substance can be determined by using the following relation:

$$V = \frac{1}{\sqrt{\mu\varepsilon}} \qquad (1)$$

where μ is the permeability and ε the permittivity of the substance. μ_0 and ε_0, the permeability and permittivity, respectively, of free space, are both constants, whose values are

$$\mu_0 = 4\pi \times 10^{-7} \text{ nt/amp}^2$$

and

$$\varepsilon_0 = 8.85 \times 10^{-12} \text{coul}^2/\text{nt} - \text{m}^2$$

Therefore, in empty space, equation (1) becomes

$$V = \frac{1}{\sqrt{\mu_0 \varepsilon_0}}$$

$$= \frac{1}{\sqrt{4\pi \times 10^{-7} \times 8.85 \times 10^{-12} \, \text{coul}^2/\text{amp}^2 - \text{m}^2}}$$

$$= 3.00 \times 10^8 \text{ m/sec} .$$

DETERMINATION OF THE DISTANCE TRAVELLED BY LIGHT IN A GIVEN TIME PERIOD

● PROBLEM 2-2

If the velocity of light is assumed to be 3×10^8 m/sec, how much time does it take the light to travel through a distance of 30 cm?

Solution: When the velocity of light v and the distance x which it has traveled are both known, then the time t required for the light to travel that distance is found by applying the equation

$$v \cdot t = x .$$

If the velocity of light is 3×10^8 m/sec and the distance it has to travel is 30 cm, or 0.30 m, then the time it takes to travel that distance is 0.30 m/3×10^8 m/sec or 1×10^{-9} sec, which is equal to 1 nanosecond.

THE VELOCITY OF LIGHT IN GLASS

● PROBLEM 2-3

What is the velocity and wavelength of light with vacuum wavelength $\lambda = 500$ mμ when measured in glass whose index of refraction at this wavelength is 1.50?

Solution: For any particular ray of light, the product of its velocity and the index of refraction of the medium it is traveling in is always constant:

$$v \cdot n = \text{constant} \tag{1}$$

Also, since $v = f\lambda$, $\lambda = \frac{v}{f}$ or λ is proportional to v. Thus,

$$\lambda \cdot n = \text{constant} \tag{2}$$

In other words, the product of the wavelength of light and the index of refraction of the medium it is traveling through is constant for a particular light ray.

Equation (1) states that

$$v_V \cdot n_V = v_G \cdot n_G \tag{3}$$

where the subscripts V and G represent vacuum and glass, respectively, and equation (2) states that

$$\lambda_V \cdot n_V = \lambda_G \cdot n_G \tag{4}$$

n_V, the index of refraction of a vacuum = 1, v_V = the speed of light in a vacuum = 3×10^8 m/sec, and n_G and λ_V are given to be 1.50 and 500 mμ, respectively.

Thus, from equation (3),

$$v_G = \frac{v_V \cdot n_V}{n_G} = \frac{(3 \times 10^8 \text{ m/sec})(1)}{1.50} = 2 \times 10^8 \text{ m/sec}$$

and from equation (4),

$$\lambda_G = \frac{\lambda_V \cdot n_V}{n_G} = \frac{(500 \text{ mμ})(1)}{1.50} = 333 \text{ mμ} .$$

METHODS USED TO MEASURE THE VELOCITY OF LIGHT

● PROBLEM 2-4

A rotating mirror experiment, to measure the speed of light, is set up on Mt. Wilson with the return mirror on Mt. San Antonia 35377 meters away. When the 8-face mirror rotates at a speed of 530 rps no shift of the light source is obtained. Calculate the velocity of light.

Solution: The distance which a beam of light travels in one round trip from Mt. Wilson to Mt. San Antonia is 2×35377 m. Each time the beam of light strikes the rotating mirror it has made one round trip. If the mirror has 8 faces and is rotating at a rate of 530 revolutions per second then the light makes 8×530 round trips per second or it travels

$(2 \times 35377 \text{ m}) \cdot (8 \times 530)$ per second,

which is equal to 3.00×10^8 m/sec.

● PROBLEM 2-5

In a Fizeau toothed-wheel experiment for obtaining the velocity of light, an eclipse of the source is first observed when the speed of the disk is 1500 rpm. (a) If the distance of the toothed wheel, which has 600 teeth, to the reflecting mirror is 4980 meters, find the velocity of light. (b) At what speed must the disk be moving for a second eclipse to be observed?

Solution:

(a) For a Fizeau toothed-wheel apparatus for measuring the speed of light, the following equation is used:

27

$$c = \frac{2\omega\ell}{\theta} \qquad\qquad (1)$$

where c is the velocity of light, ω is the angular speed of the wheel, ℓ is the length of the apparatus, and θ is the angular distance from the center of a gap to the center of a tooth. The wheel is rotating at an angular speed of $\omega = (1500 \text{ rev/min})\left(\frac{1 \text{ min}}{60 \text{ sec}}\right) = 25$ rev/sec. The angular distance from the center of a gap to the next center of a gap is $\frac{1}{600}$ rev; hence $\theta = \frac{1}{2}\left(\frac{1}{600} \text{ rev}\right) = \frac{1}{1200}$ rev; and the length of the apparatus, ℓ, is 4980 meters. Substituting this data into equation (1) gives the result

$$c = \frac{2\left(25 \frac{\text{rev}}{\text{sec}}\right)(4980\text{m})}{\left(\frac{1}{1200} \text{ rev}\right)}$$

$$c = 2.988 \times 10^8 \text{ m/s}$$

(b) If the first eclipse of the source occurs when the wheel is rotating at a rate of 1500 rpm, then the next eclipse occurs when the wheel is spinning at 3000 rpm. But this next eclipse would occur at a tooth rather than at a gap; therefore, this next eclipse would go undetected. Thus, the next detectable eclipse would occur at 4500 rpm.

● **PROBLEM 2-6**

In Anderson's method for measuring the velocity of light, the response of the photo-electric cell was a minimum when the path difference was 171.8 meters and the frequency of modulation 9.6×10^6 cps. Find the value of the velocity of light.

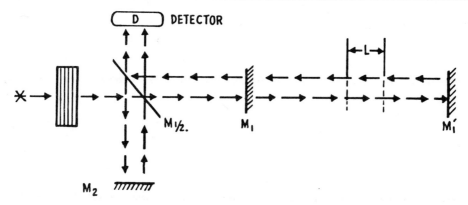

M₂ ▨▨▨

Solution: In this method, light from a light source was chopped by the Kerr cell into pulses of length L, from crest to crest, determined by the ratio of the speed of light to the frequency of interruption of the shutter, f. The light pulses, represented by arrows (bright) and gaps (dark), were divided by the half silvered mirror $M_{\frac{1}{2}}$ into two beams. One beam was reflected downwards by mirror $M_{\frac{1}{2}}$, struck mirror M_2, was reflected back through $M_{\frac{1}{2}}$, and finally traveled to the detector D. The other beam was transmitted through $M_{\frac{1}{2}}$, struck mirror M_1, was reflected back to mirror $M_{\frac{1}{2}}$, which reflected the beam to the detector D. If the mirrors M_1 and M_2 were equidistant from $M_{\frac{1}{2}}$, the two bright crests of the light flashes reached the photo-electric cell simultaneously, and a moment later the two dark troughs arrived together. Thus, the output signal fluctuated strongly at the chopping frequency.

If the mirrors M_1 and M_2 were not equidistant, but placed so that the round trip path to and from each of them differed by $\frac{L}{2}$ (or any odd multiple of $\frac{L}{2}$), the cell was illuminated alternately by light coming from mirrors M_1 and M_2. Thus, the photocell saw a steady light intensity, and no signal resulted.

The path difference is varied by moving M_1 to a position M_1'. This increases the path difference to 2 times M_1M_1' which must be an integral multiple of L.

The speed of light is given by

$$c = s\,\frac{f}{n}$$

where s is the length $(2 \times 171.8$ m$)$ by which the path has been increased, f is the chopping frequency, and n is the number of pulses of length L which are present in a total length s. This number is evaluated from taking as a rough value, $c = 3 \times 10^8$ m/sec. Thus,

$$L = \frac{c}{f} = \frac{3 \times 10^8 \text{ m}}{9.6 \times 10^6} = 31.25 \text{ m}$$

and

$$n = \frac{2 \times 171.8}{31.25} \approx 11 \ .$$

Hence,

$$c = s\,\frac{f}{n}$$

$$= \frac{343.6 \times 9.6 \times 10^6}{11} \text{ m/sec}$$

$$= 2.99 \times 10^8 \text{ m/sec} \ .$$

STELLAR ABERRATION

Find the velocity of light by considering the aberration of light from the stars, which is 20.47 seconds of arc.

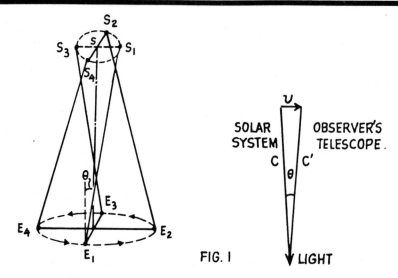

FIG. I

Solution: The aberration of light from the stars, known as stellar aberration, is the apparent systematic movement of fixed stars relative to the direction of motion of the earth in orbit and is not dependent on the earth's position in space.

The star s appears to be at s_1, s_2, s_3 and s_4 for positions of the earth E_1, E_2, E_3 and E_4, respectively, as shown in Figure 1. The telescope must be tilted by an angle θ to receive the light from the star.

The angular shift in the apparent position of stars is shown in Figure 1 to be given by the relation

$$\tan\theta = \frac{v}{c} \qquad (1)$$

where v is the velocity of the earth in its orbit and c is the velocity of light. Now

$$v = \frac{\text{circumference of the earth's orbit}}{\text{period of the earth's orbit}} = \frac{2\pi R}{T} \qquad (2)$$

where $R = 93 \times 10^6$ miles and T = 365 days. Hence,

$$v = \frac{(2\pi)(93 \times 10^6 \text{ miles})}{(365 \text{ days})\left(24 \frac{\text{hours}}{\text{day}}\right)\left(60 \frac{\text{min}}{\text{hour}}\right)\left(60 \frac{\text{sec}}{\text{min}}\right)} = 18.53 \frac{\text{miles}}{\text{sec}}$$

Since θ is small, the approximation $\tan\theta = \theta$ is valid.

Therefore, equation (1) becomes $\theta = \frac{v}{c}$ or $c = \frac{v}{\theta}$ and substituting for v and for θ gives

$$c = \frac{18.53 \frac{miles}{sec}}{(20.47 \ sec)\left(\frac{1 \ min}{60 \ sec}\right)\left(\frac{1 \ degree}{60 \ min}\right)\left(\frac{\pi \ radians}{180 \ degrees}\right)}$$

$$= 186717 \frac{miles}{sec}$$

● **PROBLEM 2-8**

If the radius of the Earth's orbit is 1.497×10^8 km calculate the magnitude of stellar aberration.

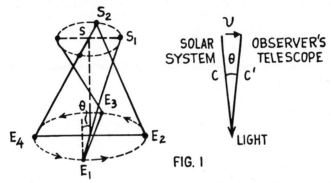

FIG. I

Solution: Since the stellar aberration is due to the apparent systematic movement of fixed stars relative to the direction of motion of the earth in its orbit and is not dependent on the earth's position in space, it can be inferred from Figure 1 that

$$\tan \theta = \frac{v}{c} \tag{1}$$

where v is the velocity of the earth in its orbit and c is the velocity of light.

$$v = \frac{\text{the circumference of the earth's orbit}}{\text{the period of the earth's orbit}} = \frac{2\pi R}{T}$$

where $R = 1.497 \times 10^{11}$ m, and T = 365 days.   Hence,

$$v = \frac{(2\pi)(1.497 \times 10^{11} \ m)}{(365 \ days)\left(24 \frac{hours}{day}\right)\left(60 \frac{min}{hour}\right)\left(60 \frac{sec}{min}\right)}$$

$$= 2.983 \times 10^4 \ m/sec$$

Thus, substituting the value just computed for v along with the known value for c into equation (1) gives

$$\tan \theta = \frac{v}{c} = \frac{2.983 \times 10^4 \ m/sec}{2.998 \times 10^8 \ m/sec} = 9.95 \times 10^{-5} \ rad \ .$$

31

Since θ is small, the approximation $\tan \theta = \theta$ is valid, and so,

$$\theta = (9.95 \times 10^{-5} \text{ rad}) \left(\frac{180 \text{ degrees}}{\pi \text{ rad}}\right)\left(\frac{60 \text{ min}}{\text{degree}}\right)\left(\frac{60 \text{ sec}}{\text{min}}\right)$$

$$= 20.52 \text{ seconds of arc} .$$

STANDING WAVES

An oscillator which emits high frequency waves at 0.26 GHz is set up in front of a large plane metal reflector. Standing waves are formed with nodes 57.5 cm apart. Neglecting the refractive index of air, compute the velocity of light.

Solution: Standing waves are obtained by superposition of two wave trains of the same frequency and wavelength but traveling in opposite directions. Two such waves are

$$y_1 = r \sin 2\pi \left(\frac{t}{T} - \frac{x}{\lambda}\right)$$

$$y_2 = r \sin 2\pi \left(\frac{t}{T} + \frac{x}{\lambda}\right)$$

where λ is the wavelength of light used, r represents the maximum amplitude of the waves, and T denotes the period of the waves.

The resultant is given by

$$y = y_1 + y_2 = r\left[\sin 2\pi \left(\frac{t}{T} - \frac{x}{\lambda}\right) + \sin 2\pi \left(\frac{t}{T} + \frac{x}{\lambda}\right)\right] \qquad (1)$$

Using the trigonometric identity

$$\sin A + \sin B = 2 \sin \left(\frac{A+B}{2}\right) \cos \left(\frac{A-B}{2}\right) \qquad (2)$$

Taking $A = 2\pi \left(\frac{t}{T} - \frac{x}{\lambda}\right)$ and $B = 2\pi \left(\frac{t}{T} + \frac{x}{\lambda}\right)$, equation (1) becomes

$$y = 2r \sin \left[\frac{2\pi}{2}\left(\frac{t}{T} - \frac{x}{\lambda} + \frac{t}{T} + \frac{x}{\lambda}\right)\right] \cos \left[\frac{2\pi}{2}\left(\frac{t}{T} - \frac{x}{\lambda} - \left(\frac{t}{T} + \frac{x}{\lambda}\right)\right)\right]$$

$$= 2r \sin \left(\frac{2\pi t}{T}\right) \cos\left(-\frac{2\pi x}{\lambda}\right) \qquad (3)$$

Since $\cos \theta = \cos(-\theta)$, equation (3) can be rewritten as

$$y = 2r \sin \left(\frac{2\pi t}{T}\right) \cos \left(\frac{2\pi x}{\lambda}\right) \qquad (4)$$

The nodes are given by the condition $y = 0$ for all t. Applying this condition to equation (4) gives the result $0 = 2r \sin\left(\frac{2\pi t}{T}\right) \cos\left(\frac{2\pi x}{\lambda}\right)$. Since $\cos\frac{m\pi}{2} = 0$, where m is an odd integer, $\frac{2\pi x}{\lambda} = \frac{m\pi}{2}$ and so, $x = \frac{m\pi\lambda}{4\pi} = \frac{m\lambda}{4}$. Thus $y = 0$ for $x = \frac{\lambda}{4}$, $\frac{3\lambda}{4}$, $\frac{5\lambda}{4}$, etc., and so, the distance between two successive nodes is $\frac{3\lambda}{4} - \frac{\lambda}{4} = \frac{\lambda}{2}$.

Hence, $\lambda = 2 \times 57.5$ cm $= 115$ cm. The velocity v is given by the relation

$$v = f\lambda \tag{5}$$

where f represents the frequency of the waves.

Substituting the given value for f and the value just computed for λ into equation (5) gives

$$v = 0.26 \times 10^9 \times 115 \text{ cm/sec}$$

$$v = 2.99 \times 10^{10} \text{ cm/sec .}$$

● **PROBLEM 2-10**

An oscillator of frequency 2.3×10^8 Hz is set up near a plane metal reflector, and the distance between adjacent nodes in the standing waves produced is found to be 65 cm. From this data, compute the velocity of light.

Solution: Standing waves giving rise to nodes and loops are obtained by superposition of two wave trains of the same frequency and amplitude but traveling in opposite directions. Two such waves may be represented as follows:

$$y_1 = r \sin 2\pi\left(\frac{t}{T} - \frac{x}{\lambda}\right) \tag{1}$$

$$y_2 = r \sin 2\pi\left(\frac{t}{T} + \frac{x}{\lambda}\right) \tag{2}$$

The resultant is given by

$$y = y_1 + y_2 = r\left[\sin 2\pi\left(\frac{t}{T} - \frac{x}{\lambda}\right) + \sin 2\pi\left(\frac{t}{T} + \frac{x}{\lambda}\right)\right] \tag{3}$$

Using the trigonometric identity for the sum of the sines of two angles,

$$\sin A + \sin B = 2 \sin\left(\frac{A+B}{2}\right)\cos\left(\frac{A-B}{2}\right) \tag{4}$$

and letting

$$A = 2\pi\left(\frac{t}{T} - \frac{x}{\lambda}\right) \text{ and } B = 2\pi\left(\frac{t}{T} + \frac{x}{\lambda}\right) ,$$

equation (3) becomes

$$y = 2r \sin\left[\frac{2\pi}{2}\left(\frac{t}{T} - \frac{x}{\lambda} + \frac{t}{T} + \frac{x}{\lambda}\right)\right] \cos\left[\frac{2\pi}{2}\left(\frac{t}{T} - \frac{x}{\lambda} - \left(\frac{t}{T} + \frac{x}{\lambda}\right)\right)\right]$$

$$= 2r \sin\left(\frac{2\pi t}{T}\right) \cos\left(-\frac{2\pi x}{\lambda}\right) \tag{5}$$

Since $\cos\theta = \cos(-\theta)$, equation (5) becomes

$$y = 2r \sin\left(\frac{2\pi t}{T}\right) \cos\left(\frac{2\pi x}{\lambda}\right) \tag{6}$$

The nodes are given by $y = 0$ for all t. Applying this condition to equation (6) gives

$$0 = 2r \sin\left(\frac{2\pi t}{T}\right) \cos\left(\frac{2\pi x}{\lambda}\right) .$$

This is satisfied when $\frac{2\pi x}{\lambda} = \frac{m\pi}{2}$, where m is an odd integer. Then

$$x = \frac{m\pi\lambda}{4\pi} = \frac{m\lambda}{4} .$$

Thus, $y = 0$ when $x = \frac{\lambda}{4}$, $\frac{3\lambda}{4}$, $\frac{5\lambda}{4}$,.... Therefore, the distance between two nodes is $\left(\frac{3\lambda}{4} - \frac{\lambda}{4}\right) = \frac{\lambda}{2}$.

Hence $\lambda = 2 \times 65$ cm $= 130$ cm. The velocity v of the wave is given by the relation

$$v = f\lambda, \tag{7}$$

where f denotes the frequency of the wave. Substituting the known values for f and λ into equation (7) gives

$$v = 2.3 \times 10^8 \times 130 \text{ cm/sec}$$

$$= 2.99 \times 10^{10} \text{ cm/sec} .$$

CHAPTER 3

PHYSICAL PROPERTIES OF LIGHT

THE DOPPLER EFFECT

A laser emits a monochromatic light beam, of wavelength λ, which falls normally on a mirror moving at velocity V. What is the beat frequency between the incident and reflected light?

Solution: When a source of light is in motion relative to an observer or vice versa, the light waves exhibit a change in frequency as seen by that observer. This phenomenon is known as the Doppler effect, and the Doppler shift for light is given as

$$\nu_{observed} = \nu \sqrt{\frac{c \pm v}{c \mp v}} \qquad (1)$$

where ν is the frequency of the light in an inertial frame of reference, v is the speed of the source relative to the observer, and c is the speed of light. In this problem v is the speed of the mirror. Let us choose the mirror to be moving away from the laser, so that it absorbs the light as if it were an observer moving away at speed v; it then re-emits the light as if it were a source moving away at speed v. In both cases the source and observer are separating from one another, so the frequency decreases. To get $\nu_{observed} < \nu$, we need the lower signs in equation (1).

Now, when the mirror absorbs the light, we have

$$\nu_{absorbed} = \nu \sqrt{\frac{c - v}{c + v}} \qquad (2)$$

Similarly, when it re-emits the light, the frequency shift is given by

$$\nu_{emitted} = \nu_{absorbed} \sqrt{\frac{c - v}{c + v}} = \nu \left(\frac{c - v}{c + v}\right) . \qquad (3)$$

The beat frequency is the difference in frequencies between the incident and reflected light:

$$\nu_{beat} = \nu - \nu_{emitted}$$

$$\nu_{beat} = \nu - \nu \left(\frac{c - v}{c + v}\right)$$

35

$$= \nu\left[1 - \frac{c - v}{c + v}\right]$$

$$= \nu\left[\frac{2v}{c + v}\right]$$

$$\nu_{beat} = \frac{c}{\lambda}\left[\frac{2v}{c + v}\right]$$

when $v \ll c$, then $c + v \cong c$. In this case $\nu_{beat} \cong \frac{2v}{\lambda}$.

● PROBLEM 3-2

The Milky Way galaxy rotates once in 200 million years, and our sun is located about 30,000 light years from the galactic center. As a result, the earth is moving through space relative to the other galaxies. What is the observed Doppler shift in Å of the hydrogen line of 6563 Å for light coming from other galaxies? Consider two cases: a) The line of observation is in the direction of the earth's motion; b) The line of observation is perpendicular to the direction of the earth's motion. Ignore other causes of observed Doppler effects.

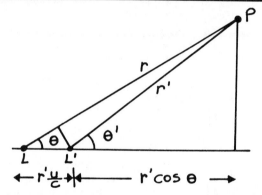

Solution: The relativistic Doppler shift is given by the expression

$$\nu' = \nu\sqrt{\frac{1 - u/c}{1 + u/c}}$$

Multiplying both the numerator and denominator by the factor $\sqrt{1 - u/c}$, one obtains the expression

$$\nu' = \nu\sqrt{\frac{1 - u/c}{1 - (u/c)^2}}$$

where ν' is the observed frequency of light of frequency ν in the frame of reference of the source; u is the relative source-observer velocity, and c is the speed of light.

For case (a), the light is travelling parallel to the earth's motion, and u is given by $u = R\Omega$, with $R = 30,000$ light-years, and

$$\Omega = \frac{2\pi}{200(10^6)} \quad \text{rad/year.}$$

Thus,

$$u = \frac{30,000(2\pi)}{200(10^6)} \quad \text{light-years (rad/year)}$$

36

$= 9.425(10^{-4})c$ (where c represents the speed
of light) or
$$\left(\frac{u}{c}\right) = 9.425(10^{-4}).$$

Now since $u \ll c$, $\nu' \simeq \nu \{1 - (u/c)\}$, or, since $\nu' = c/\lambda'$ and
$\nu = c/\lambda$ (λ = the wavelength of light),

$$\frac{1}{\lambda'} \simeq \frac{1}{\lambda} \{1 - (u/c)\}, \text{ with } \lambda = 6563\text{Å} .$$

Thus, $\lambda' = 6569.2$ Å, or $\Delta\lambda = \lambda' - \lambda = 6.2$ Å .

b) Where the line of observation is perpendicular to the direction of
the earth's motion, the observed frequency shift, which is purely a
relativistic effect, is called the transverse Doppler effect. The
frequency shift is given by the expression

$$\nu = \nu'[1 - (u/c)^2]^{\frac{1}{2}}.$$

The derivation of this effect is indicated in the figure. The generalized
Doppler shift is given by

$$\nu = \nu' \frac{1 + (u/c)\cos\theta'}{\sqrt{1 - (u/c)^2}}$$

where, as indicated, the observer (on the earth) is located at point P
at rest in the unprimed coordinate system, and the source of light is
at rest in the primed system. For transverse observation,

$$\theta = \frac{\pi}{2} ,$$

$$\cos\theta' = -\frac{u}{c}$$

Thus,
$$\nu = \nu' \frac{1 - (u/c)^2}{\sqrt{1 - (u/c)^2}} = \nu'[1 - (u/c)^2]^{\frac{1}{2}}$$

or

$$\frac{1}{\lambda} = \frac{1}{\lambda'} [1 - (u/c)^2]^{\frac{1}{2}}, \text{ with } (u/c) = 9.425(10^{-4}).$$

Thus, $\lambda = 6563.003$ Å , or $\Delta\lambda = 0.003$ Å.

● **PROBLEM** 3-3

What is the Doppler width of the hydrogen line H_α ($\lambda = 6563$ Å) in a
laboratory discharge tube operating at a temperature of $200°C$? Give
the results in frequency units and wavelength units.

Solution: For a luminous gas, the atoms are moving with a Maxwellian
distribution of velocities. Therefore, a spectral line emitted by a
gas must comprise a range of frequencies symmetrically distributed
about the frequency emitted by the atom when at rest; this range increases with increasing temperature. We define the full width at
half intensity, Δ, to be the separation between two points of the
spectral line at which the intensity is one-half as great as it is at
its maximum. The brightness of a line a distance $\lambda' - \lambda$ from the
center is proportional to

$$e^{-b(\lambda' - \lambda)^2}$$

where b is a constant dependent on the temperature and on the mass
of the atom. The width, Δ, if it is due entirely to the Doppler ef-

fect, is

$$\Delta = 0.72\left(10^{-6}\right) \lambda \sqrt{\frac{T}{M}}$$

where T is the absolute temperature and M is the atomic weight of
the radiating atom.
Substituting the values for T and M into the above equation, one
obtains

$$\Delta = 0.72\left(10^{-6}\right) \; 6563 \; \text{Å} \sqrt{\frac{473}{1}} = 0.103 \; \text{Å} \; .$$

Further,

$$c = f\lambda$$

(c = the speed of light), or since $c/f = \lambda$, $\Delta\lambda = -\frac{c}{f^2} \Delta f$. Thus,

$$\Delta f = -\frac{f^2}{c} \Delta\lambda \; ,$$

with

$$f = \frac{c}{\lambda} = \frac{3 \times 10^8 \; \text{m/sec}}{6563 \times 10^{-10} \text{m}} = 4.571 \times 10^{14} \; \text{sec}^{-1} \; .$$

Therefore,

$$\Delta f = \frac{\left(4.571 \times 10^{14} \; \text{sec}^{-1}\right)^2}{\left(3 \times 10^8 \; \text{m/sec}\right)} \; (.103 \; \text{Å})$$

or,

$$\Delta f = 7.17 \times 10^9 \; \text{Hz}.$$

● **PROBLEM** 3-4

Light may be incident at an angle of 40° on a plane mirror moving toward the source at a velocity v = 0.15 c. Find: a) the angle of reflection, and b) the wavelength of the reflected light, assuming the incident light has a wavelength of 550 nm.

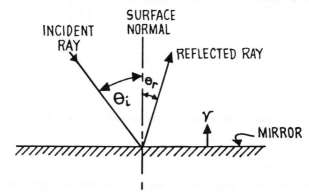

Solution: a) The law of reflection modified for the Doppler effect is
given by

$$\frac{\sin \theta_i}{\cos \theta_i + v/c} = \frac{\sin \theta_r}{\cos \theta_r - v/c} \; . \tag{1}$$

Substitution of $\theta_i = 40°$, v/c = 0.15   results in

$$\cos \theta_r = 0.15 + 1.43 \sin \theta_r \; ; \tag{2}$$

squaring both sides of equation (2) and using the trigonometric identity
$\cos^2\theta = 1 - \sin^2\theta$ gives

$$3.03 \sin^2\theta_r + 0.43 \sin\theta_r - 0.98 = 0.$$

Solving for $\sin\theta_r$ using the quadratic formula,

$$\sin\theta_r = \frac{-0.43 \overset{+}{-} \sqrt{(.43)^2 + 4(3.03)(0.98)}}{2(3.03)} \tag{3}$$

$$\sin\theta_r = 0.50, \text{ or}$$
$$\theta_r = 30° .$$

(Note: The positive solution to equation (3) is used since θ_r is obviously less than $90°$.)

b) If the direction of motion of a source of light moving with velocity v and the direction from which it is seen subtend an angle θ, the Doppler shifted wavelength λ' is related to the wavelength λ emitted by the source through the expression

$$\lambda' = \lambda \left[\frac{1 - (v'/c)\cos\theta}{\sqrt{1 - (v'/c)^2}} \right]. \tag{4}$$

In the problem the observer sees a reflection of the source in a mirror moving with velocity v; since the image seen in a moving mirror moves with twice the velocity of the mirror, $v' = 2v$; using $v/c = 0.15$, $\lambda = 550$ nm, and $\theta = 30°$, equation (4) gives

$$\lambda' = 427 \text{ nm.}$$

ENERGY AND MOMENTUM OF LIGHT

● **PROBLEM 3-5**

A parallel beam of light of radiant energy density 6.4×10^4 J/m^3 is incident on a plane mirror. What is a) the momentum acting upon the mirror and b) the force exerted upon it during 5 seconds illumination?

Solution: The momentum of light is given by the de Broglie relation as

$$p = \frac{h}{\lambda} = \frac{hc}{\lambda} \times \frac{1}{c} = \frac{h\nu}{c} = \frac{E}{c} , \tag{1}$$

where h is Planck's constant, λ, c, and ν are the wavelength, speed, and frequency of light, respectively, and E is the energy of the light beam. Knowing the energy of the beam, we can find the momentum exerted by the beam. If this beam impinges on a mirror the change in momentum will be twice the incident momentum (no energy lost in reflection, direction of momentum changes), or considering a volume of 1 cubic meter and a mirror surface of 1 square meter,

$$\text{change in momentum} = 2E/c = \frac{2 \times 6.4 \times 10^4}{3 \times 10^8} = 4.28 \times 10^{-4} \text{ kgm/s.} \tag{2}$$

Now, force is defined as the rate of change of momentum, so the force exerted on the mirror is given by

$$F = \frac{\Delta p}{\Delta t} = \frac{4.28 \times 10^{-4}}{5} = 8.58 \times 10^{-5} \text{ N/m}^2. \tag{3}$$

We will now use dimensional analysis to see how the units were arrived at: for the first equation we had

$$momentum = \frac{Energy}{speed}$$

$$= \frac{J}{m/sec}$$

$$= \frac{N \cdot m}{m/sec}$$

$$= \frac{kg\text{-}m/sec^2}{1/sec}$$

$$= kg\text{-}m/sec$$

In the second equation,

$$Force = \frac{momentum}{time}$$

$$= \frac{kg\text{-}m/sec}{sec}$$

$$= kg\text{-}m/sec^2 = N$$

Since this was the force exerted on one square meter of the mirror's surface, the units become N/m^2.

● **PROBLEM 3-6**

Find the momentum density (momentum per unit volume) in a beam of sunlight.

Solution: Each photon in a beam of sunlight carries momentum p given by

$$p = E/c , \tag{1}$$

where E, the energy of the photon, can be found from its frequency f;

$$E = hf. \tag{2}$$

Since

$$f = c/\lambda , \tag{3}$$

using $\lambda = 5 \times 10^{-7}$ meters and $c = 3 \times 10^8$ m/sec gives $E \simeq 4 \times 10^{-19}$ Joules and $p = 1.33 \times 10^{-27}$ kg-m/sec, for each photon. To find the number of photons per unit volume (and hence the momentum density by multiplying this number by p obtained above), we use the known fact that the average flux density for sunlight is about 1400 watts/m², i.e., on each square meter of the earth's surface there are incident 1400 Joules of energy each second. This energy must be carried by the photons contained between the earth's surface and a height equal to the distance a photon can travel in one second, i.e., a height $H = c \cdot 1$ sec = 3×10^8 meters. Thus in a box of base area equal to 1 square meter and height 3×10^8 m there must be

$$1400 \text{ Joules} \times \frac{1 \text{ photon}}{4 \times 10^{-19} \text{ Joules}} = 3.5 \times 10^{21} \text{ photons;}$$

in a box one meter high, (i.e., of volume one cubic meter) there would then be

$$\frac{3.5 \times 10^{21} \text{ photons}}{3 \times 10^8 \text{ m}^3} = 1.2 \times 10^{13} \text{ photons/m}^3 .$$

The momentum density is then

$$1.2 \times 10^{13} \frac{photons}{m^3} \times \frac{1.33 \times 10^{-27} \ kg\text{-}m/sec}{photon} = \frac{1.6 \times 10^{-14} \ kg\text{-}m/sec}{m^3}$$

● **PROBLEM 3-7**

A flashlight of mass M floats in space, at rest with respect to the "fixed stars". It is turned on for 1 hr., emitting 1W of light in a parallel beam. How fast is it going at the end of the hour with respect to the fixed stars? (Velocity is not an absolute quantity and must be measured with respect to some inertial frame.)

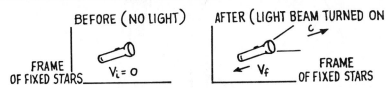

BEFORE (NO LIGHT)   AFTER (LIGHT BEAM TURNED ON

FRAME OF FIXED STARS $V_i = 0$ V_f FRAME OF FIXED STARS

(V_i AND V_f REPRESENT THE INITIAL AND FINAL VELOCITIES OF THE FLASHLIGHT, RESPECTIVELY)-

Solution: This problem can be solved by momentum conservation: the initial momentum of the flashlight is MV_i , the final momentum of the flashlight is MV_f. Light, though massless, has the property of momentum such that $P = U/c$ where U is the energy of the light. Here we are concerned with a beam of light. To calculate the energy of a beam we can use 2 methods;

    a) if the beam has an energy per unit volume, ϵ , and a volume V then $U = \epsilon V$,

    b) if the beam has a power output P, which we know is defined as energy per unit time, and it is on for a time T, then the total energy $U = PT$.

    In our problem we have the latter case. Therefore:

Total momentum initially is $P_T = MV_i + 0$,

However, with respect to the fixed stars $V_i = 0$, so P_T initially is 0.

    Total momentum finally is $P_T = MV_f + \frac{PT}{c}$.

These must be equal; so $0 = MV_f + \frac{PT}{c}$, or solving for V_f we have

$$V_f = -\frac{PT}{Mc} = -\frac{(1 \ W)(3600 \ sec)}{M(3 \times 10^8 \ m/sec)} .$$

Dimensionally, a watt $= \frac{kg\text{-}m^2}{sec^3}$.

$$V_f = \frac{\left(\frac{kg\text{-}m^2}{sec^3}\right)(sec)}{(kg)(m/sec)} = m/sec,$$

which is the units of velocity. Thus, $V_f = -\frac{1}{M}\left(1.2 \times 10^{-5}\right)m/sec$.

The minus sign merely signifies that the flashlight and the light beam move in opposite directions. Incidentally, the volume of the beam is its cross-sectional area times cT.

How many photons are there in 1 mm^3 of monochromatic light of 488 nm wavelength, whose beam has a radiant power flux density of 20 watts/cm^2 and a cross-sectional area of 1 cm^2?

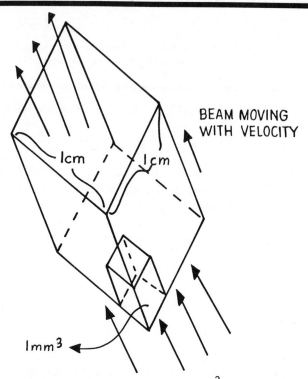

BEAM MOVING
WITH VELOCITY

Icm

Icm

1mm^3

Solution: The idea is to find the energy in 1mm^3 of the beam and divide it by the energy per photon. The result will be the number of photons per mm^3.

$$\left[\frac{\text{Energy}}{\text{mm}^3}\right] \Big/ \left[\frac{\text{Energy}}{\text{Photon}}\right] = \frac{\text{Photons}}{\text{mm}^3}$$

What is the energy of one photon?

The energy of a photon, denoted as E_1, is given by hf where h is Planck's constant and f is the frequency of the light. The frequency is related to the wavelength λ through the equation $f\lambda = c$, where c is the speed of light. By rearranging we get $f = c/\lambda$.

$$E_1 = hf = \frac{hc}{\lambda}.$$

All the work will be done in the mks (meter-kilogram-sec) system. All non-mks units will have to be converted. We also need to know the following 3 things:

    a) 1 nm = 10^{-9} m

    b) $c = 3 \times 10^8$ m/sec

    c) $h = 6.625 \times 10^{-34}$ joule-sec.

$$E_1 = \frac{hc}{\lambda} = \frac{\left(6.625 \times 10^{-34} \text{ joule-sec}\right)\left(3 \times 10^8 \text{ m/sec}\right)}{\left(4.88 \times 10^{-7} \text{ m}\right)}$$

$$E_1 = 4.1 \times 10^{-19} \text{ joules}$$

42

The diagram indicates the situation. The beam traveling with velocity c has a flux of 20 watts/cm² . Call this flux F.

$$F = \frac{Power}{area} = \frac{Energy}{(area)(time)}$$

If we want the energy enclosed in 1 mm³ of the beam we have $\varepsilon_T = FAt$ where A is the arc of one surface of the 1 mm³ volume, and t is the time required for the beam to travel 1mm.

$$t = \frac{1mm}{c} = \frac{(.001\ m)}{\left(3 \times 10^8\ m/sec\right)} = 3.3 \times 10^{-12}\ sec.$$

$$F = \left(20\ \frac{watts}{cm^2}\right)\left(\frac{1\ cm^2}{1 \times 10^{-4} m^2}\right) = 20 \times 10^4\ \frac{watts}{m^2} = 20 \times 10^4\ \frac{joules}{m^2 - sec}$$

$$\varepsilon_T = \left(20 \times 10^4\ \frac{joules}{m^2 - sec}\right)\left(1 \times 10^{-6}\ m^2\right)\left(3.3 \times 10^{-12}\ sec\right)$$

$$\varepsilon_T = 6.6 \times 10^{-13}\ joules$$

To obtain the number of photons per mm³, we just calculate

$$\frac{\varepsilon_T}{E_1} = \frac{6.6 \times 10^{-13}}{4.1 \times 10^{-19}} = 1.6 \times 10^6.$$

Therefore there are 1.6×10^6 photons/mm³ .

THE PHOTOELECTRIC EFFECT

● **PROBLEM 3-9**

Ultraviolet light of 300 nm wavelength strikes the surface of a material which has a work function of 2.0 eV. What is the velocity of the electrons emitted from the surface?

Solution: Using the equation $c = \nu\lambda$, where ν and λ represent the frequency and wavelength of light, respectively, and c is the speed of light,

$$\nu = \frac{c}{\lambda} = \frac{3 \times 10^8\ m/sec}{3 \times 10^{-7}\ m} = 10^{15}\ sec^{-1} = 10^{15}\ Hz\ .$$

Converting the work function of 2.0 eV to 3.2×10^{-19} J by use of the relationship 1 eV = 1.6×10^{-19} J, and using K.E. = $h\nu$ - w , we have

$$K.E. = \left(6.63 \times 10^{-34}\ J/sec\right)\left(10^{15}\ sec^{-1}\right) - 3.2 \times 10^{-19}\ J$$

$$= 3.43 \times 10^{-19}\ J$$

where h is Planck's constant.
    Now the velocity can be found by using

$$K.E. = \tfrac{1}{2}\ mv^2\ ,$$

where the mass of an electron, m, is 9.1×10^{-31} kg. Hence,

$$3.43 \times 10^{-19}\ J = \tfrac{1}{2} \cdot \left(9.1 \times 10^{-31}\ kg\right) v^2$$

and so,

$$v = 0.87 \times 10^6\ m/sec.$$

Photoelectrons of kinetic energy 2 eV are emitted from a cesium surface; the work function $\left(\text{or } W_f\right) = 1.8$ eV. What is the longest wavelength of light which could have produced such emission?

Solution: The photoelectric effect is produced when a metal surface is bombarded by photons. The photon possessing energy $hf = h\dot{c}/\lambda$ (where h is Plancks' constant, and f, λ, and c are the frequency, wavelength, and speed of light, respectively) imparts energy to the metal's electrons. If the photon energy just equals the energy needed to free the electron from the surface we term it the work function energy W_f.

This is the minimum photonic energy needed to remove the electron. The frequency of the photon needed for W_f is termed the threshold frequency f_0, W_f is given by the equation $W_f = hf_0$.

If the incoming photon has more energy than W_f, the electron ejected possesses kinetic energy as well. The following equation expresses these facts:

$$E_{Photon} = hf = \frac{hc}{\lambda} = W_f + E_k \text{ ,}$$

where E_k represents the kinetic energy of the emitted electron.

In this problem, $E_k = 2eV$ and $W_f = 1.8eV$. From the equation $E_{Photon} = hf = \frac{hc}{\lambda}$, it is apparent that the longest wavelength (λ) of light corresponds to the smallest incoming photon energy required for electron ejection at $E_k = 2eV$.

$$\frac{hc}{\lambda} = \left(W_f + E_k\right) \Rightarrow \lambda = \frac{hc}{\left(W_f + E_k\right)} \text{ .}$$

Substituting for h and c,

$$\lambda = \frac{(6.625 \times 10^{-34} \text{ joule-sec})(3 \times 10^{8} \text{ m/sec})}{\left(W_f + E_k\right)}$$

$$= \frac{1.99 \times 10^{-25} \text{ j-m}}{W_f + E_k}$$

therefore, $W_f + E_k = 3.8$ eV and 1 eV $= 1.6 \times 10^{-19}$ joules;

$$W_f + E_k = (3.8eV)\left(\frac{1.6 \times 10^{-19} \text{ joules}}{1eV}\right) = 6.08 \times 10^{-19} \text{ joules.}$$

$$\lambda = \frac{(1.99 \times 10^{-25} \text{ j-m})}{\left(6.08 \times 10^{-19} \text{ j}\right)} = 3.27 \times 10^{-7} \text{ m}$$

$1nm = 10^{-9}$ m.

Therefore

$$\lambda = 327 \text{ nm .}$$

THE POYNTING VECTOR

A light wave is traveling in glass of index of refraction 1.5. If the amplitude of the electric field of the lightwave is 100 volts/meter, what is the magnitude of the Poynting vector?

Solution: One of the important characteristics of an electromagnetic wave is that it can transport energy from point to point. The rate of energy flow per unit area in a plane electromagnetic wave can be described by the vector $\vec{S}$ called the Poynting vector. We define $\vec{S}$ as

$$\vec{S} = \frac{1}{\mu_0} \vec{E} \times \vec{B} \tag{1}$$

where $\mu_0 = 4\pi \times 10^{-7}$ wb/amp-m, $\vec{E}$ and $\vec{B}$ refer to the instantaneous values of the electric and magnetic fields respectively, and S is given in units of watts/meters^2. In addition, we know that the magnitudes of the electric and magnetic fields are related by the following expression when the wave is traveling in a vacuum:

$$E = VB \tag{2}$$

where V is the speed of the wave.

In the given problem, we have light traveling through glass of index of refraction 1.5. The speed of the light wave is thus reduced and is found from the definition of the index of refraction:

$$n = \frac{c}{V} = \frac{\text{speed of light in a vacuum}}{\text{speed of light in given medium}} ;$$

hence,

$$V = \frac{c}{n} = \frac{3 \times 10^8 \text{ m/sec}}{1.5} = 2 \times 10^8 \text{ m/sec} .$$

We are given the amplitude of the electric field, so we can find the amplitude of the magnetic field:

$$E = 100 \text{ volts/meter.}$$

Using equation (2), where V is now the speed of the wave in glass, we have

$$B = \frac{E}{V} = \frac{100}{2 \times 10^8} = 50 \times 10^{-8} = 5 \times 10^{-7} .$$

Then the magnitude of the Poynting vector is given by

$$S = \frac{1}{\mu_0} EB$$

$$= \left(\frac{1}{4\pi \times 10^{-7}} \right)(100)\left(5 \times 10^{-7} \right)$$

$$S = 39.8 \text{ w/m}^2 .$$

It is important to note that this is the maximum value, since the magnitude of E was given as a maximum value ("amplitude" implies E_{max}). To obtain the average value of S, we use $\bar{S} = \frac{1}{2\mu_0} E_{max} B_{max}$, the magnitude of the Poynting vector then becomes $S = 19.9 \text{ w/m}^2 .$

The solar constant, the power due to radiation from the sun falling on the earth's atmosphere, is 1.35 kW·m^{-2}. What are the magnitudes of $\vec{E}$ and $\vec{B}$ for the electromagnetic waves emitted from the sun at the position of the earth?

Solution: Starting with the electromagnetic waves at the earth, it is possible to determine $\vec{E}$ and $\vec{B}$ by two methods. (a) The Poynting vector

$$\vec{S} = \frac{1}{\mu_0} \vec{E} \times \vec{B}$$

gives the energy flow across any section of the field per unit area per unit time.

Here, $\vec{E}$ and $\vec{B}$ are the instantaneous electric field and magnetic induction, respectively, at a point of space, and μ_0 is the permeability of free space. If we approximate the sun as a point source of light, then we realize that it radiates electromagnetic waves in all directions uniformly. However, the distance between earth and sun is very large, and we may approximate the electromagnetic waves arriving at the surface of the earth as plane waves. For this type of wave, $\vec{E}$ and $\vec{B}$ are perpendicular. Thus

$$\left| \vec{S} \right| = \left| \frac{1}{\mu_0} \vec{E} \times \vec{B} \right| = EH = 1.35 \times 10^3 \text{ W·m}^{-2}$$

where we have used the fact that $|\vec{B}| = |\vec{H}\mu_0|$ in vacuum. ($\vec{H}$ is the magnetic field intensity.)

But in the electromagnetic field in vacuum, $\epsilon_0 E^2 = \mu_0 H^2$, or $E\sqrt{\epsilon_0/\mu_0} = H$. Then

$$E \times \sqrt{\epsilon_0/\mu_0} \; E = EH = 1.35 \times 10^3 \text{ W·m}^{-2}$$

or

$$E^2 = \sqrt{\mu_0/\epsilon_0} \times 1.35 \times 10^3 \text{ W·m}^{-2}$$

$$= 377 \; \Omega \times 1.35 \times 10^3 \text{ W·m}^{-2} . \quad [\text{where, } \Omega = \text{ohm}]$$

$$E = \sqrt{5.09 \times 10^5} \text{ V·m}^{-1} = 0.71 \times 10^3 \text{ V·m}^{-1} .$$

Similarly,

$$B = \mu_0 H = \frac{\mu_0 \left(1.35 \times 10^3 \text{ W·m}^{-2} \right)}{E} .$$

Substituting for μ_0 and E,

$$B = \frac{\left(4\pi \times 10^{-7} \text{ Weber·A}^{-1}\text{·m}^{-1} \right) \left(1.35 \times 10^3 \text{ W·m}^{-2} \right)}{.71 \times 10^3 \text{ V·m}^{-1}}$$

$$B = 2.39 \times 10^{-6} \frac{\text{Weber·W·A}^{-1}\text{·m}^{-2}}{V} .$$

But $1 \text{ W} = 1 \text{ J·s}^{-1}$ and $1 \text{ V} = 1 \text{ J·C}^{-1}$ [C $\equiv$ coulomb]

$$B = 2.39 \times 10^{-6} \frac{\text{Weber·J·s}^{-1}\text{·A}^{-1}\text{·m}^{-2}}{J\text{·C}^{-1}}$$

since $1 \text{ amp(A)} = 1 \text{ cs}^{-1}$ $\qquad B = 2.39 \times 10^{-6} \text{ Weber·m}^{-2} .$

(b) The electromagnetic energy density (or, energy per unit volume) in an electromagnetic field in vacuum is $\mu_0 H^2 = \epsilon_0 E^2$. The energy falling on $1\ m^2$ of the earth's atmosphere in 1 second is the energy initially contained in a cylinder $1\ m^2$ in cross section and 3×10^8 m in length; all this energy travels to the end of the cylinder in the space of 1 second. Hence the energy density near the earth is

$$\mu_0 H^2 = \epsilon_0 E^2 = \frac{1.35 \times 10^3\ \text{W}\cdot\text{m}^{-2}}{3 \times 10^8\ \text{m}\cdot\text{s}^{-1}}$$

Here, ϵ_0 is the permittivity of free space.

$$E^2 = \frac{1.35 \times 10^3\ \text{W}\cdot\text{m}^{-2}}{8.85 \times 10^{-12}\ \text{c}^2\cdot\text{N}^{-1}\cdot\text{m}^{-2} \times 3 \times 10^8\ \text{m}\cdot\text{s}^{-1}}$$

$$E^2 = \frac{1.35 \times 10^7}{26.55}\ \frac{\text{W}}{\text{c}^2\cdot\text{N}^{-1}\cdot\text{m}\cdot\text{s}^{-1}} .$$

But $1\ \text{W} = 1\ \text{J}\cdot\text{s}^{-1} = 1\ \text{N}\cdot\text{m}\cdot\text{s}^{-1}$; therefore,

$$E^2 = 5.085 \times 10^5\ \text{N/c}^2\text{N}^{-1} = 5.085 \times 10^5\ \text{N}^2/\text{c}^2$$

or

$$E = .71 \times 10^3\ \text{N}\cdot\text{c}^{-1} = .71 \times 10^3\ \text{V}\cdot\text{m}^{-1} .$$

Also,

$$\mu_0 H^2 = \frac{B^2}{\mu_0} = \frac{1.35 \times 10^3\ \text{W}\cdot\text{m}^{-2}}{3 \times 10^8\ \text{m}\cdot\text{s}^{-1}}$$

or

$$B^2 = \frac{4\pi \times 10^{-7}\ \text{N}\cdot\text{A}^{-2} \times 1.35 \times 10^3\ \text{W}\cdot\text{m}^{-2}}{3 \times 10^8\ \text{m}\cdot\text{s}^{-1}}$$

$$B = 2.36 \times 10^{-6}\ \text{Wb}\cdot\text{m}^{-2} .$$

CERENKOV RADIATION

Cerenkov radiation can be loosely compared to the shock wave caused by a speed boat traveling in shallow water. If the boat moves at 60 km/hr and if the bow wave has an apex angle of $30°$, what is h, the depth of the water?

(Phase velocity of water waves $v_{ph} = \sqrt{gh}$)

Solution: From an appropriate optics text we find that the angle of Cerenkov radiation is given by

$$\sin \theta = \frac{c}{nv} \tag{1}$$

where θ is the limiting angle of the cone of Cerenkov radiation, c is the velocity of light, n is the index of refraction of the medium, and v is the velocity of light in the medium of the particle emitting the radiation. c/n then represents the phase velocity of light in the medium. We can then relate this to the bow wave of a speed boat, where θ will represent the angle that the edge of the bow wave makes with the direction of motion of the speed boat; v is the velocity of the speed boat and c/n is the phase velocity of the water waves. Now the phase velocity of the water waves is found to depend on the depth of the water in which the waves are produced and is given in this problem as

$$v_{ph} = \sqrt{gh}.$$ (2)

Converting 60 km/hr to m/s,

$$\frac{60 \text{ km}}{\text{hr}} \times \frac{10^3 \text{ m}}{\text{km}} \times \frac{1 \text{ hr}}{3600 \text{ sec}}$$

$$= 16.66 \text{ m/s};$$ (3)

we get from (1) and (2),

$$\sin \theta = \frac{\sqrt{gh}}{v}.$$ (4)

Substituting for θ, g, and v,

$$\sin 30^\circ = \frac{1}{2} = \sqrt{\frac{9.8 \text{ h}}{16.66}}$$ (5)

$$h = \frac{(16.66)^2}{4 \times 9.8} = 7 \text{ m}.$$ (6)

● **PROBLEM 3-14**

A source emitting waves travels through a medium with a velocity of v, which is greater than the velocity V with which a wave disturbance travels in the medium. a) Apply Huygen's principle to show that a conical wave surface is produced. b) Illustrate with a diagram. c) Find an expression for the angle between the two "bow" waves formed. d) Given the relativity constraint that no body can move at speeds exceeding c, the speed of light, is this concept of any physical significance for light?

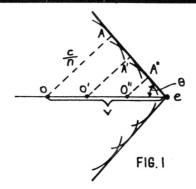

FIG. 1

Solution: Looking at Figure 1 we start with the source of wave motion at O which proceeds through O', O", and e with a velocity v. While at O the source emits waves which travel with velocity $V = c/n$ spherically from O. While at O' and O" and in between the source also emits waves which travel with velocity V spherically from O' and O", respectively. When the source reaches e, the waves emitted from O will have reached A, those waves emitted from O' will have reached A', those waves emitted from O" will have reached A", and those waves emitted from e will still be at e. From a Huygen's construction of the resulting wave fronts, the line $\overline{AA'A''e}$ represents the resulting wave progressing through the medium. If we consider the medium to be three dimensional and isotropic, then the wave front will be that cone resulting from a rotation of the line $\overline{AA'A''e}$ about the axis represented by the direction of the velocity.

Since $\overline{OA} \perp \overline{AA'A''e}$, triangle OAe is a right triangle and

$$\text{Sin } \theta = V/v$$ (1)

or the total angle of the cone is then

$$2\theta = 2 \sin^{-1} V/v .\tag{2}$$

As we developed equation (1), we said that the wave propagation velocity was $V = c/n$; or for light, the phase velocity of electromagnetic radiation in the medium. So we can also write equation (1) as

$$\sin \theta = \frac{c}{nv} .\tag{3}$$

Then, defining

$$v/c = \beta , \text{ equation (3) becomes}$$

$$\sin \theta = \frac{1}{n\beta} .\tag{4}$$

Since the speed of light is reduced in a medium to $V = c/n$, $n > 1$, it is indeed possible to create these wave fronts. This type of radiation is known as Cerenkov radiation and is used extensively in high energy particle physics to measure the velocity of particles.

TOTAL REFLECTION OF LIGHT

● **PROBLEM** 3-15

A beam of light is totally reflected in a 45-90-45 degree glass prism ($n = 1.5$) as shown in the diagram. The wavelength of the light is 5000Å. (a) What is the distance into air at which the amplitude of the external wave is e^{-1} of its value at the surface? (b) What is the ratio of the intensity of the external wave at a distance of 1 mm to that at the surface?

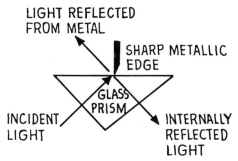

LIGHT REFLECTED
FROM METAL

SHARP METALLIC
EDGE

GLASS
PRISM

INCIDENT
LIGHT

INTERNALLY
REFLECTED
LIGHT

Solution: (a) From the electromagnetic theory of reflection and refraction the expression for the amplitude of the transmitted wave is known to be of the form

$$Ae^{-\alpha y}e^{i(kx - \omega t)}\tag{1}$$

where

$$\alpha = k \sqrt{\frac{\sin^2 \theta}{n^2} - 1} ;\tag{2}$$

k represents the angular wavenumber $2\pi/\lambda$, and ω represents the angular frequency. The amplitude will thus be reduced by a factor of e^{-1} if $\alpha y = 1$, or $y = \alpha^{-1}$. Substitution of $k = 2\pi/5 \times 10^{-4}$ mm, $\theta = 45°$, and $n = (1.5)^{-1}$ (the index of refraction of the second medium (air) relative to the first), into equation (2) gives

$$\alpha = \left(\frac{2\pi}{5 \times 10^{-4} \text{ mm}}\right) \sqrt{\frac{\sin^2(45°)}{\frac{1}{(1.5)^2}} - 1}$$

49

$$= \frac{2\pi}{5 \times 10^{-4} \text{mm}} \quad \sqrt{1.125 - 1}$$

Hence, $y = \alpha^{-1} = \dfrac{5 \times 10^{-4} \text{ mm}}{2\pi\sqrt{1.125 - 1}}$

$$y = 2.3 \times 10^{-4} \text{ mm}.$$

(b) The intensity of a wave is proportional to the square of the amplitude; hence if R represents the ratio of the intensity at $^{\cdots} = 1$ mm to that at $y = 0$,

$$R = \frac{e^{-2\alpha(1 \text{ mm})}}{e^{-2\alpha(0 \text{ mm})}} = e^{-2\alpha(1 \text{ mm})};$$

using $\alpha = \left(2.3 \times 10^{-4}\right)^{-1}$ from part (a),

$$R = e^{-8.7 \times 10^{3}}; \text{ rewriting in powers of ten, i.e.,}$$

setting

$$e^{-8.7 \times 10^{3}} = 10^{x} \tag{3}$$

and solving for x by taking the natural logarithm of both sides of equation (3),

$$x = \frac{-8.7 \times 10^{3}}{\ln 10} \approx -3800 ,$$

so

$$R = 10^{-3800}$$

(a considerable reduction in intensity).

THE LORENTZ TRANSFORMATIONS

• **PROBLEM** 3-16

Show how the Lorentz transformations correctly describe the experimentally demonstrated fact that the same light pulse is seen to spread out in a spherical wave front for two observers moving relative to each other.

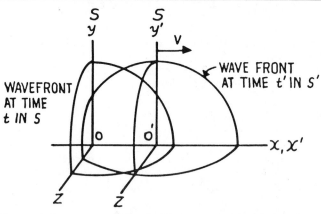

Solution: We must base our calculations on Einstein's postulates; namely,
   1) All laws of physics, including the Maxwell equations, are invariant in all inertial reference frames.
   2) The speed of light, {c}, measured in any inertial frame will be

invariant.

In the following diagram, at time $t = 0$ in the S frame and time $t' = 0$ in the S' frame the origins of both coincide and a light pulse is emitted at that origin. The S' frame is moving with velocity $\vec{v}$ to the right.

An observer in either frame sees his frame as inertial. If a pulse of light is emitted from the origin of an inertial reference frame S_i at time $t_i = 0$, at some later time t_i the original wave front of the pulse will be a spherical shell whose radius equals ct_i, where $c =$ the speed of light. Using analytic geometry we know a sphere is represented in Cartesian coordinates by $x_i^2 + y_i^2 + z_i^2 = r^2$ in this S_i frame. Thus by equating we have $x_i^2 + y_i^2 + z_i^2 = c^2 t_i^2$.

Now we apply this to our situation described by the diagram. The S frame has coordinates (x,y,z,t) and the S' frame has coordinates (x',y',z',t').

We have just stated that both frames are inertial, so in the S frame,

$$x^2 + y^2 + z^2 = c^2 t^2, \tag{1}$$

and in the S' frame

$$x'^2 + y'^2 + z'^2 = c^2 t'^2. \tag{2}$$

[Note that the speed of light c is the same in both frames]. But how is it possible that two observers who are at the same place when a light pulse is emitted and who then travel apart at some constant speed v later both observe the light wave front to be a sphere with themselves at the center?

This would be geometrically impossible if the two observers meant the same thing when they specified the time at which they located the wave front. If the two observers' ideas of when two events are simultaneous do not coincide, this paradoxical result can be accounted for. Equations (1) and (2) can be written in the form

$$c^2 t^2 - (x^2 + y^2 + z^2) = 0$$

$$c^2 t'^2 - (x'^2 + y'^2 + z'^2) = 0$$

which implies that the value of this combination of time and coordinates has the same value, zero, in all inertial coordinate systems whose origins coincide at time zero.

The Lorentz transformations are given by

$$t' = \gamma\left[t - \frac{xv}{c^2}\right]$$

$$x' = \gamma\left[x - vt\right]$$

$$y' = y$$

$$z' = z.$$

The inverse transformations are given by

$$t = \gamma\left[t' + \frac{x'v}{c^2}\right]$$

$$x = \gamma\left[x' + vt'\right]$$

$$y = y'$$

$$z = z'.$$

where $\gamma = \dfrac{1}{\sqrt{1 - v^2/c^2}}$ and the primed frame is moving to the right, which we have.

We want to show that by using these transformations on the S frame we get the same kind of spherical wave form in the S' system. In the S' frame, $x^2 + y^2 + z^2 = c^2t^2$. By substituting in the inverse transformations we get

$$\gamma^2[x' + vt']^2 + y'^2 + z'^2 = c^2\gamma^2\left[t' + \frac{x'v}{c^2}\right]^2 .$$

By expanding the above equation, we now have

$$\gamma^2[x'^2 + 2x'vt' + v^2t'^2] + y'^2 + z'^2 = c^2\gamma^2\left[t'^2 + 2t'\frac{x'v}{c^2} + \frac{x'^2v^2}{c^4}\right].$$

Now by moving the y'^2 and z'^2 terms to the other side of the above equation, and regrouping γ^2 terms we have

$$\gamma^2\left[x'^2 + 2x'vt' + v^2t'^2 - c^2t'^2 - 2t'x'v - \frac{x'^2v^2}{c^2}\right] = -y'^2 - z'^2 .$$

We can simplify this equation to yield the following:

$$\gamma^2\left[x'^2 + v^2t'^2 - c^2t'^2 - \frac{x'^2v^2}{c^2}\right] = -y'^2 - z'^2 .$$

Within the brackets, the x'^2 and t'^2 terms can be factored out

$$\gamma^2\left[x'^2\left(1 - \frac{v^2}{c^2}\right) + t'^2(v^2 - c^2)\right] = -y'^2 - z'^2$$

$$1 - \frac{v^2}{c^2} = \frac{c^2 - v^2}{c^2} = \frac{1}{c^2}(c^2 - v^2) = -\frac{1}{c^2}(v^2 - c^2).$$

By making this substitution we have

$$\gamma^2\left[-\frac{x'^2}{c^2}(v^2 - c^2) + t'^2(v^2 - c^2)\right] = -y'^2 - z'^2 .$$

Now factoring out $(v^2 - c^2)$ gives the result

$$\gamma^2(v^2 - c^2)\left[t'^2 - \frac{x'^2}{c^2}\right] = -y'^2 - z'^2$$

$$\gamma^2 = \frac{1}{\left(1 - \frac{v^2}{c^2}\right)} = \frac{c^2}{c^2 - v^2} = -\frac{c^2}{v^2 - c^2} .$$

Substituting this value for γ^2 into the above equation yields

$$-\frac{(v^2 - c^2)}{(v^2 - c^2)} c^2\left[t'^2 - \frac{x'^2}{c^2}\right] = -y'^2 - z'^2$$

or,

$$- c^2t'^2 + x'^2 = -y'^2 - z'^2$$

$$x'^2 + y'^2 + z'^2 = c^2t'^2 .$$

This was the equation that the S' observer used to describe his view of the light pulse. It may seem a bit strange that both see spherical waves, but the Lorentz transformations show this to be true. The acceptance of this comes with the acceptance of the fact that time and space are dependent on the particular inertial frame one is in.

CHAPTER 4

RECTILINEAR PROPAGATION OF LIGHT

THE PINHOLE CAMERA

If the sensitive plate of a pinhole camera is 20 cm from the pinhole, what should be the diameter of the pinhole, according to Abney's formula?

Assume that the photographic film used has its highest sensitivity at a wavelength of 450 nm.

Solution: In essence, a pinhole camera can be described as a Fresnel lens, such that as seen by the photographic film the pinhole has a proper fractional Fresnel zone to provide focusing. An equation which can be used in this problem is

Abney's formula, which is as follows:

$$D = 1.9 \sqrt{a'\lambda} \qquad (1)$$

where a' is the distance from the pinhole to the film, λ is the wavelength for which the film used has its highest sensitivity and D is the diameter of the pinhole. Hence, substituting the given values for a' and λ into equation (1) gives the result:

$$D = 1.9 \sqrt{.20 \times 450 \times 10^{-9} m} =$$

$$5.7 \times 10^{-4} m = 0.57 \text{ mm}$$

● **PROBLEM** 4-2

An object 6 inches high is placed in front of a pinhole camera at a distance of 6 feet from the aperture. What is the size of the inverted image on the ground glass screen if the length of the camera-box is 1 foot?

Solution: From the figure, it can be seen from the two

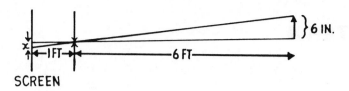

SCREEN

similar triangles that the following relation is valid:

$$\frac{6 \text{ ft}}{6 \text{ in}} = \frac{1 \text{ ft}}{x}$$

Hence, x = 1 in. and so, the size of the inverted image on the screen is 1 in.

THE ILLUMINATION OF LIGHT

PROBLEM 4-3

An opaque globe, 1 foot in diameter, is interposed between an arc lamp and a white wall. If the wall is 12 feet from the lamp and the center of the globe is 3 feet from the lamp, what is the area of the shadow on the wall?

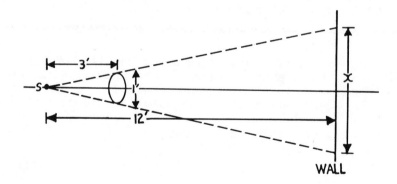

WALL

Solution: Assume that the source of light given in this problem is a point source. In this problem, the size of the shadow on the wall is proportional to the distance from the wall to the source of light. From the similar triangles shown in the figure, the following relation holds true:

$$\frac{12 \text{ ft}}{x} = \frac{3 \text{ ft}}{1 \text{ ft}}$$

Solving for the diameter of the shadow, x, gives

$$x = 4 \text{ ft.}$$

The area of the shadow is $= \pi R^2$, where R represents the radius of the shadow. Then, the area of the shadow =

$$\left(\frac{4 \text{ ft}}{2}\right)^2 \cdot \pi = 4\pi \text{ ft}^2 \cong 12.57 \text{ ft}^2$$

Light from the sun is reflected on a tiny plane mirror
measuring 2 mm x 2 mm in size. What is the shape
of the illuminated area on a screen (a) 1 cm away
and (b) 2 m away from the mirror?

Solution: When light is reflected by a small mirror onto
a screen, the shape of the illuminated area of the screen
depends upon the distance between the mirror and the screen.
If the distance is small, relative to the size of the mirror, then the shape of the illuminated area on the screen
will resemble that of the mirror. If the screen is far
away from the mirror then the illuminated area becomes circular in shape.

   In this problem, the mirror measures 2 mm x 2 mm
in size. The illuminated area on the screen at a distance of 1 cm will be rectangular in shape. In order
for its shape to be that of an exact square, the light
would have to be reflected exactly perpendicularly to
the mirror. If the mirror is moved to a distance of 2
meters away from the screen, the illuminated area on
the screen will be circular in shape.

● **PROBLEM** 4-5

What is the apparent angular elevation of the sun when a
telephone pole 15 feet high casts a shadow 20 feet long on
a horizontal pavement?

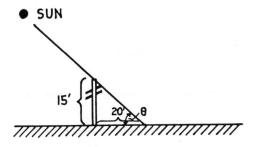

Solution: This problem can be solved trigonometrically, by
examining the figure. Given the height of the pole and the
length of the shadow which it casts, the angle of elevation
of the sun, θ, can be found from the following relation (see
figure):

$$\tan \theta = \frac{15}{20} \quad ,$$

hence, $\theta = \tan^{-1}\left(\frac{3}{4}\right) = 36°52'12".$

VERGENCE

What are the vergences for light at points at the following distances from a light source: 100 cm, 33.3 cm, 400 mm, 25 cm, 0.50 m, and 100 mm?

Solution: Vergence is defined to be the reciprocal of the distance from a reference point to a point of vergence. In this problem the point of vergence is the light source and the reference point is a point that is a given distance away from the source. The vergence is positive when the rays of light are diverging, and it is negative for converging rays of light. The vergence of light at a given distance from the source is equal to the curvature of the wave front at that distance from the source.

Using the data in this problem, the vergence can be calculated in terms of diopters, which are equivalent to units of m^{-1}. Thus, the distances are converted to meters before taking their reciprocals. The following table indicates the results:

Given distance	100 cm	33.3 cm	400 mm	25 cm	0.50 m	100 mm
distance in m	1.00 m	0.33 m	0.40 m	0.25 m	0.50 m	0.10 m
vergence (diopters)	1	3	2.5	4	2	10

THE UMBRA AND PENUMBRA

Discuss the type of shadow formed by an extended source.

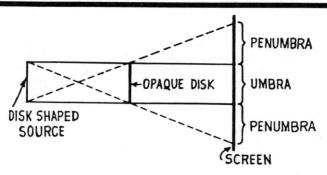

56

Solution: If the source is of finite size instead of being a point, the shadow is divided into a central part, called the umbra, which is uniformly dark, and a peripheral part called the penumbra, which is graded from dark at its inner edge to bright at its outer edge, where it becomes equal in brightness to the part of the screen that falls outside of the shadow. In the figure, the source is a bright disk of finite size, and the object is an opaque disk which throws its shadow on the screen. The umbra of the shadow is disk-shaped, and the penumbra is annular (ring-shaped).

● **PROBLEM** 4-8

Describe the two portions of the shadow of an object illuminated by a source of small dimensions and explain what relationship they have to partial and total solar eclipses.

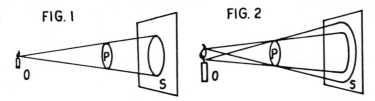

FIG. I   FIG. 2

Solution: Probably one of the first optical phenomena to be noted was that the shadow of an object illuminated by a source of small dimensions has the same shape as the object and that the edges of the shadow are the extensions of straight lines from the source tangent to the edges of the object. Apart from diffraction effects, the formation of shadows can be treated satisfactorily in terms of a ray picture.

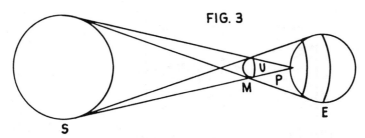

FIG. 3

Point 0 in Fig. 1 represents a point source of light. That is, the dimensions of the source are small in comparison with other distances involved. S is a screen and P is a circular obstacle between the source and the screen. The area of the screen, bounded by rays from the source tangent to the edges of the obstacle, is called the geometrical shadow of the obstacle.

If the source is not sufficiently small to be considered a point, as in Fig. 2, the shadow consists of two portions. The region behind the obstacle which receives no light from the source is called the umbra. This is surrounded by the penumbra, within which a part of the source is screened by the obstacle. The fuzzy appearance of the edges of a shadow cast by a frosted bulb incandescent lamp is due to the penumbra. An observer within the umbra cannot see any part of the source, one within the penumbra can see a portion of the source, while from points outside the penumbra the entire source can be seen.

The phenomenon of a partial or total solar eclipse is caused by the passage of a portion of the earth's surface within the penumbra or umbra of the shadow of the moon, cast by the sun. In Fig. 3 (obviously not to scale) S, M, and E represent the sun, moon, and earth, respectively. The moon's shadow in space consists of a conical umbra U surrounded by a penumbra P. When a portion of the umbra near the tip sweeps over the earth's surface, the solar eclipse will be total for all observers within it. Within a band on either side lying in the penumbra, the eclipse will be only a partial one. Eclipses of the moon arise in a similar manner when the relative positions of sun, earth, and moon are such that the moon lies within the shadow of the earth.

● **PROBLEM** 4-9

An opaque circular disk is interposed between a screen and a luminous disk of greater size. The straight line joining the centers of the disks is perpendicular to the faces of the disks and to the plane of the screen. The radius of the luminous disk is r, the distance between the disks is d, and the distance of the screen from the opaque disk is X. Show that the width of the penumbra ring projected on the screen is equal to 2rX/d, and that it is therefore independent of the diameter of the opaque object.

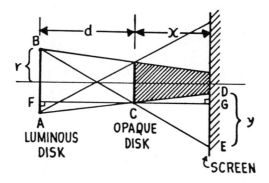

Solution: If a source is not sufficiently small to be considered a point, the shadow formed by the opaque disk consists of two portions, the umbra and the penumbra. The region behind the opaque disk which receives no light from the source is called the umbra, whereas the penumbra is the region surrounding the umbra within which a part of the source is screened by the opaque disk.

Consider the situation where the umbra reaches the screen and the penumbra is in the shape of a washer, as shown by the figure. The radius of the luminous disk is r.

Thus, the length of the line segment $\overline{AB}$ is 2r. In addition, it is also given that the distance between the two disks is d and the distance between the opaque disk and the screen is X. The width of the penumbra is represented as Y in the figure. Triangles ABC and CDE are similar, so the following relation is valid:

$$\overline{AB}/\overline{FC} = \overline{DE}/\overline{CG} \tag{1}$$

where $\overline{FC}$ is the altitude of triangle ABC and $\overline{CG}$ is the altitude of triangle CDE. Substituting the given data into equation (1) gives

$$\frac{2 \cdot r}{d} = \frac{Y}{X}$$

Hence

$$Y = \frac{2rX}{d} \; ,$$

and is independent of the size of the opaque disk.

Now, when the umbra does not reach the screen, the penumbra is just a dark circular disk that is not independent of the size of the opaque disk. Thus, the formula for the width of the penumbra is valid only when an umbra is present at the screen.

● **PROBLEM** 4-10

The diameters of the sun, earth, and moon are 864,000 miles, 7920 miles, and 2160 miles, respectively. A solar eclipse occurs at a moment when the earth to sun distance is 92,900,000 miles and the earth to moon distance is 226,000 miles. Compute the length of the conical umbra of the moon's shadow and compare it with the distance from the moon to the earth's surface.

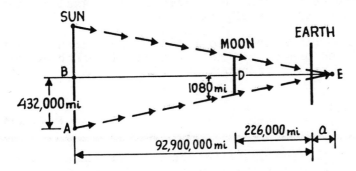

Solution: Triangles ABE and CDE, shown in the figure, are similar triangles. Thus, the following relation holds:

$$\frac{\overline{AB}}{\overline{BE}} = \frac{\overline{CD}}{\overline{DE}}$$

$\overline{AB}$ = the radius of the sun = $\frac{1}{2}$ (864,000 miles) = 432,000 miles;

$\overline{BE}$ = the distance from the earth to the sun + a (where a is shown in the figure) = 92,900,000 miles + a;

$\overline{CD}$ = the radius of the moon = $\frac{1}{2}$ (2160 miles) = 1080 miles;

$\overline{DE}$ = the length of the conical umbra = the distance from the moon to the earth + a = 226,000 miles + a.

Thus, the above relation becomes

$$\frac{432,000}{92,900,000 + a} = \frac{1080}{226,000 + a}$$

Cross-multiplying gives

$$(432,000)(226,000 + a) = (1080)(92,900,000 + a)$$

or,

$$97632 \times 10^6 + 432a \times 10^3 = 100332 \times 10^6 + 1080a.$$

Thus,

$$432 \times 10^3 - 1080)a = (100332 - 97632) \times 10^6$$

and so,

$$430920a = 2700 \times 10^6$$

or

$$a \cong 6266 \text{ miles.}$$

Hence, the length of the umbra = (226,000 + a) miles = 232,226 miles.

The difference between the length of the umbra and distance between the moon and earth is very small; thus, the earth is at the tip of the umbra.

Under the given conditions and if the earth is assumed to be flat, the shadow of the umbra on the earth would be a circle with a radius of about 29 miles.

ASTRONOMY

● **PROBLEM** 4-11

Artificial satellites can often be seen as bright objects high in the sky long after sunset. What must be the minimum altitude of a satellite moving above the earth's equator for it to be still visible directly overhead two hours after sunset?

Solution: Let the circle with center O shown in figure 1

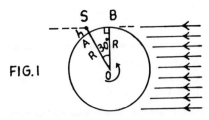

FIG.1

represent the plane of a section of the earth, parallel to the equator and viewed from the south pole. This means that the earth is rotating about its own axis in a counter-clockwise direction. Since it takes 24 hours to make one complete revolution, any point on the equator or on the circumference of this circle will rotate through

$$\frac{360°}{24 \text{ hours}}$$

or 15° each hour.

Assume that the observer is at point B at the time of sunset. (The sun's rays are falling on the earth from the right and are parallel.)

Two hours after sunset, the observer would have moved to the new position A and any point overhead would lie along the radius OA.

The minimum altitude at which a satellite would be visible is obtained by finding the point of intersection of the solar rays grazing the earth's surface at B and extended radius OA. This point is S and is a distance h above the observer at A.

Since the solar rays are perpendicular to the surface of the earth, the triangle OBS shown in figure 1 is a right triangle.

From figure 1,

$$\cos 30° = \frac{\overline{OB}}{\overline{OS}} = \frac{R}{R + h}$$

where R is the radius of the earth. Thus,

$$\frac{R + h}{R} = \frac{1}{\cos 30°}$$

or

$$1 + \frac{h}{R} = \frac{1}{\cos 30°} = \frac{1}{0.866} \cong 1.1547$$

Hence,

$$h = (1.1547 - 1)R = 0.1547R.$$

R is approximately equal to 6400 Km. Thus,

$$h = (0.1547)(6400 \text{ Km}) \cong 990 \text{ Km}.$$

61

With the aid of diagrams, explain why (a) a moon rising in the east at midnight cannot be a full moon and why (b) a new moon cannot be seen for long after dark.

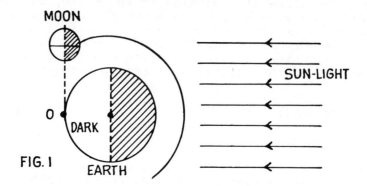

FIG. 1

Solution: (a) In order to understand why a moon rising in the east at midnight cannot be a full moon, refer to figure 1.

As depicted in figure 1, at midnight, the observer on the earth is at position O while the moon rising in the east is directly over point O. The part of the moon that is illuminated by sunlight and observed from O is the part of the figure which is shaded. This is clearly not a full moon. The rest of the moon that is illuminated by the sunlight is not seen from O. Hence, a full moon cannot be seen at midnight while rising in the east.

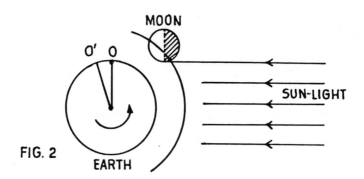

FIG. 2

(b) A new moon is only seen when the moon is close to a line joining the earth and sun. As shown in figure 2, a new moon is seen by the observer at O only at or near sunset. After darkness has arrived, the position of the observer has shifted to O' due to the rotation of the earth. The motion of the moon is negligible during this time and hence, the moon remains more or less stationary. The illuminated area of the moon is then no longer visible to the observer at O'.

CHAPTER 5

REFRACTION

HUYGEN'S PRINCIPLE

A wave front, which has amplitude A = 1 arbitrary unit, is advancing due East. Considering the obliquity factor, what are the amplitudes of secondary Huygen's wavelets, originating at a given point on the wave front and then traveling West, North West, North, North-East, and East?

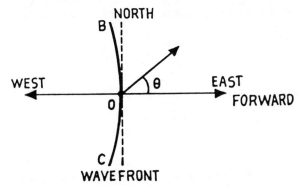

Solution: According to Huygen's principle, one regards each point on the wave front as the source of secondary wavelets. The secondary wavelets do not have uniform amplitude in all directions and to conform to the practical situation that no light goes in the opposite direction, one introduces the obliquity factor $(1 + \cos\theta)/2$ to be multiplied by the amplitude in order to calculate the amplitude in any direction making an angle θ with the forward direction.

Now let 0 be the source of wavelets on the original wave front BC, as shown in the figure.

For the secondary wavelet traveling West,

$$\theta = 180°$$

Thus,

$$\text{Amplitude} = \frac{1(1 + \cos 180°)}{2} = \frac{1}{2}(1 - 1) = 0$$

for the secondary wavelet traveling Northwest,

$$\theta = 135°$$

Thus,

$$\text{Amplitude} = 1(1 + \cos 135°)/2.$$

$$= 1(1 - .707)/2$$

$$= 0.15$$

For the secondary wavelets traveling north

$$\theta = 90°$$

Thus,

$$\text{Amplitude} = \frac{1(1 + \cos 90°)}{2}$$

$$= \frac{1(1 + 0)}{2}$$

$$= 0.5$$

For the secondary wavelets traveling north-east

$$\theta = 45°$$

Thus

$$\text{Amplitude} = 1(1 + \cos 45°)/2$$

$$= 1(1 + .707)/2$$

$$= 0.85$$

For the secondary wavelets traveling east

$$\theta = 0°$$

Thus,

$$\text{Amplitude} = \frac{1(1 + \cos 0°)}{2}$$

$$= 1(1 + 1)/2$$

$$= 1.$$

● **PROBLEM** 5-2

Explain how the earth's atmosphere alters light rays.

Solution: The velocity of light in all material substances is less than its velocity in free space and in a gas the

64

velocity decreases as the density increases. The density of
the earth's atmosphere is greatest at the surface of the
earth and decreases with increasing elevation. As a result,
light waves entering the earth's atmosphere are continuously
deviated as shown in Fig. 1. The line A-A' represents a

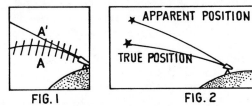

FIG. 1   FIG. 2

wave front in the light from the sun or a star. The density
of the air at the lower portion of the wave front is greater
than that at the upper portion. Hence the lower portion of
the wave always travels more slowly than the upper portion
and Huygens' construction leads to the shift in the direction
of the wave front as shown. An observer at the earth's surface sees the light source in the direction of the tangent to
the rays when they reach the earth and concludes that the object is nearer the zenith than its true position.

Rays entering the earth's atmosphere horizontally are
"lifted" by atmospheric refraction through about 0.5°. This
is very nearly equal to the angle subtended by the sun's disk,
so that when the sun appears to be just above the horizon at
sunrise or sunset, it is, geometrically, just below it.
Furthermore, since the sun requires about two minutes to move
(apparently) a distance equal to its own diameter, the day (at
the equator) is lengthened by about two minutes at both sunrise
and sunset. At higher latitudes the increase is even greater.
The necessary correction for atmospheric refraction must be
made by every navigator in the process of "shooting" the sun or
any other heavenly body.

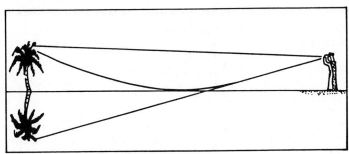

FIG. 3

The deviation of light by atmospheric refraction decreases
with increasing angle of elevation of the light above horizontal, falling to zero for light incident normally on the earth's
surface. Since rays from the upper portion of the sun's disk
are incident at a slightly greater angle than those from the
lower part, they are refracted to a smaller extent. This accounts for the slightly flattened appearance of the sun at sunset or sunrise, the lower portion being lifted more than the
upper.

Another phenomenon produced by atmospheric refraction is
the mirage, illustrated in Fig. 3. The conditions necessary

for its production require that the air nearer the surface of the ground shall be less dense than that above, a situation which is sometimes found over an area intensely heated by the sun's rays. Light from the upper portion of an object may reach the eye of an observer by the two paths shown in the figure, with the result that the object is seen in its actual position, together with its inverted image below it, as though a reflecting surface lay between the object and observer. The weary traveler in the desert interprets the reflecting surface as a body of water. This same phenomenon accounts for the "wet" appearance of the surface of a smooth highway under a hot sun, when a rise in the road ahead permits it to be seen at a glancing angle. Mirages are also produced when the reverse conditions arise , which is sometimes the case over

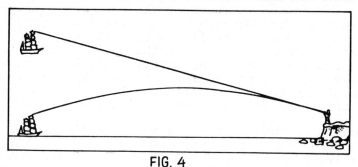

FIG. 4

large bodies of water. Objects at a distance appear to be lifted above their true positions. This phenomenon is known as "looming." (Fig. 4.)

SNELL'S LAW

● **PROBLEM** 5-3

At a water-glass interface let the upper medium be water of index 1.33 and the lower one to be glass of index 1.50.

(a) Let the incident ray, traveling from the water medium to the glass medium, be at an angle of 45° with the normal. What is the angle of refraction?

(b) Suppose the light is incident from below on the same boundary, but at an angle of incidence of 38.8°. Find the angle of refraction.

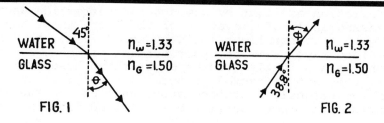

Solution: (a) To find the angle of refraction in the first case (see Fig. 1), one must apply the law of refraction (Snell's law),

$$n_w \cdot \sin 45° = n_G \cdot \sin \theta$$

to obtain $\theta = 38.8°$

(b) Again, one must apply the law of refraction to Fig. 2

$$n_G \cdot \sin 38.8° = n_w \cdot \sin \phi$$

to get $\phi = 45°$

Thus we see that if the direction of a ray of light is reversed, it will retrace its original path.

● **PROBLEM** 5-4

A light ray passes through two materials with the parameters indicated in figure 1.
Where does the light ray hit the screen?

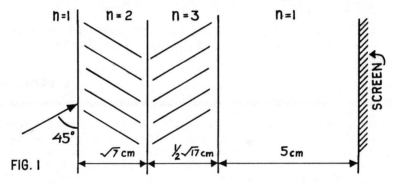

FIG. 1

Solution: Using the law of refraction we have:

$$n_A \cdot \sin 45° = n_B \cdot \sin \phi_B$$

$$\frac{1}{\sqrt{2}} = 2 \sin \phi_B$$

$$\phi_B = 21°$$

Similarly, $\phi_C = 14°$

Using $n_A \cdot \sin 45° = n_B \cdot \sin \phi_B = n_C \cdot \sin \phi_C = n_D \cdot \sin \phi_D$

$$n_A \cdot \sin 45° = n_D \cdot \sin \phi_D$$

$$\phi_D = 45°$$

Applying trigonometry, we have

$$a = \sqrt{7} \cdot \tan \phi_B = \sqrt{7} \cdot \tan 21°$$

$$b = \frac{1}{2} \sqrt{17} \cdot \tan \phi_C = \frac{1}{2} \sqrt{17} \cdot \tan 14°$$

$$c = 5 \cdot \tan\phi_D = 5 \cdot \tan 45°$$

and since $y = a + b + c$ then

$$y = \sqrt{7} \cdot \tan 21° + \frac{1}{2} \sqrt{17} \cdot \tan 14° + 5 \cdot \tan 45°$$

$$y = 1.0 + 0.5 + 5.0 = 6.5 \text{ cm}$$

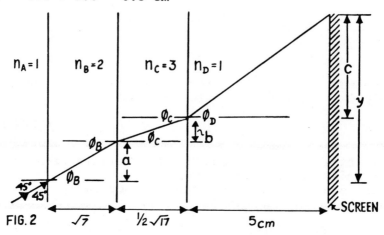

FIG. 2

So the light ray will strike the screen 6.5 cm above the level of the point where it initially struck the first surface.

● **PROBLEM** 5-5

A man standing symmetrically in front of a plane mirror with beveled edges can see three images of his eyes when he is 3 ft. from the mirror (see figure (A)). The mirror is silvered on the back, is 2½ feet wide, and is made of glass of refractive index 1.54. What is the angle of bevel of the edges?

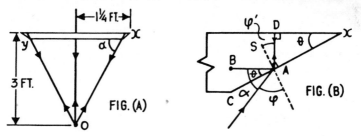

FIG. (A)   FIG. (B)

Solution: The man can only see an image of his eyes if light leaves them, strikes the mirror, and is reflected back along the same path. The central image is thus formed by light traversing the perpendicular from his eyes to the mirror. The outer images are formed by light striking the beveled edges at the point A (see figure (B)) at an angle of incidence φ such that the angle of refraction φ' makes the refracted ray strike the silvered surface normally (at point D in Fig. (B)). This must be the case if the ray of light is to leave the beveled edge by the same path with which it arrived. The angle φ' lies between the normal to the beveled edge and the normal to the back surface. Since ∢ SAX = 90° (see figure (B))

$$\varphi' + ∢ DAX = 90°$$

But ∢ DAX = 90° - θ because △ADX is a right triangle and all of

the internal angles of a triangle add up to $180°$.
Hence, $\varphi' = 90° - 90° + \theta = \theta$.

Draw BA, a construction line at A parallel to the back of the mirror. Angle BAC is also equal to θ.

But by Snell's Law, $n_1 \sin \varphi = n \sin \varphi'$, where n_1 is the refractive index of air ($n_1 = 1$) and n is that of glass. Then $\sin \varphi = n \sin \varphi' = n \sin \theta$. $\qquad$ (1)

Also, $\alpha = \theta + (90 - \varphi)$. (See figure (B)). Thus, $\varphi = 90 + \theta - \alpha = 90 - (\alpha - \theta)$. Now we can write (from equation (1)),

$$\sin[90 - (\alpha - \theta)] = n \sin \theta.$$

But $\sin(90 - \psi) = \cos \psi$ and therefore, we have
$$\cos(\alpha - \theta) = n \sin \theta.$$
By the trigonometric relation for the cosine of the difference of two angles, $\cos(\alpha - \theta) = \cos \alpha \cos \theta + \sin \alpha \sin \theta = n \sin \theta$. Dividing both sides by $\cos \theta$ gives
$$\cos \alpha + \sin \alpha \tan \theta = n \tan \theta$$

$$\cos \alpha = \tan \theta \, [n - \sin \alpha]$$

$$\tan \theta = \frac{\cos \alpha}{n - \sin \alpha} \qquad (2)$$

We need to find the angle θ. Looking at figure (A)),

$$\cos \alpha = \frac{1\frac{1}{4} \text{ ft.}}{\sqrt{(1\frac{1}{4} \text{ ft.})^2 + (3 \text{ ft.})^2}} = \frac{5}{13}$$

and

$$\sin \alpha = \frac{3 \text{ ft.}}{\sqrt{(1\frac{1}{4} \text{ ft.})^2 + (3 \text{ ft.})^2}} = \frac{12}{13}$$

or, alternatively, we know from the pythagorean triple 5,12,13 that if $\cos x = 5/13$ then $\sin x = 12/13$.

From equation (2),

$$\tan \theta = \frac{5/13}{1.54 - (12/13)} = 0.625.$$

Then θ, the angle of bevel, is given by

$$\theta = \arctan(.625)$$

or

$$\theta = 32°.$$

● **PROBLEM 5-6**

An optic fiber may have a core of dense flint, $n_1 = 1.66$, and a coating of crown glass, $n_2 = 1.52$. What is the highest angular aperture (half angle of the cone of light entering the fiber) for light that is transmitted through the straight fiber?

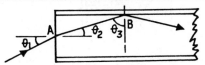

Solution: The figure shows a cross-section of the fiber; a ray is incident on the end of the fiber at point A with angle of incidence θ_1 , refracted into the fiber at angle θ_2 , and strikes the core-coating interface at point B at an angle θ_3 ; θ_3 must be equal to (or greater than) the critical angle for the ray to be totally reflected down the fiber. Note that if θ_1 is increased, θ_3 will decrease; thus, setting θ_3 equal to the critical angle and solving for θ_1 will yield the largest value of θ_1 which permits light to be transmitted through the fiber.

Snell's law applied at point A gives

$$\frac{\sin\theta_1}{\sin\theta_2} = n_1 \tag{1}$$

and the condition for total internal reflection at point B is

$$\sin\theta_3 = n_2/n_1 . \tag{2}$$

From geometry, $\theta_2 = 90° - \theta_3$, so $\sin\theta_3 = \cos\theta_2 = n_2/n_1$, and therefore

$$\sin\theta_2 = \sqrt{1 - \cos^2\theta_2} = \sqrt{1 - \left(\frac{n_2}{n_1}\right)^2} \tag{3}$$

Using equation (3) for $\sin\theta_2$ in equation (1) gives

$$\sin\theta_1 = \sqrt{n_1^2 - n_2^2} . \tag{4}$$

Substitution of $n_1 = 1.66$ and $n_2 = 1.52$ gives $\sin\theta_1 = 0.67$, or $\theta_1 = 42°$.

● **PROBLEM** 5-7

What is the least radius through which an optic fiber of core diameter 0.05 mm may be bent without serious loss of light? The refractive index of the core is 1.66, of the sheath 1.52.

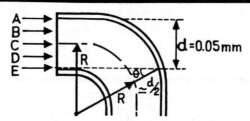

Solution: The figure shows a cross-section of the optic fiber. The collimated incident light is represented by parallel rays A, B, C, D, and E. Of the rays shown, ray E will strike the core-sheath interface with the smallest

70

angle of incidence; if this angle is set equal to the critical angle, all rays will necessarily be totally re-flected at the interface, thus reducing losses to a mini-mum. Since the sine of the critical angle is given by the ratio of the indices of refraction of the two media in-volved,

$$\sin \theta = n_2/n_1 . \tag{1}$$

But from the geometry shown in the figure, another relation is available for θ,

$$\sin \theta \approx \frac{R - d/2}{R + d/2} . \tag{2}$$

Eliminating $\sin \theta$ between equations (1) and (2) and solving for R,

$$R = \frac{d}{2} \left(\frac{n_1 + n_2}{n_1 - n_2} \right) .$$

Substitution of the given values of n_1, n_2, and d gives

$$R = 0.57 \text{ mm.}$$

● **PROBLEM** 5-8

A glass plate 1 inch thick, of index 1.50, having plane parallel faces, is held horizontally 4 inches above a printed page. Find the position of the image of the page, formed by small angle of incidence rays only.

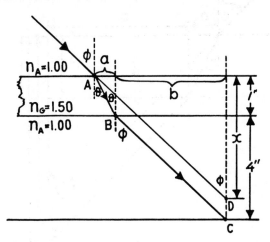

Solution: The actual path of the light ray is represented by $\overline{ABC}$, the source being at point C, but the eye does not account for the refraction of the beam. To the eye, the image appears to be at point D, which is x cm deep.

From the figure,

$$a = \tan \theta$$

$$b = 4 \cdot \tan \phi$$

$$a+b = x \cdot \tan\phi = \tan\theta + 4 \cdot \tan\phi \qquad (1)$$

Using the law of refraction we have $n_A \sin\phi = n_G \sin\theta = 1.5 \sin\theta$. Assuming that both θ and ϕ are very small, the small angle approximation, $\sin\theta = \tan\theta$ can be made. Then

$$1.5 \cdot \tan \theta = \tan \phi$$

and $\qquad \tan \theta = 0.67 \cdot \tan \phi$

substituting into (1), we get

$$x \cdot \tan\phi = 0.67 \cdot \tan + 4 \cdot \tan\phi .$$

Cancelling out the $\tan\phi$'s we get

$$x = 4.67 \text{ inches.}$$

Then, the image of the page is located 4.67 inches below the top of the glass plate.

● **PROBLEM** 5-9

What will be the effect on the apparent length of an object if a slab of transparent material with plane parallel sides is interposed at right angles to the line of vision?

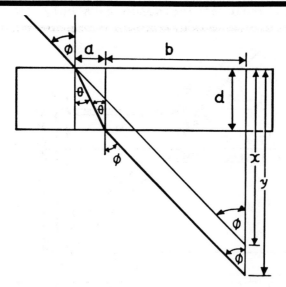

Solution: Let d be the thickness of the material and n, its index of refraction.

In this problem, we will try to find how much closer the object appears to be. Let y be the distance from the object to the front side of the slab, and x be the apparent distance. φ is the angle of incidence on the first surface, so it is also the angle of refraction, or the angle of emergence, at the second surface. θ is the angle of refraction at the first surface and, similarly, the angle of incidence at the second surface. We start by applying some basic trigonometry.

$$a = d \cdot \tan \theta \tag{1}$$

$$b = (y-d) \cdot \tan \phi \tag{2}$$

$$a + b = x \cdot \tan \phi \tag{3}$$

Then $a + b = x \cdot \tan \phi = d \cdot \tan \theta + (y-d) \cdot \tan \phi$ (4)

Now we apply the law of refraction to get

$$\sin \phi = n \cdot \sin \theta. \tag{5}$$

Assuming that φ and θ are very small, we can change (5) to tan φ = n · tan θ by using the small angle approximation given by

$$\sin \alpha = \tan \alpha = \alpha$$

Then $\qquad \tan \theta = \dfrac{1}{n} \cdot \tan \phi.$ (6)

If we substitute (6) into (4) we get

$$x \cdot \tan\phi = \frac{d}{n} \cdot \tan\phi + (y-d) \cdot \tan\phi.$$

Dividing through by tanφ, we get:

$$x = \frac{d}{n} + y-d$$

so $\qquad y-x = d - \dfrac{d}{n} = d\left(1-\dfrac{1}{n}\right) = \dfrac{d(n-1)}{n}$

Thus the image appears to be a distance of $\dfrac{d(n-1)}{n}$ units closer to the observer.

● **PROBLEM 5-10**

A block of flint glass, of refractive index 1.65 and of depth 5 cm, rests on the bottom of a beaker of water. The surface of the water is 10 cm above the top surface of the glass block. What is the apparent depth of a scratch on the inside of the bottom of the beaker below the surface of the water?

Solution: The scratch is actually 15 cm deep but to the eye it seems to be x cm deep because the eye does not take into account the refraction of the light ray at each surface.

From the law of refraction it is known that

$$n_A \cdot \sin \phi = n_\omega \cdot \sin \theta = n_F \cdot \sin \gamma.$$

Putting in the indices of refraction n_A, n_ω, and n_F, we have

$$\sin \phi = 1.33 \cdot \sin \theta = 1.65 \cdot \sin \gamma. \qquad (1)$$

From the figure,
$$a = 10 \cdot \tan \theta$$

$$b = 5 \cdot \tan \gamma$$

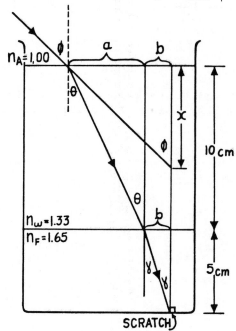

$$a + b = x \cdot \tan \phi = 10 \cdot \tan \theta + 5 \cdot \tan \gamma. \qquad (2)$$

If θ and γ are very small, then we can use the small angle approximation, which says that

$$\sin \beta = \beta = \tan \beta.$$ Then equation (1)
becomes

$$1.33 \cdot \tan \theta = 1.65 \cdot \tan \gamma$$

So
$$10 \cdot \tan \theta = \frac{16.5}{1.33} \cdot \tan \gamma \cong 12.4 \tan \gamma$$

Substituting back into equation (2) gives us:

$$x \tan\phi = 10 \tan\theta + 5 \tan\gamma \cong (12.4 + 5) \tan\gamma$$

or
$$x \cdot \tan \phi = 17.4 \cdot \tan \gamma \qquad (3)$$

Dividing (1) by (3) results in

$$\frac{\sin \phi}{x \tan \phi} = \frac{1.65 \sin \gamma}{17.4 \tan \gamma}$$

and so, $\frac{\cos \phi}{x} = \frac{1.65}{17.4} \cdot \cos \gamma.$

If ϕ and γ are very small, then

$$\cos \phi, \cos \gamma \approx 1$$

So we have $\frac{1}{x} = \frac{1.65}{17.4}$

$$x = 10.5 \text{ cm.}$$

Thus the apparent depth of the scratch is 10.5 cm.

THE CRITICAL ANGLE

● PROBLEM 5-11

A ray of light is incident on the left vertical face of a glass cube of index 1.50, as shown in the figure. The plane of incidence is the plane of the paper, and the cube is surrounded by water. At what maximum angle must the ray be incident on the left vertical surface of the cube if total internal reflection is to occur at the top surface? Water has an index of 1.33.

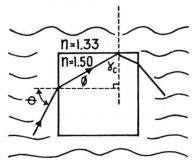

Solution: To find the incident angle at which there is total internal reflection of the ray at the top surface of the cube, we must find its critical angle using the law of refraction.

$$1.50 \cdot \sin \gamma_c = 1.33 \cdot \sin 90°.$$

So $\gamma_c = 62.5°.$

Then $\phi = 27.5$ because ϕ and γ_c are the complementary angles of a right triangle. So using the law of refraction, we have:

$$1.33 \cdot \sin \Theta = 1.50 \cdot \sin \phi.$$

Substituting in $\phi = 27.5$ and solving for Θ we have

$$\Theta = 31.4° \qquad \text{for total internal reflection.}$$

● **PROBLEM** 5-12

A semicylinder such as is shown in sectional view is constructed of glass of refractive index 1.65, and its flat
horizontal upper surface supports a drop of liquid (also
shown). For light directed radially toward the drop, total
internal reflection is found to occur with critical angle
$\Theta_c = 58°$. What is the refractive index of the liquid?

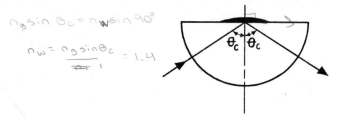

$n_g \sin \Theta_c = n_w \sin 90°$

$n_w = \dfrac{n_g \sin \Theta_c}{1} = 1.4$

Solution: It can be proven that if a beam of light strikes
a surface perpendicularly then there is no bending of the
beam of light (no refraction) as it passes that surface.

Then as this ray of light enters the cylindrical surface of the glass it is perpendicular to that surface so
there is no refraction at the surface.

For a critical angle of 58°, we use the law of refraction and get

$$1.65 \cdot \sin 58° = n_o \sin 90° = n_o$$

so $\qquad n_o = 1.40.$

● **PROBLEM** 5-13

A point light source is 2 inches below a water-air surface.
Compute the angles of refraction of rays from the source
with incident angles of 10°, 20°, 30°, 40°, and show these
rays in a diagram.

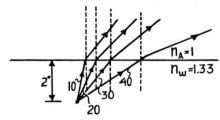

$n_A = 1$
$n_w = 1.33$

2" 10° 40 30 20

Solution: We must first find the critical angle so we can
check if there is any total internal reflection. Using the

law of refraction, we have:

$$n_W \cdot \sin \phi_C = n_A \cdot \sin 90°$$

$$\phi_C = 48.8°$$

Since the given angles of incidence never exceed the critical angle, all four rays are refracted. To find each angle of refraction, we must, once again, use the law of refraction,

$$1.33 \cdot \sin 10° = 1 \cdot \sin \phi_r$$

to get $\phi_r = 13.4°$ for an angle of incidence of 10°.

Similarly, the angles of refraction for the other angles of incidence are: 27.1°, 41.7° and 58.7° respectively.

Notice that the angle of refraction is independent of the distance of the source from the surface, and depends only on the angle of incidence and the refractive indices of the mediums in question.

● **PROBLEM 5-14**

A fish looks upward at an unobstructed overcast sky. What total angle does the sky appear to subtend? Water has an index of 1.33.

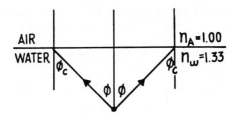

Solution: First the critical angle for the surface between water and air must be found using the law of refraction.

$$n_W \cdot \sin \phi_C = n_A \cdot \sin 90°$$

$$\phi_C = 48.8°$$

Once we know that ϕ_C is 48.8° we also know that ϕ is also 48.8° because these angles are alternate interior angles. To the fish, the sky tends to subtend an angle of $2 \cdot \phi$ which says that the fish's field of vision (upward) is 97.6°. Note that this is independent of the depth of the fish.

A small pebble lies at the bottom of a tank of water. Determine the size of a piece of cardboard which, when floating on the surface of the water, directly above the pebble, totally obscures the latter from view.

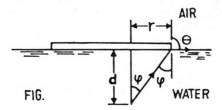

FIG.

Solution: We can consider the pebble as a point source of light. If the cardboard is big enough for its purpose, then all rays of light from the pebble which would be refracted into the air at the surface must be blocked off by the cardboard, and all rays striking the surface of the water outside the cardboard must be totally internally reflected (see figure).

The cardboard must obviously be circular, and, if its center is directly above the pebble, a ray of light striking the edge of the cardboard must do so at an angle $\varphi \geq$ the critical angle.

By Snell's Law, traveling from pebble to edge of cardboard

$$n_w \sin \varphi = n_a \sin \theta$$

where φ is the angle of incidence, θ is the angle of refraction, n_a is the index of refraction of air ($n_a = 1$) and n_w is that of water. Then,

$$n_w \sin \varphi = 1$$

because $\theta = 90°$ for total internal reflection, which satisfies the requirement that φ be a critical angle. Therefore, using the figure,

$$\sin \varphi = \frac{r}{\sqrt{r^2 + d^2}} .$$

Hence, $n_w \dfrac{r}{\sqrt{r^2 + d^2}} = 1$ Squaring both sides and cross-multiplying gives

$$r^2 + d^2 = n_w^2 r^2 \quad \text{or} \quad r^2 = \frac{d^2}{n_w^2 - 1} .$$

Thus a circular piece of cardboard with a radius given by $r = \dfrac{d}{\sqrt{n_w^2 - 1}}$

will totally obscure the pebble from view.

● **PROBLEM** 5-16

A skin diver shines his flashlight at the surface of the water so that the beam makes an angle of 60° with the vertical. ($n_{water} = 1.33$)

(a) Where does the beam go? Assume there is no reflected beam if there is a transmitted one.

(b) Oil of index 1.2 is now spread on the water. Where does the beam go?

(c) Many layers of oil are spread on the water, as shown in Fig. 1. Sketch the path of the beam.

(d) The air over a blacktop road is hottest near the road surface. The index of air away from the surface is 1.0003. An observer sees the road surface only if he looks down at an angle of 89° or more. What is the index of air at the surface?

FIG. I

$n = 1.00 \rightarrow$
$1.05 \rightarrow$
$1.10 \rightarrow$
$1.15 \rightarrow$
$1.20 \rightarrow$
$1.25 \rightarrow$
$1.33 \rightarrow$

Solution: (a) As the incident wave makes contact with the surface of the water it may be refracted, or it may be totally reflected if the incident angle is greater than the critical angle.

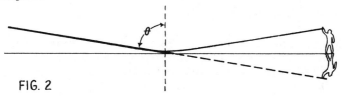

FIG. 2

The critical angle can be found by solving the equation

$$n_w \sin\phi_c = 1 \quad \text{for} \quad \phi_c. \quad \text{So } \phi_c = 49°$$

The incident angle of 60° is greater than the critical angle; thus there is total internal reflection, which means that the ray of light will be reflected as if the surface was a mirror.

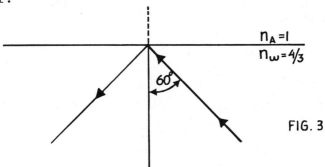

$n_A = 1$
$n_w = 4/3$

60°

FIG. 3

(b) We must use the law of refraction to find the critical angles of both surfaces. For the lower surface:

$$n_w \sin\phi_c = n_o \cdot \sin 90° \text{ where } n_o \text{ represents the}$$
index of refraction of the oil

79

$\phi_c = 64$

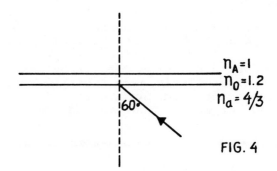

FIG. 4

$n_A = 1$
$n_0 = 1.2$
$n_a = 4/3$

Thus the incident ray will be refracted and transmitted to the second surface since the angle of incidence is less than ϕ_c.

Similarly, the critical angle for the upper surface is 56°. Now we must find the angle of refraction of the lower surface, which is also equal to the angle of incidence of the upper surface

$$n_w \cdot \sin 60° = n_0 \cdot \sin\phi$$

$$\phi = 74°$$

Since the incident angle of 74° for the upper surface is greater than its critical angle, there will be total internal reflection at the upper surface.

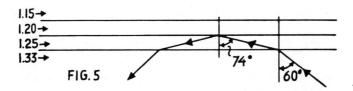

1.15→
1.20→
1.25→
1.33→

FIG. 5

74°

60°

(c) At the surface, which seperates the indices of refraction 1.33 and 1.25, the critical angle, using the law of refraction is

$$1.33 \sin\phi_c = 1.25 \sin 90°,$$

or $$\phi_c = \sin^{-1}\left(\frac{1.25}{1.33}\right) \cong 70°$$

The angle of the refracted beam is computed as follows:

$$1.33 \sin 60° = 1.25 \sin\theta.$$

Then, $$\theta \cong \sin^{-1}\left(\frac{(1.33) \sin 60°}{1.25}\right) \cong 67.5°$$

For the next surface, the critical angle is about 74° and the angle of the refracted beam slightly larger than 74°. Therefore the beam of light will be totally reflected at the second surface and will emerge at an angle equal to the original angle of incidence.

(d) Using the law of refraction and given that the
critical angle is 89°, we can find the index of refraction
of the air just above the hot pavement by

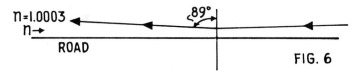

FIG. 6

$$1.0003 \cdot \sin 89° = n \cdot \sin 90°$$

Solving, we have,

$$n = 1.0001 .$$

● **PROBLEM** 5-17

The index of refraction of silver for X-rays of wavelength 1.279 Å is 0.9999785. Calculate the grazing angle
(between the incident ray and the surface) smaller than that
for which total reflection will occur for X-rays incident on
a silver surface.

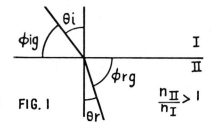

FIG. 1

$$\frac{n_{II}}{n_I} > 1$$

Solution: Snell's law states that

$$\frac{\sin\theta_i}{\sin\theta_r} = n$$

where θ_i is the angle of incidence. The angle is measured
from the incoming ray to the normal to the surface. θ_r is
the angle of refraction, measured to the normal and n is the
relative index of refraction between the two media.   If we
look at figure 1, we see that we can write Snell's law in
terms of the angle between the ray and the tangent to the
surface, ϕ_{ig}, rather than θ_i.

From figure 1, $\theta_i = 90 - \phi_{ig}$ and $\theta_r = 90 - \phi_{rg}$.   Therefore
$\sin\theta_i = \sin(90 - \phi_{ig}) = \sin 90 \cos\phi_{ig} - \cos 90 \sin\phi_{ig} = \cos\phi_{ig}$;
similarly, $\sin\theta_r = \cos\phi_{rg}$. Therefore, Snell's law becomes:

$$\frac{\cos\phi_{ig}}{\cos\phi_{rg}} = n$$

Now if the index of refraction in region II is less than that

81

in region I then there will be a critical angle above which rays will not be able to go from region I to region II giving rise to internal reflection. This critical angle can then be defined by the angle $\phi_{rg} = 0$, or then the equation for ϕ_{cg} is

$$\cos\phi_{cg} = n$$

and in this problem n = 0.9999785

so $$\cos\phi_{cg} = 0.9999785$$

or $$\phi_{cg} = 0°\ 22'32"\ .$$

REFRACTIVE INDICES

● **PROBLEM** 5-18

Show that the optical length of a light path, defined as the geometrical length times the refractive index of the medium in which the light is moving, is the equivalent distance which the light would have traveled in a vacuum.

Solution: Suppose that light travels a distance ℓ in a medium of refractive index n. The optical length is then

optical length = $n\ell$

and, since n = c/v where c and v represent the speed of light in a vacuum and in the given medium, respectively, substituting for n in the preceding equation gives

optical length = $c\ell/v$.

But light travels with constant velocity in the medium, and hence $\ell/v = t$, where t is the time taken to traverse the light path.

$$n\ell = \frac{c\ell}{v} = ct = \ell_0$$

where ℓ_0 is the distance the light would have traveled at velocity c, that is, in a vacuum. Thus the optical length is the equivalent distance which the light would have traveled in the same time in a vacuum.

● **PROBLEM** 5-19

A large piece of plastic of nonuniform refractive index is made in the form of a doughnut. The inside diameter (the diameter of the hole) is 34 cm and the outside diameter is 46 cm; the annular body of the doughnut is circular. If the mean refractive index of the plastic is 1.6, what refractive index gradient is necessary to keep a beam of light traveling along the center of the plastic ring? Express this in terms of the refractive index at the outside and inside periphery of the doughnut.

Solution: From the theory of Schlieren optics it is known that a ray traverses a stratified medium in an arc with the radius of curvature determined by the index gradient. For example, for the case illustrated in the figure shown, in

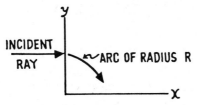

which a plane wave is incident from the left onto a medium occupying the region x > 0, where in the medium the index n(y) decreases vertically, a given incident ray will curve downward as shown with a radius of curvature R given by

$$R = n \frac{1}{dn/dy} \qquad (1)$$

In this problem the ray is to travel a circular path of radius $R = \frac{\text{mean diameter}}{4} = \frac{34 \text{ cm} + 46 \text{ cm}}{4} = 20 \text{ cm}$. The average balue of the index between y = 17 cm and y = 23 cm is given as 1.6, so (assuming a uniform gradient),

$$\frac{n(17) + n(23)}{2} = 1.6 \qquad (2)$$

Note that n(17) does not mean n times 17, but rather the value of n at y = 17.

Also, if the gradient is uniform,

$$(dn/dy) = \frac{n(17) - n(23)}{(23 - 17) \text{ cm}} . \qquad (3)$$

Combining equations (1) and (3),

$$\frac{n(17) - n(23)}{(23 - 17) \text{ cm}} = \frac{1.6}{20 \text{ cm}} , \text{ or}$$

$$n(17) - n(23) = 0.48. \qquad (4)$$

Equations (2) and (4) can now be solved for the two unknowns n(17) and n(23), giving n(17) = 1.84, n(23) = 1.36. Thus the refractive index at the outside of the doughnut is 1.36 and that at the inside is 1.84.

● **PROBLEM** 5-20

In classical dispersion theory introduction of a damping term, $m\gamma \vec{r}$, into the equation of motion of a bound electron results in the necessity of introducing a complex index of refraction $\hat{n} = n + ik$. Analysis results in two equations relating n, the real part of $\hat{n}$, and k, the complex part:

$$n^2 - k^2 = 1 + \frac{Ne^2}{m\varepsilon_o} \frac{w_o^2 - w^2}{\left(w_o^2 - w^2\right)^2 + \gamma^2 w^2} \qquad (1)$$

83

and

$$2nk = \frac{Ne^2}{m\varepsilon_o} \frac{\gamma w_o w}{\left(w_o^2 - w^2\right)^2 + \gamma^2 w^2} \quad ; \tag{2}$$

w_o is the resonant frequency of the electron, N the number of electrons per unit volume, m and e the electron mass and charge respectively. Show that if $k \ll n$, equations (1) and (2) reduce to

$$n \simeq 1 + \frac{Ne^2}{2m\varepsilon_o} \left(\frac{1}{w_o^2 - w^2}\right) \tag{3}$$

and

$$k \simeq \frac{Ne^2}{2m\varepsilon_o} \left(\frac{\gamma w w_o}{w_o^2 - w^2}\right) \tag{4}$$

Solution: If $k \ll n$, the index of refraction is nearly real, and since it is the introduction of the damping term $m\gamma \vec{r}$ into the equation of motion,

$$m\ddot{\vec{r}} + m\gamma \dot{\vec{r}} + k\vec{r} = - e\vec{E},$$

that results in a complex index, we must assume the damping term is small, i.e., $\gamma \ll 1$. Then γ and k are negligible in comparison with n, so equation (1) becomes

$$n^2 \simeq 1 + \frac{Ne^2}{m\varepsilon_o} \frac{1}{w_o^2 - w^2} . \tag{5}$$

Noting that $n^2 - 1 = (n-1)(n+1)$, and remembering from dispersion theory that equations (1) and (2) predict that $k < n$ only if $|n-1| \ll 1$, then

$$n^2 - 1 \simeq (n-1) \ (2); \tag{6}$$

Substitution of equation (6) into (5) gives

$$n \simeq 1 + \frac{Ne^2}{2m\varepsilon_o} \frac{1}{\left(w_o^2 - w^2\right)} . \tag{7}$$

Likewise, if $|n-1| \ll 1$, n does not differ greatly from 1, so $2nk \simeq 2k$, and equation (2) becomes

$$k \simeq \frac{Ne^2}{2m\varepsilon_o} \frac{\gamma w w_o}{\left(w_o^2 - w^2\right)} . \tag{8}$$

Such approximations would be valid, for example, for gases of relatively low densities.

84

A microscope is placed vertically above a small vessel and focused on a mark on the base of the vessel. A layer of transparent liquid of depth d is poured into the vessel, and then it is found by refocusing the microscope that the image of the mark has been displaced through a distance x. Show that the index of refraction of the liquid is equal to d/(d-x).

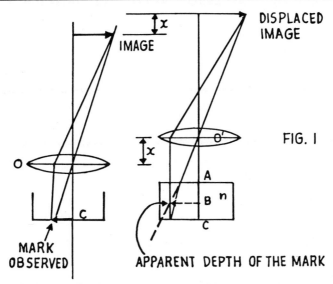

FIG. I

Solution: When the microscope is refocused, the image is displaced a distance x, and so the objective lens that focuses the image is raised a distance x (see figure 1). Because of refraction due to the liquid, the mark no longer appears located at its actual depth d in the vessel, but

instead appears suspended in the liquid at depth d'. From the law of refraction, the index of refraction is given by the ratio of these depths:

$$n = \frac{d}{d'} \qquad (1)$$

Now, referring to figure 1, the displacement of the image, x, can be expressed as the distance between the original and refocused positions of the lens:

$$x = \overline{oo}' \qquad (2)$$

Studying figure 1 will show that this distance can be expressed in many ways:

$$x = \overline{oo}'$$

$$= \overline{o'c} - \overline{oc}$$

$$= \overline{o'A} + d - \overline{oc}$$

85

$$= o'A + d - o'B$$

$$= o'A + d - (o'A + d')$$

$$x = d - d' \tag{3}$$

Solving (3) for d' gives:

$$d' = d - x \tag{4}$$

Thus, $d - x$ can be substituted for d' in equation (1), and hence,

$$n = \frac{d}{d - x}$$

● **PROBLEM** 5-22

Find the index of refraction for a glass whose dielectric constant is 2.5 .

Solution: Maxwell's equation for the curl of the electric field can be expressed as:

$$\nabla \times E = -\mu \frac{\partial H}{\partial t} , \tag{1}$$

where μ is the permeability of the glass and H represents the magnetic field.

Taking the curl of both sides of equation (1) gives:

$$\nabla \times (\nabla \times E) = \nabla \times \left[-\mu \frac{\partial H}{\partial t} \right] \tag{2}$$

The vector operator on the right side of equation (2) can interchange with the partial time derivative:

$$\nabla \times (\nabla \times E) = -\mu \frac{\partial}{\partial t} (\nabla \times H)$$

$$= -\mu \frac{\partial}{\partial t} \left(J + \varepsilon \frac{\partial E}{\partial t} \right) ,$$

where ε is the permittivity of the glass and J is the current density, by Maxwell's equation for the curl of the magnetic field. Assuming J is not a function of t, and using the vector identity

$$\nabla \times (\nabla \times E) = \nabla (\nabla \cdot E) - \nabla^2 (E) ,$$

since $\nabla \cdot E = 0$ (Maxwell's equation),

$$\nabla^2 E = \mu \varepsilon \frac{\partial^2 E}{\partial t^2} \tag{3}$$

For a plane wave propagating itself along the positive

x-axis, equation (3) can be reduced to one dimension:

$$\frac{\partial^2 E}{\partial x^2} = \mu \ \varepsilon \ \frac{\partial^2 E}{\partial t^2} \tag{4}$$

Now since E is an arbitrary vector function, it can be expressed as another arbitrary vector function:

$$E = F\left(t - \frac{x}{v}\right) \tag{5}$$

Substituting equation (5) into equation (4) and carrying out the partial differentiation immediately gives the result:

$$\frac{1}{v^2} = \mu \ \varepsilon$$

or:

$$v = \frac{1}{\sqrt{\mu \ \varepsilon}} \tag{6}$$

From the definition of the index of refraction,

$$v = \frac{c}{n} \tag{7}$$

where n = index of refraction and c = speed of light.

Using the expression for v in (7) in (6) gives:

$$\frac{c}{n} = \frac{1}{\sqrt{\mu \ \varepsilon}}$$

rearranging yields:

$$n = c\sqrt{\mu \ \varepsilon} \tag{8}$$

For glass, $\mu \approx \mu_o$ and $\varepsilon = K\varepsilon_o$, where K = dielectric constant and μ_o and ε_o are the permeability and the permittivity, respectively, of the vacuum. Using these values in equation (8) yields:

$$n = \sqrt{K \ \varepsilon_o \ \mu_o} \quad (c) \tag{9}$$

In free space the speed of light is just:

$$c = \frac{1}{\sqrt{\mu_o \ \varepsilon_o}} \tag{10}$$

Substitution of (10) into (9) gives:

$$n = \sqrt{K \ \varepsilon_o \ \mu_o} \ \left(\frac{1}{\sqrt{\mu_o \ \varepsilon_o}}\right) = \sqrt{K}$$

The dielectric constant, K, is given as 2.5; hence,

$$n = \sqrt{2.5} = 1.58$$

TRANSVERSE DISPLACEMENT

A ray of light is incident at an angle of 60° on one surface of a glass plate 2 cm thick, of index 1.50. The medium on either side of the plate is air. Find the transverse displacement between the incident and emergent rays.

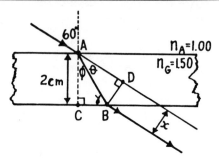

Solution: The transverse displacement between the incident and emergent ray of light is represented by x in the above diagram. Once the angle of refraction ϕ is found, we can apply some basic laws of trigonometry to find the displacement x.

Using the law of refraction to find ϕ we have:

$$n_A \cdot \sin 60° = n_G \cdot \sin \phi$$

so $\phi = 35.3°$ and $\gamma = 90 - \phi = 54.7°$

Now we use the law of sines on triangle ABC to find the length of segment $\overline{AB}$.

$$\frac{\overline{AB}}{\sin 90°} = \frac{2 \text{ cm}}{\sin 54.7°}$$

$$\overline{AB} = 2.45 \text{ cm}$$

Once again, using the law of sines on triangle ABD, we have:

$$\frac{2.45 \text{ cm}}{\sin 90°} = \frac{x}{\sin \theta}$$

Since $\phi + \theta = 60°$ (see figure), $\theta = 24.7°$.

So $x = (2.45)(\sin 24.7°) \text{ cm} \cong 1.02 \text{ cm}$.

A slab of transparent plastic measures $2 \times 10 \times 60 \text{ mm}^3$ in size. If the refractive index of the plastic varies monotonically in the lengthwise direction from 1.4 to 1.56, how much will a beam of collimated light, incident normally, be deflected at a distance of 1 m from the plastic?

Solution: From the theory of Schlieren optics, the incident ray will, upon entering the stratified medium, describe an arc of radius R determined by the index gradient
according to the relation

$$R = n \frac{1}{dn/dy} .$$ (1)

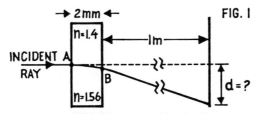

FIG. I

(In the figure the positive y axis is up.)   Once R is
determined, the distance d follows from Snell's law applied at the second surface of the plastic and the laws of
geometry.   Since n varies with y monotonically,

$$\frac{dn}{dy} = \frac{1.56 - 1.4}{60 \text{ mm}} = 2.7 \times 10^{-3} \text{ mm}^{-1} ;$$

at the center of the incident beam, $n = \frac{1.40 + 1.56}{2} = 1.48;$

then, from equation (1), $R = 5.48 \times 10^2$ mm.

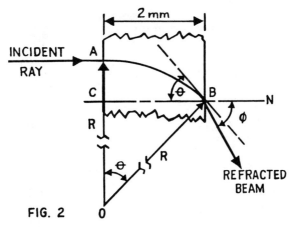

FIG. 2

Figure 2 shows the passage of the ray through the
slab in greater detail.   N represents the surface normal
at the point where the curving beam strikes the second
surface of the slab, θ the angle of incidence, and ϕ the
final angle of refraction out of the slab.   From Figure 2,
triangle BOC,

$$\sin \theta = \frac{2}{R} = 3.6 \times 10^{-3}.$$

Applying Snell's law at point B,

$$\frac{\sin \theta}{\sin \phi} = \frac{1}{n(B)} ;$$

89

since R is so large very little error is made if we assume $n(B) \simeq n(A) = 1.48$, and then

$$\sin \phi = (1.48)(3.6 \times 10^{-3}) = 5.4 \times 10^{-3}.$$

Then from geometry, assuming that point B very nearly lies directly opposite point A, and setting $\sin \phi \simeq \tan \phi$ since $\sin \phi$ is so small,

$$d \simeq (1 \text{ m}) \sin \phi = 5.4 \text{ mm}.$$

IMGAGES

● **PROBLEM** 5-25

An object viewed normally through a plate of glass (n=1.5) with plane parallel faces appears to be five-sixths of an inch nearer than it really is. How thick is the glass?

Solution: If an object is viewed through a transparent material with plane parallel faces, then the object seems to be $\dfrac{d(n-1)}{n}$ closer than it actually is, where d is the thickness of the material and n is its index of refraction.

So, in this problem, if the index of refraction is 1.5 and the object viewed through it seems to be $\dfrac{5}{6}$ inch closer than it actually is, then we have:

$$\frac{5}{6} = \frac{d(n-1)}{n} \ .$$

Substituting for n:

$$\frac{5}{6} = \frac{d(1.5-1)}{1.5}$$

and d = 2.5 inches. So in order for an object to be seen $\dfrac{5}{6}$ inch closer than it actually is through a plate glass of index 1.5, the glass must be 2.5 inches thick.

● **PROBLEM** 5-26

Show that the correct formula, when considering "back surface" mirrors, for the distance of the image behind the reflecting surface is

$$D' = D - t(1 - 2/n),$$

where D is the object distance to the front of the glass, t is the thickness of the glass, n is the relative index of refraction of the glass.

Solution: First construct a ray diagram picture of this problem (see figure 1). A ray from the object A proceeds to G

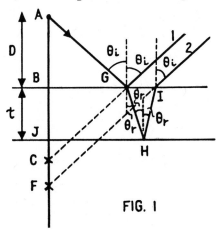

FIG. I

and is reflected at G in the direction of 1. Another part of
the ray is refracted and proceeds to H, I, and the direction
2. Looking back from the direction of 1 and 2 the object
appears to be located at C and F, respectively. So C is the
image of A in a reflection from the front surface and F is
the image of A in the rear surface. The distance we wish to
determine is $\overline{JF}$. Now from triangles AGB and BGC, $\sphericalangle AGB = \sphericalangle BGC$
because they are both complements of the angle θ_i . There-
fore, $\overline{BC}$ = D. Also looking at triangle GHI, $\overline{GI} = 2t\,\tan\theta_r$.
From triangle ABG, $\overline{BG} = D\,\tan\theta_i$ and from triangle FIB,
$\overline{BF}\,\tan\theta_i = \overline{BI}$.

Now we note that BIF = θ_i and BGC is also equal to θ_i.
Then we can write

$$\frac{\overline{BI}}{\overline{BF}} = \frac{\overline{BG}}{\overline{BC}} \qquad \text{or}$$

$$\frac{\overline{BG} + \overline{GI}}{\overline{BF}} = \frac{\overline{BG}}{D} \tag{1}$$

since $\overline{BI} = \overline{BG} + \overline{GI}$ and $\overline{BC}$ = D.

Rearranging,

$$\frac{\overline{BG}}{\overline{BF}} - \frac{\overline{BG}}{D} = -\frac{\overline{GI}}{\overline{BF}} \tag{2}$$

and substituting for $\overline{GI}$

$$\frac{\overline{BG}}{\overline{BF}} - \frac{\overline{BG}}{D} = -\frac{2t\,\tan\theta_r}{\overline{BF}} \tag{3}$$

$$= \frac{-\,2t\,\sin\theta_r}{\overline{BF}\,\cos\theta_r} \tag{4}$$

91

Using Snell's law $(\sin\theta_i / \sin\theta_r = n)$

$$\frac{\overline{BG}}{\overline{BF}} - \frac{\overline{BG}}{D} - \frac{2t\,\sin\theta_i}{n\,\overline{BF}\,\cos\theta_r}; \quad \overline{BG} = D\,\tan\theta_i = \frac{D\,\sin\theta_i}{\cos\theta_i}.$$

Therefore, $\sin\theta_i = \dfrac{\overline{BG}}{D}\cos\theta_i$, and so,

$$\frac{\overline{BG}}{\overline{BF}} - \frac{\overline{BG}}{D} = -\frac{2t\,\overline{BG}\,\cos\theta_i}{Dn\,\overline{BF}\,\cos\theta_r} \tag{5}$$

Factoring out and cancelling $\overline{BG}$ on both sides of equation (5) gives,

$$\frac{1}{\overline{BF}} - \frac{1}{D} = -\frac{2t}{nD\,\overline{BF}}\frac{\cos\theta_i}{\cos\theta_r} \tag{6}$$

or $\left(1 + \dfrac{2t}{nD}\dfrac{\cos\theta_i}{\cos\theta_r}\right)\dfrac{1}{\overline{BF}} = \dfrac{1}{D}$ \hfill (7)

$$\overline{BF} = D\left(1 + \frac{2t}{nD}\frac{\cos\theta_i}{\cos\theta_r}\right) \tag{8}$$

The distance we wish to find is

$$\overline{JF} = \overline{BF} - \overline{BJ} = \overline{BF} - t \tag{9}$$

and substituting into equation (8)

$$\overline{JF} + t = D\left(1 + \frac{2t}{nD}\frac{\cos\theta_i}{\cos\theta_r}\right) \tag{10}$$

$$\overline{JF} = D\left(1 + \frac{2t}{nD}\frac{\cos\theta_i}{\cos\theta_r}\right) - t$$

$$= D + \frac{2t}{n}\frac{\cos\theta_i}{\cos\theta_r} - t$$

$$\overline{JF} = D - t\left(1 - \frac{2}{n}\frac{\cos\theta_i}{\cos\theta_r}\right) \tag{11}$$

If we now take the limit $\theta_i \to 0$ then $\theta_r \to 0$ and $\dfrac{\cos\theta_i}{\cos\theta_r} \to 1$ so equation (11) becomes

$$\overline{JF} = D - t(1 - 2/n) .$$

What is the percentage of angular magnification when one views an object at 33 cm through a pane of glass 5 mm thick?

Solution: The angular magnification provided by a plane (not curved) pane of glass is given by

$$A.M. (\%) = \left(\frac{t}{p}\right)\left[\frac{(n-1)}{n}\right](100\%)$$

where t is the thickness of the pane, p is the distance from the observer to the object and n is the relative index of refraction.

Taking n = 1.5 and substituting the given values for t and p,

$$AM(\%) = \left[\frac{.5}{33} \quad \frac{1.5-1}{1.5}\right] \cdot 100\% = 0.5\%.$$

PHASE CHANGES

Refer to the figure below:

a) If $n_2 > n_1$ and $n_2 > n_3$, will a 180° phase change occur on reflection? If so, at which boundary?

b) If $n_3 > n_2 > n_1$, at which boundary will a phase change occur?

c) If $n_1 > n_2$ and $n_3 > n_2$, at which boundary will a phase change occur?

d) If $n_1 > n_2 > n_3$, at which boundary will a phase change occur?

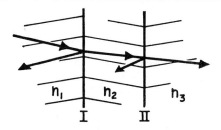

Solution: When reflection occurs from an interface beyond which the medium has a lower index of refraction than the medium which the light is in initially, the reflected wave undergoes no phase change; when the medium beyond the interface has a higher index, there is a phase change of π. The transmitted wave does not experience a phase change in either case.

With reference to the figure:

(a)   if $n_2 > n_1$, and $n_2 > n_3$, there will be a 180° phase change for light rays entering from the left at boundary I, but no phase change at boundary II.

(b)   If $n_3 > n_2 > n_1$, light entering from the left will experience a 180° phase change at each of the boundaries I and II.

(c)   If $n_1 > n_2$ and $n_3 > n_2$, there will be a 180° phase change at boundary II.

(d)   If $n_1 > n_2 > n_3$, light entering from the left will not experience any phase changes in passing through boundaries I and II.

CHAPTER 6

REFRACTION AT CURVED SURFACES

DETERMINATION OF IMAGE POSITIONS

Show that when doing problems with a virtual object and
trying to find the position of the image, we cannot simplify the problem and assume the object to be real.

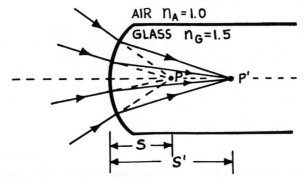

Solution: Let converging rays of light strike a spherical,
glass, refracting surface whose radius of curvature is 40 mm
and whose index of refraction is 1.5, as shown in the figure.
Without the glass, the incident rays would converge at point
P, which is 20 mm to the right of the spherical surface, but
the glass refracts the rays and they converge at P' instead.

The proper method of finding the position of P' is to
let P be a virtual object and use the lens equation,

$$\frac{n_A}{S} + \frac{n_G}{S'} = \frac{n_G - n_A}{R}$$

where n_A and n_G are the indices of refraction of the air and
glass, respectively, R is the radius of curvature of the
glass surface, and S and S' are the object and image distances from the surface, respectively. Letting S = - 20 mm
(because it's a virtual image), n_A = 1.0, n_G = 1.5, and

R = 40 mm, we have

$$\frac{1.0}{-20 \text{ mm}} + \frac{1.5}{S'} = \frac{1.5 - 1}{40 \text{ mm}}$$

Hence, $S' = 24$ mm.

Thus, the image appears 24 mm to the right of the spherical surface.

   If we try to simplify the problem by assuming the object to be real and the image virtual, the lens equation becomes

$$\frac{n_G}{S} + \frac{n_A}{S'} = \frac{n_A - n_G}{R}$$

where $n_G = 1.5$, $n_A = 1.0$, $S = + 20$ mm, and $R = - 40$ mm (because the refracting surface is now concave rather than convex). Now the rays of light diverge from point P to form a virtual image at point P'. If this is a valid procedure for this type of problem, then the virtual image at P' should also be 24 mm to the right of the surface of the glass. Solving the above equation, we have

$$\frac{1.5}{20 \text{ mm}} + \frac{1.0}{S'} = \frac{1.0 - 1.5}{-40 \text{ mm}} \quad ,$$

hence $S' = - 16$ mm. Therefore the virtual image, if the object at P is real, is 16 mm to the right of the surface. This solution does not agree with the first one. Therefore, the two methods of solving this problem were not equivalent, because in the first method converging rays were incident on the convex side of the refracting surface, while in the presumed equivalent method, diverging rays were incident on the concave side of the surface.

● **PROBLEM** 6-2

A solid glass sphere of radius R and index of refraction 1.50 is silvered over one hemisphere. A small object is located on the axis of the sphere at a distance 2R from the unsilvered surface. Find the position of the image formed by the refracting and reflecting surfaces.

Solution: To solve this problem, the small aperture equation for a spherical surface is used:

$$\frac{n_1}{s_1} + \frac{n_2}{s_2} = \frac{n_2 - n_1}{R} \tag{1}$$

where n_1 and n_2 are the indices of refraction on the two sides of the spherical interface, s_1 is the object distance, s_2 is the image distance, and R is the radius of curvature of the surface. In addition, $(n_2 - n_1)/R$ is the effective

focal length of the spherical interface.   Recall that the
focal length of a spherical mirror of radius R is R/2.

To find successively the image formed by each interface from the object of the previous interface, first substitute the following given values into equation (1):

$$s_1 = 2R \ , \ n_1 = 1.0 \text{ and } n_2 = 1.5$$

Then, equation (1) becomes

$$\frac{1}{2R} + \frac{1.5}{s_2} = \frac{1.5 - 1}{R}$$

$$\frac{1.5}{s_2} = \frac{1}{2R} - \frac{1}{2R} = 0$$

$$s_2 = \infty$$

This means that the image created by the first surface of
the original object is an infinite distance from the intersection of the axis with the first spherical interface.
This also means that the rays from the initial object will
be parallel to the mirror's axis as they encounter the
mirror.   Therefore, the mirror's image will be at a distance
R/2 from the mirror (the focal point of the mirror).   This
image will then be a distance

$$R + \frac{R}{2} = 3R/2$$

from the spherical glass surface.   Now we can use equation
(1) a second time:

$$\frac{1.5}{3R/2} + \frac{1}{s_2} = \frac{1 - 1.5}{-R}$$

$$\frac{1}{s_2} = -1/2R$$

or $$s_2 = -2R \ .$$

Remembering sign conventions, this means that the final
image will be virtual, located at a distance of 2R from
the spherical glass surface, or in other words, at the
vertex of the mirror surface.

● PROBLEM 6-3

A small air-bubble is imbedded in a glass sphere at a distance of 5.98 cm from the nearest point on the surface.
What will be the apparent depth of the bubble, viewed from
this side of the sphere, if the radius of the sphere is
7.03 cm, and the index of refraction of the glass is 1.42?

Solution: For this problem, we will use the following

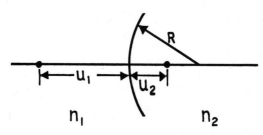

equation for refraction at a spherical surface, noting that this equation holds only for small distances from the optic axis:

$$\frac{n_1}{u_1} + \frac{n_2}{u_2} = \frac{n_2 - n_1}{R} \tag{1}$$

where the n's represent the indices of refraction in the respective media, the u's the respective distances of the object and image from the intersection of the optical axis and the spherical surface, and R is the radius of the spherical surface. In the figure, u_1 , u_2 and R are shown as being positive.

Substituting the given values

$u_2 = 5.98$ cm, $n_1 = 1.0$, $n_2 = 1.42$ and $R = 7.03$ cm

into equation (1) gives

$$\frac{1}{u_1} + \frac{1.42}{5.98} = \frac{1.42 - 1}{7.03} \tag{2}$$

$$\frac{1}{u_1} = \frac{0.42}{7.03} - \frac{1.42}{5.98} = 0.059 - 0.237 = -0.178 \tag{3}$$

or $u_1 = -5.62$ cm.

Since u_1 is negative, a virtual image of the air bubble is formed at a distance of 5.62 cm to the right of the glass surface.

● **PROBLEM 6-4**

A small bubble in a sphere (radius 2.5 cm) of glass (n = 1.5) appears, when looked at along the radius of the sphere, to be 1.25 cm from the surface nearer the eye. What is its actual position? If the image is 1 mm wide, what is the bubble's true diameter? What is the longitudinal magnification?

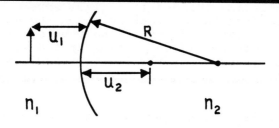

Solution: The equation for the refraction at a spherical surface will be used in this problem, noting that this equation holds only for small distances from the optical axis:

$$\frac{n_1}{u_1} + \frac{n_2}{u_2} = \frac{n_2 - n_1}{R} \tag{1}$$

where the n's represent the indices of refraction in the respective media, the u's the respective distances of the object and image from the intersection of the optic axis and the spherical surface and R is the radius of curvature of the spherical surface. In the figure, u_1, u_2 and R are shown as if they were positive.

Substituting the given values

$u_1 = -1.25$ cm; $n_1 = 1.0$, $n_2 = 1.5$, and R = 2.5 cm

into equation (1) gives

$$\frac{1}{-1.25} + \frac{1.5}{u_2} = \frac{1.5 - 1}{2.5} = \frac{.5}{2.5} = \frac{1}{5}$$

$$\frac{1.5}{u_2} = \frac{1}{5} + 4/5 = 1$$

$$u_2 = 1.5 \text{ cm },$$

or, the bubble is located at a distance of 1.5 cm from the glass surface.

Since we also want to find the size of the bubble whose apparent size is 1 mm, we use

$$M = \frac{u_2}{u_1} = \frac{1.5}{1.25} = 1.2$$

where M represents the magnification and

$$\frac{\text{image size}}{\text{object size}} = M; \quad \text{object size} = \frac{1}{1.2} = 0.83 \text{ mm }.$$

To find the longitudinal magnification, we need to find the image distances for the front and back of the bubble.

$$u_2 \text{ front} = 15 - \frac{0.83}{2} = 14.58 \text{ mm}$$

$$u_2 \text{ back} = 15 + \frac{0.83}{2} = 15.41 \text{ mm }.$$

Applying equation (1) for both u_2 front and u_2 back gives the following results:

$$\frac{1}{u_{1 \text{ front}}} + \frac{1.5}{14.58 \text{ mm}} = \frac{1.5 - 1}{25 \text{ mm}}$$

$$\frac{1}{u_{1 \text{ front}}} = \frac{1}{50} - 0.102 = 0.02 - 0.102 = -0.082 \text{ mm}^{-1}$$

$$u_{1 \text{ front}} = -12.20 \text{ mm}$$

$$\frac{1}{u_{1 \text{ back}}} + \frac{1.5}{15.41 \text{ mm}} = \frac{1.5 - 1}{25 \text{ mm}}$$

$$\frac{1}{u_{1 \text{ back}}} = 0.02 - 0.097 = -0.077 \text{ mm}^{-1}$$

$$u_{1 \text{ back}} = -12.99$$

and

$$u_{1 \text{ front}} - u_{1 \text{ back}} = 0.79 \text{ mm} .$$

Since the diameter of the bubble is 0.83 mm, the longitudinal magnification is

$$\frac{0.79}{0.83} = 0.95.$$

● **PROBLEM** 6-5

A thin biconvex lens has surfaces of equal radius of curvature, 15 cm, made of glass with index of refraction 1.5. One of the lens surfaces is silvered, so that it acts as a mirror, and an object is placed 40 cm from the lens on the other side. Find the position of the image of this object.

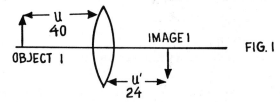

FIG. I

Solution: For this problem, three solutions will be presented. Solution (1) will be to use the thin lens/mirror equation, successively treating the problem as three optical elements with zero separation; solution (2) will be to use the thin lens/mirror equation, successively treating the problem as three optical elements with a separation d, and then let the separation d approach zero; and solution (3) will be to use the small aperture refraction equation

$$\frac{n_1}{u} + \frac{n_2}{u'} = \frac{n_2 - n_1}{R} \tag{1}$$

(n_1 and n_2 denote the indices of refraction of the media, u and u' represent the object and image distances from the curved surface, respectively, and R is the radius of curvature of the curved surface) successively for each of the three curved surfaces, with zero separation at each surface.

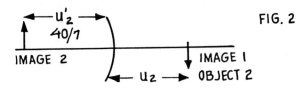

FIG. 2

Solution (1):

For the biconvex lens we can find the focal length f_ℓ of the lens from the lens makers formula:

$$\frac{1}{f_\ell} = (n - 1)(1/R_1 - 1/R_2)$$

$$= (1.5 - 1)\left(\frac{1}{15} - 1/-15\right) = \frac{1}{15} \tag{2}$$

$$f_\ell = 15 \text{ cm};$$

for the mirror, $f_m = R/2 = 15/2 = 7.5$ cm.

Now, the thin lens/mirror equation,

$$\frac{1}{u} + \frac{1}{u'} = 1/f$$

applied to the incident rays on the biconvex lens, yields

$$\frac{1}{40} + \frac{1}{u_1'} = 1/15$$

$$1/u_1' = \frac{1}{15} - 1/40 = \frac{40 - 15}{40 \times 15} = \frac{1}{24}$$

$$u_1' = 24 \text{ cm}.$$

This then will be the image of the object in the first encounter with the biconvex lens and is the object for the mirror. Now we must be careful about the sign convention of the thin lens/mirror equation. $u' = 24$ cm says that the first image formed is to the right of the biconvex lens (see figure 1), so the object distance u_2 for the mirror is -24 cm. Applying the thin lens/mirror equation again yields

$$\frac{1}{u_2} + \frac{1}{u_2'} = \frac{1}{f_m}$$

101

or

$$\frac{1}{-24} + \frac{1}{u_2'} = \frac{2}{15}$$

$$\frac{1}{u_2'} = \frac{2}{15} + \frac{1}{24} = \frac{48 + 15}{15 \times 24} = 7/40$$

$$u_2' = 40/7 \text{ cm .}$$

This image, by sign convention, will be to the left of the mirror (see figure 2). Hence, u_3 for the second pass through the lens is $-40/7$ cm. Applying the thin lens/mirror equation again yields

$$\frac{1}{-40/7} + \frac{1}{u_3'} = 1/15$$

$$\frac{1}{u_3'} = \frac{1}{15} + \frac{7}{40} = \frac{40 + 7 \times 15}{40 \times 15} = \frac{29}{120}$$

$$u_3' = \frac{120}{29} = 4.14 \text{ cm .}$$

That is, since we are passing back through the lens, a real image is formed 4.14 cm in front of the lens.

Solution (2):

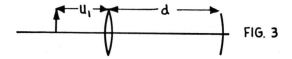

FIG. 3

Here our optical system looks as shown in figure 3. Ultimately, d will be allowed to approach zero. Thus, the first time the light passes through the lens, the image distance will be 24 cm, as in solution (1). Now the object distance for the mirror is d−24 and applying the thin lens/mirror equation,

$$\frac{1}{d - 24} + \frac{1}{u_2'} = 2/15$$

$$\frac{1}{u_2'} = \frac{2}{15} - \frac{1}{d - 24} = \frac{(2d-48)-15}{15(d - 24)} = \frac{2d - 63}{15(d - 24)}$$

$$u_2' = \frac{15(d - 24)}{2d - 63}$$

Now the object distance for the second pass through the lens will be $d - u_2'$ or

102

$$u_3 = d - \frac{15d - 360}{2d - 63} = \frac{2d^2 - 63d - 15d + 360}{2d - 63} \quad .$$

Simplifying this expression for u_3 and applying the thin lens/mirror equation yields

$$\frac{2d - 63}{2d^2 - 78d + 360} + \frac{1}{u_3'} = \frac{1}{15}$$

or

$$\frac{1}{u_3'} = \frac{1}{15} - \frac{2d - 63}{2d^2 - 78d + 360} =$$

$$\frac{2d^2 - 78d + 360 - 30d + 945}{30d^2 - 1170d + 5400}$$

$$u_3' = \frac{30d^2 - 1170d + 5400}{2d^2 - 108d + 1305}$$

Letting d approach zero,

$$u_3' = \frac{5400}{1305} = 4.14 \text{ cm} \quad .$$

In this case we again need to look at the sign convention which tells us that a positive value will be to the left of the lens. Therefore, this is the same answer as solution (1).

Solution (3):

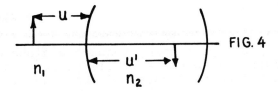

FIG. 4

Considering figure 4, equation (1) yields

$$\frac{1}{40} + \frac{1.5}{u_1'} = \frac{1.5 - 1}{15}$$

$$\frac{1.5}{u_1'} = \frac{1}{30} - 1/40$$

or solving for u_1' ,

$$u_1' = 180 \text{ cm}.$$

Now consider the mirror. With our sign convention, u_2 is -180 cm. Thus, solving for the image distance in the

103

mirror gives:

$$\frac{1}{-180} + \frac{1}{u_2{'}} = \frac{2}{15}$$

$$\frac{1}{u_2{'}} = \frac{2}{15} + \frac{1}{180}$$

$$u_2{'} = \frac{36}{5} \text{ cm.}$$

Now the curved surface is again considered and with our sign convention,

$$u_3 = -36/5; \quad R = -15.$$

Again applying the lens equation,

$$\frac{1.5}{-36/5} + \frac{1}{u_3{'}} = \frac{1 - 1.5}{-15}$$

$$\frac{1}{u_3{'}} = \frac{1}{30} + \frac{7.5}{36} = \frac{36 + 225}{30 \times 36} \; ;$$

$$u_3{'} = \frac{30 \times 36}{261} = 4.14 \text{ cm.}$$

Thus, each method of solving this problem yields the same result.

● **PROBLEM** 6-6

Show that the sun's rays passing through a globe of water (n = 1.33), 6 inches in diameter, will be converged to a focus 6.05 inches from the center of the sphere.

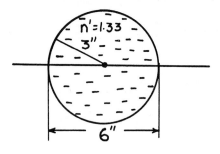

Solution: This problem can be solved by considering what happens at each refracting surface. The sunlight falling on the first surface creates an image given by the equation

$$\frac{n}{S} + \frac{n'}{S'} = \frac{n' - n}{R}$$

where n is the refractive index of the first medium (air; n = 1), n' is the refractive index of the second medium (water; n' = 1.33), S is the object distance (S = ∞ for the sun's rays), S' is the image distance from the vertex of the first surface, and R is the radius of curvature of the first surface. Substituting the given values for n, n', S and R into the preceding equation,

$$\frac{1.0}{\infty} + \frac{1.33}{S'} = \frac{1.33 - 1.0}{3"}$$

or $$\frac{1}{S'} = \frac{0.33}{3" \times 1.33}$$

$$S' = 12.09"$$

Hence, the image is formed at a distance of 12.09" from the first surface or (12.09" - 6") from the second surface. This image now acts as the object for the second surface. Hence, again using the preceding equation,

$$\frac{1.0}{S"} - \frac{1.33}{(12.09" - 6")} = \frac{0.33}{3"}$$

where S" is the image distance from the vertex of the second surface. Solving for S" gives the result

$$S" = 3.05".$$

Hence the sun's rays converge at 3" + 3.05" = 6.05" from the center of the globe.

● **PROBLEM 6-7**

A glass rod (n = 1.50) is 10 cm long between vertices. The left end is a convex hemispherical surface of radius 5 cm, the right end is a convex hemispherical surface with radius 10 cm. An arrow 1 mm long is placed 20 cm to the left of the left end, an axis oriented at right angles to the axis. (a) What is the object distance for the right surface? (b) Is the object real or virtual? (c) What is the image position from the right surface? (d) Is the image real or virtual? (e) What is the magnification of the whole rod?

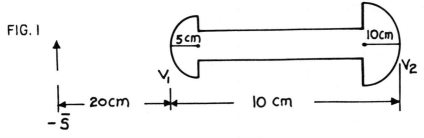
FIG. I

105

Solution: (a) The glass rod is shown in figure 1. The problem is solved easily by considering the refraction at the left surface first and the refraction at the right surface next. The object distance for the first surface (V_1) is $-\overline{s}$ $(= +20\,cm)$. Considering the refraction at the first surface, the image is formed at a distance s_1' from the first surface given by the following equation:

$$\frac{n}{s_1'} - \frac{1}{\overline{s}} = \frac{n-1}{R_1} \tag{1}$$

where n is the refractive index of the glass rod and R_1 is the radius of curvature of the first surface. Substituting the given values for n, $\overline{s}$ and R, into equation (1),

$$\frac{1.5}{s_1'} = \frac{0.5}{5} - \frac{1}{20} \, .$$

Hence $s_1' = \dfrac{100 \times 1.5}{10 - 5} = 30\,cm$ from V_1 or $-20\,cm$ from the right surface V_2. This is the object distance for the second surface (V_2). (b) The object is obviously virtual with respect to the second surface. (c) Now applying equation (1) at the second surface,

$$\frac{1}{\overline{s}'} - \frac{n}{s_{o_2}} = \frac{1-n}{R_2}$$

where $\overline{s}'$ is the image distance from the second surface, and s_{o_2} is the object distance with respect to the second surface (-20 cm)

$$\frac{1}{\overline{s}'} = \frac{0.5}{10} + \frac{1.5}{20} \, .$$

Solving for $\overline{s}'$ yields the result $\overline{s}' = 8\,cm$ from V_2. (d) the image is obviously real. (e) The linear lateral magnification may be obtained by taking the product of the magnifications produced by the two refracting surfaces. Thus, for the first surface,

$$m_1 = \frac{s_1'}{n\overline{s}} = \frac{-30\,cm}{1.5 \times 20} = -1$$

For the second surface,

$$m_2 = \frac{n\overline{s}'}{s_1' - t} = \frac{+1.5 \times 8}{20} = 0.6$$

(t denotes the length of the rod.)

Hence $m = m_1 m_2 = -0.6$.

106

A plane mirror is suspended vertically at the center of a large spherical flask filled with water (the index of refraction for water is 1.33). The diameter of the flask is 10 inches. An observer whose eye is 35 inches from the mirror sees an image of his own eye. Where is the image seen?

Solution: For this problem, we will use the single surface refraction equation locating the image distance u' from the object distance u, the radius of curvature R, and the indices of refraction n and n'. This equation is:

$$\frac{n}{u} + \frac{n'}{u'} = \frac{n' - n}{R} \tag{1}$$

Equation (1) can be applied for each surface the rays contact in turn, until a final image is formed. Initially, $n = 1$, $n' = 4/3$, the radius of curvature of the spherical flask, R, $= \frac{10 \text{ inches}}{2} = 5$ inches, and the radius of curvature of the mirror is infinite. Since $u_1 = 30$ inches (the distance of the eye from the surface of the flask), substituting into equation (1) gives the result

$$\frac{1}{30} + \frac{4/3}{u_1'} = \frac{4/3 - 1}{5} = \frac{1}{15}$$

$$\frac{4}{3u_1'} = \frac{1}{15} - \frac{1}{30} = \frac{1}{30}$$

$$\frac{3u_1'}{4} = 30$$

$$u_1' = \frac{4}{3} \times 30 = 40 \text{ inches}$$

u_1' is measured from the front surface of the flask, and so, the image is 35 inches behind the mirror. Reflection of this image places the next image 35 inches in front of the mirror, which is 30 inches outside the flask surface. Therefore u_2 is a virtual object, or $u_2 = -30$ inches.

Applying equation (1) again, this time with $n = \frac{4}{3}$ and $n' = 1$ (going from the flask into air),

$$\frac{4/3}{-30} + \frac{1}{u_2'} = \frac{1 - 4/3}{-5} = \frac{1}{15}$$

$$\frac{1}{u_2'} = \frac{4}{90} + \frac{1}{15} = \frac{10}{90}$$

$$u_2' = 9 \text{ inches}$$

The final image, u_2', is 9 inches outside the flask. Since the original object was 30 inches from the flask, the final image is 21 inches from the original object.

● **PROBLEM** 6-9

Light originates at an axial point object 40 cm to the left of a long glass rod of index 1.6. The end of the rod is ground and polished to a convex spherical surface of radius 6 cm. Find the image distance.

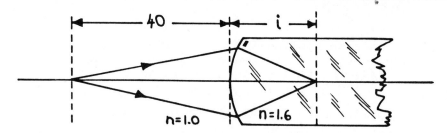

Solution: When light is refracted from a point object at a spherical surface, apply the relationship

$$\frac{n_1}{o} + \frac{n_2}{i} = \frac{n_2 - n_1}{r}$$

where n_1 is the index of the medium from which the light source originates, n_2 is the index of the medium where the image appears, o is the object's distance from the surface, i is the image's distance from the surface, and r is the radius of curvature of the surface.

In the given example, n_1 is assumed to be 1 (n = 1 for air), n_2 = 1.6, o = 40 cm, and r = 6 cm. Substituting these given values into the equation gives:

$$\frac{1}{40 \text{ cm}} + \frac{1.6}{i} = \frac{1.6-1}{6 \text{ cm}} \quad .$$

Solving for i gives us i = 21.3 cm.

The image distance i is positive, which implies that the image is real. If i was negative, then it would be a virtual image.

● **PROBLEM** 6-10

One end of a cylindrical glass rod of index of refraction 1.50 is ground and polished to a hemispherical surface of radius R = 20mm. An object in the form of an arrow 1mm

108

high, at right angles to the axis of the rod, is located 80mm to the left of the vertex of the surface. Find the position and magnification of the image if the rod is in (a) air and (b) water of index 1.33. (c) Find the first and second focal lengths of the spherical surface in air.

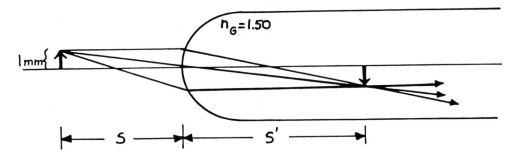

Solution: (a)   For the given data, $n_A = 1.00$, $n_G = 1.50$, $s = 80mm$, $R = 20mm$, and using the equation

$$\frac{n_A}{s} + \frac{n_G}{s'} = \frac{n_G - n_A}{R} \tag{1}$$

(s' is the image distance from the glass surface) we have

$$\frac{1.00}{80mm} + \frac{1.50}{s'} = \frac{1.50 - 1.00}{20mm}$$

hence s' = 120mm. The image is 120mm to the right of the surface of the glass rod and since s' is positive, the image is real.

The magnification, m, of the image inside the glass rod can be found by applying the formula,

$$m = -\frac{n_A \times s'}{n_G \times s} \tag{2}$$

$$m = -\frac{1.00 \times 120mm}{1.50 \times 80mm} = -1 \; .$$

Hence the image formed is the same size as the object but inverted because the magnification is negative.

(b)   For the glass rod in water, equation (1) becomes

$$\frac{n_W}{s} + \frac{n_G}{s'} = \frac{n_G - n_W}{R}$$

where n_W is the index of water, 1.33. Now, using the data for this part of the problem, we have

$$\frac{1.33}{80mm} + \frac{1.50}{s'} = \frac{1.50 - 1.33}{20mm}$$

Thus, s' = -185mm. Hence, when the glass rod is immersed in water of index 1.33, a virtual image will appear about 185mm to the left of the surface of the glass.

Using equation (2), the magnification, m, is

$$m = -\frac{n_W \times s'}{n_G \times s} = -\frac{1.33 \times (-185mm)}{1.50 \times 80mm} \sim +2$$

Since the magnification is positive, the image is erect and it is twice the height of the object.

(c) The first focal length, which is to the left of the surface, is found by applying the equation

$$\frac{n_A}{s} + \frac{n_G}{s'} = \frac{n_A}{f_1}$$

where f_1 is the first focal length and we use the object and image distances of the rod when it was in air. This gives us

$$\frac{1.00}{80mm} + \frac{1.50}{120mm} = \frac{1.00}{f_1} \quad ;$$

hence f_1 = 40mm.

The second focal length, which is to the right of the surface, is found by applying

$$\frac{n_A}{s} + \frac{n_G}{s'} = \frac{n_G}{f_2}$$

and this gives us

$$\frac{1.00}{80mm} + \frac{1.50}{120mm} = \frac{1.50}{f_2}$$

so f_2 = 60mm. Hence, the first focal point lies 40mm to the left of the surface and the second focal point lies 60mm to the right of the surface, when the glass rod is in air.

● **PROBLEM 6-11**

A small fish is at the center of a spherical fish bowl 1 ft. in diameter. Find the position and the lateral magnification of the image of the fish, seen by an observer outside the bowl.

Solution: In the figure, OS = a represents the small fish,

110

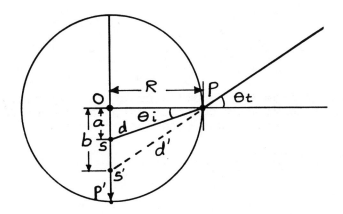

R is the radius of the sphere, OS' = b is the apparent size of the fish, θ_i is the angle of incidence (measured from the normal), and θ_t is the angle of refraction.

First we want to determine the ratio b/a. To do this, we notice from the figure that geometrically,

$$b = R \tan \theta_t \qquad (1)$$

$$a = R \tan \theta_i \qquad (2)$$

or, dividing equation (1) by equation (2),

$$b/a = \frac{\tan \theta_t}{\tan \theta_i} \qquad (3)$$

Remembering that $\tan A = \sin A / \cos A$ (4)

$$b/a = \frac{\sin \theta_t}{\sin \theta_i} \frac{\cos \theta_i}{\cos \theta_t} \qquad (5)$$

Snell's law of refraction

$$n_t \sin \theta_t = n_i \sin \theta_i$$

allows us to write equation (5) as

$$b/a = \frac{n_i}{n_t} \frac{\cos \theta_i}{\cos \theta_t} \qquad (6)$$

At this point, it would be helpful if the approximation $\frac{\cos \theta_i}{\cos \theta_t} = 1$ was valid.

From the figure, by the Pythagorean Theorem,

$$d^2 = a^2 + R^2 \qquad (7)$$

$$d'^2 = b^2 + R^2 \qquad (8)$$

111

and

$$\cos \theta_i = \frac{R}{\sqrt{a^2 + R^2}} \tag{9}$$

Factoring out R from the denominator of the expression on the right hand side of equation (9), and cancelling out the R's in numerator and denominator gives

$$\cos \theta_i = \frac{1}{\sqrt{1 + a^2/R^2}} \tag{10}$$

Similarly,

$$\cos \theta_t = \frac{1}{\sqrt{1 + b^2/R^2}} \tag{11}$$

Dividing equation (11) by equation (10) gives:

$$\frac{\cos \theta_t}{\cos \theta_i} = \sqrt{\frac{1 + a^2/R^2}{1 + b^2/R^2}} \tag{12}$$

Now, if the fish is small and the sphere is large,

$$a^2/R^2 \sim b^2/R^2 \ll 1$$

so

$$\cos \theta_t/\cos \theta_i \sim 1 \tag{13}$$

and equation (6) becomes

$$b/a = n_i/n_t . \tag{14}$$

In our problem, $n_i = 1.33$ (the index of refraction of water), $n_t = 1.0$, and $R = 0.5$ ft. Pick the small fish for example to be of size $a = 0.25$ inch. Then

$$a/R = 1/24 \quad \text{or} \quad a^2/R^2 = 1.7 \times 10^{-3}$$

so the approximation made in equation (13) is valid. Therefore the magnification is

$$\text{Magnification} = b/a = n_i/n_t = 1.33 . \tag{15}$$

Now to find where the image is located, one ray from S, namely SP, when refracted is represented by ray S'P. Another ray which can be used is ray SP'. Since it is radial, it will not be refracted, so S'P' represents the so called "refracted ray," and both S'P' and S'P intersect at S'. Thus, the image plane is the line which bisects the sphere. This means that the image distance is 1/2 the diameter of the sphere, or - 0.5 ft., obeying the usual sign conventions.

112

Another way to find the image point is to make use of an approximation first, which says that the small fish is a point at the center of the sphere. Then all rays from the fish are radial and are not refracted at the spherical surface since the radial rays are normally incident at the surface (i.e., $\theta_i = 0$ and therefore $\theta_t = 0$). Since the radial rays are not refracted, the observer sees them to be converging to the center of the sphere. So, again the image distance is - 0.5 ft.

● PROBLEM 6-12

A piece of capillary glass tubing has an outside diameter of 7mm. The tubing appears to have a diameter of 1mm inside when looked at through the glass wall. What is its real diameter (n = 1.5)?

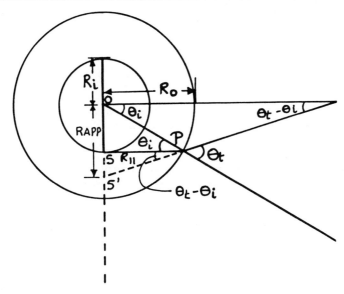

Solution: In the figure, R_i represents the radius of the capillary; R_o represents the outer radius of the glass tube; R_{app} represents the apparent radius of the capillary as seen from outside, θ_i is the angle of incidence, and θ_t is the angle of refraction. We will look at a ray which leaves from S and travels to P before being refracted at the surface. Since a radius vector is always perpendicular to a circle, θ_i and θ_t in the figure are the angle of incidence and angle of refraction respectively. By geometry, other angles in the figure can be determined.

We want to get the ratio R_{app}/R_i. To do this, we notice by geometry that

$$\frac{R_i}{R_o} = \sin\theta_i \tag{1}$$

113

$$\frac{R_{11}}{R_o} = \cos\theta_i \qquad (2)$$

$$R_{app} - R_i = R_{11} \tan(\theta_t - \theta_i) \qquad (3)$$

Solving equations (1) and (2) for R_i and R_{11}, respectively $R_i = R_o \sin\theta_i$ and $R_{11} = R_o \cos\theta_i$. Substituting for R_i and R_{11} in equation (3) gives $R_{app} - R_o \sin\theta_i$

$$= R_o \cos\theta_i \tan(\theta_t - \theta_i) \qquad \text{or}$$

$$R_{app} = R_o(\sin\theta_i + \cos\theta_i \tan(\theta_t - \theta_i)).$$

Dividing through by R_o gives

$$R_{app}/R_o = \sin\theta_i + \cos\theta_i \tan(\theta_t - \theta_i) \qquad (4)$$

Expressing $\tan(\theta_t - \theta_i)$ as $\dfrac{\sin(\theta_t - \theta_i)}{\cos(\theta_t - \theta_i)}$ equation (4) becomes

$$R_{app}/R_o = \sin\theta_i + \cos\theta_i \frac{\sin(\theta_t - \theta_i)}{\cos(\theta_t - \theta_i)} \qquad (5)$$

$$= \frac{\sin\theta_i \cos(\theta_t - \theta_i) + \cos\theta_i \sin(\theta_t - \theta_i)}{\cos(\theta_t - \theta_i)} \qquad (6)$$

Using the following trigonometric identity

$$\sin A \cos B + \cos A \sin B = \sin(A + B) \qquad (7)$$

equation (6) becomes

$$\frac{R_{app}}{R_o} = \frac{\sin(\theta_i + \theta_t - \theta_i)}{\cos(\theta_t - \theta_i)} \qquad (8)$$

or

$$\frac{R_{app}}{R_o} = \frac{\sin\theta_t}{\cos(\theta_t - \theta_i)} \qquad (9)$$

Dividing equation (9) by equation (1) gives

$$\frac{R_{app}}{R_i} = \frac{\sin\theta_t/\sin\theta_i}{\cos(\theta_t - \theta_i)} \qquad (10)$$

By Snell's law ($n_t \sin\theta_t = n_i \sin\theta_i$), equation (10) becomes

$$\frac{R_{app}}{R_i} = \frac{n_i/n_t}{\cos(\theta_t - \theta_i)} \qquad (11)$$

114

Substituting the given values $n_i = 1.5$ and $n_t = 1.0$ into equation (11) gives

$$\frac{R_{app}}{R_i} = \frac{1.5}{\cos(\theta_t - \theta_i)} \tag{12}$$

To eliminate the $\cos(\theta_t - \theta_i)$ term, we make use of approximations. If it can be shown that $\theta_t - \theta_i \cong 0°$, then $\cos(\theta_t - \theta_i) \cong 1$. R_o and R_{app} are given to be $\frac{7}{2}$ mm and $\frac{1}{2}$ mm, respectively. In addition, it is evident from the figure that $R_i < R_{app}$. Therefore, from equation (1),

$$\sin\theta_i = \frac{R_i}{R_o} < \frac{R_{app}}{R_o} = \frac{1}{7} = 0.143.$$

Hence,

$$\theta_i < 8°$$

$$\cos\theta_i \sim 0.989$$

Taking $\cos\theta_i = 1$ introduces approximately a 1% error. Then equation (11) becomes

$$\frac{R_{app}}{R_i} = \frac{n_i}{n_t} = 1.5$$

and

$$R_i = \frac{R_{app}}{1.5} = 0.33\text{mm}.$$

Hence, the real diameter is $2(0.33)$ mm = 0.66 mm. That the image of S is at S' can be seen by looking at a ray proceeding from S along the radius vector OSS'. At the surface this ray will not be refracted, so we will have an image of S at S'.

THE METHOD OF CHANGE OF CURVATURE OF WAVEFRONT

• PROBLEM 6-13

Plane waves, traveling in air, fall on a convex surface with radius of curvature 20 cm, separating air from glass. Find, by the method of change of curvature of wave front, at what point the waves are brought to a focus. (Index of refraction for glass = 1.64)

Solution: First, the sagittal equation must be derived.

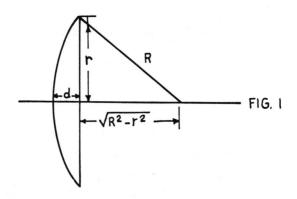

FIG. I

Looking at figure 1, we see that

$$d = R - \sqrt{R^2 - r^2} \tag{1}$$

Factoring out R from the radical sign gives

$$d = R - R\sqrt{1 - r^2/R^2} \tag{2}$$

The binomial theorem states:

$$(1 + x)^n = 1 + nx + \frac{n(n - 1)x^2}{2!} + \ldots \tag{3}$$

Therefore,

$$\sqrt{1 - r^2/R^2} = (1 - r^2/R^2)^{\frac{1}{2}} = 1 - \frac{r^2}{2R^2} + \ldots \tag{4}$$

Neglecting higher order terms,

$$d = R - R\left(1 - \frac{r^2}{2R^2}\right) = R - R + \frac{r^2}{2R} \tag{5}$$

Thus,

$$d = \frac{r^2}{2R} \tag{6}$$

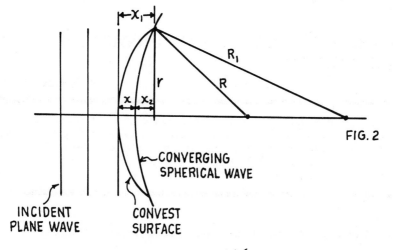

FIG. 2

CONVERGING
SPHERICAL WAVE

INCIDENT
PLANE WAVE

CONVEST
SURFACE

116

Figure 2 shows what happens when a plane wave interacts with a convex surface. When the plane wave is in
air, all parts of the plane wave move to the right with
velocity c (the speed of light in air). When the part of
the plane wave on the axis first encounters the convex
surface, the part of the plane wave off the axis will continue to move with a velocity c while that part of the
wave on the axis moves with a velocity c_m (the speed of
light in the medium). Since the index of refraction, n,
$= c / c_m$, this can be used to determine the relative positions of the wave front when the off axis part of the plane
wave interacts with the convex surface. Fermat's principle
of least action tells us that the time necessary for the
wave to move a distance x in the medium x is the same
amount of time necessary for the wave to move a distance
x_1 in air, or

$$\frac{x_1}{c} = \frac{x}{c_m} \tag{7}$$

or

$$x = \frac{x_1}{c/c_m} = \frac{x_1}{n} \tag{8}$$

Now, making use of equation (6) and figure 2,

$$x_1 = \frac{r^2}{2R} \tag{9}$$

$$x_2 = \frac{r^2}{2R_1} \tag{10}$$

where R is the radius of curvature of the convex surface
and R_1 is the radius of curvature of the wave surface in
the medium. R_1 will represent the location of the con-
vergence of the spherical wavefront.

From figure 2,

$$x_1 - x_2 = x \tag{11}$$

Substituting the expression on the right hand sides of
equations (8), (9), and (10), for x, x_1, and x_2, respectively,

$$\frac{r^2}{2R} - \frac{r^2}{2R_1} = \frac{r^2}{2Rn} \tag{12}$$

Then

$$\frac{r^2}{2R_1} = \frac{r^2}{2R} - \frac{r^2}{2Rn} = \frac{r^2}{2R}\left(1 - \frac{1}{n}\right) = \frac{r^2}{2R}\left(\frac{n-1}{n}\right) \tag{13}$$

117

Then, solving for R_1 yields

$$R_1 = \frac{n}{n - 1} R \qquad (14)$$

Substituting the given values for n and R into equation (14)

$$R_1 = \frac{1.64}{1.64 - 1} \times 20 \text{ cm} = \frac{20 \times 1.64}{.64} = 51.3 \text{ cm}$$

● **PROBLEM** 6-14

A water tank is closed at one end by a very thin glass window, curved outward, with radius of curvature equal to 20 cm, and at the other end by a very thin window of plane glass. The distance from window to window is 164.6 cm. A small bright source is placed on the central axis of these windows at a distance of 100 cm outside the curved window. Find, by the method of change of curvature of wave front, the position of the image of the source. (The index of refraction of water = 1.33.)

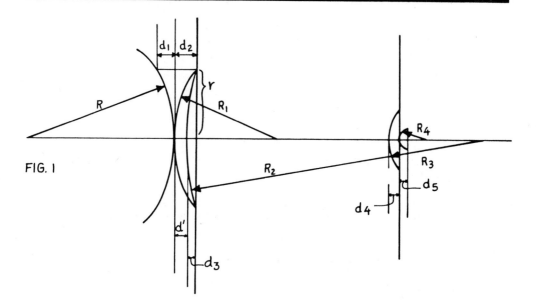

FIG. 1

Solution: Figure 1 shows a wave front diagram for this problem. From Fermat's principle of least action, while the off axis part of the wave front is traveling a distance $d_1 + d_2$, the on axis part of the wave will travel a distance d' related by

$$t = \frac{d_1 + d_2}{c} = \frac{d'}{c_m} \qquad (1)$$

where c is the velocity of light in air, and c_m is the velocity of light in the medium and t is the time required to move towards the right. The index of refraction for the medium is $n = c/c_m$. From the sagittal equation

118

derived in the preceding problem,

$$d_1 = \frac{r^2}{2R} \tag{2}$$

$$d_2 = \frac{r^2}{2R_1} \tag{3}$$

where $r = \frac{1}{2}$ the vertical height of the glass window.

From equations (1), (2), and (3),

$$d' = \frac{1}{n} \frac{r^2}{2} \left(\frac{1}{R} + \frac{1}{R_1} \right) \tag{4}$$

From figure 1, we can see that

$$d_3 = d_2 - d'$$

Then, from equations (3) and (4),

$$d_3 = \frac{r^2}{2} \left[\frac{1}{R_1} - \frac{1}{n} \left(\frac{1}{R} + \frac{1}{R_1} \right) \right] \tag{5}$$

From the sagittal equation,

$$d_3 = \frac{r^2}{2} \frac{1}{R_2} \tag{6}$$

Solving for $\frac{1}{R_2}$,

$$\frac{1}{R_2} = \frac{2d_3}{r^2} \tag{7}$$

Substituting the expression for d_3 given by equation (5) into equation (7),

$$\frac{1}{R_2} = \frac{1}{R_1} - \frac{1}{n} \left(\frac{1}{R} + \frac{1}{R_1} \right) \tag{8}$$

This spherical wave front will then converge to form an image of the object at a point R_2 from the convex surface. Substituting the given values

$$n = 1.33, \ R = 100 \text{ cm and } R_1 = 20 \text{ cm}$$

into equation (8) gives $R_2 = 2.05$ meters. Our problem states that the length of the water tank is 164.6 cm; therefore, what happens to the converging wave front when it reaches the right end of the water tank must be considered. Looking at figure 1, we see that

$$R_3 = R_2 - \ell$$

where ℓ represents the distance from window to window.

Substituting in the values for R_2 and ℓ gives

$$R_3 = (2.05 - 1.646) \text{ m} = .404 \text{ m} \tag{9}$$

Now we have the reverse of what happened at the left of the tank. While the spherically converging wave on the axis moves a distance d_4 in water, the off axis point moves a distance d_5 in air. By Fermat's principle,

$$\frac{d_4}{c_m} = \frac{d_5}{c} \tag{10}$$

or $\quad d_5 = nd_4 \tag{11}$

The sagittal equations are

$$d_5 = \frac{r^2}{2R_4} \tag{12}$$

and

$$d_4 = \frac{r^2}{2R_3} \tag{13}$$

Substituting the expressions for d_5 and d_4 (from equations (12) and (13), respectively) into equation (11),

$$\frac{r^2}{2R_4} = \frac{nr^2}{2R_3} \tag{14}$$

Solving for R_4,

$$R_4 = \frac{R_3}{n} \tag{15}$$

Substituting for R_3 and n,

$$R_4 = \frac{.404}{1.33} \text{ m}$$

or $\quad R_4 = .304 \text{ m} = 30.4 \text{ cm.}$

Hence, the image of the source is located 30.4 cm beyond the plane window

DERIVATIONS

• PROBLEM 6-15

A surface of curvature c separates media of refractive indices n and n'. Show that the conjugate (positions of object and image points) distance equation for this surface is

$$\frac{n}{\ell} + \frac{n'}{\ell'} = (n' - n)c,$$

where ℓ and ℓ' are the object and image distances, respectively.

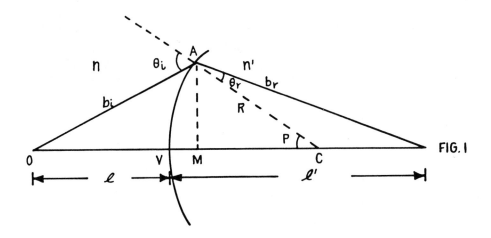

FIG. I

Solution: Figure 1 shows the refracting surface element separating the object space and the image space with indices of refraction n and n' respectively. The curvature $c = \frac{1}{R}$ where R is the radius of curvature of the refracting element. Distances are positive when taken from O to V in the object space and from I to V in the image space. A ray from an axial point O is refracted at A in accordance with Snell's law, and proceeds to the axial image point I. Let the object distance be ℓ and the image distance be ℓ', as shown in figure 1, measured from V. Let the path length of the incident ray OA = b_i and let the path length of the refracted ray AI = b_r.

Considering triangle OAC, the law of Sines gives

$$\frac{\sin\theta_i}{\sin\rho} = \frac{\ell + R}{b_i} \tag{1}$$

Considering triangle IAC, the law of Sines gives

$$\frac{\sin\theta_r}{\sin\rho} = \frac{\ell' - R}{b_r}. \tag{2}$$

Dividing equation (1) by equation (2), we have

$$\frac{\sin\theta_i}{\sin\theta_r} = \frac{\ell + R}{\ell' - R}\frac{b_r}{b_i} \tag{3}$$

121

Snell's law of refraction states:

$$n \sin\theta_i = n' \sin\theta_r \tag{4}$$

Hence, substituting $\dfrac{n'}{n}$ for $\dfrac{\sin\theta_i}{\sin\theta_r}$ in equation (3)

$$\frac{\ell + R}{\ell' - R} \cdot \frac{b_r}{b_i} = \frac{n'}{n} \tag{5}$$

In a general case, b_r and b_i can be related to ℓ, ℓ', and the distances AM and VM. However when an important assumption is made, namely that the distance AM is small compared to ℓ and ℓ', then to a sufficient degree of approximation,

$$b_r = \ell' \quad \text{and} \quad b_i = \ell$$

Then equation (5) becomes

$$\frac{\ell + R}{\ell' - R} \frac{\ell'}{\ell} = \frac{n'}{n}$$

Cross-multiplying gives

$$n\ell'(\ell + R) = n'\ell(\ell' - R)$$

Expanding,

$$n\ell\ell' + nR\ell' = n'\ell\ell' - n'R\ell$$

Dividing both sides by $\ell\ell'R$ gives

$$\frac{n}{R} + \frac{n}{\ell} = \frac{n'}{R} - \frac{n'}{\ell'}$$

or

$$\frac{n}{\ell} + \frac{n'}{\ell'} = c(n' - n)$$

● **PROBLEM** 6-16

The curved surface of a glass hemisphere is silvered. Rays coming from a luminous point at a distance u from the plane surface are refracted into the glass reflected from the concave spherical surface, and refracted at the plane surface back into the air. If r denotes the radius of the spherical surface and n the index of refraction of the glass, show that

$$\frac{1}{u} + \frac{1}{u'} + \frac{2n}{r} = 0$$

where u' denotes the distance of the image from the plane surface.

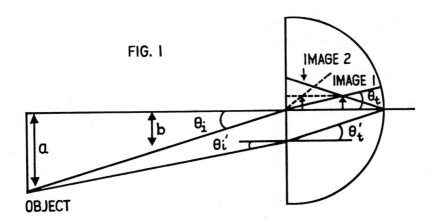

FIG. I

IMAGE 2
IMAGE I

θ_t

θ_i

θ_i'

θ_t'

b

a

OBJECT

Solution: This problem can be solved by two methods.
Method 1: First, the small aperture equation for refractive media states:

$$\frac{n_1}{u} + \frac{n_2}{u'} = \frac{n_2 - n_1}{R} \qquad (1)$$

where the n's represent the indices of refraction of the
materials at the interface, u and u' are the object and
image distances, respectively, from the interface, and R
is the radius of curvature of the surface. For a mirror,

$$\frac{1}{u} + \frac{1}{u'} = \frac{2}{R} \qquad (2)$$

Secondly, we will look at ray diagrams and use Snell's
law:

$$n_1 \sin\theta_1 = n_2 \sin\theta_2 \qquad (3)$$

where the θ's represent the angles the ray makes with the
normal to the surfaces and the n's are the indices of refraction. The law of reflection states

$$\theta_i = \theta_r \qquad (4)$$

where θ_i and θ_r represent the angles of incidence and reflection, respectively.

At the plane surface, $1/R = 0$ so equation (1)
yields

$$\frac{1}{u_1} + \frac{n}{u_1'} = 0$$

(n_1 = the index of refraction of air = 1);

$$u_1' = -nu_1 \qquad (5)$$

123

For the mirror,

$$u_2 = R - u_1' = R + nu_1 \tag{6}$$

Substituting this value for u_2 into equation (2),

$$\frac{1}{R + nu_1} + \frac{1}{u_2'} = \frac{2}{R}$$

$$\frac{1}{u_2'} = \frac{2}{R} - \frac{1}{R + nu_1} = \frac{R + 2nu_1}{R(R + nu_1)}$$

$$u_2' = \frac{R(R + nu_1)}{R + 2nu_1} \tag{7}$$

At the plane surface,

$$u_3 = R - u_2'$$

Substituting the expression for u_2' given by equation (7) into this equation,

$$u_3 = R - \frac{R(R + nu_1)}{R + 2nu_1} = R\left(1 - \frac{R + nu_1}{R + 2nu_1}\right)$$

$$= \frac{Rnu_1}{R + 2nu_1} \tag{8}$$

Using equation (1) again,

$$\frac{n}{u_3} + \frac{1}{u_3'} = \frac{n-1}{R} = 0$$

$$\frac{n(R + 2nu_1)}{nRu_1} + \frac{1}{u_3'} = 0 \quad ; \quad \frac{1}{u_3'} = -\left(\frac{R + 2nu_1}{Ru_1}\right)$$

Cross multiplying,

$$-Ru_1 = Ru_3' + 2nu_1u_3'$$

or

$$Ru_3' + Ru_1 + 2nu_3'u_1 = 0 \tag{9}$$

Dividing equation (9) by $Ru_3'u_1$ yields

$$\frac{1}{u_1} + \frac{1}{u_3'} + \frac{2n}{R} = 0 \tag{10}$$

124

Letting $u_1 = u$, the initial object distance, and $u_3' = u'$, the final image position, equation (10) becomes

$$\frac{1}{u} + \frac{1}{u'} + \frac{2n}{R} = 0 \tag{11}$$

as required.

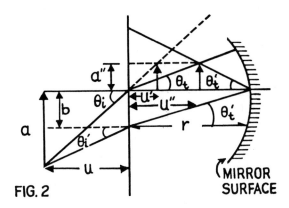

FIG. 2

Method 2: In figure 1, we choose a ray from the object which will encounter the flat hemispherical surface at the axis of symmetry. This ray will be refracted at the surface but will proceed along the radius of the hemisphere. Since a radius vector is normal to the surface of a sphere, this ray will be reflected at the mirror surface back along its radius and retrace its path to the flat surface, and thus, to the original object point.

For a second ray, choose that ray from the object which when refracted at the flat hemispherical surface will be directed to the intersection of the axis of symmetry and the mirror. This ray will be reflected symmetrically and finally refracted at the flat surface.

These two rays intersect and a real image is produced in the glass at a distance u" from the flat surface. However, further consideration shows that this real image produces a virtual image, the location of which we seek since this is the image visible from outside the glass.

From this image point u", draw a third ray parallel to the axis of symmetry which will then be normal to the flat hemispherical surface and be undeviated as it leaves the hemisphere.

If we look at the first ray and the third ray which we chose, we see that the rays leaving the hemisphere are diverging and so we have a virtual image formed which will be at the intersection of the rays at the final image point u' (see figure 1).

From figures 1 and 2 the following geometric relationships exist:

125

$$\sin\theta_i = \frac{a}{(u^2 + a^2)^{\frac{1}{2}}} \quad \text{(a)} \qquad\qquad \sin\theta_i' = \frac{a - b}{[(a - b)^2 + u^2]^{\frac{1}{2}}} \quad \text{(e)}$$

$$\sin\theta_t = \frac{a''}{(a''^2 + u''^2)^{\frac{1}{2}}} \quad \text{(b)} \qquad \sin\theta_t' = \frac{b}{(b^2 + r^2)^{\frac{1}{2}}} \quad \text{(f)}$$

$$\sin\theta_i = \frac{a''}{(u'^2 + a''^2)^{\frac{1}{2}}} \quad \text{(c)} \qquad \sin\theta_t' = \frac{a''}{[(r - u'')^2 + a''^2]^{\frac{1}{2}}} \quad \text{(g)}$$

$$\sin\theta_t = \frac{\sin\theta_i}{n} \quad \text{(d)}$$

Again, from Snell's law,

$$\sin\theta_t' = \frac{\sin\theta_i'}{n} \quad \text{(h)}$$

From (a), $\sin\theta_i = \dfrac{a}{(a^2 + u^2)^{\frac{1}{2}}}$.

From (c), $\sin\theta_i = \dfrac{a''}{(u'^2 + a''^2)^{\frac{1}{2}}}$;

therefore,

$$\sin\theta_i = \frac{a}{(a^2 + u^2)^{\frac{1}{2}}} = \frac{a''}{(u'^2 + a''^2)^{\frac{1}{2}}} = n\sin\theta_t$$

[by (d)] $\quad = \dfrac{na''}{(a''^2 + u''^2)^{\frac{1}{2}}} \qquad$ [by (b)]

From (f) and (g),

$$\sin\theta_t' = \frac{b}{(b^2 + r^2)^{\frac{1}{2}}} = \frac{a''}{[(r - u'')^2 + a''^2]^{\frac{1}{2}}} =$$

$$\frac{1}{n}\sin\theta_i' \quad \text{[from (h)]} = \frac{a - b}{n[(a - b)^2 + u^2]^{\frac{1}{2}}} \quad \text{[from (e)]}$$

Now we need to eliminate a'', u'', b and a from these relationships and keep u, u', r, n. It has been shown that

$$\frac{a}{(a^2 + u^2)^{\frac{1}{2}}} = \frac{a''}{(u'^2 + a''^2)^{\frac{1}{2}}}$$

Squaring both sides of this equation gives

$$\frac{a^2}{a^2 + u^2} = \frac{a''^2}{u'^2 + a''^2}$$

126

Cross-multiplying gives

$$a^2(u'^2 + a''^2) = a''^2(a^2 + u^2)$$

or,

$$a^2u'^2 + a^2a''^2 = a''^2a^2 + a''^2u^2$$

The $a^2a''^2$ terms drop out, leaving

$$a^2u'^2 = a''^2u^2$$

or

$$a'' = a\frac{u'}{u} \qquad\qquad (12)$$

In addition, from (b), (c) and (d),

$$\frac{a''}{(a''^2 + u''^2)^{\frac{1}{2}}} = \frac{1}{n} \frac{a''}{(u'^2 + a''^2)^{\frac{1}{2}}}$$

The a" terms in the numerators cancel, and squaring both sides,

$$\frac{1}{a''^2 + u''^2} = \frac{1}{n^2(u'^2 + a''^2)}$$

Hence,

$$n^2u'^2 + n^2a''^2 = a''^2 + u''^2$$

or

$$u''^2 = (n^2 - 1)a''^2 + n^2u'^2 = (n^2 - 1)a^2\frac{u'^2}{u^2} + n^2u'^2$$

$$= c^2 \text{ [from equation (12)]} \qquad\qquad (13)$$

where c^2 is used to consolidate the writing of terms.

From (f) and (g),

$$\frac{b^2}{b^2 + r^2} = \frac{a''^2}{[(r - u'')^2 + a''^2]}$$

Cross-multiplying gives

$$b^2[(r - u'')^2 + a''^2] = a''^2b^2 + a''^2r^2$$

Then

$$b^2a''^2 + b^2(r - u'')^2 = b^2a''^2 + a''^2r^2$$

127

The $b^2 a''^2$ terms cancel and so,

$$b^2 = \frac{a''^2 r^2}{(r - u'')^2} = \frac{a''^2 r^2}{(r - c)^2} = \frac{a^2 u'^2 r^2}{u^2 (r - c)^2}$$

[from equation (12)]

Hence,

$$b = \frac{aru'}{u(r - c)} \tag{14}$$

Similarly,

$$n^2 u'^2 = \frac{1}{u^2} (ur - ru' - uc)^2 \left[1 - \frac{(n^2 - 1) a^2 u'^2}{u^2 (r - c)^2} \right] \tag{15}$$

In this last equation, using small aperture, let a go to 0. As a result, c goes to nu' [from equation (13)]. So, equation (15) becomes

$$n^2 u'^2 u^2 = (ur - ru' - nu'u)^2$$

or, taking the square root of both sides,

$$nu'u = ur - ru' - nu'u$$

Then,

$$2nu'u = ur - ru'$$

Dividing both sides of this equation by u'ur gives

$$\frac{2n}{r} = \frac{1}{u'} - \frac{1}{u}$$

or

$$\frac{1}{u} + \frac{1}{(-u')} + \frac{2n}{r} = 0$$

Now, as we have drawn figure 2, u' is inside the glass hemisphere and is a virtual image. Therefore to be consistent with the first method, we must substitute u' = -u'. Thus,

$$\frac{1}{u} + \frac{1}{u'} + \frac{2n}{r} = 0$$

PARTIAL REFLECTION

● **PROBLEM 6-17**

The index of refraction of a refracting sphere in air is

128

$\sqrt{3}$. A ray of light, entering the sphere at an angle of incidence of 60° and passing over to the other side, is there partly reflected and partly refracted.

(a) Show that the reflected ray and the emergent ray are at right angles to each other.

(b) Show that the refracted ray will cross the sphere and be refracted back into the air in a direction exactly opposite to the direction in which the ray was going before it entered the sphere.

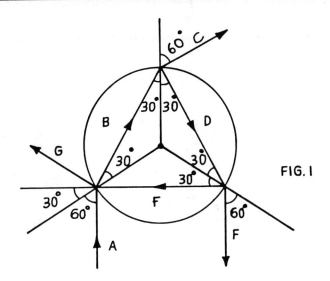

FIG. I

Solution: Let a light ray be incident on a sphere of index of refraction $\sqrt{3}$ at an angle of incidence of 60°. This is indicated as ray A in figure 1. By Snell's law of refraction,

       n sin i = n' sin r

where n and n' are the indices of refraction in the two media, i is the angle of incidence, measured with respect to the normal, a radius vector in this case, and r is the angle of refraction, we can find the path of the refracted ray B as follows:

    1 sin 60° = $\sqrt{3}$ sin r

       r = 30°

When ray B again strikes the spherical surface, ray B and the two radius vectors form an isosceles triangle, so the interior angle as shown on the figure is 30° and applying Snell's law again, the exterior angle for ray C can be shown to be 60°. The reflected ray G makes an angle of 60° with respect to the normal, by the law of reflection (the angle of incidence = the angle of reflection). Likewise, ray D will be at an angle of 30° to the radius vector. Where ray D strikes the surface, we have a similar condition

129

to ray B striking the surface so rays E and F will be as
shown.

Then, since a straight line contains 180 degrees,
60 + 30 + the angle between C and D = 180 and so, the
angle between C and D = 90°.   In addition, it can easily
be determined that A and E are antiparallel.

THE RAINBOW

● PROBLEM 6-18

Describe how a rainbow is produced.

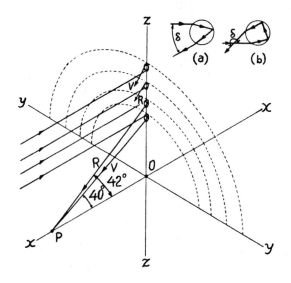

Solution: The rainbow is produced by the combined effects
of refraction, dispersion, and internal reflection of sunlight by drops of rain.   When conditions for its observation are favorable, two bows may be seen, the inner being
called the primary bow and the outer the secondary bow.
The inner bow, which is the brighter of the two, is red on
the outside and violet on the inside, while in the more
faint outer bow, the colors are reversed.   The primary bow
is produced in the following manner.   Assume that the sun's
rays are horizontal, and consider a ray striking a raindrop
as shown in figure (a).   This ray is refracted at the first
surface and is in part reflected at the second surface,
passing out again at the front surface as shown.   An exact
computation of the course of such a ray is exceedingly
laborious but the French scientist Descartes computed the
paths of some thousands of rays incident at different points
on the surface of a raindrop and showed that if a ray of any
given color were incident at such a point that its deviation
was a maximum, all other rays of the same color which struck
the surface of the drop in the immediate neighborhood of
this point would be reflected in a direction very close to
that of the first.   The angle of maximum deviation of red
light is 138°, or the angle δ, shown in the figure, is equal

to 180° - 138° = 42°. The corresponding angle for violet light is 40°, while that for other colors lies intermediate between these.

Consider now an observer at P. The X-Y plane is horizontal and sunlight is coming from the left parallel to the X-axis. All drops which lie on a circle subtending an angle of 42° at P and with the center at O will reflect red light strongly to P. All those on a circle subtending an angle of 40° at P will reflect violet light strongly, while those occupying intermediate positions will reflect the intermediate colors of the spectrum.

The point O, the center of the circular arc of the bow, may be considered the shadow of P on the Y-Z plane. As the sun rises above the horizon the point O moves down, and hence with increasing elevation of the sun a smaller and smaller part of the bow is visible. Evidently an observer at ground level cannot see the primary bow when the sun is more than 42° above the horizon. If the observer is in an elevated position, however, the point O moves up and more and more of the bow may be seen. In fact, it is not uncommon for a complete circular rainbow to be seen from an airplane.

The secondary bow is produced by two internal reflections, as shown in figure (b). As before, the light which is reflected in any particular direction consists largely of the color for which that direction is the angle of maximum deviation. Since the angle of deviation is here the angle δ and since the violet is deviated more than the red, the violet rays in the secondary bow are deflected down at a steeper angle than the red and the secondary bow is red on the inside and violet on the outside edge. The corresponding angles are 50.5° for the red and 54° for violet.

CHAPTER 7

DIOPTICS

REFRACTING POWER

> The radius of curvature of the front surface of the cornea of the human eye is about 7.7 mm and the radius of curvature for the back surface is about 6.8 mm. The index of refraction of the cornea is 1.376 and for the aqueous humor it is 1.336. Find the dioptric power of the front and back surfaces of the cornea.

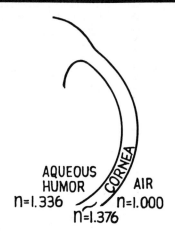

AQUEOUS HUMOR
n=1.336

CORNEA

AIR
n=1.000

n=1.376

Solution: The dioptric power, D, of a surface is found by using the equation

$$D = \frac{n_b - n_a}{R_s} \tag{1}$$

where n_b is the index of refraction of the second medium, n_a is the index of refraction of the first medium (the medium which the light is incident upon), and R_s is the radius of curvature of the surface. For the front surface of the cornea, $n_b = 1.376$, $n_a = 1.000$, and $R_s = 0.0077$ m.

Substituting these values into equation (1) gives

$$D = \frac{1.376 - 1.000}{0.0077 \text{ m}} \cong 48.8 \text{ m}^{-1}$$

or $D = 48.8$ diopters. For the back surface of the cornea,

$$n_b = 1.336, \quad n_a = 1.376, \quad \text{and} \quad R_s = 0.0068 \text{ m} .$$

Substituting these values into equation (1) gives

$$D = \frac{1.336 - 1.376}{0.0068 \text{ m}} \cong -5.9 \text{ m}^{-1}$$

or $D = -5.9$ diopters.

● **PROBLEM** 7-2

Given a biconvex lens in air, the radius of the front
surface, R_1 , $= 6.25$ cm, the radius of the back surface,
R_2 , $= -8.33$ cm, the thickness of the lens, $t = 12.0$ mm,
and the index of refraction of the lens, n_L , $= 1.5$.   There
is an object 50 cm from the front surface of the lens.
What is (a) the true power of the lens, (b) the positions
of the first and second principal points, (c) the position
of the image, and (d) the magnification?

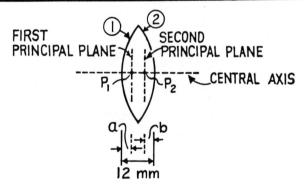

Solution: Since the lens used in this problem has a thickness of 12 mm, the equations for a thin lens cannot be
used because they only hold for lenses of negligible thicknesses.

(a)   To find the true power of the lens, D, it is necessary
to first find the power of each surface, D_1 and D_2 , and
then to use the following equation:

$$D = D_1 + D_2 - \frac{D_1 \cdot D_2 \cdot t}{n_L} \tag{1}$$

where t is the thickness and n_L is the index of refraction
of the lens.

133

The power of the first surface is found by making use of the relation

$$D_1 = \frac{n_L - n_A}{R_1} \; ,$$

where n_A is the index of refraction of air $\cong 1$.

Hence,

$$D_1 = \frac{1.5 - 1.0}{0.0625 \text{ m}} = 8.0 \text{ m}^{-1}$$

or

$$D_1 = 8.0 \text{ diopters.}$$

The power of the second surface can be found by using the relation

$$D_2 = \frac{n_A - n_L}{R_2}$$

Hence,

$$D_2 = \frac{1.0 - 1.5}{-0.0833 \text{ m}} \cong 6.0 \text{ m}^{-1}$$

or

$$D_2 \cong 6.0 \text{ diopters.}$$

Now, substituting the values computed for D_1 and D_2 along with the given value for t into equation (1) gives

$$D = 8.0 + 6.0 - \frac{(8.0)(6.0)(0.012)}{(1.5)} \text{ diopters} =$$

$$13.62 \text{ diopters.}$$

Hence, the true power of the lens is 13.62 diopters or 13.62 m^{-1}.

(b) For thick lenses, the first and second principal points are the points where the first and second principal planes and the central axis intersect. These points are represented by P_1 and P_2 in the figure. The distance from the first principal point, P_1 , to the first surface (along the central axis) is represented by a and the distance from the second principal point, P_2 , to the second surface is represented by b. a and b can be found by using the formulas

$$a = \frac{f \cdot \left(1 - n_L\right) \cdot t}{R_2 \cdot n_L} \qquad\qquad (2)$$

and

$$b = \frac{f \cdot \left(n_L - 1\right) \cdot t}{R_1 \cdot n_L} \tag{3}$$

where f is the focal length of the lens, which is the reciprocal of the power of the lens. So the focal length, f,
is

$$f = \frac{1}{D} = \frac{1}{13.62 \text{ m}^{-1}} = 0.0734 \text{ m} = 7.34 \text{ cm.}$$

Substituting into equation (2) for f, n_L, t and R_2
gives the result

$$a = \frac{(7.34 \text{ cm})(1.0 - 1.5)(1.20 \text{ cm})}{(-8.33 \text{ cm})(1.5)} = 0.35 \text{ cm}$$

and similarly, equation (3) becomes

$$b = \frac{(7.34 \text{ cm})(1.5 - 1.0)(1.20 \text{ cm})}{(6.25 \text{ cm})(1.5)} = 0.47 \text{ cm}$$

(c) The position of the image can be found by applying the
lens equation,

$$\frac{1}{0} + \frac{1}{i} = \frac{1}{f} \tag{4}$$

where 0 is the distance of the object from the first principal point, i is the distance of the image from the second
principal point, and f is the focal length of the lens.
Since the object is given to be 50 cm from the front surface
of the lens, the object distance, 0, is equal to

50 cm + 0.35 cm = 50.35 cm.

Substituting the value 0 = 50.35 cm into equation (4)
gives

$$\frac{1}{50.35 \text{ cm}} + \frac{1}{i} = \frac{1}{7.34 \text{ cm}} \quad .$$

Hence,

$$i = \frac{(7.34)(50.35)}{50.35 - 7.34} \cong 8.59 \text{ cm.}$$

The image is 8.59 cm to the right of the second principal
point or (8.59 - 0.47) cm = 8.12 cm to the right of the
second surface of the lens.

(d) The magnification, m, of a thick lens is the same as
the magnification for a thin lens, and thus can be found by

making use of the following expression:

$$m = -\frac{i}{0} = -\frac{8.59 \text{ cm}}{50.35 \text{ cm}} \cong -0.171 \ .$$

Thus, the image is approximately 0.171 times as large as the object, and the minus sign indicates that it is inverted.

● **PROBLEM** 7-3

Calculate the powers of the glass surfaces in air whose radii of curvature are 40 cm, 250 mm, 10 cm, 70 mm, and 2 cm, if the index of refraction of the glass is 1.50.

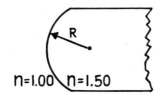

Solution: The figure shown is of the glass surface in air. To find the power of the surface, D, in diopters (m^{-1}) the following equation must be used:

$$D = (n - 1) \frac{1}{R}$$

where n is the index of refraction of the glass and R is the radius of curvature of the glass surface. Given that n = 1.5 and that the radii are 0.4 m, 0.25 m, 0.1 m, 0.07 m, and 0.02 m, the powers can be computed to be D = 1.25, 2.00, 5.00, 7.14 and 25.00 diopters, respectively.

● **PROBLEM** 7-4

What is the refracting power of a spherical refracting surface of radius 20 cm separating air (n = 1) from glass (n = 1.5, where n denotes the index of refraction of the medium)?

Solution: The power of a spherical refracting surface can be found from the following equation:

$$D = (n - 1) \frac{1}{R} \ ,$$

where D is the refracting power, n is the index of refraction of the glass surface, and R is the radius of curvature of the surface. Substituting the given values

R = 20 cm = 0.20 m and n = 1.5

into the equation gives the result

$$D = (1.5 - 1) \frac{1}{0.20 \text{ m}} = 2.5 \text{ m}^{-1} \text{ or } 2.5 \text{ diopters.}$$

A spherical glass surface having a radius of curvature of 20 mm is immersed in water. What is the power of the surface in water (n_{water} = 1.333, n_{glass} = 1.50; n represents index of refraction)?

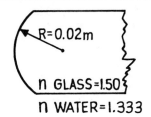

R=0.02m

n GLASS=1.50

n WATER=1.333

Solution: The power of the surface when immersed in water can be found by applying the following equation:

$$D = (n - 1) \frac{1}{R}$$

where D is the power of the surface, R is the radius of curvature of the glass surface, and n is the relative index of refraction; that is, the ratio of the index of refraction of the glass to the index of refraction of the medium in which the glass is immersed. In this problem, n is equal to

$$\frac{1.50}{1.333}$$

or   1.125.

Substituting the values n = 1.125 and R = 0.02 m into the above equation gives the result

$$D = (1.125 - 1) \frac{1}{0.02 \text{ m}} = 6.25 \text{ m}^{-1}$$

Since power is expressed in diopters when the radius of curvature of the lens is expressed in meters, the power of this surface is 6.25 diopters.

The refractive power of a thin plano-convex lens made of glass of index of refraction 1.5 is 20 diopters. Find the radius of curvature of the curved surface of the lens.

Solution: The power of a lens, expressed in dipoters, is the reciprocal of the focal length, expressed in meters. The equation relating the focal length f of a lens to its radii of curvature R_1 and R_2 and its refractive index n is the following:

$$\frac{1}{f} = (n - 1)\left(\frac{1}{R_1} - \frac{1}{R_2}\right) \tag{1}$$

Thus the power D is given by the following equation:

$$D = (n - 1)\left(\frac{1}{R_1} - \frac{1}{R_2}\right) \qquad (2)$$

Substituting the given values

n = 1.50, D = 20 diopters or 20 m^{-1} and $R_2 = \infty$

(The radius of curvature of the plane side of the lens) into equation (2) gives the result

$$20 \ m^{-1} = (1.50 - 1) \frac{1}{R_1} \ .$$

Solving for R_1 gives $R_1 = \dfrac{.50}{20 \ m^{-1}}$

$$= .025 \ m$$

$$= 2.5 \ cm.$$

● **PROBLEM** 7-7

What is the refracting power of a concave mirror of radius 20 cm when the reflecting surface is in contact with (a) air (n = 1) and (b) water (n = 1.33; n denotes index of refraction)?

Solution: The power of a lens or a mirror is the reciprocal of its focal length. When the focal length is expressed in meters, the power is expressed in diopters.

(a) The focal length of a mirror in air (n = 1) is half the radius of curvature of the mirror. Thus the focal length of the mirror in air is $\frac{1}{2}$ · (20 cm) or 0.1 m. Hence, the power of the mirror is $\frac{1}{0.1 \ m}$ or 10 diopters.

(b) If the mirror is immersed in a medium other than air, the focal length of the mirror is still half the radius of curvature of the mirror, but the power is the product of the reciprocal of the focal length and the index of refraction of the medium. So, the power of the lens is

$$\frac{1}{\frac{1}{2} \ (0.20 \ m)} \ (1.333) = 13.33 \ diopters.$$

● **PROBLEM** 7-8

A concave lens with focal length 12 cm is placed in contact with a convex lens of focal length 7.5 cm. Find the refracting power of the combination.

Solution: When two lenses of focal lengths f_1 and f_2 are placed in contact with each other, the resulting focal length f can be calculated as follows;

$$\frac{1}{f} = \frac{1}{f_1} + \frac{1}{f_2} \text{ .}$$

The refracting power of the combination of the lenses is the reciprocal of the focal length of the combination of the two. Thus the refracting power of the combination, D, is given by the following equation:

$$D = \frac{1}{f_1} + \frac{1}{f_2} \text{ ,}$$

where f_1 and f_2 are the focal lengths of the two lenses. f_1 is equal to +0.12 m since it is the focal length of a concave lens and f_2 is equal to -0.075 m since it is the focal length of a convex lens. Substituting into the above equation gives

$$D = \frac{1}{0.12 \text{ m}} + \frac{1}{-0.075 \text{ m}} = -5m^{-1}$$

When the focal lengths of the lenses are expressed in meters the power is expressed in diopters; hence the refracting power of the combination of the two lenses is -5 diopters.

● PROBLEM 7-9

If one holds a lens 50 cm from a flash lamp and finds that an image of the lamp is sharply focused at a distance of 16.6 cm from the lens, what is the power of the lens?

Solution: The power of a lens is the reciprocal of its focal length (when expressed in meters). Thus the power of the lens, P is given as follows:

$$P = \frac{100}{f}$$

where f is the focal length in centimeters. A lens in air is said to have a power of 1 diopter when its focal length is 1 meter. Given that the object distance, S = +50 cm and that the image distance, S', = + 16.6 cm, the lens equation

$$\frac{1}{f} = \frac{1}{S} + \frac{1}{S'} \text{ ,}$$

gives the result

$$\frac{1}{f} = \frac{1}{50 \text{ cm}} + \frac{1}{16.6 \text{ cm}} \cong 0.08 \text{ cm}^{-1} \text{ .}$$

Hence,

$$P = \frac{100}{f} = 8 \text{ diopters.}$$

A lens-gauge graduated in diopters for glass with index of refraction 1.5 is used to measure the power of a thin double convex lens made of glass with index of refraction 1.6. The readings on the dial are +4 diopters for both surfaces of the convex lens. Find the refractive power of the lens, assuming that its thickness is negligible.

Solution: Since the lens-gauge is graduated for glass of index of refraction 1.5, the readings obtained for each surface must use n = 1.5. The power of the two surfaces of a lens is defined as follows:

$$P_1 = \frac{n - 1}{r_1} = 4$$

and

$$P_2 = \frac{1 - n}{r_2} = 4$$

Hence, the total power of the lens, P, is given as follows:

$$P = P_1 + P_2 =$$

$$\frac{n - 1}{r_1} + \frac{1 - n}{r_2}$$

$$= (n - 1) \left(\frac{1}{r_1} - \frac{1}{r_2} \right) \tag{1}$$

Thus, since P = 4 + 4 = 8,

$$(n - 1) \left(\frac{1}{r_1} - \frac{1}{r_2} \right) = 8$$

Solving for

$$\frac{1}{r_1} - \frac{1}{r_2}$$

and substituting n = 1.5 gives the result

$$\frac{1}{r_1} - \frac{1}{r_2} = \frac{8}{n - 1}$$

$$= \frac{8}{1.5 - 1}$$

$$= 16$$

Therefore, from equation (1), if n = 1.6, then

$$P = (1.6 - 1) \left(\frac{1}{r_1} - \frac{1}{r_2} \right)$$

= 0.6 x 16

= 9.6 diopters.

● **PROBLEM** 7-11

What is the prismatic effect of a lens of power +4 diopters decentered 0.75 cm?

FIG. I

Solution: Prismatic effects are produced by mounting a
lens in front of an eye so that the optical center of the
lens is displaced from the normal intersection point of
the visual axis.

Consider a lens of power F decentered through a distance y. The axis of the lens is GAF'. A ray parallel
to the axis, incident at a height y, is deviated toward
the principal focus F', i.e., through an angle equivalent
to the deviation produced by a prism of power y/f' prism
diopters if y is in cm and f' is the focal length in
meters.

Prismatic Power = yF

= 0.75 x 4 prism-diopters

= 3 prism-diopters

● **PROBLEM** 7-12

The refracting power of a symmetric glass lens
(n = 1.5, where n represents index of refraction) surrounded by air (n = 1) is +10 diopters, and its thickness is 0.5 cm. Determine the radius of the first
surface.

FIG. I

$(-S,0)$ V_1 V_2 $(S'',0)$

$\longmapsto t \longleftarrow$

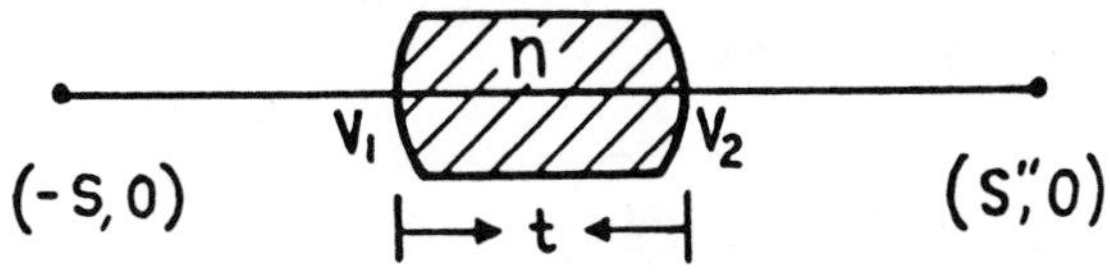

Solution: The magnitudes of the radii of curvature for
the two faces of a symmetric lens are equal. Let this
magnitude be $|r|$. Then the first surface has a radius
of curvature of r and the second surface has a radius of
curvature of -r. The refracting power measured in
diopters is the reciprocal of the focal length of the
lens, expressed in meters. Hence, the focal length

$$f = \frac{1}{10 \text{ m}^{-1}} = .1 \text{ m} = 10 \text{ cm.}$$

141

The problem of finding the focal length in terms of the thickness and the radius of curvature can be solved by considering the refraction of light at the two surfaces of the lens consecutively. Consider an object at a distance of -s from the first surface as shown in fig. 1.

The refraction equation applied to the first face is

$$\frac{n}{s'} - \frac{1}{s} = \frac{n-1}{|r|} \tag{1}$$

where s' is the image distance from the first surface of the lens. The image s' acts as the object for the second surface and hence,

$$\frac{1}{s''} - \frac{n}{s'-t} = \frac{(n-1)}{|r|} \tag{2}$$

where s" denotes the image distance from the second surface of the lens and t is the thickness of the lens.

Let $\dfrac{n-1}{|r|} = \dfrac{-1}{f}$.

Now it is desired to eliminate s' from equations (1) and (2). From equation (1),

$$s' = \frac{n}{\frac{1}{s} - \frac{1}{f}}$$

Substituting

$$s' = \frac{n}{\frac{1}{s} - \frac{1}{f}}$$

and

$$\frac{(n-1)}{|r|} = \frac{-1}{f}$$

into equation (2) gives

$$\frac{1}{s''} - \frac{n}{\dfrac{n}{\frac{1}{s} - \frac{1}{f}} - t} = \frac{-1}{f} .$$

This is equivalent to the following:

$$\frac{1}{s''} - \frac{1}{\dfrac{1}{\frac{1}{s} - \frac{1}{f}} - t/n} = -\frac{1}{f} \tag{3}$$

Hence,

$$\frac{1}{\dfrac{1}{\frac{1}{s} - \frac{1}{f}} - \dfrac{t}{n}} = \frac{1}{s''} + \frac{1}{f}$$

and so

$$\frac{1}{(\frac{1}{s} - \frac{1}{f})} - \frac{t}{n} = \frac{1}{(\frac{1}{s''} + \frac{1}{f})}$$

Thus,

$$t = \frac{n}{\frac{1}{s} - \frac{1}{f}} - \frac{n}{\frac{1}{s''} + \frac{1}{f}} \qquad (4)$$

Equation (3) can be rewritten as follows:

$$\frac{1}{s''} - \frac{1}{\dfrac{sf}{f - s} - \dfrac{t}{n}} = - \frac{1}{f}$$

or

$$\frac{1}{s''} - \frac{1}{\dfrac{nsf - t(f - s)}{n(f - s)}} = - \frac{1}{f}$$

Hence,

$$\frac{1}{s''} + \frac{n(s - f)}{nsf - t(f - s)} = - \frac{1}{f}$$

and so,

$$\frac{nsf - t(f - s) + ns''(s - f)}{s''nsf - s''t(f - s)} = \frac{-1}{f} \; .$$

Cross-multiplying gives the result

$$s''nsf - s''t(f - s) = - nsf^2 + tf(f - s) - ns''f(s - f).$$

Expanding this equation gives

$$s''nsf - s''tf + s''ts = - nsf^2 + tf^2 - tfs$$

$$- ns''fs + ns''f^2 \; .$$

This is equivalent to the following:

$$ss''(nf + t + nf) = s''(tf + nf^2) - s(nf^2 + tf) + tf^2$$

or

$$ss'' = \frac{f(nf + t)s''}{2nf + t} - \frac{f(nf + t)s}{2nf + t} + \frac{tf^2}{2nf + t}$$

This can be rearranged to yield the following equation:

143

$$ss" + \frac{f(nf + t)s}{2nf + t} - \frac{f(nf + t)s"}{2nf + t} - \frac{tf^2}{2nf + t} = 0 \qquad (5)$$

Here s is measured with respect to V_1 and s" is measured with respect to V_2. The second principal focal length f' is defined in terms of object and image distances measured from principal points such that

$$\frac{1}{s" - h'} - \frac{1}{s - h} = \frac{1}{f'}$$

where h and h' are the distances of the first and second surfaces of the lens from the principal planes, respectively or

$$\frac{s - h - s" + h'}{(s" - h')(s - h)} = \frac{1}{f'} \ .$$

Cross-multiplying gives the result

$$sf' - hf' - s"f' + h'f' = s"s - h's - hs" + hh'$$

and so,

$$ss" - (f' + h')s + (f' - h)s" + f'(h - h') + hh'$$
$$= 0 \ . \qquad (6)$$

Solving equations (5) and (6) for ss" and equating the expressions obtained gives the result

$$\frac{-f(nf + t)s}{2nf + t} + \frac{f(nf + t)}{2nf + t}\,s" + \frac{tf^2}{2nf + t}$$

$$= (f' + h')s - (f' - h)s" - f'(h - h') - hh' \ .$$

Equating the terms with like coefficients (s, s", and 1, respectively) gives

$$f' + h' = - \frac{f(nf + t)}{2nf + t} \qquad (7)$$

$$f' - h = - \frac{f(nf + t)}{2nf + t} \qquad (8)$$

$$f'(h - h') + hh' = \frac{-tf^2}{2nf + t} \qquad (9)$$

However, from equations (7) and (8),

$$h = f' + \frac{f(nf + t)}{2nf + t} \qquad (10)$$

and

$$h' = -f' - \frac{f(nf + t)}{2nf + t} \qquad (11)$$

Thus,

$$h - h' = 2f' + \frac{2f(nf + t)}{2nf + t} \quad ,$$

And in addition, from equations (10) and (11),

$$hh' = -\left(f' + \frac{f(nf + t)}{2nf + t} \right)^2 .$$

Substituting these expressions for $h - h'$ and hh' into equation (9) gives

$$2f'^2 + \frac{2f(nf + t)}{2nf + t} f' - \left(f' + \frac{f(nf + t)}{2nf + t} \right)^2$$

$$= - \frac{tf^2}{(2nf + t)}$$

Expanding this equation gives

$$2f'^2 + \frac{2f(fn + t)f'}{2nf + t} - f'^2 - \frac{2f(nf + t)f'}{2nf + t}$$

$$- \frac{f^2(nf + t)^2}{(2nf + t)^2} = - \frac{tf^2}{2nf + t}$$

or

$$f'^2 - \frac{f^2(nf + t)^2}{(2nf + t)^2} = - \frac{tf^2}{2nf + t}$$

Now, placing each term of this equation over a common denominator

$$((2nf + t)^2),$$

the above equation becomes

$$f'^2 (2nf + t)^2 - f^2 (nf + t)^2 = -tf^2 (2nf + t)$$

or

$$f'^2 (2nf + t)^2 - f^2 (n^2 f^2 + 2nft + t^2)$$

$$= - 2nf^3 t - t^2 f^2 .$$

Hence,

$$f'^2 (2nf + t)^2 - n^2 f^4 - 2nf^3 t - f^2 t^2$$

$$= -2nf^3 t - f^2 t^2 .$$

The $-2nf^3 t$ and $-f^2 t^2$ terms cancel and so,

$$f'^2 = \frac{n^2 f^4}{(2nf + t)^2}$$

Taking the square root of both sides of this equation gives

$$f' = \pm \frac{nf^2}{2nf + t}$$

$$= \pm \frac{n}{\dfrac{2n}{f} + \dfrac{t}{f^2}}$$

when $t = 0$ $\quad f' = -\dfrac{f}{2}$; hence,

$$f' = - \frac{n}{\dfrac{2n}{f} + \dfrac{t}{f^2}}$$

or

$$-\frac{2}{f} - \frac{t}{nf^2} = \frac{1}{f'} \tag{12}$$

Using the relation

$$\frac{(n-1)}{|r|} = -\frac{1}{f} ,$$

where r represents the radius of curvature of the first surface of the lens, equation (12) becomes

$$\frac{2(n-1)}{|r|} - \frac{t(n-1)^2}{n|r|^2} = \frac{1}{f'}$$

Placing both terms of the left hand side of this equation over the denominator $|r|^2$ gives the result

$$\frac{2(n-1)|r| - \dfrac{t(n-1)^2}{n}}{|r|^2} = \frac{1}{f'}$$

Cross-multiplying and neglecting the absolute value signs,

$$2(n-1)r\,f' - \frac{t(n-1)^2}{n}\,f' = r^2$$

or

$$r^2 - 2f'(n-1)\,r + \frac{t}{n}(n-1)^2 f' = 0 \tag{13}$$

The refracting power D, the thickness t, and the index of refraction n are given to be +10 diopters, 0.5 cm, and 1.5, respectively. The focal length

$$f' = \frac{1}{D} = 0.1\ m = 10\ cm.$$

Now, substituting for f', n, and t in equation (13) gives

$$r^2 - 2(10\ cm)(1.5 - 1)r + \frac{(0.5\ cm)}{1.5}(1.5-1)^2(10\ cm) = 0$$

146

or

$$r^2 - 10r + 0.8333 = 0$$

Using the quadratic formula,

$$r = \frac{10 \pm \sqrt{100 - 3.3332}}{2} \text{ cm} \cong (5 + 4.916) \text{ cm}$$

$$= 9.916 \text{ cm}.$$

IMAGE POSITION

● **PROBLEM** 7-13

The cornea of the eye is a convex mirror, and the high-light usually seen in it is a reflected image. Suppose that a circular object 20 cm in diameter is located 40 cm from the eye. If the radius of the cornea is 0.8 cm, how far is the virtual image from the cornea and what is its size?

Solution: The thin lens/mirror equation is as follows:

$$\frac{1}{0} + \frac{1}{i} = \frac{2}{R} , \tag{1}$$

where R is the radius of curvature of the surface, and 0 and i are the object and image distances, respectively. Substituting the given values 0 = 40 cm and R = -0.8 cm (the minus sign is due to the fact that the mirror is convex) into equation (1) gives the result

$$\frac{1}{40 \text{ cm}} + \frac{1}{i} = \frac{2}{-0.8 \text{ cm}}$$

hence i ≅ -0.396 cm. The magnification, m, of the image is given by the expression

$$m = -\frac{i}{0} = \frac{0.396 \text{ cm}}{40 \text{ cm}} = 0.0099.$$

Thus, the image is virtual, located about 4 mm inside the cornea, and it is magnified by a factor of 0.0099, which makes it seem to be erect and (20 cm)(.0099) ≅ 2 mm in diameter.

CHAPTER 8

OPHTHALMIC OPTICS

EFFECTIVE, VERTEX, AND TRUE POWERS

● PROBLEM 8-1

An ophthalmic prescription calls for corrective glasses of -4.50 m^{-1} refractive power to be worn 14mm in front of the cornea, the customary position of spectacle lenses. If the patient chooses to wear contact lenses instead, what prescription would be needed for them?

Solution: In this case, the power of the new lens would be the same as the effective power of the prescription lens at the cornea.

$$P_{eff} = \frac{P_1}{1 - dP_1} ,$$

where d represents the distance from the cornea to the glasses and P_1 represents the refractive power of the glasses. Then, substituting the given values for d and P_1 into the above equation gives the result

$$P_{eff} = \frac{-4.50}{1 - .014(-4.50)}$$

$$= \frac{-4.50}{1 + .063}$$

$$= -4.23 \text{ m}^{-1} .$$

Therefore, if the patient chooses to wear contact lenses instead of glasses, the lenses should both have a refractive power of -4.23 m^{-1}.

● PROBLEM 8-2

A corrective lens of refractive power -10.00 diopters corrects a myopic eye. What would be the effective power of this lens if it were 12mm. from the eye?

Solution: The effective power of a lens placed at a distance d from another lens is given by

$$P_{eff} = \frac{P_1}{1 - dP_1} \cdot$$

For a positive lens, P_{eff} increases as d decreases, but for a negative lens, P_{eff} decreases as d decreases.

$$P_{eff} = \frac{P_1}{1 - dP_1}$$

$$= \frac{-10}{1 - .012(-10)}$$

$$= \frac{-10}{1 + .12}$$

$$= -8.93 \text{ diopters.}$$

● **PROBLEM** 8-3

A trial-case sphere has a front surface power of 6.50 diopters, a thickness of 4mm, and a back surface power of -12.00 diopters (n = 1.50). Calculate the vertex power. What is the true power of the lens?

Solution: For a thick lens, the true power P is given by

$$P = P_1 + P_2 - \frac{d}{n} P_1 P_2 , \qquad (1)$$

where P_1 is the power of the front surface, P_2 is the power of the back surface, d is the thickness of the lens and n is the refractive index of the lens.

Substituting the given values for P_1, P_2, d and n into equation (1) gives the result

$$P = 6.50 - 12.00 - \frac{.004}{1.50} (6.50)(-12.00)$$

$$= 6.50 - 12.00 + 0.21$$

$$= -5.29 \text{ diopters .}$$

The vertex power, Pv, is given by

$$Pv = \frac{P}{1 - dP_1/n} \qquad (2)$$

$$= - \frac{5.29}{1 - \frac{.004(6.50)}{1.50}}$$

$$= - \frac{5.29}{1 - .017}$$

$$= -5.38 \text{ diopters.}$$

FAR POINT OF EYE

The far point of a certain eye is 1 meter in front of the eye. What lens should be used to see clearly an object at infinity?

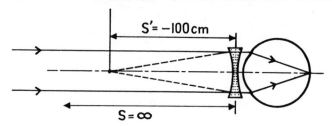

Solution: Assume that the image is to be formed at the far point. Then, using the lens equation

$$\frac{1}{f} = \frac{1}{0} + \frac{1}{i} \ ,$$

substituting in the given values, $0 = \infty$ and $i = -100$cm, we have

$$\frac{1}{f} = \frac{1}{\infty} + \frac{1}{-100\text{cm}} \ ,$$

or

$$f = -100 \text{ cm.}$$

Therefore, a diverging lens which has a focal length of 100 cm is needed.

Determine the positions of the far point for eyes corrected by lenses at a distance of 15 mm and having refractive powers of +5, -8, +10, and -15 diopters. The focal length of the cornea = 1 meter.

Solution: We know that for a system of two lenses, the first lens of power P_1 has an effective power P_{eff} at the second lens given by

$$P_{eff} = \frac{P_1}{1 - dP_1}$$

where d is the distance in meters between the two lenses. (a) For the lens $P_1 = +5$ diopters:

$$P_{eff} = \frac{5}{1 - .015 \times 5}$$

$$= \frac{5}{1 - .075}$$

$$= \frac{5}{.925}$$

$$= 5.41 \text{ diopters.}$$

The far point is the position of the object with respect to the lens with effective power P_{eff} when the lens is placed at the cornea and the image is formed at infinity. Using the lens equation

$$\frac{1}{S_0} + \frac{1}{S_i} = \frac{1}{f_{eff}} \; ,$$

$$\frac{1}{S_0} + \frac{1}{\infty} = \frac{P_{eff}}{100} \; (cm^{-1})$$

Thus,

$$S_0 = \frac{100}{P_{eff}} = \frac{100}{5.41}$$

$$= 18.5 \; cm.$$

(b) For the lens with $P_1 = -8$ diopters:

$$P_{eff} = \frac{P_1}{1 - dP_1}$$

$$= \frac{-8}{1 - .015(-8)}$$

$$= \frac{-8}{1 + .12}$$

$$= -7.14 \; diopters.$$

Thus,

$$f_{eff} = -\frac{100}{7.14}$$

$$= -14.0 \; cm.$$

Using the lens equation

$$\frac{1}{S_0} + \frac{1}{S_i} = \frac{1}{f_{eff}} \; ,$$

$$\frac{1}{S_0} + \frac{1}{\infty} = -\frac{1}{14.0} \; .$$

Hence, $S_0 = -14.0 \; cm$.

(c) For the lens with $P_1 = +10$ diopters:

$$P_{eff} = \frac{P_1}{1 - dP_1}$$

$$= \frac{10}{1 - .015 \times 10}$$

$$= \frac{10}{1 - .15}$$

$$= 11.76 \; diopters.$$

Thus,

$$f_{eff} = \frac{100}{11.76}$$

$$= 8.5 \; cm.$$

From the lens equation,

$$\frac{1}{S_0} + \frac{1}{S_i} = \frac{1}{f_{eff}}$$

$$\frac{1}{S_0} + \frac{1}{\infty} = \frac{1}{8.5}$$

Hence, $S_0 = 8.5 \; cm.$

(d) $P_1 = -15$ diopters:

$$P_{eff} = \frac{P_1}{1 - dP_1}$$

$$P_{eff} = \frac{-15}{1 - .015(-15)}$$

$$= \frac{-15}{1.225}$$

$$= -12.24 \text{ diopters.}$$

Thus,

$$f_{eff} = \frac{100}{P_{eff}}$$

$$= \frac{100}{-12.24}$$

$$= -8.17 \text{ cm.}$$

Hence

$$\frac{1}{S_0} + \frac{1}{\infty} = \frac{1}{f_{eff}}$$

$$S_0 = f_{eff} = -8.17 \text{ cm.}$$

NEAR POINT OF EYE

The near point of a certain eye is 100 cm in front of the eye. What lens should be used to see clearly an object 25 cm in front of the eye?

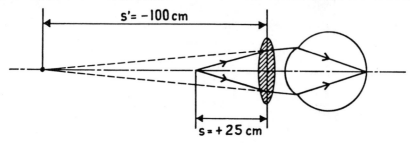

Solution: Using the lens equation $\frac{1}{f} = \frac{1}{0} + \frac{1}{i}$, where f is the focal length of the lens, 0 is the object distance, and i the image distance, substituting the given values 0 = 25 cm and i = -100 cm (the negative sign is due to the fact that the image is on the same side of the lens as the object), we have,

$$\frac{1}{f} = \frac{1}{25 cm} + \frac{1}{-100 cm} ,$$

$$f = 33 \text{ cm.}$$

Hence, a converging lens with a focal length of 33 cm is required.

(1) Where is the near point of an eye for which a spectacle lens of power +2 diopters is prescribed?
(2) Where is the far point of an eye for which a spectacle lens of power −0.5 diopter is prescribed for distant vision?

Solution: (1) A spectacle lens of positive power is used for those eyes which focus rays from infinity behind the retina. This reduces the focal length of the combination of the two lenses. In order to see the nearest object placed at a distance S_0, the object distance from the lens, its image must be formed at infinity. If the image distance is denoted by S_i, then $S_i = \infty$. This is a virtual image and is seen clearly by the eye.

Using the lens formula, we have

$$\frac{1}{S_0} + \frac{1}{S_i} = \frac{1}{f}$$

Hence,

$$\frac{1}{S_0} + \frac{1}{\infty} = \frac{1}{f}$$

or

$$S_0 = f = \frac{100 \text{ cm}}{2 \text{ diopters}}$$

$$= 50 \text{ cm.}$$

(2) For an eye for which a spectacle of Power $= -0.5$ diopters is pre-scribed for distant vision, the image of an object placed at infinity must be formed at its nearest point. Hence, when $S_0 = \infty$, S_i must be negative and is obtained from the lens equation.

$$\frac{1}{S_0} + \frac{1}{S_i} = \frac{1}{f} = \frac{P}{100}$$

Hence,

$$\frac{1}{\infty} + \frac{1}{S_i} = \frac{1}{f} = \frac{-0.5}{100}$$

and so,

$$S_i = f = -200 \text{ cm.}$$

RESOLVING POWER OF EYE

● **PROBLEM** 8-8

The resolving power of the eye is 1 minute of arc. What is the cor-responding dimension on the retina?

Solution: Angular resolving power of a circular aperture of diameter d is given by the following formula:

$$\text{Ang. R.P.} = \theta = 1.22 \frac{\lambda}{d},$$

where λ is the wavelength of light. For the eye, the nodal points for the eye lens lie 17.1mm in front of the retina since the direction of any ray remains unchanged when passing through the nodal points.

Hence the dimension on the retina will be the angular resolving power multiplied by this distance, or

$$R = \theta \,(\text{rad})\,(17.1)$$

$$= \frac{1}{60} \times \frac{\pi}{180} \times 17.1$$

$$\cong .5 \times 10^{-2} \text{ mm.} = 5\mu \text{ (microns).}$$

LEAST DISTANCE
FOR DISTINCT VISION

(1) A man decides to test his eyesight with the aid of a small mirror. When he stands in front of the mirror he finds that he can see himself clearly, with his eyes relaxed, at a maximum distance of 1m from the mirror. He then reduces his distance from the mirror and finds that with an effort of accomodation he can continue to see himself clearly down to a distance of 15cm from the mirror. What spectacle lenses should he wear in order to be able to see very distant objects clearly? What is his least distance for distinct vision when wearing these?

(2) An object is placed 60cm. in front of a concave mirror of radius of curvature 1m. When not wearing spectacles what is the maximum distance the man may stand away from the mirror while still seeing clearly the image of the object formed by the mirror?

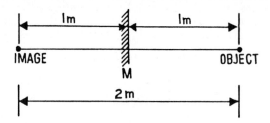

Solution: (1) In order to see distant objects with the help of spectacles, the image distance must be the maximum distance of distinct vision for objects at infinity. The maximum distance of distinct vision for the eye, as shown in the figure , is 2m.
   The lens equation states

$$\frac{1}{p} + \frac{1}{q} = \frac{1}{f} ,$$

where p and q denote the object and image distances, respectively, from the lens, and f represents the focal length of the lens.

$$p = \infty$$
$$q = -2m$$

(Image is on the same side as the object). Therefore,

$$\frac{1}{\infty} + \frac{1}{-2m} = \frac{1}{f}$$

so,

$$f = -2m .$$

The lens is a diverging lens. With the glasses, his nearest distance of distinct vision is obtained by taking q = -30cm , f = -2m = -200cm

$$\frac{1}{p} + \frac{1}{q} = \frac{1}{f} \text{ gives}$$

$$\frac{1}{p} + \frac{1}{-30} = \frac{1}{-200}$$

or

$$\frac{1}{p} = - \frac{1}{200} + \frac{1}{30}$$

Then,
$$\frac{1}{p} = \frac{-3 + 20}{600}$$
$$= \frac{17}{600}$$

Therefore,
$$p = \frac{600}{17}$$
$$= 35.3 \text{cm.}$$

(2)   Using the mirror formula
$$\frac{1}{p} + \frac{1}{q} = \frac{1}{f} = \frac{2}{R} ,$$

and substituting the given values $p = 60\text{cm.}$ and $f = R/2 = 50\text{cm.}$, we have
$$\frac{1}{60} + \frac{1}{q} = \frac{1}{50}$$

therefore,
$$\frac{1}{q} = \frac{1}{50} - \frac{1}{60}$$

or
$$\frac{1}{q} \simeq \frac{1}{300}$$

Therefore,
$$q = 300 \text{cm.}$$

Hence the image is formed 300cm from the mirror. In order to see it clearly, the man must be 200cm. from the image or 500cm. from the mirror.

IMAGE SEPARATION

● **PROBLEM** 8-10

The separation of the headlights on a car is about 150cm. When the car is 30 meters away, what is the separation of the images of the lights on the retina?

Solution: While each person's eye is different, we can use a "standard" eye which approximates the average of all human eyes. The "standard" eye has a strength of +60 diopters when viewing objects a large distance from the eye. Using the thin lens equation we find that 30 meters is equivalent to a large distance from the eye for a +60 diopter lens. Diopters are the units which the inverse of the focal length is expressed in terms of when the focal length is measured in meters.

The magnification is given by
$$M = \frac{u'}{u} = \frac{I}{0} \tag{1}$$

where u' is the image distance, u is the object distance, I is the image size and 0 is the object size. Since we have determined that 30 meters is equivalent to a large distance from the eye, u' will be the focal length of the eye lens, determined from the lens equation $1/u + 1/u' = 1/f$, or
$$\frac{1}{30\text{m}} + \frac{1}{u'} = 60\text{m}^{-1} ,$$

155

where f is the focal length of the eye. $u' \cong 1/60m = .0167m.$
Substituting into equation (1),

$$\frac{.0167}{30} = \frac{I}{1.5}$$

Solving for I,

$$I = 8.33 \times 10^{-4} \, m = .833 \, mm.$$

● **PROBLEM** 8-11

The angular width of the blind spot is $6°$.
a)   What is the width of the blind spot on the retina?
b)   What is the width of area on a tangent screen at a distance of 2
     meters from the eye?

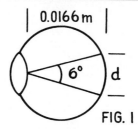

FIG. 1

Solution: a) As stated in the previous problem, the "standard" eye
has a strength of +60 diopter when viewing objects a large distance
from the eye. Using the thin lens equation

$$\frac{1}{u} + \frac{1}{u'} = \frac{1}{f}$$

where u is the object distance, u' is the image distance (eye lens
to retina in this problem) and f is the focal length. We then find

$$\frac{1}{\infty} + \frac{1}{u'} = \frac{1}{f} = 60$$

$$u' = 0.0166m.$$

From figure 1, we have the geometry of the blind spot, so d, the
diameter of the blind spot, is

$$\frac{d}{0.0166} = \tan 6°$$

Solving for d,

$$d = 1.8 \times 10^{-3} m = 1.8mm$$

Therefore, the width of the blind spot on the retina = 1.8mm.

b) We can express the magnification of a lens by

$$m = \frac{u'}{u} = \frac{I}{0}$$

where u' is the image distance, u is the object distance, I is the
image size, and 0 is the object size. Solving for 0,

$$0 = \frac{Iu}{u'}$$

Substituting the given value u = 2 meters and the computed values

$I = 1.8 \times 10^{-3}$ m, and $u' = 0.0166$ m into the above equation,

$$0 = \frac{1.8 \times 10^{-3} \times 2}{.0166} \text{m} = 21 \text{ cm.}$$

THE OPHTHALMOMETER

● **PROBLEM** 8-12

What principles of optics does an ophthalmometer use to measure the radius of the cornea of the eye?

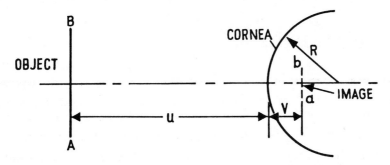

Solution: An ophthalmometer is an instrument an ophthalmologist uses to measure the radius of curvature of the cornea of the eye. The cornea is the first refracting surface of the eye. Rays of light that enter the eye are first refracted by the cornea.

An ophthalmometer utilizes the two following equations to calculate the radius of curvature of the cornea,

$$\frac{1}{V} + \frac{1}{u} = \frac{2}{R} \quad \text{(the lens equation)} (1)$$

and

$$\frac{\overline{ab}}{\overline{AB}} = \frac{I}{0} = \frac{V}{u} \qquad (2)$$

In the latter equation, I is the size of the image and 0 is the size of the object, V and u represent the image and object distances from the lens (as shown in the figure). We can eliminate V by solving for $1/V$ in equation (2) and substituting this value into equation (1). Hence, we have

$$\frac{0}{I \cdot u} + \frac{1}{u} = \frac{2}{R} ,$$

from which the radius, $R = \frac{2 \cdot u \cdot I}{0 + I}$. Usually, however, the size of the object 0 is so much larger than that of the image I that I can be neglected in comparison to 0. Therefore,

$$R \cong \frac{2 \cdot u \cdot I}{0}$$

In the ophthalmometer, the size of the image is measured by an optical doubling device and the object size 0 and the object distance u are directly measured by the instrument. Thus, R can be determined by the previous equation.

CHAPTER 9

INTERFERENCE

PHASE DIFFERENCES

Find the phase difference between light reflected from the inner and outer surfaces of a deposit of magnesium fluoride (n = 1.38) 1000 Å thick on a lens surface (a) for violet light of wavelength 4000 Å (b) for red light of wavelength 7000 Å. (Neglect variations of n with λ.)

<u>Solution</u>: We want to investigate the phase difference of 400 nm and 700 nm light in air as it reflects from the front and back surfaces of a thin coating (index of refraction, n = 1.38) on a lens surface (typically n = 1.5). The total phase difference will be composed of differences in phase shifts on reflection plus the difference in path lengths. Since at the front surface the ray goes from n = 1.00 to n = 1.38 and at the rear surface the ray goes from n = 1.38 to n = 1.5 whatever phase shift occurs at the front surface will also occur at the back surface, so the phase shift difference will be zero. The ray reflected from the back surface will travel twice the thickness of the coating. So we want to find how many wavelengths of 400 nm and 700 nm are equal to 2 x 100 nm.

However the light is travelling in MgF_2 , so we need to find the equivalent wavelenth of 400 nm and 700 nm in MgF_2. Now,

$$f\lambda = c \qquad (1)$$

where f, the frequency of vibration is constant in all materials, λ is the wavelength in the medium and c is the velocity of light in the medium. Also

$$\frac{c_{vacuum}}{c_{medium}} = n . \qquad (2)$$

158

The ratio of vacuum velocity of light to velocity of light in the medium is just the index of refraction. Combining equations (1) and (2) yields,

$$\lambda_{medium} = \frac{\lambda \text{ air}}{n_{medium}} \tag{3}$$

$$\lambda_{MgF_2} \ 400 \ mm = \frac{400 \times 10^{-9}}{1.38} = 2.89 \times 10^{-7} \ m$$

$$\lambda_{MgF_2} \ 700 \ nm = \frac{700 \times 10^{-9}}{1.38} = 5.07 \times 10^{-7} \ m$$

or, the fractional wavelength path difference is

$$fwp_{400 \ nm} = \frac{2 \times 10^{-7}}{2.89 \times 10^{-7}} = 0.689$$

$$fwp_{700 \ nm} = \frac{2 \times 10^{-7}}{5.07 \times 10^{-7}} = 0.394,$$

If we denote the phase difference by ϕ,

then ϕ = fwp x 360° (or fwp x 2π, with the result expressed in radians).

So, $\phi_{400 \ nm}$ = 0.689 x 360° = 248°

and $\phi_{700 \ nm}$ = 0.394 x 360° = 142°

are the phase differences for parts (a) and (b), respectively, of this problem.

PATH DIFFERENCES

● **PROBLEM** 9-2

Two rectangular pieces of plane glass are placed one upon the other with a thin strip of paper between them at one edge. When illuminated by sodium light at normal incidence bright and dark interference bands are formed, ten of each per centimeter in length. Find the angle which the wedge makes with the horizontal.

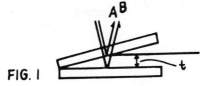

FIG. I

Solution: In this problem we wish to investigate the path difference between a ray which is reflected from the bottom surface of the top piece of glass, and a ray which is reflected from the top surface of the bottom piece of glass

(see Figure 1). We shall consider that both rays A and B
are incident normal to the surfaces (only a small approximation). We can see that ray B travels an extra distance
2t in the gap between the plates. Therefore we would say
that 2t must be equal to some integer, m, times the wavelength of light to have a maximum, and $2t = (2m + 1)(\lambda/2)$ to
have a minimum. However, if we recall the Fresnel equations
for refraction,

$$r_\perp = \frac{n_i \cos \theta_i - n_t \cos \theta_t}{n_i \cos \theta_i + n_t \cos \theta_t} \tag{1}$$

and

$$r_{||} = \frac{n_t \cos \theta_i - n_i \cos \theta_t}{n_i \cos \theta_t + n_t \cos \theta_i} \tag{2}$$

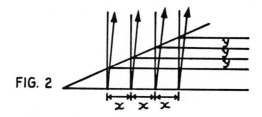

FIG. 2

where the r's are the amplitude reflection coefficients, the
i's refer to the incident material medium and the t's to the
transmitted material medium; the n's are the indices of refraction in the appropriate medium, and the thetas are the
angles of the rays with respect to the normal to the surface.
As suggested above, we are going to look at normally incident
rays; so

$$\theta_i = \theta_t = 0.$$

Then,

$$-r_\perp = r_{||} = \frac{n_t - n_i}{n_t + n_i}, \tag{3}$$

so we can see that ray A is then phase shifted half a wavelength from the incident ray and ray B has zero phase shift
from its incident ray, conditions which hold for either
parallel or perpendicular components of the E vector. So
our condition for phase difference between ray A and B after
reflection is

$$2t + \lambda/2 = m\lambda + \lambda/2 \text{ minimum} \tag{4}$$

$$2t = m\lambda \tag{5}$$

and

$$2t + \lambda/2 = m\lambda \text{ maximum} \tag{6}$$

$$2t = (2m - 1)\lambda/2 \tag{7}$$

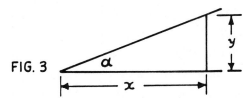

FIG. 3

Looking at Figure 2 we see our problem says for a distance in the x direction of 1 cm we can have ten interference bands or, for every x = 1/10 cm we have the m in equation 7 increasing by 1, or from Figure 3; 2y must be one wavelength of light in length for a shift of 0.1 cm change in x.

Then,

$$\tan \alpha = y/x = \frac{\lambda/2}{x}$$

since sodium light has wavelength

= 589 nm, $\tan \alpha =$

$$\frac{589 \times 10^{-9}\,m}{2 \times \left(.1 \times 10^{-2}\right)m} = 2.95 \times 10^{-4}$$

and $\alpha_{in\ radians} = 2.95 \times 10^{-4}$ radians.

YOUNG'S EXPERIMENT

● **PROBLEM** 9-3

In a Young's experiment the distance d between the slits is 0.1 mm and the perpendicular distance to the screen is 50 cm. Compute the distance on the screen between maxima for violet light (λ = 400 mμ) and red light (λ = 700 mμ).

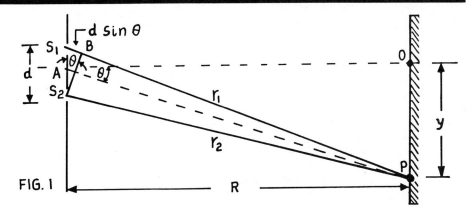

FIG. 1

Solution: Figure 1 illustrates Young's experiment. Consider the point P on the screen in a direction making an angle θ with the axis of the system. With P as a center and PS_2 as a radius, strike an arc intersecting PS_1 at B.

If the distance R from slits to screen is large in comparison with the distance d between the slits, the arc S_2B can be considered a straight line at right angles to PS_2, PA, and PS_1. Then the triangle BS_1S_2 is a right triangle, similar to POA, and the distance S_1B equals $d\sin\theta$. This latter distance is the difference in path length $r_1 - r_2$ between the waves reaching P from the two slits. The waves spreading out from S_1 and S_2 necessarily start out in phase but they may not be in phase at P because of this difference in length of path. Complete reinforcement will take place at the point P only when the path difference is some integral number of wavelengths. Thus,

$$d\sin\theta = m\lambda \qquad (m = 1,2,3\ldots) \qquad (1)$$

for complete reinforcement. Now, if point P is at the center of the m-th fringe, the distance y_m from the zeroth to the m-th fringe is (from Figure 1)

$$y_m = R\tan\theta_m . \qquad (2)$$

Since the angle θ_m for all values of m is extremely small, we can use the approximation $\tan\theta_m \cong \sin\theta_m$ so,

$$y_m = R\sin\theta_m . \qquad (3)$$

Therefore, from eqs. (1) and (3),

$$y_m = R \frac{m\lambda}{d} . \qquad (4)$$

In the given problem,

$$d = .1 \text{ mm} = 10^5 \text{ m}\mu$$
$$R = 50 \text{ cm} = 5 \times 10^8 \text{ m}\mu$$
$$\lambda_1 = 400 \text{ m}\mu$$
$$\lambda_2 = 700 \text{ m}\mu .$$

Then from eq. (4)

$$y_{m_1} = (5 \times 10^8)m(400)/10^5 \text{ m}\mu$$
$$= 2m \text{ millimeters} \qquad (y_{m_1} = 0,2,4,6,8\ldots)$$

$$y_{m_2} = (5 \times 10^8)m(700)/10^5 \text{ m}\mu$$
$$= 3.5m \text{ millimeters}. \qquad (y_{m_2} = 0,3.5,7,10.5\ldots)$$

So the distance on the screen between maxima for violet light is 2 mm and the distance between maxima for red light is 3.5 mm.

162

In an interference experiment of the Young type, the
distance between the slits is 1/2 mm.   The wavelength
of the light is 6000Å.   If it is desired to have a fringe
spacing of 1 mm at the screen, what is the corresponding
screen distance?

Solution: Figure 1 illustrates Young's interference
experiment.   Light of a single wavelength is incident on
two slits, a distance d apart.   This produces a relative
maximum at point P when,

$$d \cdot \sin \theta = m \cdot \lambda \qquad\qquad (1)$$

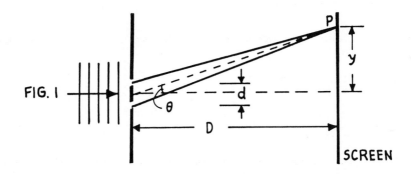

FIG. 1

where d is the slit distance, θ is the angle shown in
Figure 1, m is the order number, and λ is the wavelength
of the incident light.

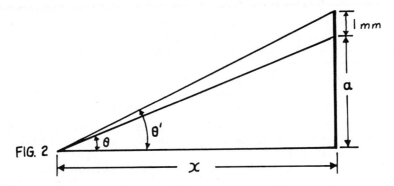

FIG. 2

If the fringe spacing on the screen is 1 mm, then
according to Figure 2 we have,

$$\tan \theta = \frac{a}{x} \qquad\qquad (2)$$

and

$$\tan \theta' = \frac{1 \text{ mm} + a}{x} . \qquad\qquad (3)$$

If we assume that θ is small we can make the approximation

163

$$\tan\theta = \sin\theta \quad ;$$

thus, from equations (2) and (3) we have:

$$\sin\theta = \frac{a}{x} \tag{4}$$

and

$$\sin\theta' = \frac{1 \text{ mm } + a}{x} \quad . \tag{5}$$

Applying equation (1) to equations (4) and (5), we have

$$\frac{m \cdot \lambda}{d} = \frac{a}{x} \tag{6}$$

and

$$\frac{m' \cdot \lambda}{d} = \frac{1 \text{ mm } + a}{x} \quad . \tag{7}$$

Combining these two equations by solving for a and substituting, we get,

$$\frac{m'\lambda}{d} = \frac{1 \text{ mm}}{x} + \frac{m\lambda}{d} \quad ,$$

$$x = \frac{d}{\lambda(m'-m)} \text{ mm}, \tag{8}$$

where (m'-m) = 1 because the maximas are next to each other. Letting d = 0.5 mm. and λ = 6000Å = 6×10^{-4} mm, then the screen distance, x, is 833 mm or about 83 cm.

● **PROBLEM** 9-5

A Young's experiment is set up with the following characteristics: Monochromatic source (λ = 0.55µ), slit separation d = 3.3 mm, distance from slits to screen D = 3m (see figure).
1) Calculate the fringe spacing.
2) Place a sheet of glass with plane parallel faces and thickness e = 0.01 mm in front of slit F_1.
   a) Determine the direction of the displacement of the fringes and the formula giving the relationship for their displacement.
   b) Knowing that the fringes are displaced by 4.73 ± .01 mm find the index of refraction of the glass and its error.

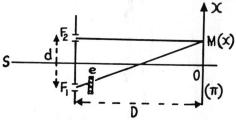

Solution: Here we need to concentrate on the interference

between two slits. From a standard optics text we find that the intensity of the interference pattern on N slits is,

$$I = \frac{I_o}{N^2} \frac{\sin^2 N\delta}{\sin^2 \delta} \tag{1}$$

where I_o is the initial intensity; I is the intensity at the screen; N is the number of slits; and δ is given by,

$$\delta = \frac{\pi d}{\lambda} \sin \theta \tag{2}$$

where λ is the wavelength of coherent monochromatic light from the source; d is the slit separation, and θ is the angle between the normal to the slit system and the point on the screen. For small angles, $\sin\theta = x/D$ where x is the distance from the center of the screen to a point at which we wish to measure the intensity and D is the distance from slits to screen.

Substituting into equation (2) gives the result

$$\delta = \frac{\pi d}{\lambda} \frac{x}{D} \tag{3}$$

For two slits N = 2. Substituting this into equation (1) we realize we can expand the $\sin^2 2\delta$ term because,

$$\sin 2\delta = 2 \sin\delta \cos\delta . \tag{4}$$

Squaring both sides results in,

$$\sin^2 2\delta = 4 \sin^2\delta \cos^2\delta . \tag{5}$$

Substituting this into equation (1) and cancelling terms,

$$I = I_o \cos^2\delta . \tag{6}$$

The fringe spacing i is the distance between two maxima or two minima. We therefore let $i = x_2 - x_1$ and $\delta = \pi$. Applying equation (3),

$$\pi = \frac{\pi d i}{\lambda D} . \tag{7}$$

Solving for i,

$$i = \frac{\lambda D}{d} . \tag{8}$$

Substituting the given values for λ, D, and d into equation (8),

$$i = \frac{(.55 \times 10^{-6})(3)}{3.3 \cdot 10^{-3}} = 5 \times 10^{-4} m . \tag{9}$$

Now we insert a sheet of glass of thickness 0.01 mm and index of refraction n in front of one of the slits. The light of this slit will now travel a different optical distance to a position x on the screen. Initially before the glass plate was inserted in front of the slit, the path difference was,

$$\delta_1 = F_1M - F_2M = x\frac{\lambda}{i} \quad .\qquad(10)$$

The glass plate will add an additional path difference (n - 1)e so the new path difference is,

$$\delta = x\frac{\lambda}{i} + (n-1)e \qquad(11)$$

so, the new δ for a maximum will be $p\lambda$ (p being an integer) or,

$$p\lambda = x\frac{\lambda}{i} + (n-1)e \quad .\qquad(12)$$

Solving for x,

$$x = \frac{i}{\lambda}\left[p\lambda - (n-1)e\right] \qquad(13)$$

so the shift in fringes will be the change in x:

$$\Delta x = -\frac{i}{\lambda}(n-1)e \quad .\qquad(14)$$

To measure the index of refraction we solve for n:

$$n = 1 - \frac{\lambda}{i}\frac{\Delta x}{e} \quad .\qquad(15)$$

So we do the measurement as follows. Observe the fringe system with no glass plate, record the positions x of the maxima, then insert the glass plate, record the new positions of the maxima and determine the shift Δx of the maxima. In our problem $\Delta x = -4.73$ mm, substituting values into equation (15),

$$n = 1 - \frac{0.55 \times 10^{-3}}{0.5}\frac{(-4.73)}{10^{-2}} = 1.5203 \quad .\qquad(16)$$

To determine the error in n we want to look at the relationship $d(\Delta x)/\Delta x$. Differentiating equation (15) we have

$$dn = -\frac{\lambda}{ie}d(\Delta x) \quad .\qquad(17)$$

Solving equation (14) for $-\frac{\lambda}{ie}$,

$$-\frac{\lambda}{ie} = \frac{n-1}{\Delta x} \quad .\qquad(18)$$

Substituting for $-\frac{\lambda}{ie}$ in equation (17),

$$dn = (n-1) \frac{d(\Delta x)}{\Delta x} \ .$$

Substituting values

$$dn = 0.5 \ \frac{2 \times 10^{-2}}{4.73} = 2 \times 10^{-3},$$

so $n = 1.520 \pm 0.002$.

● **PROBLEM 9-6**

Calculate the interference pattern that would be obtained if three slits (equally spaced) instead of two were used in Young's experiment.

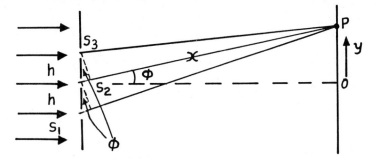

Solution: Let the spacing between the slits be h, as shown in the figure. Let the amplitude at P due to the wave coming from S_2 be given by,

$$E_1 = E_o \ e^{i(\omega t - kx)} \ . \tag{1}$$

Since the distance between S_1 and P is greater than that between S_2 and P, we calculate the difference between the two distances by dropping a perpendicular from S_2 on $S_1 P$. If $S_2 P$ makes an angle ϕ with the normal to the slit line,

$$S_1 P - S_2 P = h \sin \phi \ .$$

Hence, the amplitude at P due to the wave coming from S_1 can be written as,

$$E_2 = E_o \ e^{i(\omega t - kx - kh \sin \phi)} \ . \tag{2}$$

Similarly, we can write the amplitude of the wave at P arriving from S_3, keeping in mind that this path length is less than x by $h \sin \phi$. Thus,

$$E_3 = E_o \ e^{i(\omega t - k[x - h \sin \phi])}$$

$$= E_o \ e^{i(\omega t - kx + kh \sin \phi)} \ . \tag{3}$$

Hence, the total amplitude at P is,

$$E = E_1 + E_2 + E_3$$

$$= E_o \, e^{i(\omega t - kx)} \left[1 + e^{-ikh \sin \phi} + e^{ikh \sin \phi} \right] .$$

After making use of Euler's equations, $e^{ix} = \cos x + i \sin x$ and $e^{-ix} = \cos x - i \sin x$,

$$E = E_o \, e^{i(\omega t - kx)} \left[1 + 2 \cos (kh \sin \phi) \right] \qquad (4)$$

where k is the propagation vector $\left(\frac{2\pi}{\lambda} \right)$.

Hence, the intensity at P is given by the square of E. Therefore,

$$I = \left| E \right|^2 = EE^*,$$

where E* denotes the complex conjugate of E,

$$E_o \, e^{-i(\omega t - kx)} \left[1 + 2 \cos (kh \sin \phi) \right] .$$

Then,

$$I = \left\{ E_o \, e^{-i(\omega t - kx)} \left[1 + 2 \cos (kh \sin \phi) \right] \right\}$$

$$\times \left\{ E_o \, e^{i(\omega t - kx)} \left[1 + 2 \cos (kh \sin \phi) \right] \right\}$$

$$= E_o^2 \left\{ 1 + 2 \cos (kh \sin \phi) \right\}^2$$

$$= I_o \left\{ 1 + 4 \cos^2 (kh \sin \phi) + 4 \cos (kh \sin \phi) \right\}$$

$$= I_o \left\{ 1 + 4 \cos^2 \theta + 4 \cos \theta \right\} \qquad (5)$$

where $\theta = (kh \sin \phi = \dfrac{kh \, y}{x}$. $\qquad (6)$

Now $\cos^2 \theta = \dfrac{\cos 2\theta + 1}{2}$ (Trig. identity.)

After substituting for $\cos^2 \theta$, equation (5) becomes,

$$I = I_o \left[1 + 4 \left(\frac{\cos 2\theta + 1}{2} \right) + 4 \cos \theta \right]$$

$$= I_o \left[1 + 2 + 2 \cos 2\theta + 4 \cos \theta \right]$$

$$= I_o \left[3 + 4 \cos \theta + 2 \cos 2\theta \right] .$$

DOUBLE-SLIT EXPERIMENTS

A double slit experiment is performed, with the modifi-
cation that following slit A is a half wave plate with
fast axis along the slit, and following slit B is a
half wave plate with fast axis perpendicular to the slit.
The light is unpolarized. What is the position of the
dark fringes?

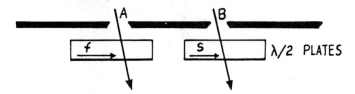

Solution: In this case, although the light is never
polarized, the birefringent material will make a
difference. Consider first that component of the light
which is polarized along the slit (say, vertically); the
path through the half wave plate over slit B contains,
say, N wavelengths. That through slit A then contains
N + 1/2 wavelengths, with the result that the symmetric
center point $(L_A = L_B)$, $\left(\text{where } L_A \text{ and } L_B \text{ represent the}\right)$
distances from plates A and B, respectively, to the point
of observation) is now a dark fringe and the equal time
(or equal number of wavelengths, m = 0) point has shifted
half a fringe toward A.

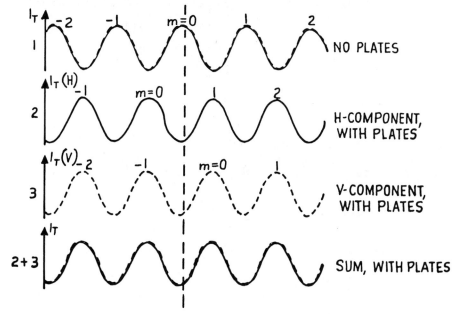

   The horizontal polarization component (H) does not,
of course, interfere with the vertical one, since vectors
can cancel only if they are collinear. This fringe
pattern also shifts, this time half a fringe toward B.
The result is, as shown, a restored fringe pattern, with
a dark fringe at the center.

169

In a double slit interference experiment the distance between the slits is 0.05 cm and the screen is 2 meters from the slits. The light is yellow light from a sodium lamp and it has a wavelength of 5.89×10^{-5} cm. What is the distance between the fringes?

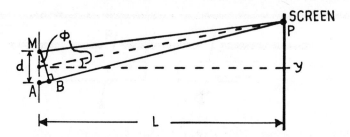

Solution: To find the distance between fringes in the double slit experiment, we must first derive the formulas for the location of the maxima and minima of the fringe pattern. Let us examine this experiment in more detail.

Light is incident on the 2 slits from the left (see figure). MP and AP represent 2 rays of light, one from each slit, arriving at P. Typically, L >> d, we may consider MP to be equal to BP. Assuming that the light rays emerging from the slits are in phase, the two light rays arriving at P will be out of phase because light from A must travel the extra distance AB when compared with light from M. If this path difference (AB = d sinφ) is equal to an even number of half wavelengths, P will be a maximum point. If AB equals an odd number of half wavelengths, P will be a minimum point. Hence,

For a maximum, $\sin\phi = (2n)\dfrac{\lambda}{2d}$ (n = 0,1,2,...).

For a minimum, $\sin\phi = (2n+1)\dfrac{\lambda}{2d}$ (n = 0,1,2,...).

Therefore, the angular location of adjacent maxima on the screen (say the nth and (n+1)th maxima), is

$$\sin\left(\phi_{n+1}\right) = \frac{\left(2(n+1)\right)\lambda}{2d} = \frac{(n+1)\lambda}{d} \qquad (1)$$

$$\sin\left(\phi_{n}\right) = \frac{(2n)\lambda}{2d} = \frac{n\lambda}{d}$$

But, if φ is small,

$$\sin\left(\phi_{n+1}\right) \approx \tan\left(\phi_{n+1}\right)$$

$$\sin\left(\phi_{n}\right) \approx \tan\left(\phi_{n}\right).$$

Hence, using equation (1) and the figure,

170

$$\frac{Y_{n+1}}{L} = \frac{(n+1)\lambda}{d} ,$$

where Y_{n+1} = the distance from the central maximum to the n+1'st bright fringe.

$$\frac{Y_n}{L} = \frac{n\lambda}{d} ;$$

hence,

$$Y_{n+1} - Y_n = \frac{(n+1)\lambda L}{d} - \frac{n\lambda L}{d}$$

$$Y_{n+1} - Y_n = \frac{\lambda L}{d} .$$

This is the screen separation of 2 adjacent maxima. If

$\lambda = 5.89 \times 10^{-5}$ cm

L = 200 cm

d = 0.05 cm,

then the distance between fringes is given by,

$$Y_{n+1} - Y_n = \frac{\left(5.89 \times 10^{-5} \times 200\right)\text{cm}^2}{0.05 \text{ cm}}$$

$$= .233 \text{ cm.}$$

WIENER'S EXPERIMENT

● **PROBLEM** 9-9

Standing waves of light are produced, as in Wiener's experiment, by reflecting light normally from a plane mirror.

If the light has a wavelength of 5461 Å, find the number of dark bands per centimeter on the photographic plate when it is inclined at a) 0.5° to the reflecting surface, b) 10°.

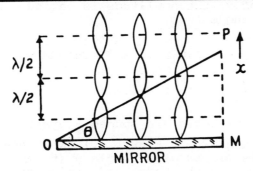

FIG. I

Solution: Consider Wiener's experiment shown in Figure 1. The standing wave pattern is set up with light of wavelength λ by reflecting it normally from the plane mirror.

The standing waves are obtained by the superposition of two wave trains of equal amplitude but travelling in opposite direction. These may be represented by,

$$y_1 = r \sin 2\pi \left(\frac{t}{T} - \frac{x}{\lambda} \right) \tag{1}$$

and

$$y_2 = r \sin 2\pi \left(\frac{t}{T} + \frac{x}{\lambda} \right), \tag{2}$$

where r is the amplitude of the wave trains and T is the period of the waves.

Adding equations (1) and (2), we obtain the resultant,

$$y = y_1 + y_2 = r \left[\sin 2\pi \left(\frac{t}{T} - \frac{x}{\lambda} \right) + \sin 2\pi \left(\frac{t}{T} + \frac{x}{\lambda} \right) \right]$$

$$\sin 2\pi \left(\frac{t}{T} - \frac{x}{\lambda} \right) = \sin \left(2\pi \frac{t}{T} \right) \cos \left(2\pi \frac{x}{\lambda} \right) - \cos \left(\frac{2\pi t}{T} \right) \sin \left(\frac{2\pi x}{\lambda} \right)$$

and $\sin 2\pi \left(\frac{t}{T} + \frac{x}{\lambda} \right) = \sin \left(\frac{2\pi t}{T} \right) \cos \left(\frac{2\pi x}{\lambda} \right)$

$$+ \cos \left(2\pi \frac{t}{T} \right) \sin \left(\frac{2\pi x}{\lambda} \right),$$

results which follow from the double-angle formulas.

Therefore,

$$\sin 2\pi \left(\frac{t}{T} - \frac{x}{\lambda} \right) + \sin 2\pi \left(\frac{t}{T} + \frac{x}{\lambda} \right)$$

$$= 2 \sin \left(\frac{2\pi t}{T} \right) \cos \left(\frac{2\pi x}{\lambda} \right).$$

Then, since $\cos (y) = \cos (-y)$,

$$y = 2r \cos \left(- \frac{2\pi x}{\lambda} \right) \sin \left(2\pi \frac{t}{T} \right).$$

For any value of x, the amplitude is periodic and has maximum value (antinodes) for

$$x = n \frac{\lambda}{2} ; \quad n = 1,2, \ldots \text{ and minimum value (nodes) for}$$

$$x = (2n + 1) \frac{\lambda}{4} ; \quad n = 0,1, \ldots$$

The nodes and anti-nodes are spaced $\frac{\lambda}{2}$ apart. (The anti-nodal planes are shown in Figure 1.) Now when a photographic plate is placed at an angle θ (to OM as shown in Figure 1), it crosses the nodes and antinodes formed. The light will affect the plate and darken it only when an antinode falls on the plate. Where there is a node, the plate is not affected and no blackening will be observed.

If L is the length of the photographic plate, the antinodes occur whenever

$$L \sin \theta = n \frac{\lambda}{2} .$$

Hence, the number of antinodes/cm on the plate =

$$\frac{2 L \sin \theta}{L\lambda} = \frac{2 \sin \theta}{\lambda}$$

When $\theta = 0.5°$, the number of antinodes or dark spots = 319.6 per cm. When $\theta = 10°$, the number of antinodes is 6360 per cm.

THE FABRY-PEROT INTERFEROMETER AND ETALON

● PROBLEM 9-10

The plates of a Fabry-Perot etalon are held strictly parallel at a distance of 1 cm. This etalon is placed between two identical converging lenses L_1 and L_2 having focal length 15 cm. A monochromatic source 1 cm in diameter is placed at the principal focus of L_1 ($\lambda = 0.49\mu$). Take the index of refraction of air equal to 1 . If an opaque screen which covers half the surface of the plates is placed between the plates, what change is observed in the etalon fringes focused by L_2 at the plane F'?

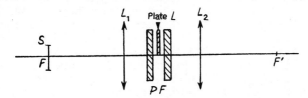

Solution: It is clear from the figure that circular fringes will be observed on the screen at F'. These would be complete circles. The lenses are used to collimate the beam and make the beam as close to the normal to the interferometer surfaces as possible.

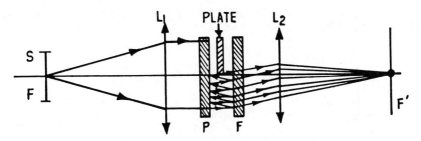

The effect of introduction of an opaque screen covering one half of the surface of the interferometer plates is to reduce the number of multiple internal

173

reflections by 50 percent and hence reduce the intensity of the fringes by an equal amount. No change in the fringe pattern would be observed as no new path difference is introduced by the opaque screen.

● **PROBLEM** 9-11

Calculate the ratio of full width at half-maximum to the separation between maxima (as a function of the phase difference) for a Fabry-Perot etalon with the reflectance R = 0.5, 0.8, 0.9, 0.98.

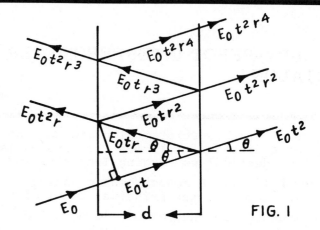

FIG. I

Solution: The Fabry-Perot etalon consists essentially of two optically flat, partially reflecting plates of glass or quartz. The plates are held fixed by spacers. The beam incident on the first plate is partially reflected and partially transmitted. The transmitted beam is subsequently reflected back and forth between the two plates, as shown in Figure 1, where r is the coefficient of reflection and t is the coefficient of transmission. The geometric path difference between any two successive transmitted rays is 2d cos θ, where d is the separation between the plates and θ is the angle either the transmitted or reflected ray makes with the surface normal. The corresponding phase difference between two successive rays is

$$\delta = \frac{4\pi}{\lambda} d \cos \theta$$

where λ is the wavelength of the light. Then summing the amplitudes of the transmitted rays

$$E_T = E_o t^2 \left(1 + r^2 e^{i\delta} + r^4 e^{2i\delta} + \dots \right)$$

$$= E_o t^2 \sum_{k=0}^{\infty} r^{2K} e^{iK\delta} = \frac{E_o t^2}{1 - r^2 e^{i\delta}}$$

$$E_T = E_o t^2 + E_o t^2 r^2 e^{i\delta} + \dots \qquad (1)$$

174

The intensity is then given by,

$$I_T = |E_T|^2 = \frac{I_o |t^4|}{|1 - r^2 e^{i\delta}|^2}$$

where $|E_o|^2 = I_o$

is the intensity of the incident beam. In general there will be a phase change on reflection and hence we can write

$$r = |r| e^{i\delta_r/2}$$

where $\delta_r/2$ is the phase change on a single reflection. If $R = |r|^2 = rr^*$ and $T = |t|^2 = tt^*$ (r^* and t^* denote the complex conjugates of r and t, respectively), then

$$I_T = I_o \frac{T^2}{|1 - Re^{i\Delta}|^2} \, ,$$

where $\Delta = \delta + \delta_r$ is the total phase change.

$$\left|1 - Re^{i\Delta}\right|^2 = \left(1 - Re^{i\Delta}\right)\left(1 - Re^{-i\Delta}\right) =$$

$$1 - R\left(e^{i\Delta} + e^{-i\Delta}\right) + R^2 \, .$$

Euler's equations state that $e^{i\Delta} = \cos \Delta + i \sin \Delta$ and $e^{-i\Delta} = \cos \Delta - i \sin \Delta$.

Then, $\left|1 - Re^{i\Delta}\right|^2 = 1 - 2R \cos \Delta + R^2$.

Therefore,

$$I_T = \frac{I_o \, T^2}{1 + R^2 - 2R \cos \Delta}$$

$$\cos \Delta = \cos\left(\frac{\Delta}{2} + \frac{\Delta}{2}\right) = \cos^2 \frac{\Delta}{2} - \sin^2 \frac{\Delta}{2} \, .$$

$$\cos^2 \frac{\Delta}{2} = 1 - \sin^2 \frac{\Delta}{2} \, , \quad so$$

$$\cos \Delta = 1 - 2 \sin^2 \Delta /2 \, .$$

$$I_T = I_o \frac{T^2}{\left(1 - R\right)^2 + 4R \sin^2 \frac{\Delta}{2}} \, .$$

Factoring out $(1 - R)^2$ from the denominator of this expression,

$$I_T = \frac{I_o \, T^2}{(1 - R)^2} \frac{1}{1 + \frac{4R}{(1 - R)^2} \sin^2 \Delta/2} \, .$$

175

Thus, the intensity varies as

$$\frac{1}{1 + F \sin^2 \Delta/2}$$

where $F = \dfrac{4R}{(1 - R)^2}$.

F is referred to as the coefficient of finesse. I_T attains its maximum value for

$$\sin^2 \frac{\Delta}{2} = 0, \text{ or for } \Delta = 2m\pi .$$

Then,

$$\frac{I_T}{I_{Tmax}} = \frac{\left(\dfrac{I_o T^2}{(1 - R)^2}\right)\left(\dfrac{1}{1 + \dfrac{4R}{(1 - R)^2} \sin^2 \dfrac{\Delta}{2}}\right)}{\dfrac{I_o T^2}{(1 - R)^2}} =$$

$$\frac{1}{1 + \dfrac{4R}{(1 - R)^2} \sin^2 \Delta/2} ,$$

as shown in Fig. 2.

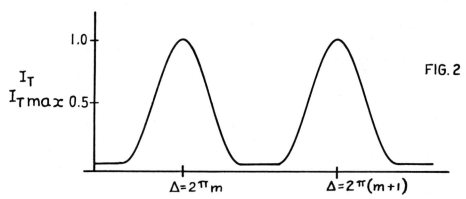

FIG. 2

I_T/I_{Tmax} will be $\frac{1}{2}$ when

$$\frac{1}{2} = \frac{1}{1 + \dfrac{4R}{(1 - R)^2} \sin^2 \left(\dfrac{\Delta_{1/2}}{2}\right)} .$$

Then,

$$1 + \dfrac{4R}{(1 - R)^2} \sin^2 \left(\dfrac{\Delta_{1/2}}{2}\right) = 2 .$$

176

So,

$$\frac{4R}{(1 - R)^2} \sin^2\left(\frac{\Delta_{1/2}}{2}\right) = 1, \text{ and}$$

$$\sin^2\left(\frac{\Delta_{1/2}}{2}\right) = \frac{1}{\dfrac{4R}{(1 - R)^2}} = \frac{1}{F} \quad .$$

Taking the square root of both sides gives the result

$$\sin\left(\frac{\Delta_{1/2}}{2}\right) = \frac{1}{\sqrt{F}} \quad .$$

Hence, $\Delta_{1/2} = 2 \sin^{-1}\left(\frac{1}{\sqrt{F}}\right) \quad .$

Full width at half maximum is $2\Delta_{1/2} = 4 \sin^{-1}\left(\frac{1}{\sqrt{F}}\right)$

The adjacent maxima are separated by 2π. Hence the ratio of full width half maximum to the separation between maxima is,

$$f = \frac{4 \sin^{-1}\left(\frac{1}{\sqrt{F}}\right)}{2\pi}$$

$$f = \frac{2}{\pi} \sin^{-1}\left(\frac{1}{\sqrt{F}}\right) \quad .$$

Since $F = \dfrac{4R}{(1 - R)^2}$ is large we can say that

$\sin^{-1}\left(\frac{1}{\sqrt{F}}\right)$ is approximately equal to $\frac{1}{\sqrt{F}}$.

Then,

$$f = \frac{2}{\pi\sqrt{F}}$$

R	F	f
0.5	8	0.225
0.8	80	0.071
0.9	360	0.0335
0.98	9800	0.00643

The reflecting power of the silvered surfaces of a Fabry-Perot etalon is 64%. Find the minimum intensity halfway between the maxima for the transmitted fringes.

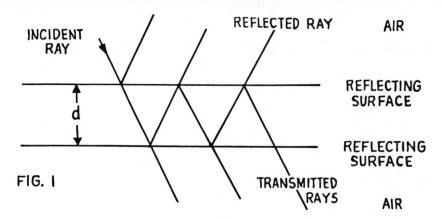

FIG. I

Solution: Figure 1 shows a Fabry-Perot etalon. It is an optical device that provides an interference pattern resulting from multiple transmission-reflection of an incident beam of monochromatic light. The angle of incidence is exaggerated so that the path of the rays are easily seen. Normally it is used with the angle of incidence zero.

If we now look at zero incident angle, the incident ray is reflected and transmitted at the first surface such that the reflected ray can be represented by an electric field $E_i = r'e^{i\omega t}$ and the transmitted ray by an electric field $E_i = t'e^{i\omega t}$, where E_i is incident electric field, r' and t' are the reflection and transmission coefficients at the first surface respectively, ω is the angular frequency of the monochromatic light and t is time. Using r" and t" as reflection and transmission coefficients for the second surface and δ as the phase shift caused by the path difference, and including any relative phase change at the two surfaces in r", we can write for the set of reflections and transmissions

$$E_{1r} = E_i r' \, e^{i\omega t}$$

$$E_{2r} = E_i t' r'' t'' e^{i(\omega t - \delta)}$$

$$E_{3r} = E_i t' r'' r'' r'' t'' e^{i(\omega t - 2\delta)}$$

$$\vdots$$

$$E_{Nr} = E_i t' r''^{(2N-3)} t'' e^{i(\omega t - (N-1)\delta)}$$

$$E_{1t} = E_i t' t'' e^{i\omega t}$$

$$E_{2t} = E_i t' r'' r'' t'' e^{i(\omega t - \delta)}$$

$$E_{3t} = E_i t' r'' r'' r'' r'' t'' e^{i(\omega t - 2\delta)}$$

$$\vdots$$

$$E_{Nt} = E_i t' t'' r''^{2(N-1)} e^{i(\omega t - (N-1)\delta)}$$

to find the amplitude of either the reflected or transmitted pattern we have only then to add all the amplitudes. For the reflected amplitude this is

$$E_r = E_i e^{i\omega t} \left\{ r' + r'' t' t'' e^{-i\delta} \left[1 + \left(r''^2 e^{-i\delta} \right) + \left(r''^2 e^{-i\delta} \right)^2 + \right.\right.$$
$$\left.\left. \cdots \left(r''^2 e^{-i\delta} \right)^{N-2} \right] \right\}$$

now if $r''^2 e^{-i\delta} < 1$ and we let the number of reflections N become infinite,

since

$$\sum_{k=0}^{\infty} a^k = \frac{1}{1-a} \quad , \quad \text{the series} \sum_{k=0}^{\infty} \left(r''^2 e^{-i\delta} \right)^k$$

converges to

$$\frac{1}{1 - r''^2 e^{-i\delta}}$$

so,

$$E_r = E_i e^{i\omega t} \left[r' + \frac{r'' t' t'' e^{-i\delta}}{1 - r''^2 e^{-i\delta}} \right].$$

Doing the equivalent sum on the transmitted rays yields,

$$E_t = E_i e^{i\omega t} t' t'' \left\{ 1 + r''^2 e^{-i\delta} + \left(r''^2 e^{-i\delta} \right)^2 + \left(r''^2 e^{-i\delta} \right)^4 + \right.$$
$$\left. \cdots \left(r''^2 e^{-i\delta} \right)^{N-1} \right\}$$

$$= E_i e^{i\omega t} t' t'' \left[\frac{1}{1 - r''^2 e^{-i\delta}} \right].$$

Now from the Fresnel equation matching the boundary conditions we have $r' = -r''$ and $t' t'' = 1 - r'^2$ so we can write ,

$$E_r = E_i e^{i\omega t}\left[r'\left(1 - \frac{\left(1 - r'^2\right)e^{-i\delta}}{1 - r'^2 e^{-i\delta}}\right)\right]$$

$$= E_i r' e^{i\omega t}\left[\frac{1 - r'^2 e^{-i\delta} - e^{-i\delta} + r'^2 e^{-i\delta}}{1 - r'^2 e^{-i\delta}}\right]$$

$$= E_i e^{i\omega t}\left[\frac{r'\left(1 - e^{-i\delta}\right)}{\left(k_1 - r'^2 e^{-i\delta}\right)}\right]$$

and

$$E_t = E_i e^{i\omega t}\left[\frac{1 - r'^2}{1 - r'^2 e^{-i\delta}}\right] \ .$$

To find the intensity of the reflected and transmitted rays we must form the product $E_r E_r^*$ and $E_t E_t^*$, where E_r^* and E_t^* denote the complex conjugates of E_r and E_t , respectively. For the reflected rays, if we denote $I_i = E_i^2$,

$$I_r = I_i r'^2 \left[\frac{1 - e^{-i\delta}}{1 - r'^2 e^{-i\delta}} \cdot \frac{1 - e^{i\delta}}{1 - r'^2 e^{i\delta}}\right]$$

$$= I_i r'^2 \ \frac{2 - \left(e^{-i\delta} + e^{i\delta}\right)}{1 + r'^4 - r'^2\left(e^{-i\delta} + e^{i\delta}\right)}$$

$$= \frac{2 I_i r'^2 (1 - \cos \delta)}{1 + r'^4 - 2r'^2 \cos \delta}$$

and for the transmitted intensity

$$I_t = I_i \left[\frac{1 - r'^2}{1 - r'^2 e^{-i\delta}} \cdot \frac{1 - r'^2}{1 - r'^2 e^{i\delta}}\right]$$

$$= I_i \ \frac{\left(1 - r'^2\right)^2}{1 + r'^4 - 2r'^2 \cos \delta} \ .$$

Dividing both numerator and denominator of both I_r and I_t by $\left(1 - r'^2\right)^2$ and using the identity

$$\cos \delta = 1 - 2 \sin^2 \frac{\delta}{2}$$

we have

$$I_r = \frac{I_i\left(\frac{2r'}{1 - r'^2}\right)^2 \sin^2 \frac{\delta}{2}}{1 + \left(\frac{2r'}{1 - r'^2}\right)^2 \sin^2 \frac{\delta}{2}}$$

180

$$I_t = I_i \frac{1}{1 + \left(\dfrac{2r'}{1 - r'^2}\right)^2 \sin^2 \frac{\delta}{2}}$$

In this problem we have a reflecting power of 64%, which says that $r'^2 = 0.64$ and we want to find the transmitted intensity halfway between the maxima for the transmitted fringes. This means we want to find the minimum transmitted intensity which occurs when the path difference, related to δ, yields $\sin^2 \delta/2 = 1$. Then since the reflectance $R = |r'|^2$,

$$\frac{I_t}{I_i} = \frac{1}{1 + \left(\dfrac{2r'}{1 - r'^2}\right)^2} = \frac{1}{1 + \dfrac{4r'^2}{(1 - r'^2)^2}} = \frac{1}{1 + \dfrac{4R}{(1 - R)^2}}$$

$$\frac{I_t}{I_i} = \frac{1}{1 + \dfrac{(4)(.64)}{(1 - .64)^2}} = \frac{1}{1 + \dfrac{2.56}{(.36)^2}} = \frac{1}{1 + 19.75}$$

$$= 0.0482$$

● **PROBLEM** 9-13

A "solid" Fabry-Perot interferometer consists merely of a 2 cm slab of high index material ($n = 4.5$). Calculate a) the fringe contrast and b) the resolving power.

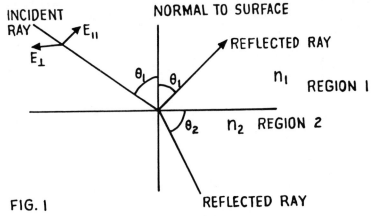

FIG. 1

Solution: The intensity of the transmitted beam in a Fabry-Perot etalon is given as,

$$I_t = I_i \frac{1}{1 + \left(\dfrac{2r}{1 - r^2}\right)^2 \sin^2 \left(\dfrac{\delta}{2}\right)} \qquad (1)$$

In this problem we first want to determine the fringe

contrast; namely the contrast between the intensity of the fringe when at maximum intensity and the intensity of the fringe when at minimum intensity. In equation (1) r represents the reflection coefficient, δ the path difference of the multiply reflected rays, and the I's represent the incident and transmitted intensities. By considering equation (1) we can see that the maximum of the function occurs when $\sin^2 \delta/2 = 0$ and the minimum when $\sin^2 \delta/2 = 1$ so the maximum

$$\frac{\left(I_t\right)_{max}}{I_i} = 1$$

and the minimum intensity is ,

$$\frac{\left(I_t\right)_{min}}{I_i} = \frac{1}{1 + \dfrac{4r^2}{\left(1 - r^2\right)^2}} \tag{2}$$

$$= \frac{\left(1 - r^2\right)^2}{\left(1 - r^2\right)^2 + 4r^2} \tag{3}$$

$$= \frac{\left(1 - r^2\right)^2}{1 - 2r^2 + r^4 + 4r^2} \tag{4}$$

$$= \frac{\left(1 - r^2\right)^2}{\left(1 + r^2\right)^2} . \tag{5}$$

Now we need to determine the reflection coefficient. For this we need to look at the boundary conditions on the electric and magnetic field which lead to the Fresnel equations,

$$r_\perp = \left|\frac{E_r}{E_i}\right|_\perp = \frac{n_1 \cos \theta_1 - n_2 \cos \theta_2}{n_1 \cos \theta_1 + n_2 \cos \theta_2} \tag{6}$$

$$r_\| = \left|\frac{E_r}{E_i}\right|_\| = \frac{n_2 \cos \theta_1 - n_1 \cos \theta_2}{n_1 \cos \theta_2 + n_2 \cos \theta_1} \tag{7}$$

$$t_\perp = \left|\frac{E_t}{E_i}\right|_\perp = \frac{2n_1 \cos \theta_1}{n_1 \cos \theta_1 + n_2 \cos \theta_2} \tag{8}$$

$$t_\| = \left|\frac{E_t}{E_i}\right|_\| = \frac{2n_1 \cos \theta_1}{n_1 \cos \theta_2 + n_2 \cos \theta_1} \tag{9}$$

where, with respect to Figure 1, subscripts 1 and 2 refer to quantities in regions 1 and 2, n's are the indices of refraction in the two regions, and θ the angle with respect to the normal of the rays at the surface. $\|$ represents the properties when the incident electric field is in the plane of incidence and ⊥ represents the properties when the incident electric field is perpendicular to the plane of incidence.

In a Fabry-Perot etalon, θ is normally zero so the reflection coefficients reduce to

$$r_\perp = \frac{n_1 - n_2}{n_1 + n_2} \tag{10}$$

and

$$r_{||} = \frac{n_2 - n_1}{n_1 + n_2} = - r_\perp \tag{11}$$

in this problem $n_1 = 1.0$; $n_2 = 4.5$ so $r_{||} = 3.5/5.5 = 0.6363...$
..... so the fringe contrast is,

$$\frac{I_{t\ max}}{I_{t\ min}} = \frac{1}{\left(\frac{1 - r^2}{1 + r^2}\right)^2} = \left(\frac{1 + (0.6363\ ....)^2}{1 - (0.6363\ ....)^2}\right)^2$$

$$= \left(\frac{1 + .4049}{1 - .4049}\right)^2 \tag{12}$$

$$= 2.36$$

which says the intensity at a maximum is 2.36 times the intensity at the minimum.

To find the resolving power, defined as $\lambda/\Delta\lambda$, we can investigate equation (1) using the additional relation

$$\delta = \frac{4\pi}{\lambda}\ nd\ \cos\ \theta \tag{13}$$

where δ refers to the path difference.

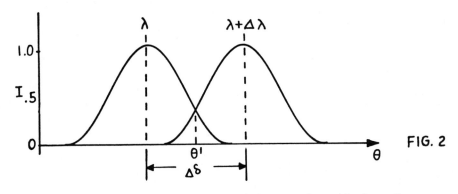

FIG. 2

Consider two sources, one with wavelength λ and a second with wavelength $\lambda + \Delta\lambda$, where from equations (1) and (3) the intensity pattern appears as shown in Figure 2. So

183

we can decide that two sources are just resolved when both λ and $\lambda + \Delta\lambda$ have an intensity equal to half the maximum intensity at θ, in Figure 2. From equation (1) this says that,

$$\left(\frac{2r}{1 - r^2}\right)^2 \sin^2(\delta/2) = 1 \tag{14}$$

or,

$$\sin \delta/2 = \frac{1 - r^2}{2r} \tag{15}$$

or, with our definition of $\Delta\delta$

$$\sin \frac{\Delta\delta}{4} = \frac{1 - r^2}{2r} \tag{16}$$

now a maximum will occur when δ in equation (13) has a value of $2m\pi$ and so we expect $\Delta\delta$ to be very close to a maximum; therefore, $\Delta\delta/4$ will represent a small angle and we can replace $\sin \Delta\delta/4$ by $\Delta\delta/4$ or

$$\frac{\Delta\delta}{4} \sim \frac{1 - r^2}{2r} \quad . \tag{17}$$

We can also differentiate equation (13) to yield,

$$\Delta\delta = -\frac{4\pi n d}{\lambda} \sin \theta \Delta\theta \quad . \tag{18}$$

The condition for a maximum, $\delta = m2\pi$ causes equation (13) to become

$$m\lambda = 2nd \cos \theta \tag{19}$$

and differentiating yields

$$m\Delta\lambda = -2nd \sin \theta \Delta\theta \quad . \tag{20}$$

We can combine equations (17), (18), (19) and (20) as follows: From equations (19) and (20),

$$\frac{\lambda}{\Delta\lambda} = -\frac{\cos \theta}{\sin \theta \Delta\theta} \quad .$$

From equation (18),

$$\sin \theta \Delta\theta = -\frac{\lambda \Delta\delta}{4\pi n d}$$

and from equation (17),

$$\Delta\delta = \frac{4\left(1 - r^2\right)}{2r} = \frac{2\left(1 - r^2\right)}{r} \quad .$$

Substituting for $\sin\theta\Delta\theta$ and $\Delta\delta$, we have

$$\frac{\lambda}{\Delta\lambda} = \frac{\cos\,\theta\,(4\pi nd)}{\lambda\Delta\delta} = \frac{4\pi ndr\,\cos\,\theta}{2\lambda\left(1-r^2\right)}\,;$$

therefore,

$$\frac{\lambda}{\Delta\lambda} = \frac{2nd}{\lambda}\,\frac{\pi r}{\left(1-r^2\right)}\,\cos\,\theta\quad. \tag{21}$$

Since a Fabry-Perot is used with $\theta \cong 0$ and we have calculated r in the first part of the problem then,

$$\frac{\lambda}{\Delta\lambda} = \frac{2 \times 4.5 \times 2 \times 10^{-2}\,\pi\,(.6363\,\ldots)}{\lambda\left(1-\left(.6363\,\ldots\right)^2\right)}$$

$$= \frac{0.604}{\lambda}$$

where λ is measured in meters and for a wavelength of say 500 nm,

$$\frac{\lambda}{\Delta\lambda} = 1.21 \times 10^6\quad.$$

THE MICHELSON INTERFEROMETER

● PROBLEM 9-14

When the movable mirror of a Michelson's interferometer is shifted a certain distance, 200 fringes are observed to pass a given point in the field of view. If light of wavelength 6.24×10^{-5} cm is used, determine how far the mirror was moved.

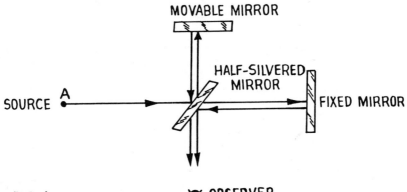

FIG. I   ▽ OBSERVER

Solution: Figure 1 is a diagram indicating the principal features of the Michelson interferometer. It is known for this piece of equipment that if m fringes cross the observer's field of view when the movable mirror is moved a distance x, then the following relation is true:

$$2x = m\lambda,$$

where λ = the wavelength of light used.

Here we have m = 200 and $\lambda = 6.24 \times 10^{-5}$ cm. Then,

$$x = \frac{m\lambda}{2} = \frac{200 \times 6.24 \times 10^{-5}}{2} \text{ cm}$$

$$= 6.24 \times 10^{-3} \text{ cm} = 6.24 \times 10^{-2} \text{ mm} .$$

Thus, the mirror was moved .0624 mm.

● **PROBLEM** 9-15

A Michelson interferometer is adjusted so that white light fringes are in the field of view. Sodium light is substituted and one mirror moved until the fringes reach minimum visibility. How far is the mirror moved?

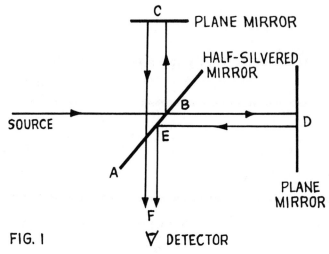

FIG. I

Solution: A Michelson interferometer is shown in figure 1. A ray from the source can then be traced through the interferometer. At B the ray is split and the transmitted portion proceeds to D, and is reflected back to E, where a portion is reflected to F. The portion that is reflected at B proceeds to C, is reflected to E, and a portion is transmitted to F. The interference pattern that is observed at F will depend on the path difference $\overline{BDE}$ - $\overline{BCE}$. If this optical path difference is an integer number of wavelengths of the source light, a maximum will occur at F and if the path difference is an odd integer number of half-wavelengths, a minimum will occur there. So at F we will see a pattern of maxima and minima (fringes). However white light has all wavelengths, so we will have an overlapping of fringes for each of the wavelengths represented and therefore the only time we will be able to distinguish fringes will be if the path difference is zero.

186

For minimum visibility for sodium light (consider sodium light to be primarily the 589.0 nm and 589.6 nm doublet) we will need to have a maximum of one of the lines to be located at the minimum of the other line. In essence then, we want to find the distance d, a measure of how far the mirror must be moved so that,

$$2d = m\lambda_1 \quad ; \quad \text{maximum for } \lambda_1 \tag{1}$$

and

$$2d = (m + 1/2)\lambda_2 \quad ; \quad \text{minima for } \lambda_2, \tag{2}$$

where λ_1 and λ_2 represent the two wavelengths of sodium light.

From equation (1), $m = \dfrac{2d}{\lambda_1}$, and substituting for m in equation (2)

$$2d = \left(\frac{2d}{\lambda_1} + \frac{1}{2}\right)\lambda_2 \tag{3}$$

or,

$$2d\left(1 - \frac{\lambda_2}{\lambda_1}\right) = \frac{\lambda_2}{2} \tag{4}$$

Then,

$$d = \frac{\lambda_2}{4(1 - \lambda_2/\lambda_1)} \tag{5}$$

So, after substituting the values for λ_1 and λ_2 into (5),

$$d = \frac{589.0 \times 10^{-9}}{4\left(1 - \frac{589.0 \times 10^{-9}}{589.6 \times 10^{-9}}\right)} = 1.45 \times 10^{-4} m = 0.0145 \text{ cm}.$$

THE MACH-ZENDER INTERFEROMETER

● **PROBLEM** 9-16

The apparatus shown in Figure 1 is a Mach-Zender interferometer. Both beam splitters transmit 90% and reflect 10% of the light intensity incident on them. Mirror 2 is not parallel to the others, by the angle δ.
1) What pattern does observer A see?
2) What pattern does observer B see?
3) If a half-wave plate with its fast axis vertical is inserted in the beam at C, and one with its fast axis horizontal is inserted in the beam at C', what does the observer A see?

Solution: Figure 2 shows two sets of rays traversing the interferometer when all four optical surfaces are parallel. If mirror 2 is tilted by an angle δ the incident ray on mirror 2 then follows the rays labeled (1), (2), (3), (4),

187

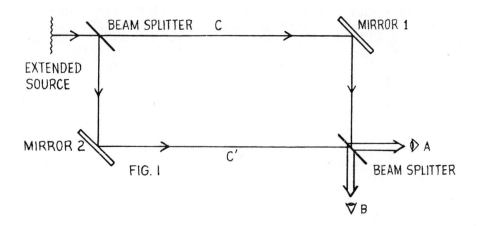

EXTENDED
SOURCE

BEAM SPLITTER   C

MIRROR 1

MIRROR 2

C'

FIG. I

BEAM SPLITTER

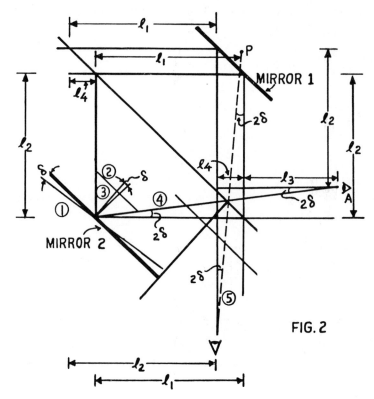

FIG. 2

and (5) through the remainder of the interferometer.

Let us now consider what A sees for an optical path difference between two sets of rays. From the first beam splitter to mirror 1 to the second beam splitter to A the path length is

$$\ell_1 + \ell_2 + \ell_3 + \ell_4$$

The other path (from the first beam splitter to mirror two to the second beam splitter to A) yields

$$\ell_4 + \ell_2 + (\ell_3 + \ell_1)/\cos 2\delta$$

and the path difference is then

$$\left(\ell_1 + \ell_3\right)\left(1 - \frac{1}{\cos 2\delta}\right) \quad .$$

The path difference B sees will be the same as that which A sees. So there will be phase differences for both observer A and observer B and so fringes will occur. To determine the intensity of the fringes seen we must make use of the fact that the beam splitters do not yield equal intensities.

For A the beam progressing through mirror 1 is transmitted in the first beam splitter and reflected at the second beam splitter so its intensity is $0.9 \times 0.1\ I_o = 0.09\ I_o$. For the beam progressing by mirror 2 there is reflection at the first beam splitter and transmission at the second beam splitter, so its intensity is $0.1 \times 0.9\ I_o = 0.09\ I_o$. So A sees two interfering beams of equal intensity with resulting $I_{max} = 0.18\ I_o$ and $I_{min} = 0$.

For B the beam progressing via mirror 1 is transmitted in both beam splitters so its intensity is $0.9 \times 0.9\ I_o = 0.81\ I_o$. For the beam passing through mirror 2 both beam splitters reflect the beam so the intensity is $0.1 \times 0.1\ I_o = 0.01\ I_o$. So B sees two interfering beams of different intensities with resulting $I_{max} = 0.82\ I_o$ and $I_{min} = 0.80\ I_o$.

Since visibility, V, is a common way to express the variation in the fringe pattern and is defined as

$$V = \frac{I_{max} - I_{min}}{I_{max} + I_{min}}$$

A sees $V = 1$ and B sees $V \doteq 0.012$.

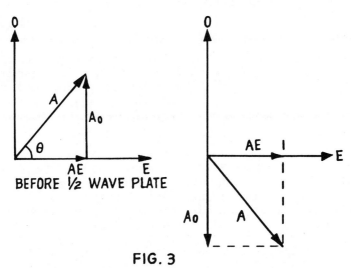

BEFORE ½ WAVE PLATE

FIG. 3

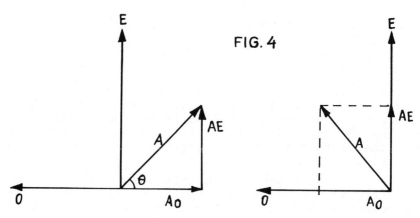

FIG. 4

If we insert half wave plates in the upper and lower arms of the interferometer, we suspect that polarization will result. In the top leg, if we have an "individual photon" polarized at some angle with respect to the E axis of the half wave plate, we have in figure 3 a polarized vector A with components A_O and A_E respectively along the ordinary and extraordinary axis. After passing through the half wave plate the A_E component

is a half wavelength out of phase with the A_O component or the resulting A vector is rotated 90^0 clockwise. In the bottom leg we see in figure 4 that a similar condition occurs with the A vector rotated 90^0 counterclockwise. Now when these recombine at A [it has been shown that the intensities were equal and had a fringe pattern,] we see that we have introduced through the two half-wave plates an additional half wave-length phase difference. Therefore the fringes will be shifted by half a fringe; namely, the former bright spots are now dark and the former dark spots are bright. In our polarization decomposition we defined the A vector arbitrarily so that for all "individual photons" there will be an extra half wavelength phase shift.

THE LUMMER-GEHRCKE PLATE

● **PROBLEM** 9-17

A Lummer-Gehrcke plate 1 cm thick is used for studying sodium light, $\lambda = 5893\text{Å}$. If the index of refraction is 1.52, find the order of interference nearest the faces of the plate.

Solution: A Lummer-Gehrcke plate is shown in Figure 1. Allow a ray of sodium light to enter along the incident ray. The angle θ is chosen so that the incident ray is internally reflected at the second surface of the prism, and since the prism and the plate have the same index of refraction, ray 1 is not deviated as it enters the plate. However, at the bottom of the plate, its angle of incidence is less than the critical angle so the ray splits into transmitted ray 2 and reflected ray 3. At the upper plate

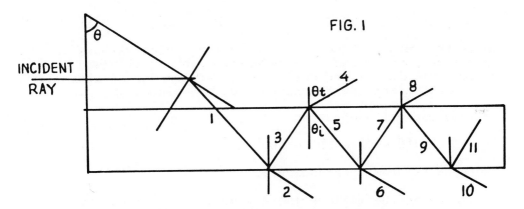

FIG. I

surface ray 3 further splits into transmitted ray 4 and
reflected ray 5. This splitting continues as the split
reflected ray progresses down the plate. A careful
observation of the geometry shows that rays 4 and 8, etc.,
emerge parallel to each other and also rays 2, 6 and 10,
etc., emerge parallel to each other. Also from ray 3 to
ray 8 there are two internal reflections and likewise from
ray 1 to ray 6. This means that the phase difference
between rays 4 and 8 and also between rays 2 and 6 are
due to the difference in path length only.

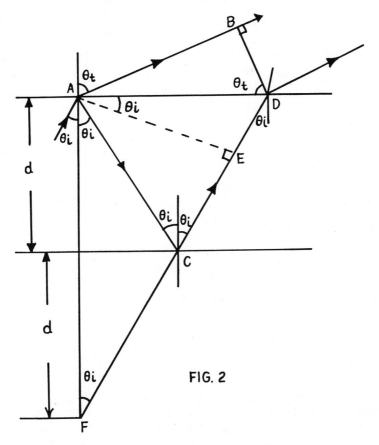

FIG. 2

Let us now look at Figure 2. We then want to find
the path difference

$$\Delta = n(\overline{ACD}) - \overline{AB} \tag{1}$$

(n is the relative index of refraction) which will determine whether our Lummer-Gehrcke plate will yield a maximum or minimum or something in between for a particular wavelength λ and the thickness d of the plate.

We can write equation (1) as

$$\Delta = n(\overline{AC} + \overline{CE} + \overline{ED}) - \overline{AB} \tag{2}$$

where $\overline{AE}$ is drawn perpendicular to $\overline{CD}$.

Tracing the various angles equal to θ_i it becomes clear that ⧣ DAE = θ_i. Thus $\overline{ED} = \overline{AD} \sin\theta_i$ while $\overline{AB} = \overline{AD} \sin\theta_t$. From Snell's law, $\sin\theta_i/\sin\theta_t = n_{air}/n_{glass} = 1/n$, so that

$$\frac{\overline{ED}}{\sin\theta_i} = \frac{\overline{AB}}{\sin\theta_t} \quad \text{becomes}$$

$$\frac{\overline{ED}}{\overline{AB}} = \frac{\sin\theta_i}{\sin\theta_t} = \frac{1}{n}$$

$$n\overline{ED} = \overline{AB} . \tag{3}$$

The path difference is then

$$\Delta = n(\overline{AC} + \overline{CE}) . \tag{4}$$

Examining triangle FAE we see that

$$\overline{FE} = 2d \cos\theta_i$$

and since $\overline{FC} = \overline{AC}$,

equation (4) becomes

$$\Delta = n(\overline{FC} + \overline{CE}) = n\overline{FE}$$

or $\quad \Delta = n(2d \cos\theta_i).$ \hfill (5)

For a maximum the path difference must be an integer number of wavelengths or

$$m\lambda = 2nd \cos\theta_i \tag{6}$$

where m is the order of interference.

In this problem we want to find the order of interference nearest the faces of the plate. Now the critical angle is that internal angle θ_i for which the exterior angle θ_t will be $90°$, so we want to use in equation (6), $\theta_i = \theta_{critical}$. From Snell's law

$$\sin\theta_c = \frac{1}{n} = \frac{1}{1.52} \tag{7}$$

$$\theta_c = 41.14° \tag{8}$$

or from equation (6),

$$m = \frac{2nd\ \cos\ 41.14°}{\lambda} \tag{9}$$

$$= \frac{2 \times 1.52 \times 10^{-2} \times 0.7531}{589.3 \times 10^{-9}} \tag{10}$$

$$= 38849 \tag{11}$$

remembering that m must be an integer.

FRESNEL'S DOUBLE MIRRORS

● **PROBLEM** 9-18

A laser beam illuminates two mirrors, as shown in Figure 1. If we assume that the beam consists of strictly monochromatic plane waves and has a circular cross section of 10cm diameter, what interference pattern do we see at a distance of 5m from the mirrors? The angle between the mirrors is 0.01 rad.

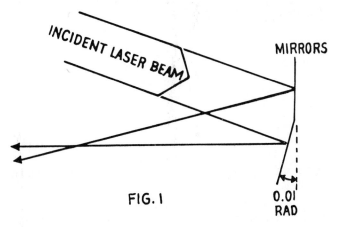

FIG. 1

Solution: This arrangement, known as Fresnel's double mirrors, allows two plane-wave fronts to overlap. The two reflected half-beams (semicircular in cross section) interfere where they overlap, giving a pattern like that sketched in Figure 2. In the region of overlap, where fringes are formed by the intersection of plane-wave fronts, we may find the fringe spacing by the equation

$$D = \frac{\lambda/2}{\sin(\alpha/2)} \quad .$$

This equation may be found by assuming that the two triangles

193

FIG. 2

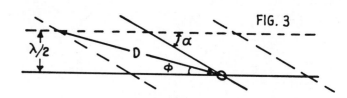

FIG. 3

formed by the diagonal of length D shown in Figure 3 are isosceles. Then $\phi = \frac{\alpha}{2}$ and the equation follows geometrically (α is the angle between the mirrors). For our small angle, $D = \lambda/\alpha$, since for very small α, $\sin\left(\frac{\alpha}{2}\right)$ is approximately equal to $\frac{\alpha}{2}$. We can formulate our problem as a two-source one. The fringes may be thought of as due to two point sources at some large distance L away and separated by the angle α. Then

$$d = 2L \sin\frac{\alpha}{2} \quad \text{and} \quad I = I_o \cos^2\left[\frac{\pi d}{\lambda} \sin\theta\right]$$

$$= I_o \cos^2\left[\frac{2\pi}{\lambda}L \sin\theta \sin\frac{\alpha}{2}\right]$$

This gives us a fringe spacing of $D = (\lambda/2)/\sin(\alpha/2)$, which agrees with the other result. Since L and θ are arbitrary, we might replace them by a measured position along the detection plane (a film, perhaps): $Y = L \sin\theta$. Then

$$I = I_o \cos^2\left(\frac{2\pi}{\lambda} Y \sin\frac{\alpha}{2}\right).$$

It is given that d = 10cm, Y = 5m, and α = 0.01 rad = 0.57°. Hence,

$$I = I_o \cos^2\left[\frac{2\pi}{\lambda}(5m) \sin\left[\frac{0.57°}{2}\right]\right]$$

$$= I_o \cos^2\left[\frac{8.95}{\lambda}\right],$$

where λ is the wavelength of the laser beam, expressed in meters.

Notice that the geometry here is the difficulty rather than the concepts of interference. This is why such approximations as that of small angles are so important. A more exact solution contributes nothing to our understanding of the physics.

HAIDINGER FRINGES

● **PROBLEM** 9-19

Haidinger fringes are observed with a 2-mm thick slab of index n = 1.600 having accurately flat surfaces. The light used has λ = 5000 Å. Calculate the maximum order at the

center of the circular fringe pattern. How many bright
fringes are observed within a cone of 1/30 radian of the
normal to the surface?

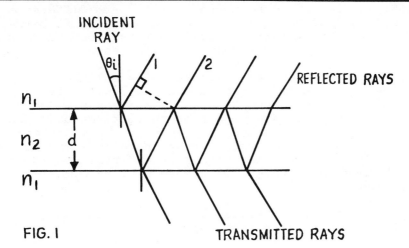

FIG. I

Solution: Haidinger fringes are the interference pattern
of maxima and minima that are formed with multiple reflections and transmissions from an optically flat-parallel
set of surfaces when the angle of incidence onto the plate
is zero (See figure 1). Our condition of maxima or minima
then relates to the optical path difference between successive rays (say 1 and 2). It can be shown geometrically
that

$$2d \cos \theta = m \lambda_{medium} \qquad \text{maxima} \qquad (1)$$

$$= (m + \tfrac{1}{2}) \lambda_{medium} \qquad \text{minima} \qquad (2)$$

for the transmitted rays, and

$$2d \cos \theta = (m + \tfrac{1}{2}) \lambda_{medium} \qquad \text{maxima} \qquad (3)$$

$$= m \lambda_{medium} \qquad \text{minima} \qquad (4)$$

for the reflected rays, where d is the thickness of the slab.

Now we need to investigate the apparent difference between the transmitted and reflected maxima. First, since
the incident rays are split on transmission and reflection,
if the transmitted rays form a maximum then the reflected
rays will form a minimum (from conservation of energy).
Also we must recognize that there is the possibility of a
phase change as the rays interact at the surface. In reflection, the Fresnel equations, which are the result of
matching boundary conditions between the electric and magnetic fields at the boundary of the interface, tell us that
an E-M wave parallel to the plane of incidence will have a
phase change of π (half-wavelength) when the index of refraction of the incident ray medium is greater than that of
the refracted ray medium, and zero when the index of refraction
of the incident ray medium is less than the refracted ray medium.

195

For an E-M wave perpendicular to the plane of incidence the reverse is true.

Looking again at figure 1, we see that ray 1 has π phase change on reflection and ray 2 has 0 phase change on reflection, so in addition to the optical path difference there is an additional half-wavelength phase shift between rays 1 and 2. It is further noted that rays beyond 2 have 0 phase shift plus the optical path difference from ray 2.

So if the optical path difference is an integer number of wavelengths, the reflected rays 1 and 2 will have a half-wavelength phase difference and yield a minimum. Conversely, on transmission there are a pair of reflections occurring between all transmitted rays and therefore only the optical path difference will control whether there is a maximum or minimum. Namely, when the optical path difference is an integral number of wavelengths, there will be a maximum on transmission.

Now the relations between velocity c, frequency f, wavelength λ, and index of refraction n are

$$f\lambda = c \tag{5}$$

$$n = \frac{c_{air}}{c_{medium}} \tag{6}$$

and the frequency remains constant in any medium. So for λ_{air} = 500 nm, the wavelength in the slab is

$$\lambda_{medium} = \frac{\lambda_{air}}{n} = \frac{500.0 \times 10^{-9}}{1.6} \tag{7}$$

$$= 312.5 \text{ nm} \tag{8}$$

Since Haidinger fringes are formed with θ = 0°, equation (1) will yield the maximum order for reflection at the center and the maximum order for transmission will be 0.5 larger. So

$$2d \cos 0 = m \lambda_{medium} \tag{9}$$

$$m = \frac{2d}{\lambda_{medium}} = \frac{2 \times 2 \times 10^{-3}}{312.5 \times 10^{-9}} \tag{10}$$

$$m = 12800 \tag{11}$$

$$m + \frac{1}{2} = 12800.5 \tag{12}$$

is the answer to part one.

For the second part, we use equation (4) with θ = 1/30 radian to get

$$2d \cos (1/30 \text{ radian}) = m_1 \lambda_{medium} \tag{13}$$

$$m_1 = \frac{2 \times 2 \times 10^{-3} \times .99944}{312.5 \times 10^{-9}} \tag{14}$$

$$m_1 = 12792.89$$

196

and the difference between m and m_1 is the number of bright fringes that will be observed. Note that here we can use a decimal number of fringes, since we can estimate that we are between maxima by a certain fraction.

$$\Delta m = 12800 - 12792.89 = 7.11 \text{ bright fringes.}$$

INTERFERENCE FILTERS

● **PROBLEM** 9-20

A fourth-order interference filter (path difference 7λ where λ is the wavelength of light used) is chosen to transmit a narrow band of light of wavelength 4000Å. Find, neglecting dispersion, what other bands are transmitted in the visible region.

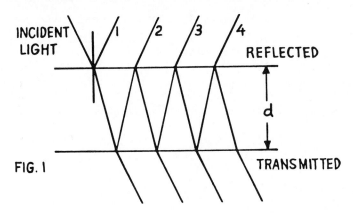

FIG. 1

Solution: An interference filter to transmit a narrow band ($\Delta\lambda$ small) of light appears in Figure 1, where the angle of incidence of the light is exaggerated. We want to look at an angle of incidence equal to zero, but to understand what is happening to the rays we must look at a finite angle of incidence.

It is known that the phase condition for reflection in the denser (n larger) medium at a boundary is such that the reflected ray is phase shifted by a half wavelength. It is seen from the figure that each reflected ray goes through an odd number of reflections so that the net effect of the reflections is to leave the reflected rays out of phase by 180°. Therefore the reflected beam will be a maximum when twice the thickness is an odd integer multiple of a half wavelength. By energy conservation, if the reflected intensity is a maximum, then the transmitted intensity is a minimum.

Similarly the reflected beam will be a minimum when twice the thickness is an even integer multiple of a half wavelength. Once again, by energy conservation, if the reflected beam is a minimum, the transmitted beam will be a maximum.

The order of the interference filter is then related

to the odd integer multiple, so that first order corresponds to odd integer multiple one, second order corresponds to odd integer multiple three, third order corresponds to odd integer multiple five and fourth order corresponds to odd integer multiple seven. In a similar way we look at the harmonics of a standing wave.

In this problem, for $\lambda = 400$ nm, our path difference in the interferometer is 7λ or 2800 nm. Now if $n\lambda = 2800$ nm, where n is an integer, we will have a maximum in the transmitted intensity. We must find those corresponding wavelengths which are in the visible spectrum (400-700 nm). We then want to investigate

$$n_1 \lambda_1 = 2800 \text{ nm} .$$

Clearly, for n_1 an integer greater than 7, the light will not be in the visible range, so we want to look at n_1 less than 7. If n_1 is less than 4 then the resulting wavelength again will not be in the visible range. Therefore we are left with $n_1 = 4,5,6$ which yields for λ_1

$$\frac{2800}{6} ; \quad \frac{2800}{5} ; \quad \frac{2800}{4}$$

or

466.6nm, 560 nm, and 700 nm.

INTERFERENCE FRINGES

How many fringes are formed per millimeter if light beams of wavelength 632.8 nm intersect at an angle of 5°?

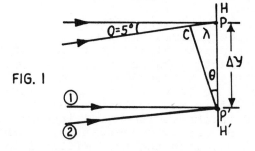

FIG. I

Solution: Figure 1 shows the two monochromatic beams of the same wavelength and inclined to each other at an angle θ. These two beams interfere on the photographic plate HH', producing bright and dark lines. Since the beam (1) is seen to be in constant phase across the surface of the hologram plane, the interference pattern, or fringes, will be separated by an amount Δy, whenever the path difference between the two beams is one wavelength

From the triangle CPP',

$$\sin\theta = \frac{CP}{PP'} = \frac{\lambda}{\Delta y}.$$

Therefore,

$$\Delta y = \frac{\lambda}{\sin\theta}.$$

Hence the number of fringes per mm is equal to

$$\frac{1}{\Delta y\,(mm)} = \frac{\sin\theta}{\lambda\,(mm)}$$

$$= \frac{\sin 5°}{6.328 \times 10^{-4}}$$

$$= 138\,(mm)^{-1}$$

● **PROBLEM** 9-22

Interference fringes are produced in a thin wedge-shaped film of cellophane of index of refraction 1.4. If the angle which the film makes with the horizontal is 20 sec. of arc, and the distance between fringes is 0.25 cm, find the wavelength of light.

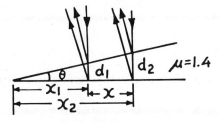

Solution: The optical path difference between two beams reflected from the two surfaces of a wedge shaped film, at normal incidence, is 2 μd where μ is the refractive index of the film and d is the height of the film, at a distance of x from its vertex.

For two successive fringes separated by a distance x, we can write the condition for a maximum:

$$2\,\mu d_1 = n\lambda$$

and

$$2\,\mu d_2 = (n + 1)\lambda.$$

On subtracting the top equation from the bottom equation,

$$2\,\mu(d_2 - d_1) = \lambda \qquad\qquad (1)$$

but

$$d_2 = x_2\theta$$

and

$$d_1 = x_1\theta$$

199

(since θ is small, tan θ ≃ θ)

Therefore,

$$d_2 - d_1 = (x_2 - x_1)\theta \tag{2}$$

Substituting the expression found for $d_2 - d_1$ from equation (2) into equation (1), we have

$$2\,\mu\theta(x_2 - x_1) = \lambda \tag{3}$$

but $\quad (x_2 - x_1) = 0.25$ cm

and $\qquad \theta = 20$ sec. of arc

$$= \frac{20}{60 \times 60} \times \frac{\pi}{180°} \text{ rad}$$

$$= 9.696 \times 10^{-5} \text{ rad.}$$

Therefore, from equation (3),

$$\lambda = 2 \times 1.4 \times 9.696 \times 10^{-5} \times 0.25 \text{ cm}$$

$$= 6.787 \times 10^{-5} \text{ cm}$$

$$= 6787 \text{ Å}$$

● **PROBLEM** 9-23

With two slits spaced 0.2 mm apart, and a screen at a distance of ℓ = 1 m, the third bright fringe is found to be displaced a distance h = 7.5 mm from the central fringe. Find the wavelength λ of the light used. See the figure.

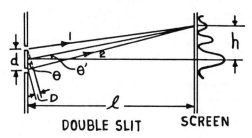

DOUBLE SLIT   SCREEN

Solution: When the difference D between the path lengths of the rays 1 and 2 is an integral multiple of the wavelength λ, one obtains a maximum (bright fringe) of the interference pattern on the screen. From the figure we see that

$$D = d \sin\theta \ .$$

If ℓ is much larger than the distance between the two slits, we see that θ' ≈ θ, where θ' relates the position of the maximum on the screen to the distance between slits and the screen,

$$\tan \theta' = \frac{h}{\ell} .$$

The approximation $\ell \gg d$ also means that θ is small; for which case we have

$$\tan \theta' \simeq \sin\theta' .$$

Therefore, for the third maximum to occur at h, D must be 3λ;

$$D = d \sin\theta = 3\lambda$$

or

$$\sin\theta \simeq \sin\theta' = \frac{3\lambda}{d} .$$

Therefore, since $\sin\theta' \simeq \tan\theta' = \frac{h}{\ell}$, $\frac{h}{\ell} = \frac{3\lambda}{d}$,

$$\frac{h}{\ell} = \frac{3\lambda}{d} ,$$

which gives λ as

$$\lambda = \frac{dh}{3\ell}$$

$$= \frac{0.75 \text{ cm} \times 0.02 \text{ cm}}{3 \times 100 \text{ cm}}$$

$$= 5 \times 10^{-5} \text{ cm}$$

$$= 500 \times 10^{-9} \text{ m}$$

$$= 500 \text{ nm}.$$

● **PROBLEM 9-24**

Light falls on two parallel slits separated by 0.2 mm. If interference fringes on a screen 75 cm away have a spacing of 2.2 mm, what is the wavelength of the light used?

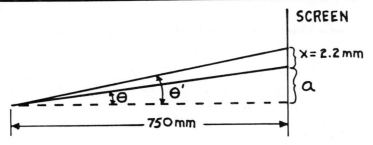

Solution: The fringes on the screen 750 mm away from the

201

slit can be seen if the condition

$$d \sin\theta = m\lambda \tag{1}$$

holds; d is the spacing between the two slits, λ is the wavelength of the light in air, and m is the order number. When θ, in equation (1), is small, we can make the approximation $\sin\theta = \tan\theta$; therefore equation (1) becomes

$$d \tan\theta = m\lambda \tag{2}$$

and

$$d \tan\theta' = (m+1)\lambda, \tag{3}$$

for two consecutive interference fringes.

From the figure,

$$\tan\theta = \frac{a}{750}$$

and

$$\tan\theta' = \frac{x + a}{750} = \frac{2.2 + a}{750} \quad ,$$

so equations (2) and (3) become

$$\frac{0.2a}{750} = m\lambda \tag{4}$$

and

$$\frac{0.2(2.2 + a)}{750} = (m+1)\lambda \quad , \tag{5}$$

since d = 0.2 mm. Now solving for a in equation (4), we have

$$a = 3750m\lambda$$

and substituting this into equation (5), we have

$$\frac{0.2(2.2 + 3750m\lambda)}{750} = (m+1)\lambda$$

from which the wavelength λ is found to be 5.87×10^{-4} mm.

● **PROBLEM** 9-25

Parallel white light is incident on two very narrow but parallel slits for which d, the slit separation, = 1 mm. A 1 meter focus lens is used to focus the interference fringes on a screen. If a small hole is made in this screen 3 mm from the central white fringe and the light examined by a spectroscope, what wavelengths between 4000 Å and 8000 Å will be missing?

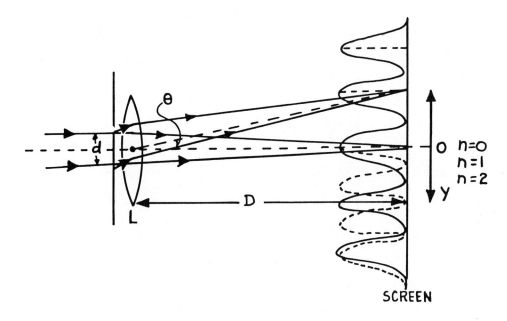

Solution: Maximum intensities for a wavelength λ are produced at those values of y which satisfy the equation

$$d \sin \theta = n\lambda ; \qquad n = \text{integer} .$$

For small θ,

$$\sin \theta \simeq \theta \simeq \tan \theta = \frac{y}{D} ,$$

where y and D are as shown in the figure.

Therefore,

$$d \frac{y}{D} = n\lambda$$

or

$$y = n \frac{\lambda D}{d} .$$

and minima are produced when

$$y = \left(n + \frac{1}{2} \right) \frac{\lambda D}{d} .$$

Now when a hole is made 3 mm from the central maxima, those wavelengths would be missing which have a minima at y = 3 mm.

Then $\lambda_{\text{min}} = \dfrac{dy}{\left(n + \frac{1}{2} \right) D}$, where

$$d = 1 \text{ mm} = 10^{-3} \text{ m}$$

$$y = 3 \text{ mm} = 3 \times 10^{-3} \text{ m}$$

$$D = 1 \text{ m}$$

203

Therefore,

$$\lambda_{min} = \frac{10^{-3} \times 3 \times 10^{-3}}{\left(n + \frac{1}{2}\right)(1)} \text{ m}$$

$$= \frac{3 \times 10^{-6}}{n + \frac{1}{2}} \text{ m} \quad .$$

All values of n which produce λ_{min} between 4000 Å
= 4 x 10^{-7}m and 8000 Å = 8 x 10^{-7}m will be missing.
Hence, for n = 1,

$$\lambda = \frac{3 \times 10^{-6}}{\frac{3}{2}} = 2 \times 10^{-6} = 20 \times 10^{-7} \text{ m} \quad ;$$

for n = 2,

$$\lambda = \frac{3 \times 10^{-6}}{\frac{5}{2}} = \frac{6}{5} \times 10^{-6} = 12 \times 10^{-7} \text{ m} \quad ;$$

for n = 3,

$$\lambda = \frac{3 \times 10^{-6}}{(7/2)} = \frac{6 \times 10^{-6}}{7} = 8.57 \times 10^{-7} \text{ m} \quad ;$$

for n = 4,

$$\lambda = \frac{3 \times 10^{-6}}{(9/2)} = \frac{6 \times 10^{-6}}{9} = 6.667 \times 10^{-7} \text{ m} ;$$

for n = 5,

$$\lambda = \frac{3 \times 10^{-6}}{(\frac{11}{2})} = \frac{6 \times 10^{-6}}{11} = 5.454 \times 10^{-7} \text{m};$$

for n = 6,

$$\lambda = \frac{3 \times 10^{-6}}{(13/2)} = \frac{6 \times 10^{-6}}{13} = 4.615 \times 10^{-7} \text{ m} \quad .$$

Hence, wavelengths 4615 Å, 5454 Å and 6667 Å will be absent
in the spectrograph.

● **PROBLEM 9-26**

A single dust particle acts like an isotropic scatterer.
Such a particle is on the front (unsilvered) surface of a
mirror so that one may observe the light scattered directly
from the particle and that scattered to the mirror and back.
Find the observed interference pattern.

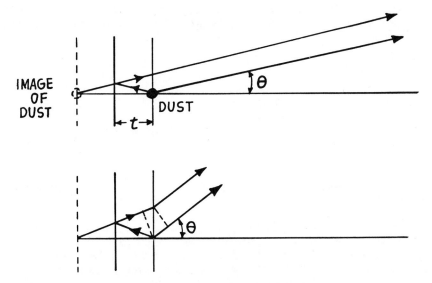

Solution: From the figure, we see that the dust and its image form two coherent sources, separated by a distance 2t. First neglect refraction at the surface. At an angle θ from the normal, the two light paths differ in length by 2nt cosθ, where n is the index of the glass. So the bright fringes occur at 2nt cosθ = mλ. Since only θ is specified, all the rays with this angle form a cone of revolution about the normal, and the fringes appear circular. Close to θ = 0 the fringe separation is large, but as θ increases, the fringes get closer together. Thus fringes are actually observable only close to the normal.

If we include refraction, the condition becomes

$$m\lambda = 2nt\sqrt{n^2 - \sin^2\theta}\ , \text{ because } \cos\theta \text{ becomes } \sqrt{n^2 - \sin^2\theta}\ .$$

● **PROBLEM** 9-27

The focal length of a Billet split lens is 12 cm and the separation between the lens halves is 0.4 mm. If the split lens is placed 30 cm from a narrow slit illuminated by sodium light (λ = 5893Å), what will be the fringe spacing on a screen held 1 m from the lens? Assume that the center of the slit is 0.2 mm below the bottom edge of the top lens half.

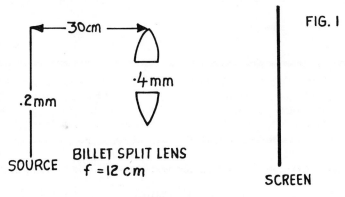

FIG. I

30cm

·4mm

.2mm

SOURCE

BILLET SPLIT LENS
f =12 cm

SCREEN

Solution: Figure 1 shows the arrangement of a Billet split lens. The lens will form an image of the source according to the thin lens formula

$$\frac{1}{u} + \frac{1}{u'} = \frac{1}{f} \ .$$

Substituting the given values u = 30 cm and f = 12 cm into the above equation gives

$$\frac{1}{30} + \frac{1}{u'} = \frac{1}{12}$$

Hence, the image will be formed u' = 20 cm to the right of the Billet lens.

Since the lens is split, two images will be formed of the source, at a position (100 - 20) cm or 80 cm from the screen. We now need to find the spacing between these two images. For this we can use the relation

$$\frac{I}{O} = \frac{u'}{u}$$

where I is the image size, and O is the object size, u is the object distance and u' is the image distance. Now at the slit the center of the original slit is 0.2 mm below the axis of the bottom edge of the top lens, so O = 0.2 mm so

$$I = O \frac{u'}{u} = 0.2 \times 10^{-3} \times \frac{20 \times 10^{-2}}{30 \times 10^{-2}} = 1.33 \times 10^{-4} \text{ m},$$

or the spacing of the image of the slit is $2 \times 1.33 \times 10^{-4}$ m $= 2.66 \times 10^{-4}$ m. Now for constructive interference to occur,

$$n\lambda = \frac{dy}{\ell}$$

where n is an integer, d is the slit spacing, y is the distance from the central point on the screen to the first secondary maximum, and ℓ is the distance from the double slit image to the screen. Then, taking n = 1, the fringe spacing is

$$y = \frac{\lambda \ell}{d} = \frac{589.3 \times 10^{-9} \times .8}{2.66 \times 10^{-4}} = 1.77 \times 10^{-3} \text{ m}$$

$$= 1.77 \text{ mm}$$

● **PROBLEM** 9-28

Two glass plates are nearly in contact and make a small angle θ with each other. Show that the fringes produced by interference in the air film have a spacing equal to $\lambda/2\theta$ if the light is incident normally and has wavelength λ.

Solution: Let θ be the angle between the two glass plates

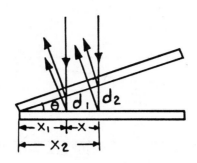

and let x_1 and x_2 be the distances from the edge of the wedge of two consecutive fringes, as shown in the figure.

If d_1 and d_2 denote the air gaps for these two fringes, then

$$2d_1 = n\lambda \tag{1}$$

and

$$2d_2 = (n+1)\lambda \tag{2}$$

where λ is the wavelength and n is an integer.   Subtracting (1) from (2)

$$2(d_2 - d_1) = \lambda \ . \tag{3}$$

From the figure, $\tan\theta = \dfrac{d_1}{x_1} = \dfrac{d_2}{x_2}$.   Assuming θ to be very small, the approximation $\tan\theta \simeq \theta$ can be made.   Therefore,

$$d_2 - d_1 = \theta(x_2 - x_1)$$

$$= \theta x \tag{4}$$

where

$$x = (x_2 - x_1)$$

Substituting for $d_2 - d_1$ into equation (3),

$$2\theta x = \lambda$$

Then,

$$x = \frac{\lambda}{2\theta} \ .$$

● **PROBLEM** 9-29

Two beams of radio waves of frequency 3MHz intersect at an angle of 10°.   What is the interference-fringe spacing?

Solution: Figure 1 shows the two waves of frequency 3MHz

207

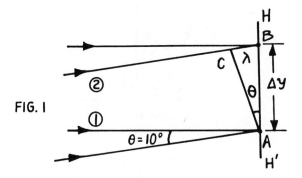

FIG. I

intersecting on a plane HH' and inclined to each other at an angle of 10°. The successive maxima will be formed at a distance Δy whenever the path difference between them is one wavelength. Hence from the triangle ABC,

$$\sin\theta = \frac{CB}{AB} = \frac{\lambda}{\Delta y}$$. where λ is the wavelength of light used.

Therefore,

$$\Delta y = \frac{\lambda}{\sin\theta} = \frac{c}{f \sin\theta}$$

where c is the velocity of light and f is the frequency.

Then, substituting the given values for f and θ and the known value for c(3×10^8 m/sec) into the preceding equation, we get $\Delta y = \dfrac{3 \times 10^8 \text{ m/sec}}{3 \times 10^6 \text{Hz} \sin 10°} \approx 576$ meters.

● **PROBLEM** 9-30

Suppose that the plates shown in figure 1a are 10 cm wide and are separated at one edge by 0.1 mm. The plates are made of glass with n = 1.50, and the space between them is filled with an oil having n = 1.33. Taking λ = 500 nm, compute the spacing between interference fringes. Is the fringe at the line of contact dark or bright?

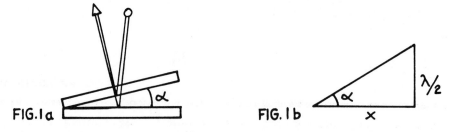

FIG.1a   FIG.1b

Solution: If the phase difference between the rays reflecting from the top surface and the bottom surface can be found, then the points where constructive and destructive interference between the rays occurs can be determined.

Destructive interference will occur when the phase difference, related to the wavelength, λ, of the light, is $(2m + 1)\lambda/2$, where m is an integer including 0. Constructive interference will occur when the phase difference is $m\lambda$. The phase difference results from the differences in path lengths and difference in phase shifts. Since there is a phase difference equivalent to half a wavelength between two rays, the first being reflected at a surface as the ray goes from high index of refraction to a low index of refraction and the second ray which goes from low index of refraction to high index of refraction, we do not need to remember which ray has the equivalent half wavelength phase shift and which ray has the zero phase shift because we are comparing the total phase difference between the rays.

In order to concentrate on where along the wedge we will have constructive interference, we need

$$m\lambda = 2t + \lambda/2 \tag{1}$$

where t is the thickness of the wedge at the point of constructive interference. The next point along the wedge which will give constructive interference will be

$$(m + 1)\lambda = 2t_1 + \lambda/2 \tag{2}$$

and subtracting equation (1) from equation (2) gives

$$2t_1 - 2t = \lambda$$

or

$$t_1 - t = \lambda/2 \ .$$

Now looking at Figure 1b, since we can determine α from the data of the problem and λ is given, we have

$$(\lambda/2)/x = \tan\alpha \ ,$$

where x represents the fringe spacing; hence,

$$x = \frac{\lambda}{2 \ \tan\alpha} \ . \tag{3}$$

Now we need to determine the wavelength in oil with index of refraction n; relative to the wavelength in air, 500 nm. First we have the relations

$$f\lambda = c$$

$$\frac{c_{vacuum}}{c_{medium}} = n$$

where f is the frequency of light, a constant for any material, c the velocity of light in the medium, λ the wavelength of light in the medium and n the index of refraction of the medium. So

$$\lambda_{medium} = \frac{\lambda_{vacuum}}{n_{medium}}$$

and so the wavelength in oil is

$$\lambda_{oil} = \frac{500 \times 10^{-9}}{1.33} = 3.75 \times 10^{-7} \text{ m}$$

Substituting into equation (3), where $\tan\alpha = \dfrac{\text{plate separation}}{\text{plate width}}$

$= \dfrac{0.1 \text{ mm}}{10 \text{ cm}} = \dfrac{0.1 \times 10^{-3} \text{m}}{0.1 \text{ m}}$, we have

$$x = \frac{3.75 \times 10^{-7}}{2 \times \dfrac{0.1 \times 10^{-3}}{0.1}} = 1.88 \times 10^{-4} \text{ m} = 0.188 \text{ mm} \; .$$

To determine whether the line of contact is bright or dark
we can look at equation (1) in which $2t + \lambda/2$ is the phase
difference between the two rays. With $t = 0$, which is the
situation at the line of contact, the phase difference is
$\lambda/2$, so destructive interference occurs and the fringe at
the line of contact is dark.

● **PROBLEM** 9-31

Two identical sources are far apart, but still a large number of wavelengths from an observer. Thus the Fraunhofer
condition is satisfied; but the approximation of parallel
rays from the sources is not. Find the fringe spacing near
the observation point when a) observer and sources are
nearly collinear, b) observer and sources are at the vertices
of an equilateral triangle, and c) observer and sources lie
on the circumference of a circle with sources on a diameter.

FIG. I

FIG. 2

Solution: All the wave fronts are plane, since the distances are large. In (a) the fringe at the observer might
be bright or dark, depending on the value of d.

A little to the side of the axis the rays from S_1 and S_2
are nearly parallel, where S_1 and S_2 represent the two
sources as shown in Figure 1 (P represents the point of
observation), and the next fringe occurs at $d \cos \theta_1 = \lambda$.

210

The actual fringe spacing, in terms of the distance to source 2, is

$$D = L_2 \sin \theta_1.$$

Since $\cos \theta_1 = \frac{\lambda}{d}$, $\sin \theta_1 = \sqrt{1 - \cos^2 \theta_1} = \frac{\sqrt{d^2 - \lambda^2}}{d}$.

Hence, $D = L_2 \dfrac{\sqrt{d^2 - \lambda^2}}{d} \simeq \left[1 - \frac{1}{2} \frac{\lambda^2}{d^2}\right] L_2$,

where L_2 represents the distance from S_2 to P. Similarly, L_1 represents the distance from S_1 to P. D is the length of the fringe spacing.

An alternative arrangement is that shown in Figure 2. Again the fringe at P is not determined, but the spacing is:

$$L_1 \tan \theta_1 = L_2 \tan \theta_1' \text{ and } \frac{L_1}{\sin \theta_1} + \frac{L_2}{\sin \theta_1'} = \lambda$$

where, as usual, the subscript 1 refers to the point one fringe away from the center. Again we take small angles (since the general problem yields the equation of a conic). Then

$$\tan \theta \simeq \sin \theta \simeq \theta,$$

and

$$\frac{L_1}{\theta_1} + \frac{L_2}{\theta_1'} = \lambda \ ; \quad L_1\theta_1 = L_2\theta_1' = D.$$

$$D = \frac{L_1^2 + L_2^2}{\lambda}.$$

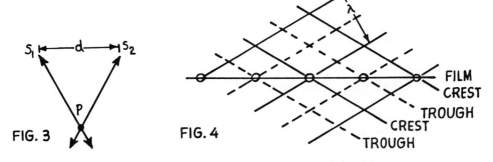

FIG. 3

FIG. 4

FILM
CREST
TROUGH
CREST
TROUGH

In (b) we have a single geometric arrangement as shown in Figures 3 and 4. The wave fronts intersect as shown, with bright fringes marked by circles. These are easily shown to be separated by $D = \lambda$.

In (c) the wave fronts always intersect at right

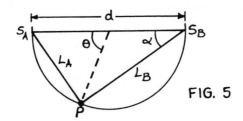

FIG. 5

angles. We can think of the observer here as a strip of film along the circumference. Thus the spacing D is an arc length. From Figure 5,

$$L_A = d \sin \alpha = d \sin \frac{\theta}{2} \qquad L_B = d \cos \frac{\theta}{2} .$$

$$L_A - L_B = N\lambda , \qquad L_{A_1} - L_{B_1} = (N + 1)\lambda ,$$

where the subscript 1 refers to the next fringe. Subtracting,

$$\Delta (L_A - L_B) = \lambda , \qquad \Delta L_A = d \left(\sin \frac{\theta_1}{2} - \sin \frac{\theta}{2} \right) = \frac{d}{2} \Delta\theta \cos \frac{\theta}{2} .$$

$$\Delta L_B = d \left(\cos \frac{\theta_1}{2} - \cos \frac{\theta}{2} \right) = - \frac{d}{2} \Delta\theta \sin \frac{\theta}{2}$$

Here $\Delta x \equiv x_1 - x$, and we can find Δ (sin or cos) by trigonometry, using the small-angle approximations, or by differentiation. So

$$\lambda = \Delta L_A - \Delta L_B = \frac{1}{2} d\Delta\theta \left(\sin \frac{\theta}{2} + \cos \frac{\theta}{2} \right) .$$

The fringe spacing is $D = \frac{1}{2} d\Delta\theta$, so we can write

$$D = \frac{\lambda}{(\sin \frac{1}{2}\theta + \cos \frac{1}{2}\theta)} ,$$

which is easily confirmed at $\theta = 0$, π, and $\pi/2$.

Notice that we have used three different approaches to these solutions. In (a) we have found the (small) angle be-tween the m = 0 and the m = 1 fringe. In (b) we have measured the actual distance between wave-front intersec-tions in a fixed geometry, and in (c) we have used the path-length difference to arrive at a general expression.

212

INTERFERENCE DISTRIBUTIONS

A satellite circling the Earth is transmitting microwaves of 15 cm wavelength. When the satellite is above a ground station which has two antennas connected together 100 m apart and located in the plane of the orbit, a signal is received that fluctuates in intensity with a period of 1/10 sec. If we know that the satellite is 400 km high, and if we neglect the curvature of the Earth, what is the velocity of the satellite?

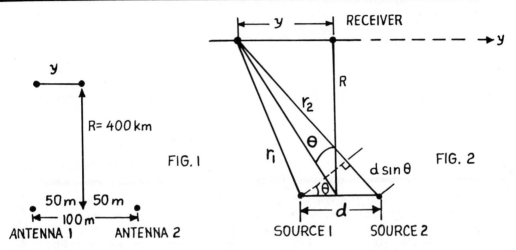

FIG. 1

FIG. 2

Solution: Let us look at this problem as a stationary source of 15 cm microwaves 400 km from two receiving antennas separated by 100 meters as seen in Figure 1. In this figure y represents the distance the source is away from a symmetric position with respect to the two antennas. If y = 0, the signal received from antenna 1 is in phase with the signal received from antenna 2 and connecting the two antennas will yield a signal with intensity equal to twice the intensity of either signal. If we now let y be different from zero there will be a phase difference in the signals received at antennas 1 and 2 until for some value of y the phase difference will be equal to half a wavelength so the sum of the signals received at the antennas will be zero.

Now if we allow the satellite to move with a velocity v along a line parallel to the line joining the two antennas, we will find a varying signal whose period of variation will be related to v.

So from Figure 2, we see that to find the phase difference we need to determine $r_2 - r_1$. If at a point y distant from the symmetry point we construct a circle of radius r_1 we see that $r_2 - r_1$ is just d sinθ. So when

$$d \sin\theta = n\lambda$$

where λ is the wavelength of the source, we have a maximum of order n, an integer, and when

$$d \sin\theta = (2n+1)\left(\lambda/2\right)$$

we have a minimum. In an approximation of small angles, $\sin\theta \approx \tan\theta = y/R$, so the maxima will occur at

$$y = R \sin\theta = \frac{n\lambda R}{d}.$$

What we want is the velocity $v = dy/dt$ and since the maxima are related to different orders n of the interference pattern, then

$$\frac{dy}{dt} = \left(\frac{dn}{dt}\right)\left(\frac{dy}{dn}\right) = \frac{dn}{dt}\frac{\lambda R}{d}.$$

Now dn/dt is the number of fringe maxima that pass the receiver per second or the reciprocal of the period of fluctuation in intensity and so is 10 per second. Therefore

$$\frac{dy}{dt} = 10 \times \frac{(15 \times 10^{-2})(400 \times 10^{3})}{100} \; m/s = 6 \; km/s.$$

● **PROBLEM** 9-33

The radius of curvature of the convex surface of a plano-convex lens is 200 cm. The lens is placed convex side down on the concave surface of a plano-concave lens with radius of curvature of 400 cm. The lenses are illuminated from above with red light of wavelength 625 mµ. Find the diameter of the third bright ring in the interference pattern of the reflected light.

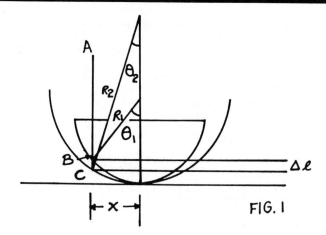

FIG. I

Solution: Figure 1 shows the geometry of this problem. A beam of light travels from A to B where part of it is reflected and the remainder proceeds to C where part of it is reflected. The parts reflected at B and C can then interfere and will exhibit constructive or destructive interference depending on whether the total phase difference between the two reflected beams is $m\lambda$ or $(2m + 1)\lambda/2$; where m is an integer and λ is the wavelength of the light used.

214

Since reflection at B is a reflection at a glass-air interface and reflection at C is a reflection at an air-glass
interface. and since the reflection at C has an extra path
length of $2\Delta\ell$, where $\Delta\ell$ is the distance between points B
and C, our condition for a bright ring is

$$2\Delta\ell + \lambda/2 = m\lambda \tag{1}$$

and since we want the third bright ring, $m = 3$. So

$$\Delta\ell = \frac{\lambda}{2} (m - 1/2) = (\lambda/2)(3 - 1/2) = \frac{5\lambda}{4} \tag{2}$$

In order to find x, the following relations can be established:

$$\frac{x}{R_1} = \sin\theta_1 \quad ; \quad \frac{x}{R_2} = \sin\theta_2 \tag{3}$$

and

$$\Delta\ell = R_2 \cos\theta_2 - (R_2 - R_1) - R_1 \cos\theta_1 \tag{4}$$

From equation (3)

$$R_1 \sin\theta_1 = R_2 \sin\theta_2 \tag{5}$$

and by squaring both sides and using the trigonometric
identity

$$\sin^2\theta + \cos^2\theta = 1$$

we obtain

$$R_2 \cos\theta_2 = \left(R_2^2 - R_1^2 + R_1^2 \cos^2\theta_1 \right)^{\frac{1}{2}} \tag{6}$$

so from equation (4),

$$\Delta\ell = \left(R_2^2 - R_1^2 + R_1^2 \cos^2\theta_1 \right)^{1/2} - (R_2 - R_1) - R_1 \cos\theta_1 \; . \tag{7}$$

Rearranging and squaring to eliminate the square root
term,

$$\left(R_2^2 - R_1^2 + R_1^2 \cos^2\theta_1 \right)^{1/2} =$$

$$\Delta\ell + (R_2 - R_1) + R_1 \cos\theta_1 \tag{8}$$

$$R_2^2 - R_1^2 + R_1^2 \cos^2\theta_1 =$$

$$(\Delta\ell)^2 + (R_2 - R_1)^2 + R_1^2 \cos^2\theta_1 \tag{9}$$

$$+ 2\Delta\ell(R_2 - R_1) + 2\Delta\ell \, R_1 \cos\theta_1 + 2(R_2 - R_1)R_1 \cos\theta_1 \, .$$

The $R_1{}^2 \cos^2 \theta_1$ terms cancel one another, and we are left with

$$R_2{}^2 - R_1{}^2 = (\Delta\ell)^2 + (R_2 - R_1)^2 + 2\Delta\ell(R_2 - R_1)$$

$$+ [2\Delta\ell R_1 + 2(R_2 - R_1)R_1] \cos\theta_1 \, . \qquad (10)$$

Solving for $\cos\theta_1$ yields the following result:

$$\cos\theta_1 = \frac{R_2{}^2 - R_1{}^2 - (\Delta\ell)^2 - (R_2 - R_1)^2 - 2\Delta\ell(R_2 - R_1)}{2\Delta\ell R_1 + 2(R_2 - R_1)R_1}$$

$$(11)$$

Therefore,

$$\cos\theta_1 = \frac{- (\Delta\ell)^2 + 2R_1(R_2 - R_1) - 2\Delta\ell(R_2 - R_1)}{2\Delta\ell R_1 + 2R_1(R_2 - R_1)} \qquad (12)$$

Substituting the following data:

$$R_1 = 2m \, , \quad R_2 = 4m, \text{ and } \Delta\ell = \frac{5}{4}(6.25 \times 10^{-7} \text{ m})$$

(see equation (2)), into equation (12) yields the result

$$\theta_1 = 0.0716°.$$

Since

$$x = R_1 \sin\theta_1 \, ,$$

$$x = 2\sin(0.0716°) = (2)(1.24 \times 10^{-3}) = 2.5 \times 10^{-3} \text{ m} = 2.5 \text{ mm}$$

will be the radius of the third bright spot. Hence, the diameter of the third bright ring is 5.0 mm.

● **PROBLEM 9-34**

Prove that the formula giving the intensity for the interference pattern from two coherent point sources is

$$A^2 = I = 2a^2(1 + \cos \delta),$$

where a is the amplitude of each source separately, and δ is the difference in phase of the wave train from each source at the point where the intensity is measured.

<u>Solution:</u> Consider any particle P which is disturbed as a result of wave motion coming from two sources S_1 and S_2

216

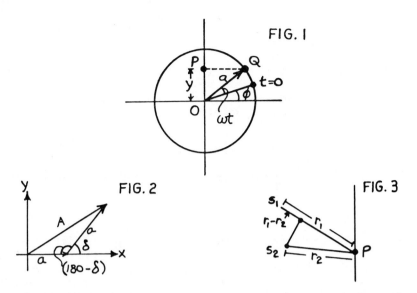

FIG. I

FIG. 2

FIG. 3

which are of equal amplitude, have the same period, and are
in phase. The problem is to find the resultant disturbance
at P. We shall approach this problem in two different ways:
first graphically using phasors, and then analytically.

I.   Each source, S_1 and S_2 , produces a sinusoidally-
varying electric field at point P. The equation of this
field is of the form of simple harmonic motion, that is
$$y = a \sin (\omega t + \phi).$$

We can represent the instantaneous value of a quantity that
varies sinusoidally with time by the projection onto a vertical axis of a vector of length corresponding to the amplitude of the quantity and rotating counterclockwise with angular velocity ω. These rotating vectors are called phasors
and are illustrated in Figure 1.

The point Q moves in a circle of radius equal to the
amplitude a, with constant angular velocity ω. Then the
position vector of this point, $\overrightarrow{OQ}$, having length = a, rotates with constant angular velocity ω about point O. Let
the vector $\overrightarrow{OQ}$ make an angle with the horizontal axis, at
time t=0, equal to the initial phase angle ϕ. Point P is
the projection of point Q onto the vertical axis and, as
$\overrightarrow{OQ}$ rotates, point P oscillates along the axis. Let y represent the length of OP. At any time t, the angle between
the radius $\overrightarrow{OQ}$ and the horizontal axis is $\omega t + \phi$, and
$y = a \sin(\omega t + \phi)$.

Now, to find the amplitude of the resulting E field,
we represent each sinusoidal field as a phasor. The appropriate diagram is shown in Figure 2.

In Fig. 2, a is the amplitude of each of the two
fields, A is the amplitude of the resultant, and δ is the
phase difference of the two disturbances on reaching P.

Applying the law of cosines, we find
$$A^2 = a^2 + a^2 - 2aa \cos(180 - \delta)$$

217

$$A^2 = 2a^2 + 2a^2 \cos \delta$$

$$A^2 = 2a^2(1 + \cos \delta) = I$$

If we wish to determine the points at which I is a minimum or a maximum, we employ the following method:

The fields arriving at P differ in phase by an amount proportional to the path difference $(r_1 - r_2)$, where r_1 and r_2 are shown in Figure 3. In general, it is known that

$$\delta = \frac{2\pi}{\lambda}(r_1 - r_2),$$

where λ represents the wavelength of light.

When the path difference is λ, then $\delta = 2\pi$. At this point, $\cos \delta = 1$ and the intensity is a maximum given by $A = 2a$. More generally, when $(r_1 - r_2) = n\lambda$, n an integer, the intensity is a maximum. Similarly, when $(r_1 - r_2) = \lambda/2$, then $\delta = \pi$ and $\cos \delta = -1$. At this point $I = 0$. Again, if the path difference is $\lambda/2$, $\frac{3\lambda}{2}$, $\frac{5\lambda}{2}$ .... or in general, $(2n + 1)\frac{\lambda}{2}$ where n = 0,1,2,3, ..., the intensity is a minimum.

To summarize, the intensity at any point resulting from the simultaneous disturbances from two sources of equal amplitude, frequency, and phase angle, is given by

$$I = 2a^2(1 + \cos \delta)$$

where a is the amplitude of each of the two disturbances and δ is their phase difference when arriving at the point in question. The intensity is a maximum when the difference in path lengths is an integral number of whole wavelengths, and is a minimum when the path difference is an odd number of half wavelengths.

II. We wish to obtain the same result by a purely analytical method of solution. If we consider the point P, then $y_1 = a \sin(\omega t + \phi_1)$ is the disturbance reaching P from S_1, and $y_2 = a \sin(\omega t + \phi_2)$ is the disturbance reaching P from S_2. ϕ_1 and ϕ_2 are the phase angles corresponding to y_1 and y_2, respectively. Then $\delta = \phi_1 - \phi_2$. The resultant disturbance at P is given by

$$y = y_1 + y_2 = a \sin(\omega t + \phi_1) + a \sin(\omega t + \phi_2)$$

Then using the trigonometric identity

$$\sin(\alpha + \beta) = \sin \alpha \cos \beta + \cos \alpha \sin \beta$$

we have

$$y = a \sin \omega t \cos \phi_1 + a \sin \phi_1 \cos \omega t +$$

$$a \sin \omega t \cos \phi_2 + a \sin \phi_2 \cos \omega t$$

Factoring out $\sin \omega t$ and $\cos \omega t$,

$$y = \sin \omega t[a \cos \phi_1 + a \cos \phi_2] + \cos \omega t[a \sin \phi_1 + a \sin \phi_2]$$

Now let
$$a \cos \phi_1 + a \cos \phi_2 = A \cos \theta \qquad (1)$$

and
$$a \sin \phi_1 + a \sin \phi_2 = A \sin \theta \qquad (2)$$

then
$$y = A \cos \theta \sin \omega t + A \sin \theta \cos \omega t$$

$$y = A \sin(\omega t + \theta)$$

Note that this is the simple harmonic motion form of the resultant disturbance. The intensity is given by

$$I = A^2$$

To find A^2 we square equations (1) and (2) and add:

$$A^2(\cos^2\theta + \sin^2\theta) = (a \cos\phi_1 + a \cos\phi_2)^2 + (a \sin\phi_1 + a \sin\phi_2)^2$$

$\cos^2\theta + \sin^2\theta = 1$. Therefore,

$$A^2 = a^2(\cos^2\phi_1 + \cos^2\phi_2 + 2 \cos\phi_1 \cos\phi_2 + \sin^2\phi_1 + \sin^2\phi_2 +$$

$$2 \sin\phi_1 \sin\phi_2)$$

Again making use of the trigonometric identity
$$\cos^2\theta + \sin^2\theta = 1 ,$$

$$A^2 = a^2[2 + 2 \cos\phi_1 \cos\phi_2 + 2 \sin\phi_1 \sin\phi_2]$$

$$= 2a^2[1 + \cos(\phi_1 - \phi_2)]$$

$$A^2 = 2a^2(1 + \cos\delta) = I, \text{ where } \delta = \phi_1 - \phi_2$$

THIN FILMS

● PROBLEM 9-35

A wedge-shaped vertical soap film (index 1.33), 2.75 cm × 2.75 cm, is illuminated normally by red light of wavelength 600 mμ (in vacuum). The upper edge of the film is observed to be black when viewed by reflected light. Six horizontal bright bands appear to traverse the film, the center of the sixth bright band coinciding with the bottom of the film. Find the angle of the wedge.

Solution: As shown in the figure, let us assume that x

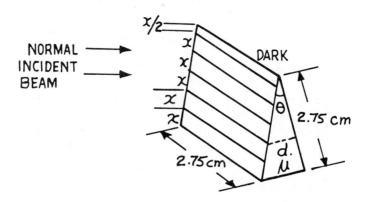

denotes the distance between two successive bright fringes.
The dark fringe lies midway between the two bright fringes.
Hence the length of the film is to be divided in such a way
that the bright fringe lies at the bottom of the film.
Hence

$$\frac{x}{2} + 5x = 2.75 \text{ cm}$$

or

$$x = 0.5 \text{ cm} = (x_n - x_{n-1})$$

The optical path length between two beams reflected
from the two surfaces of the film is

$$2\mu d \ ,$$

where μ is the refractive index of the film medium and d
is the thickness of the film. For a bright fringe

$$2\mu d = n\lambda_{vac} \ , \text{ and n is an integer.}$$

where λ_{vac} is the wavelength of light measured in
centimeters. Therefore, for two successive fringes

$$2\mu(d_2 - d_1) = \lambda_{vac}$$

$$d_i = \theta x_i \text{ (i is an integer); so}$$

$$2\mu\theta(x_2 - x_1) = \lambda_{vac}$$

Thus,

$$\theta = \frac{\lambda_{vac}}{2\mu(x_2 - x_1)}$$

$$= \frac{\lambda_{vac}}{2\mu x}$$

$$= \frac{6 \times 10^{-5}}{2 \times 1.33 \times 0.5}$$

$$= 4.5 \times 10^{-5} \text{ rad} .$$

● **PROBLEM** 9-36

Derive a relation describing the interference effects observed when light is reflected from a thin film (see Figure A).

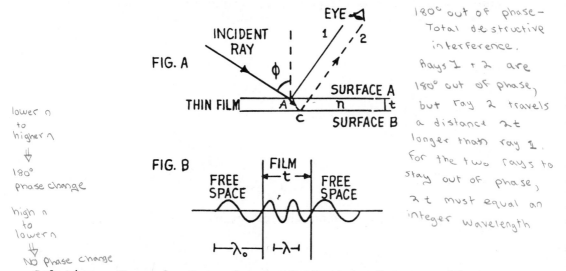

EYE

INCIDENT RAY

FIG. A

1 2

ϕ

SURFACE A

THIN FILM   A n t

c SURFACE B

FILM

FIG. B t

FREE SPACE   FREE SPACE

λ_0 λ

Handwritten annotations:

lower n to higher n ⇩ 180° phase change

high n to lower n ⇩ No phase change

180° out of phase— Total destructive interference.

Rays 1 + 2 are 180° out of phase, but ray 2 travels a distance 2t longer than ray 1. For the two rays to stay out of phase, 2t must equal an integer wavelength

Solution: In order to understand the interference effects produced by a thin film, we trace the path of an incident ray of light, as shown in Figure (A). The incident ray first encounters surface A, where it is partially reflected and partially absorbed. Since the refractive index of the film is greater than the refractive index of air, the reflected ray undergoes a 180° phase change. The transmitted part of the incident ray now encounters interface B, where it is partially reflected and partially absorbed. However, this time the reflected ray undergoes no phase change since it is traveling from a region of high refractive index to a region of low refractive index. Hence, rays 1 and 2 differ in phase by 180°, or $\lambda_0/2$ where

λ_0 is the wavelength of the incident light in free space.

In addition to the 180° phase change due to reflection, ray 2 travels a distance 2t greater than ray 1. (This holds only if the rays shown are incident at an angle ϕ which is very small.) Then, if we want to observe destructive interference, the distance 2t must contain an integral number of wavelengths, $N\lambda$, where $N = 0,1,2,\ldots$. But, λ is not the wavelength of the light in free space, but rather, the wavelength of light in the film (see Figure (B)). However, the wavelengths λ_0 and λ are related. By definition of the refractive index of the film,

$n = c/v$

221

where c is the speed of light in free space, and v is its speed in the film. If λ_0 and f_0 are the free space wavelength and frequency of light, we may write

$$c = \lambda_0 f_0$$

Similarly,

$$v = \lambda f$$

where λ and f are the wavelength and frequency of light in the film. But the frequency of light is the same in all media. Then

$$v = \lambda f_0$$

Hence

$$n = \frac{\lambda_0 f_0}{\lambda f_0} = \frac{\lambda_0}{\lambda}$$

and

$$\lambda_0 = n\lambda$$

Combining this fact with the previous discussion, we obtain

$$2t = N\lambda = \frac{N\lambda_0}{n} \qquad N = 0,1,2,\ldots \qquad \text{destructive interference}$$

$$2t = (N + \tfrac{1}{2})\lambda = \frac{(N + \tfrac{1}{2})\lambda_0}{n} \qquad N = 0,1,2,\ldots \qquad \text{constructive interference}$$

or

$$t = \frac{N\lambda_0}{2n} \qquad N = 0,1,2,\ldots \qquad \text{destructive interference}$$

$$t = \frac{(N + \tfrac{1}{2})\lambda_0}{2n} \qquad N = 0,1,2,\ldots \qquad \text{constructive interference}$$

● **PROBLEM 9-37**

a) Find the thickness of a soap film ($n = 1.33$) for a strong first-order reflection of yellow light, $\lambda = 600\,m\mu$ (in vacuum). Assume normal incidence. b) What is the wavelength of the light in the film?

Solution: a) Assuming that the light ray, i, strikes the soap film at near-normal incidence (note that the figure is exaggerated), to get a strong first order reflection off the soap film, the relative phase difference between

222

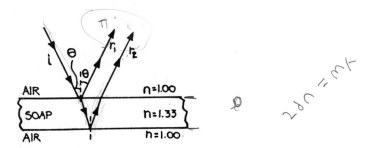

the reflected rays r_1 and r_2 must be zero, or the change of phase of r_1 must be equal to the change of phase of r_2.

The phase change for r_1 is $\frac{1}{2}\lambda$ as it is reflected off the top surface of the soap film and the phase change for r_2 is the extra optical path length it travels through the soap film, which is equal to 2dn, where d is the thickness of the film and n its index of refraction. Setting these phase changes equal to each other, we have

$$\frac{1}{2}\lambda = 2dn$$

where $\lambda = 600$ mμ and n = 1.33. Therefore, the thickness d of the soap film for a strong reflection of yellow light must be

$$d = \frac{1}{4}\frac{(600m\mu)}{1.33} = 113 \ m\mu.$$

b)   The wavelength of the light in the film is found by dividing the wavelength in air (or vacuum) by the index of refraction of the film.

$$\lambda_{film} = \frac{\lambda_{air}}{n_{film}} = \frac{600m\mu}{1.33} = 451 \ m\mu \ .$$

● **PROBLEM** 9-38

A plane wave of monochromatic light falls normally on a uniformly thin film of oil which covers a glass plate. The wavelength of the source can be varied continuously. Complete destructive interference of the reflected light is observed for wavelengths of 5000Å and 7000Å and for no wavelengths in between.   If the index of refraction of the oil is 1.30 and that of the glass is 1.50, find the thickness of the oil film.

Solution: Using the formula for complete destructive interference we have, 2d = (m + ½)λ_o where d is the thickness of the oil, λ_o is the wavelength in air, and m is an integer.   At the wavelengths where there is total destructive interference, since $\lambda_{oil} = \lambda_{air}/n_{oil}$, we have

$$2d = \left(m + \frac{1}{2}\right)\frac{7000}{1.3} \ \text{Å} \tag{1}$$

223

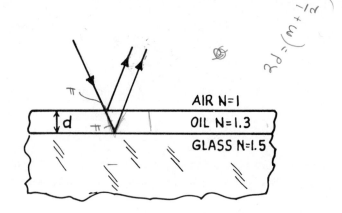

AIR N=1

OIL N=1.3

GLASS N=1.5

and

$$2d = \left(m + 1 + \frac{1}{2} \right) \frac{5000}{1.3} \text{ Å} \qquad (2)$$

We added 1 to m because that is where the next complete destructive interference of the reflected light occurs.

$$\text{Then } 2d = \left(m + \frac{1}{2} \right) \frac{7000}{1.3} = \left(m + \frac{3}{2} \right) \frac{5000}{1.3} \text{ , and}$$

$$\frac{7000m}{1.3} + \frac{3500}{1.3} = \frac{5000m}{1.3} + \frac{7500}{1.3} \text{ .}$$

$$\text{Therefore, } \frac{2000m}{1.3} = \frac{4000}{1.3} \text{ , and } m = \left(\frac{4000}{1.3} \right) \left(\frac{1.3}{2000} \right) = 2.$$

Substituting this value for m back into equation (1),

$$d = \frac{\left(\frac{5}{2} \right) \left(\frac{7000}{1.3} \right) \text{Å}}{2} \approx 6731 \text{Å.} \quad \text{Hence, the thickness of the oil}$$

film is 6731Å.

● **PROBLEM** 9-39

When a thin flake of glass, with index of refraction = 1.5, is introduced into the path of one of the interfering beams in an arrangement such as the biprism, the position of the central bright fringe becomes that normally occupied by the fifth. If the wavelength used is 6×10^{-5} cm, find the thickness of the glass.

Solution: In the original arrangement without the glass flake, if C is in the position of the fifth bright fringe, then

$$BC - AC = 5\lambda \text{ ,}$$

where A, B, and C are shown in Figure 1 and where λ is the wavelength in air.

But with the glass flake present, we have

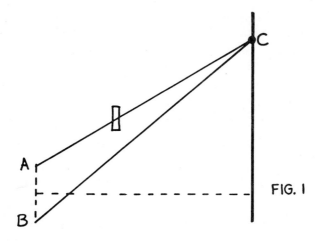

FIG. I

BC - AC = 0 .

Therefore, if t(cm) is the required thickness of the glass, replacing t(cm) of air by t(cm) of glass must lengthen the optical path AC by 5λ.

But t(cm) of glass = 1.5t(cm) of air. Therefore the path change is (1.5 - 1)t(cm) of air. Hence

(1.5 - 1)t = 5λ

so

t = 6 × 10^{-4} cm .

Note that when given the index of refraction of a thin piece of glass, and the wavelength of the light, the thickness can be found. Conversely, when given the thickness and the wavelength, the index of refraction can be found.

● **PROBLEM** 9-40

A thin film with n = 1.40 for light of wavelength 5890Å is placed in one arm of a Michelson interferometer. If this causes a shift of seven fringes, what is the film thickness?

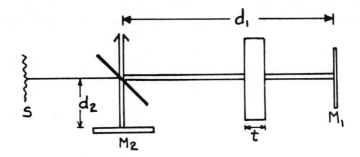

Solution: The light coming from the source S is divided into two beams by the plate of glass shown in the figure

225

accompanying this problem. One beam is transmitted and eventually hits mirror M_1, at which point it is reflected back to the plate and is reflected to the observer. The second beam is reflected to mirror M_2, reflected back to the plate by M_2, and then transmitted to the observer. Then there will be a bright fringe when the number of wavelengths in $2d_1$, minus the number in $2d_2$, is an integer, where d_1 and d_2 are shown in the figure. If the number of

wavelengths in $2d_2 = \dfrac{2d_2}{\lambda_{vac}}$ and the number of wavelengths in

$2d_1 = \dfrac{2(d_1 - t)}{\lambda_{vac}} + \dfrac{2t}{\lambda_{film}}$, then since $n = \dfrac{c}{v} = \dfrac{f\lambda_{vac}}{f\lambda_{film}} = \dfrac{\lambda_{vac}}{\lambda_{film}}$,

a bright fringe occurs when $\dfrac{2(d_1 - t - d_2)}{\lambda_{vac}} + \dfrac{2t}{\lambda_{vac}}\, n = m$,

where m = the number of fringes shifted as a result of the presence of the film. Therefore, in this problem, m = 7.

Before the film was present, $\dfrac{2(d_1 - d_2)}{\lambda_{vac}} = m - 7.$

Subtracting the second equation from the first,

$7 = \dfrac{2t}{\lambda_{vac}}\,(n-1).$ So $t = \dfrac{7\lambda_{vac}}{2(n-1)}$, and after substituting

the values for λ_{vac} and n given in this problem into the above equation, one determines that t = 5.150 μm.

A simple way to look at this is: taking out $2t/\lambda_{vac}$ wavelengths and putting in $2tn/\lambda_{vac}$ wavelengths resulted in seven more wavelengths. So $t(n-1) = 3.5\,\lambda_{vac}$.

● **PROBLEM** 9-41

An oil film (n = 1.42) spread on a plate of glass (n = 1.58) shows minimum return of blue light of 400 nm incident at 45°. What is the least thickness the oil film can have? What other thicknesses are possible?

Solution: Figure 1 shows the geometry of this problem. First we need to determine the path difference between ray A and ray B as they are reflected from the two oil surfaces. The path difference as seen from Figure 1 is

$\Delta \ell = 2\ell_2 - \ell_1$.

Let us spend some time with geometry to find this in terms of the thickness t, the index of refraction n and the incident angle θ_i . First we see that

226

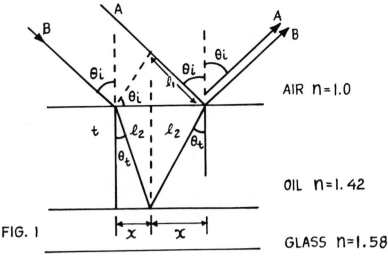

FIG. 1

$$\frac{t}{\ell_2} = \cos\theta_t \qquad (1)$$

$$\frac{x}{\ell_2} = \sin\theta_t \qquad (2)$$

$$\frac{\ell_1}{2x} = \sin\theta_i \qquad (3)$$

From equation (1),

$$2\ell_2 = \frac{2t}{\cos\theta_t} \qquad (4)$$

and

since $x = t \cdot \dfrac{\sin\theta_t}{\cos\theta_t}$ (from equations (1) and (2)),

$$\ell_1 = 2 \ x \ \sin\theta_i = 2t \ \frac{\sin\theta_t}{\cos\theta_t} \ \sin\theta_i \qquad (5)$$

Snell's law states:

$$\frac{\sin\theta_i}{\sin\theta_t} = n_{oil} \qquad (6)$$

so substituting for $\sin\theta_t$ in equation (5),

$$\ell_1 = 2t \ \frac{\sin^2\theta_i}{n_{oil} \ \cos\theta_t} \qquad (7)$$

The relationship between the frequency of vibration, f, the wavelength in the medium, λ, and the velocity of light in the medium, c_m, is

$$f\lambda_m = c_m \qquad (8)$$

227

and

$$\frac{c_{vacuum}}{c_{medium}} = n_{medium} \tag{9}$$

Using equations (8) and (9),

$$\lambda_m = \frac{c_{medium}}{f} = \frac{c_{medium}}{c_{vacuum}/\lambda_{vacuum}} = \frac{\lambda_{vacuum}}{n_{medium}} \tag{10}$$

so the number of wavelengths in the path length $2\ell_2$ is

$$\frac{2\ell_2}{\lambda_{oil}} = \frac{2\ell_2}{\lambda_{air}/n_{oil}} = \frac{2\ell_2 \, n_{oil}}{\lambda_{air}} = \frac{2t \, n_{oil}}{\lambda_{air} \, \cos\theta_t} \tag{11}$$

(from equation (4))

and the number of wavelengths in path length ℓ_1 is

$$\frac{\ell_1}{\lambda_{air}} = \frac{2t \, \sin^2\theta_i}{n_{oil} \, \lambda_{air} \, \cos\theta_t} \tag{12}$$

(from equation (7))

or

$$\frac{\Delta\ell}{\lambda_{air}} = \frac{2t}{\lambda_{air} \cos\theta_t} \left(n_{oil} - \frac{\sin^2\theta_i}{n_{oil}} \right) \tag{13}$$

Factoring out $\frac{1}{n_{oil}}$ gives the following result:

$$\frac{\Delta\ell}{\lambda_{air}} = \frac{2t}{n_{oil} \, \lambda_{air} \, \cos\theta_t} \left(n_{oil}^2 - \sin^2\theta_i \right), \tag{14}$$

and since $\cos^2\theta + \sin^2\theta = 1$

$$\frac{\Delta\ell}{\lambda_{air}} = \frac{2t}{\lambda_{air} \, n_{oil}} \frac{\left(n_{oil}^2 - \sin^2\theta_i \right)}{\left(1 - \sin^2\theta_t \right)^{1/2}} \tag{15}$$

and using Snell's law again (equation 6),

$$\frac{\Delta\ell}{\lambda_{air}} = \frac{2t}{\lambda_{air} \, n_{oil}} \frac{\left(n_{oil}^2 - \sin^2\theta_i \right)}{\left(1 - \frac{\sin^2\theta_i}{n_{oil}^2} \right)^{1/2}} \tag{16}$$

We must also consider any phase shift of the light as it reflects from the air-oil interface and also the oil-glass interface. Since from Figure 1, the indices increase

228

downward in the figure regardless of what phase shift occurs at the air-oil interface, the same phase shift will occur at the oil-glass interface, so the difference in phase shift will be zero. So our total phase difference between the two rays A and B will be the path difference expressed by equation (16) in fractions of a wavelength.

Since at an angle of 45° we observe a minimum, then

$$\frac{\Delta \ell}{\lambda_{air}} = \frac{(2m + 1)}{2} \qquad (17)$$

where m is an integer, 0,1,2,3, etc. Namely, that if the path difference is an odd multiple of half a wavelength, the waves will destructively interfere, or combining with equation (16),

$$t = \frac{(2m + 1)}{2} \cdot \frac{\lambda_{air}}{2} \cdot \frac{(n_{oil})\left(1 - \frac{\sin^2 \theta_i}{n_{oil}^2}\right)^{1/2}}{(n_{oil}^2 - \sin^2 \theta_i)} \qquad (18)$$

$$= (2m + 1) \frac{400 \times 10^{-9} \text{ m}}{4} \cdot \frac{(1.42)\left(1 - \frac{\sin^2 45°}{1.42^2}\right)^{1/2}}{(1.42^2 - \sin^2 45°)}$$

$$= (2m + 1) \times 8.12 \times 10^{-8} \text{ meters}$$

So for various m :

m	t in meters x 10^{-8}
0	8.12
1	24.4
2	40.6
3	56.8

NEWTON'S RINGS

● PROBLEM 9-42

When a flat plate of glass and a lens are placed in contact, a distinctive interference pattern, known as Newton's Rings, is observed. (See Figure A.) Derive a formula giving the location of the fringes of the interference pattern relative to the center of the lens. (See Figure B.)

Solution: Destructive interference will result when the

229

FIG. (A) INTERFERENCE PATTERN

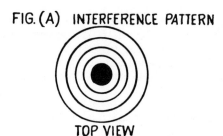

TOP VIEW

FIG. (B)

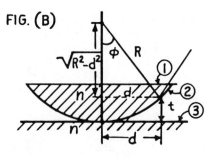

waves reflected from the apparatus shown in Figure B are 180° out of phase. Let us trace the path of an incident ray. The ray will be partially reflected and partially transmitted at surface (1). When a ray of light is transmitted from a region of low refractive index to a medium of higher refractive index, it undergoes a phase change of 180°. Hence, the ray reflected at surface (1) is 180° out of phase with the incident ray. The transmitted ray next encounters surface (2). At this surface there is no phase change, since the light leaves an area of high refractive index and enters a region of low refractive index. In addition, part of this light is reflected at surface (2). The light transmitted at surface (2) next encounters surface (3) and is reflected with a 180° or $\lambda/2$ phase change. (λ is the wavelength of the light.) Hence, the ray reflected at (2) and the ray reflected at (3) are 180° out of phase.

Now, the ray reflected at (3) travels a distance 2t greater than the ray reflected at (2). We will see destructive interference whenever 2t is an integral number of wavelengths, since the additional $\lambda/2$ required for destruction is provided by the phase change due to reflection. Hence

$$2t = n\lambda \qquad n = 0,1,2,\ldots \qquad \text{destructive interference} \qquad (1)$$

$$2t = (n + 1/2)\lambda \qquad n = 0,1,2,\ldots \qquad \text{constructive interference}$$

We must now find the location of the interference fringes in terms of the geometry of Figure B.

From Figure B,

$$t = R - \sqrt{R^2 - d^2} \qquad (2)$$

Then

$$t = R - R\sqrt{1 - d^2/R^2}$$

Factoring out R,

$$t = R\left(1 - \sqrt{1 - d^2/R^2}\right) \qquad (3)$$

But d << R and d/R << 1. (This means that the radius of

230

curvature of the lens is large.) We may therefore
approximate the square root in (3) by the binomial theorem
$(1 + x)^n = 1 + nx + \dfrac{n(n - 1)}{2!} x^2 + \dots$. Therefore,

choosing $x = \dfrac{-d^2}{R^2}$ and $n = \dfrac{1}{2}$,

$$\sqrt{1 - d^2/R^2} \approx 1 - d^2/2R^2 .$$ (4)

Substituting this expression for $\sqrt{1 - d^2/R^2}$ into equation
(3),

$$t = R(1 - 1 + d^2/2R^2)$$

$$t = d^2/2R$$

$$d = \sqrt{2tR}$$

Using (1),

$$d = \sqrt{n\lambda R} \qquad\qquad n = 0,1,2,\dots \qquad \text{destructive interference}$$

$$d = \sqrt{(n + \tfrac{1}{2})\lambda R} \qquad n = 0,1,2,\dots \qquad \text{constructive interference}$$

The first equation locates the dark rings relative to the
center of the lens, and the second equation locates the
bright rings.

● **PROBLEM 9-43**

Newton's rings are formed between the convergent crown and
divergent flint glass elements of an uncemented achromatic
doublet. When seen by reflection through the flint element
there is a dark fringe at the center, and the fourth bright
fringe has a radius of 1.6 cm. If the radius of curvature
of the crown glass interface is 50 cm, and the incident
light is nearly normal, what is the radius of curvature of
the flint glass face next to it? Assume a wavelength of
5500Å.

Solution: A nearly normal monochromatic beam is incident
on the divergent lens. At the center of the lens interference takes place between the two beams, one reflected
from the flint glass-air boundary and the other reflected
from the air-crown glass boundary. Due to the phase change
introduced in the second beam and no air gap, the two beams
interfere destructively and give rise to a dark spot.

As we move away from the center point C, the air gap
increases. We see constructive interference or bright
rings at a distance r from the center C when the air gap
increases by $\dfrac{\lambda}{4}$ because the second beam travels this gap

231

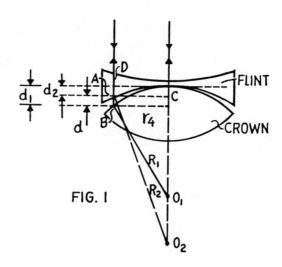

FIG. I

twice and hence travels an additional distance of $2(\frac{\lambda}{4}) = \frac{\lambda}{2}$.

Each time the air gap increases by $\frac{\lambda}{2}$, another bright ring appears. Hence for the fourth bright ring, the air gap, d, must be equal to $3(\frac{\lambda}{2}) + \frac{\lambda}{4}$, or

$$d = \frac{7\lambda}{4} \qquad (1)$$

Using the sagittal relation for the two surfaces with radii R_1 and R_2, we can write

$$d_1(2R_1 - d_1) = r_4^2 ; \qquad (2)$$

where r_4 = the radius of the fourth bright ring.

Since d_1 is assumed to be much less than $2R_1$

$$d_1 \approx \frac{r_4^2}{2R_1} \qquad (3)$$

Similarly,

$$d_2 \approx \frac{r_4^2}{2R_2} \qquad (4)$$

Therefore,

$$d = d_1 - d_2 = \frac{r_4^2}{2}\left[\frac{1}{R_1} - \frac{1}{R_2}\right]$$

Rearranging this equation so as to solve for R_2,

$$\frac{1}{R_1} - \frac{1}{R_2} = \frac{2d}{r_4^2} , \text{ and } \frac{1}{R_2} = \frac{1}{R_1} - \frac{2d}{r_4^2} . \text{ Then } R_2 = \left[\frac{1}{R_1} - \frac{2d}{r_4^2} \right]^{-1} ,$$

and so, substituting $d = \frac{7\lambda}{4}$ [equation (1)] and the values given for R_1, r_4 and λ, we get

$$R_2 = \left[\frac{1}{50cm} - \frac{(2)(7)(5.5 \times 10^{-5}cm)}{4(1.6)^2} \right]^{-1} \approx 50.02 \text{ cm}$$

● **PROBLEM** 9-44

Newton's rings are observed when a plano-convex lens is placed convex side down on a plane glass surface and the system is illuminated from above by monochromatic light. The radius of the first bright ring is 1 mm. a) If the radius of the convex surface is 4 m, what is the wavelength of light used? b) If the space between the glass surfaces is filled with water, what is the radius of the first bright ring?

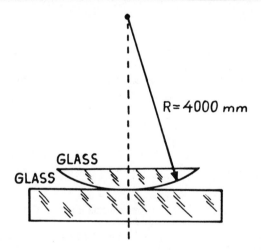

$R = 4000$ mm

GLASS

GLASS

<u>Solution</u>: Whenever a plano-convex lens is placed convex side down on a plane glass surface and Newton's rings are observed, we can always apply the equation

$$r = \sqrt{(m + \tfrac{1}{2})\lambda R} \tag{1}$$

where r is the radius of the ring, m is the order number, λ is the wavelength of the incident light, and R is the radius of curvature of the lens.

a)   Solving for λ in equation (1) we have $\lambda = \frac{r^2}{(m + \tfrac{1}{2})R}$ and substituting $r = 1$ mm, $m = 0$, and $R = 4000$ mm gives us $\lambda = 500 \times 10^{-6}$ mm $= 500$ mμ. Note that m = 0 rather than 1 because we used the radius of the dark circle as the first ring.

b)   Filling the space between the glass surfaces with water just changes the wavelength of the light as it travels between the glass surfaces, so equation (1) becomes

$$r = \sqrt{\left(m + \frac{1}{2}\right) \frac{\lambda}{n} R} \quad ,$$

where n is the refractive index of water = 1.33

$$r = \sqrt{\left(0 + \frac{1}{2}\right)\left(\frac{500 \times 10^{-6}\,mm}{1.33}\right)\left(4000mm\right)} \quad ,$$

r =   0.867 mm.

● **PROBLEM 9-45**

Newton's rings are seen in transmitted light of 500 nm. The diameter of the 20th bright ring is found to be 4 mm.
a) What is the radius of curvature of the lens?
b) What is the diameter of the 30th bright ring?

Solution: For Newton's rings we use the equation

$$r = \sqrt{(m + \frac{1}{2}) \lambda R} \tag{1}$$

to find the positions of the circular rings, where r is the radius of the circular rings, m the order number, λ is the wavelength of the light, and R is the radius of curvature of the lens.

a)   Solving for R in equation (1), we have $R = \frac{r^2}{(m + \frac{1}{2}) \lambda}$.

Using the data r = 2mm, m = 20, and λ = 500 × 10^{-6} mm, the radius of curvature of the lens, R, is found to be 390 mm or 39 cm.

b)   Using equation (1), the diameter of the 30th bright ring is $2\sqrt{(30 + \frac{1}{2})(500 \times 10^{-6}mm)(390mm)}$ or 4.9 mm.

● **PROBLEM 9-46**

In order to obtain Newton's rings, a plano-convex lens of R = 100 cm is placed on a plano-concave lens as shown in Figure 1.   If, using green light of λ = 550 nm, the 20th dark ring, seen in the direction of the incident light, has a radius of 20 mm, what is the radius of curvature of the concave lens surface?

Solution: Let d be the thickness of the air film at a distance x from the point of contact.   A dark ring is observed in the direction of the incident light if $d = \frac{m\lambda}{2}$, where m is the order of the fringe and λ is the wavelength of light

FIG. 1

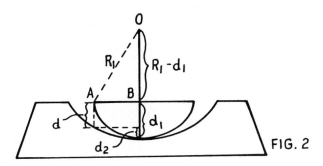

FIG. 2

used. From Figure 2 it can be determined that d is given by

$$d = d_1 - d_2 .$$

Now considering the triangle OAB formed by the first surface, we have

$$R_1^2 = x^2 + (R_1 - d_1)^2 , \qquad (1)$$

where R_1 is the radius of curvature of the first surface. Similarly, considering the second surface with radius of curvature R_2 ,

$$R_2^2 = x^2 + (R_2 - d_2)^2 \qquad (2)$$

Since d_1 and d_2 are small compared to R_1 and R_2, equations (1) and (2) can be solved for d_1 and d_2 as follows.

$$R_1^2 = x^2 + R_1^2 - 2R_1d_1 + d_1^2 \approx x^2 + R_1^2 - 2R_1d_1$$

Then the R_1^2 terms cancel one another and so, $d_1 \approx \dfrac{x^2}{2R_1}$.

Similarly,

$$d_2 = \frac{x^2}{2R_2}$$

Hence the condition for the dark fringe is

$$d = d_1 - d_2 = \frac{x^2}{2}\left(\frac{1}{R_1} - \frac{1}{R_2}\right) = \frac{m\lambda}{2} .$$

Therefore,

$$x^2\left(\frac{1}{R_1} - \frac{1}{R_2}\right) = m\lambda$$

and so

$$\frac{1}{R_2} = \frac{1}{R_1} - \frac{m\lambda}{x^2} \qquad (3)$$

Since x is the radius of the 20th fringe, m = 20 and substituting the given values for R_1 , λ, and x into equation
(3), it is found that

$$\frac{1}{R_2} = \frac{1}{100 \text{ cm}} - \frac{20 \text{ x } (550 \text{ x } 10^{-7}) \text{ cm}}{(2 \text{ cm})^2}$$

$$R_2 = 102.8 \text{ cm}.$$

CHAPTER 10

APPLIED INTERFEROMETRY

THE INDEX OF REFRACTION

● **PROBLEM** 10-1

> The removal of all the air from tube A, as shown in the figure, corresponds to a shift of 150 fringes in the telescope of the Rayleigh Refractometer. If the wavelength in air is 0.00004 cm and the tube is 20 cm long, find the index of refraction of air.

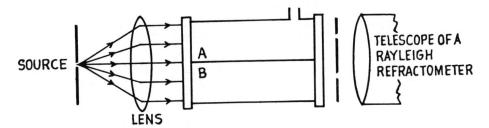

Solution: There are three methods of solving this problem.

Method I: A shift of 150 fringes means that a bright fringe changes from bright to dark and back again to bright 150 times, which corresponds to a path change of 150 wavelengths (of the light in air). Since the tube is 20 cm long, the path length of the wave in A with air is 20 cm or 20 · n cm in a vacuum, where n represents the index of refraction of air. After removal of all of the air from tube A, the path length = 20 cm in a vacuum. Thus, the difference in the path lengths = (20 · n - 20) cm. The path change brought about by removing the air in tube A is also equal to 150 wavelengths. Thus,

(20 · n - 20) cm vacuum = 150 wavelengths

20 · (n - 1) cm vacuum = 150 x 0.00004 cm air

20 · (n - 1) cm vacuum = 150 x 0.00004 x n cm vacuum

Solving for the index of refraction of air gives

237

n = 1.0003.

Method II: The number of wavelengths in 20 cm air is $\left(20 \text{ cm}/0.00004 \dfrac{\text{cm}}{\text{wavelength}}\right)$ and the number of wavelengths in 20 cm vacuum is $\left(20 \text{ cm}/\left(0.00004 \cdot n \dfrac{\text{cm}}{\text{wavelength}}\right)\right)$, so the change in the number of wavelengths when the air is removed is

$$\dfrac{20 \text{ cm}}{0.00004 \text{ cm/wavelength}} - \dfrac{20 \text{ cm}}{0.00004 \cdot n \text{ cm/wavelength}}$$

The shift in fringes is equal to 150, a change of 150 wavelengths. Therefore, 150 wavelengths $= \dfrac{20 \text{ cm}}{0.00004 \text{ cm/wavelength}} - \dfrac{20 \text{ cm}}{0.00004 \cdot n \text{ cm/wavelength}}$.

Factoring out $\dfrac{20}{0.00004}$ from the expression to the right of the equal sign gives

$$150 = \dfrac{20}{0.00004}(1 - \dfrac{1}{n}) = 5 \times 10^5 (\dfrac{n - 1}{n}).$$

Hence, $5 \times 10^5 n - 150n = 5 \times 10^5$

or $n = \dfrac{5 \times 10^5}{5 \times 10^5 - 150} \cong 1.0003.$

Method III: Let V = velocity of light in a vacuum.
V_a = velocity of light in air.
Then $V = n \cdot V_a$, where n is the index of refraction of air.

Then, the time required for the light to travel 20 cm in air is $\dfrac{20}{V_a}$, which is also equal to $\dfrac{20 \cdot n}{V}$, and the time required for the light to travel 20 cm in the vacuum is $\dfrac{20}{V}$. Thus, the difference in the time required for the light to travel 20 cm in air and vacuum is $\dfrac{20}{V} \cdot (n - 1)$. This difference is also equal to the time corresponding to a path difference of 150 wavelengths, which is 150 T, where T is the time it takes to travel one wavelength. Thus,

$$150 \cdot T = \dfrac{20}{V} \cdot (n - 1).$$

However, λ (in vacuum) = V $\cdot$ T, which is also equal to 0.00004 x n.
Therefore

$$\dfrac{20}{V} \cdot (n - 1) = \dfrac{150 \times 0.00004 \cdot n}{V}$$

$$20 \cdot (n - 1) = 150 \times 0.00004 \cdot n \, ,$$

and so,

$$20n - 20 = .006n, \text{ and } n = \frac{20}{19.994} \cong 1.0003 \, .$$

● **PROBLEM** 10-2

One of the tubes of a Rayleigh refractometer is filled
with air, the other is evacuated. Then the second tube
is filled with air at the same temperature and pressure
as the first tube. During this process 98 fringes are
seen to pass the field of view. What is the index of
refraction of the air if sodium light is used and the
tubes are each 20 cm long?

Solution: The optical path length of the light ray in
the 20 cm tube filled with air is 20n cm vacuum, where
n represents the index of refraction of air, and the optical path length in vacuum is 20 cm vacuum, so the difference between them, (20n - 20) cm vacuum, should equal
the length occupied by 98 wavelengths (fringes). Since
the wavelength of sodium light is 589 nm or 5.89×10^{-5} cm
and there is a shift of 98 fringes, the distance that the
path length is shifted is $(98)(5.89 \times 10^{-5} n)$ cm
vacuum. Thus,

$$20n - 20 = (98)(5.89 \times 10^{-5}n) \, .$$

Solving for n gives n $\cong$ 1.00029.

● **PROBLEM** 10-3

A double slit apparatus is used to measure the indices
of refraction of gases. The slits are illuminated by
monochromatic plane waves from the left. To the right
of the slits are two identical glass containers A and B
each of inside thickness ℓ (see the accompanying Figure).
With both containers evacuated, a bright fringe appears
at point P on a screen in the focal plane of a converging
lens, just past the cubicals. A gas is then admitted to
A, resulting in a shift of 20 fringes at P. Light of
wavelength λ is used.

    1)   Which way do the fringes move?
    2)   What is the index of refraction of the gas?

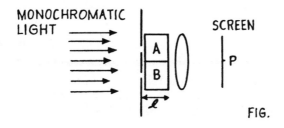

MONOCHROMATIC LIGHT   SCREEN

A

B

P

ℓ

FIG.

Solution: The double slit apparatus is shown in the figure. With no gas in either cell A or cell B, both cells contain equal numbers of wavelengths of light and the central fringe falls at the symmetric point P. After gas is admitted to cell A, there are $\ell n/\lambda$ wavelengths in cell A but only ℓ/λ in cell B, where n is the index of refraction of the gas. Therefore, the central fringe is shifted towards cell A, to the position previously occupied by the 20th fringe. Thus, cell A now contains 20 more wavelengths than does cell B and so,

$$\frac{\ell n}{\lambda} = \frac{\ell}{\lambda} + 20$$

or, dividing both sides of this equation by $\frac{\ell}{\lambda}$,

$$n = 1 + \frac{20\lambda}{\ell} = \text{the index of refraction of the gas.}$$

• **PROBLEM 10-4**

The two tubes in a Jamin refractometer are 30 cm long. One contains a gas at a low pressure and the other a vacuum. If on removing the gas a shift of 10 fringes of red light λ_{vac} = 6000A° is counted, what is the index of refraction of the gas?

Solution: In a Jamin refractometer, split coherent light is allowed to pass through two tubes of equal length and different indices of refraction and then recombine. If the optical path difference in the two tubes is one wavelength, then a shift of one fringe will occur. If a gas of index of refraction n is now placed in one tube and a vacuum in the other, the path difference is

$$(n - 1)\ell = m\lambda \tag{1}$$

where ℓ is the length of the tubes, m is the number of shifted fringes and λ is the wavelength of the light used. Then, substituting ℓ = 30 cm = .3m, m = 10, and λ = 6000A° into equation (1) gives

$$(n - 1)(.3) = 10 \times 600 \times 10^{-9}$$

Then,

$$n - 1 = 2 \times 10^{-5}$$

and so,

$$n = 1.00002$$

• **PROBLEM 10-5**

A Fabry-Perot etalon is adjusted so that for a wavelength of 5461A°, interference fringes are observed in a telescope focused for infinity. The etalon, of thickness

1.01 cm, is enclosed in a box with transparent windows from which the air can be exhausted. It is found that there is a shift of one fringe when the pressure is changed by 6.46 cm Hg. Find the index of refraction of the air at room temperature and at the original pressure, which was 77 cm Hg.

Solution: In a Fabry-Perot etalon, the light beam passes twice through the space between the plates before it re-combines; so for a physical spacing of ℓ between plates, the optical path length between sets of beams is $2\,n\ell$, where n is the index of refraction. In order for the sets of beams to recombine to yield a maximum, the optical path length $2n\ell$ must be equal to an integer K times the wavelength λ of light used. Therefore with air in the space between the plates, the relation is

$$2n_1\ell = K\lambda$$

and at the new pressure,

$$2n_2\ell = (K + 1)\lambda$$

since there is a shift of one fringe. Eliminating K from the two equations yields

$$n_2 - n_1 = \frac{1}{2\ell}[(K + 1)\lambda - K\lambda] = \frac{\lambda}{2\ell} = \frac{546.1 \times 10^{-9}}{2 \times 1.01 \times 10^{-2}}$$

$$= 2.71 \times 10^{-5}$$

Since the index of refraction is proportional to pressure,

$$\frac{\Delta P}{P_o} = \frac{n_2 - n_1}{n_1 - n_{vac}} ,$$

where ΔP and P_o represent the change in pressure, and the original pressure, respectively.

$$n_1 = n_{vac} + \frac{n_2 - n_1}{\Delta P/P_o} = 1 + \frac{2.71 \times 10^{-5}}{6.46/77}$$

$$n_{air\,77cm} = 1 + 3.23 \times 10^{-4} = 1.000323$$

● PROBLEM 10-6

A brine solution, placed in a cuvette of 4 mm inside width, is left to settle for a while. When examined in light of 500 nm wavelength in an interferometer, it is found that the fringe pattern, adjusted for vertical fringes, shows a shift of 16 fringes for the bottom part of the liquid as compared with the top. If the average refractive index of the solution is 1.462 and the distribution of the solution is linear, find (a) the two refractive indices and (b) the ratio of the densities at the top and bottom of the solution.

241

Solution: (a) In an interferometer, the split light beam will pass through the cuvette twice. Thus, the conditions of interference are (a) at the top, the optical path length is $2 n_1 \ell = m\lambda$ and (b) at the bottom the optical path length is $2 n_2 \ell = (m + 16)\lambda$, where ℓ is the thickness of the cuvette, n_1 is the index of refraction of the brine solution at the top of the cuvette and n_2 is the index of refraction of the brine solution at the bottom of the cuvette, m is an integer to provide constructive inter- ference and λ is the wavelength of the light used.

Subtracting (a) from (b) gives

$$2\ell(n_2 - n_1) = 16\lambda$$

$$n_2 - n_1 = \frac{16\lambda}{2\ell}.$$

Substituting the given values $\lambda = 500$ nm and $\ell = 4$ mm gives

$$n_2 - n_1 = \frac{16 \times 500 \times 10^{-9}}{2 \times 4 \times 10^{-3}} = 1 \times 10^{-3} \tag{1}$$

Now, since the average value of n for the brine solution is 1.462 and the distribution of the solution is linear,

$$\frac{n_1 + n_2}{2} = 1.462 \tag{2}$$

From equation (1), $n_2 = 1 \times 10^{-3} + n_1$ and substituting this value for n_2 into equation (2) gives

$$n_1 + 1 \times 10^{-3} + n_1 = 2.924$$

or,

$$n_1 = \frac{(2.924 - 1 \times 10^{-3})}{2} = 1.4615$$

Then, from equation (1), $n_2 = 1 \times 10^{-3} + 1.4615$

$$= 1.4625.$$

(b) It is known that

$$n - 1 \propto \sqrt{N}$$

where n is the index of refraction and N is the number of atoms per unit volume, which is proportional to the density of the solution.

Hence,

$$\frac{n_1 - 1}{n_2 - 1} = \sqrt{\frac{d_1}{d_2}}$$

and substituting the computed values for n_1 and n_2 into this equation gives

$$\left(\frac{.4615}{.4625}\right)^2 = \frac{d_1}{d_2}$$

or

$$\frac{d_1}{d_2} \cong 0.996$$

FRINGE DISTORTION

While examining the surface of a polished workpiece by interferometry using thallium light of wavelength 535 nm, it is found that in a certain area on the surface the fringes are distorted by 0.4 of the distance between the undistorted fringes. What is the depth, or elevation, of the defect?

Solution: In interferometry, if the mirror is moved a distance of Δs, and a shift of one fringe results, the relation between Δs and λ, the wavelength of light used, is the following:

$$\Delta s = \lambda/2 \tag{1}$$

In this problem it is given that $\lambda = 535$ nm. Therefore, equation (1) becomes

$$\Delta s = \frac{535 \times 10^{-9}m}{2} = 2.675 \times 10^{-7}m$$

For a distortion of 0.4 fringe, the depth (or elevation of the distortion is $0.4\Delta s = 0.4 \times 2.675 \times 10^{-7}m = 1.07 \times 10^{-4}mm$.

A 5 cm thick transparent sample is examined interferometrically using green light of 550 nm. If an accuracy of 1 part in 2 million is desired, to what fraction, in percent, of a fringe width (width of fringe + interval) must any distortions be measured? Is this possible?

Solution: Using an interferometer, it is desired to measure a sample 5 cm thick to 1 part in 2 million, or to be able to measure a length of $\frac{5 \times 10^{-2}m}{2 \times 10^6} = 2.5 \times 10^{-8}m$. Light of wavelength 550 nm or $5.5 \times 10^{-7}m$ is to be used. Thus, it is necessary to measure $\frac{2.5 \times 10^{-8}}{5.5 \times 10^{-7}} \cong 0.045$ wavelengths

of green light. Now, if the sample accepts two beams of
coherent light, one beam which passes through 5 cm of
sample and the other going through an equivalent distance,
and then the two beams are recombined as in an interferometer, a set of fringes will be produced as output. Now,
if there is a variation of 2.5×10^{-8}m = 2.5×10^{-6}cm in
the 5 cm sample there will be a distortion of 4.5%, which
should be detectable. If on the other hand, a Michelson
interferometer is used and the 5 cm sample is placed in
one arm of the Michelson interferometer, then the imperfections will cause the beam to pass through the sample
twice, resulting in a distortion of the fringes of 9% of
the fringe separation.

FRINGE DISAPPEARANCE

● **PROBLEM** 10-9

Michelson's stellar interferometer is used to measure the
diameter of Jupiter's satellite Europa. The diameter of
Europa is 1980 miles, and at the time of measurement it was
4.829×10^8 miles from the earth. At what separation of the
two apertures over the telescope objective would the fringes
first disappear?   (Assume λ = 5600 A°.)

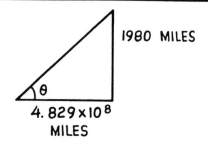

1980 MILES

θ

4.829×10⁸
MILES

Solution: Rayleigh's criterion can be used in this problem
since it is desired to distinguish between two distant point
objects whose angular separation is small. Rayleigh's criterion states the following:

$$\sin \theta = 1.22 \frac{\lambda}{d} \tag{1}$$

where θ is the angular separation between the two distant
point objects, λ is the wavelength of the light from the
objects, and d is the diameter of the circular aperture
being used. When the angular separation is sufficiently
small, $\sin \theta$ can be replaced by $\tan \theta$ in equation (1)
since as θ approaches 0, $\tan \theta$ approaches $\sin \theta$. Thus,
equation (1) becomes

$$\tan \theta = 1.22 \frac{\lambda}{d} \tag{2}$$

In this problem the diameter of Europa, 1980 miles,
will be taken for the distance between the two objects. In
addition, given that Europa is 4.829×10^8 miles from the

aperture (see the figure) then

$$\tan \theta = \frac{1980 \, \text{mi}}{4.829 \times 10^8 \, \text{mi}} .$$

Solving equation (2) for d gives

$$d = \frac{(1.22) \, \lambda}{\tan \theta} \qquad (3)$$

and

$$\lambda = 5600 \, \text{A}^\circ = 5600 \times 10^{-8} \, \text{cm}.$$

Substituting

$$\frac{1980}{4.829 \times 10^8}$$

for tan θ in equation (3) gives the result

$$d = \frac{(1.22)(5600 \times 10^{-8} \, \text{cm})(4.829 \times 10^8)}{(1980)}$$

or

$$d = 16.66 \, \text{cm}.$$

● **PROBLEM** 10-10

In an experiment with a stellar interferometer, the fringes from the star Betelgeuse had zero visibility for a wavelength in the middle of the visible spectrum for a separation of the mirrors of 3m. Estimate the angle subtended by Betelgeuse in arc seconds.

Solution: The visibility, V, is defined as follows:

$$V = \frac{I_{max} - I_{min}}{I_{max} + I_{min}} \qquad (1)$$

where I_{max} is the light intensity at a maximum and I_{min} is the light intensity at a minimum of an interference-diffraction pattern. The light generated at different points on a star is incoherent. Assuming that the star is equivalent to a circular aperture and that each element of area of the star contributes an equal amount to the illumination at the stellar interferometer, all of the contributions over the surface of the circular aperture can be added to find

$$V = 2 \left| \frac{J_1 \left(\pi h \theta / \bar{\lambda}_o \right)}{\pi h \theta / \bar{\lambda}_o} \right| \qquad (2)$$

where h is the separation of the mirrors in the stellar interferometer; θ is the angle subtended by the star; $\overline{\lambda}_o$ is the mean wavelength of light from that star and J_1 is the first order Bessel function. For a reference which gives a derivation of this result, see "Optics," Hecht and Zajac, Addison Wesley, 1974, pages 435-6.

Since it is given that the visibility is zero when the separation h is 3 meters, it is necessary to find the first zero of the Bessel function, J_1. Consultation with tables of Bessel functions indicates that the zero occurs when

$$\frac{\pi h \theta}{\overline{\lambda}_o} = 3.83 \tag{3}$$

Solving equation (3) for θ gives

$$\theta = \frac{3.83 \, \overline{\lambda}_o}{\pi h} = \frac{1.22 \, \overline{\lambda}_o}{h} \tag{4}$$

Assuming that the visible spectrum goes from $\lambda = 400$ nm to $\lambda = 700$ nm, a wavelength in the middle of the visible spectrum $\cong 550$ nm.

Substituting this value into equation (4) along with the given value h = 3 m gives

$$\theta = \frac{(1.22)(550 \times 10^{-9} \, m)}{3m} \cong$$

$$22.4 \times 10^{-8} \text{ radians} \left(\frac{180 \text{ degrees}}{\pi \text{ radians}}\right)\left(\frac{3600 \text{ seconds}}{\text{degree}}\right)$$

$$\cong 0.046 \text{ second of arc.}$$

● **PROBLEM** 10-11

When Michelson and Peace measured the diameter of the star α Orionis, they observed the first disappearance of interference fringes at a mirror separation of 3.065 m. If the effective wavelength of the light from this star is assumed to be 575 nm, what is the angular diameter, in radians and in arc seconds, of the star disk?

Solution: The visibility, V, is defined as follows:

$$V = \frac{I_{max} - I_{min}}{I_{max} + I_{min}} \tag{1}$$

where I_{max} is the light intensity at a maximum, and I_{min}

is the light intensity at a minimum, of an interference-diffraction pattern. The light generated at the different points on a star is incoherent. Assuming that the star is equivalent to a circular aperture and that each element of area of the star contributes an equal amount to the illumination of the stellar interferometer, the contributions over the surface of the circular aperture can be added to yield the following result:

$$V = 2 \left| \frac{J_1 \left(\pi h\theta / \overline{\lambda}_o \right)}{\pi h\theta / \overline{\lambda}_o} \right| \qquad (2)$$

where h is the separation of the mirrors in the stellar interferometer; θ is the angle subtended by the star; $\overline{\lambda}_o$ is the mean wavelength from the star and J_1 is the first order Bessel function.

Since it is given that the visibility is zero when the separation h is 3.065 meters, it is necessary to find the first zero of the Bessel function, J_1. Consulting a table of Bessel functions, it is found that this zero occurs when

$$\frac{\pi h\theta}{\overline{\lambda}_o} = 3.83 \qquad (3)$$

Solving equation (3) for θ gives the result

$$\theta = \frac{3.83 \, \overline{\lambda}_o}{\pi h} = \frac{1.22 \, \overline{\lambda}_o}{h} \, .$$

Substituting in the given values for $\overline{\lambda}_o$ and h gives

$$\theta = \frac{1.22 \times 575 \times 10^{-9}}{3.065}$$

or

$$\theta = 2.29 \times 10^{-7} \text{ radians}$$

$$= (2.29 \times 10^{-7} \text{ radians}) \left(\frac{180 \text{ degrees}}{\pi \text{ radians}} \right) \left(\frac{3600 \text{ seconds}}{\text{degree}} \right)$$

$$= 0.047 \text{ second of arc.}$$

● **PROBLEM** 10-12

A large telescope is focused on a double star and the interference pattern is observed when an adjustable double slit is placed in front of the objective. The distance between the centers of the components of the double slit is gradually increased until the fringes disappear. If this distance is 57.5 cm, find the angular separation of the two components of the double star. (Take mean λ = 5550A°.)

Solution: The visibility, V, is defined as follows:

$$V = \frac{I \max - I \min}{I \max + I \min}$$ (1)

where I_{max} is the light intensity at a maximum and I_{min} is the light intensity at a minimum of an interference-diffraction pattern. The light generated at different points on a star is incoherent. By using a double slit in front of the telescope, it is then necessary to add up all of the contributions across the slits due to the two separated stars. This leads to the following equation for the visibility of the fringes (see "Optics," Hecht and Zajac, Addison Wesley, 1974, page 427):

$$V = \left| \frac{\sin\left(\frac{2\pi h\theta}{\bar{\lambda}o}\right)}{2\pi h\theta/\bar{\lambda}o} \right|$$ (2)

where h is the separation of the slits, θ is the angular separation of the two stars in radians, and $\bar{\lambda}o$ is the mean wavelength of the light from the stars.

When the fringes disappear, V = 0.
Thus,

$$\frac{2\pi h\theta}{\bar{\lambda}o} = \pi$$ (3)

and solving equation (3) for θ gives

$$\theta = \frac{\bar{\lambda}o}{2h}$$ (4)

Substituting the given values for $\bar{\lambda}o$ and h into equation (4) gives

$$\theta = \frac{555 \times 10^{-9}}{2 \times 57.5 \times 10^{-2}}$$

$$= (4.82 \times 10^{-7} \text{ radians}) \left(\frac{180 \text{ degrees}}{\pi \text{ radians}}\right)\left(\frac{3600 \text{ seconds}}{\text{degree}}\right)$$

$$\cong 0.1 \text{ second of arc.}$$

CONSTRUCTIVE AND DESTRUCTIVE INTERFERENCE OF LIGHT

● **PROBLEM** 10-13

A thin lens of long focal length is supported horizontally a short distance above the flat polished end of a steel cylinder. The cylinder is 5 cm high and its lower end is rigidly held. Newton's rings are produced between the lens and the upper end of the cylinder, using normally incident light of wavelength 6000 Å, and viewed from above by means of a microscope. When the temperature of the cylinder is raised by 25 degrees Centigrade, 50 rings move past the cross-wires of the microscope. What is

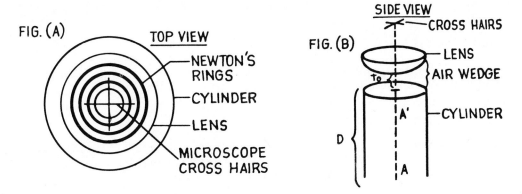

FIG. (A)

TOP VIEW

NEWTON'S RINGS

CYLINDER

LENS

MICROSCOPE CROSS HAIRS

SIDE VIEW

FIG. (B)

CROSS HAIRS

LENS

AIR WEDGE

CYLINDER

Solution: Initially, the cylinder has a length D, and a gap of length t_0 exists between the top of the cylinder and the bottom surface of the lens in the portion of the air wedge viewed in the microscope at the same position as the cross-wires. (Technically, t_0 is the distance of the lens from the cylinder as measured along axis AA' in figure (B). However, since the lens is thin, t_0 is the distance of any point on the bottom surface of the lens from the top of the cylinder). Let us now see how interference fringes are produced.

Light is incident upon the lens from above. Light is transmitted through both lens surfaces with no phase change. However, the light reflected from the bottom lens surface and the top of the cylinder are 180° (or $\frac{\lambda}{2}$, where λ is the wavelength of light used) out of phase. This phase change is due to the reflection of light from the cylinder. In addition, the wave reflected from the cylinder travels a distance $2t_0$ greater than the ray reflected from the lens in traversing the air gap. If this distance is equal to an odd number of half-wavelengths (odd because the waves are already $\lambda/2$ out of phase due to reflection) constructive interference will occur. Hence,

Constructive
Interference $2t_0 = (2n + 1)\dfrac{\lambda}{2}$ $(n = 0, 1, 2, \ldots)$

or $\qquad 2t_0 = (n + 1/2)\lambda$ $(n = 0, 1, 2 \ldots)$

Hence, for a bright fringe to appear at the crosswires, $2t_0 = (n + 1/2)\lambda$, where n is an unknown integer.

After one heats the cylinder through a temperature difference T, the length of the cylinder is $D(1 + \alpha T)$, where α is the coefficient of linear expansion of steel, and the gap between the cylinder and the lens will have been reduced to t, where $t_0 - t = D(1 + \alpha T) - D = D\alpha T$.

If a bright fringe is again seen at the position of the cross-wires, then similarly, $2t = (m + 1/2)\lambda$, where m is an integer. $(m \neq n)$

Therefore,

$$2(t_0 - t) = 2t_0 - 2t$$
$$= (n + 1/2)\lambda - (m + 1/2)\lambda$$
$$= (n - m)\lambda,$$

and so, $2(t_0 - t) = 2D\alpha T = (n - m)\lambda$

During the heating process, $(n - m)$ bright fringes must have passed over the cross-wires. Thus, since

$$\alpha = \frac{(n - m)\lambda}{2DT},$$

the given values $n - m = 50$, $\lambda = 6000\overset{\circ}{A} = 6 \times 10^{-5}$ cm, $D = 5$ cm., and $T = 25$ degrees Centigrade, may be substituted into this equation to give

$$\alpha = \frac{50 \times 6 \times 10^{-5} \text{ cm}}{2 \times 5 \text{ cm} \times 25 \text{ C deg}}$$

$$= 1.2 \times 10^{-5} \text{ per } °C.$$

● **PROBLEM** 10-14

Lenses are often coated to reduce reflections. How thick should a coating of index n = 1.70 be if reflections from the coating surface interfere destructively with those from the coating-glass interface for a wavelength in the center of the visible spectrum (say yellow light of wavelength 550 nm)? The index of refraction of glass = 1.50.

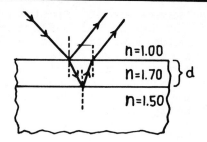

Solution: Assume that light strikes the surface of the coating at near-normal incidence. Some of the light is transmitted through the coating and some is reflected by the coating, as shown in the figure. Some of the light that is transmitted through the coating is reflected by the glass. In addition, some light is also transmitted through the glass.

There is a phase displacement of 180° or $\frac{1}{2}\lambda$ (where λ represents the wavelength of light) when the incident ray is reflected from the upper surface, and a phase displacement of 2dn (where d represents the thickness of the coating) due to the optical path difference (for normal incidence) of the two reflected rays. When the total phase displacement is $\frac{1}{2}\lambda$, $\frac{3}{2}\lambda$, $\frac{5}{2}\lambda$, etc., there is

250

complete destructive interference upon reflection.   So
the minimum thickness of the coating of index of refraction
n = 1.70 is found by applying the equation,

$$\frac{1}{2}\lambda + 2dn = \frac{3}{2}\lambda \qquad (1)$$

where λ is the wavelength of the incident light in air,
d is the thickness of the coating, and n is the index of
refraction of the coating.

Solving equation (1) for d and substituting the
given values λ = 550 nm. and n = 1.70 gives

$$d = \frac{\frac{3}{2}.(550 \text{ nm}) - \frac{1}{2}.(550 \text{ nm})}{2(1.70)} = 162 \text{ nm}.$$

Hence, the minimum thickness of the coating on the lens
required to produce destructive interference upon reflection
is 162 nm.   Minimum reflection is also produced for
coating thicknesses equal to multiples of 162 nm., such
as 324 nm., 486 nm, 648 nm, etc.   However, since a thicker
coating minimizes the transmitted light, a thickness of
162 nm is the most practical and economical thickness
which can be used.

● **PROBLEM** 10-15

Two semi-metallized sheets of glass are separated by a
material of fixed length e with a constant index of
refraction n.   (a) If the interference filter is to have
one pass band between wavelengths of 4000A° and 7500 A°,
with a maximum transmission at λ = 5500A°, determine
the possible values for the spacing length e.   Assume
that the spacing material is cryolite with index of
refraction n = 1.35.   (b) How is the wavelength of the
transmission maximum changed when parallel rays fall on
the filter at an angle of incidence r rather than normal
incidence?

METALLIC LAYER

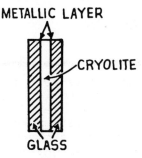

CRYOLITE

GLASS

Solution: (a)   The transmission maxima correspond to
constructive interference, that is, to path differences

$$\delta = 2ne = k_0\lambda_0 = \ldots = k\lambda \qquad (1)$$

where $k_0, \ldots, k$ are integers giving the interference
order for wavelengths $\lambda_0, \ldots, \lambda$.

From equation (1), a transmission maximum for the

251

filter can be found for thicknesses of cryolite such that

$$e = k_v \frac{\lambda_0}{2n} = k_v e_0 \tag{2}$$

Substituting the given values $\lambda_0 = 5500 A°$ and $n = 1.35$ into equation (2) gives

$$e = k_v \times \frac{5500 A°}{2 \times 1.35} = k_0 \times 2037 A°.$$

The following chart can be constructed by solving for k in equation (2) for λ_1 (7500A°), λ_2 (4000A°), and multiples of e_0;

e	λ_1	λ_0	λ_2	Number of pass bands
e_0	k = 0.73	k_0 = 1	k = 1.37	1
$2e_0$	k = 1.46	k_0 = 2	k = 2.74	1
$3e_0$	k = 2.19	k_0 = 3	k = 4.11	2

From this chart it can be seen that only the spacings $e = e_0 = 2037 A°$ and $e = 2e_0 = 4074 A°$ give but one pass band.

(b) The path difference becomes:

$$\delta = 2ne \cos r = k_0 \lambda_0'. \tag{3}$$

Compare this expression with equation (1). One finds the same interference order for shorter wavelengths.

$$\lambda_0' < \lambda_0 .$$

When the filter is inclined, the pass bands shift toward shorter wavelengths.

DOUBLET SEPARATION

● **PROBLEM** 10-16

A Michelson interferometer is used for measuring the separation of a doublet of atomic emission lines. The average wavelength of the doublet is known to be 676 nm. Periodic variations of the fringe contrast are found whenever one of the mirrors is moved through a distance of 0.44 mm. What are the two wavelengths of the doublet?

Solution: When the Michelson interferometer is adjusted so that fringes can be seen, the path length difference in the two arms of the interferometer is an integral number of wavelengths. As one mirror is moved a distance Δx, the optical path length is changed by $2\Delta x$. Thus, with a doublet line structure rather than a monochromatic line, when one mirror is moved a distance of Δx from the maximum intensity of the fringes to the next position where there is a maximum intensity of the fringes, the relation between Δx and the shorter wavelength of the doublet, λ_2 , is

$$m\lambda_2 = 2\Delta x \tag{1}$$

where m is an integer, and for the longer wavelength λ_1

$$(m - 1)\lambda_1 = 2\Delta x \tag{2}$$

Using equation (1) and using the relations

$$\lambda_2 = \lambda_o - \frac{\Delta\lambda}{2}$$

and

$$\lambda_1 = \lambda_o + \frac{\Delta\lambda}{2} \quad ,$$

where λ_o is the average wavelength of the doublet, and making the approximation $\lambda_2 = \lambda_o$ in equation (1),

$$m = \frac{2\Delta x}{\lambda_o} = \frac{2 \times .44 \times 10^{-3}}{676 \times 10^{-9}} = 1301.775 \cong 1302$$

since m is an integer.

Equating the expressions for $2\Delta x$ to the left of the equal sign in equations (1) and (2) gives

$$m\lambda_2 = (m - 1)\lambda_1$$

$$m\left(\lambda_o - \frac{\Delta\lambda}{2}\right) = (m - 1)\left(\lambda_o + \frac{\Delta\lambda}{2}\right)$$

$$m\lambda_o - \frac{m\Delta\lambda}{2} = m\lambda_o + \frac{m\Delta\lambda}{2} - \lambda_o - \frac{\Delta\lambda}{2}$$

$$m\Delta\lambda = \lambda_o + \frac{\Delta\lambda}{2}$$

Neglecting the $\Delta\lambda/2$ term, which is negligible compared to the $m\Delta\lambda$ and λ_o terms,

$$\Delta\lambda = \frac{\lambda_o}{m} = \frac{676 \times 10^{-9}}{1302} = 5.19 \times 10^{-10} \text{ m} = .519 \text{ nm.}$$

Then,

$$\lambda_2 = \lambda_o - \frac{\Delta\lambda}{2} = 675.74 \text{ nm}$$

$$\lambda_1 = \lambda_o + \frac{\Delta\lambda}{2} = 676.26 \text{ nm}$$

CHAPTER 11

DIFFRACTION

DETERMINATION OF PHASE DIFFERENCES BETWEEN RAYS OF LIGHT

● **PROBLEM** 11-1

A rectangular aperture of width 0.67 mm is set up immediately in front of an objective lens of focal length 60 cm. If light of wavelength 5.36 x 10^{-5} cm is used, find the difference in phase between the rays from the two edges of the aperture arriving at a point P which is in the focal plane of the lens and 0.1 mm to the side of the principal focus.

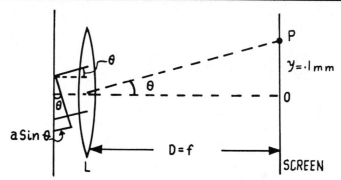

Solution: Width of the aperture a = 0.67mm = 0.67 x 10^{-3} m
Wavelength λ   = 5.36 x 10^{-7}m
Distance from the edge of the aperture to the
screen (D)   = f = 0.60m.

Hence the diffraction angle θ shown in the figure is given by

$$\tan \theta \approx \theta \text{ (for small } \theta) = \frac{y}{f} = \frac{0.1 \times 10^{-3}}{.60}$$

$$= 1.66 \times 10^{-4} \text{ rad.}$$

The path difference between the two beams originating at

the top and bottom of the aperture and going in a direction θ with respect to the normal to the aperture is   a sin θ.

Hence the phase difference is

$$\delta = \frac{2\pi}{\lambda} \text{ (path difference) rad.}$$

$$= \frac{2\pi}{\lambda} a \sin\theta \approx \frac{2\pi}{\lambda} (a\theta) \text{ rad.   Since } \theta \text{ is small.}$$

$$\delta = \frac{2\pi}{5.36 \times 10^{-7}} [0.67 \times 10^{-3} \times 1.66 \times 10^{-4}] \text{ rad.}$$

$$= \frac{2\cancel{\pi} \times 1.112 \times 10^{-7}}{5.36 \times 10^{-7}} \times (\frac{180}{\cancel{\pi}}) \text{ degrees.}$$

$$= \underline{\underline{75°.}}$$

FRAUNHOFER DIFFRACTION

● **PROBLEM** 11-2

Parallel light of wavelength 5461Å is incident normally on a slit 1 mm wide. If a lens of 100 cm focal length is mounted just behind the slit and the light focused on a screen, what will be the distance in millimeters from the center of the diffraction pattern to a) the first minimum, b) the first secondary maximum, c) the third minimum.

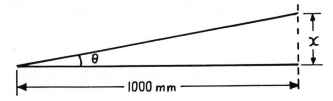

Solution: The positions of the minima of a diffraction pattern are found by applying the equation

$$a \cdot \sin\theta = m\lambda \tag{1}$$

where a is the width of the aperture, θ is the angle by which the incident beam is diffracted, m is the order for the diffraction pattern, and λ is the wavelength of the incident light.

a) For the first minimum, equation (1) becomes

$$(1mm) \cdot \sin\theta = (1)(5.461 \times 10^{-4}mm)$$

from which $\sin \theta = 5.461 \times 10^{-4}$. If the focal length of the lens is 1000 mm then we can assume that the distance from the slit to the screen, where the beam is focused is also 1000 mm as shown in the figure.

Since $\tan \phi \approx \sin \phi$ at very small angles, we can use that approximation in the figure to get

$$\tan \theta = \sin \theta = \frac{x}{1000mm} \qquad (2)$$

$$5.461 \times 10^{-4} = \frac{x}{1000mm}$$

from which $x = 0.546$ mm.

b)   Even though equation (1) is for the minima of a diffraction pattern, the maxima may be found about half way between each minima.   Therefore, a very close approximation to the positions of the maxima is

$$a \cdot \sin \theta = \left(m + \frac{1}{2}\right)\lambda. \qquad (3)$$

For the first secondary maximum, we have (from equation (3)),

$$(1mm) \cdot \sin \theta = \left(1 + \frac{1}{2}\right) \cdot (5.461 \times 10^{-4} \text{ mm})$$

and $\sin \theta = 8.192 \times 10^{-4}$.

From equation (2), the distance from the center of the diffraction pattern to the first secondary maximum is 0.819 mm.

c)   For the distance from the center to the third minimum of the diffraction pattern, we apply equation (1) with m = 3:

$$(1mm) \sin \theta = 3(5.461 \times 10^{-4} mm)$$

$$\sin \theta = 1.638 \times 10^{-3}$$

Now if we apply equation (2), we have

$$\sin \theta = \frac{x}{1000mm}$$

$$1.638 \times 10^{-3} = \frac{x}{1000mm}$$

$$x = 1.638 \text{ mm.}$$

256

If the parallel light in the previous problem is produced
by a slit at the focus of a lens of focal length 20 cm,
how wide could this first slit be before details of the
pattern would begin to be lost?

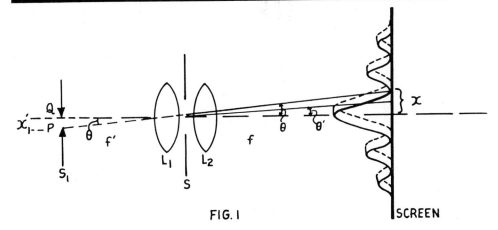

FIG. I   SCREEN

Solution: In the previous problem, it has been shown that
the first minimum appears at a distance of 0.546 mm from
the central maximum when a slit, 1 mm wide, is illuminated
by a parallel beam of light of wavelength 5461Å and the
diffracted beam is focused by a lens of 100 cm focal length.

The angular separation between the first minimum and central
maximum was found to be

$$a \sin \theta = \lambda \quad \text{or for small } \theta,$$

$$\theta = \frac{\lambda}{a} = \frac{x}{f} . \tag{1}$$

The last equality comes from examination of figure 1.
λ is the wavelength of light used, a the slit width, f is
the focal length of the lens placed between the slit and
the screen, and x is the distance between the central
maximum and the first minimum.

Substituting the values for λ and a into equation (1)

$$\theta = \frac{5461 \times 10^{-10}}{1 \times 10^{-3}} = 5.461 \times 10^{-4} \text{ radians} \tag{2}$$

If the slit S_1, producing the parallel monochromatic beam
is made wider (represented as PQ in Fig. 1), the diffraction pattern would be produced by each element of the slit
and the resultant pattern will be the sum of a large number
of these patterns displaced by an infinitesimal amount
with respect to each other.   This is shown in figure 1.

When the slit S_1 is widened to the width x_1' such that the maximum from one extreme point of this slit falls on the first minimum of the other extreme point, the intensity distribution will not show any pattern and will be completely lost.

If x_1' is the width of the slit S_1 and f' is the focal length of the lens L_1, then $\frac{x_1'}{f'}$ is the angular width of the slit S_1 for complete discordance of the fringes on the screen. This must then be equal to θ.

The value of the slit width for which the pattern would not be seriously impaired or before which the details of the pattern would begin to be lost depends upon our criteria for clear fringes. A good working rule is to permit a maximum discordance of the fringes of about 1/4 of that for the first disappearance.

Hence

$$\frac{x_1'}{f'} = \frac{\theta}{4} = \frac{5.461 \times 10^{-4}}{4} = 1.365 \times 10^{-4} \text{ rad.}$$

Hence, $x_1' = 1.365 \times 10^{-4}$ $f' = 1.365 \times 10^{-4} \times 20$ cm

$$= 2.730 \cdot 10^{-3} \text{ cm.}$$

● **PROBLEM 11-4**

What is the diameter of the central image, i.e., the diameter of the first dark ring, formed on the retina of the eye, of a distant point object? Assume the wavelength is 5500 Å, and consider the diameter of the exit pupil of the eye to be 2.2 mm and its distance from the retina to be 20 mm.

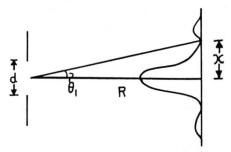

Solution: The exit pupil of the eye acts as a circular aperture and the Airy's disc pattern is formed on the retina. The radius of the first dark ring of the pattern subtends an angle at the center of the exit pupil given by

$$\sin \theta_1 = \frac{1.22 \lambda}{d} \qquad \text{where}$$

λ is the wave length of the light used, d is the diameter of the exit pupil (the circular aperture), and θ_1 is as shown in the figure. If x is the radius of the first dark ring and R is the distance between the aperture and the screen, then from the figure

$$\frac{x}{R} = \text{Tan } \theta_1$$

Since the approximation $\text{Tan } \theta_1 = \theta_1 = \text{Sin } \theta_1$ can be made for small angles,

$$x = \frac{1.22 \ R \ \lambda}{d}$$

Hence the diameter of the first dark ring is $\dfrac{2 \times 1.22 \ R \ \lambda}{d}$

or $\quad \dfrac{2 \times 1.22 \times 2 \text{ cm} \times 5.5 \times 10^{-5} \text{ cm}}{0.22 \text{ cm}}$

$$= 1.22 \times 10^{-3} \text{ cm.}$$

● **PROBLEM 11-5**

The interference pattern of two identical narrow slits separated by a distance d = 0.1mm is observed on a screen at a distance of 1m from the plane of the slits. The slits are illuminated by monochromatic light of wave length 590 mμ. Five bright bands are observed on each side of the central maximum, but beyond these bands the intensity is very weak. Calculate the approximate width of each of the slits.

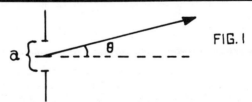

FIG. I

Solution: When a single slit has a width, a, as in figure (1), such that

$$a \sin \theta = m\lambda \tag{1}$$

where θ is the angle from the center of the slit to the position on the screen being observed, m is an integer, and λ is the wavelength of the light being used, then at that point there will be a diffraction minimum. When two slits of very small width are spaced a distance d apart such that

$$d \sin \theta = m_1 \lambda \tag{2}$$

then at that point there will be an interference maximum. If we have two slits, whose slit widths a are not too small, then the interference pattern will be modified by

259

the diffraction of the slit.

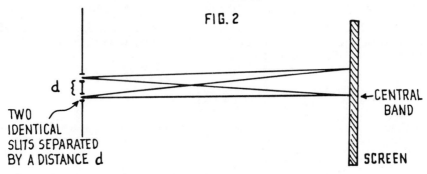

FIG. 2

d {I

TWO
IDENTICAL
SLITS SEPARATED
BY A DISTANCE d

←CENTRAL
BAND

SCREEN

In this problem we have five bright bands on each side of
the central maximum. If the width of the slits, a, is much
smaller than the separation of the slits, then the angle θ
we find for the first minimum of diffraction will be much
larger than the angle for the first minimum of the interference pattern. So we then estimate that an integer $m_1 =$
5 for interference will correspond to an integer $m = 1$
for diffraction at the same angle θ. In other words, the
fifth interference maximum in a two slit aperture has the
same angle θ as the first diffraction maximum in a single
slit aperture.

Thus, from equations (1) and (2)

$$\sin \theta = \frac{m\lambda}{a} = \frac{1\lambda}{a} = \frac{m_1\lambda}{d} = \frac{5\lambda}{d}$$

or
$$\frac{\lambda}{a} = \frac{5\lambda}{d}$$

Then
$$a = \frac{d}{5} = \frac{0.1mm}{5} = 0.02mm.$$

● **PROBLEM 11-6**

A single slit is illuminated by light of wavelength 500nm.
A diffraction pattern is formed on a screen 50cm away
from the slit, and the distance between the first and third
minima in the pattern is found to be 2mm. What is the
width of the slit?

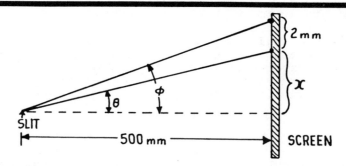

2mm

x

ϕ

θ

SLIT

500 mm

SCREEN

Solution: The minima of a diffraction pattern can be
found by applying the equation

260

$$a \cdot \sin \theta = m\lambda \tag{1}$$

where a is the slit width, θ is the angle the light ray makes with the axis, m is the order number, and λ is the wavelength.

Applying equation (1) to the two light rays shown in the figure we have

$$a \cdot \sin \theta = 1 \cdot (500 \times 10^{-6} mm) \tag{2}$$

and $$a \cdot \sin \phi = 3 \cdot (500 \times 10^{-6} mm). \tag{3}$$

If the angles θ and ϕ are sufficiently small, we can make the approximations $\sin \theta = \tan \theta$ and $\sin \phi = \tan \phi$, which gives us

$$a \cdot \tan \theta = 5.0 \times 10^{-4} mm \tag{4}$$

and $$a \cdot \tan \phi = 1.5 \times 10^{-3} mm. \tag{5}$$

From the figure, $\tan \theta = \dfrac{x}{500mm}$ and $\tan \phi = \dfrac{2mm + x}{500mm}$. Substituting for $\tan \theta$ and $\tan \phi$ in equations (4) and (5), respectively, we have

$$\frac{ax}{500mm} = 5.0 \times 10^{-4} mm \tag{6}$$

and $$\frac{a(2mm + x)}{500mm} = 1.5 \times 10^{-3} mm. \tag{7}$$

Solving equation (6) for x gives the result $x = \dfrac{.25mm^2}{a}$. Substituting into equation (7),

$$\frac{a \left(2mm + \dfrac{.25mm^2}{a}\right)}{500mm} = 1.5 \times 10^{-3} mm.$$

Then $2a$ mm $+ .25mm^2 = .75mm^2$

and $a = \dfrac{.50mm^2}{2mm} = .25mm.$

● **PROBLEM** 11-7

A laser beam (694nm wavelength) is used in measuring variations in the size of the moon by timing its return from mirror systems on the moon. If the beam is expanded to 1m diameter and collimated, estimate its size at the moon. (Moon's distance $\sim 3.8 \times 10^5$ km.)

Solution: This problem consists of a circular aperture, of diameter one meter, of coherent parallel light. A

261

screen is then placed 3.8×10^5 km away from the circular aperture and we wish to determine the diameter of the diffracted spot (to the first diffraction minimum) at the screen. From any standard optics text that covers Fraunhofer diffraction of a circular aperture,

$$r = \frac{1.22R\lambda}{D}$$

where r is the radius of the first minimum of the circular aperture Fraunhofer diffraction; R is the distance from the aperture to the screen; λ is the wavelength of the light used and D is the diameter of the aperture. Therefore the diameter of the spot on the moon to the first minimum is

$$d = 2r = \frac{2.44 \times (3.8 \times 10^5 \times 10^3 m)(694 \times 10^{-9} m)}{1 \ m}$$

$$= 643m \approx 0.643km.$$

● **PROBLEM 11-8**

A single slit, illuminated by red light of 650nm, gives first order Fraunhofer diffraction minima that have angular distances of $\theta = 5°$ from the optic axis. How wide is the slit?

Solution: When light is incident on the edge of a slit it is bent slightly as it passes through that slit. For a minimum to occur the following equation must be satisfied:

$$a \cdot \sin \theta = m\lambda, \qquad\qquad (1)$$

where a is the width of the slit, θ is the angle at which the light ray is bent, λ is the wavelength of the light, and m is the order number.

If $\lambda = 650nm = 6.5 \times 10^{-4}$ mm, m = 1, and $\theta = 5°$, then substituting the values of θ, m, and λ into equation (1),

$$a = \frac{(1)(6.5 \times 10^{-4} mm.)}{\sin(5°)} \approx 7.45 \times 10^{-3} mm.$$

● **PROBLEM 11-9**

In a single-slit diffraction experiment, the slit is 0.1mm wide and is illuminated by monochromatic light with a wavelength of 500nm. The diffraction pattern is observed on a screen 10m away. What is the spacing between successive minima in the pattern?

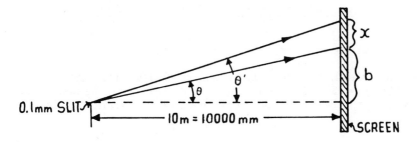

Solution: The monochromatic light produces minima on the screen when

$$a \cdot \sin \theta = m\lambda \qquad (1)$$

where a is the width of the slit, m is the order number, λ is the wavelength of the monochromatic light and θ is as shown in the figure.   For two successive minima of the diffraction pattern, we have, from equation (1),

$$a \cdot \sin \theta = m\lambda \qquad (2)$$

and $a \cdot \sin \theta' = (m+1)\lambda$ (θ' is indicated in the figure)   (3)

If the angles θ and θ' are sufficiently small, because of the large distance between the slit and screen, then we can make the following approximations:

$$\sin \theta = \tan \theta = \frac{b}{10000mm} \qquad (4)$$

and $$\sin \theta' = \tan \theta' = \frac{x + b}{10000mm} . \qquad (5)$$

When the expressions given for $\sin \theta$ and $\sin \theta'$ in equations (4) and (5) are substituted back into equations (2) and (3), respectively, we have

$$a \cdot \left(\frac{b}{10,000mm} \right) = m\lambda \qquad (6)$$

and $$a \cdot \left(\frac{x + b}{10,000mm} \right) = (m+1)\lambda. \qquad (7)$$

From equation (7),

$$x + b = \frac{(m+1)(10,000mm)\lambda}{a} .$$

Solving for b in equation (6),

$$b = \frac{m\lambda(10,000mm)}{a}$$

Substituting for b into the preceding equation,

263

$$x = \frac{10,000(m+1)\lambda - 10,000m\lambda}{a} = \frac{10,000\lambda}{a} \quad ,$$

where x will be expressed in millimeters.

Since the width of the slit, a, is 0.1mm and the wavelength, λ, is 500ņm = 5 x 10^{-4}mm, then the distance between two successive minima of the diffraction pattern, x, is 50mm or 5cm.

● **PROBLEM** 11-10

A slit 0.25mm wide is placed in front of a positive lens and illuminated by plane waves of wavelength 500mµ. In the Fraunhofer diffraction pattern formed in the focal plane of the lens, the distance from the third minimum on the left to the third minimum on the right is found to be 3mm. Find the focal length of the lens.

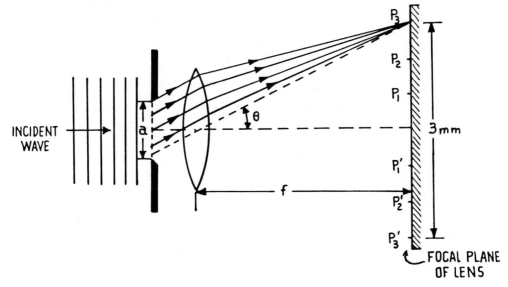

Solution: In the figure, in order to find the position of any minimum on the focal plane, we must apply the following equation.

$$a \cdot \sin \theta = m\lambda \tag{1}$$

where a is the slit width, m the order number, λ the wavelength of light and θ is as shown in the figure. The problem states that the distance between the third minima on both sides of the axis is 3mm; thus the distance from the third minimum on either side of the central maximum to the central maximum is 1.5mm. If the width of the slit, a, is 0.25mm, the order number m is 3, the wavelength λ is 5.0 x 10^{-4}mm and θ is small enough to make the approximation sin θ = tan θ, then equation (1) becomes

$$(0.25\text{mm}) \cdot (\tan \theta) = 3 \cdot (5 \times 10^{-4}\text{mm})$$

$$(0.25)\left(\frac{1.5}{f}\right) = 1.5 \times 10^{-3},$$

where the relation $\tan \theta = \frac{1.5mm}{f}$ can be determined from the figure. Solving for the focal length of the lens,

$$f = 250mm = 25cm.$$

Find the value of I/I_0 for the first diagonal maximum of the Fraunhofer diffraction pattern of a circular aperture.

Solution: For Fraunhofer diffraction, any standard optics text tells us that the electric field intensity E for an aperture can be written as

$$E = \frac{E_A \; e^{i(\omega t - kR)}}{R} \iint\limits_{aperture} e^{ik(Yy+Zz)} dS$$

where E_A is the electric field at the aperture, $\omega = 2\pi f$, $k = 2\pi/\lambda$, λ is the wavelength of the light used, R is the distance from the aperture to the screen, y,z are coordinates of the aperture and Y,Z are coordinates of the screen. The intensity pattern on the screen will then be $1/2 \; E \; E^*$ where E^* is the complex conjugate of E. Now if we carry out the integral for a circular aperture we find

$$E = \frac{E_A \; e^{i(\omega t - kR)}}{R} \; 2\pi a^2 \left(\frac{R}{kaq}\right) J_1\left(\frac{kaq}{R}\right)$$

where $J_1\left(\frac{kaq}{R}\right)$ is a first order Bessel function, a is the radius of the aperture and q is the radial distance from a centered point on the screen.

Then the intensity

$$I = \tfrac{1}{2} E \; E^* = \frac{1}{2}\left[\frac{E_A \; e^{i(\omega t - kR)}}{R} \; 2\pi a^2 \left(\frac{R}{kaq}\right) J_1\left(\frac{kaq}{R}\right)\right]$$

$$\times \left[\frac{E_A \; e^{-i(\omega t - kR)}}{R} \; 2\pi a^2 \left(\frac{R}{kaq}\right) J_1\left(\frac{kaq}{R}\right)\right],$$

and so,

$$I = \frac{2E_A^2 A^2}{R^2}\left[\frac{J_1(kaq/R)}{(kaq/R)}\right]^2 , \quad \text{where } A = \pi a^2.$$

265

$$I = I(0) \left[\frac{2J_1(kaq/R)}{(kaq/R)} \right]^2 , \text{ where } I(0) = \frac{E_A^2 A^2}{2R^2} .$$

For $q = 0$, $I = I(0)$. To find the intensity of the first maximum we need to find the value of q for which $J_1(kaq/R)$ is a maximum and the value of J_1 at that point. From a set of tables we find the first maximum occurs for $(kaq/R) = 5.136$, at which point $J_1(kaq/R) = -0.3397$ or

$$I_{1st\ max} = I(0) \left[\frac{2 \times .3397}{5.136} \right]^2 = I(0) \times .0175$$

so

$$\frac{I_{1st\ max}}{I_{q\ =\ 0}} = 0.175$$

Find the half-angular breadth of the central bright band in the Fraunhofer diffraction pattern of a slit 14×10^{-5} cm wide, when the slit is illuminated by a parallel beam of monochromatic light of wavelength a) 400 mμ, b) 700 mμ.

Solution: The intensity pattern in diffraction by a single slit varies as

$$\left[\frac{\sin\beta}{\beta} \right]^2$$

where $\beta = \frac{\pi D \sin \alpha}{\lambda}$ and D is the slit width, λ is the wavelength of light used and α is the angle of observation measured from the perpendicular to the slit. We are interested in the minima so we want $\sin \beta = 0$ or $\pi = \beta = \frac{\pi D \sin \alpha}{\lambda}$

or $\qquad \sin \alpha_1 = \frac{\lambda_1}{D} = \frac{400 \times 10^{-9}}{14 \times 10^{-7}} = \frac{4}{14}$

$$\alpha_1 = 16.6°$$

$$\sin \alpha_2 = \frac{\lambda_2}{D} = \frac{700 \times 10^{-9}}{14 \times 10^{-7}} = \frac{1}{2}$$

$$\alpha_2 = 30°$$

A distant sodium street lamp seen through a woven nylon curtain appears to be accompanied by a series of "images" spaced 0.3° apart. What is the spacing of the nylon fibers? (λ_{Na} = 5893 Å)

Solution: Here we have Fraunhofer diffraction; the source and the screen are both far from the aperture. We will assume that the weaving of the curtain is the same both vertically and horizontally. From any standard optics text that includes Fraunhofer diffraction of a rectangular aperture we find that the intensity of light behaves as

$$I = C \; \frac{\sin^2\alpha}{\alpha^2} \frac{\sin^2\beta}{\beta^2} \; , \text{ where C is a constant.}$$

and $\quad \alpha = \frac{\pi b}{\lambda} \sin\theta; \quad \beta = \frac{\pi d \sin\theta}{\lambda} \;$, and

b and d are dimensions of the aperture, λ is the wavelength and θ is the angle from the aperture-screen perpendicular axis to the screen point at which the intensity is sought. α and β represent the path difference of the light from the aperture. To have maxima, the path differences must have a difference of an integer number of wavelengths and for minima the path differences must be odd multiples of a half-wavelength.

As we look at our intensity equation we see that successive maxima will occur with $\alpha = \frac{\pi}{2}$, $\frac{3\pi}{2}$, $\frac{5\pi}{2}$ . . . and for successive minima for $\alpha = \pi$, 2π; 3π. Note that $\alpha = 0$ yields a maximum (i.e. $\lim\limits_{\alpha \to 0} \frac{\sin\alpha}{\alpha} = 1$, which can be seen by applying L'Hospital's rule:

$$\lim_{\alpha \to 0} \frac{\sin\alpha}{\alpha} = \lim_{\alpha \to 0} \frac{\cos\alpha}{1} = 1).$$

In this case the angular difference in θ between two minima is 0.3°. We expect both maxima and minima to be reasonably evenly spaced so we choose the easier one to calculate. The first two minima occur for $\alpha = \pi$ and $\alpha = 2\pi$. Therefore, substituting first π and then 2π into the expression for α,

$$\alpha = \pi = \frac{\pi b}{\lambda} \sin\theta$$

$$2\pi = \frac{\pi b}{\lambda} \sin\theta_1.$$

Solving for $\sin\theta$ and $\sin\theta_1$,

267

$$\sin \theta = \frac{\lambda}{b}$$

$$\sin \theta_1 = \frac{2\lambda}{b}$$

$$\sin \theta_1 - \sin \theta = \frac{\lambda}{b}$$

For small values of θ_1 and θ, we can expand $\sin \theta \approx$

$\theta - \frac{\theta^3}{3!} + \ldots$ (the Taylor series expansion of $\sin \theta$)

and keep only the first term.

$$\theta_1 - \theta = \frac{\lambda}{b}$$

$\theta_1 - \theta$ must be measured in radians so

$$\theta_1 - \theta = 0.3 \times \frac{\pi}{180} = 5.23 \times 10^{-3} \text{ rad.}$$

and

$$b = \frac{\lambda}{\theta_1 - \theta} = \frac{5893 \times 10^{-8}}{5.23 \times 10^{-3}} \text{ cm} = 0.0112 \text{cm}$$

$$= 1.12 \times 10^{-2} \text{ cm.}$$

FRESNEL DIFFRACTION

● **PROBLEM** 11-14

(a) In a diffraction experiment a point source is used 5m from the diffracting aperture. If the aperture is 1mm in diameter, determine whether Fraunhofer or Fresnel diffraction applies when the screen-to-aperture distance is a) 10cm, b) 50cm, c) 5m. Take λ = 5000Å.

(b) An aperture 5mm in diameter diffracts light of wavelength 0.5μm. How far away must a screen be placed to show the far-field diffraction pattern?

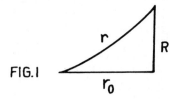

FIG.I

Solution: a) The difference between Fraunhofer (far-field) and Fresnel diffraction is that in Fraunhofer diffraction we can treat all points at the surface of the aperture as being in phase and look at the phase change from aperture to screen, while in Fresnel diffraction we do not have all points at the surface in phase.

So we must determine at what point in source-aperture distance and aperture-screen distance the phase of the light does not vary over the surface. With Fresnel diffraction we divide the aperture into circular zones, each zone boundary producing a half-wavelength path difference from the previous zone. Now if the screen or source is at such a distance that the aperture size is equal to or less than the radius of the first Fresnel zone we would not expect to see a difference between Fresnel and Fraunhofer diffraction. Then looking at figure 1 we need to determine the radius of the first Fresnel zone. We want

$$r - r_o = \frac{\lambda}{2}$$

and from the figure we have

$$R^2 = r^2 - r_o^2 = (r - r_o)(r + r_o), \text{ where R is the}$$

aperture radius and r_o is the screen-aperture distance.

$$R^2 = \frac{\lambda}{2}(r + r_o) \approx \lambda r_o \quad \text{(since } \lambda \text{ is small in com-}$$

parison to r and r_o)

or $\qquad r_o = \frac{R^2}{\lambda}$ $\hspace{3cm}$ (2)

so if r_o is greater than R^2/λ we expect Fraunhofer diffraction and if r_o is less than R^2/λ we anticipate Fresnel diffraction. So then in our problem

$$\frac{R^2}{\lambda} = \frac{\left(\frac{10^{-3}}{2}\right)^2}{500 \times 10^{-9}} = 0.5\text{m}$$

so with the source 5 meters away the diffraction pattern is Fraunhofer-like. With a screen-aperture distance of 10cm or 0.1 meter the diffraction pattern clearly is Fresnel since $r_o < \frac{R^2}{\lambda}$; at 50cm or 0.5m $r_o = \frac{R^2}{\lambda}$. In this case, it would probably be best to consider the resulting diffraction pattern to be Fresnel.

b) From equation (2), since to show a far-field or Fraunhofer diffraction pattern, the minimum screen-aperture distance is $\frac{R^2}{\lambda}$,

$$r_o \approx \frac{R^2}{\lambda}$$

and $\qquad R = \frac{1}{2}(5 \times 10^{-3}\text{m}),$

$$\lambda = 0.5 \times 10^{-6}\text{m}$$

we have

$$r_o \cong \frac{\left[\frac{1}{2}(5 \times 10^{-3} m)\right]^2}{0.5 \times 10^{-6} m} = 12.5 m.$$

Monochromatic light of wavelength 400mμ from a distant point source falls on an opaque plate in which there is a small circular opening. As a screen is moved toward the plate from a large distance away, the Fresnel diffraction pattern on the screen first has a dark center when the distance from plate to screen is 160cm. Find the diameter of the central disk in the diffraction pattern if a lens of focal length 160cm is placed just to the right of the circular opening.

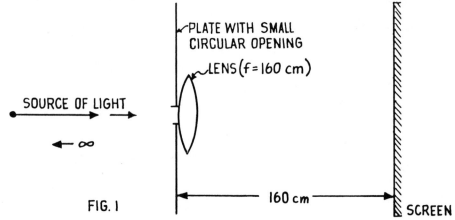

FIG. 1

Solution: We have a circular aperture illuminated by coherent light from a source infinitely distant from the aperture. This implies that all points on the aperture are in phase with all other points. We now place a screen an infinite distance from the aperture and slowly move it towards the aperture observing the center spot of the screen. At some distance the path length from the light at the circumference of the aperture will be just one wavelength out of phase with light from the center of the aperture, which can be represented algebraically as $R_1 = R_o + \lambda$ in figure (2). We have learned from our study of diffraction that this is just the condition for destructive interference. Now if we move the screen closer to the aperture, the center of the screen will have a bright spot when the path difference between a circumferential ray and a central ray is $3\lambda/2$ and dark when there is a 2λ path difference, etc. Each of the path differences defines the edges of Fresnel zones.

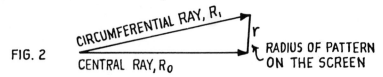

FIG. 2

Looking at figure (2) for our problem when R_o is 160cm, r

270

will just be the outer radius of the second Fresnel zone. From figure (2),

$$R_1^2 = R_o^2 + r^2 \tag{1}$$

and $\quad R_1 = R_o + \lambda \quad$ because there is destructive interference at R_o = 160cm. $\tag{2}$

Substituting for R_1 in equation (1) yields

$$R_o^2 + 2\lambda R_o + \lambda^2 = R_o^2 + r^2$$

The R_o^2 terms cancel, and so,

$$r^2 = 2\lambda R_o + \lambda^2$$

or

$$r = \sqrt{\lambda^2 + 2\lambda R_o}$$

$$= \left[(400 \times 10^{-9}m)^2 + 2 \times 400 \times 10^{-9}m \times 1.6m\right]^{1/2}$$

$$= 1.13 \times 10^{-3}m, \tag{3}$$

which is the radius of the aperture. If we now place a 160cm focal length lens on the screen side of the aperture, the lens will convert an infinite distance on the screen side to a point 160cm from the aperture (as in figure (1)). Stating it another way, the screen at 160cm from the aperture with a 160cm focal length lens will produce a Fraunhofer diffraction pattern of the source. Now from any standard optics text Fraunhofer diffraction of a circular aperture is

$$\frac{d/2}{\ell} = \frac{1.22\lambda}{2r} \tag{4}$$

where d is the diameter of the central disk; ℓ is the distance from the aperture; λ is the wavelength of the light used and r is the radius of the aperture. Now solving for the diameter of the central disk we have

$$d = \frac{\ell \times 1.22 \times \lambda}{r}$$

where ℓ = 1.6m, λ = 400x10^{-9}m, and r = 1.13x10^{-3}m.

Hence $\quad d = \dfrac{1.6m \times 1.22 \times 400 \times 10^{-9}m}{1.13 \times 10^{-3}m} = 6.91 \times 10^{-4}m.$

A point source S (λ = 5000Å) is placed 1m from an aperture consisting of a hole of 1mm radius in which there is
a circular opaque obstacle whose radius is 1/2mm, as
shown in figure 1.   The receiving point P is 1m from the
aperture.   What is the intensity at P compared to the
intensity if the aperture were removed?

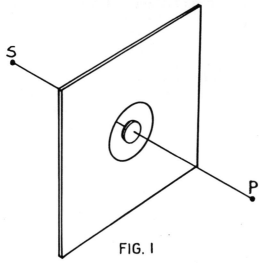

FIG. I

Solution: From the geometry of figure (2), let us calcu-
late ρ_1, ρ_2, r_1 and r_2 using the values of ρ_o, r_o, a_1, a_2
and λ, the wavelength of light used, as given in this
problem.   From figure 2,

$$\rho_1^2 = a_1^2 + \rho_o^2$$

$$\rho_2^2 = a_2^2 + \rho_o^2$$

$$r_1^2 = a_1^2 + r_o^2$$

$$r_2^2 = a_2^2 + r_o^2$$

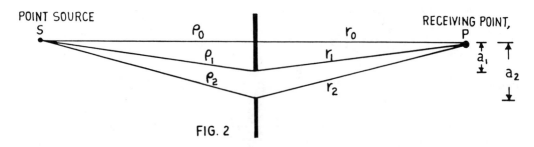

FIG. 2

In this problem, $\rho_o = 1m$, $r_o = 1m$, $a_1 = 1/2mm$, and $a_2 = 1mm$. Then

$$\rho_1 - \rho_o = r_1 - r_o = \sqrt{a_1^2 + r_o^2} - r_o$$

$$= \sqrt{(0.5 \times 10^{-3})^2 + 1} - 1 = 1.25 \times 10^{-7}m$$

$$\rho_2 - \rho_o = r_2 - r_o = \sqrt{a_2^2 + r_o^2} - r_o$$

$$= \sqrt{(1 \times 10^{-3})^2 + 1} - 1 = 5 \times 10^{-7}m$$

so the path difference between $(\rho_1 + r_1)$ and $(\rho_o + r_o)$ is
$(\rho_1 + r_1) - (\rho_o + r_o) = \rho_1 - \rho_o + r_1 - r_o = 2(\rho_1 - \rho_o)$

or

$$\frac{2(\rho_1 - \rho_o)}{\lambda} = \frac{2 \times 1.25 \times 10^{-7}}{5 \times 10^{-7}} = \frac{1}{2}$$

and similarly

$$\frac{2(\rho_2 - \rho_o)}{\lambda} = \frac{2 \times 5 \times 10^{-7}}{5 \times 10^{-7}} = 2$$

We have found that the path difference between a "central" ray and the inner edge of the opening is $1/2\lambda$ and to the outer edge of the opening is 2λ. Since these are small integers of a half wavelength, it appears that we have Fresnel zones. In Fresnel diffraction Fresnel zones are built such that each boundary of the Fresnel zone has just a half wavelength path difference (source to detector). Then if we have two adjacent Fresnel zones open between source and detector, the intensity at the detector will be zero. Since in this problem we have three Fresnel zones open we expect a maximum (bright spot) at the detector point P.

Now that we have noticed that there are three Fresnel zones and we have a maximum with the aperture in place, we need to determine how to get the ratio of the intensity at P with the aperture in place to the intensity with nothing between the source and P. The intensity of light at a point in space is proportional to the square of the electric field vector, E, at that point. In addition, we can find that the electric vector at a point a distance $\rho_o + r_o$ from a point source can be written as

$$E = \frac{\varepsilon_o}{(\rho_o + r_o)} \cos\left(\omega t - k(\rho_o + r_o)\right) \tag{1}$$

273

where ε_o is the electric vector at the source point, $(\rho_o + r_o)$ is the distance between source and detector; ω is the angular frequency of the light; t is the time; and k is the propagation vector of the light. It can be found in an optics textbook that for a single Fresnel zone we can express the electric field vector at the detector for the ℓth Fresnel zone as

$$E_\ell = (-1)^{\ell+1} \frac{2\varepsilon_o}{(\rho_o + r_o)} \cos\left(\omega t - k\left(\rho_o + r_o\right)\right) \qquad (2)$$

with the notation as in equation (1), except that now ρ_o represents the source-aperture distance and r_o represents the aperture-detector distance.

Since we have established that in our problem the open part of the aperture consists of the second, third and fourth Fresnel zones, we can find the total electric field vector at the detector by summing the contributions of each of the three Fresnel zones or

$$\sum_{\rho=2}^{4} E_\rho = \left[(-1)^3 + (-1)^4 + (-1)^5\right] \frac{2\varepsilon_o}{\rho_o + r_o} \cos\left(\omega t - k\left(\rho_o + r_o\right)\right)$$

$$= \frac{-2\varepsilon_o}{\rho_o + r_o} \cos\left(\omega t - k\left(\rho_o + r_o\right)\right) \qquad (3)$$

and since the intensity is proportional to the square of the electric field vector

$$\frac{I_{\text{aperture}}}{I_{\text{no aperture}}} = \frac{\left(\sum_{\ell=2}^{4} E_\ell\right)^2}{E^2} = 4$$

● **PROBLEM** 11-17

Monochromatic light of wavelength 563.3 mμ originates at a distant point source and passes through a circular opening. The Fresnel diffraction pattern is observed on a screen 1m beyond the opening. Find the diameter of the circular opening if it exposes   a) the central Fresnel zone only,   b) the first four Fresnel zones.

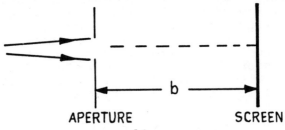

APERTURE   SCREEN

Solution: $\lambda = 5633 \times 10^{-10}$ m.

Let a be the distance from the source to the aperture and b be the distance from the screen to the aperture so that

$$a \to \infty$$

$$b = 1m.$$

(a) If there are m zones involved in the opening and if r_m is the radius of the mth zone, then

$$r_m^2 \left[\frac{a + b}{2ab} \right] = m\frac{\lambda}{2} \; .$$

Now for first zone m = 1.

Therefore,

$$\frac{r_1^2}{2} \left[\frac{1}{a} + \frac{1}{b} \right] = \frac{\lambda}{2} \; .$$

Let $a \to \infty$

Thus, $\frac{1}{a} \to 0.$

Then $\frac{r_1^2}{2b} = \frac{\lambda}{2}$

or $r_1^2 = b\lambda$

$$r_1 = \sqrt{b\lambda} = \sqrt{5633 \times 1 \times 10^{-10}} \; m$$

$$= 7.505 \times 10^{-4} \; m$$

$$= .7505 \; mm.$$

Therefore, the diameter of the opening $= 2r_1 = 1.50$ mm.

(b) For the first four zones

$$\frac{r_4^2}{2b} = \frac{4\lambda}{2} \; .$$

Therefore, $r_4 = \sqrt{4b\lambda} = 1.50$ mm.

Therefore, the diameter of the opening $= 2r_4 = 3.00$ mm.

FRESNEL ZONES

● **PROBLEM** 11-18

A zone lens is made for use with soft X-rays of wave-

length λ = 40Å. What should be the outside diameter of
the zone plate if it is to contain 25 zones and if details
10×10^{-3} mm in size are to be resolved? What role does
the wavelength play in this context?

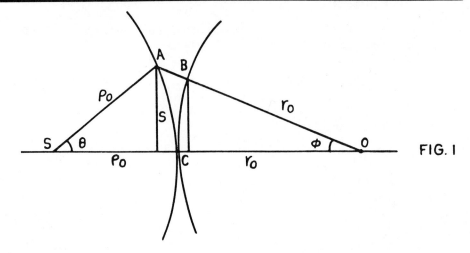

FIG. 1

Solution: A zone plate is a device where successive circular annular regions of an aperture are covered so that
at the screen the difference in path length varies in such
a way that there is never any component of light which can
cause destructive interference at the screen; only those
terms which can cause constructive interference reach the
screen.

So our first job is to determine the radius of a Fresnel
zone, defined as the radius of that aperture which will
allow paths that differ only by half a wavelength. Let
us refer to figure 1. We want to find the appropriate
points A such that the path SABO is just an integer multiple
of a half-wavelength longer than the path SCO. We see
that is just the distance AB. ρ_o and r_o (ρ_o and r_o as
indicated in figure 1) will be large with respect to s so
we can determine AB as the sum of the sagittas and for
small angles θ and ϕ the sagitta formula will yield

$$AB = \frac{s^2}{2\rho_o} + \frac{s^2}{2r_o} = \frac{s^2}{2} \left(\frac{1}{\rho_o} + \frac{1}{r_o} \right) \tag{1}$$

So the radius s_m of the mth Fresnel zone will be given by
the condition

$$\frac{m\lambda}{2} = \frac{s_m^2}{2} \left(\frac{1}{\rho_o} + \frac{1}{r_o} \right) \tag{2}$$

or

$$\frac{1}{\rho_o} + \frac{1}{r_o} = \frac{m\lambda}{s_m^2} = \frac{1}{s_m^2/m\lambda} \tag{3}$$

276

now ρ_o is just the object distance from the aperture and r_o is just the image distance so we have the equivalent of a lens if we define the focal length as

$$f = \frac{s_m^2}{m\lambda} \tag{4}$$

Since in this problem we want to resolve details of size 10×10^{-3}mm we see that we have a resolving power problem of circular objects. We remember that to resolve two objects our Rayleigh condition indicates that the central maximum intensity of one object must fall on the first minimum of the other object or then using the Fraunhofer diffraction of a circular aperture we have

$$\Delta\phi = \frac{1.22\lambda}{D} \tag{5}$$

and

$$\Delta\phi = \frac{\Delta\ell}{R} \tag{6}$$

where $\Delta\phi$ is the minimum angular resolution for a circular aperture of diameter D and wavelength λ; $\Delta\ell$ is the linear distance resolved on a screen which is a distance R from the aperture. Now if we have a lens of focal length f in the optical system then the lens will provide focusing, so we want to put our screen at the focal length from the lens. Then R = f, and the minimum linear resolution will then be

$$\Delta\ell = \frac{1.22f\lambda}{D} \tag{7}$$

and since we are using a Fresnel zone lens

$$f = \frac{s_m^2}{m\lambda} \quad \text{and} \quad D = 2s_m$$

$$\Delta\ell = \frac{1.22}{2s_m} \frac{s_m^2}{m\lambda} \lambda = \frac{0.61 s_m}{m}$$

$$s_m = \frac{m\Delta\ell}{0.61} = \frac{25 \times 10 \times 10^{-3} \text{mm}}{0.61} = 0.41\text{mm}.$$

Hence, $D = 2s_m = 0.82$mm

and we see that it is independent of the wavelength of the light used.

● **PROBLEM** 11-19

The eighth boundary of a zone plate has a diameter of 5mm. What is its principal focal length for light of

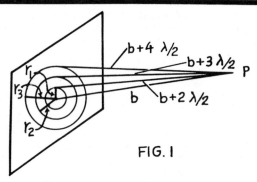

FIG. 1

Solution: Fresnel diffraction concerns itself with the
patterns resulting when there are no lenses employed and
the distances involved are small or the sizes of the
apertures are large.   A zone plate is a clear example of
Fresnel diffraction.   Consider a plane wave of wavelength
λ as shown in figure 1.   To find the resultant effect at
P of all the secondary wavelets on the wavefront, there is
drawn a series of concentric circles, whose radii r_1, r_2,
... r_n satisfy

$$r_n^2 = (b + \frac{n\lambda}{2})^2 - b^2 \tag{1}$$

where r_n is the radius of the nth circle and b is the
perpendicular distance from P to the center of the series
of circles.   Each circle is then a half wavelength farther
from P than its smaller neighboring circle.   The wave-
front is thus divided into half-period zones.   These
zones have the property that the ratio of the area of the
n^{th} zone to the mean distance of this zone from P is a
constant $\pi\lambda$.   Expanding equation (1),

$$r_n^2 = b^2 + bn\lambda + \frac{n^2\lambda^2}{4} - b^2 = nb\lambda + \frac{n^2\lambda^2}{4} \, .$$

Since λ is small compared to b, the $n^2\lambda^2/4$ term can be
neglected and so,

$$r_n^2 \approx nb\lambda \tag{2}$$

Thus, the radii are proportional to $\sqrt{n}$.   By drawing on a
white paper concentric circles whose radii are proportional
to $\sqrt{n}$, n = 1,2,3,......, blackening out every other zone,
say the even ones, and photographing the remaining set so
that the negative shows a very much diminished image of
the ring set, a zone plate is obtained.   By allowing the
plane monochromatic waves to fall on the zone plate and
placing a screen on the emergent side at such a distance
that actual Fresnel zones coincide with the zones appearing on the zone plate, the light coming through the unblackened area is all in phase, having a resulting

amplitude $A = A_1 + A_3 + A_5 + \ldots$, where A_i = the amplitude of the light coming through the ith unblackened zone.
Thus a very large intensity is produced on the axis of
the zone plate at the screen position. The zone plate
acts as a lens whose focal length is given by $b = r_n^2/n\lambda$
(follows from equation (2)).

$$b = \frac{(0.25)^2}{8 \times 5000 \times 10^{-8}} \text{ cm} = 156 \text{ cm}.$$

This is the principal focal length giving maximum intensity.
There are a series of foci with decreasing intensity as we
go toward the zone plate on the axis. The next one occurs
when the image distance is decreased so that the first
zone of the zone plate contains 3 actual half period
elements. The focal length is

$$\left(\frac{r_1}{\sqrt{3}}\right)^2 \frac{1}{\lambda} = \frac{b}{3} = 52.1 \text{ cm}.$$

In the same way there is still less bright focus at $b/5$ =
31.2 cm.

● **PROBLEM** 11-20

A circular opening of radius 0.8mm in an opaque screen is
illuminated by plane waves of monochromatic light and the
emergent light allowed to fall on a movable screen. As
the screen is gradually brought toward the aperture, it is
found that a succession of alternately light and dark
spots appear at the center of the diffraction patterns.

a)   If a bright spot appears for the second time when the
distance from the screen to the position of the screen
required for a bright spot to appear for the first time
is 36.2 cm, find the wavelength of the light.

b)   If a dark spot appears for the second time when the
distance between the screen and the position of the screen
required for a dark spot to appear for the first time is
36.2 cm, find the wavelength of the light.
c)   Find at what distance from the screen to the aperture
a bright spot appeared for the first time (refer to part
(a)).
d)   Find at what distance from the screen to the aperture
a dark spot appeared for the first time (refer to part
(b)).

Solution: As the screen is moved toward the aperture, a
bright spot is seen at the center of the diffraction
pattern when the screen is at a distance say b_1 from the
aperture.   If λ is the wavelength of the light used and
r_1 is the radius of the circular opening, then from the
equation

279

$$m\,\frac{\lambda}{2} = \frac{r_m^2}{2}\,[\frac{1}{a} + \frac{1}{b}]$$

where m is the number of the zones in the opening and r_m is the radius of the mth zone the bright and dark spots can be located. When m is odd, we get maximum intensity and when m is even, we get minimum intensity. a and b represent the distances from the source and the screen, respectively, to the aperture.

Now, since the source is at an infinite distance from the aperture, $a \to \infty$ and r_m = radius of the opening = $.8\times10^{-3}$m for all m.

Hence, $m\lambda = \dfrac{r_m^2}{b}$.

Therefore, $b_1 = \dfrac{r_1^2}{\lambda}$ 1st bright spot

$b_2 = \dfrac{r_2^2}{2\lambda} = \dfrac{r_1^2}{2\lambda}$ dark spot

$b_3 = \dfrac{r_3^2}{3\lambda} = \dfrac{r_1^2}{3\lambda}$ bright spot

$b_4 = \dfrac{r_4^2}{4\lambda} = \dfrac{r_1^2}{4\lambda}$ dark spot

(a)   For the bright spots:

$$b_1 - b_3 = \frac{r_1^2}{\lambda} - \frac{r_1^2}{3\lambda} = \frac{2r_1^2}{3\lambda} .$$

Then $\lambda = \dfrac{2r_1^2}{3\Delta b}$, where $\Delta b = b_1 - b_3 = 36.2$ cm.

Therefore, substituting in the given values for Δb and r_1,

$$\lambda = \frac{(2)(0.8\times10^{-3})^2 m}{3(.362)} \approx 1.17\times10^{-6}m \approx 1170m\mu .$$

(b)   For the dark spots:

$$b_2 - b_4 = \Delta b = .362 = \frac{r_1^2}{2\lambda} - \frac{r_1^2}{4\lambda} = \frac{r_1^2}{4\lambda}$$

Then $\lambda = \dfrac{r_1^2}{4\Delta b}$. Therefore, $\lambda = \dfrac{r_1^2}{4 \times .362} = \dfrac{(.8\times10^{-3})^2}{1.448}$

$$= 442 \; m\mu .$$

(c) The first bright spot appeared at b_1.

$$b_1 = \frac{r_1^2}{\lambda} = \frac{(.8x10^{-3})^2 m^2}{1.17x10^{-6} m} \approx 54.7 \text{ cm.}$$

(d) First dark spot appeared at b_2.

$$b_2 = \frac{r_1^2}{2\lambda} = \frac{(.8x10^{-3})^2}{2x442x10^{-9}} = \frac{.64x10^3}{884} = \frac{640}{884} = .724m$$

$$= 72.4 \text{ cm.}$$

THE CORNU SPIRAL

● **PROBLEM** 11-21

Using an arrangement like that of Figure 1, prove that
the intensity at P, if the obstacle AO is removed, is four
times the intensity at this point with the obstacle in the
position shown.

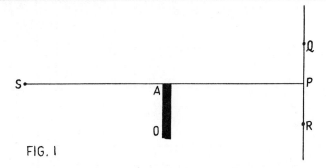

FIG. I

Solution: With the obstacle removed, the whole wave-
front is effective, and the resultant amplitude at P =
AB, in Figure 2, which represents the Cornu Spiral.

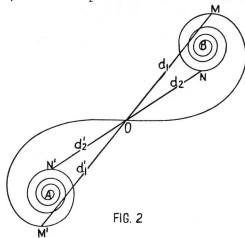

FIG. 2

With the obstacle in position, the resultant amplitude at

281

P = OB, in Figure 2.   Since the distance OB = the distance
AO, the distance AB = twice the distance OB.   Then, since
the intensity is proportional to the square of the amplitude, the required ratio

$$= \frac{AB^2}{OB^2} = \frac{4OB^2}{OB^2} = \frac{4}{1} \ .$$

● **PROBLEM** 11-22

Using Cornu's spiral plot a straight-edge diffraction
pattern where ρ_o = 100cm, r_o = 200cm, and λ = 6000Å   (ρ_o
is the distance from source to obstacle, r_o is the distance
from obstacle to screen, and λ is the wavelength of light),
plot intensity against distance x as measured on the screen.
Label the distances x for the first three maxima.

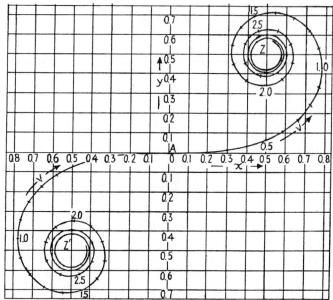

FIG. I – CORNU'S SPIRAL, A PLOT OF THE FRESNEL INTEGRALS

Solution: Use of the Cornu spiral is helpful in solving
problems in Fresnel diffraction (i.e., when source and
screen are not infinitely distant from the aperture
plane).   The electric field at a point on the screen is
given by

$$E_p = \frac{E_o}{2(\rho_o+r_o)} \ e^{i(k(\rho_o+r_o)-\omega t)} \int_{u_1}^{u_2} e^{\frac{i\pi u^2}{2}} du \int_{v_1}^{v_2} e^{\frac{i\pi v^2}{2}} dv$$

where E_o is the source strength; ρ_o is the distance from

282

the source to the aperture surface; r_o is the distance
from the aperture surface to the screen, $k = 2\pi/\lambda$; λ the
wavelength; $\omega = 2\pi f$; f the frequency; t is the time
variable and

$$u \equiv y \left[\frac{2(\rho_o + r_o)}{\lambda \rho_o r_o} \right]^{1/2}$$

$$v \equiv z \left[\frac{2(\rho_o + r_o)}{\lambda \rho_o r_o} \right]^{1/2}$$

where y and z are the coordinates of the aperture surface
representing regions where light can pass from the source
to screen. u_1, u_2, v_1 and v_2 then represent the limits of
the aperture on the aperture surface. The Cornu spiral
then represents the two integrals. To find the intensity
pattern we need to square the resultant electric field.

To utilize the Cornu spiral we determine first the values
of u_1, u_2, v_1, and v_2 from the data given in the problem.
To investigate the pattern seen on the screen we then
determine the vectors from the Cornu spiral represented
by a particular point on the screen and the square of the
resultant vector will tell us the intensity at that point
on the screen.

For this problem, since we have a straight edge we need
only work with the y coordinate. Then we need only to
determine u_1 and u_2

$$u = y \left[\frac{2(\rho_o + r_o)}{\lambda \rho_o r_o} \right]^{1/2}$$

$$= y \left[\frac{2(100+200)}{6000 \times 10^{-8} \times 100 \times 200} \right]^{1/2}$$

$$= y \, (500)^{1/2} = 22.36y$$

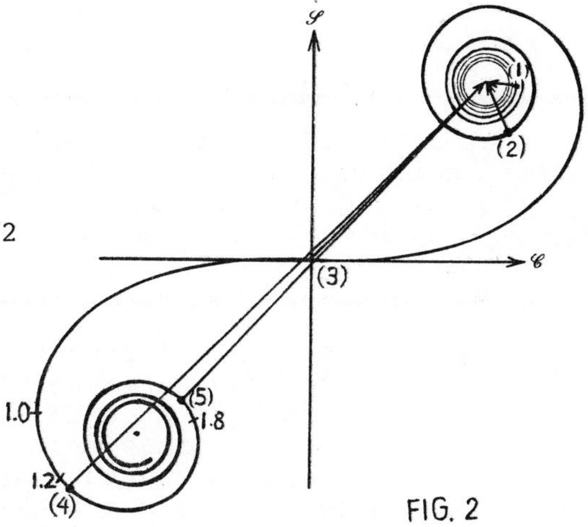

FIG. 2

so one of our points on the Cornu spiral (u_2) corresponds to y → ∞ or u_2 = ∞. u_1 will then depend on where we are located along the screen. If we are at a point in line with the edge of the screen and the source point y = 0; u_1 = 0, then our vector will start at u_2 = ∞ and go to u_1 = 0. This is equivalent to the vector labelled (3) in figure 2 and intensity point labelled (3) in figure 3. As

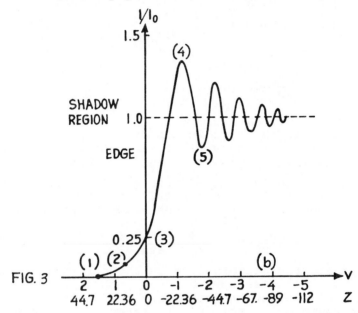

FIG. 3

we move into the shadow u_1 moves toward point (2) in figures 2 and 3. As we move into the light region we move to points (4) and (5). As we move from point (3) to (2) to (1) we can see that the vector monotonically shortens so intensity decreases monotonically. On the other hand as we progress from point (3) to (4) to (5) we see that there are maxima and minima to the vectors and therefore maxima and minima in the intensity pattern.

● **PROBLEM 11-23**

Fresnel diffraction is observed behind a wire 15 milli-meters thick which is placed 2 meters from the light source and 3 meters from the screen. If light of λ = 630 nm is used, what length C on the Cornu spiral represents the thickness of the wire?

Solution: In Fresnel diffraction we realize that since either the source or the screen is not a "large" distance away from the aperture causing the diffraction pattern, the phase of all the paths from a source point or screen point centered on the aperture are not the same so we must deal with phase differences as well as with the path dif-ferences for various paths (source-aperture-screen). This leads (see any optics text dealing with Fresnel diffrac-tion) to an expression of the electric field at a screen point P of the form

$$E_p = \frac{E_o e^{-i\omega t}}{\rho_o r_o \lambda} \int_{y_1}^{y_2} \int_{z_1}^{z_2} e^{ik(\rho+r)} dydz \qquad (1)$$

where ρ_o represents the distance from source to the center of the aperture; r_o represents the distance from center of the screen to center of the aperture; ρ and r similar distances from source and screen to some point within the aperture, λ is the wavelength of the light; ω the angular frequency of the electromagnetic wave, $k = 2\pi/\lambda$, and the y, z, dy, dz represent integration over the entire region of the aperture. Since this is a tedious integral to do, a set of dimensionless variables is then introduced, u in terms of the variable y, and v in terms of the variable z

$$u \equiv y \left[\frac{2(\rho_o+r_o)}{\lambda \rho_o r_o} \right]^{1/2} \quad ; \quad v = z \left[\frac{2(\rho_o+r_o)}{\lambda \rho_o r_o} \right]^{1/2} \qquad (2)$$

which converts E_p into

$$E_p = \frac{E_o}{2(\rho_o+r_o)} e^{i(k(\rho_o+r_o)-\omega t)} \int_{u_1}^{u_2} e^{\frac{i\pi u^2}{2}} du \int_{v_1}^{v_2} e^{\frac{i\pi v^2}{2}} dv \qquad (3)$$

and with the further definition of the Fresnel integrals as

$$C(\omega) \equiv \int_o^\omega \cos \frac{\pi \omega'^2}{2} d\omega' ; \quad S(\omega) = \int_o^\omega \sin \frac{\pi \omega'^2}{2} d\omega' \qquad (4)$$

we can write

$$\int_o^\omega e^{\frac{i\pi\omega'^2}{2}} d\omega' = C(\omega) + iS(\omega) \qquad (5)$$

by making use of Euler's equation

$$e^{ix} = \cos x + i \sin x$$

so we can then write

$$E_p = E_u [C(u) + iS(u)] \Big|_{u_1}^{u_2} [C(v) + iS(v)] \Big|_{v_1}^{v_2} \quad , \qquad (6)$$

285

where
$$E_u = \frac{E_o}{2(\rho_o + r_o)} e^{i(k(\rho_o + r_o) - \omega t)}$$

by standard calculus notation. By plotting the Fresnel integrals in the complex plane with $C(\omega)$ along the x axis

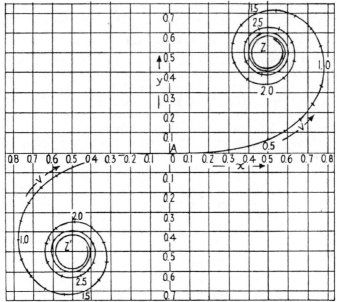

FIG. 1 — CORNU'S SPIRAL, A PLOT OF THE FRESNEL INTEGRALS

and $S(\omega)$ along the y axis, a Cornu spiral is obtained for use with Fresnel diffraction of a rectangular aperture.

To apply this to a real problem we then need to find the u_1, u_2, v_1, v_2 which are properties of the aperture and wavelengths and distance and then find the length between the two pairs of points u_1, u_2 and v_1, v_2 and perform the operation of equation (6) to determine the field strength at that point. By squaring the field strength we can determine the intensity at any point.

So in this problem we are asked to determine v for z = 15 mil; ρ_o = 2m; r_o = 3m and λ = 630nm. So we have

$$v = (15 \times 10^{-3} \times 2.54 \times 10^{-2}) \left[\frac{2(2+3)}{2 \times 3 \times 630 \times 10^{-9}} \right]^{1/2}$$

$$= 3.81 \times 10^{-4} \times 1.626 \times 10^{3} = 0.62$$

so on the screen our pattern will then be represented the square of the lengths between two points on the Cornu spiral separated by 0.62. So if v_1 is 0, v_2 is 0.62, and from the Cornu spiral we have a reasonably long length (large intensity). If on the other hand we start at the

286

equivalent position $v_1 = 1.5$ then $v_2 = 2.12$ and from our
Cornu spiral we have a small length (small intensity).
The starting points v_1 represent positions with respect to
the center point of the screen.

DOUBLE-SLIT DIFFRACTION

● **PROBLEM** 11-24

A two-slit diffraction setup is made with two slits 0.05mm
wide, spaced 0.2mm between centers.
1)   How many maxima in the two-slit interference pattern
appear between the first minima of the fringe envelope
(the single-slit diffraction pattern) on either side of
the central maximum?
2)   If the wavelength is 500nm, what is the angular separation between the second and third fringes in the interference pattern?
3)   What is the ratio of the intensity of the second
fringe to the side of the center to that of the central
fringe?

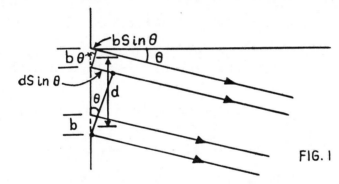

FIG. I

Solution: (1) In figure 1, b is the width of each slit
= .05mm and d is the spacing between slits = .2mm.

The amplitude of the light wave arriving at a distance x
from the slit plane and along the direction making an angle
θ with the normal to the slit plane is given by

$$y = 2A_o \frac{\sin \beta}{\beta} \cos \gamma \sin (\omega t - kx) \tag{1}$$

where $A_o = \frac{constant}{k}$, and ω is the frequency and k is the
wave vector.

The intensity is then proportional to the square of the
amplitude in (1) and we have

$$I = 4A_o^2 \frac{\sin^2 \beta}{\beta^2} \cos^2 \gamma \tag{2}$$

287

A is the amplitude of the light arriving at the screen due to one slit alone,

$$\beta = \frac{\pi}{\lambda} b \sin \theta, \text{ where } \lambda \text{ is the wavelength} \quad (3)$$
$$\text{of the light used, and } \theta$$
$$\text{is shown in Figure 1 ,}$$

and
$$\gamma = \frac{\pi}{\lambda} d \sin \theta. \quad (4)$$

$\frac{Sin^2 \beta}{\beta^2}$ represents the intensity distribution due to diffraction from a single slit. It gives maximum intensity whenever $\beta = \frac{\pi}{2}$, $\frac{3\pi}{2}$, $\frac{5\pi}{2}$ ....

or
$$b \sin \theta = \frac{\lambda}{2}, \frac{3\lambda}{2}, \frac{5\lambda}{2} \ldots \quad (5a)$$

and gives minimum intensity whenever $\beta = \pi$, 2π, 3π, ...

or
$$b \sin \theta = \lambda, 2\lambda, 3\lambda \ldots. \quad (5b)$$
$$= p\lambda \qquad p = 1,2,3,4\ldots.$$

$cos^2 \gamma$ is characteristic of the interference pattern produced by two beams of equal intensity and phase difference $\delta = 2\gamma$.

This gives maximum intensity whenever $\gamma = 0$, π, 2π, 3π ...

or
$$d \sin \theta = 0, \lambda, 2\lambda, 3\lambda\ldots \quad (6a)$$
$$= m\lambda$$

and minimum intensity when

$$\gamma = \pi/2, 3\pi/2, 5\pi/2, \ldots$$

or
$$d \sin \theta = \frac{\lambda}{2}, \frac{3\lambda}{2}, \frac{5\lambda}{2}, \ldots \quad (6b)$$
$$= (m + \frac{1}{2})\lambda. \qquad m = 0,1,2,3\ldots.$$

This shows that β and γ are not independent for a minimum of intensity as seen from equations (5b) and (6b). Actually in terms of width and separation of slits

$$\frac{\gamma}{\beta} = \frac{\frac{\pi}{\lambda} d \sin \theta}{\frac{\pi}{\lambda} b \sin \theta} = \frac{d}{b} .$$

Whenever $\frac{d}{b}$ is an integer, then for certain directions, both conditions for diffraction minima and interference maxima are satisfied

if $\qquad$ d sin θ = mλ $\qquad\qquad\qquad\qquad$ maxima

and $\qquad$ b sin θ = pλ $\qquad\qquad\qquad\qquad$ minima.

Then $\frac{d}{b} = \frac{m}{p}$ = ratio of two integers, and certain orders would be missing.

In our case

$$\frac{d}{b} = \frac{0.2}{.05} = 4$$

Hence orders 4, 8, 12, 16 would be missing. This then gives total number of maxima between the two diffraction minima on either side of central maximum as (3+3+1)=7.

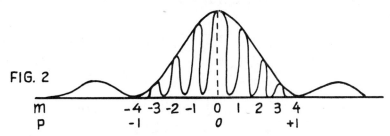

FIG. 2

m $\qquad\qquad$ -4 -3 -2 -1 $\quad$ 0 $\quad$ 1 $\,$ 2 $\,$ 3 $\,$ 4

p $\qquad\qquad\qquad$ -1 $\qquad\qquad$ 0 $\qquad\qquad$ +1

(2) Since the interference peaks are equally spaced, we can write for the second and third fringe

$$\text{d sin } \theta_2 = 2\lambda$$

$$\text{d sin } \theta_3 = 3\lambda$$

Subtracting, d(sin θ_3 - sin θ_2) = λ.

If θ_2, θ_3 are small, sin θ ≈ θ

and $\qquad$ d($\theta_3 - \theta_2$) ≈ λ

or $\qquad$ Δθ ≈ $\frac{\lambda}{d}$

or angular separation Δθ = $\frac{\lambda}{d}$ = $\frac{5\text{x}10^{-4}\text{mm}}{0.2 \text{ mm}}$ = 2.5x10^{-3} rad.

(3) To calculate the ratio of intensity of the second fringe to the side of the center to that of the central fringe, we realize that for the second fringe

$$\text{d sin } \theta = 2\lambda$$

289

or $\qquad \sin \theta = \frac{2\lambda}{d}$.

and $\qquad \beta = \frac{\pi}{\lambda} b \sin \theta = \frac{\pi}{\lambda} b \cdot \left(\frac{2\lambda}{d}\right) = 2\pi \frac{b}{d} = 2\pi \left(\frac{1}{4}\right) = \frac{\pi}{2}$.

and $\qquad \gamma = \frac{\pi}{\lambda} d \sin \theta = \frac{\pi}{\lambda} d \left(\frac{2\lambda}{d}\right) = 2\pi$.

Therefore,

$$I(\text{second fringe}) = 4A_o^2 \frac{\sin^2\beta}{\beta^2} \cos^2\gamma$$

$$= 4A_o^2 \frac{\sin^2\left(\frac{\pi}{2}\right)}{\left(\frac{\pi}{2}\right)^2} \cos^2(2\pi)$$

$$= 4A_o^2 \left(\frac{2}{\pi}\right)^2$$

and $\qquad I(\text{central fringe}) = 4A_o^2 \qquad$ because $\gamma = 0$,
$$\beta = 0 ,$$
$$\text{and } \frac{\sin\beta}{\beta} = 1$$

$\left(\text{since by L'Hospital's rule, } \lim_{\beta \to 0} \frac{\sin\beta}{\beta} = \lim_{\beta \to 0} \cos\beta \to 1\right)$.

Therefore,

$$\frac{I(\text{second fringe})}{I(\text{central fringe})} = \left(\frac{2}{\pi}\right)^2 = 0.405.$$

DIFFRACTION GRATINGS

● **PROBLEM** 11-25

The limits of the visible spectrum are approximately 400mμ for violet to 700mμ for red.
(a) Find the angular separation of the first order visible spectrum produced by a plane grating having 15,000 lines per inch, when light is incident normally on the grating.
(b) Show that the violet of the third order visible spectrum overlaps the red of the second order.
(c) What is the maximum slit width d, if the complete second order spectrum is to be formed?

Solution: (a) When light strikes the grating, different wavelengths will be scattered at different angles. In this problem, we are asked to find the angle covered by the first order visible spectrum. To find the specific angle at which each wavelength is scattered, we use the equation

290

$$d \cdot \sin \theta = m \cdot \lambda \tag{1}$$

where d is the grating spacing, θ is the angle at which the light is diffracted from the normal, m is the order number, and λ is the wavelength of the light in air.

We take the two extreme wavelengths (400mµ and 700mµ) to find the positions of the two ends of the first order spectrum. We must first find the grating spacing,

$$d = \frac{2.54 \text{ cm/inch}}{15,000 \text{ lines/inch}} = 1.69 \times 10^{-4} \text{ cm.}$$

Now, using equation (1) and letting m = 1 for the first order spectrum and $\lambda = 400$mµ $= 4 \times 10^{-5}$cm, we have

$$\sin \theta = \frac{(1) \cdot (4 \times 10^{-5} \text{cm})}{(1.69 \times 10^{-4} \text{cm})} = 0.237.$$

so $\theta = 13°40'$.

To locate the angular position on the spectrum due to the 700mµ wave, we have

$$\sin \theta = \frac{(1) \cdot (7 \times 10^{-5} \text{cm})}{(1.69 \times 10^{-4} \text{cm})} = 0.414,$$

so $\theta = 24° \, 30'$. Therefore, the angular separation of the first order visible spectrum is about

$$24°30' - 13°40' = 10°50'.$$

(b)   To show that the violet of the third order visible spectrum overlaps the red of the second order visible spectrum, we must find the angular position of the red and violet. If the red is at a greater angular position then the third order spectrum overlaps the second order spectrum.

Again, we use equation (1) to find the angular positions. For the red of the second order spectrum, we have

$$\sin \theta = \frac{(2)(7 \times 10^{-5} \text{cm})}{(1.69 \times 10^{-4} \text{cm})} = 0.828,$$

so $\theta \approx 56°$. For the violet of the third order spectrum, we have

$$\sin \theta = \frac{(3)(4 \times 10^{-5} \text{cm})}{(1.69 \times 10^{-4} \text{cm})} = 0.710,$$

so $\theta \approx 45°$.

Since the angular position for violet of the third order is less than the angular position for red of the second order, the third order spectrum will overlap the second. In general, it can be easily shown that the third order will always overlap the second, whatever the grating spacing may be.

(c) For the complete second order spectrum to be formed, the half angular separation of the central diffraction band must be at least as great as the maximum angle of deviation of the second order spectrum. It should actually be slightly greater because the intensity falls to zero at the edge of the diffraction band.

To find the maximum angle of deviation of the second order spectrum, we use wavelength λ = 700mμ and equation (1).

$$\sin \theta = \frac{(2)(7x10^{-5}cm)}{(1.69x10^{-4}cm)} = 0.828$$

$\theta = 56°$.

To find the half angular separation of the central diffraction band, we use

$$\sin \alpha = \frac{\lambda}{d} \tag{2}$$

where α is the half angular separation, λ is the wavelength of the light in air, and d is the grating spacing. Choosing the largest wavelength, 700mμ, and setting $\alpha = \theta$ in equation (2), we have

$$\sin 56° = \frac{7x10^{-5}cm}{d}$$

hence $d = 0.85x10^{-4}cm$.

So the maximum slit width d is $0.85x10^{-4}cm$ if the complete second order spectrum is to be formed.

● **PROBLEM** 11-26

A grating has 100 lines. What is the ratio of the intensity of a primary maximum to that of the first secondary maximum?

Solution: From any standard optics text we find that the intensity distribution of a grating is

$$I = \frac{I(0)}{N^2} \left(\frac{\sin\beta}{\beta}\right)^2 \left(\frac{\sin N\alpha}{\sin\alpha}\right)^2$$

where N is the number of slits, $\beta = \frac{\pi d}{\lambda} \sin \delta$, $\alpha =$

$\frac{\pi a}{\lambda}$ sin δ with λ the wavelength of the light used, d the width of each slit of the grating, a the spacing of the slits and δ the angle of interference-diffraction from a perpendicular to the grating. Since we are interested in the maxima we want $(\sin N\alpha)^2 = 1$ or for the first secondary maximum

$$N\alpha = \frac{3\pi}{2}$$

or

$$I = \frac{I(0)}{N^2} \left(\frac{\sin\beta}{\beta}\right)^2 \left(\frac{1}{\sin\alpha}\right)^2$$

Now for large N, since $\alpha = \frac{3\pi}{2N}$, α is small and we can replace sinα by α. Therefore,

$$I \approx \frac{I(0)}{N^2} \left(\frac{\sin\beta}{\beta}\right)^2 \frac{1}{\alpha^2} = \frac{I(0)}{N^2} \left(\frac{\sin\beta}{\beta}\right)^2 \left(\frac{2N}{3\pi}\right)^2$$

$$I = I(0) \left(\frac{\sin\beta}{\beta}\right)^2 \left(\frac{2}{3\pi}\right)^2$$

or

$$\frac{I_{1st\ sec\ max}}{I_{primary\ max}} = \left(\frac{2}{3\pi}\right)^2 = 0.045$$

roughly independent of the number of lines in the grating.

● **PROBLEM 11-27**

When a fairly coarse diffraction grating is placed on the table of a spectrometer adjusted in the usual way, and the slit is illuminated with sodium light ($\lambda = 5.89 \times 10^{-5}$ cm), a large number of diffraction orders are observed. If the angular separation between the central and the 20th order is 15°10', find the number of grating elements in 1 cm.

Solution: We note that

$$\lambda = 5.89 \times 10^{-7} m$$

$$\theta = 15°10'$$

$$m = 20$$

If S is the grating constant, then the grating equation for normal incidence is

$$S \sin \theta = m\lambda$$

Therefore,

$$S = \frac{m\lambda}{\sin \theta} = \frac{20 \times 5.89 \times 10^{-7}}{\sin(15°10')} = \frac{20 \times 5.89 \times 10^{-7}}{.2616}$$

$$= 450 \times 10^{-7}m = 4.50 \times 10^{-3}cm.$$

Hence number of elements/cm $= \frac{1}{S} = \frac{1}{4.5 \times 10^{-3}} = 222.$

• **PROBLEM** 11-28

The images of two wavelengths λ_1 and λ_2, which differ by a small amount, are observed in the first-order spectrum produced by a grating. If θ is the mean deflection and $\Delta\theta$ the angular separation of the two beams, prove that

$$\Delta\theta = \frac{\lambda_2 - \lambda_1}{s \cos \theta}$$ where s = grating constant.

Solution: Starting from the grating equation

$$s \sin \theta = m\lambda$$

where θ is the angle of diffraction, m is the order of diffraction, and s is the grating constant,
for m = 1
$$s \sin \theta = \lambda$$
for λ_1: $s \sin \theta_1 = \lambda_1$
for λ_2: $s \sin \theta_2 = \lambda_2$

Let $\lambda_2 > \lambda_1$. Then $\theta_2 > \theta_1$.

Let $\theta_2 = \theta_1 + \Delta\theta$.

Then, $s \sin \theta_2 = s \sin (\theta_1 + \Delta\theta) = \lambda_2$

or $\sin (\theta_1 + \Delta\theta) = \frac{\lambda_2}{s}$

or $\sin \theta_1 \cos \Delta\theta + \cos \theta_1 \sin \Delta\theta = \frac{\lambda_2}{s}.$

When $\Delta\theta$ is small,

$$\cos \Delta\theta \approx 1 \quad \text{and}$$

$$\sin \Delta\theta \approx \Delta\theta.$$

Therefore, $\sin \theta_1 \cdot 1 + \cos \theta_1 \Delta\theta = \frac{\lambda_2}{s}.$

$$\cos \theta_1 \Delta\theta = \frac{\lambda_2}{s} - \sin \theta_1$$

From the grating equation, $\sin \theta_1 = \frac{\lambda_1}{s}$. Therefore,

$$\cos \theta_1 \, \Delta\theta = \frac{\lambda_2}{s} - \frac{\lambda_1}{s} = \frac{\lambda_2 - \lambda_1}{s} \ .$$

Thus, $\quad \Delta\theta = \dfrac{\lambda_2 - \lambda_1}{s \cos \theta_1} \ .$

Since $\theta_1 \approx \theta$, $\Delta\theta = \dfrac{\lambda_2 - \lambda_1}{s \cos \theta}$

● **PROBLEM** 11-29

Prove that in the Rowland mounting shown the distance SP is proportional to the wavelength focused at P in the first order.

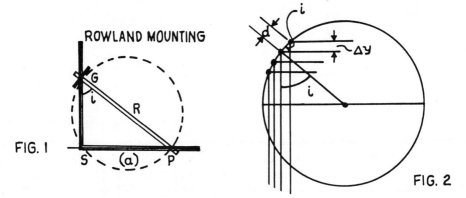

ROWLAND MOUNTING

FIG. 1

FIG. 2

Solution: In this problem we wish to find the path difference between a set of rays leaving S parallel to each other and in phase with each other at S that are reflected at the grating G and focused at P as shown in Figure 1. In this experimental arrangement, the middle of the grating must always be perpendicular to GP, thus insuring that all rays GP will have the same path length since R = GP is the radius of the grating (namely, P is the center of curvature of the grating). The path differences of the various parallel rays from S that strike the grating must be determined. As seen from S, the grating is as shown in figure 2, which is oversized to indicate the different parallel rays and the angle i (the angle that the incident path makes to the radial vector at the middle of the grating). From the drawing we can see that the angle between the horizontal and the arc segment is also i so that

$$\Delta y = d \sin i$$

where d is the distance along the arc between lines of the grating. From Figure 1 we see that

$$\sin i = \frac{\overline{SP}}{R}$$

so that the path difference Δy is related to $\overline{SP}$ as follows:

295

$$\Delta y = \frac{d}{R} \overline{SP}$$

Therefore, the total path difference between adjacent optical paths starting parallel at S and reflected at adjacent lines on the grating at G and focused at P is just

$$\Delta y = \frac{d}{R} \overline{SP}$$

Now to have a bright spot at P, all of the successive path differences Δy must be some integer multiple of the wavelength of the light.

Then, $m\lambda = \frac{d}{R} \overline{SP}$ where m is a positive integer.

So the wavelength is

$$\lambda = \frac{d}{mR} \overline{SP} \propto \overline{SP}$$

as required.

● **PROBLEM** 11-30

A certain diffraction grating has 5000 lines/cm. For a certain spectrum line a maximum is observed at 30° to the normal. What are the possible wavelengths of the line?

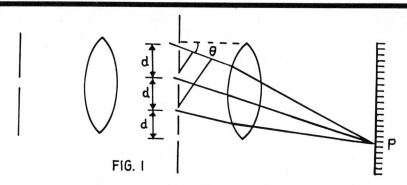

FIG. I

Solution: Consider the grating shown in figure 1. The slits of the grating are separated by a distance d. The wavelets diverging from the slits in the grating start out in phase but travel along different paths in reaching the screen. The path difference between two successive slits is d sin θ, where θ is as shown in figure 1. If this path difference is a multiple of a wavelength, the point P at the screen will be bright.

Thus   d sin θ = nλ   n = 1,2....

$$\lambda = \frac{d \sin \theta}{n}$$

Since there are 5000 lines/cm

$$d = \frac{1}{5000} \ cm$$

Substituting $d = \frac{1}{5000}$ cm and $\theta = 30°$ into the above equation for λ,

$$\lambda = \left(\frac{1}{5000} \ cm\right)\left(\sin \ 30°\right)\left(\frac{1}{n}\right)\left(10^7 nm/cm\right)$$

$$= \frac{1000}{n} \ \text{nanometers.}$$

● **PROBLEM** 11-31

A parallel beam of light comprising the wavelength range between 350mμ and 750mμ is incident normally on a plane transmission grating. Just beyond the grating is a lens of focal length 150cm. The width of the first-order spectrum, in the focal plane of the lens, is 6cm. What is the grating spacing?

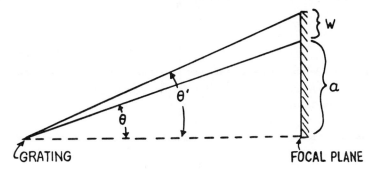

GRATING   FOCAL PLANE

Solution: A diffraction grating is an array of parallel equidistant slits which produces a diffraction pattern on a screen when it is struck by parallel light. Maxima of the diffraction pattern are produced when

$$d \cdot \sin \ \theta = m\lambda \qquad (1)$$

where d is the grating spacing, m is the order number, λ is the wavelength of the incident light, and θ is as shown in the figure.

For the lower limit of the wavelength range, we have, using equation (1),

$$d \cdot \sin \ \theta = 3.5 \times 10^{-4} mm \qquad (2)$$

and for the upper limit,

$$d \cdot \sin \ \theta' = 7.5 \times 10^{-4} mm \qquad (3)$$

If the angles θ and θ' are small, which they should be since we are only considering the first-order spectrum,

297

we can make the approximation

$$\sin \theta \overset{\sim}{\sim} \tan \theta = \frac{a}{1500mm}$$

and $\quad \sin \theta' = \tan \theta' = \frac{w + a}{1500mm}$, where w and a are as

shown in the figure.   Substituting for $\sin \theta$ and $\sin \theta'$
in equations (2) and (3), we have

$$\frac{da}{1500} = 3.5 \times 10^{-4} \tag{4}$$

and $\quad \frac{d(w+a)}{1500} = 7.5 \times 10^{-4}. \tag{5}$

Combining equations (4) and (5) leads to

$$\frac{d(w+a)}{da} = \frac{7.5 \times 10^{-4}}{3.5 \times 10^{-4}}$$

from which $\frac{w}{a} = \frac{7.5}{3.5} - 1.$

Since w = 60mm then a = 52.5mm, so from equation (4), the
grating spacing

$$d = 0.01mm.$$

● **PROBLEM** 11-32

How must a grating of alternating transmitting and opaque
spaces be constructed so that every third order will be
"missing"?

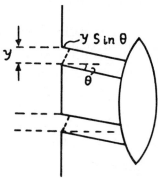

Solution: A diffraction grating consists of a number of
apertures of finite width a alternating with adjacent
opaque regions of width b.   The intensity of the transmitted beam through the diffraction grating can be obtained by using the Fresnel-Kirchoff formula applied to
Fraunhoffer diffraction.   The formula relates the
amplitude of the diffracted light to the integral of
the phase factor $e^{iky \sin \theta}$ over the aperture. where y sin θ
is the phase difference between two wave trains separated
by a distance y as shown in the figure and k is the wave

number, $= \frac{2\pi}{\lambda}$; λ the wavelength of the transmitted beam. Thus the amplitude U is given by

$$U = \int_A e^{iky \sin \theta} \, dy \; . \tag{1}$$

If there are N slits in the diffraction grating, then

$$U = \int_o^a + \int_h^{h+a} + \int_{2h}^{2h+a} + \cdots + \int_{(N-1)h}^{(N-1)h+a} e^{iky \sin \theta} \, dy \tag{2}$$

where $\quad h = a + b$ \hfill (3)

This integral can be easily evaluated since

$$\int_o^a e^{iky \sin \theta} \, dy = \frac{1}{i \, k \, \sin \theta} \left[e^{iky \sin \theta} \right]_o^a$$

$$= \frac{e^{ika \sin \theta} - 1}{i \, k \, \sin \theta} \tag{4}$$

Hence

$$U = \frac{(e^{ika \sin \theta} - 1)}{i \, k \, \sin \theta} \left[1 + e^{ikh \sin \theta} + e^{2ikh \sin \theta} \right.$$

$$\left. + \cdots + e^{ik(N-1)h \sin \theta} \right] \tag{5}$$

The term in square brackets is a geometric series and can be summed readily using the relation

$$\sum_{n=0}^{N-1} x^n = \frac{1 - x^N}{1 - x} \; .$$

Therefore,

$$1 + e^{ikh \sin \theta} + e^{2ikh \sin \theta} + \cdots$$

$$+ e^{ik(N-1)h \sin \theta} = \sum_{n=0}^{N-1} e^{ikhn \sin \theta}$$

$$= \frac{1 - e^{ikhN \sin \theta}}{1 - e^{ikh \sin \theta}} \quad , \text{ and so,}$$

$$U = \frac{\left(e^{ika \sin \theta} - 1 \right)}{ik \sin \theta} \frac{\left(1 - e^{ikNh \sin \theta} \right)}{\left(1 - e^{ikh \sin \theta} \right)} \tag{6}$$

The intensity is proportional to $|U|^2$. $|U|^2 = U \cdot U*$, where U* is the complex conjugate of U.

$$|U|^2 = \left[\frac{\left(e^{ika \sin \theta} - 1\right)}{ik \sin \theta} \frac{\left(1 - e^{ikNh \sin \theta}\right)}{1 - e^{ikh \sin \theta}}\right]$$

$$\cdot \left[\frac{\left(e^{-ika \sin \theta} - 1\right)}{-ik \sin \theta} \frac{\left(1 - e^{-ikNh \sin \theta}\right)}{\left(1 - e^{-ikh \sin \theta}\right)}\right] \quad (7)$$

$$\left(\frac{e^{ika \sin \theta} - 1}{ik \sin \theta}\right)\left(\frac{e^{-ika \sin \theta} - 1}{-ik \sin \theta}\right)$$

$$= \frac{1 - \left(e^{ika \sin \theta} + e^{-ika \sin \theta}\right) + 1}{k^2 \sin^2 \theta} \quad (8)$$

From Euler's equations, $e^{ik\phi} + e^{-ik\phi} = 2 \cos k\phi$. In addition, $2 \cos k\phi = 2 \cos \left(\frac{1}{2} k\phi + \frac{1}{2} k\phi\right)$
$= 2\left[\cos^2\left(\frac{1}{2} k\phi\right) - \sin^2\left(\frac{1}{2} k\phi\right)\right] = 2\left[1 - 2\sin^2\left(\frac{1}{2} k\phi\right)\right]$.
Therefore, $e^{ika \sin \theta} + e^{-ika \sin \theta}$

$= 2\left[1 - 2\sin^2\left(\frac{1}{2} ka \sin \theta\right)\right]$ and substituting back into equation (8),

$$\left(\frac{e^{ika \sin \theta} - 1}{ik \sin \theta}\right)\left(\frac{e^{-ika \sin \theta} - 1}{-ik \sin \theta}\right) = \frac{2\sin^2\left(\frac{1}{2} ka \sin \theta\right)}{\frac{1}{2} k^2 \sin^2 \theta}$$

$$= A\left(\frac{\sin \beta}{\beta}\right)^2, \text{ where } \beta = \frac{1}{2} ka \sin \theta \text{ and A is a}$$

constant, $= a^2$.

Similarly, it can be shown that

$$\left|\frac{1 - e^{ikNh \sin \theta}}{1 - e^{ikh \sin \theta}}\right|\left|\frac{1 - e^{-ikNh \sin \theta}}{1 - e^{-ikh \sin \theta}}\right| = B\left(\frac{\sin N\gamma}{N \sin \gamma}\right)^2,$$

where $\gamma = \frac{1}{2} kh \sin \theta$ and B is a constant.

Then since $I = C|U|^2$, C a constant,

$$I = I_o \left(\frac{\sin \beta}{\beta}\right)^2 \left(\frac{\sin N\gamma}{N \sin \gamma}\right)^2 \qquad (9)$$

where I_o is another constant.

The first term gives the amount of light from each aperture reaching any point and the second term gives the interference between disturbances from N apertures.

If a principal maximum as given by the term $\left(\frac{\sin N\gamma}{N \sin \gamma}\right)^2$ coincides with the minimum of the first term $\left(\frac{\sin \beta}{\beta}\right)^2$, then the principal maximum of that order will be absent. The principal maxima occur at

$$\gamma = n\pi \qquad\qquad n = 0,1,2... \qquad (10)$$

Therefore, principal maxima occur for

$$\frac{1}{2} kh \sin \theta = n\pi \quad \text{or} \quad h \sin \theta = \frac{2n\pi}{k} = n\lambda \qquad (11)$$

The minima occur at

$$\beta = m\pi \qquad\qquad m = 0,1,2... \qquad (12)$$

or $\qquad a \sin \theta = m\lambda \qquad\qquad\qquad\qquad (13)$

Hence the missing orders occur when

$$\sin \theta = \frac{n\lambda}{h} = \frac{m\lambda}{a} \quad \text{or when}$$

$$\frac{h}{a} = \frac{n}{m} \qquad\qquad n \text{ and } m \text{ integers}$$

$$\frac{a + b}{a} = \frac{n}{m} \qquad\qquad (14)$$

For example, when $a = b$ the missing orders are given by

$$n = 2m.$$

For the third order to be missing

$$n = 3m \qquad\qquad \text{and}$$

$$\frac{a + b}{a} = \frac{3m}{m} \qquad\qquad (15)$$

$$a + b = 3a$$
$$b = 2a \qquad\qquad (16)$$

RESOLVING POWER

Find the theoretical resolving power of a transmission echelon of 30 plates each 1cm thick. Assume an index of refraction $\mu = 1.50$ and a wavelength of 4000 Å with $d\mu/d\lambda = -900$ cm^{-1}.

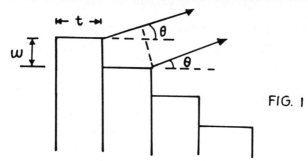

FIG. 1

Solution: A transmission echelon consists of a pile of plane parallel plates of equal thickness as shown in figure 1, each plate projecting behind the one preceding it by a small width ω. The incident plane wave front is diffracted at each step at an angle θ with respect to the normal to the face of the glass plate. The path dif- ference at angle θ between two successive diffracted beams is $(\mu-1)t+\omega\theta$. Here t is the thickness of the plate and μ is the refractive index. When the path difference is equal to $m\lambda$, interference is obtained. The equation for the echelon then is

$$(\mu-1)t + \omega\theta = m\lambda \tag{1}$$

where m is the order of the interference pattern for a single step (m an integer). The resolving power then is given by

$$R = \frac{\lambda}{\Delta\lambda} = \frac{d\theta}{d\lambda} \cdot \frac{\lambda}{d\theta} = Da$$

where a is the total aperture and $D = \frac{d\theta}{d\lambda}$ is called the dispersion. The total aperture is given by $a = N\omega$ where N is the number of plates.

Differentiating equation (1) with respect to λ gives the result $t\frac{d\mu}{d\lambda} + \omega\frac{d\theta}{d\lambda} = m$. Therefore, solving this equation for $\frac{d\theta}{d\lambda}$ yields:

$$D = \frac{d\theta}{d\lambda} = \frac{m}{\omega} - \frac{t}{\omega}\frac{d\mu}{d\lambda} \tag{2}$$

For small angles, $\theta \approx 0$; so the $\omega\theta$ term in equation (1) can be neglected. Then

$$m = \frac{(\mu-1)t}{\lambda} \tag{3}$$

Hence,

$$R = N\omega \left(\frac{m}{\omega} - \frac{t}{\omega} \frac{d\mu}{d\lambda} \right) = Nm - Nt \frac{d\mu}{d\lambda}$$

$$= N\frac{(\mu-1)t}{\lambda} - Nt \frac{d\mu}{d\lambda}$$

$$= \frac{30(1.5-1)(1cm)}{4 \times 10^{-5} cm} + (30)(1cm)\left(\frac{900}{cm}\right)$$

$$= 4.02 \times 10^{5}$$

HALF PERIOD ELEMENTS

● PROBLEM 11-34

Plane waves of monochromatic light fall normally on an
opaque screen containing an adjustable circular aperture.
The size of the aperture is altered so that, with respect
to a point P on the axis the aperture successively contains:
(a) $1\frac{1}{2}$ half-period elements (H.P.E.); (b) 1 H.P.E. ; (c)
$\frac{1}{2}$ H.P.E.; (d) $\frac{1}{4}$ H.P.E.   If the resultant intensity at P
in case (b) is taken as 1, find the intensity at P in
each of the other cases.

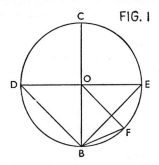

FIG. I

Solution: In Fig. 1 let BC = d_1 represent the resultant
amplitude at P due to the first H.P.E.   In Fig. 1 the arc
BFEC is proportional to the area of the first H.P.E.   Hence,
the arc BECD is proportional to $1\frac{1}{2}$ H.P.E.; the arc BFE
to 1/2 H.P.E.; and the arc BF (where BF = FE) to 1/4 H.P.E.

The corresponding amplitudes are the lengths of the line
segments drawn from point B to the endpoints of the arcs
corresponding to each number of half period elements.
These amplitudes are BD, for $1\frac{1}{2}$ H.P.E.; BE for 1/2
H.P.E.; and BF for 1/4 H.P.E.

Since OB $= \frac{BC}{2} = \frac{d_1}{2}$, and since DO also $= \frac{d_1}{2}$ (the radius of the circle centered at O shown in Figure 1), by simple geometry, using triangle BOD, it follows at once that BD

$$= \sqrt{\left(\frac{d_1}{2}\right)^2 + \left(\frac{d_1}{2}\right)^2} = \sqrt{\frac{d_1^2}{2}}$$

$= d_1/\sqrt{2}$. Also BE $= d_1/\sqrt{2}$, and using triangle BOF,

$$BF = d_1 \tan 22.5° = 0.414d_1 .$$

Hence, since the intensity varies as the square of the amplitude, and we are given that $d_1^2 = 1$, the four required intensities are (a) $|BD|^2 = 0.5$, (b) $|BC|^2 = 1$, (c) $|BE|^2 = 0.5$, and (d) $|BF|^2 = (0.414)^2 \approx 0.17$.

THE COLOR OF THE SKY

● **PROBLEM** 11-35

Why does the sky appear to be blue?

Solution: As visible (white) light travels from the sun to an observer on the earth, it is scattered by the earth's atmosphere. It has been verified by measurements made in spaceships and satellites above the atmosphere, that without the atmosphere, the sky would appear to be black except when looking directly at the sun.

Scattering occurs when waves encounter particles whose sizes are comparable with the wavelengths of light. Since the particles in the atmosphere are extremely fine dust particles whose sizes are close to that of the smaller wavelengths of visible light, the blue and violet colors are scattered much more than the reds. Even though both blue and violet lights are scattered, we see blue because, due to the sun's radiation pattern, the blue light emitted by the sun is more intense than light of any other color; so there is more blue light to be scattered than violet. Evidence that it is not only the particles of dust that scatter the light comes from the fact that over the oceans, where there are much fewer dust particles than over land, the sky still appears blue. This suggests that there are other particles in the atmosphere that scatter light other than dust. It has been shown through direct experimentation that it is possible for molecules of a gas to scatter light. Since the molecules of a gas are very small, they scatter light with small wavelengths which are, again, blue and violet.

THE HUYGEN-FRESNEL THEORY

A black screen with a circular opening of radius a is located in the xy-plane, with center at the origin. It is irradiated by a plane wave

$$\psi = \exp(ikz), \quad k = \frac{2\pi}{\lambda} \quad (\lambda = \text{the wavelength of the light used})$$

Determine the approximate zeros of intensity on the positive z-axis for z>>a.

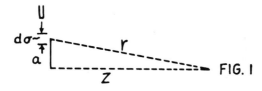

FIG. I

Solution: The amplitude of the wave on the positive z-axis which is transmitted through the opening is given by

$$\psi = A_o \int \frac{d\sigma\, e^{ikr}}{r} \quad ,$$

where $d\sigma$ is an element of surface area of the opening and r is the distance from $d\sigma$ to the observation point. This expression follows from the simple version of Huygen-Fresnel theory where the obliquity factor is taken constant (valid for (a/z)<<1). Using $d\sigma = 2\pi\rho d\rho = 2\pi r dr$,

$$\psi = A_o \int_z^{\sqrt{a^2+z^2}} \frac{e^{ikr}}{r} 2\pi r dr \quad , \quad \text{where the limits}$$

z and $\sqrt{a^2+z^2}$ are obtained as follows: The integration ranges between the minimum and maximum distances of r from the point of observation to the opening, which from inspection of Figure 1 are seen to be r = z and r = $\sqrt{a^2+z^2}$, respectively.

Then
$$\psi = 2\pi A_o \int_z^{\sqrt{a^2+z^2}} e^{ikr} dr = \frac{2\pi A_o}{ik} e^{ikr} \Big|_z^{\sqrt{a^2+z^2}}$$

$\lambda = \frac{2\pi}{k}$ and $\frac{1}{i} = -i$; therefore,

$$\psi = -iA_o\lambda\{\exp\left(ik\sqrt{a^2+z^2}\right) - \exp(ikz)\}$$

which has zeros for $\sqrt{a^2+z^2} = z + n\lambda$. This is so since
exp(ik(z+nλ)) - exp(ikz) = exp(ikz)exp(iknλ) - exp(ikz)
= exp(ikz)[exp(iknλ) - 1].

Since $\frac{2\pi}{k} = \lambda$, exp(iknλ) = exp(2πni). exp(2πni) =

cos(2πn) + i sin (2πn) = 1 for all integer values of n.
Then exp(ik(z+nλ)) - exp(ikz) = exp(ikz)(1-1) = 0.
n is a positive integer, thus $a^2+z^2 = z^2+2zn\lambda + n^2\lambda^2$. The
z^2 terms cancel and $a^2 = 2zn\lambda + n^2\lambda^2$. Therefore, z =
$\left(a^2 - n^2\lambda^2\right)/2n\lambda$.

CHAPTER 12

RESOLUTION

GRATINGS

● **PROBLEM** 12-1

> A grating has 1000 lines/mm of width. How wide must the grating be in order to resolve the mode structure of a laser beam of wavelength 6328 Å? The frequency difference between the modes is 450 MHz?

Solution: The resolution of a diffraction grating is given by the expression

$$R = \frac{\lambda}{\delta\lambda} = mN,$$

where N is the total number of lines required, and m is the order of the interference pattern.

Since $c = \nu\lambda$ (c = the speed of light in a vacuum, and ν and λ represent the frequency and wavelength, respectively, of light),

$$\nu = c\left(\frac{1}{\lambda}\right)$$

Differentiating ν with respect to λ gives the result

$$\delta\nu = \frac{-c}{\lambda^2}\,\delta\lambda$$

Then, since $\delta\nu = 450$ MHz,

$$= 450\ (10^6)\ \text{Hz},$$

ignoring the minus sign,

$$\delta\lambda = \frac{\delta\nu\lambda^2}{c} = \frac{\left(450 \times 10^6\ \text{sec}^{-1}\right)\left(6328\ \overset{\circ}{\text{A}}\right)^2\left(10^{-8}\ \frac{\text{cm}}{\overset{\circ}{\text{A}}}\right)^2}{3 \times 10^{10}\ \text{cm/sec}}$$

$$= 6.007 \times 10^{-11} \text{ cm} = 0.006 \text{ Å}$$

If m = 1,

$$N = \frac{6328 \text{ Å} \left(10^{-8} \frac{\text{cm}}{\text{Å}}\right)}{6.007 \times 10^{-11} \text{ cm}} = 1.053 \times 10^6 \text{ lines}$$

Therefore the width must be:

$$W = \frac{N}{1000 \text{ lines/mm}} = \frac{1.053 \times 10^6 \text{ lines}}{10^3 \text{ lines/mm}}$$

$$W = 1053 \text{ mm} \cong 105 \text{ cm}.$$

● **PROBLEM 12-2**

The two sodium D lines are about 6Å apart.   If only a grating with 400 rulings is available,

(a) What is the lowest order possible in which D lines are resolved?

(b) How wide must the grating be?

Solution: (a) The formula relating resolving power, $\frac{\lambda}{\Delta\lambda}$, to the grating is $mN = \frac{\lambda}{\Delta\lambda}$ where m is the diffraction order and N is the number of lines. For sodium light, λ = 589 nm, $\Delta\lambda$ = (589.6 - 589) nm = 0.6nm, and N is given to be 400. Therefore, substituting these values in the above equation and solving for m gives the result

$$m = \frac{589 \text{ nm}}{(.6\text{nm}) \ 400} = 2.45.$$

However, the order must be an integer, so the lowest order at which the D lines are resolved is the smallest integer above 2.45, namely, 3.

(b) As we have seen, the resolving power depends only on the number of lines of the grating and the order used; so the physical width of the grating is immaterial and is governed by how far apart we decide to rule the slits.

● **PROBLEM 12-3**

The wavelengths of the sodium D lines are 589.593 mμ and 588.996 mμ.

(a) What is the minimum number of lines a grating must have in order to resolve these lines in the first order spectrum?

(b) How large a prism is needed to resolve these lines, if the rate of change of index with wavelength, at a wavelength of 589 mµ, is 5.30 x 10^{-5} per millimicron?

Solution: (a) Use the formula

$$N = \frac{\lambda}{m\Delta\lambda}$$

where N is the number of lines in a grating, λ is the wavelength of light passing through the grating, $\Delta\lambda$ is the difference in wavelengths of light passing through the grating, and m is the order.   Using λ = 588.996 mµ, m = 1, and $\Delta\lambda$ = 589.593 mµ - 588.996 mµ = 0.597 mµ, the result is

$$N = \frac{588.996 \text{ mµ}}{0.597 \text{ mµ}} = 987 \text{ lines.}$$

(b) The formula used in this part of the problem is

$$B = \frac{\lambda}{\Delta\lambda\left(\frac{dn}{d\lambda}\right)}$$

where B is the size of the prism, λ is the wavelength of light passing through the grating, $\Delta\lambda$ is the difference in wavelengths of light passing through the grating and $\frac{dn}{d\lambda}$ is the rate of change of the index with respect to wavelength.   Substituting the given data into the equation results in:

$$B = \frac{589 \text{ mµ}}{0.597 \text{ mµ x } 5.30 \text{ x } 10^{-5} \text{ mµ}^{-1}}$$

$$B = 1.87 \text{ x } 10^{7} \text{ mµ} = 1.87 \text{ cm.}$$

● **PROBLEM** 12-4

The sodium doublet has wavelengths of 589.0 nm and 589.6 nm. If a diffraction grating is blazed so as to be used best in the second order, at least how many lines must the grating have in order to resolve the doublet?

Solution: The chromatic resolving power of any optical instrument is defined as $\lambda/\Delta\lambda$ where λ is the wavelength of the primary spectral line and $\Delta\lambda$ is the difference in wavelengths between the two spectral lines to be resolved.

Now for N slits, neglecting diffraction, the intensity of radiation as a function of the angle θ, measured from the normal of the plane of the slits, is

$$I(\theta) \text{ is proportional to } \left(\frac{\sin N\alpha}{\sin \alpha}\right)^{2} \qquad (1)$$

309

where

$$\alpha = \frac{\pi a}{\lambda} \sin \theta \qquad (2)$$

a is the slit separation, and λ is the wavelength of the monochromatic light. Clearly the minima will occur whenever $(\sin N\alpha/\sin \alpha)^2 = 0$ or when $N\alpha$ is an integer multiple of π.

To get maximum resolution the maximum of the 589.0 nm line must coincide with the minimum of the 589.6 nm line, or vice-versa (the Rayleigh condition for resolution).

Defining the angular dispersion as $\Delta\theta/\Delta\lambda$; and with a grating the relation between θ and λ is

$$m\lambda = a \sin \theta \qquad (3)$$

Now differentiating equation (3) with respect to θ yields

$$m\Delta\lambda = a \cos \theta \Delta\theta \qquad (4)$$

or

$$\Delta\theta = \frac{m\Delta\lambda}{a \cos \theta} \qquad (5)$$

Differentiating equation (2) with respect to θ gives

$$\Delta\alpha = \frac{\pi a}{\lambda} \cos \theta \Delta\theta \qquad (6)$$

and the conditions on maxima and minima require that

$\Delta\alpha = \pi/N$, i.e., $\Delta\alpha$ represents the effective width of the spectral line as the angular distance between zeros of intensity on either side of a principal maximum. Therefore equation (6) can be written as follows:

$$\frac{\pi}{N} = \frac{\pi a}{\lambda} \cos \theta \Delta\theta \qquad (7)$$

or

$$\Delta\theta = \frac{\lambda}{Na \cos \theta} \qquad (8)$$

and equating the expressions given for $\Delta\theta$ in equations (5) and (8) gives

$$\frac{\lambda}{Na \cos \theta} = \frac{m\Delta\lambda}{a \cos \theta} \qquad (9)$$

or

$$\frac{\lambda}{\Delta\lambda} = mN. \qquad (10)$$

Substituting the given values $\lambda = 589$ nm, $\Delta\lambda = 0.6$ nm, and $m = 2$ into equation (10) gives the result

$$N = \frac{\lambda}{\Delta\lambda m} = \frac{589.0 \text{ nm}}{(0.6 \text{ nm})(2)} = 491 \text{ lines.}$$

310

A grating 1 cm wide has 4000 lines/cm. Half of it is illuminated by a line source S at the focus of lens L_1. Spectra are recorded on a film F at the focus of lens L_2. The line source emits light of two wavelengths λ_1 = 6400.0 Å and λ_2 = 6400.5 Å, and the focal length of L_2 is 1 m.

    (a) At what angle θ is the third-order spectrum of light of wavelength λ_1 formed?

    (b) What is the distance between the third order spectra of λ_1 and λ_2 on the film F?

    (c) Are these two wavelengths resolved in third order?

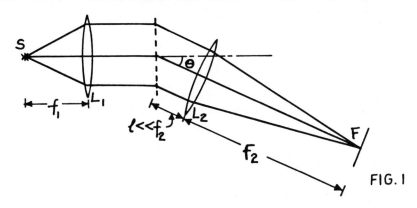

FIG. I

<u>Solution:</u> (a) The principal maxima for gratings, assuming that the incident light falls on the grating at right angles, is given by the equation

$$d \sin \theta = m \cdot \lambda \qquad\qquad (1)$$

where d is the distance between each slit of the grating, m is the order of the particular principal maximum, and λ is the wavelength of the incident ray in air.

    Substituting the given values (d = $\frac{1}{4000}$ cm, the order m = 3, and the wavelength λ = 6400.0 Å = 6.4000 x 10^{-5} cm) into equation (1), gives the following result:

$$\left(\frac{1}{4000} \text{ cm}\right) \sin \theta = (3)(6.4000 \times 10^{-5} \text{ cm}),$$

$$\sin \theta = 0.768$$

from which $\qquad\qquad \theta = 50.175°$

If λ = 6400.5 Å = 6.4005 x 10^{-5} cm was used in equation (1) and solved for the angle, the result would be θ = 50.180°. Therefore such a small difference in wavelengths results in a very small difference in the positions of their maxima.

311

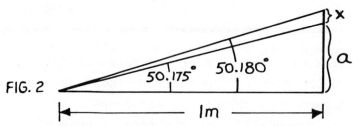

FIG. 2

(b) Since the distance between the gratings and the screen is about the same as the focal length of L_2 , and the angle between the two spectras is also known, then by simple laws of trigonometry, the distance between the two spectras can be found, as illustrated by Figure 2.

$$\tan 50.175° = \frac{a}{1 \text{ m}} \tag{2}$$

$$\tan 50.180° = \frac{x + a}{1 \text{ m}} \tag{3}$$

Solving for x in equation (2) and (3) gives:

$$x = \tan 50.180° - \tan 50.175° = 2.128 \times 10^{-4} \text{ meters}$$

$$= 0.2128 \text{ millimeters}$$

(c)   To find whether the lines are resolved in the third order, it is necessary to find whether or not

$$\Delta\lambda > \frac{\lambda}{Nm} \ .$$

N denotes the number of lines of the grating which are illuminated.   Here, since it is given that half of the grating is illuminated by the source S,

$$N = \frac{1}{2} \ (1 \text{ cm}) \left(\frac{4000 \text{ lines}}{\text{cm}}\right) = 2000 \text{ lines.}$$

If $\Delta\lambda$ is $> \frac{\lambda}{Nm}$, then the two wavelengths are resolved.   We know that $\Delta\lambda = 6400.5 \text{ Å} - 6400.0 \text{ Å} = 0.5 \text{ Å}.$ Now,

$$\frac{\lambda}{Nm} = \frac{6400 \text{ Å}}{2000 \cdot 3} = 1.07 \text{ Å} \ .$$

Since $\Delta\lambda$ is not $> \frac{\lambda}{Nm}$, the lines are not resolved.   If we illuminated the whole grating, and went to the fourth order, they would be resolved.

THE FABRY-PEROT INTERFEROMETER

● **PROBLEM** 12-6

What is the resolving power of a Fabry-Perot interferometer, in which the mirror separation is 15 mm, for a reflecting power of 75%? For a reflecting power of 90%? (Assume $\lambda = 5000$ Å.)

Solution: The resolving power of a Fabry-Perot interferometer is given by

$$R = \frac{\lambda}{\delta\lambda} = \frac{2.6 \; p_o \; \sqrt{r}}{1 - r} \quad ,$$

where $p_o = 2d/\lambda$, d is the separation of the mirrors of the interferometer, and r is the reflection coefficient of the surface film. Here $r = 0.75$, $d = 15$ mm $= 1.5$ cm, and $\lambda = 5000 \; \overset{o}{A} \left(10^{-8} \; \frac{cm}{\overset{o}{A}} \right) = 5 \times 10^{-5}$ cm.

Then

$$R = \frac{2.6 \left[\dfrac{2(1.5 \; cm)}{5 \times 10^{-5} \; cm} \right] \sqrt{0.75}}{1 - 0.75}$$

$$R = 540,400 \quad .$$

If $r = 0.90$, then

$$R = \frac{2.6 \left[\dfrac{2(1.5 \; cm)}{5 \times 10^{-5} \; cm} \right] \sqrt{0.90}}{1 - 0.90}$$

$$R = 1,479,946 \quad .$$

● **PROBLEM** 12-7

A certain spectral line at 3440 $\overset{o}{A}$ is actually a doublet with a separation of 0.0063 $\overset{o}{A}$. If the mirrors of a Fabry-Perot interferometer have a reflecting power of 85%, what must their separation be in order to resolve the doublet? What resolving power is indicated? Assume the width of each component is less than 0.002 $\overset{o}{A}$.

Solution: The resolving power of a Fabry-Perot interferometer is given by the expression

$$R = \frac{\lambda}{\delta\lambda} = \frac{2.6 \; p_o \; \sqrt{r}}{1 - r}$$

where

$$p_o = \frac{2d}{\lambda} \quad ;$$

d is the separation of the mirrors of the interferometer, and r is the reflection coefficient of the surface film. Here, $r = 0.85$.

The above equation is based on the Rayleigh criterion

313

and assumes that the intensity contributed by one bright fringe falls off to $4/\pi^2$ at the midway point between the two maxima. That is, the expression for the intensity in the interference pattern for light differing in phase by δ from light at the central maximum is given by

$$I = \quad I = \frac{I_{max}}{1 + \left[4r^2/\left(1-r^2\right)^2\right]\sin^2(\delta/2)}$$

The resolving power is given by

$$\frac{I}{I_{max}} = \frac{4}{\pi^2} = 0.405 = \frac{1}{1 + F\sin^2(\delta/2)} \quad ,$$

where $F = \dfrac{4r^2}{\left(1-r^2\right)^2}$ and is called the coefficient of finesse.

In this case,

$$\frac{\lambda}{\Delta\lambda} = \frac{3440\ \overset{\circ}{A}}{0.0063\ \overset{\circ}{A}} = \frac{(2.6)\left(\frac{2d}{\lambda}\right)\sqrt{r}}{1-r} = 5.46 \times 10^5$$

Solving for d yields

$$d = \frac{(3440\ \overset{\circ}{A})\,(1 - .85)\,(3440\ \overset{\circ}{A})}{(0.0063\ \overset{\circ}{A})\,(2.6)\,(2)\,(\sqrt{0.85})}$$

$$d = 5.877 \times 10^7\ \overset{\circ}{A}\left(10^{-8}\ \frac{cm}{\overset{\circ}{A}}\right) = 0.588\ cm$$

Thus, the mirrors must be 0.588 cm apart, and the resolving power is 5.46×10^5.

● **PROBLEM** 12-8

A Fabry-Perot interferometer is to be used to resolve the mode structure of a He-Ne laser operating at 6328 $\overset{\circ}{A}$. The frequency separation between the modes is 150 MHZ. What plate spacing is required in (a) R = 0.9; (b) R = 0.999 (where R denotes the reflectance of the mirrors)?

Solution: From another problem, it is known that the transmitted intensity in a Fabry-Perot interferometer is given by the equation

$$I_t = \frac{I_i}{1 + \left(\frac{2r}{1-r^2}\right)^2\sin^2(\delta/2)} \tag{1}$$

314

$$\delta = \frac{4\pi}{\lambda} nd \cos \theta \tag{2}$$

where I_t is the transmitted intensity, I_i is the incident intensity, r is the reflection coefficient (R, the reflecting power is equal to $|r|^2$), δ is the optical path difference between successively multiple reflected rays, n is the index of refraction of the interferometer, d is the thickness, λ is the wavelength of light used, and θ is the angle of refraction in the interferometer.

Resolving power can be measured such that if the primary wavelength λ has a transmitted intensity equal to $0.5\ I_i$ at some angle θ, then the resolved wavelength $\lambda + \Delta\lambda$ will also have a transmitted intensity of $0.5\ I_i$ at the same angle θ. From equation (1), this condition states

$$\left(\frac{2r}{1-r^2}\right)^2 \sin^2\left(\delta/2\right) = 1 \tag{3}$$

$$\sin\left(\delta/2\right) = \frac{1-r^2}{2r} \tag{4}$$

If the fringes are reasonably sharp, the change of $\delta/2$ from a multiple of π will be small and the sine can be replaced by its argument. If in addition, $\Delta\delta$ is defined as the change in path length in going from the maximum of λ to the maximum of $\lambda + \Delta\lambda$, then to move to the position of half intensity $\delta = \frac{\Delta\delta}{2}$, equation (4) becomes

$$\sin \frac{1}{2} \frac{\Delta\delta}{2} \sim \frac{\Delta\delta}{4} = \frac{1-r^2}{2r} \tag{5}$$

differentiating δ as given by equation (2) with respect to θ yields

$$\Delta\delta = -\frac{4\pi nd}{\lambda} \sin\theta\ \Delta\theta \tag{6}$$

and if the maximum for $\lambda + \Delta\lambda$ is to occur at this same angular separation $\Delta\theta$, then since the condition for a maximum is

$$m\lambda = 2nd \cos\theta \tag{7}$$

differentiating with respect to θ yields

$$m\Delta\lambda = -2nd \sin\theta\ \Delta\theta \tag{8}$$

Dividing equation (7) by equation (8) gives the result

$$\frac{\lambda}{\Delta\lambda} = \frac{2nd \cos\theta}{-2nd \sin\theta\ \Delta\theta} = \frac{-\cos\theta}{\sin\theta\ \Delta\theta}.$$

Now substituting the expression for $\sin\theta\ \Delta\theta$ given by equation (6),

315

$$\frac{\lambda}{\Delta\lambda} = \frac{-\cos\theta}{-\lambda\Delta\delta}(4\pi nd) = \frac{4\pi nd}{\lambda\Delta\delta}\cos\theta.$$

Substituting $\Delta\delta = 4\left(\frac{1-r^2}{2r}\right)$ (from equation (5)),

$$\frac{\lambda}{\Delta\lambda} = \frac{4\pi nd\ (2r)}{4\lambda(1-r^2)}\cos\theta = \frac{2nd}{\lambda}\frac{\pi r}{(1-r^2)}\cos\theta \qquad (9)$$

Now with nearly normal incidence, $\cos\theta \cong 1$; and with a Fabry-Perot interferometer as two silvered films in air, $n = 1$; thus, remembering that the definition of resolving power is $\lambda/\Delta\lambda$, equation (9) becomes

$$RP = \frac{\lambda}{\Delta\lambda} = \frac{2\,d\,\pi\,r}{\lambda(1-r^2)} \qquad (10)$$

The following relation is also known:

$$f\lambda = c, \qquad (11)$$

where f, λ, and c represent the frequency, wavelength, and speed, respectively, of light.

Thus, for $\lambda = 632.8$ nm, the frequency is

$$f = c/\lambda = \frac{3 \times 10^8}{632.8 \times 10^{-9}} = 4.74 \times 10^{14} \text{ hertz} \qquad (12)$$

From equation (11) we also find by differentiating with respect to λ,

$$\Delta f = \frac{c\,\Delta\,\lambda}{\lambda^2} = f\frac{\Delta\lambda}{\lambda} \qquad (13)$$

(ignoring minus signs)

or $\quad \dfrac{\lambda}{\Delta\lambda} = \dfrac{f}{\Delta f} = \dfrac{4.74 \times 10^{14}}{150 \times 10^6} = 3.16 \times 10^6 \qquad (14)$

Now, part (a) of the problem says $R = r^2 = 0.9$ so from equations (10) and (14)

$$d = \frac{f}{\Delta f}\frac{\lambda(1-R)}{2\pi\sqrt{R}}$$

$$= \frac{3.16 \times 10^6 \times 632.8 \times 10^{-9} \times .1}{2\pi\sqrt{.9}} = 0.0335 \text{ m}$$

$$= 3.35 \text{ cm}$$

316

and for part (b), R = 0.999 and

$$d = \frac{3.16 \times 10^6 \times 6.32.8 \times 10^{-9}(.001)}{2\pi\sqrt{.999}} = 3.18 \times 10^{-4} \text{ m}$$

$$= 0.318 \text{ mm.}$$

● **PROBLEM** 12-9

A Fabry-Perot interferometer is used with yellow light of two wavelengths of equal intensity $\lambda_1 = 6000$ Å, and $\lambda_2 = 5994$ Å. At what approximate value of the total order number, m, will they be just resolvable if R = 0.85?

Solution: In a Fabry-Perot interferometer the fringes are observed when the phase difference

$$\Delta = \frac{4\pi d}{\lambda}$$

is a multiple of 2π, where λ is the wavelength of light used and d is the separation between the two reflecting surfaces. Equating 2π to $\frac{4\pi d}{\lambda}$ gives the result

$$m\lambda = 2d \tag{1}$$

where m is an integer.
    Differentiating equation (1) gives

$$m\Delta\lambda + \lambda\Delta m = 0 \tag{2}$$

Hence

$$\frac{\lambda}{\Delta\lambda} = \frac{m}{\Delta m} \quad , \tag{3}$$

where the omitted minus sign signifies that the order number increases as λ decreases. When λ changes by 2π, m changes by 1, and the result is

$$\frac{2\pi}{(\Delta' - \Delta)} = \frac{1}{\Delta m} \tag{4}$$

Solving for Δm in equation (4) yields

$$\Delta m = \frac{\Delta' - \Delta}{2\pi} \quad .$$

Substituting this value for Δm into equation (3) gives the result

$$\frac{\lambda}{\Delta\lambda} = \frac{2\pi m}{\Delta' - \Delta} \tag{5}$$

317

As the wavelength difference increases, the mth order fringe for one wavelength λ will approach the $(m + 1)^{st}$ order of the other wavelength λ'. Thus, the order to which the two lines are resolvable will be yielded by equation (5) with $\Delta' - \Delta$ corresponding to the minimum resolvable phase increment satisfying the Rayleigh Criterion.

$$m = \frac{1}{2\pi} \, 2.076 \, \frac{(1 - R)}{\sqrt{R}} \, \frac{\lambda}{\Delta\lambda} \tag{6}$$

$$= \frac{6000 \, \overset{\circ}{A}}{6\overset{\circ}{A}} \, \frac{(1 - 0.85)}{\sqrt{0.85}} \, \frac{2.076}{2\pi} \approx 54$$

Another criterion, called the Taylor Criterion, states that the two lines are resolved if the two separate intensity curves intersect at

$$I = \frac{1}{2} \, I_{max}$$

in the same order. Then the separation of the maxima in the mth order is equal to the full width at half maximum. (see Fig.)

Half width at half maximum is given by $\Delta_{1/2}$, so

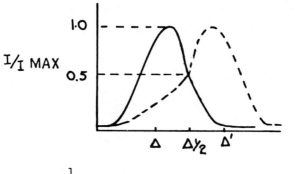

$$\frac{1}{2} = \frac{1}{1 + F \, \sin^2\left(\frac{\Delta_{(1/2)}}{2}\right)} \tag{7}$$

$F = \dfrac{4R}{(1 - R)^2}$ and is known as the coefficient of finesse.

For small angles $\Delta_{1/2}$, $\sin \Delta_{1/2}$ is approximately equal to $\Delta_{1/2}$ and so, equation (7) becomes $\dfrac{1}{2} = \dfrac{1}{1 + F\left(\frac{\Delta_{1/2}}{2}\right)^2}$.

Then $1 + F\left(\dfrac{\Delta^2_{1/2}}{4}\right) = 2$ and so, $\Delta_{1/2} = \dfrac{2}{\sqrt{F}}$

Hence,

$$\Delta' - \Delta = 2\Delta_{1/2} = 2 \times \frac{2}{\sqrt{F}} = \frac{2(1 - R)}{\sqrt{R}}$$

318

from the equation $\Delta = \frac{4\pi}{\lambda} d$, $\frac{1}{\lambda} = \frac{1}{4\pi d} \Delta$ and so,

$$\frac{1}{\lambda'} - \frac{1}{\lambda} = \frac{1}{4\pi d} (\Delta' - \Delta) = \frac{1}{4\pi d} \left[\frac{2(1 - R)}{\sqrt{R}} \right] = \frac{1}{2\pi d} \frac{(1 - R)}{\sqrt{R}}$$

$$\frac{\Delta\lambda}{\lambda} = \frac{\lambda}{2\pi d} \frac{(1 - R)}{\sqrt{R}}$$

From equation (1), $d = \frac{m\lambda}{2}$ and so, $\frac{\Delta\lambda}{\lambda} = \frac{1}{\pi m} \frac{(1 - R)}{\sqrt{R}}$

where m is the order of the fringe.

Solving for m,

$$m = \frac{\lambda}{\Delta\lambda} \frac{1}{\pi} \frac{(1 - R)}{\sqrt{R}}$$

$$= \frac{6000 \overset{\circ}{A}}{6 \overset{\circ}{A}} \frac{1}{\pi} \frac{0.15}{\sqrt{0.85}} = 51.78$$

$$= 52$$

Thus the result depends on the criterion chosen.

• **PROBLEM** 12-10

A Fabry-Perot interferometer has a plate spacing d and a plate reflectance R. Find the minimum frequency difference, $f - f'$, and the corresponding minimum wavelength difference, $\lambda - \lambda'$, between two barely resolvable spectrum lines.

Solution: A Fabry-Perot interferometer consists of two optically flat, partially reflecting plates of glass or quartz. The separation between the plates, d, can be varied mechanically. The interferometer is very useful in determining the fine structure of spectral lines, and also serves as a resonant cavity for a laser. The incident beam with intensity I_o is split into multiple beams which are partially reflected and transmitted.

If R is the reflectance and T is the transmittance, then the transmitted beam has an intensity of

$$I_T = I_o \frac{T^2}{|1 - Re^{i\Delta}|^2} \tag{1}$$

where Δ is the total phase change due to partial reflection and partial transmission and is related to d by the equation

$$\Delta = \frac{4\pi}{\lambda} d \cos \theta + \delta_r .$$

Here δ_r is the phase change due to partial reflection.

319

Then,

$$\frac{I_T}{I_o} = \frac{T^2}{\left(1 - Re^{i\Delta}\right)\left(1 - Re^{-i\Delta}\right)} \quad ,$$

where

$1 - Re^{-i\Delta}$ is the complex conjugate of $1 - Re^{i\Delta}$

Expanding,

$$\frac{I_T}{I_o} = \frac{T^2}{1 - R\left(e^{i\Delta} + e^{-i\Delta}\right) + R^2} \quad .$$

Using Euler's equations, $e^{i\Delta} = \cos \Delta + i \sin \Delta$, and $e^{-i\Delta}$
$= \cos \Delta - i \sin \Delta$,

$$\frac{I_T}{I_o} = \frac{T^2}{1 - 2R \cos \Delta + R^2}$$

adding and subtracting 2R from the denominator gives the
result

$$\frac{I_T}{I_o} = \frac{T^2}{(1 - R)^2 + 2R(1 - \cos \Delta)}$$

$$= \frac{T^2}{(1 - R)^2} \times \frac{1}{1 + \frac{2R}{(1 - R)^2}(1 - \cos \Delta)}$$

$$\cos \Delta = \cos \left(\frac{\Delta}{2} + \frac{\Delta}{2}\right) = \cos^2 \frac{\Delta}{2} - \sin^2 \frac{\Delta}{2} = 1 - 2 \sin^2 \frac{\Delta}{2}$$

(making use of the trigonometric identity $\sin^2\theta + \cos^2\theta = 1$)
and so,

$$\frac{I_T}{I_o} = \frac{T^2}{(1 - R)^2} \frac{1}{1 + \frac{4R}{(1 - R)^2} \sin^2 \frac{\Delta}{2}} \tag{2}$$

If $I_{T_{max}}$ is the maximum transmitted intensity, then

$$I_{T_{max}} = I_o \frac{T^2}{(1 - R)^2} \qquad \text{occurs at } \Delta = 2m\pi \tag{3}$$

Then,

$$\frac{I_T}{I_{T_{max}}} = \frac{\dfrac{I_T}{I_o}}{\dfrac{I_{T_{max}}}{I_o}} \quad .$$

Substituting in the expression for $\frac{I_T}{I_o}$ and $\frac{I_{T_{max}}}{I_o}$ given in

equations (2) and (3) respectively, $\frac{I_T}{I_{T_{max}}} =$

$$\left[1 + \frac{4R}{(1 - R)^2} \sin^2 (\Delta/2) \right]^{-1} \qquad (5)$$

Now, assuming the spectrum consists of two closely spaced frequencies with equal intensity, the intensity of the resultant fringe pattern will be a combination of the two fringe systems corresponding to the two frequencies (see fig. 1).

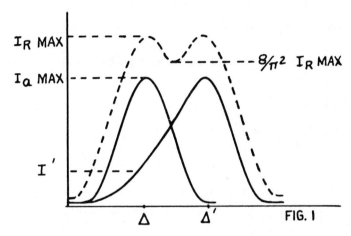

FIG. 1

The two individual fringe systems peak at Δ and Δ' given by

$$\Delta = \frac{4\pi d}{\lambda}$$

and $\Delta' = \frac{4\pi d}{\lambda'}$, where normal viewing is assumed. Both

peaks having equal intensity, the resultant shown in figure 1 also peaks at Δ and Δ' with equal irradiance.

$$I_{R_{max}} = I_{a_{max}} + I'$$

where I' is the intensity of the second fringe at the first peak position. Since the intensities of the two peaks are equal, the intensity of the second fringe at the first peak position is the same as the intensity of the first fringe at the second peak position Δ'.

$$I_{R_{max}} = I_{a_{max}} + I_{a_{max}} \left[1 + \frac{4R}{(1 - R)^2} \sin^2 \frac{\Delta' - \Delta}{2} \right]^{-1} \qquad (6)$$

The intensity at the saddle point is

321

$$I_S = 2 I_{a_{max}} \left[1 + \frac{4R}{(1 - R)^2} \sin^2 \frac{\Delta' - \Delta}{4} \right]^{-1} \tag{7}$$

because the intensities of the two fringe systems are equal and the saddle point occurs at

$$\frac{\Delta' - \Delta}{2} .$$

Using the Rayleigh Criterion,

$$\frac{I_{R_{max}}}{I_S} = \frac{\pi^2}{8} \approx \frac{1}{.81} \tag{8}$$

and making use of the small angle approximation

$$\sin \theta \sim \theta \text{ and equations (6), (7) and (8),}$$

the result obtained is:

$$I_S = .81 \ I_{R_{max}} \quad \text{or}$$

$$\frac{2}{1 + F \left(\frac{(\Delta' - \Delta)}{4} \right)^2} = 0.81 \left[1 + \frac{1}{1 + F \left(\frac{(\Delta' - \Delta)}{2} \right)^2} \right]$$

where

$$F = \frac{4R}{(1 - R)^2} .$$

$$\frac{2}{0.81} = \left[1 + \frac{1}{1 + F \left(\frac{\Delta' - \Delta}{2} \right)^2} \right] \left[1 + F \left(\frac{\Delta' - \Delta}{4} \right)^2 \right] =$$

$$1 + \frac{F}{16} (\Delta' - \Delta)^2 + \frac{1 + \frac{F(\Delta' - \Delta)^2}{16}}{1 + \frac{F(\Delta' - \Delta)^2}{4}}$$

multiplying both sides of this equation by

$$1 + F \left(\frac{\Delta' - \Delta}{4} \right)^2$$

gives the result

$$\frac{2}{0.81} \left(1 + \frac{F(\Delta' - \Delta)^2}{4} \right) = 1 + \frac{F(\Delta' - \Delta)^2}{4} + \frac{F}{16} (\Delta' - \Delta)^2$$

$$+ \frac{F^2}{64} (\Delta' - \Delta)^4 + 1 + \frac{F(\Delta' - \Delta)^2}{16}$$

Expanding this equation,

$$\frac{2}{0.81} + \frac{F(\Delta' - \Delta)^2}{1.62} = 2 + \frac{3F(\Delta' - \Delta)^2}{8} + \frac{F^2}{64} (\Delta' - \Delta)^4$$

or

$$\frac{F^2}{64} (\Delta' - \Delta)^4 + F\left(\frac{3}{8} - \frac{1}{1.62}\right) (\Delta' - \Delta)^2 + \left(2 - \frac{2}{0.81}\right) = 0 .$$

Multiplying both sides of this equation by 64 gives the result

$$F^2(\Delta' - \Delta)^4 - 15.5 \, F(\Delta' - \Delta)^2 - 30.016 = 0$$

This is a quadratic in $(\Delta' - \Delta)^2$ and can be solved easily by the use of the quadratic formula,

$$(\Delta' - \Delta)^2 = \frac{-b \pm \sqrt{b^2 - 4ac}}{2a} ,$$

where a, b, and c are the coefficients multiplying

$(\Delta' - \Delta)^4$ $(\Delta' - \Delta)^2$ and 1, respectively, in the above

equation. Substituting the values a $= F^2$, b $= (-15.5F)$

and C $= -30.016$ into the quadratic equation gives the result

$$(\Delta' - \Delta)^2 \cong \frac{17.24}{F^2} ,$$

where the positive physical root is taken.

Then

$$\Delta' - \Delta \cong \frac{4.152}{\sqrt{F}} \sim \frac{2.076}{\sqrt{R}} (1 - R)$$

This is the minimum phase increment separating two just resolvable fringes. Also,

$$\frac{1}{\lambda'} - \frac{1}{\lambda} = \frac{2.076}{4\pi} \frac{1}{d} \frac{(1 - R)}{\sqrt{R}}$$

or

$$\Delta\lambda = \frac{0.17\lambda^2}{d} \frac{(1 - R)}{\sqrt{R}}$$

where the minus sign which indicates only that the order

323

increases when λ decreases, is omitted. In addition, since

$$f = c/\lambda$$

(f and c are the frequency and speed, respectively, of light), the answer immediately obtained is

$$\Delta f = 0.17 \frac{c}{d} \frac{(1 - R)}{\sqrt{R}} .$$

PRISMS

● **PROBLEM** 12-11

(a) What is the smallest wavelength difference that can be resolved at a wavelength of 500 mµ by a prism spectrometer using an equiangular prism 5 cm on a side, constructed of the silicate flint glass whose dispersion curve is given in the graph? (b) What is the width of a grating ruled with 2000 lines/cm that has the same limit of resolution in the second order as does the prism?

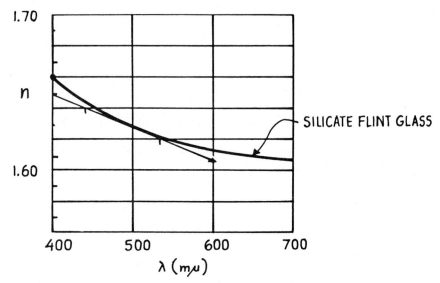

Solution: (a) The resolving power of a prism is given by

$$\frac{\lambda}{\delta\lambda} = B \frac{dn}{d\lambda}$$

where B is the length of the base, = 5 cm,

$$\lambda = 500 \text{ mµ} \left(10^{-7} \frac{cm}{mµ}\right) = 5 \times 10^{-5} \text{ cm}$$

and from the graph (using a tangent line at λ = 500 mµ to obtain the slope) we obtain

$$\frac{dn}{d\lambda} = \frac{1.650 - 1.615}{(600 - 400)\text{mµ}} = 1.75 \times 10^{-4} \text{ mµ}^{-1}$$

324

$$= 1.75 \times 10^3 \text{ cm}^{-1}$$

Then

$$\delta\lambda = \lambda \Big/ B\left(\frac{dn}{d\lambda}\right) = \frac{(5 \times 10^{-5} \text{ cm})}{(5 \text{ cm})(1.75 \times 10^3 \text{ cm}^{-1})} = 5.71 \times 10^{-9} \text{ cm}$$

$$\delta\lambda = 5.71 \times 10^{-2} \text{ m}\mu$$

(b) The resolving power of a grating and of a prism is defined by the ratio $\lambda/\delta\lambda$, where $\delta\lambda$ is the smallest wavelength difference that produces resolved images. For a diffraction grating,

$$\lambda/\delta\lambda = mN \ ,$$

where N is the total number of lines of the grating and m is the order of the interference pattern.

Thus if $mN = \lambda/\delta\lambda = B\frac{d\mu}{d\lambda} = 5 \text{ cm } (1.75 \times 10^3 \text{ cm}^{-1}) = 2N$

then

$$N = 4375 \text{ Lines, and}$$

the grating width $= \dfrac{4375 \text{ lines}}{2000 \text{ lines/cm}}$

$$= 2.19 \text{ cm}.$$

● **PROBLEM 12-12**

Calculate the chromatic resolving power of a prism having

$$\frac{d\mu}{d\lambda} = -1200$$

(where μ denotes the refractive index of the prism and λ the wavelength of light in cm), and a base of 5 cm.

Will this be adequate to resolve the sodium D lines, the wavelengths of which are 5890 Å and 5896 Å?

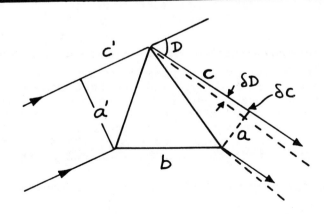

Solution: From the figure, $c + c' = \mu b$. since any optical path between the two successive positions a' and a of the wavefront, must be the same. Now suppose the wavelength is decreased by $\delta\lambda$, the optical path length of the base of the prism is then $(\mu + \delta\mu)b$ and the emergent wavefront must now turn through an angle $\delta D = \frac{\lambda}{a}$ in order that the image it forms may be just resolved (i.e., the criterion for the resolution is given by $\delta D = \lambda/a$). Since $\delta D = \delta c/a$, this increases the length of the upper ray by a length λ

Then

$$c + c' + \lambda = (\mu + \delta\mu)b$$

Subtracting the equation $c + c' = \mu b$ from this equation gives the result $\lambda = b\delta\mu$

or

$$\frac{\lambda}{\Delta\lambda} = \frac{bd\mu}{\mu}$$

which is a general relationship for the resolving power of a prism.

If $\frac{d\mu}{d\lambda} = -1200$, and b = 5 cm,

then

$$\frac{\lambda}{\delta\lambda} = b\frac{du}{d\lambda} = 5(1200) = 6000$$

since

$$\frac{\lambda}{\delta\lambda} = 6000,$$

the sodium D lines, which have a separation of 6 Å clearly can be resolved.

● **PROBLEM** 12-13

The slit of a spectrometer is replaced by two narrow slits whose centers are 0.03 cm apart, and the spectrometer is adjusted in the usual way. The focal length of the collimator is 20 cm. If an adjustable rectangular aperture is placed in front of the objective and gradually narrowed, find the maximum width of this aperture at which it is no longer possible to detect two images, when yellow sodium light is used.

Solution: Two images can be detected until the width of

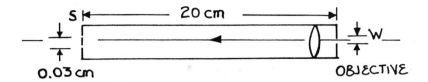

S |← —————— 20 cm —————— →| W
OBJECTIVE
0.03 cm

the single slit diffraction pattern, given by

$$\theta = \lambda/W \ ,$$

becomes equal to or greater than the separation of the two slits, namely 0.03 cm.

From the figure, trigonometrically,

$$\tan \theta = \frac{\text{opposite}}{\text{adjacent}} = \frac{0.03 \ \text{cm}}{20 \ \text{cm}} \approx \theta$$

(this approximation is valid for small θ).

So:

$$\theta = \frac{0.03 \ \text{cm}}{20 \ \text{cm}} = (1.5 \times 10^{-3}) = \frac{\lambda}{W}$$

Yellow sodium light has a wavelength

$\lambda = 5890 \ \overset{\circ}{A}$, so solving for the width W gives:

$$W = \frac{\lambda}{(1.5 \times 10^{-3})} = \frac{5890 \ \overset{\circ}{A} \left(10^{-8} \ \frac{\text{cm}}{\overset{\circ}{A}} \right)}{(1.5 \times 10^{-3})}$$

$$W = 0.039 \ \text{cm} = 0.39 \ \text{mm}$$

● **PROBLEM** 12-14

What will be the dispersion of a 60° prism made of light flint at 7000 $\overset{\circ}{A}$? At 4000 $\overset{\circ}{A}$? If the prism face is completely filled with light, how wide must it be if the sodium doublet (5890 $\overset{\circ}{A}$ and 5896 $\overset{\circ}{A}$) is to be exactly resolved? For light flint $n_{4000 \ \overset{\circ}{A}} = 1.593$, $n_{6000 \ \overset{\circ}{A}} = 1.573$, and $n_{7000 \ \overset{\circ}{A}} = 1.568$ (where n denotes the index of refraction).

Solution: The angular dispersion of a prism is $d\theta/d\lambda$ where θ is the angle of incidence into the prism.   This can be written as

$$d\theta/d\lambda = (d\theta/dn)(dn/d\lambda) \tag{1}$$

and from tables, $dn/d\lambda$ for any glass prism can be found, so $d\theta/dn$ must be determined in order to find $d\theta/d\lambda$.   If θ is the angle of incidence and ϕ is the angle of refraction,

327

then Snell's law states:

$$n = \frac{\sin \theta}{\sin \phi} \tag{2}$$

For the special case of minimum deviation, $\phi = \alpha/2$ where α is the prism angle. Then ϕ is a constant, so, differentiating n with respect to θ,

$$\frac{dn}{d\theta} = \frac{\cos \theta}{\sin \phi} \tag{3}$$

$$\frac{d\theta}{dn} = \frac{\sin \phi}{\cos \theta} = \frac{\sin \alpha/2}{\cos \theta} \ . \tag{4}$$

This is the rate of change of θ at the first surface; because of the symmetry at minimum deviation the total rate of change will be 2 $d\theta/dn$, so equation (1) becomes

$$\frac{d\theta}{d\lambda} = \frac{2 \sin \alpha/2}{\cos \theta} \ dn/d\lambda \ . \tag{5}$$

Now at minimum deviation,

$$n = \frac{\sin \theta}{\sin \alpha/2} \tag{6}$$

Therefore, from the value of n at wavelengths of 400, 600, and 700 nm, we can find cos θ:

$$\sin \theta_{400} = n \sin \alpha/2 = 1.593 \sin\left(60/2\right) = 1.593 \times 1/2$$

$$. = 0.7965$$

$$\cos \theta_{400} = \sqrt{1 - \sin^2 \theta_{400}} = 0.605$$

$$\sin \theta_{600} = 1.573 \times 1/2 = 0.7865$$

$$\cos \theta_{600} = \sqrt{1 - \sin^2 \theta_{600}} = 0.618$$

$$\sin \theta_{700} = 1.568 \times 1/2 = 0.784$$

$$\cos \theta_{700} = \sqrt{1 - \sin^2 \theta_{700}} = 0.621 \ .$$

Thus we have at λ = 700 nm,

$$\frac{d\theta}{dn} = 2 \ \frac{\sin 60/2}{0.621} = 1.610$$

at λ = 600 nm,

$$\frac{d\theta}{dn} = 2 \ \frac{\sin 60/2}{0.618} = 1.618$$

and at λ = 400 nm,

$$\frac{d\theta}{dn} = 2 \ \frac{\sin 60/2}{0.605} = 1.653 \ .$$

From a table of indices of refraction of glass; for light flint:

λ nm	dn/dλ (cm^{-1})
400	1880
589	577
700	351

Using the values of $\frac{dn}{d\lambda}$ from this table in equation (5) gives the dispersions: for λ_{nm} = 400,

$$\frac{d\theta}{d\lambda} = 3108 \text{ radians/cm;}$$

for λ_{nm} = 700, $\frac{d\theta}{d\lambda}$ = 565 radians/cm.

Now to find the length of the side of the prism to resolve the sodium doublet, use

$$\frac{\lambda}{\Delta\lambda} = B\left(dn/d\lambda\right) \tag{7}$$

where $\Delta\lambda$ is the separation of the spectral lines and B is the length of the side of the prism.

Thus,

$$B = \frac{\lambda/\Delta\lambda}{dn/d\lambda} = \frac{589 \text{ nm}/.6 \text{ nm}}{577 \text{ cm}^{-1}} = 1.7 \text{ cm} .$$

RESOLVING POWER

• **PROBLEM** 12-15

Assuming that the resolving power of the eye is one minute of arc, at what distance can a black circle 6 inches in diameter be seen on a white background?

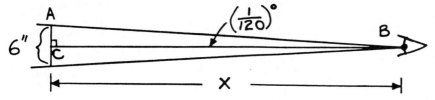

Solution: If the resolving power of the eye is one minute of arc, then that is equivalent to an angle of $\left(\frac{1}{60}\right)^\circ$. In the figure, the distance X is found trigonometrically. In right triangle ABC, we have

$$\tan\left(\frac{1}{120}\right)^\circ = \frac{\text{opposite side}}{\text{adjacent side}} = \frac{3 \text{ in.}}{X}$$

from which X is found to be approximately 20,626.5 inches or

X = 1719 feet.

If a normal eye cannot separate two objects (or images) subtending an angle of less than 1.5 minutes, approximate the magnifying power that is necessary to make use (visually) of the full resolving power of a telescope whose objective has a diameter of 40 inches. (Assume a mean wavelength of 5.5×10^{-5} cm.)

Solution: The minimum angle of resolution for a telescope is given by the Rayleigh criterion, $\theta_1 = 1.220 \ \lambda/a$ where a is the diameter of the circular aperture which limits the beam from the primary image (in this case, 40 inches) and $\lambda = 5.5 \ (10^{-5})$ cm. The magnifying power of a telescope is defined as the ratio between the angle subtended at the eye by the final image, θ_1, and the angle subtended at the eye by the object itself, θ. That is, $M = \theta/\theta_1$. The minimum value of θ_1 is given by $\theta_1 = 1.220 \ \lambda/a$, and the minimum value of θ is 1.5 minutes or $4.363 \ (10^{-4})$ radians.

Thus,

$$M = \frac{\theta}{\theta_1} = \frac{\theta a}{1.220\lambda} =$$

$$\frac{(4.363 \times 10^{-4} \text{ radians}) (40 \text{ inches} \left[\frac{2.54 \text{ cm}}{\text{inch}} \right])}{(1.220)(5.5 \times 10^{-5} \text{ cm})}$$

or   M = 660.6 .

All except a narrow ring around the periphery of a telescope objective is masked off by an opaque disk coaxial with the telescope placed directly in front of it (see figure 1).

(a) Does this produce a dark patch in the central region of the image of a distant object formed in the focal plane of the telescope?

(b) How, if at all, will the presence of the disk in front of the light affect the resolving power? Explain your answer with the aid of phasor diagrams.

Solution: (a) The effect of the presence of an opaque disk

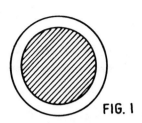

FIG. 1

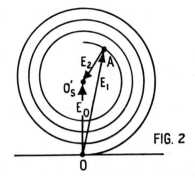

FIG. 2

in front of telescope objective, which leaves a narrow transparent annular region, can be understood by applying Babinet's principle. It states that the scalar optical disturbance at any image point through an unobstructed aperture is equal to the sum of scalar optical disturbances from two complementary screens whose apertures add up to the unobstructed aperture.

If E_0 is the scalar optical disturbance at the image center due to the total aperture of the telescope, and E_1 is the scalar optical disturbance at the image center due to a smaller aperture, then the scalar optical disturbance, E_2, produced at the image center due to an opaque disk whose diameter is the same as the smaller aperture, and placed in the telescope is $E_2 = E_0 - E_1$.

Now, E_2 is not zero unless $E_0 = E_1$; hence some light will always be present in the central region of the image so long as the opaque disk does not cover the lens completely.

In terms of phasor diagram, this is shown in figure 2.

If E_0 represents the amplitude of the disturbance due to the unobstructed telescope objective and A represents the point on the edge of the opaque disk, then $AO's = E_2$ represents the optical disturbance due to the transparent ring and is not zero.

(b) Since the resolving power of a telescope depends upon the aperture of the objective, it will be affected by the presence of the disk in front of the aperture.

The minimum resolvable angular separation is given by

$$\Delta\theta = 1.22 \frac{\lambda}{D}$$

and the resolving power for an image forming system is generally defined as $\frac{1}{\Delta\theta}$.

Therefore,

$$R \cdot P = \frac{D}{1.22 \ \lambda}$$

331

Hence, a reduction in diameter D implies a reduction in the Resolving Power.

AIRY PATTERNS

Plot a graph of the light intensity across the center line of two star images of equal intensities. Assume the centers are separated by a distance equal to the radius of the first dark ring of the Airy pattern.

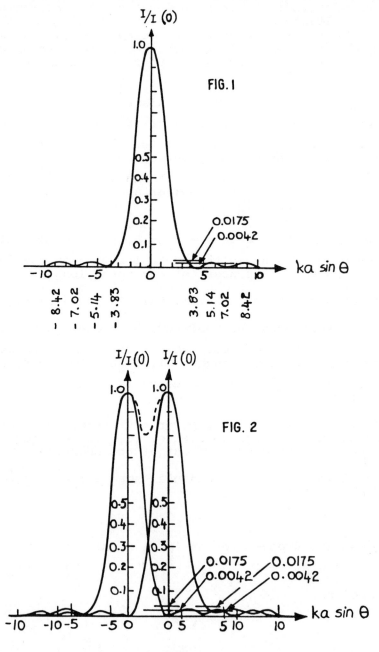

FIG. 1

FIG. 2

Solution: Two stars of equal light intensity will produce
incoherent light, so at a detector the resultant pattern
will be the sum of the intensities of the light. Thus, in
figure 1 we have an Airy pattern for one star. The other
star will also have an Airy pattern but it will be displaced
from the first star by the radius of the first dark ring.
Figure 2 is then the superposition of the Airy pattern of
the two stars. To find the intensity of the combination,
we need only add the ordinates of the two curves. Outside the two maxima is essentially just the intensity pattern of one star while between the two maxima there is a
substantial interaction of the two intensities, but still a
detectable minimum, as shown by the dashed line in figure 2.

● **PROBLEM** 12-19

Neglecting the effects of irregularities of refraction in
the earth's atmosphere, calculate the linear separation of
two objects on the moon's surface that could just barely be
resolved by the 200-inch Mount Palomar telescope.

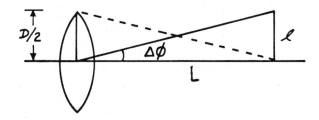

Solution: According to Rayleigh's Criterion, two Airy patterns are just barely resolvable when the central peak of
one coincides with the first minimum of the other.
This just corresponds to a separation equivalent to the
angular radius of the Airy disk:

$$(\Delta\phi)_{min} = \frac{1.22\ \lambda}{D}$$

where λ is the wavelength of light and D is the diameter of
the objective.

If L is the distance between the moon and the earth
then

$$(\Delta\phi_{min}) \cong \tan\ (\Delta\phi)$$

(this approximation is valid for small $\Delta\phi$) $= \frac{\ell}{L}$

where ℓ is the linear separation between two objects on
the moon's surface. Hence, assuming L = 3.86 x 10^{10} cm and
λ = 5500 Å gives:

$$\ell = \frac{1.22\ \lambda L}{D}$$

$$= \frac{1.22(550\ x\ 10^{-9}\ m)\ ((3.86\ x\ 10^{10}\ cm)\ (1\ m/100\ cm))}{(200\ inches)\ (2.54\ cm/inch)}$$

ℓ = 0.51 meters

333

Two pinholes 1.5 mm apart are placed in front of a bright light source and viewed through a telescope with its objective stopped down to a diameter of 4 mm. What is the maximum distance from the telescope at which the pinholes can be resolved? Assume $\lambda = 550$ nm.

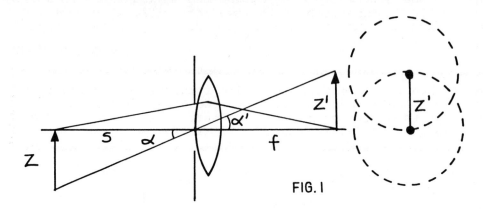

FIG. I

Solution: The two pinholes separated by a distance Z placed at a distance S from the objective produce the images separated by Z' at a distance f from the objective. The image consists of two circular Airy discs produced by the diffraction at the circular aperture of the objective, whose diameter is D. The radius of the Airy disc is

$$1.22 \; \frac{f\lambda}{D}$$

where λ is the wavelength of light used. According to the Rayleigh criterion, the two images are just resolvable when the radius of the Airy disc is equal to the separation between the two images:

$$z' = 1.22 \; \frac{f\lambda}{D} \tag{1}$$

From basic optics,

$$\frac{z'}{f} = \frac{Z}{S} \tag{2}$$

Combining equations (1) and (2) to solve for S gives:

$$S = \frac{ZD}{1.22\lambda} = \frac{0.15 \text{ cm x } 0.4 \text{ cm}}{1.22 \text{ x } 550 \text{ x } 10^{-7} \text{ cm}}$$

$$= 894.19 \text{ cm} \approx 900 \text{ cm} .$$

334

DETERMINATION OF OBJECT AND IMAGE SIZES

● **PROBLEM** 12-21

An object on the stage of a microscope is examined by light of wavelength 410 nm. The numerical aperture of the objective is 0.5 and normal magnification is used. Find the diameter of the object if its geometrical image is the same size as the central disk in the diffraction pattern that a point object would produce.

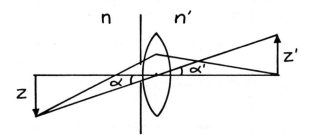

Solution: If the object is in a medium of refractive index n and the image is formed in a medium of index of refraction n', Snells law states:

$$n' \sin \alpha' = n \sin \alpha$$

where α and α' are the angles of incidence and refraction, respectively.

Given that the image diameter is the same as that of the central disk in the diffraction pattern,

$$z' = \frac{0.61\lambda}{n' \sin \alpha'} \tag{1}$$

Using Abbe's sine condition,

$$\frac{z'}{z} = \frac{n \sin \alpha}{n' \sin \alpha'} \tag{2}$$

Equations (1) and (2) give:

$$z = z' \left(\frac{n' \sin \alpha'}{n \sin \alpha} \right) = \left(\frac{0.61\lambda}{n' \sin \alpha'} \right) \left(\frac{n' \sin \alpha'}{n \sin \alpha} \right) =$$

$$\frac{0.61\lambda}{n \sin \alpha} .$$

The quantity $n \sin \alpha$ is called the numerical aperture of the objective. Assuming normal incidence, $\alpha = 90°$ and $\sin \alpha = 1$,

$$z = \frac{0.61 \times 410 \times 10^{-7}}{0.5} \text{ cm} = 500.2 \text{ nm}.$$

Normal magnification means that the size of the retinal
image is increased by the ratio of the Maximum Numerical
Aperture of the objective to the maximum numerical aperture
of the eye. Thus, the size of the image is enhanced
250 x 0.5 = 125 times.

● **PROBLEM** 12-22

The headlights of a distant automobile may be considered as
point sources. The distance between the two headlights is
1.5 m and the automobile is 6000m (about 4 mi) away.

(a) What is the distance between the centers of the
images of the sources on the retina?

(b) What is the radius of the central diffraction disk
of each image?

(c) What is the maximum distance at which the headlights
could be resolved? Assume a wavelength of 550 mµ and a
pupillary radius of 1 mm.

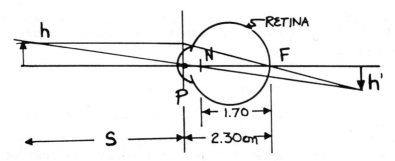

Solution: (a) The relaxed eye is adjusted to focus distant
objects on the retina, which is a distance of about 2.30 cm
from the principal plane, and 1.70 cm from the nodal point
(see figure).   Thus the magnification

$$m = \frac{image\ size}{object\ size} = h'/h = 1.70\ cm/s.$$

Here S = 6000 m$\left(10^2\ \frac{cm}{m}\right)$= 6 x 10^5 cm and h = 1.5 m $\left(10^2\ \frac{cm}{m}\right)$

   = 1.5 x 10^2 cm

So the distance between the centers of the images of the
sources on the retina is:

$$h' = h\left(\frac{1.70\ cm}{S}\right) = \frac{(1.5\ x\ 10^2\ cm)\ (1.70\ cm)}{(6\ x\ 10^5\ cm)}$$

$$h' = 4.25\ x\ 10^{-4}\ cm$$

(b) The first minimum in the diffraction pattern of a
circular aperture of diameter d, assuming Fraunhofer conditions, is given by sin θ = 1.22 λ/d. For small θ, this

336

minimum reduces to $\theta = 1.22$ /d where

$\lambda = 550$ (10^{-7}) cm and d $= 0.2$ cm,

since the pupillary radius $= 1$ mm.

Thus,

$$\theta = \frac{1.22 \ (550) \ (10^{-7}) \ cm}{0.2 \ cm} = 3.355 \ (10^{-4}) \ rad$$

Since $S' = 2.30$ cm, the radius of the diffraction disk is given by

$$r = (\theta)S' = 7.7 \ (10^{-4}) \ cm$$

(c) The Rayleigh criterion states that two objects can be resolved if they have an angular separation given by $\theta_R = 1.22 \ \lambda/d = 3.355 \ (10^{-4})$ rad.

Thus, $\theta_R = 3.355 \ (10^{-4}) = 1.5$ meters/S

or $\qquad$ S $= 4471$ meters.

COMPUTATION OF APERTURE DIAMETERS

● **PROBLEM** 12-23

What diameter of aperture, of a telescope, would be required to resolve the components of a double star, whose linear separation is 100 million Km and whose distance from the earth is 10 light years? $(\lambda = 5000 \ \overset{\circ}{A})$.

EARTH $\qquad \theta \qquad$ 10 LIGHT YEARS $\qquad 10^8 km$

Solution: First determine the angular separation of the two stars as seen from the earth.

From the figure and simple trigonometry:

$$\tan \theta = \frac{opposite \ side}{adjacent \ side} \approx \theta$$

(since θ is small, this approximation is valid).

$$\theta = \frac{\left(10^8 \ km\right) \left(10^3 \ \frac{m}{km}\right)}{10 \ yr \ \left(3 \times 10^8 \ \frac{m}{sec}\right)\left(3600 \ \frac{sec}{hr}\right)\left(24 \ \frac{hr}{day}\right)\left(365.25 \ \frac{days}{yr}\right)}$$

$\theta = 1.056 \times 10^{-6}$ radians

Now the Rayleigh criterion for resolution is:

$$\theta_R = 1.22 \frac{\lambda}{d}$$

where λ is the wavelength of light observed and d is the telescope diameter.

Solving for d gives:

$$d = \frac{1.22\lambda}{\theta_R}$$

$$= \frac{(1.22)(5000 \text{ Å } [10^{-8} \text{ cm/Å}])}{(1.056 \times 10^{-6} \text{ rad})}$$

$$d = 57.8 \text{ cm}$$

● **PROBLEM 12-24**

In a pin hole camera the distance of the pin hole from the photographic plate is 10 cm. What is the diameter of the pinhole that should be made to obtain the sharpest resolution of the image of the sun ($\lambda \approx 5000$ Å)?

Solution: Consider a source of light P on the sun. The image of this source is spread over a region of linear dimension $\delta x = D + \ell(\lambda/D)$, where D is the pin hole diameter. The first term in δx is due to the spread of rays over the pinhole opening. As a result of diffraction there is a spread in angle of approximately λ/D upon passing through the opening, and hence an additional increment in δx of about $(\lambda/D)\ell$.

The sharpest resolution occurs when δx is a minimum. In order to find the minimum value for δx, differentiate the equation

$$\delta x = D + \ell(\lambda/D)$$

with respect to D and equate it to zero.

$$\frac{d(\delta x)}{dD} = 1 - \frac{\ell\lambda}{D^2} = 0 .$$

Then $D^2 = \ell\lambda$ or $D = (\ell\lambda)^{1/2}$. Substituting in the given values $\ell = 10$ cm and $\lambda = 5000$Å $= 5000 \times 10^{-8}$ cm, gives the result $D = 0.0224$ cm $= 0.224$ mm.

Hence, to obtain the sharpest resolution of the image

of the sun, the diameter of the pinhole should be about
0.22 mm.

ANGULAR SEPARATION

● **PROBLEM** 12-25

Find the angular separation, in seconds of arc, of the
closest double star which can be resolved by the Mount
Wilson reflecting telescope, which has a mirror 100 inches
in diameter.

Solution: For a circular aperture, the Rayleigh condition
for resolution is:

$$\theta = \frac{1.22\lambda}{a} \qquad (1)$$

where θ is the minimum angle in radians for resolution, λ
is the wavelength of the light used, and a is the diameter
of the aperture. Taking λ = 5600 Å and a = 100 inches
gives:

$$\theta = \frac{(1.22)[5600 \text{ Å}(10^{-8} \text{ cm/Å})]}{(100 \text{ inches})(2.54 \text{ cm/inch})}$$

$$= 2.69 \times 10^{-7} \text{ radians} = 5.55 \times 10^{-2} \text{ seconds of arc.}$$

ANGULAR RESOLUTION

● **PROBLEM** 12-26

What is the theoretical limit on angular resolution for
telescopes with objective diameters of 100 mm, 1 m, and
5m   (λ = 550 nm)?

Solution: Rayleigh's criterion for resolving two objects
states that two equally bright objects (point sources) could
just be resolved by an optical system if the central maximum
of the diffraction pattern of one source coincides with the
first minimum of the other. This is equivalent to the condition that the distance between the centers of the diffraction patterns must equal the radius of the central disk of
the Airy pattern. This happens when the angular resolution is

$$\sin \alpha \stackrel{\sim}{\sim} \alpha$$

(this approximation is valid for small α) $= \dfrac{1.22 \ \lambda}{D}$

where D is the diameter of the objective, and λ is the
wavelength of light used.

Given λ = 550 $\times$ 10^{-7} cm, for D = 100 mm,

$$\alpha = \frac{1.22 \times 550 \times 10^{-7} \text{ cm}}{100 \times 10^{-1} \text{ cm}} = 6.71 \times 10^{-6} \text{ rad}$$

for D = 1 m,

$$\alpha = \frac{1.22 \times 550 \times 10^{-7} \text{ cm}}{100 \text{ cm}} = 6.71 \times 10^{-7} \text{ rad}$$

for D = 5 m,

$$\alpha = \frac{1.22 \times 550 \times 10^{-7} \text{ cm}}{500 \text{ cm}} = 1.34 \times 10^{-7} \text{ rad} .$$

CHAPTER 13

ABSORPTION AND SCATTERING

TRANSMITTANCE

• **PROBLEM** 13-1

A certain type of glass has an absorption coefficient of $\alpha = 0.05$ mm^{-1}. What percentage of light is transmitted through a plate 4 mm thick?

<u>Solution</u>: When light passes through an absorber, its intensity is reduced according to the following equation:

$$I = I_o e^{-\alpha x}$$

where I is the light intensity after travelling a distance x through the absorber, I_o is the incident intensity of light, and α is the absorption coefficient.

Then

$$\frac{I}{I_o} = e^{-\alpha x}$$

and

$$\frac{I}{I_o} \times 100 = \text{percentage of light transmitted.}$$

In this problem, $\alpha = 0.05$ mm^{-1} and x = 4 mm.

Then

$$\frac{I}{I_o} = e^{-(.05)(4)} = .8187$$

and thus, the percentage of light transmitted is

81.87%.

A 0.1 mm thick neutral density filter gives 70% transmission. If the filter were 2 mm thick, what would be its transmittance?

Solution: Upon passing through an absorber, the intensity of a light beam is reduced according to the following equation:

$$I = I_o e^{-\alpha x} \qquad (1)$$

where I is the light intensity after traveling a distance x in the absorber, I_o is the incident intensity of the light, and α is the absorption coefficient. The transmittance of an absorber is the percentage of light (intensity) that remains after passing through the absorber

$$\left(\frac{I}{I_o} \times 100 \right).$$

For the given filter, the transmittance is 70% for an absorber thickness of x = .1 mm. Then, substituting into equation (1) gives

$$\frac{I}{I_o} = e^{-\alpha(.1 \text{ mm})} = .7$$

Taking the natural log of both sides gives

$$- \alpha(.1 \text{ mm}) = \ln(.7)$$

$$- \alpha(.1 \text{ mm}) = - .357$$

$$\alpha = \frac{.357}{.1 \text{ mm}}$$

$$\alpha = 3.57 \text{ mm}^{-1}$$

Then, if the filter were 2 mm thick (x = 2), its transmittance would be given by equation (1):

$$\frac{I}{I_o} \times 100 = e^{-\alpha x} \times 100 = e^{-(3.57)(2)} \times 100$$

$$= 7.93 \times 10^{-2} \cong .08$$

Thus, the transmittance = .08%.

Visible light is incident on a medium whose coefficient of absorption is $\alpha = 0.10 \text{ cm}^{-1}$. Find the ratios of the ampli-

tude and intensity of the light after traveling distances
of 5 cm, 10 cm, 25 cm, and 50 cm in the medium compared to
their values initially.

Solution: When electromagnetic radiation (of which light
is one form) strikes a material, the intensity of the beam
is reduced according to the following equation:

$$I = I_o e^{-\alpha x} \tag{1}$$

where I_o is the light intensity incident on the absorber, I is the light intensity at a distance x from the front
surface, and α is the absorption coefficient (whose units
are length^{-1}). Solving equation (1) for the fraction of
the original intensity that is still present after traveling
a distance x in the absorber gives

$$\frac{I}{I_o} = e^{-\alpha x} \tag{2}$$

Substituting the given values for x and α into equation (2)
gives

$$\left.\frac{I}{I_o}\right|_{x\ =\ 5\ cm} = e^{-(.10)(5)} = .606$$

$$\left.\frac{I}{I_o}\right|_{x\ =\ 10\ cm} = e^{-(.10)(10)} = .368$$

$$\left.\frac{I}{I_o}\right|_{x\ =\ 25\ cm} = e^{-(.10)(25)} = .082$$

$$\left.\frac{I}{I_o}\right|_{x\ =\ 50\ cm} = e^{-(.10)(50)} = .007 \ .$$

In general, the instantaneous intensity, I, of an electromagnetic wave is given by

$$I = \varepsilon_o E^2 C \tag{3}$$

where ε_o is the permittivity of free space, C is the
speed of the wave, and E is the amplitude of the wave's
electric field. Then equating the expressions for I given
by equations (1) and (3) gives

$$I_o e^{-\alpha x} = \varepsilon_o E^2 C$$

Solving for E gives the following result:

$$E = \sqrt{\frac{I_o e^{-\alpha x}}{\varepsilon_o C}} \qquad\qquad (4)$$

When $I = I_o$, $E = E_o$ (upon making contact with the absorber); so from eq. (3)

$$I_o = \varepsilon_o E_o^2 C \quad .$$

Solving for E_o gives

$$E_o = \sqrt{\frac{I_o}{\varepsilon_o C}} \quad . \qquad\qquad (5)$$

Equation (4) can then be written as

$$E = \sqrt{\frac{I_o}{\varepsilon_o C}} \; \sqrt{e^{-\alpha x}}$$

$$E = E_o \sqrt{e^{-\alpha x}}$$

$$\frac{E}{E_o} = \sqrt{e^{-\alpha x}} \quad .$$

Substituting for $e^{-\alpha x}$ from equation (2) gives

$$\frac{E}{E_o} = \sqrt{\frac{I}{I_o}}$$

Then,

$$\frac{E}{E_o}\bigg|_{x = 5 \text{ cm}} = \sqrt{.606} = .778$$

$$\frac{E}{E_o}\bigg|_{x = 10 \text{ cm}} = \sqrt{.368} = .607$$

$$\frac{E}{E_o}\bigg|_{x = 25 \text{ cm}} = \sqrt{.082} = .286$$

$$\frac{E}{E_o}\bigg|_{x = 50 \text{ cm}} = \sqrt{.007} = .084$$

A collimated beam of light falls at normal incidence on a plate of glass of index n and thickness d. Develop a formula for the transmittance as a function of wavelength. Show that maxima occur at those wavelengths such that

$$\lambda_N = \frac{2nd}{N} ,$$

where λ_N is the vacuum wavelength and N is an integer. The transmission function is thus periodic (in wavenumber or frequency) and is called a "channeled spectrum ".

Solution: The transfer matrix

$$M = \begin{bmatrix} \cos Kd & \frac{-i}{n} \sin Kd \\ -i\, n \sin Kd & \cos Kd \end{bmatrix}$$

is determined from the equations

$$1 + \frac{E_o'}{E_o} = \left(\cos Kd - i\, \frac{n_T}{n} \sin Kd\right) \frac{E_T}{E_o}$$

$$\text{and } n_o - n_o \frac{E_o'}{E_o} = \left(-i\, n \sin Kd + n_T \cos Kd\right) \frac{E_T}{E_o}$$

where E_O = the amplitude of the electric vector of a beam incident upon a dielectric layer, E_O' = the amplitude of the electric vector of the reflected beam, and E_T = the amplitude of the electric vector of the beam transmitted through the glass plate. K is the angular wavenumber of the light and is equal to $\frac{2\pi}{\lambda}$, where λ = the wavelength of the light. n_o and n_T are the indices of the media bordering the dielectric (in this problem, $n_o = n_T = 1$, since it is assumed that the glass plate is surrounded on all sides by a vacuum.)

After solving for t, or $\frac{E_T}{E_o}$, the transmission coefficient, from the above equations, it is found that

$$t = \frac{2n_o}{An_o + Bn_T n_o + C + Dn_T} = \frac{2}{A + B + C + D} .$$

A, B, C, and D represent the elements of the matrix M

$$\left(M = \begin{bmatrix} A & B \\ C & D \end{bmatrix} \right)$$

Upon comparison with

$$M = \begin{bmatrix} \cos Kd & -\dfrac{i}{n} \sin Kd \\ -\, i\, n \, \sin Kd & \cos Kd \end{bmatrix} ,$$

it is clear that

$$A = D = \cos Kd, \quad B = \frac{-i}{n} \sin Kd,$$

and $C = -\, i\, n\, \sin Kd.$

Therefore,

$$t = \frac{2}{2 \cos Kd - i\left(n + \dfrac{1}{n}\right) \sin Kd} .$$

The transmittance $T = t\, t^*$ (where t^* is the complex conjugate of t) is given by

$$T = \left[\frac{2}{2 \cos Kd - i\left(n + \dfrac{1}{n}\right)\sin Kd}\right]\left[\frac{2}{2 \cos Kd + i\left(n + \dfrac{1}{n}\right)\sin Kd}\right]$$

$$= \frac{4}{4 \cos^2 Kd + \left(n + \dfrac{1}{n}\right)^2 \sin^2 Kd} =$$

$$\frac{1}{\cos^2 Kd + \left(\dfrac{n^2 + 1}{2n}\right)^2 \sin^2 Kd}$$

Using the trigonometric identity

$$\cos^2 Kd + \sin^2 Kd = 1, \quad \cos^2 Kd = 1 - \sin^2 Kd ,$$

and so,

$$T = \frac{1}{1 + \left[\left(\dfrac{n^2 + 1}{2n}\right)^2 - 1\right] \sin^2 Kd} =$$

$$\frac{1}{1 + \left[\dfrac{n^4 + 2n^2 + 1 - 4n^2}{4n^2}\right] \sin^2 Kd} =$$

$$\frac{1}{1 + \left(\dfrac{n^2 - 1}{2n}\right)^2 \sin^2 Kd} .$$

Therefore,

$$T = \frac{1}{1 + \left(\dfrac{n^2 - 1}{2n}\right)^2 \sin^2 Kd} ,$$

where

$$K = \frac{2\pi}{\lambda}$$

(λ = the wavelength of the incident beam of light).

The maximum transmittance occurs for $\sin^2 Kd = 0$, which implies that $Kd = N\pi$ or

$$K = \frac{N\pi}{d} \, ,$$

where N = an integer. The wave number K is also given by

$$K = \frac{2\pi}{\lambda} = \frac{2\pi n}{\lambda_N}$$

where λ_N = the vacuum wavelength.

Equating these two expressions for K gives

$$\frac{2\not\pi nd}{\lambda_N} = N\not\pi \, .$$

Therefore,

$$\lambda_N = \frac{2nd}{N}$$

is the condition required for maximum transmittance.

● PROBLEM 13-5

A collimated beam of light of wavelength λ falls at normal incidence on a plate of glass of index of refraction n and thickness d. Give a formula for the fraction of the incident intensity that is transmitted. Find the numerical value of the transmittance for

(a) λ_{vac} = 5000.0000 Å and

(b) λ_{vac} = 5000.0416 Å , n = 1.5, d = 1 cm.

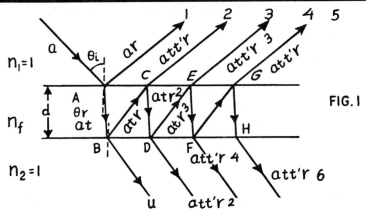

FIG. 1

Solution: Consider the plate of glass of index of refraction n and thickness d shown in Figure 1.

Let a be the amplitude of the incident beam (not its intensity) striking the surface at A at an angle of incidence θ_i.

Let 'r' be the fraction of the light amplitude which is reflected and let 't' be the fraction of the light amplitude which is transmitted. Then the amplitude of the first reflected beam is ar and the amplitude of the first refracted beam is at. At the second surface at B, part of the beam is reflected with amplitude atr and part transmitted to U with amplitude att', where t' represents the complex conjugate of t. This process is repeated every time the beam strikes the surface, giving rise to two sets of parallel rays, one on each side of the glass.

In each of these sets, of course, the intensity decreases rapidly from one ray to the next.

The optical path difference between any two successive rays emerging from the first surface is equivalent to n(ABC) - AJ, as shown in Figure 2.

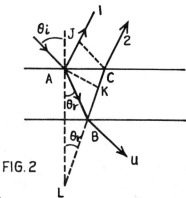

FIG. 2

(THE DOTTED LINES ARE THE TWO SUCCESSIVE POSITIONS OF A WAVE FRONT REFLECTED FROM THE LOWER SURFACE.)

Since AB = LB,

the path difference Δ is given by the following expression:

$$\Delta = n(LC) - AJ$$

$$= n(LK + KC) - AJ .$$

But nKC = AJ.

Hence,

$$\Delta = nLK$$

$$= n(2d \cos\theta_r)$$

where θ_r is the angle the refracted beam of light makes with the normal. Ray 1 undergoes a phase change of π radians at reflection while ray 2 does not, since it is internally reflected. Thus, the expression for the interference between rays 1 and 2 is

$$2\text{nd } \cos\theta_r = m\lambda \quad \text{minima.}$$

and

$$2\text{nd } \cos\theta_r = \left(m + \frac{1}{2}\right)\lambda \quad \text{maxima.}$$

Here, rays 1 and 2 will be in phase but rays 3, 5, 7, ... will be out of phase with 2, 4, 6 ..... Since ray 2 is more intense than rays 3 and 4, each of which is more intense than 5, etc., these pairs cannot cancel each other, and since the stronger series of rays combines with ray 1, the strongest of all, there will be a maximum of intensity.

For the minimum of intensity, ray 2 is out of phase with ray 1, but ray 1 has a considerably greater amplitude than does ray 2, so that these two will not completely annul each other. Adding rays 3, 4, 5 which are all in phase, gives the amplitude which is just sufficient to make up the difference and to produce complete darkness at the minima.

Using complex notation for the amplitudes of the transmitted rays which have the same phase differences between successive rays, the amplitude of the transmitted beam can be written as follows:

$$Ae^{i\theta} = att' + att'r^2e^{i\delta} + att'r^4e^{i2\delta}$$

$$+ att'r^6e^{i3\delta} + \ldots$$

where

$$\delta = \frac{2\pi}{\lambda}\Delta$$

$$= \left(\frac{2\pi}{\lambda}\right)(2\text{nd }\cos\theta_r)$$

$$= \frac{4\pi nd \cos\theta_r}{\lambda}$$

and θ is the angle subtended with respect to the x-axis.

Therefore,

$$Ae^{i\theta} = att'\left\{1 + r^2e^{i\delta} + r^4e^{i2\delta} + r^6e^{i3\delta} + \ldots\right\}.$$

$$tt' = |t|^2 = 1 - r^2 \quad \text{and}$$

$$1 + r^2e^{i\delta} + r^4e^{i2\delta} + r^6e^{i3\delta} + \ldots$$

$$= \sum_{K=0}^{\infty} r^{2K}e^{i\delta K} = \frac{1}{1 - r^2e^{i\delta}}.$$

Hence,

$$Ae^{i\theta} = a\left(1 - r^2\right)\left\{\frac{1}{1 - r^2e^{i\delta}}\right\}.$$

Then, I_T = Intensity of the transmitted beam

$$= |Ae^{i\theta}|^2$$

$$= \left\{\left(\frac{a(1 - r^2)}{1 - r^2 e^{i\delta}}\right)\left(\frac{a(1 - r^2)}{1 - r^2 e^{-i\delta}}\right)\right\}$$

$\left(\dfrac{a(1 - r^2)}{1 - r^2 e^{-i\delta}}\right)$ is the complex conjugate of $\left(\dfrac{a(1 - r^2)}{1 - r^2 e^{i\delta}}\right)$.

Hence,

$$I_T = \frac{a^2(1 - r^2)2}{1 + r^4 - r^2\{e^{i\delta} + e^{-i\delta}\}} \, .$$

Euler's equations state:

$$e^{i\delta} = \cos\delta + i\,\sin\delta \quad \text{and}$$

$$e^{-i\delta} = \cos\delta - i\,\sin\delta \, .$$

Thus, $e^{i\delta} + e^{-i\delta} = \cos\delta + i\,\sin\delta + \cos\delta - i\,\sin\delta$

$$= 2\,\cos\delta \, .$$

In addition, $a^2 = I_o$, the intensity of the incident beam of light. Then, the preceding equation becomes

$$I_T = \frac{I_o(1 - r^2)2}{1 + r^4 - 2r^2\,\cos\delta} \, .$$

Adding and subtracting $2r^2$ in the denominator gives

$$I_T = \frac{I_o(1 - r^2)^2}{1 + r^4 - 2r^2 + 2r^2 - 2r^2\,\cos\delta}$$

$$= \frac{I_o(1 - r^2)^2}{(1 - r^2)^2 + 2r^2(1 - \cos\delta)} \, .$$

$$\cos\delta = \cos\left(\frac{\delta}{2} + \frac{\delta}{2}\right) = \cos^2\frac{\delta}{2} - \sin^2\frac{\delta}{2} \, .$$

By the trigonometric identity

$$\cos^2\frac{\delta}{2} + \sin^2\frac{\delta}{2} = 1, \quad \cos^2\frac{\delta}{2} = 1 - \sin^2\frac{\delta}{2}$$

and so,

$$\cos\delta = 1 - 2\sin^2\frac{\delta}{2} \quad.$$

Substituting this expression for $\cos\delta$ into the above equation gives

$$I_T = \frac{I_o\left(1 - r^2\right)^2}{\left(1 - r^2\right)^2 + 4r^2\sin^2\frac{\delta}{2}} \quad.$$

Dividing both numerator and denominator by $\left(1 - r^2\right)^2$ and substituting the expression

$$\frac{4\pi nd\,\cos\theta_r}{\lambda}$$

for δ gives

$$I_T = \frac{I_o}{1 + \dfrac{4r^2}{\left(1 - r^2\right)^2}\sin^2\left[\dfrac{2\pi nd\,\cos\theta_r}{\lambda}\right]} \quad.$$

For normal incidence,

$$\theta_i = 0 \quad.$$

Then $\theta_r = 0$, or $\cos\theta_r = 1$.

Thus,

$$I_T = \frac{I_o}{1 + \dfrac{4r^2}{\left(1 - r^2\right)^2}\sin^2\left(\dfrac{2\pi nd}{\lambda}\right)}$$

and so,

$$\frac{I_T}{I_o} = T = \frac{1}{1 + \dfrac{4R}{(1 - R)^2}\sin^2\left(\dfrac{2\pi nd}{\lambda}\right)}$$

where $R = r^2$ (the reflectance).

For normal incidence

$$R = \frac{(n - 1)^2}{(n + 1)^2} \quad.$$

(a) For the case $n = 1.5$, $d = 1$ cm

and

$$\lambda_{vac} = 5000.0000 \ \mathring{A} \ ,$$

$$R = \left(\frac{1.5 - 1}{1.5 + 1}\right)^2 = \frac{.25}{6.25} = .04 \quad.$$

351

$$\frac{I_T}{I_O} = T = \frac{1}{1 + \frac{4(.04)}{(1 - .04)^2} \sin^2 \left[\frac{2\pi(1.5).01}{5 \times 10^{-7}}\right]}$$

$$= \frac{1}{1 + \frac{0.16}{.9216} \sin^2 [108 \times 10^5]}$$

108×10^5 is a multiple of $360°$ or 2π radians. Since

$$\sin(2\pi m) = 0$$

where m is an integer, $\sin^2 (108 \times 10^5) = \sin(108 \times 10^5) = 0$.

Thus, $T = 1$.

(b)   when $\lambda_{vac} = 5000.0416$ Å,

$$\frac{I_T}{I_O} = T = \frac{1}{1 + \frac{.16}{.9216} \sin^2 \left[\frac{2\pi \times 1.5 \times 10^{-2}}{5000.0416 \times 10^{-10}} \times \frac{180}{\pi}\right]}$$

$$= \frac{1}{1 + .1736 \times 1} = \frac{1}{1.1736} = 0.85$$

REFLECTANCE

● **PROBLEM** 13-6

A crystal reflects 70% at the wavelength of its residual rays, and 4% at adjacent wavelengths. How many reflections are necessary in order that the residual ray shall be 100 times as intense as the light of adjacent wavelengths?

Solution: The intensity of the light after n reflections is proportional to $(R)^n$, where R denotes the reflectance of the crystal.

Hence, for the two wavelengths, the ratio of the intensities after n reflections is

$$\frac{(0.7)^n}{(.04)^n} = \frac{100}{1}$$

or

$$\left(\frac{0.7}{.04}\right)^n = 100 ,$$

and so,

$$(17.5)^n = 100.$$

Taking the base 10 logarithm of both sides gives

$$n \log 17.5 = \log 100 = 2.$$

Thus,

$$n = \frac{2}{\log 17.5}$$

$$= 1.6.$$

Hence the intensity of the residual rays is 100 times as strong as that of the adjacent light after 2 reflections since $1.6 \approx 2$.

● **PROBLEM** 13-7

What is the reflectance for light of normal incidence at a water-glass boundary if the glass is (a) crown of $n = 1.523$ and (b) flint of $n = 1.62$?

Solution: (a) At normal incidence, the reflectance at a boundary separating two media of refractive indices n_1 and n_2 is given by the equation

$$R = \frac{\left(n_2 - n_1 \right)^2}{\left(n_2 + n_1 \right)^2} \ .$$

In this case,

n_1 (the refractive index of water) = 1.333

and n_2 (the refractive index of crown glass) = 1.523

Thus,

$$R = \frac{(1.523 - 1.333)^2}{(1.523 + 1.333)^2}$$

$$= \frac{(.19)^2}{(2.856)^2}$$

$$= \frac{3.61 \times 10^{-2}}{8.157}$$

$$= 0.44 \times 10^{-2} \quad \text{or} \quad 0.44\%$$

(b) Here,

$$n_1 = 1.333 \quad \text{and}$$

353

n_2 (the refractive index of flint glass) $= 1.62$.

Thus,

$$R = \frac{\left(n_2 - n_1\right)^2}{\left(n_2 + n_1\right)^2}$$

$$= \frac{(1.62 - 1.333)^2}{(1.62 + 1.333)^2}$$

$$= \frac{(.287)^2}{(2.953)^2}$$

$$= \frac{8.237 \times 10^{-2}}{8.720}$$

$$= 0.94 \times 10^{-2}$$

or $R = 0.94\%$.

● **PROBLEM** 13-8

Calculate the reflectance of a quarter-wave antireflecting film of magnesium fluoride ($n = 1.35$) coated on an optical glass surface of index 1.52.

Solution: For the case of a film of index n and thickness ℓ placed on a glass substrate of index n_T , the coefficient of reflection, r, is given by the expression

$$r = \frac{An_o + Bn_T n_o - C - Dn_T}{An_o + Bn_T n_o + C + Dn_T} \text{ ,}$$

where $A = D = \cos K\ell$, $B = \frac{-i}{n} \sin K\ell$,

$C = - i n \sin K\ell$, and n_o is the index of refraction of the surrounding medium.

In this problem, the optical thickness of the film is $\frac{1}{4}$ wavelength, so $K\ell = \frac{\pi}{2}$. Therefore, $A = D = \cos \frac{\pi}{2} = 0$,

$B = \frac{-i}{n} \sin \frac{\pi}{2} = \frac{-i}{n}$, and $C = - i n \sin \frac{\pi}{2} = - i n$.

It then follows from substituting the values determined above for A, B, C, and D into the expression for r that

$$r = \frac{\frac{-i}{n} n_T n_o + i n}{\frac{-i}{n} n_T n_o - i n} \text{ .}$$

n_o is assumed to be 1 since the light passes from air to

the film.

Therefore,

$$r = \frac{\dfrac{-i\, n_T}{n} + i\, n}{\dfrac{-i n_T}{n} - i\, n} = \frac{\dfrac{n_T}{n} - n}{\dfrac{n_T}{n} + n}$$

$$= \frac{n_T - n^2}{n_T + n^2}$$

The reflectance is given by $R = rr*$, where $r* = $ the complex conjugate of r. In this case, $r* = r$ and so,

$$R = r^2 = \frac{\left(n_T - n^2\right)^2}{\left(n_T + n^2\right)^2} \, ,$$

and after substituting the values $n = 1.35$ and $n_T = 1.52$ into this equation, we obtain the result

$$R \simeq 0.0079 \simeq 0.8\%$$

● **PROBLEM** 13-9

Find the peak reflectance of a high-reflecting multilayer film consisting of eight layers of high-low index material (four of each) of indices $n_L = 1.4$ and $n_H = 2.8$.

Solution: In order to obtain a high value of reflectance in a multilayer film, a stack of alternate layers of high index of refraction n_H, and low index of refraction n_L, materials is used. The thickness of each layer is $\frac{1}{4}$ wavelength or $\frac{1}{4}$ $(2\pi) = \frac{\pi}{2}$. Then $K\ell = \frac{\pi}{2}$ and so, the transfer matrix

$$M = \begin{bmatrix} \cos K\ell & \dfrac{-i}{n}\, \sin K\ell \\ -i\, n\, \sin K\ell & \cos K\ell \end{bmatrix}$$

reduces to the matrices

$$\begin{bmatrix} 0 & \dfrac{-i}{n_L} \\ -i\, n_L & 0 \end{bmatrix}$$

and

$$\begin{bmatrix} 0 & \dfrac{-i}{n_H} \\ -i\, n_H & 0 \end{bmatrix}$$

for the high (n_H) and low (n_L) index materials, respectively. The overall transfer matrix for two such layers (one of index n_L and one of index n_H) is calculated by multiplying the individual transfer matrices corresponding to each layer. Then, M =

$$
\begin{bmatrix} 0 & \dfrac{-i}{n_L} \\ -i\,n_L & 0 \end{bmatrix}
\begin{bmatrix} 0 & \dfrac{-i}{n_H} \\ -i\,n_H & 0 \end{bmatrix}
= \begin{bmatrix} \dfrac{-n_H}{n_L} & 0 \\ 0 & \dfrac{-n_L}{n_H} \end{bmatrix} .
$$

If instead of two layers, a stack of 2N layers is used, the transfer matrix of the complete multilayer film is

$$
\begin{bmatrix} \dfrac{-n_H}{n_L} & 0 \\ 0 & \dfrac{-n_L}{n_H} \end{bmatrix}^N
= \begin{bmatrix} \left(\dfrac{-n_H}{n_L}\right)^N & 0 \\ 0 & \left(\dfrac{-n_L}{n_H}\right)^N \end{bmatrix} .
$$

The coefficient of reflection r is given as

$$
r = \frac{An_O + Bn_T n_O - C - Dn_T}{An_O + Bn_T n_O + C + Dn_T}
$$

where

$$
M = \begin{bmatrix} A & B \\ C & D \end{bmatrix}
$$

and n_T and n_O represent the indices of refraction corresponding to the media surrounding the film. In this problem, since we merely wish to determine the reflectance of the film, we can set $n_T = n_O = 1$. In addition, after comparison with the transfer matrix of the complete multilayer film, we determine that

$$
A = \left(\frac{-n_H}{n_L}\right)^N, \quad B = C = 0, \quad \text{and} \quad D = \left(\frac{-n_L}{n_H}\right)^N ,
$$

and that

$$
r = \frac{\left(\dfrac{-n_H}{n_L}\right)^N - \left(\dfrac{-n_L}{n_H}\right)^N}{\left(\dfrac{-n_H}{n_L}\right)^N + \left(\dfrac{-n_L}{n_H}\right)^N}
$$

The reflectance $R = |r|^2 =$

$$\left[\frac{\left(\dfrac{-n_H}{n_L}\right)^N - \left(\dfrac{-n_L}{n_H}\right)^N}{\left(\dfrac{-n_H}{n_L}\right)^N + \left(\dfrac{-n_L}{n_H}\right)^N}\right]^2 = \left[\frac{\dfrac{\left(\dfrac{-n_H}{n_L}\right)^N}{\left(\dfrac{-n_L}{n_H}\right)^N} - 1}{\dfrac{\left(\dfrac{-n_H}{n_L}\right)^N}{\left(\dfrac{-n_L}{n_H}\right)^N} + 1}\right]^2 = \left[\frac{\left(\dfrac{-n_H}{n_L}\right)^{2N} - 1}{\left(\dfrac{-n_H}{n_L}\right)^{2N} + 1}\right]^2$$

Upon substitution of the values $n_L = 1.4$, $n_H = 2.8$, and $N = 4$ into the preceding equation, we see that

$$R = \left[\frac{(-2)^8 - 1}{(-2)^8 + 1}\right]^2 = \left(\frac{256 - 1}{256 + 1}\right)^2 = \left(\frac{255}{257}\right)^2 \approx (.992)^2 \approx .984.$$

Therefore, the peak reflectance of the multilayer film is approximately .984.

● **PROBLEM** 13-10

For aluminum at $\lambda = 5500$ Å, $n = 1.15$, and $K = 3.2$, where n and K are the real and complex parts, respectively, of the index of refraction, find the reflectance, the absorption coefficient, and the phase change on reflection at normal incidence.

Solution: The reflectance R is the ratio of reflected to incident energy. Since the energy is the product of the complex amplitude with its conjugate, and since the complex amplitudes for incident and reflected waves are given by the Fresnel equations, R can be found. From the Fresnel equations for normal incidence,

$$A_r = A_i \frac{\hat{n} - 1}{\hat{n} + 1}, \tag{1}$$

where A_i and A_r are the complex amplitudes of the incident and reflected waves, respectively, and where the circumflex over the index of refraction n indicates that the index of refraction is complex; i.e.,

$$\hat{n} = n - jK, \quad (j = \sqrt{-1}). \tag{2}$$

Then

$$R = \frac{A_r A_r^*}{A_i^2} = \frac{\hat{n} - 1}{\hat{n} + 1} \frac{\hat{n}^* - 1}{\hat{n}^* + 1},$$

where * denotes a complex conjugate. Then, from equation

(2), $\hat{n} = n - jK$ and $\hat{n}^* = n + jK$, and substituting these expressions into the preceding equation gives

$$R = \frac{[(n - 1) - jK][(n - 1) + jK]}{[(n + 1) - jK][(n + 1) + jK]} = \frac{(n - 1)^2 + K^2}{(n + 1)^2 + K^2} . \quad (3)$$

Substitution of the given values yields

$$R = \frac{(1.15 - 1)^2 + (3.2)^2}{(1.15 + 1)^2 + (3.2)^2} = 0.69$$

The absorption coefficient α can be found by comparing Lambert's law for the decrease in light intensity with distance (z) penetrated into a medium,

$$I = I_o e^{-\alpha z} , \quad (4)$$

with the equation for the intensity obtained from the solution of Maxwell's equations. Maxwell's equations predict that for a wave (field) traveling through a medium in the z-direction,

$$A = A_o e^{j(\omega t - \hat{K}z)} \quad (5)$$

where

$$\hat{K} = \frac{\omega}{c} \hat{n} = \frac{\omega}{c} (n - jK) . \quad (6)$$

Substitution of the expression for $\hat{K}$ found in equation (6) into equation (5) gives

$$A = A_o e^{j(\omega t - \frac{\omega n}{c} z + \frac{\omega}{c} jKz)}$$

$$= A_o e^{\frac{-\omega K}{c} z} e^{j\omega(t - \frac{n}{c} z)} .$$

Thus the wave amplitude decreases exponentially with distance z, and since the intensity is proportional to the square of the field amplitude,

$$I = I_o e^{\frac{-2\omega K}{c} z} . \quad (7)$$

Comparing equations (4) and (7),

$$\alpha = \frac{2\omega K}{c} . \quad (8)$$

Substituting $K = 3.2$ and using $\omega = \frac{2\pi c}{\lambda}$ yields

$$\alpha = \frac{4\pi K}{\lambda} = \frac{(4\pi)(3.2)}{5500 \times 10^{-8} cm} = 7.3 \times 10^5 \ cm^{-1} .$$

To find the phase change on reflection, note that the amplitude ratio A_r/A_i is a complex number and can be put

358

into the standard form $Ce^{i\gamma}$; once this is done, the phase change ϕ is just $\tan^{-1}\gamma$. To get the amplitude ratio into the form $Ce^{i\gamma}$, write it as a real part + an imaginary part, $a + jb$; then γ is simply b/a. Using $\hat{n} = n - jK$,

$$\frac{A_r}{A_i} = \frac{\hat{n} - 1}{\hat{n} + 1} \quad \text{(from equation (1))}$$

$$= \frac{n - 1 - jK}{n + 1 - jK} \; .$$

Multiplying both numerator and denominator by the complex conjugate of $n + 1 - jK$, $n + 1 + jK$, gives

$$\frac{A_r}{A_i} = \left[\frac{(n - 1) - jK}{(n + 1) - jK}\right]\left[\frac{(n + 1) + jK}{(n + 1) + jK}\right]$$

$$= \frac{n^2 + K^2 - 1 - 2jK}{n^2 + K^2 + 2n + 1} = \frac{n^2 + K^2 - 1}{n^2 + K^2 + 2n + 1}$$

$$- j \; \frac{2K}{n^2 + K^2 + 2n + 1} \; .$$

Then, $\qquad \phi = \tan^{-1} \dfrac{b}{a}$

$$a = \frac{n^2 + K^2 - 1}{n^2 + K^2 + 2n + 1} \quad \text{and} \quad b = \frac{-2K}{n^2 + K^2 + 2n + 1} \; .$$

Hence,

$$\phi = \tan^{-1}\left[\left(\frac{-2K}{n^2 + K^2 + 2n + 1}\right)\left(\frac{n^2 + K^2 + 2n + 1}{n^2 + K^2 - 1}\right)\right]$$

$$= \tan^{-1}\left(\frac{-2K}{n^2 + K^2 - 1}\right)$$

$$= \tan^{-1}\left[\frac{(-2)(3.2)}{(1.15)^2 + (3.2)^2 - 1}\right]$$

$$= \tan^{-1} \; (-0.606) = -31.2 .$$

$$\tan (\pi + (-\theta)) = \frac{\sin (\pi + (-\theta))}{\cos (\pi + (-\theta))} =$$

$$\frac{\sin \pi \cos (-\theta) + \cos \pi \sin (-\theta)}{\cos \pi \cos (-\theta) - \sin \pi \sin (-\theta)}$$

by the double angle formulas for the sine and cosine.

Thus,

$$\tan (\pi - \theta) = \frac{-\sin (-\theta)}{-\cos (-\theta)} = \tan (-\theta) .$$

Hence,

$$\tan (-31.2°) = \tan (180° - 31.2°) = \tan (148.8).$$

Thus,
$$\phi = 148.8° .$$

OPTICAL DENSITIES

A metallic coating absorbs 88% of the incident light. A thin film has one half the optical density of the coating. What is the transmittance of the film?

Solution: Since A = 88% = 0.88,

$$T = 1 - A = .12.$$

The optical density O.D. is defined as follows:

$$O.D. = \log_{10} \left(\frac{I_O}{I_T} \right) = \frac{1}{2.303} \ln \left(\frac{I_O}{I_T} \right)$$

where I_O and I_T represent the intensities of the incident and transmitted beams of the light, respectively.

$$\frac{I_T}{I_O} = T; \text{ hence, O.D.} = \frac{1}{2.303} \ln \left(\frac{1}{T} \right)$$

or, the optical density of the metallic coating is

$$O.D. = \frac{1}{2.303} \ln \left(\frac{1}{0.12} \right)$$

$$O.D. = \frac{2.1203}{2.303} = 0.9207 .$$

O.D. of the thin film = $\frac{0.9207}{2}$ = .46035 .

Hence,

$$.46035 = \frac{1}{2.303} \ln \left(\frac{1}{T} \right)$$

$$\ln \left(\frac{1}{T} \right) = 2.303 \times .46035 = 1.0601 .$$

Taking the exponential of both sides of this equation gives

$$\frac{1}{T} = e^{1.0601} \quad \text{or,}$$

$$\frac{1}{T} = 2.887 .$$

Then,

$$T = \frac{1}{2.887} = 0.346 = 34.6\% .$$

(1) If 22% of the incident light is transmitted through a given sample, what is the absorbtance and what is the optical density of the sample?

(2) What are the optical densities corresponding to transmittances of 52%, 98%, and 2%?

Solution: (1) The intensity of the transmitted beam, I_T, is related to the intensity of the incident beam, I_o, the thickness of the sample, d, and the absorption coefficient, α (alpha), by the equation

$$I_T = I_o e^{-\alpha d} .$$

The transmittance of the sample is defined as

$$T = \frac{I_T}{I_o} .$$

The absorbtance of the sample is defined as $A = (1 - T)$.

The optical density O.D. is defined as

$$O.D. = \log_{10}\left(\frac{I_o}{I_T}\right) = \frac{1}{2.303} \ln\left(\frac{I_o}{I_T}\right) = \frac{\alpha d}{2.303} .$$

Hence if $T = 22\% = 0.22$,

$A = 1 - T = 1 - 0.22 = 0.78 = 78\%$.

$$O.D. = \frac{1}{2.303} \ln\left(\frac{I_o}{I_T}\right) = \frac{1}{2.303} \ln\left(\frac{1}{T}\right)$$

$$= \frac{1}{2.303} \ln\left(\frac{1}{.22}\right)$$

$$= \frac{1}{2.303} \ln(4.545)$$

$$= \frac{1.5141}{2.303}$$

$$= 0.6575 \ .$$

(2) When T = 0.52,

$$O.D. \ = \frac{1}{2.303} \ \ell n \left(\frac{1}{0.52} \right)$$

$$= \frac{0.6539}{2.303}$$

$$= 0.2839 \ .$$

When T = 98% = 0.98,

$$O.D. \ = \frac{1}{2.303} \ \ell n \left(\frac{1}{0.98} \right)$$

$$= \frac{.0202}{2.303}$$

$$= .0088 \ .$$

When T = 2% = .02,

$$O.D. \ = \frac{1}{2.303} \ \ell n \left(\frac{1}{.02} \right)$$

$$= \frac{3.9120}{2.303}$$

$$= 1.6987.$$

THE FABRY-PEROT INTERFEROMETER

● **PROBLEM** 13-13

The plates of a Fabry-Perot interferometer are coated with silver of such a thickness that for each plate the reflectance is 0.9, the transmittance is 0.05, and the absorption is 0.05. Find the maximum and minimum fractional transmittance of the interferometer.

Solution: A Fabry-Perot interferometer consists of two optically flat, partially reflecting plates of glass or quartz with their reflecting surfaces held parallel. It employs multiple-beam interference, meaning that multiple reflection takes place between the two plates, as shown in the figure.

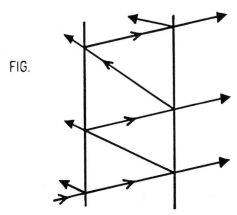

FIG.

The formula for the total intensity I_T of the transmitted light is

$$I_T = I_o \; \frac{T^2}{(1 - R)^2} \; \frac{1}{1 + F \sin^2\left(\Delta/2\right)}$$

where $F = \dfrac{4R}{(1 - R)^2}$,

I_o = the initial intensity of the primary beam, and Δ = the total phase change between two successive beams.

$$\frac{I_{T(max)}}{I_o} = F_{max}$$, the maximum fractional transmittance

and can be found by setting the term

$1 + F \sin^2\left(\Delta/2\right)$ equal to its minimum value. This can be done by setting $\Delta = 0$. Then

$$F_{max} = \frac{T^2}{(1 - R)^2} \; .$$

In this problem, $T = 0.05$ and $R = 0.9$, so

$$F_{max} = \frac{(0.05)^2}{(.1)^2} = \frac{25 \times 10^{-4}}{10^{-2}} = 0.25 \; .$$

The minimum fractional transmittance can be determined by setting

$$1 + F \sin^2\left(\Delta/2\right)$$

to its maximum value. This is done when $\Delta = \pi$. Therefore,

$$F_{min} = \frac{I_{T(min)}}{I_o} = \frac{T^2}{(1 - R)^2} \; \frac{1}{1 + \dfrac{4R}{(1 - R)^2}}$$

$$= \frac{T^2}{(1 - R)^2 + 4R} = \frac{T^2}{1 - 2R + R^2 + 4R} =$$

$$\frac{T^2}{R^2 + 2R + 1} = \frac{T^2}{(R + 1)^2} = \frac{(0.05)^2}{(1.9)^2} = \frac{25 \times 10^{-4}}{3.61}$$

$$\approx 0.0007 \ .$$

RAYLEIGH SCATTERING

If light of wavelength 635 nm causes a certain amount of Rayleigh scattering, light of what wavelength will give exactly 10 times as much scattering?

Solution: In Rayleigh scattering, the intensity I of the scattered light is inversely proportional to the fourth power of the wavelength of light used.

$$\text{or } I_s(\lambda) \propto \frac{1}{\lambda^4}$$

$$\text{Now } I_s(635 \text{ nm}) \propto \frac{1}{(635 \text{ nm})^4} \ .$$

$$\text{Hence } \frac{I_s(\lambda)}{I_s(635 \text{ nm})} = \frac{\frac{1}{\lambda^4}}{\frac{1}{(635 \text{ nm})^4}} = \frac{(635 \text{ nm})^4}{\lambda^4} = 10 \ .$$

Solving for λ^4 gives

$$\lambda^4 = \frac{(635 \text{ nm})^4}{10}$$

$$\text{or} \quad \lambda = \frac{635 \text{ nm}}{\sqrt[4]{10}}$$

$$= \frac{635 \text{ nm}}{1.778}$$

$$= 357 \text{ nm}.$$

What is the ratio of intensities of Rayleigh scattering for the two hydrogen lines λ_1 = 410 nm and λ_2 = 656 nm?

Solution: Since the intensity I of the scattered beam is inversely proportional to the fourth power of the wavelength, the following is true:

$$\frac{I(410\ nm)}{I(656\ nm)} = \frac{(656\ nm)^4}{(410\ nm)^4}$$

$$= \frac{18.52 \times 10^{10}}{2.826 \times 10^{10}}$$

$$= \frac{6.55}{1}$$

Hence, the intensity ratio at the two wavelengths is 6.55:1.

CHAPTER 14

POLARIZATION

ROTATION OF THE PLANE OF POLARIZATION OF LIGHT

● **PROBLEM** 14-1

Calculate the required thickness of a quartz plate cut perpendicular to the optic axis which will produce a rotation of the blue mercury line λ = 435.8 nm, by 180°.

Solution: We will use in this problem the relationship

$$\beta = \frac{\pi d (|n_L - n_R|)}{\lambda_o}$$

where β is the rotation of the plane of linear polarization in radians for a thickness d of optically active material whose indices of refraction for right and left circularly polarization are n_R and n_L, respectively, at the wavelength of the entering light in a vacuum, λ_o.

So, after rearranging the above equation, and after finding n_L and n_R from optical constants tables which yields $\qquad |n_L - n_R| \cong 1 \times 10^{-4}$

We have

$$d = \frac{\beta \lambda_o}{\pi (n_L - n_R)} = \frac{\pi \times 435.8 \times 10^{-9}}{\pi \times (1 \times 10^{-4})} \; m = 4.36 \; mm.$$

● **PROBLEM** 14-2

From the specific rotation of quartz for λ = 508.582 nm, β = 29.728 Deg/mm, compute the difference in refractive index $(n_L - n_R)$, setting the thickness of the quartz plate = 1 mm.

Solution: For this problem we can use the relation

$$\beta = \frac{\pi d}{\lambda_o} \, (|n_L - n_R|)$$

where β is the rotation of the plane of polarization (linear polarization) in radians, d is the thickness of the quartz plate, λ_o is the wavelength of light in vacuum, n_L is the index of refraction for left circular polarization and n_R is the index of refraction for right circular polarization.

Thus,

$\beta = (29.728 \text{ Deg/mm}) \, (1 \text{ mm}) = 29.728 \text{ Deg}$

Substituting the given values into the above equation yields

$$|n_L - n_R| = \frac{\beta \lambda_o}{\pi d} = \frac{(29.728 \text{ Deg}) \left(\frac{\pi \text{ rad}}{180 \text{ Deg}}\right) (508.582 \times 10^{-9} \text{m})}{(\pi \text{ rad}) (10^{-3} \text{m})}$$

$$= 8.4 \times 10^{-5}.$$

● **PROBLEM** 14-3

From the indices of refraction given below, calculate the rotation of the plane of polarization for violet light λ = 396.0 nm, in a quartz plate cut perpendicular to the optic axis and 1 mm thick.

λ	n_R	n_L
396.0 nm	1.55810	1.55821

(Refractive Indices for Quartz)

Solution: Quartz, when in crystal form, is optically active. This means that right circularly polarized light travelling parallel to the optic axis will have a different index of refraction (n_R), than left circularly polarized light (n_L).

Since plane polarized light can be formed by the proper combination of right and left circularly polarized light, as plane polarized light progresses through quartz parallel to the optic axis, the plane of polarization will rotate.

Right circularly polarized light will have a wavelength in quartz $\lambda_R = \frac{\lambda}{n_R}$ and left circularly polarized will have a wavelength in quartz of $\lambda_L = \frac{\lambda}{n_L}$. Thus, in a distance d there will be d/λ_R and d/λ_L waves of right and left circularly polarized light, respectively, or, when the light emerges

367

from the quartz crystal, there will be a difference in the number of waves of right and left circularly polarized light equal to

$$\frac{d}{\lambda_L} - \frac{d}{\lambda_R} = d\left(\frac{1}{\lambda_L} - \frac{1}{\lambda_R}\right) = \frac{d}{\lambda}\left[n_L - n_R\right] = \text{path difference.}$$

This path difference, expressed as a phase angle is

$$\beta = \frac{2\pi d}{\lambda} (n_L - n_R) \ ,$$

where β is measured in radians. Inserting values we have

$$\beta = \frac{2\pi(10^{-3})}{396.0 \times 10^{-9}} (1.55821 - 1.55810) = 1.745 \text{ radians}$$
$$= 100° \ .$$

The rotation of the plane of polarization, being a linear superposition of the left and right circular polarized light, will be just half the angular path difference so that

$$\theta = \beta/2 = 50°.$$

● **PROBLEM 14-4**

A solution of camphor in alcohol in a tube 20 cm long rotates the plane of vibration of light passing through it 33°. What must the density of camphor be in the solution? The specific rotation of camphor is +54°.

Solution: $\delta = \frac{10 \ \theta}{\ell d}$.

In this problem, $\delta = 54°$

$\theta = 33°$

$\ell = 20$ cm

Then the density of camphor in the solution, d, is given by

$$d = \frac{10 \ \theta}{\ell \delta}$$

$$= \frac{10(33)}{20(54)}$$

$$= .306 \text{ grams per cc.}$$

● **PROBLEM 14-5**

A plate of crystal quartz cut with its faces perpendicular to the optic axis is found to exactly annul the rotation of the plane of polarization of sodium light produced by a 10 cm length of a 20% solution of maltose. Calculate the thickness of the quartz plate. [δ] for maltose = 144°. (Specific rotation is defined as the rotation produced by a 10 cm column of liquid with a 1 gram/cubic centimeter active substance.)

Solution: We know that the specific rotation δ, is given by

$$\delta = \frac{10\ \theta}{\ell d}$$

where θ is the rotation of the plane of polarization, ℓ is the length of solution column in cm, and d is the number of grams per cubic centimeter.

Now for our problem

$$\ell = 10 \text{ cm}$$

$$d = 0.2$$

$$\delta = 144°$$

$$\therefore \qquad \theta = \frac{\delta\ \ell\ d}{10}$$

$$= \frac{144 \times 10 \times 0.2}{10}$$

$$= 28.8°$$

For a crystal quartz plate, the phase difference, δ, between the left-handed and right-handed polarized beam is given by

$$\delta = \frac{2\pi}{\lambda} t(n_L - n_R) \ .$$

where t is the thickness of the plate and n_L and n_R are the refractive indices for left-handed and right-handed polarized beams, respectively.

For crystal quartz, the phase difference or angle of rotation for sodium light is 21.72°/mm. Hence the thickness of the quartz plate, t, necessary to produce a rotation of 28.8 is given by

$$\frac{t}{28.8°} = \frac{1 \text{ mm}}{21.72°}$$

Therefore,

$$t = \frac{28.8}{21.72}$$

$$= 1.326 \text{ mm.}$$

● **PROBLEM 14-6**

If 4° is the magnitude of Faraday rotation for a given substance, 100 cm the distance of travel, and Verdet's constant = 3.8 x 10 -4 $\frac{\text{minutes}}{(\text{gauss -cm.})}$ and if the magnetic field is parallel to the light, what is the magnetic field strength? What if the field is normal to the light?

Solution: The faraday rotation θ, is related to the magnetic flux density B, the length of the medium the light traverses, ℓ, and the Verdet constant V, by the relation

$$\theta = B V \ell$$

where θ is given in arc minutes, B is given in gauss, V is given in $\underline{\text{minutes}}$, and ℓ is given in centimeters.
gauss-cm.

Hence for our problem $\theta = 4° = 240$ min.

$$\ell = 100 \text{ cm.}$$

$$V = 3.8 \times 10^{-4} \frac{\text{minutes}}{\text{gauss- cm.}}$$

$$B = \frac{\theta}{V\ell} = \frac{240}{3.8 \times 10^{-4} \times 100}$$

$$= 6.316 \times 10^3 \text{ gauss.}$$

When the field is normal to the light, there is no effect and hence no rotation.

● PROBLEM 14-7

A beam of linear polarized light is sent through a piece of solid glass tubing 25 cm long and 1 cm in diameter. The tubing is wound with a single layer of 250 turns of enameled copper wire along its entire length. If the Verdet constant of the glass is 0.05 $\underline{\text{min. of angle}}$, what is the
oersted - cm
amount of rotation of the plane of polarization of the light when a current of 5 amperes is flowing through the wire?

Solution: $\theta = B V \ell$

where θ is the angle of rotation, B is the magnetic field along the direction of propagation of the wave and ℓ = the length of the glass tubing.

$$B = nI \frac{\text{amp. turns}}{\text{meter}}$$

$$= 12.57 \times 10^{-3} \text{ nI oersted}$$

$$V = .05 \frac{\text{min}}{\text{oersted . cm}} = \frac{.05}{60} \frac{\text{deg.}}{\text{oersted . cm}}$$

$$\ell = 25 \text{ cm.}$$

Therefore,

$$\theta = (12.57 \times 10^{-3} \text{ oersted}) \left(\frac{1000 \text{ turns}}{\text{m}} \right) (5 \text{ amps})$$

$$\times \left(\frac{.05 \text{ deg}}{60 \text{ oersted-cm}} \right) (25 \text{ cm})$$

370

$$= \frac{12.57 \times 6.25}{60}$$

$$= 1.3°$$

POLARIZATION BY REFLECTION

● **PROBLEM** 14-8

What is the refractive index of a piece of glass if the light
of the green mercury line (5461Å) is plane-polarized when
reflected at an angle of 57° 47'?

Solution: If light is reflected obliquely from the surface
of a transparent body, such as water, or a glass plate, then
in general both the reflected and transmitted beams are found
to be partly polarized. At a particular angle of incidence,
which has been called the "polarizing angle," the reflected
light is completely plane-polarized.   The angle of incidence
θ which gives completely plane polarized reflected light is
found by applying the equation

$$\tan \theta = n,$$

which is known as Brewster's Law.   Letting the angle of
incidence θ = 57° 47' (since the angle of incidence is also
equal to the angle of reflection), in the equation it is
found that the index of refraction of the piece of glass is
n = 1.5869.

● **PROBLEM** 14-9

Derive Brewster's law.   a) Calculate the polarizing angle
for dense flint glass of index 1.9.   b) At what angle
above the horizontal must the sun be in order that sunlight
reflected from the surface of a calm body of water shall be
completely linearly polarized?   Is the plane of the
E-vector in the reflected light horizontal or vertical?

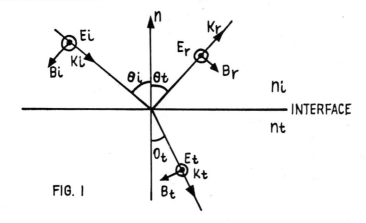

FIG. I

Solution: To investigate polarization on reflection let us first look at the Fresnel equations for reflection. The amplitude reflection coefficients for E waves perpendicular ($\perp$) and parallel ($\parallel$) are found to be

$$r_\perp = \left(\frac{E_{or}}{E_{oi}}\right)_\perp = \frac{n_i \cos \theta_i - n_t \cos \theta_t}{n_i \cos \theta_i + n_t \cos \theta_t} \tag{1}$$

$$r_\parallel = \left(\frac{E_{or}}{E_{oi}}\right)_\parallel = \frac{n_t \cos \theta_i - n_i \cos \theta_t}{n_i \cos \theta_t + n_t \cos \theta_i} \tag{2}$$

where E_{or} and E_{oi} are the amplitudes of the E wave reflected and incident respectively; the subscript i refers to the incident region; the subscript t refers to the transmitted region; n's are indices of refraction and theta's the angle between the propagation vector and the normal to the surface. By perpendicular we mean that the plane of the E vibrations is perpendicular to the plane of incidence and by parallel that the plane of the E vibrations is in the plane of incidence (see figure 1).

If we look at the numerator of equations (1) and (2), and reflect upon them a moment we discern that equation (1) can never equal zero as we vary θ_i. This result follows from Snell's law which states that $\dfrac{\sin \theta_i}{\sin \theta_t} = n_t/n_i$ (3)

However in equation (2) the numerator can be made zero when

$$n_t \cos \theta_i - n_i \cos \theta_t = 0$$

provided $n_t > n_i$

or, $$\frac{n_t}{n_i} = \frac{\cos \theta_t}{\cos \theta_i} \tag{4}$$

and from Snell's law, $$\frac{\sin \theta_i}{\sin \theta_t} = \frac{\cos \theta_t}{\cos \theta_i} \tag{5}$$

or $\sin \theta_i \cos \theta_i - \sin \theta_t \cos \theta_t = 0.$ (6)

By using the trigonometric identities

$\sin (\theta_i - \theta_t) = \sin \theta_i \cos \theta_t - \cos \theta_i \sin \theta_t$,
$\cos (\theta_i + \theta_t) = \cos \theta_i \cos \theta_t - \sin \theta_i \sin \theta_t$,
and $\sin^2 \theta_i + \cos^2 \theta_i = 1$

we can show that equation (6) is equivalent to

$$\sin (\theta_i - \theta_t) \cos (\theta_i + \theta_t) = 0 \tag{7}$$

and there will only be one angle θ_i for which equation 7 holds,
$$\theta_i + \theta_t = 90°$$

because θ_i can never be equal to θ_t in mediums of different indices.

Since θ_i and θ_t are connected through equation (3),

$$\frac{\sin \theta_i}{\sin (90 - \theta_i)} = \frac{\sin \theta_i}{\cos \theta_i} = \tan \theta_i = \frac{n_t}{n_i}$$

This is known as Brewster's law, where θ_i is the polarization angle (θ_ρ).

a) So in this problem the polarization angle is found by applying

$$\frac{n_t}{n_i} = \tan \theta_\rho = 1.9$$

$$\theta_\rho = 62°15'$$

and the plane of the E vector of the reflected polarized light is perpendicular to the plane of incidence.

b) If the index of water is 1.33, then according to Brewster's law,

$$\tan \theta_\rho = 1.33$$

$$\theta_\rho = 53.1$$

Now θ_ρ is the angle between the normal to the surface of the body cf water and the ray from the sun, so the angle from the horizontal is $90 - \theta_\rho$ or $36.9°$ and the plane of the E -vector of the reflected polarized light is perpendicular to the plane of incidence or horizontal.

● **PROBLEM 14-10**

A beam of natural light is incident on the surface of a piece of glass of index 1.523 at an angle of incidence of $70°$. a) What fraction of the incident light is reflected? b) In the reflected beam, what is the ratio of the component of the E - vector in the plane of incidence to the component of the E - vector at right angles to the plane of incidence?

Solution: Natural or unpolarized light is a mixture of waves polarized in all possible azimuths. Each wave then may be resolved into components with electric vector parallel to the plane of incidence and with electric vector perpendicular to the plane of incidence. Then the amount of reflected light is given by

$$\frac{I_r}{I_0} = \frac{1}{2} \frac{E_r^2}{E_{o\perp}^2} + \frac{1}{2} \frac{E_r^2}{E_{o\|}^2} \tag{1}$$

Where I_0 is the incident intensity, $E_{o\perp}$ is the electric vector perpendicular to the plane of incidence and $E_{o\|}$ is the electric vector parallel to the plane of incidence.

When an electromagnetic wave is incident on a boundary, the electric and magnetic fields must satisfy the boundary conditions. For the case in which the electric vector is parallel to the plane of incidence

$$E_o \parallel \cos \phi - E_r \cos r = E' \cos \phi' \qquad (2)$$

where ϕ is the angle of incidence, r is the angle of reflection and ϕ' is the angle of refraction. The magnetic
vector in this case must satisfy

$$H_{o\perp} + H_r = H' \qquad (3)$$

where H_r and H' are the reflected and transmitted magnetic vectors.

The electric and magnetic vectors are related by

$$\sqrt{\varepsilon} \ E_{o\parallel} = \sqrt{\mu} \ H_{o\perp}$$
$$\sqrt{\varepsilon} \ E_r = \sqrt{\mu} \ H_r$$
$$\sqrt{\varepsilon'} \ E' = \sqrt{\mu'} \ H'$$

where μ and ε are the permittivity and the permeability of
the 1st medium and μ' and ε' are the permittivity and permeability of the second medium. For all transparent dielectrics

$$\mu = \mu' = \mu_o$$

The index of refraction is related to ε by

$$\sqrt{\varepsilon} = n\sqrt{\varepsilon_o}$$
$$\sqrt{\varepsilon'} = n'\sqrt{\varepsilon_o}$$

Hence, the magnetic vector equation can be written as

$$nE_{o\parallel} + n \ E_r = n'E' \qquad (4)$$

The laws of reflection and refraction are

$$r = \phi \qquad (5)$$

$$n \sin \phi = n' \sin \phi' \qquad (6)$$

Hence

$$E' = \frac{\sin \phi'}{\sin \phi} E_{o\parallel} + \frac{\sin \phi'}{\sin \phi} E_r \qquad \text{from} \quad (4)$$

$$E_{o\parallel} \cos \phi - E_r \cos \phi = \left(\frac{\sin \phi'}{\sin \phi} E_{o\parallel} + \frac{\sin \phi'}{\sin \phi} E_r \right) \cos \phi'$$

$$\frac{E_r}{E_{o\parallel}} = \frac{\sin \phi \ \cos \phi - \sin \phi' \ \cos \phi'}{\sin \phi \ \cos \phi + \sin \phi' \ \cos \phi'}$$

$$= \frac{(\sin \phi \ \cos \phi' - \sin \phi' \ \cos \phi)(\cos \phi \ \cos \phi' - \sin \phi \ \sin \phi')}{(\sin \phi \ \cos \phi' + \sin \phi' \ \cos \phi)(\cos \phi \ \cos \phi' + \sin \phi \ \sin \phi')}$$

$$= \frac{\sin (\phi - \phi') \ \cos (\phi + \phi')}{\sin (\phi + \phi') \ \cos (\phi - \phi')} = \frac{\tan (\phi - \phi')}{\tan (\phi + \phi')} \qquad (7)$$

When the electric vector is perpendicular to the Plane
of incidence, we have

$$E_{o\perp} + E_r = E' \qquad (8)$$

and $- H_{o\parallel} \cos \phi + H_r \cos r = - H' \cos \phi'$

or $\quad$ $- n \cos \phi E_{o\perp} + n \cos \phi E_r = - n' \cos \phi' E'$

or $\quad$ $- n \cos \phi E_{o\perp} + n \cos \phi E_r = - n' \cos \phi' (E_{o\perp} + E_r)$

$(n' \cos \phi' + n \cos \phi) E_r = (- n' \cos \phi' + n \cos \phi) E_{o\perp}$

$$\frac{E_r}{E_{o\perp}} = \frac{n \cos \phi - n' \cos \phi'}{n' \cos \phi' + n \cos \phi}$$

$$= - \frac{\sin (\phi - \phi')}{\sin (\phi + \phi')}$$

$\therefore$ $\quad$ $\dfrac{I_r}{I_o} = \dfrac{1}{2} \dfrac{\tan^2 (\phi - \phi')}{\tan^2 (\phi + \phi')} + \dfrac{1}{2} \dfrac{\sin^2 (\phi - \phi')}{\sin^2 (\phi + \phi')}$

$$\sin \phi' = \frac{\sin \phi}{1.523} = \frac{\sin 70°}{1.523} = 0.617$$

$$\phi' = 38.097°$$

$$\frac{I_r}{I_o} = \frac{1}{2} \frac{0.3875}{9.3638} + \frac{1}{2} \frac{0.2793}{0.9035}$$

$$= 17.5\%$$

$$\frac{E_r}{E_{o\perp}} = - \frac{\sin (\phi - \phi')}{\sin (\phi + \phi')} = -0.5559 ,$$

$$\frac{E_r}{E_{o\parallel}} = \frac{\tan (\phi - \phi')}{\tan (\phi + \phi')} = - 0.2034$$

Hence $\quad$ $\dfrac{E_{o\parallel}}{E_{o\perp}} = \dfrac{\dfrac{E_r}{E_{o\perp}}}{\dfrac{E_r}{E_{o\parallel}}} = 2.73$

ANALYSIS OF STATES OF POLARIZATION OF LIGHT

● **PROBLEM** 14-11

1) Two linearly polarized waves are in phase, but have different amplitudes. At x = 0

$$\vec{E}_1 = \hat{\imath} A_1 \cos 2\pi\nu t + \hat{\jmath} B_1 \cos 2\pi\nu t,$$

$$\vec{E}_2 = \hat{\imath} A_2 \cos 2\pi\nu t + \hat{\jmath} B_2 \cos 2\pi\nu t.$$

Show that $\vec{E}_T = \vec{E}_1 + \vec{E}_2$ is also linearly polarized, and find its polarization direction.

2) Two circularly polarized waves (a right and a left) can be added to form a linearly polarized wave: At x = 0,

$$\vec{E}_1 = \hat{\imath}\, E_o \cos 2\pi\nu t + \hat{\jmath}\, E_o \sin 2\pi\nu t,$$

$$\vec{E}_2 = \hat{\imath}\, E_o \cos (2\pi\nu t + \alpha) - \hat{\jmath}\, E_o \sin (2\pi\nu t + \alpha).$$

Show that $\vec{E}_T$ is linearly polarized, and find its polarization direction.

3) An elliptically polarized wave is written (at z = 0) as

$$\vec{E}_T = \hat{\imath}\, A \sin 2\pi\nu t + \hat{\jmath}\, B \cos 2\pi\nu t.$$

Show that this can be decomposed into a linearly and a circularly polarized wave.

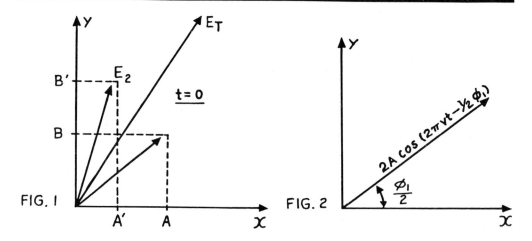

FIG. I

FIG. 2

Solution: 1) $E_1 = (\hat{\imath}A_1 + \hat{\jmath}B_1) \cos 2\pi\nu t,$

$$E_2 = (\hat{\imath}A_2 + \hat{\jmath}B_2) \cos 2\pi\nu t.$$

Now, add the components of E_1 and E_2 together to find the expression for E_T. Then, $E_T = \{\hat{\imath}(A_1 + A_2) + \hat{\jmath}(B_1 + B_2)\} \cos 2\pi\nu t.$

The point here is that the quantity in { } just specifies a vector, and the time variation is the same for all parts of it. So the vector lies along a line and changes size, but not direction. Therefore, $\vec{E}_T$ is linearly polarized.

In the case of circular polarization, this is not true, since the x and y components vary differently in time, one being large when the other is small.

2) Left: $E_1 = \hat{\imath}E_o \cos 2\pi\nu t + \hat{\jmath}E_o \sin 2\pi\nu t,$

Right: $E_2 = \hat{\imath}E_o \cos (2\pi\nu t + \alpha) - \hat{\jmath}E_o \sin (2\pi\nu t + \alpha).$

$E_T = \hat{\imath}E_o\{\cos 2\pi\nu t + \cos(2\pi\nu t + \alpha)\} + \hat{\jmath}E_o\{\sin 2\pi\nu t - \sin(2\pi\nu t + \alpha)\}$

$\cos(2\pi\nu t + \alpha) = \cos(2\pi\nu t + \frac{\alpha}{2} + \frac{\alpha}{2})$

376

Using one of the double angle formulas, we find

$\cos(2\pi\nu t + \alpha) = \cos(2\pi\nu t + \frac{\alpha}{2})\cos\frac{\alpha}{2} - \sin(2\pi\nu t + \frac{\alpha}{2})\sin\frac{\alpha}{2}$

$= \cos(2\pi\nu t + \frac{\alpha}{2})\cos\frac{\alpha}{2} - (\sin 2\pi\nu t \cos\frac{\alpha}{2} + \cos 2\pi\nu t \sin\frac{\alpha}{2})\sin\frac{\alpha}{2}$

where we have made use of the formula

$\sin(x + y) = \sin x \cos y + \cos x \sin y.$

Then, $\cos(2\pi\nu t + \alpha)$

$= \cos(2\pi\nu t + \frac{\alpha}{2})\cos\frac{\alpha}{2} - \sin 2\pi\nu t \cos\frac{\alpha}{2}\sin\frac{\alpha}{2} - \cos 2\pi\nu t \sin^2\frac{\alpha}{2}.$

Therefore, $\cos 2\pi\nu t + \cos(2\pi\nu t + \alpha)$

$= \cos 2\pi\nu t + \cos(2\pi\nu t + \frac{\alpha}{2})\cos\frac{\alpha}{2} - \sin 2\pi\nu t \cos\frac{\alpha}{2}\sin\frac{\alpha}{2}$

$- \cos 2\pi\nu t \sin^2\frac{\alpha}{2}.$

Substituting $1 - \cos^2\frac{\alpha}{2}$ for $\sin^2\frac{\alpha}{2}$ in the preceding expression yields the following result:

$\cos(2\pi\nu t) + \cos(2\pi\nu t + \alpha) = \cos(2\pi\nu t) + \cos(2\pi\nu t + \frac{\alpha}{2})\cos\frac{\alpha}{2}$

$- \sin(2\pi\nu t)\cos\frac{\alpha}{2}\sin\frac{\alpha}{2} + \cos(2\pi\nu t)\cos^2\frac{\alpha}{2} - \cos(2\pi\nu t).$

The $\cos(2\pi\nu t)$ terms cancel one another, and so,

$\cos(2\pi\nu t) + \cos(2\pi\nu t + \alpha)$

$= \cos(2\pi\nu t + \frac{\alpha}{2})\cos\frac{\alpha}{2} + \cos\frac{\alpha}{2}\left[\cos(2\pi\nu t)\cos\frac{\alpha}{2}\right.$

$\left. - \sin(2\pi\nu t)\sin\frac{\alpha}{2}\right].$

By applying the double angle formula $\cos(x + y) = \cos x \cos y - \sin x \sin y$, we have the result that $\cos(2\pi\nu t) + \cos(2\pi\nu t + \alpha)$

$= 2\cos(2\pi\nu t + \frac{\alpha}{2})\cos\frac{\alpha}{2}.$ Similarly, $\sin(2\pi\nu t) - \sin(2\pi\nu t + \alpha)$

$= 2\sin\frac{\alpha}{2}\cos(2\pi\nu t + \frac{\alpha}{2}).$

Therefore,

$$E_T = 2\hat{\imath}E_0\cos\left[2\pi\nu t + \frac{\alpha}{2}\right]\cos\frac{\alpha}{2} + 2\hat{\jmath}E_0\sin\frac{\alpha}{2}\cos\left[2\pi\nu t + \frac{\alpha}{2}\right]$$

$$= 2E_0\left[\hat{\imath}\cos\frac{\alpha}{2} + \hat{\jmath}\sin\frac{\alpha}{2}\right]\cos\left[2\pi\nu t + \frac{\alpha}{2}\right].$$

Since the two components are in phase, we can add them in a vector diagram: E_T is a vector of magnitude $2A\cos\{2\pi\nu t - (\phi_1/2)\}$ at an angle of $\phi_{1/2}$ to the y axis.

Notice that we can see some easy limiting cases in the first two lines: If $\alpha = 0$ the y components cancel out, while the x components add to $E_T = \hat{\imath}2E_0\cos(2\pi\nu t)$ ($\alpha = 2\pi$ just

377

multiplies everything by -1). If $\alpha = \pi/2$, we get $E_T =$

$2E_0$ ($\hat{\imath} \cos \frac{\pi}{4} + \hat{\jmath} \sin \frac{\pi}{4}$) $\cos (2\pi\nu t + \frac{\pi}{4})$

$= \sqrt{2}E_0 (\hat{\imath} + \hat{\jmath}) (\cos 2\pi\nu t \cos \frac{\pi}{4}$

$\qquad - \sin 2\pi\nu t \sin \frac{\pi}{4})$

$= E_0 (\hat{\imath} + \hat{\jmath}) (\cos 2\pi\nu t - \sin 2\pi\nu t)$

linearly polarized at 45 degrees.

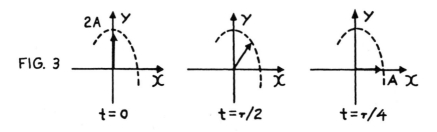

FIG. 3

$t = 0$ $t = \tau/2$ $t = \tau/4$

    3) $E = \hat{\imath}A \sin 2\pi\nu t + \hat{\jmath}B \cos 2\pi\nu t$.

First take out a circularly polarized part:

$E_0 = \hat{\imath}A \sin 2\pi\nu t + \hat{\jmath}A \cos 2\pi\nu t$.

What is left is $E_{lin} = \hat{\jmath}(B - A) \cos 2\pi\nu t$, a linearly polarized wave. To show that the original wave is elliptically polarized, draw the vector at various times, as shown in the figure.

● **PROBLEM 14-12**

Describe the polarization state of the following waves:

1) $\vec{E}_T = \hat{\imath} E_0 \sin [2\pi(z/\lambda - vt)]$

      $+ \hat{\jmath} E_0 \cos [2\pi(z/\lambda - vt)]$.

2) $\vec{E}_T = \hat{\imath} E_0 \sin [2\pi(z/\lambda + vt)]$

      $+ \hat{\jmath} E_0 \sin [2\pi(z/\lambda + vt - 1/8)]$.

3) $\vec{E}_T = \hat{\imath} E_0 \sin [2\pi(z/\lambda - vt)]$

      $- \hat{\jmath} E_0 \sin [2\pi(z/\lambda - vt)]$.

<u>Solution:</u> 1) The two components of $\vec{E}_T$ are

$E_x = E_0 \sin \left[2\pi\left(\frac{z}{\lambda} - vt)\right)\right]$, $E_y = E_0 \cos \left[2\pi\left(\frac{z}{\lambda} - vt)\right)\right]$.

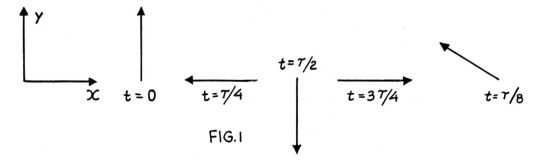

FIG.1

These are actual components of a real vector, not phasors, so we want to construct the resultant at various times and also some convenient place like $z = 0$.

t	0	$\tau/4$	$\tau/2$	$3\tau/4$	$\tau/8$ $(\tau = \frac{1}{v})$
E_x	0	$-E_o$	0	E_o	$-E_o/\sqrt{2}$
E_y	E_o	0	$-E_o$	0	$+E_o/\sqrt{2}$

The resultant vector is simply a vector of length E, rotating counterclockwise. The polarization is circular.

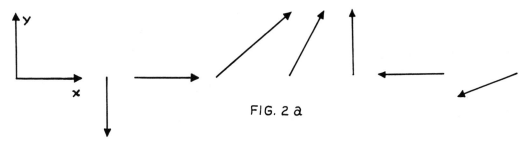

FIG. 2 a

2) The components of the given vector are

$$E_x = E_o \sin\left[2\pi\left(\frac{z}{\lambda} + vt\right)\right]$$

$$E_y = E_o \sin\left[2\pi\left(\frac{z}{\lambda} + vt - \frac{1}{8}\right)\right]$$

Again we consider the point $z = 0$ and follow the resultant as time progresses.

t	0	$\tau/8$	$2\tau/8$	$3\tau/8$	$4\tau/8$	$5\tau/8$	$6\tau/8$
E_x	0	$+E_o\sin\frac{\pi}{4}$	E_o	$E_o\sin\frac{\pi}{4}$	0	$-E_o\sin\frac{\pi}{4}$	$-E_o$
E_y	$-E_o\sin\frac{\pi}{4}$	0	$+E_o\sin\frac{\pi}{4}$	E_o	$E_o\sin\frac{\pi}{4}$	0	$-E_o\sin\frac{\pi}{4}$

The locus of the end of $E_{Resultant}$ is an ellipse at 45 degrees to the axes, as shown in figure 2b.

To find the semi-major axis, look at the time when $E_x = E_y$: this is halfway between $t = 0$ and $t = \tau/8$: $t = \tau/16$.

Hence

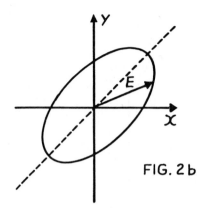

FIG. 2b

$$E_x = E_o \sin \left(\frac{\pi}{8}\right) , \quad E_y = E_o \sin \left(\frac{-\pi}{8}\right) :$$

$$E_R = E_o \sin \left(\frac{\pi}{8}\right) \sqrt{2} = 0.542 E_o$$

To find the semi-minor axis, which is $\tau/4$ later, $t = \tau/16 + \tau/4 = 5\tau/16$. So we have:

$$E_x = E_o \sin \left(\frac{5\pi}{8}\right) , \quad E_y = E_o \sin \left(\frac{3\pi}{8}\right) ,$$

$$E_R = E_o \sin \left(\frac{3\pi}{8}\right)\sqrt{2} = 1.31 E_o .$$

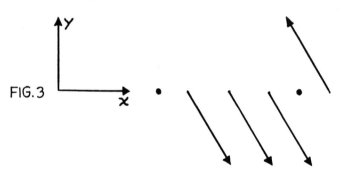

FIG. 3

3) The components of $\vec{E}_T$ are

$$E_x = E_o \sin \left[2\pi\left(\frac{x}{\lambda} - vt\right)\right] .$$

$$E_y = -E_o \sin \left[2\pi\left(\frac{z}{\lambda} - vt\right)\right] .$$

As before, z = 0 is most convenient point.

t	0	$\tau/8$	$\tau/4$	$3\tau/8$	$4\tau/8$	$5\tau/8$
E_x	0	$E_o \sin \frac{\pi}{4}$	E_o	$+E_o \sin \frac{\pi}{4}$	0	$-E_o \sin \frac{\pi}{4}$
E_y	0	$-E_o \sin \frac{\pi}{4}$	$-E_o$	$-E_o \sin \frac{\pi}{4}$	0	$E_o \sin \frac{\pi}{4}$

Thus the polarization is linear, along a line at 45 degrees
to the axes. It has amplitude $E_o/\sqrt{2}$.

EFFECT OF POLARIZERS AND ANALYZERS
ON THE TRANSMISSION OF LIGHT

● **PROBLEM** 14-13

How must a polarizer and an analyzer be oriented so that a
beam of natural light is reduced to a) 1/2, b) 1/4, c) 1/8
of its original intensity?

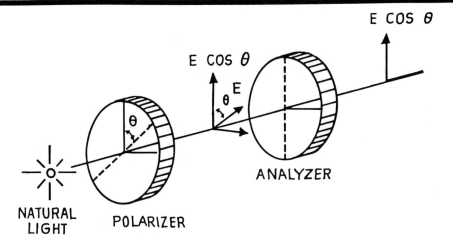

Solution: When light is incident on a polarizer (which may
be a pile of plates, a Nicol Prism or a Polaroid Sheet),
only linear light is transmitted. If this light is allowed
to pass through the analyzer (which is just another polarizer), the intensity of the transmitted light depends on
the relative orientation between the analyzer and the
polarizer. Let the transmission axis of the analyzer make
an angle θ with that of the polarizer. The linear light
transmitted by the polarizer may then be resolved into two
components, one parallel and another perpendicular to the
transmission axis of the analyzer. If the incident light
has amplitude E, only the parallel component E cos θ is
transmitted through the analyzer. Thus the transmitted
light is maximum when θ = 0 and zero when θ = 90°. At
intermediate angles, since the intensity of light is proportional to the square of the amplitude, we have

$$I_{transmitted} = I_{incident} \, Cos^2\theta$$

$$\frac{I_{transmitted}}{I_{incident}} = Cos^2\theta$$

$\dfrac{I_{transmitted}}{I_{incident}}$	Cos θ	θ
1/2	0.707	45°

381

1/4	0.5	60°
1/8	0.3535	69.3°

● **PROBLEM** 14-14

Elliptically polarized light whose Jones vector is $\begin{bmatrix} 3 \\ i \end{bmatrix}$ is sent through a quarter-wave plate, the fast axis being in the x - direction. What is the state of polarization of the emerging light?

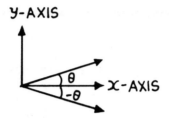

Y-AXIS

X-AXIS

Solution: The elliptically polarized light has Jones vector

$\begin{bmatrix} 3 \\ i \end{bmatrix}$ The Jones matrix for the quarter-wave plate is given by $e^{\left(i\frac{\pi}{4}\right)}\begin{pmatrix} 1 & 0 \\ 0 & -i \end{pmatrix}$ with the fast horizontal axis

The emergent light is given by

$$\begin{pmatrix} E_{tx} \\ E_{ty} \end{pmatrix} = e^{\left(i\frac{\pi}{4}\right)} \begin{bmatrix} 1 & 0 \\ 0 & -i \end{bmatrix} \begin{bmatrix} 3 \\ i \end{bmatrix}$$

$$= e^{\left(i\frac{\pi}{4}\right)} \begin{bmatrix} 3 \\ 1 \end{bmatrix}$$

Therefore, $E_t x = 3\, e^{\left(i\frac{\pi}{4}\right)}$

$$E_t y = e^{\left(i\frac{\pi}{4}\right)}$$

Hence the emerging light is plane polarized at an angle given by

$$\theta = \tan^{-1}\left[\frac{E_{ty}}{E_{tx}}\right] = \tan^{-1}\left(\frac{1}{3}\right) = 18.4° .$$

from the horizontal axis.

● **PROBLEM** 14-15

Use Jones matrices to solve each part of this problem:

(A) Determine the effect of a linear polarizer with (a) transmission axis horizontal, (b) transmission axis vertical, and (c) transmission axis at 45° to the horizontal, on light linearly polarized in the x - direction.

(B) Determine the effect of a right circular polarizer on light linearly polarized in the x - direction.

(C) Determine the effect of a quarter-wave plate with fast axis (a) vertical, (b) horizontal, and (c) at an angle of 45° to the horizontal, on right circularly polarized light.

Solution: (A) The Jones vector representing light linearly polarized in the x - direction is $\begin{bmatrix} 1 \\ 0 \end{bmatrix}$.

The Jones matrices for a linear polarizer with trans-mission axis horizontal, transmission axis vertical, and transmission axis at 45° to the horizontal, are $\begin{vmatrix} 1 & 0 \\ 0 & 0 \end{vmatrix}$, $\begin{vmatrix} 0 & 0 \\ 0 & 1 \end{vmatrix}$, and $1/2 \begin{vmatrix} 1 & 1 \\ 1 & 1 \end{vmatrix}$, respectively.

(a) $\begin{vmatrix} 1 & 0 \\ 0 & 0 \end{vmatrix} \begin{vmatrix} 1 \\ 0 \end{vmatrix} = \begin{vmatrix} 1 \\ 0 \end{vmatrix}$. Therefore, the emerging light remains linearly polarized in the horizontal direction.

(b) $\begin{vmatrix} 0 & 0 \\ 0 & 1 \end{vmatrix} \begin{vmatrix} 1 \\ 0 \end{vmatrix} = \begin{vmatrix} 0 \\ 0 \end{vmatrix}$. Therefore, no light will emerge from the polarizer.

(c) $1/2 \begin{vmatrix} 1 & 1 \\ 1 & 1 \end{vmatrix} \begin{vmatrix} 1 \\ 0 \end{vmatrix} = 1/2 \begin{vmatrix} 1 \\ 1 \end{vmatrix}$. So, the emergent light will be linearly polarized at an angle of 45° with respect to the horizontal axis.

(B) The Jones matrix which represents a right circular polarizer is $1/2 \begin{vmatrix} 1 & i \\ -i & 1 \end{vmatrix}$. $1/2 \begin{vmatrix} 1 & i \\ -i & 1 \end{vmatrix} \begin{vmatrix} 1 \\ 0 \end{vmatrix} = 1/2 \begin{vmatrix} 1 \\ -i \end{vmatrix}$.

This is the Jones vector representing right circularly polarized light.

(C) The Jones matrices representing quarter wave plates with fast axis vertical, horizontal, and at angle of 45° to the horizontal, are $\begin{vmatrix} 1 & 0 \\ 0 & -i \end{vmatrix}$, $\begin{vmatrix} 1 & 0 \\ 0 & i \end{vmatrix}$, and $\frac{1}{\sqrt{2}} \begin{vmatrix} 1 & i \\ i & 1 \end{vmatrix}$, respective-ly.

As already stated, the Jones vector representing right circularly polarized light is $\begin{vmatrix} 1 \\ -i \end{vmatrix}$.

(a) $\begin{vmatrix} 1 & 0 \\ 0 & -i \end{vmatrix} \begin{vmatrix} 1 \\ -i \end{vmatrix} = \begin{vmatrix} 1 \\ -1 \end{vmatrix}$. This represents light linearly polarized at an angle of -45° to the vertical.

(b) $\begin{vmatrix} 1 & 0 \\ 0 & i \end{vmatrix} \begin{vmatrix} 1 \\ -i \end{vmatrix} = \begin{vmatrix} 1 \\ 1 \end{vmatrix}$. This represents light linearly polarized at an angle of 45° to the vertical.

(c) $\frac{1}{\sqrt{2}} \begin{vmatrix} 1 & i \\ i & 1 \end{vmatrix} \begin{vmatrix} 1 \\ -i \end{vmatrix} = \frac{1}{\sqrt{2}} \begin{vmatrix} 2 \\ 0 \end{vmatrix}$. This represents

383

light linearly polarized in the horizontal direction.

● **PROBLEM** 14-16

A series of three parallel Polaroid disks A, B, and C are placed between a source of light and an observer. At first, A and B alone are set up, and arranged to give maximum transmission. Disk C is then added, and set relative to A and B to give zero transmission through the series. Finally, B is rotated. How does the transmission intensity vary with the angle θ through which B is turned?

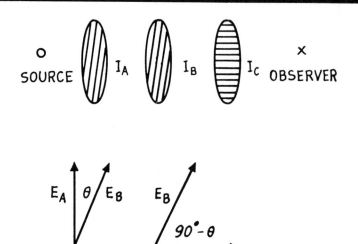

Solution: As shown in the figure accompanying this problem, A and B have their axes directed parallel to one another, and C must therefore have its axis directed perpendicularly to those of A and B so as to give zero transmission through the series of disks.

Now, assuming that disk B is rotated through an angle of θ, we have (as shown in the figure) the equation $E_B = E_A \cos \theta$, where E_B and E_A represent the electric vectors of the light relative to B and A, respectively.

Then, since the intensity I of the light beam is proportional to E^2, we have that $I_B = I_A \cos^2 \theta$.

Now, referring back again to the figure, we can see that $E_C = E_B \cos (90° - \theta) = E_B \sin \theta$, which implies that

$I_C = I_B \sin^2 \theta$. Therefore, the transmitted intensity, $I_{C'} =$

$I_B \sin^2 \theta = I_A \cos^2 \theta \sin^2 \theta$, or in other words, $I_{transmitted}$

$= I_{incident} \cos^2 \theta \sin^2 \theta$.

384

Show by means of the Jones calculus that circularly polarized light is produced by sending light through a linear polarizer and a quarter-wave plate only in the right order.

Solution: We begin with an unpolarized beam normalized so that it is represented by

$$\frac{1}{\sqrt{2}} \begin{bmatrix} 1 \\ 1 \end{bmatrix}$$

The linear polarizer is represented by

$$\frac{1}{2} \begin{bmatrix} 1 & 1 \\ 1 & 1 \end{bmatrix}$$

and the quarter wave plate is given by $e^{\left(\frac{i\pi}{4}\right)} \begin{bmatrix} 1 & 0 \\ 0 & i \end{bmatrix}$

Hence, the beam obtained after passing through a linear polarizer and a quarter-wave plate is

$$\begin{bmatrix} E_{tx} \\ E_{ty} \end{bmatrix} = \frac{e^{\left(\frac{i\pi}{4}\right)}}{2\sqrt{2}} \begin{bmatrix} 1 & 0 \\ 0 & i \end{bmatrix} \begin{bmatrix} 1 & 1 \\ 1 & 1 \end{bmatrix} \begin{bmatrix} 1 \\ 1 \end{bmatrix}$$

$$= \frac{e^{\left(i\frac{\pi}{4}\right)}}{2\sqrt{2}} \begin{bmatrix} 1 & 0 \\ 0 & i \end{bmatrix} \begin{bmatrix} 2 \\ 2 \end{bmatrix}$$

$$= \frac{e^{\left(i\frac{\pi}{4}\right)}}{\sqrt{2}} \begin{bmatrix} 1 \\ i \end{bmatrix}$$

, which is the Jones vector representation of left circularly polarized light.

If the order is reversed, then

$$\begin{bmatrix} E_{tx} \\ E_{ty} \end{bmatrix} = \frac{\exp^{\left(i\frac{\pi}{4}\right)}}{2\sqrt{2}} \begin{bmatrix} 1 & 1 \\ 1 & 1 \end{bmatrix} \begin{bmatrix} 1 & 0 \\ 0 & i \end{bmatrix} \begin{bmatrix} 1 \\ 1 \end{bmatrix}$$

$$= \frac{\exp^{\left(i\frac{\pi}{4}\right)}}{2\sqrt{2}} \begin{bmatrix} 1 & 1 \\ 1 & 1 \end{bmatrix} \begin{bmatrix} 1 \\ i \end{bmatrix}$$

$$= \frac{\exp^{\left(i\frac{\pi}{4}\right)}}{2\sqrt{2}} \begin{bmatrix} 1 + i \\ 1 + i \end{bmatrix}$$

which is not the Jones vector for circularly polarized light.

Ordinary light is incident on a pile of eight glass plates
at the polarizing angle. If the index of refraction of
each plate, n, is 1.75, find the percentage polarization
of the light transmitted.

Solution: If I_p and I_s represent the intensity components
of the light emerging from a glass plate vibrating parallel
and perpendicularly, respectively, to the plane of incidence,
the proportion of polarization is defined by the relation

$$PP = \frac{I_p - I_s}{I_p + I_s}$$

In deriving an equation for PP for a pile of plates, one
must take into account the perpendicular components of
light which by multiple reflection between the glass surfaces finally find their way through the last plate to be
observed as the transmitted beam.

The correct expression for PP is

$$PP = \frac{m}{m + \left(\dfrac{2n}{1 - n^2}\right)^2}$$

where m is the number of plates (2m surfaces) and n the refractive index. Thus, for m = 8 and n = 1.75,

$$PP = \frac{8}{8 + \left(\dfrac{3.50}{1 - (1.75)^2}\right)^2} \cong 0.735$$

$$\text{or } 73.5\%$$

Show that the effect of a half-wave plate with its axis at
an angle of θ to the polarization direction of plane-
polarized light is to rotate the plane of polarization
through 2θ.

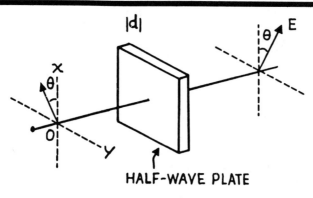

HALF-WAVE PLATE

Solution: Let us choose the fast and slow directions respectively as the OX and OY directions of a coordinate
system. Then OZ is the direction of propagation. The
surface on which the light is incident may be taken as the
XOY plane.

Let the incident beam be represented by

$$E_0 = a \cos wt \qquad\qquad (1)$$

If the plane of polarization makes an angle θ with OX, the
components Ex and Ey (polarized parallel to OY and OX respectively) may be represented by

$$Eoy = a \cos \theta \cos wt \qquad\qquad (iii)$$

$$Eox = a \sin \theta \cos wt \qquad\qquad (ii)$$

(It should be remembered that here the plane of the vector
represented by E_0 is at right angles to the plane of polarization.)

After the light has passed through a thickness z of the
plate, the components are

$$Ex = a \sin \theta \cos w \left(t - \frac{z}{b_1}\right) \qquad\qquad (iv)$$

$$Ey = a \cos \theta \cos w \left(t - \frac{z}{b_2}\right) \qquad\qquad (v)$$

where b_1 and b_2 are the fast and slow velocities, respectively. It is assumed that the propagation is normal to the
plate. This is mostly true.

The phase difference δ, between the two components on
emergence through a thickness d, is

$$\delta = \frac{2\pi}{\lambda} d(\mu_2 - \mu_1) \qquad\qquad (vi)$$

where $d(\mu_2 - \mu_1)$ is the optical path difference traversed
by the two beams and λ is the wave length in air.

Hence equations (iv) and (v) can be rewritten as

$$Ex = A \cos (wt - kz) \qquad\qquad (vii)$$

$$Ey = B \cos (wt - kz - \delta) \qquad\qquad (viii)$$

where $A = a \sin \theta$

$$B = a \cos \theta, \text{ and } k = \frac{w}{b_1}$$

Now $\dfrac{Ex}{A} = \cos (wt - kz)$

and $\dfrac{Ey}{B} = \cos (wt - kz - \delta)$

$$= \cos (wt - kz) \cos \delta + \sin (wt - kz) \sin \delta$$

$$= \frac{Ex}{A} \cos \delta + [1 - \cos^2 (wt - kz)]^{1/2} \sin \delta$$

or $\frac{Ey}{B} - \frac{Ex}{A} \cos \delta = [1 - \cos^2 (wt - kz)]^{1/2} \sin \delta$

$$= \left[1 - \left(\frac{Ex}{A}\right)^2\right]^{1/2} \sin \delta$$

squaring and rearranging, we have

$$\left(\frac{Ey}{B}\right)^2 + \left(\frac{Ex}{A}\right)^2 - \frac{2 \, Ey \, Ex \, \cos \delta}{AB} = \sin^2 \delta \qquad \text{(ix)}$$

For a half wave plate $\quad \delta = \pi$

Therefore, equation (ix) becomes

$$\left(\frac{Ey}{B}\right)^2 + \left(\frac{Ex}{A}\right)^2 + \frac{2 \, Ey \, Ex}{AB} = 0$$

or $\left(\frac{Ey}{B} + \frac{Ex}{A}\right)^2 = 0$

or $Ey = -\frac{B}{A} Ex$.

This is the equation of a plane wave which is inclined at an angle $(-\theta)$ to the fast axis. Hence the plane of polarization has been rotated from $(+\theta)$ at incidence to $(-\theta)$ at emergence or rotated through an angle of 2θ.

● **PROBLEM** 14-20

A quarter-wave plate is inserted between crossed Nicol prisms and then rotated slowly about the light beam as an axis. How many maxima and minima of the transmitted light intensity will be observed in a 360° rotation?

Solution: A Nicol Prism is an optical device made from Calcite and is used in producing and analyzing plane polarized light. It is made in such a way that it removes one of the two refracted rays by total internal reflection. When two Nicol prisms are crossed, the e-ray transmitted by the first becomes the o-ray for the second and is totally reflected. Thus no light emerges from the second Nicol, which is called the analyzer.

When a quarter wave plate is inserted between the two Nicols, the plane polarized light entering the crystal is modified by it. The emergent beam from the quarter wave plate is no longer plane polarized. This can then be decomposed into two components, one parallel to the principal axis of the analyzer and another perpendicular to the principal axis. The component that is parallel is transmitted through the analyzer.

A plane vibration of amplitude A making an angle of θ with the quarter wave plate is broken up into two compo-

388

nents, $E = A \cos \theta$ and $O = A \sin \theta$. These two components are out of phase when they arrive at the analyzer. Now only the components E' and E'' parallel to the principal plane of the analyzer are transmitted.

$$E' = E \sin \theta = A \cos \theta \sin \theta$$

$$E'' = O \cos \theta = A \sin \theta \cos \theta$$

These two waves, equal in magnitude, are in the same plane and are out of phase by $\pi/4$. They interfere with each other on emergence and the intensity is given by

$$R^2 = \left(E'\right)^2 + \left(E''\right)^2 - 2 E' E'' \cos (\pi/4)$$

$$= (A \sin \theta \cos \theta)^2 + (A \sin \theta \cos \theta)^2$$

$$- 2 A^2 \sin^2 \theta \cos^2 \theta \cos \pi/4$$

$$= 2 A^2 \sin^2 \theta \cos^2 \theta \ (1 - \cos \pi/4)$$

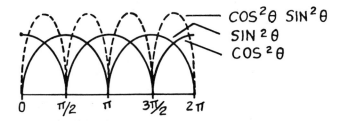

This function is shown in the figure as a function of θ. It is clear that the intensity has four minima and four maxima over a 2π rotation.

● **PROBLEM 14-21**

A horizontal beam of light traverses a tank containing water with a suspension of colloidal particles. An observer looks through a Nicol prism along a direction at right angles to the beam. By how much is the intensity of the light he sees reduced by turning the Nicol prism through an angle of 40° from the position where maximum intensity is observed?

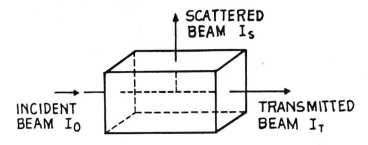

Solution: Let I_s be the intensity of the scattered beam at right angles to the incident beam. Due to the scattering

389

by the colloidal particles, this beam will be plane polarized. Let $I_{s(max)}$ be the intensity of this beam when viewed through the Nicol prism. As the Nicol prism is rotated from this position, the intensity transmitted by it is given by

$$I = I_{s(max)} \cos^2 \theta$$

where θ is the angle of rotation of the Nicol prism from its position for maximum intensity. Hence, the reduction in intensity of the beam is given by

$$I_{s(max)} - I = I_{s(max)} - I_s (max) \cos^2 40°$$

$$= I_s(max) \ [1 - \cos^2 40°]$$

Hence, the percentage of light reduced

$$= \frac{I_s (max) - I}{I_s (max)} \ \% = [1 - \cos^2 40°] \times 100$$

$$= [1 - .587] \times 100$$

$$= 41.3\%$$

● **PROBLEM** 14-22

Light passes through a polarizing and an analyzing Nicol prism. Find the percentage reduction in intensity when the analyzer is rotated through 10° a) if initially its principal plane makes an angle of 20° with that of the polarizer, b) if initially its principal plane makes an angle of 70° with that of the polarizer. (In each case the angle is increased after rotation.)

Solution: (a) Let A be the amplitude of the light transmitted by the polarizing prism along its axis. Hence the intensity distribution of the light transmitted by it at various angles θ, measured with respect to the polarizer axis is

$$I = A^2 \cos^2 \theta$$

So, the intensity transmitted by the analyzer plane placed at 20° with respect to the polarizer plane is given by

$$I_{20} = A^2 \cos^2 20$$

When the analyzer plane is rotated by 10°, the angle between the polarizer plane and the analyzer plane is 30°. The intensity transmitted is $I_{30} = A^2 \cos^2 30$.

Hence, the percentage reduction in intensity is

$$\frac{I_{20} - I_{30}}{I_{20}} \times 100 = \frac{A^2 \cos^2 20 - A^2 \cos^2 30}{A^2 \cos^2 20} \times 100$$

$$= \frac{\cos^2 20 - \cos^2 30}{\cos^2 20} \times 100$$

$$= \frac{.8830 - 0.7500}{.8830} \times 100$$

$$= 15\%$$

(b)   Repeating the above calculation where the angle changes from 70° to 80°, we have the percentage reduction in intensity

$$= \frac{I_{70} - I_{80}}{I_{70}} \times 100$$

$$= \left(1 - \frac{I_{80}}{I_{70}}\right) 100$$

$$= \left(1 - \frac{\cos^2 80}{\cos^2 70}\right) \times 100 \qquad \text{(Note: A's cancel)}$$

$$= \left(1 - \frac{.03015}{.1170}\right) \times 100$$

$$= \left(1 - .2577\right) \times 100$$

$$= 74.2\%$$

● **PROBLEM 14-23**

A number (2N + 1) of sheets of material are stacked together, each with axis rotated by $\pi/4N$ with respect to the previous one.   The first and last are polarizers, the remainder are half-wave plates.   Find the ratio of final to incident light intensity.

Solution: The first device, a polarizer, reduces intensity to $I_o/2$ and polarizes along, say, the $\theta = 0$ line.   The next device, a half-wave plate, has its axis at $\theta = \pi/4N$, and so rotates the polarization through twice this angle to $\theta = \pi/2N$.   It absorbs no energy.   The third device has its axis along $\theta = 2(\pi/4N) = \pi/2N$, so it has no effect. The next half-wave plate rotates the light another $\pi/2N$, and so forth.   Every other half-wave plate has no effect. Those N which do something rotate it through $N(\pi/2N) = \pi/2$ so that it goes through the final polarizer without loss. The final intensity is $I_f = I_o/2$.

Calculate the angular separation for the two rays refracted
at the first boundary of a Fresnel prism.   Assume the prisms
have angles of 40° - 40° - 100° with the optic axes parallel to the side opposite the 100° angle, and use the indices

given for λ = 7600Å below.

λ	n_R	n_L
760.0 nm	1.53914	1.53920

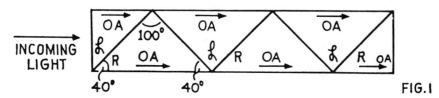

FIG.I

Solution: The Fresnel prism used in this problem is shown
in figure 1.   Since quartz, when in crystalline form, is
optically active, it will have different indices of refraction depending on the right or left circular polarization
of the incident light.   Looking at an incident beam, we
see that a light ray entering from the left will geometrically look as in figure 2.

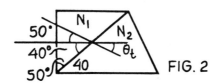

FIG. 2

Now we can use Snell's law of refraction

$n_1 \sin \theta_1 = n_2 \sin \theta_t$, where θ_1 = the angle of incidence

and θ_t = the angle of refraction.

Then $\sin \theta_t = \dfrac{n_1}{n_2} \sin \theta_1 = \dfrac{n_1}{n_2} \sin 50°$,

We have for the incident right and left circular polarized light the two conditions

$$\sin \theta_{t1} = \frac{n_L}{n_R} \sin 50°$$

and

$$\sin \theta_{t2} = \frac{n_R}{n_L} \sin 50°$$

or by substitution of the given values,

$$\sin \theta_{t1} = \frac{1.53920}{1.53914} \sin 50° = 0.766074$$

$$\sin \theta_{t2} = \frac{1.53914}{1.53920} \sin 50° = 0.766014$$

or

$$\theta_{t1} = 50.00266° \; ; \; \theta_{t2} = 49.99733°$$

and the angular separation, which is defined as the differ-
ence between θ_{t1} and θ_{t2}, is equal to 5.33 x 10^{-3} degrees.

DOUBLE REFRACTION

● **PROBLEM** 14-25

A beam of plane polarized light, for which λ = 6 x 10^{-5} cm,
falls normally on a thin piece of quartz cut so that the
optic axis lies on the surface. If n_E = 1.553 and n_O = 1.544,
find for what thickness of the crystal the difference in
phase between the E and the O beams, on emergence, is π
radians.

Solution: Use the following equation:

$$\Delta\phi = \frac{2\pi t}{\lambda} (n_E - n_O)$$

where $\Delta\phi$ is the phase difference, t is the thickness required,
λ is the wavelength, and (n_E - n_O) is the difference between the indices. Solving for the thickness t, we have:

$$t = \frac{\lambda \cdot \Delta\phi}{2\pi \cdot (n_E - n_O)}$$

and substituting the given data into the above equation,
we get:

$$t = \frac{6 \times 10^{-5} \text{ cm x } \pi}{2\pi (1.553 - 1.544)} = 0.0033 \text{ cm}$$

Hence the quartz is 0.033mm thick.

● **PROBLEM** 14-26

What minimum thickness of crystalline quartz is required
for a quarter wave plate? The indices of refraction of
quartz, for light of wavelength 589 mµ , are n_E = 1.553
and n_O = 1.544.

Solution: To find the minimum thickness required we apply

the equation $\phi_E - \phi_O = \frac{2\pi t}{\lambda} (n_E - n_O)$ (1)

where ϕ_E - ϕ_O is the phase difference, t is the thickness
of the plate, λ is the wavelength, and n_E and n_O the
indices of refraction. For a quarter wave plate, the
phase difference, ϕ_E - ϕ_O, is $\frac{\pi}{2}$.

393

Solving for t in equation (1) we have,

$$t = \frac{\lambda(\phi_E - \phi_o)}{2\pi(n_E - n_o)} \quad ,$$

and substituting in the given data, gives us

$$t = \frac{589 \text{ m}\mu \times \pi/2}{2\pi(1.553 - 1.544)}$$

$$t = 1.6 \times 10^4 \text{m}\mu = 16 \times 10^{-4} \text{ cm}.$$

Hence a thickness of at least 0.016 mm is required.

● **PROBLEM 14-27**

Plane polarized light of $\lambda = 5890\overset{\circ}{A}$ from a Nicol prism is incident normally on a plate of quartz 1mm thick and having its axis parallel to the surface. The principal section of the quartz is at 20° to that of the Nicol. The light then passes through a calcite rhomb, the principal section of which is at 90° to that of the polarizing Nicol. Calculate the relative intensity of the O and E beams.

FIG. I

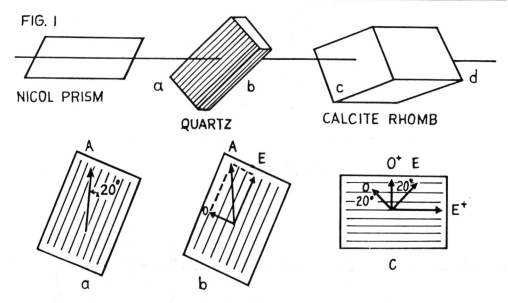

NICOL PRISM

QUARTZ

CALCITE RHOMB

Solution: Plane polarized light of amplitude A enters the quartz plate at (a). This amplitude is broken into two components, E = A cos 20° along the optic axis and O = A sin 20° perpendicular to the optic axis at (b). The optical path difference between the E and the O beams in the quartz is given by

$$\delta = \frac{2\pi}{\lambda} d\left(n_E - n_o\right), \text{ where } d = 0.1 \text{ cm., } \lambda = 5890(10^{-8}) \text{ cm,}$$

$$=$$

$n_E = 1.55330$, $n_o = 1.54425$ (n_o = the index of refraction of the O ray and n_E = the index of refraction of the E ray).

As a result of this phase difference we have, in fact, elliptically polarized light entering the calcite Rhomb at

394

(c). At (c) the amplitude components parallel to the E* axis are E sin 20° and O cos 20° .

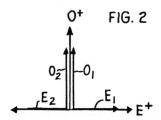

O⁺ FIG. 2

O_2 O_1

E_2 E_1 E⁺

The amplitude components parallel to the O* axis are
E cos 20° and O sin 20°

In each case the components differ in phase by δ , where δ = 97.18 radians corresponding to a net phase difference of 168°.

The following situation then exists

O_1 = E cos 20° = (A_0 cos 20°)(cos 20°) = A_0 (.883)

E_1 = E sin 20° = (A_0 cos 20°)(sin 20°) = A_0 (0.321)

O_2 = (A_0 sin 20°)(sin 20°) = A_0 (0.117)

E_2 = (A_0 sin 20°)(cos 20°) = A_0 (0.321)

To account for the 168° phase difference between the components in each case, we must add the components vectorially.

E_1 = 0.321 A_0

E_2 = 0.321 A_0

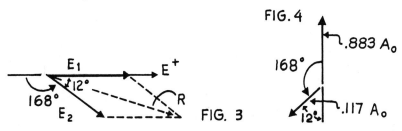

FIG.4

.883 A_0

168°

.117 A_0

12°

E_1 E⁺

12°

168° E_2 R FIG. 3

Hence, the angle opposite the side R = 168° and so,

$R^2 = E_1^2 + E_2^2 - 2E_1E_2 \cos 168°$

$\cos 168° = \cos (180 - 12)°$

$\qquad = \cos 180° \cos 12° + \sin 180° \sin 12°$

$\qquad = - \cos 12°$

Thus, $R^2 = (0.321A_0)^2 + (0.321A_0)^2 + 2(0.321A_0)^2 \cos 12°$

$\qquad = 0.4077A_0^2$

and so,

$R_{E*} = 0.6385A_0$

From figure 4, it can be seen that

$$R_{O*} = .883A_O - .117A_O \cos 12° = .7686$$

$$\frac{I_O}{I_E} = \frac{(R_{O*})^2}{(R_{E*})^2} = 1.449$$

Calculate the wave (phase) and group velocities of the O and E rays traveling in a calcite crystal perpendicular to the optic axis. Use the data given for λ = 4861 Å.

λ (A°)	μ_O	μ_E
4861.33	1.66785	1.49076
4046.56	1.68134	1.49694

Solution: The refractive index μ is the ratio of the velocity of light in vacuum to the phase velocity in the medium with refractive index μ. Hence the phase velocity v is given by

$$v = \frac{c}{\mu}$$

$$v_O = \frac{c}{\mu_O} = \frac{c}{1.66785} = 0.59957$$

$$v_e = \frac{c}{\mu_e} = \frac{c}{1.49076} = 0.67080 \text{ c.}$$

The group velocity u is related to the phase velocity v by the relation

$$u = v - \lambda \frac{dv}{d\lambda}$$

or $\quad \dfrac{1}{u} = \dfrac{1}{v} - \dfrac{\lambda}{c}\dfrac{d\mu}{d\lambda}$

where $\frac{d\mu}{d\lambda}$ is the change of refractive index μ with wavelength λ. From the given data we can obtain $\frac{d\mu}{d\lambda}$ and hence u. It is known that usually μ varies with λ according to Cauchy's relation

$$\mu = A + \frac{B}{\lambda^2} \text{ , where A and B are constants}$$

$$\frac{d\mu}{d\lambda} = \frac{-2B}{\lambda^3}$$

where
$$B = \frac{(\mu_1 - \mu_2)}{(\frac{1}{\lambda_1^2} - \frac{1}{\lambda_2^2})}$$

μ_1 is the refractive index for wave length λ_1 and μ_2 is the refractive index for wave length λ_2 . Using the data for the O-wave

$$B_O = \frac{1.68134 - 1.66785}{\frac{1}{(4046.56)^2} - \frac{1}{(4861.33)^2}} = 7.1925 \times 10^5 \text{ A°}^2$$

$\frac{d\mu}{d\lambda} = \frac{-2B}{\lambda^3}$; hence, $\frac{1}{u} = \frac{1}{v} - \frac{\lambda}{c} \frac{d\mu}{d\lambda} = \frac{1}{v} + \frac{2B}{c\lambda^2}$.

Thus, substituting into this equation for the 0-wave,

$$\frac{1}{u_O} = \frac{1}{v_O} + \frac{2}{c} \frac{7.1925 \times 10^{-11}}{(4861)^2 \, 10^{-16}}$$

$$= \frac{1}{c} \left[\frac{1}{0.6} + \frac{2 \times 7.1925 \times 10^{-11}}{(4861)^2 \, 10^{-16}} \right]$$

$u_O = 0.579c.$

similarly for the e-wave,

$$B_O = \frac{1.49694 - 1.49076}{\left[\frac{1}{(4046.56)^2} - \frac{1}{(4861.33)^2} \right]} = 3.295 \times 10^5 \text{ A°}^2$$

$$\frac{1}{u_e} = \frac{1}{v_e} + \frac{2}{c} \frac{3.295 \times 10^5}{(4861)^2}$$

$$\frac{1}{u_e} = \frac{1}{c} \left(\frac{1}{0.671} + \frac{2 \times 3.295 \times 10^5}{(4861)^2} \right)$$

$u_e = 0.659 \text{ C.}$

● **PROBLEM** 14-29

A polarizing prism of the Glan-type is to be made of quartz.
Determine the angle at which the diagonal face should be cut.

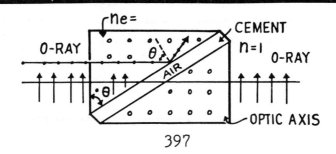

Solution: The Glan-type prism consists of two sections of natural uniaxial birefringent crystal. The optic axis is perpendicular to the plane of the figure. The ends or faces of the crystal are cut perpendicularly to the light beam. The index of refraction of the cement is such that at the angle of the cut, the ordinary wave suffers total internal reflection, whereas the extraordinary wave is transmitted with little loss.

n_O quartz $= 1.544$

n_E quartz $= 1.553$.

The O-ray sees the cement, penetrates from a lighter medium to a denser medium and hence suffers reflection and refraction.

However, the e-ray goes from a denser medium to a rarer medium and will suffer total internal reflection if the angle of incidence is greater than the critical angle.

Then the critical angle is given by

$$\sin \theta_c = \frac{1}{n_O} = \frac{1}{1.544}$$

Hence,

$$\theta_{c_1} = \sin^{-1} \left(\frac{1}{1.544} \right)$$

$$= \sin^{-1} (.647668)$$

$$= 40.366°$$

The critical angle for the e-ray is given by

$$\sin \theta_c = \frac{1}{n_E} = \frac{1}{1.553} = .643915$$

Hence,

$$\theta_{c_2} = \sin^{-1} (.643915)$$

$$= 40.084°$$

Hence the quartz prism must have its diagonal face cut such that the angle θ is halfway between θ_{c_1} and θ_{c_2}.

Thus, $\theta = \dfrac{\theta_{c1} + \theta_{c1}}{2}$

$$= (40.084 + 40.366)/2$$

$$= 40.23° \ .$$

● **PROBLEM 14-30**

A plate of quartz 0.54 mm thick is cut with its faces parallel to the axis. If a beam of plane-polarized light of wavelength 5461 Å is incident normally on the plate, what will be the phase difference between the two emergent beams ($n_O = 1.544$, $n_e = 1.553$)?

Solution: The phase difference δ between the two beams is given by

$$\delta = \frac{2\pi d}{\lambda} (n_o - n_e)$$

where λ is the wavelength, d is the thickness of the plate, and n_o and n_e are the refractive indices of quartz for the o and e ray, respectively.

Therefore, $\delta = \dfrac{-2 \times 3.142 \times 0.54 \times 10^{-3} [1.553 - 1.544]}{5.461 \times 10^{-7}}$

$= 9 \cdot 2\pi - \delta = 56.55 - 55.92 = .63$ rad $= .20\pi$

● **PROBLEM 14-31**

A ray of sodium light is incident on a calcite crystal at an angle of 70° to the normal. The optic axis lies in the surface and in the plane of incidence. Find the angles of refraction of the O and E rays.

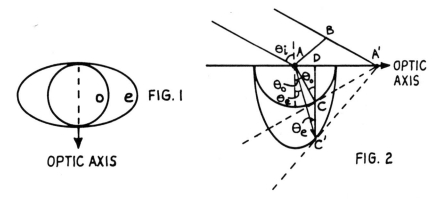

FIG. I

OPTIC AXIS

OPTIC AXIS

FIG. 2

Solution: Calcite is a negative uniaxial crystal and the wave surfaces for the ordinary (o) and the extraordinary (e) rays are shown in figure 1. The ordinary wave has the same velocity in all directions and the corresponding wavelets are spherical. The velocity of the extraordinary wave varies with direction and the wavelets are ellipsoids of revolutions. The angles of refraction are obtained by Huygen's construction for a plane wave. This construction is shown in figure 2, using the information that the optic axis is in the plane of incidence and lies on the surface. The minor axis of the e-wave ellipse lies on the surface. The section of the o-wave sphere which is a circle touches the ellipse at extremities of the minor axis.

For the ordinary wave, Snell's law is obeyed because it has the same velocity in all directions.

Hence, $\mu_o \sin \theta_o = \sin \theta_i$

Where μ_o is the ordinary refractive index, θ_o is the angle of refraction of the ordinary wave and θ_i is the angle of incidence. The wavelength of sodium light = 589.3 nm., and μ_o = 1.65836 and μ_e, the extraordinary refractive

399

index, = 1.48641. These values are obtained from a table.
Therefore,

$$\sin \theta_o = \frac{\sin 70°}{1.65836}$$

and $\theta_o = 34° \ 31'$.

Huygens construction will give us θ_e. The wave front
touching the optic axis at A reaches A' in the time the
O and E wave fronts develop, as shown in figure 2.

Drawing the tangent planes from A' to the wave surfaces
and joining the points of tangency to A we obtain the
refracted rays. A line joining the two points of contact
will cut the minor axis at right angles at D, since the
polar of any point in the chord of contact of a circle and
an ellipse having double contact is the same with regard to
both curves.

From figure 2

$$\tan \theta_o = \frac{AD}{CD}$$

$$\text{and} \quad \tan \theta_e = \frac{AD}{C'D} \ .$$

Then

$$\frac{\tan \theta_o}{\tan \theta_e} = \frac{AD}{CD} \ \frac{C'D}{AD} = \frac{C'D}{CD} =$$

the ratio of minor axis to the major axis

$$= \frac{\mu_o}{\mu_e}$$

$$\tan \theta_e = \mu_e \frac{\tan \theta_o}{\mu_o} = \frac{1.48641}{1.65836} \tan 34°31'$$

and $\theta_e = 31°99'$

● **PROBLEM** 14-32

A 30° calcite prism is cut with its refracting edge parallel to the optic axis. Find the angle of minimum deviation
for the O and E rays of sodium light (λ = 5892.90 A°,
μ_o and μ_e, the refractive indices corresponding to the
O and E rays, are 1.65836 and 1.48641, respectively.)

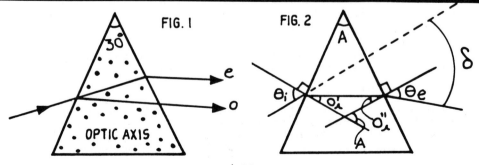

Solution: The o and e rays are refracted through the prism as shown in figure 1. The angle δ between the incident and emergent rays is known as the angle of deviation. Since the optic axis is parallel to the refracting edge, the optic axis is perpendicular to the plane of incidence. Realizing that the o and e wavelets are figures of revolution about the optic axis, it is clear that the sections for the o and e wavelets are both circular. In this plane the velocities of e- and o- rays do not depend on direction. Thus Snell's law is obeyed by both e- and o- rays.

$$\mu_e \sin \theta_e = \sin \theta_i$$

$$\mu_o \sin \theta_o = \sin \theta_i$$

where θ_i is the angle of incidence, θ_e is the angle of re-fraction of the e-ray, θ_o is the angle of refraction of the o-ray, and μ_e and μ_o represent the refractive indices cor-responding to the e and o rays, respectively. When Snell's law is obeyed, the angle of deviation is given by

$$\delta = \theta_i - \theta_r' + \theta_e - \theta_r''$$

where the angles are shown in figure 2.
Since $A = 180° - (180° - \theta_r' - \theta_r'') = \theta_r' + \theta_r''$,
as can be deduced from figure 2, this can be easily written as $\delta = \theta_i + \theta_e - A$
From Snell's law
$$\sin \theta_i = \mu \sin \theta_r'$$

$$\sin \theta_e = \mu \sin \theta_r''.$$

where μ is the index of refraction of the prism.
    To find where δ is a minimum we can differentiate the equation $\delta = \theta_i + \theta_e - A$ with respect to θ_i. Then,

$$\frac{d\delta}{d\theta_i} = 1 + \frac{d\theta_e}{d\theta_i} = 0.$$

Therefore

$$\frac{d\theta_e}{d\theta_i} = -1$$

From Snell's law, differentiating yields the following results:
$$\cos \theta_i \, d\theta_i = \mu \cos \theta_r' \, d\theta_r'$$

$$\cos \theta_e \, d\theta_e = \mu \cos \theta_r'' \, d\theta_r''.$$

Also $A = \theta_r' + \theta_r''$, hence, $\dfrac{d\delta}{d\theta_r'} = -1 - \dfrac{d\theta_r''}{d\theta_r'}$

δ is a minimum when $\dfrac{d\delta}{d\theta_r'} = 0$, or when $\dfrac{d\theta_r''}{d\theta_r'} = -1$.

Hence, $\dfrac{d\theta_i}{d\theta_e} = \dfrac{d\theta_r'}{d\theta_r''} = -1$ and so,

$$\frac{\cos \theta_i}{\cos \theta_e} = \frac{\cos \theta_r'}{\cos \theta_r''}$$

Since $\cos x = \sqrt{1-\sin^2 x}$,

$$\frac{\sqrt{1-\sin^2 \theta_i}}{\sqrt{1-\sin^2 \theta_t}} = \frac{\sqrt{1-\sin^2 \theta_r'}}{\sqrt{1-\sin^2 \theta_r''}}$$

It has already been determined that $\sin \theta_i = \mu \sin \theta_r'$ and $\sin \theta_t = \mu \sin \theta_r''$, where $\theta_t = \theta_e$.

Therefore,

$$\frac{\sqrt{1 - \sin^2 \theta_i}}{\sqrt{1 - \sin^2 \theta_t}} = \frac{\sqrt{1 - \dfrac{1}{\mu^2} \sin^2 \theta_i}}{\sqrt{1 - \dfrac{1}{\mu^2} \sin^2 \theta_t}}$$

Multiplying and dividing by μ produces the following result

$$\frac{\sqrt{1 - \sin^2 \theta_i}}{\sqrt{1 - \sin^2 \theta_t}} = \frac{\sqrt{\mu^2 - \sin^2 \theta_i}}{\sqrt{\mu^2 - \sin^2 \theta_t}}$$

After squaring both sides of this equation, we find that

$$\frac{1 - \sin^2 \theta_i}{1 - \sin^2 \theta_t} = \frac{\mu^2 - \sin^2 \theta_i}{\mu^2 - \sin^2 \theta_t} .$$

Cross multiplying yields the result

$$(1 - \sin^2 \theta_i)(\mu^2 - \sin^2 \theta_t) = (\mu^2 - \sin^2 \theta_i)(1 - \sin^2 \theta_t) .$$

Then, $\mu^2 - \mu^2 \sin^2 \theta_i - \sin^2 \theta_t + \sin^2 \theta_i \sin^2 \theta_t$

$= \mu^2 - \mu^2 \sin^2 \theta_t - \sin^2 \theta_i + \sin^2 \theta_i \sin^2 \theta_t .$

The μ^2 and $\sin^2 \theta_i \sin^2 \theta_t$ terms drop out on both sides of this equation, and so

$$-\mu^2 \sin^2 \theta_i - \sin^2 \theta_t = -\mu^2 \sin^2 \theta_t - \sin^2 \theta_i , \text{ or}$$

after collecting terms, $(1 - \mu^2)\sin^2\theta_i = (1 - \mu^2)\sin^2\theta_t$.

The only way this equation can be satisfied is for μ to $= 1$ (which only holds in a vacuum), or for $\sin^2\theta_i = \sin^2\theta_t$.

Thus $\theta_i = \theta_t$

and $\theta_r' = \theta_r''$.

This is determined from the equation

$$\frac{\cos\theta_i}{\cos\theta_t} = \frac{\cos\theta_r'}{\cos\theta_r''} . \quad \text{Since } \theta_i = \theta_t ,$$

$\cos\theta_i = \cos\theta_t$ and so,

$$\frac{\cos\theta_r'}{\cos\theta_r''} = 1 .$$

Thus the rays refract through the prism symmetrically

Then since $\delta = \theta_i - \theta_r' + \theta_t - \theta_r''$, and $A = \theta_r' + \theta_r''$,

$\delta = \theta_i + \theta_t - A$. It has been shown that $\theta_i = \theta_t$;

therefore, $\delta = 2\theta_i - A$, and

$$\theta_i = \frac{\delta + A}{2}$$

In addition, since $A = \theta_r' + \theta_r''$ and $\theta_r' = \theta_r''$,

$A = 2\theta_r'$, and so,

$$\theta_r' = \frac{A}{2} .$$

Hence, for minimum deviation

$$\sin \frac{\delta + A}{2} = \mu \sin \frac{A}{2} \quad \text{(Snell's law)}$$

$$\mu = \frac{\sin [(\delta + A)/2]}{\sin A/2}$$

Thus for ordinary and extraordinary rays,

$$\mu_o = \frac{\sin [(\delta^o + A)/2]}{\sin A/2}$$

$$\mu_e = \sin \frac{[(\delta^e + A)/2]}{\sin A/2}$$

403

Substitutuing into the above equations the given values for
A, μ_o, and μ_e, it is found that
$$\delta^o = 20°50' \; ,$$

and $\qquad \delta^e = 15°15'$

Explain the phenomenon of photoelasticity.

Solution: Ordinary glass is isotropic and exhibits no sign
of double refraction. When glass is subject to great
strain, however, it becomes doubly refracting. A convenient test of the presence of such strains is found, therefore, by placing the specimen between a crossed analyzer
and polarizer. If the glass has strains, it is doubly
refracting, two beams are transmitted, and the strains
are rendered evident by the appearance of interference
colors.

An important application of this fact has been made
to determine the distribution of stresses in solid opaque
materials used in engineering construction. To do so,
models of the material to be examined are made in glass or
in a transparent plastic substance like lucite or bakelite.
The models are then placed between analyzer and polarizer,
and from a study of the color pattern corresponding to
the strains in the transparent material, the actual stresses
can be determined. This phenomenon, with its application
in this way, is called photoelasticity.

In photoelasticity it is customary to use a circular
polariscope. This consists of a combination of the usual
polarizer and analyzer plus two quarter-wave plates, one
associated with the polarizer, the other with the analyzer.
Suppose that, before the introduction of the plates, the
analyzer and polarizer are set in the crossed position.
The introduction of a quarter-wave plate (properly oriented)
next to the polarizer gives circularly polarized light and
light is transmitted by the analyzer. A second quarter-
wave plate is now inserted in front of the analyzer and
rotated to such a position that there is again no light
transmitted through the analyzer. With this arrangement
the two quarter-wave plates have counteracted each other;
that is, they are now so placed that the component whose
phase was 90° ahead after traversing the first plate is
delayed 90° by the second, the net difference in phase between the two components now being zero. Although, as far
as extinction of transmitted light goes, the final result
is the same as if there were no quarter-wave plates, this
combination has the very great advantage that, if after
this preliminary adjustment has been made, the combination
of the analyzer and its quarter-wave plate is rotated, there
is still no light transmitted for any position.

When stresses are being examined in photoelasticity
and the specimen is placed between the polarizing and
analyzing units of a circular polariscope, it has the very

great advantage that the interference pattern remains constant for all positions of the specimen.

● **PROBLEM** 14-34

A beam of plane polarized light falls on a piece of Iceland
spar thick enough to separate the O and the E components.
If the vibration plane of the incident light makes an
angle of 20° with the principal plane of the crystal, find
the ratio of the intensity of the E beam to that of the O
beam.

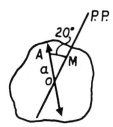

Solution: If the intensity of the original beam is proportional to a^2 or $= K^2a^2$, where K^2 is a constant, then the
amplitude of the original beam = Ka, where a is shown in
the figure.
    Since the crystal transmits vibrations only in the
principal plane (the E beam), or perpendicular to it (the
O beam), it is natural to resolve the incident disturbance
of amplitude a = OA in the figure, into one component, OM =
Ka cos 20° in the principal plane, and the other, of
amplitude AM = Ka sin 20° perpendicular to the principal
plane.   The first component will then be transmitted as
the E beam, the second as the O beam, so that we have

$$\frac{\text{amplitude of E beam}}{\text{amplitude of O beam}} = \frac{Ka \cos 20°}{Ka \sin 20°} = 2.75$$

and, therefore,

$$\frac{\text{intensity of E beam}}{\text{intensity of O beam}} = (2.75)^2 = 7.5.$$

● **PROBLEM** 14-35

A 60° quartz prism cut with the optic axis parallel to the
refracting edge throws a spectrum, focused with a lens,
on a wall 20 ft. from the prism.   With the prism set at
minimum deviation (approximately) for each ray, using
sodium light, what is the linear separation on the wall of
the sodium line formed by the ordinary and extraordinary
rays?   How does this compare with the separation of the
red and blue hydrogen lines (H_α and H_β) in the spectrum
of the ordinary ray?

Solution: Figure 1 shows the configuration used in this

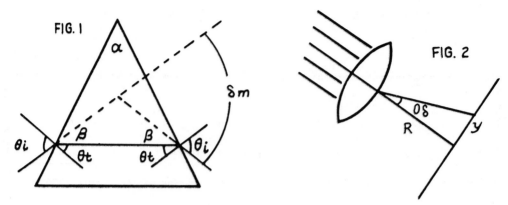

FIG. 1

FIG. 2

problem. For minimum deviation the ray in the prism is parallel to the base of the prism. By geometry we can then establish several relationships. First

$$\alpha + (90 - \theta_t) + (90 - \theta_t) = 180$$

$$\alpha/2 = \theta_t$$

$$\delta m = 2\beta \; ; \; \beta = (\theta_i - \theta_t) \tag{1}$$

$$\delta m = 2(\theta_i - \theta_t) = 2(\theta_i - \alpha/2)$$

$$\theta_i = (\delta m + \alpha)/2 . \tag{2}$$

So from Snell's law, $\quad n = \dfrac{\sin\theta_i}{\sin\theta_t} = \dfrac{\sin[(\alpha + \delta m)/2]}{\sin \alpha/2}$ (3)

Now since the prism is made of quartz, we have two indices of refraction for each wavelength. From equation (3) we can find a δm_o for the ordinary ray and a δm_e for the extraordinary ray and the difference $|\delta m_o - \delta m_e|$ will yield the angular separation. From optical tables we find that

light	wavelength	n_o	n_e
Na	589.3 nm	1.54424	1.55335
Hα	656.28 nm	1.54190	-
Hβ	486.13 nm	1.54968	-

So, substituting these values into equation (3), it is found that

$$1.54424 \sin 60/2 = \sin \frac{\delta m_o + 60}{2} \tag{4}$$

$$1.55335 \sin 60/2 = \sin \frac{\delta m_e + 60}{2} \tag{5}$$

$$1.54190 \sin 60/2 = \sin \frac{\delta m_{H\alpha} + 60}{2} \tag{6}$$

$$1.54968 \sin 60/2 = \sin \frac{\delta m_{H\beta} + 60}{2} \tag{7}$$

Solving equations 4, 5, 6, and 7 for δm_o, δm_e, δm_{H_α}, and δm_{H_β}, respectively, yields the following results:

$$\delta m_o = 41.0892°$$
$$\delta m_e = 41.9143°$$
$$\delta m_{H_\alpha} = 40.8785°$$
$$\delta m_{H_\beta} = 41.5811°$$

and $\Delta\delta m_1 = \delta m_e - \delta m_o = 0.8251° = 0.0144$ radians

$\Delta\delta m_2 = \delta m_{H_\beta} - \delta m_{H_\alpha} = 0.7026° = 0.0123$ radians.

If the incident light consists of parallel rays then the light out of the prism will also be paralel and the lens will cause these parallel rays to come to a focus at the focal point of the lens. Figure (2) shows this geometry and
$$y = R \sin (\Delta\delta) \approx R \Delta \delta \text{ for } \Delta\delta \text{ small.}$$

Thus,

$$Y_{oe} = 20 \times 0.0144 = 0.288 \text{ ft.} = 3.45 \text{ inches}$$
$$Y_{\alpha\beta} = 20 \times 0.0123 = 0.2452 \text{ ft.} = 2.94 \text{ inches.}$$

CHAPTER 15

RAY TRACING

MIRRORS

Find the image P'Q' of a point Q (where PQ represents the object) upon reflection by a spherical mirror as shown in Figure 1 by means of ray tracing. (C and F represent the center and the focal point of the mirror, respectively.)

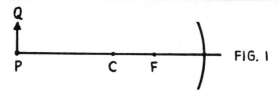

FIG. 1

Solution: Fig. 2 illustrates the graphical method applied to the formation of an image by a concave mirror. By tracing

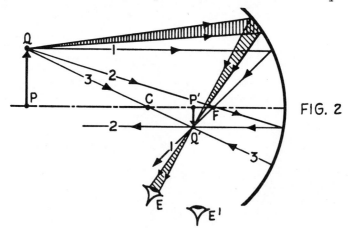

FIG. 2

the path of each of the three rays shown in Figure 2 (labeled 1, 2, and 3, respectively), one can locate the position of P'Q'. Ray 1, parallel to the axis before striking the mirror, passes through the focal point F after reflection. Ray 2, incident on the mirror after passing through the focal point, is parallel to the axis after reflection. Ray 3, incident on the mirror after passing

through the center of curvature C, strikes the mirror at
normal incidence and hence retraces its original path.
The point of intersection of any two of these rays suffices
to locate the image of the head of the arrow. Once this
point has been found, the paths of any other rays may be
traced.

The image P'Q' is a real image.

● **PROBLEM** 15-2

Using the method of ray tracing, find the position and
relative size of the image corresponding to an object
Q in figures 1-4 in the following four optical systems,
where F and F' are the focal points corresponding to the
principal planes H and H', and C is the center of curvature
corresponding to each mirror.

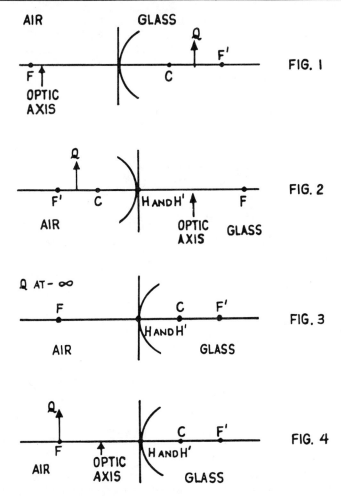

Solution: One can start with Q and draw a long, light
pencil line through it parallel to the axis without paying
any attention to what part of this line represents the path
of a ray.   At this stage, it is merely a construction line.
It crosses the secondary principal plane at V'.   A second

line is drawn through V' and F'. One can start again at Q and draw a line through Q and F to locate W in the primary focal plane. Through W a line is drawn parallel to the axis. The line through V' and F' crosses the line through W parallel to the axis at Q'. Having located Q and Q', one can use a red pencil to trace through the system the ray which in object space is directed through Q and F and also the second ray which in object space is directed through Q parallel to the axis. When Q is virtual, dotted lines can be used to show how forward extensions of the incident paths are directed through Q and when Q' is virtual, dotted lines can be used to show how backward extensions of the emerging paths are directed through Q'.

When Q' is given and Q has to be located, one can use essentially the same procedure, except that he must start at Q' and work backward.

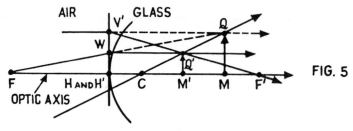

FIG. 5

It should be noted that figures 5, 6, 7, and 8 of this solution correspond to figures 1, 2, 3, and 4 of the problem.

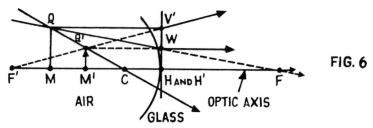

FIG. 6

In Figs. 5 and 6, the ray through the center of curvature is traced as well as the rays through F and F'. In Fig. 5 the object is virtual, and in Fig. 6 the image is virtual

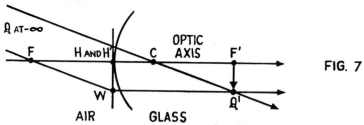

FIG. 7

In Fig. 7 Q lies at an infinite distance from the refracting surface, and one cannot trace a ray from Q parallel to the axis. However, parallel rays from Q are directed through F and C, and can be traced through the system to locate Q'.

In Fig. 8 Q' lies at an infinite distance. The ray traced through Q and C and the ray through Q parallel to the axis emerge parallel and directed toward Q'.

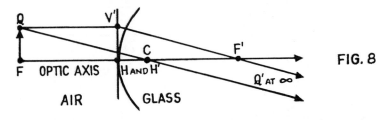

FIG. 8

● **PROBLEM** 15-3

Find the image of an object O after passing through a
mirror in each of the following eight cases, illustrated
in Figures a-h, by the method of the two ray trace procedure.   (Note: In Figures a-d, the mirror is concave;
while in Figures e-h, the mirror is convex.)

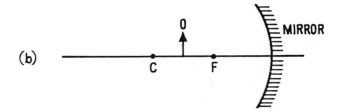

(a)

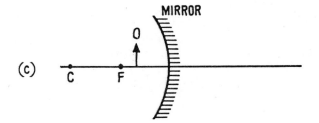

(b)

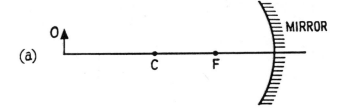

(c)

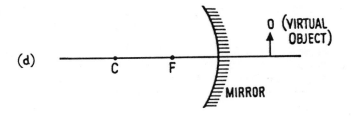

(d)

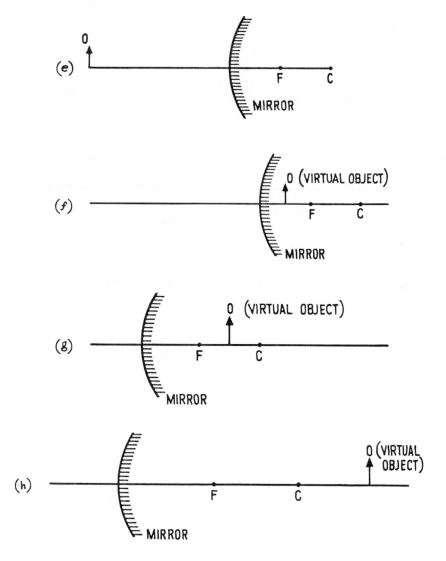

Solution: The selected-ray procedure employs only two rays. It is necessary to make one assumption: All rays emanating from an object point will converge to a single image point. If this assumption of freedom from aberration is granted, it follows that it is necessary to find only the common point of crossing of two rays. All other rays will then cross at the point, and thus that point will be the location of the image. The two rays selected, whose behavior can be readily predicted, are the following:

1. Any incident ray parallel to the optical axis, as from an infinitely distant source, must pass through the focal point after reflection. The behavior of this ray results from the definition of the focal point.

2. A ray passing through the center of rotation of the surface must be reflected back on itself since it strikes the surface perpendicularly. This means that the angle of incidence is zero and the angle of reflection must also be zero.

Image-forming mirrors are either concave or convex.
The important image characteristics are the following:

1.   Image size relative to object

2.   Image erect or inverted

3.   Image real or virtual

These image characteristics depend on the power of the
reflecting surface, whether it is concave or convex, and the
distance of the object from the surface.   A convex mirror
produces only virtual images but a concave mirror, depending
on the object distance, produces both real and virtual.
Based upon these concepts, the two rays corresponding to
figures (a) through (h) have been traced and the
image has been located in each case.   (Figures 1 through 8
correspond to figures (a) through (h).)

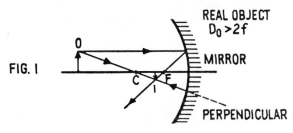

Fig. 1.   Image formation by the two ray trace procedure
by a concave mirror when the object is located more distant than the center of curvature.   The image is inverted,
real, and reduced in size.

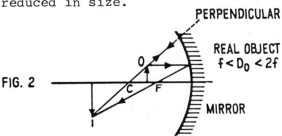

Fig. 2.   Image formation by the two ray trace procedure
by a concave mirror when the object is located between the
focal point and the center of curvature.   The image is
inverted, real, and enlarged.

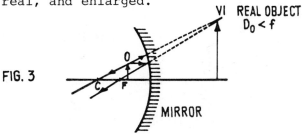

Fig. 3.   Image formation by the two ray trace procedure by
a concave mirror when the object is located closer to the
mirror than the focal point.   The image is erect, virtual,
and enlarged.

413

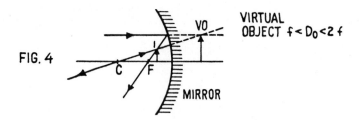

FIG. 4

VO

VIRTUAL
OBJECT $f < D_0 < 2f$

C F

MIRROR

Fig. 4. Image formation by the two ray trace procedure by
a concave mirror when the object is virtual. The image is
real, upright, and reduced in size.

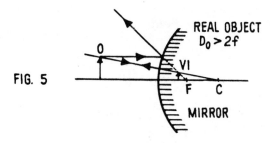

FIG. 5

O

REAL OBJECT
$D_0 > 2f$

VI

F C

MIRROR

Fig. 5. Image formation by the two ray trace procedure
by a convex mirror. The object may be located at any distance from the mirror. The image is virtual, erect, and
reduced in size.

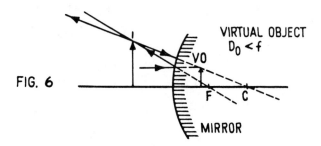

FIG. 6

VO

VIRTUAL OBJECT
$D_0 < f$

F C

MIRROR

Fig. 6. Image formation by the two ray trace procedure by
a convex mirror when the object is virtual and located
between the mirror and the focal point. The image is real,
erect, and enlarged.

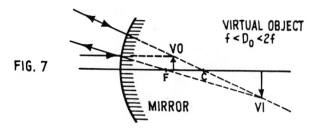

FIG. 7

VO

VIRTUAL OBJECT
$f < D_0 < 2f$

F C

MIRROR

VI

Fig. 7. Image formation by the two ray trace procedure by
a convex mirror when the object is virtual and located
between the focal point and the center of curvature. The
image is virtual, inverted, and enlarged.

414

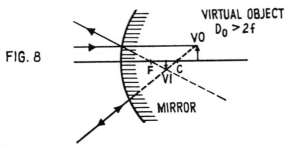

VIRTUAL OBJECT
$D_0 > 2f$

FIG. 8

VO

F C
VI

MIRROR

Fig. 8.   Image formation by the two ray trace procedure by
a convex mirror when the object is virtual and located
more distant than the center of curvature.   The image is
virtual, inverted, and reduced in size.

● **PROBLEM** 15-4

Find the position of the image of the arrow OP in Fig. 1,
formed by the plane mirrors MV and M'V.

Solution: Extend the plane of the mirror MV to m.   Construct lines from P and O perpendicular to this plane, and
make P'a = Pa, O'b = Ob.   The image of an object which
is formed by a plane mirror is virtual, meaning that the
image appears to be located at a point behind the mirror.
Because the angle of reflection is equal to the angle of
incidence, angles ePa and eP'a as shown in Figure 1, are
equal.

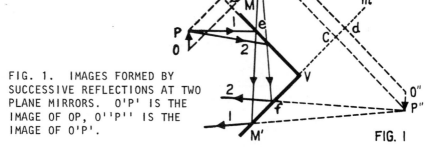

FIG. 1.   IMAGES FORMED BY
SUCCESSIVE REFLECTIONS AT TWO
PLANE MIRRORS.   O'P' IS THE
IMAGE OF OP, O''P'' IS THE
IMAGE OF O'P'.

FIG. I

Since the side $\overline{ae}$ is common to triangles Pea and
P'ea, the triangles are congruent.   Therefore, $\overline{Pa} = \overline{P'a}$,
where a is a point on the plane of the mirror.   Hence, the
image must be focused at O'P' since it is known that for
a plane mirror, the image and object distances must be
equal.   The second mirror, M'V, forms an image of this image.
Extend the plane of M'V to m'.   Construct lines from O' and
P', perpendicular to this plane, and make P''c = P'c,
O''d = O'd.   By analyzing triangles P'fc and P''fc in the
way outlined above, one finds that $\overline{P'c} = \overline{P''c}$, and therefore,
that the image of P'O' must be located at P''O''.   The
construction may be verified by drawing a few rays from P.
Ray 1, for example, may be drawn from P in any arbitrary

415

direction to the mirror MV, and its direction after reflection found from the law of reflection. When the reflected
ray is projected backward it will be found to pass through
P'. The same ray after reflection from M'V, when projected
backward, will be found to pass through P''.

LENSES

● **PROBLEM** 15-5

Define the magnifying power of a magnifying lens. Also
illustrate the difference in the size of the image of an
object O as observed by the human eye formed by a magnifier
(with O not precisely at the focal point F of the magnifier)
as compared with its size observed with unaided eye.

Solution: Magnifying power is achieved by allowing the
object of regard to be located at a distance nearer to the
observer's eye than the near point of the eye. In optics,
the accepted standard for the near point of the eye is
25 cm. Magnifying power is an angular phenomenon, and
therefore may be illustrated with only two rays. These are
the following:

1. A ray drawn from the object parallel to the optical axis
    which passes through the focal point of the magnifier
    upon emerging from it.

2. A ray through the nodal point from the object of regard.

    The simple magnifier has its greatest magnifying power
when the object is located at the first focal point of the
lens.

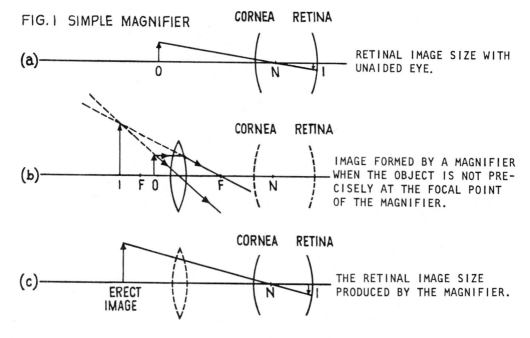

FIG. I SIMPLE MAGNIFIER

(a) CORNEA RETINA O N I RETINAL IMAGE SIZE WITH UNAIDED EYE.

(b) CORNEA RETINA I F O F N IMAGE FORMED BY A MAGNIFIER WHEN THE OBJECT IS NOT PRE- CISELY AT THE FOCAL POINT OF THE MAGNIFIER.

(c) CORNEA RETINA ERECT IMAGE N I THE RETINAL IMAGE SIZE PRODUCED BY THE MAGNIFIER.

In practice, the object is generally not located precisely at the focal point of the magnifying lens. If the departure from the focal point is small, the error introduced is not great. A situation of this type is illustrated in Figure 1. The image formed by the magnifying lens is shown together with the final size of the retinal image when the object is viewed through the magnifying lens.

When the eye is viewing without a magnifier, the object is assumed to be at the near point or 25 cm. When the observer views with the magnifier, it is also assumed that the object is located at the focal point of the magnifying lens. These assumptions result in a simplified definition of magnifying power as follows:

$$\text{M.P.} = \frac{25\ \text{cm}}{\text{focal length of magnifying lens (centimeters)}}$$

● **PROBLEM** 15-6

Determine the final image of an object 0 after passing through each of the two optical systems, (a) and (b). The optical system shown in (a) consists of two convex lenses, and the optical system shown in (b) consists of one concave and one convex lens.

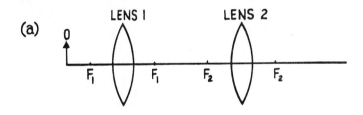

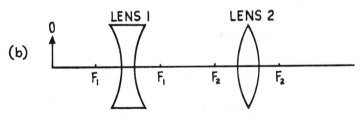

Solution: The principles of the two ray trace procedure employed for concave and convex mirrors may be applied to the problems of lenses. As in the case for mirrors, two rays are chosen whose behavior is obvious and their intersection point is determined. This is the location of the image. The two rays of predictable behavior are the following:

The first ray is one emanating from an object point traveling parallel to the optical axis and is indistinguishable from a ray from an infinite object. This ray, after refraction by the lens, must pass through the focal point.

The second ray passes directly through the center of the lens. This ray travels in a straight line and is not deviated by the lens.

Three additions are necessary to the very simple two ray trace rules employed in single lenses and mirrors. These additions are the following:

The source of light serves as the object for the first element in the optical system. After the rays pass through the initial element, the source is ignored.

The image from the first element acts as an object for the second, and so on for all succeeding elements. It makes no difference whether the images are virtual or real; they are all treated in turn as objects.

After an image has been formed by an element, that element may be disregarded.

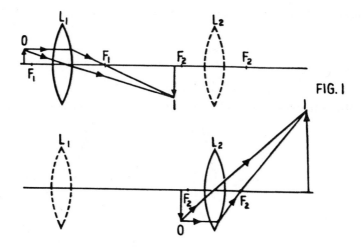

FIG. I

Figures 1 and 2 illustrate image formation by the two ray trace procedure by the optical systems shown in (a) and (b), respectively.

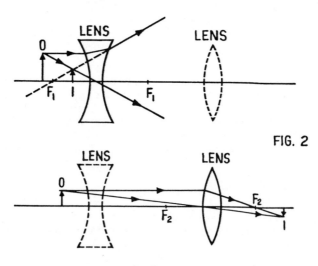

FIG. 2

418

Give a formal definition of the principal plane, nodal points, and focal points of a thick lens.

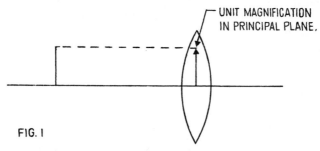

UNIT MAGNIFICATION IN PRINCIPAL PLANE.

FIG. 1

Solution: There are three pairs of cardinal points on the optical axis; the three cardinal planes, corresponding to these points, are planes perpendicular to the optical axis passing through the points. Some of the cardinal characteristics are generally referred to as planes and others as points. The cardinal planes and points commonly encountered are the principal planes, nodal points, and focal points.

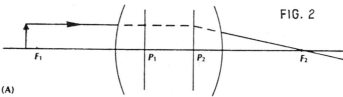

FIG. 2

(A)

THE TWO PRINCIPAL PLANES OF A THICK LENS.

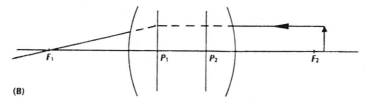

(B)

Principal Plane. A formal definition of a principal plane is that it is a plane of unit magnification (Fig. 1). However, it is best defined by reference to additional diagrams. In Figures 2 and 3, light from an object at infinity enters the lens at the left and is brought to a focus at F. In the two ray trace procedure, the ray parallel to the optical axis is assumed to be refracted at the principal plane. The principal point is located in the principal plane on the optical axis.

In an infinitely thin lens, there is one principal plane and it is assumed to be in the center of the lens. If a lens has finite thickness, there are two principal planes, designated P_1 and P_2 in Figure 2. If the incident ray from the left is extended forward and the exiting ray backwards into the lens represented by the interrupted lines in Figure 2, the point at which the extended rays intersect defines

419

the principal plane P_2. If the parallel rays are brought in from the right, another principal plane, P_1, can be defined.

Focal Point. The focal point is located on the axis of a lens. Rays from an infinitely distant object, also located on the lens axis, are brought to a focus by the lens at the focal point (Fig. 3). Another way of defining the focal point is by stating that the focal point is conjugate to an object at infinity on the optical axis.

FIG. 3

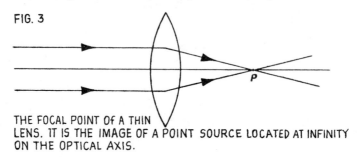

THE FOCAL POINT OF A THIN LENS. IT IS THE IMAGE OF A POINT SOURCE LOCATED AT INFINITY ON THE OPTICAL AXIS.

It is now possible to define the focal length more precisely. The focal length is the distance between the principal plane and the focal point. The focal length of a thin lens is illustrated in Figure 4. There is one

FIG. 4

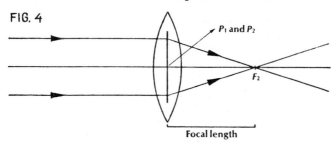

Focal length

principal plane resulting from the superposition of P_1 and P_2. In Figure 5, which shows a thick lens, the focal length is the distance between P_2 and F_2.

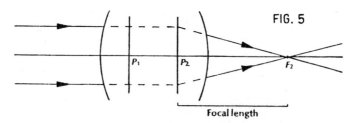

FIG. 5

Focal length

Nodal Point. The nodal point of a thin lens is characterized by no angular deviation from the initial to the final media of a refracted ray passing through the point. The angle at the first surface of the incident ray passing through the nodal point is equal to the angle of refraction

at the final surface. The incident and refracted rays are parallel.

420

Describe the differences between thin and thick lenses which must be taken into consideration when applying the techniques of ray tracing to them.

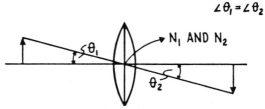

Fig. 1 The nodal points of a thin lens. They are superimposed and the ray passing through the nodal points is undeviated if the lens is infinitely thin.

Solution: In the two ray trace procedure, an infinitely thin lens has been assumed. Consequently, the ray through the nodal point may be drawn as a straight line as in Figure 1. This is one of the two rays employed in the two ray trace procedure.

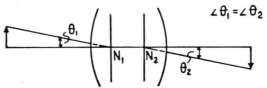

Fig. 2 The nodal points of a thick lens. The emerging ray appears to arise from the second nodal point and is parallel to the incident ray.

In thick lenses, there are two nodal points, N_1 and N_2, illustrated in Figure 2. As the thickness of the lens is increased, there is greater separation of the two nodal points. A ray entering a thick lens from the left, as in Figure 2, directed toward the first nodal point (N_1), will emerge from the lens appearing to come from the second nodal point (N_2). However, the ray directed toward the first nodal point is actually refracted at all optical surfaces within the thick lens. Snell's law is obeyed at these surfaces.

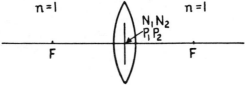

Fig. 3 The cardinal points of a thin lens in air.

In a thin lens, all nodal points and principal points are superimposed and assumed to be located in the center of the lens (Fig. 3). The principal plane will also pass through this point on the optical axis.

In most optical situations, the indices of refraction of the media of the object and image space are equal. Ordinarily this means that the object and the image are both located in air. In that situation, the first nodal point is superimposed on the first principal point and the second nodal point is superimposed on the second principal point. The ordinary thick lens is illustrated in Figure 4.

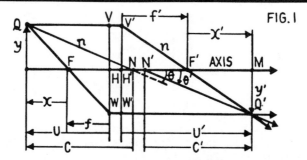

Fig. 4 The cardinal points of a thick lens in air.

● **PROBLEM** 15-9

For the cases of (a) a thick lens having two principal planes, and (b) a thin lens for which the planes coincide, illustrate the method of ray tracing.

USE OF THE NODAL POINTS AS REFERENCE POINTS.

Solution: (a)   As shown in Figure 1, one can use the nodal points to trace a ray through an optical system from an object point Q to its conjugate image point Q'. The incident ray is directed through the object point and the first nodal point N. The refracted ray emerges from the system parallel to the incident ray and directed through the second nodal point N'.

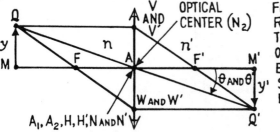

FIG. 2   USE IN RAY TRACING OF THE OPTICAL CENTER OF A THIN LENS BOUNDED ON BOTH SIDES BY THE SAME MEDIUM.

(b)   The nodal points are especially helpful in the case of a thin lens bounded on both sides by the same medium, because they coincide at the optical center. Thus, a single straight line drawn through the optical center and a given object point must pass through the conjugate image point (see Fig. 2).

422

One can use the focal points and principal planes to trace certain rays from an extra-axial object point through a single refracting surface to locate the conjugate image point. Conversely, rays can be traced backward from the image point to locate the object point.

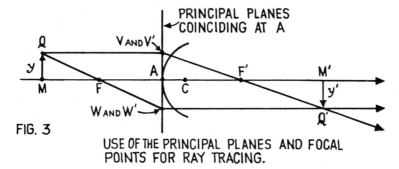

FIG. 3

USE OF THE PRINCIPAL PLANES AND FOCAL POINTS FOR RAY TRACING.

The principal planes coincide and are tangent to the surface at the vertex and may be substituted for the surface in ray tracing. In Fig. 3, a ray through Q parallel to the axis is represented as being redirected at V' through the secondary focal point. A ray through Q and F is redirected at W' parallel to the axis.

The theoretical basis for assuming that the rays may be represented as being redirected at V' and W' may be explained as follows: V' and W' are points conjugate to V and W, which lie in the secondary principal plane. V' and W' coincide with V and W because the secondary principal plane coincides with the primary principal plane and because these are conjugate planes that have unit magnification. A ray in object space directed through V must pass through V' in image space, and if the ray is parallel to the axis in object space, it must pass through F in image space. For similar reasons, the ray in object space directed through F and W must be directed through W' and Q' parallel to the axis in image space.

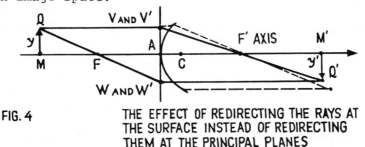

FIG. 4

THE EFFECT OF REDIRECTING THE RAYS AT THE SURFACE INSTEAD OF REDIRECTING THEM AT THE PRINCIPAL PLANES

Most students want to know why we get a different answer for the location of Q' if the rays are redirected at the surface instead of at the principal planes. This discrepancy is illustrated in Fig. 4.

If we were interested in tracing the actual paths of the rays QV and QF, it would be necessary to represent them as undeviated until they strike the surface, but these rays penetrate the surface so far from the axis that it could not be assumed that the ray QV passes through the secondary

focal point after refraction or that the ray QF proceeds
parallel to the axis after refraction.

In a sense QV and QF do not represent actual rays. A
Gaussian ray tracing diagram such as Fig. 3 is an attempt
to show what would happen if we tried to trace rays from
an object point Q that lies very close to the axis.   If
Q were very close to the axis, the rays QV and QF would
penetrate the surface close to the axis.   The distance from
the principal plane to the points of penetration at the
surface would be negligible.

If the arc representing the surface were simply left
off the diagram, it could be regarded as a diagram grossly
expanded in the vertical direction to show in more detail
what happens close to the axis.

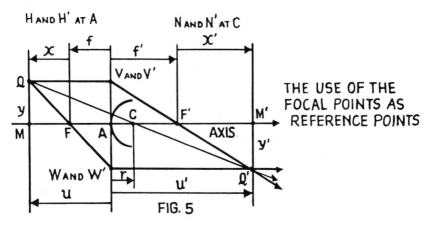

The nodal points of a single refracting surface are
very useful in ray tracing.   Since they coincide at the
center of curvature, a straight line drawn through the center
of curvature and a given object point must also pass through
the conjugate image point (see Fig. 5).

● **PROBLEM** 15-10

Show the tracing of a ray through a plano-convex lens, with
the light coming from the first focal point. By definition, the light is made parallel to the optic axis after
refraction, and the second principal plane, H_2, is tangent
to the back surface of the lens. Find the separation of
the two principal planes.

Solution: From the construction in Figure 1, it follows
that
$$f_1 = S + D - e$$
Thus,
$$e = S + D - f_1$$

Distances S and D can easily be measured, S by collima-
tion or autocollimation, and D mechanically. Turning the
lens around, f_2--and hence the location of H_2--is found in
the same way.

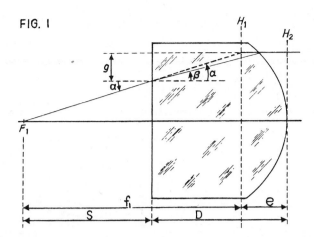

FIG. I

If we knew the location of H_1, any ray coming from F_1 could easily be traced. It can be seen from Figure 1 that

$$\tan \alpha = \frac{g}{D - e} \quad \text{and} \quad \tan \beta \cong \frac{g}{D}$$

Expressing both equations in terms of g and equating them

$$(D - e) \tan \alpha \cong D \tan \beta$$

or

$$\frac{\tan \alpha}{\tan \beta} \cong \frac{D}{D - e}$$

Since α and β are small, the following approximation is valid:

$$\frac{\tan \alpha}{\tan \beta} \cong \frac{\sin \alpha}{\sin \beta} \quad .$$

Snell's law can be written such that

$$\frac{\sin \alpha}{\sin \beta} = \frac{n_2}{n_1} \quad , \text{ where } n_2 = \text{the index of refraction}$$

in medium H_1 and n_1 = the index of refraction of the medium through which the light passes before reaching H_1. Let $\frac{n_2}{n_1}$ = n, the relative index of refraction. Therefore,

$\frac{\tan \alpha}{\tan \beta} \cong n$ and $\frac{D}{D - e} \cong n$. This implies that $D \cong (D - e)n$ and $D \cong Dn - en$. Therefore, $en \cong Dn - D = D(n-1)$, and so,

$$e \cong D \frac{n - 1}{n}$$

Therefore, for glass of n = 1.5, the separation of the two principal planes is

$$e \cong \frac{1}{3} D$$

425

TELESCOPES

State and explain the function of the basic component parts of the telescope.

FIG. I

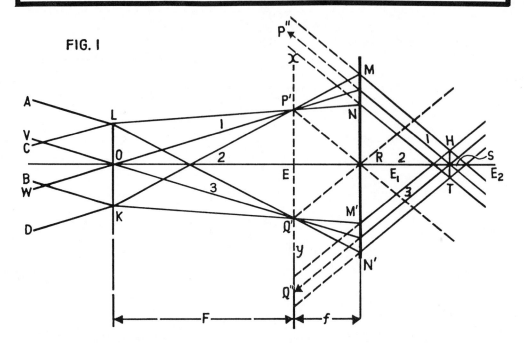

Solution: The telescope, an instrument used to observe a distant object, consists essentially of (a) the objective, a converging lens which forms a real image of the distant object in its focal plane and (b) an eyepiece, which, in the simplest case, is a single converging lens through which this real image is viewed. The eye lens, then, is used as a magnifying glass forming a virtual image at any distance between 25 cm and infinity. Since, as already noted, the eye muscles are subject to the least strain when parallel rays fall on the eye, in the work that follows we shall assume that the instrument has been adjusted so that this is the case, that is, for most comfortable vision.

Fig. 1 shows the optical paths of two bundles through such an instrument: (1) AVB, parallel rays, from a point on one side of a distant object; and (2) CWD, another parallel bundle from a point on the other side of the object. Corresponding real point images are then formed by the objective at Q' and P', so that, if a screen (or photographic plate) is placed in the plane P'Q', a sharp image of the distant object is seen (or photographed). Actually the rays spread out from P' and Q', eventually, on emergence from the eye lens, giving rise to the bundles MNHT and M'N'HT. These emergent bundles will consist of parallel rays, if ER = f, the focal length of the eye lens. When these emergent bundles fall on the eye, point images are formed on the retina and the eye sees the final virtual image at P''Q'' (at infinity).

426

Illustrate and describe the function of an astronomical telescope, indicating its important features.

Solution: An astronomical telescope is an auxiliary optical device used in conjunction with an eye or a camera to permit the eye or camera to view an inverted magnified image of a distant object. In viewing an extra-terrestrial object like a star, it is not important whether the image is upright or inverted.

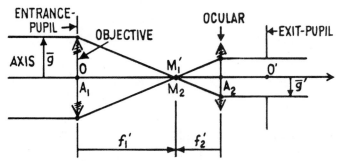

FIG.1   ASTRONOMICAL TELESCOPE. THE OBJECT POINT M LIES ON THE AXIS AT AN INFINITE DISTANCE.

As illustrated in Fig. 1, an astronomical telescope may consist of two thin convex lenses, the first of which constitutes the objective and the second the ocular. Parallel incident rays from a distant object point M on the axis come to a focus in the secondary focal plane at M'_1, and the same point serves as an object point M_2 for the ocular. The ocular can be moved in a fore and aft direction, and when it is properly focused for a normal eye, the primary focal plane of the ocular coincides with the secondary focal plane of the objective. Consequently, the rays from the point M_1' emerge from the ocular parallel.

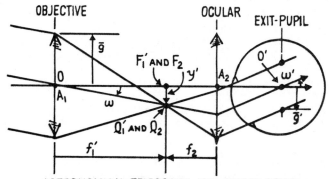

FIG. 2   ASTRONOMICAL TELESCOPE. THE OBJECT POINT Q LIES OFF THE AXIS AT AN INFINITE DISTANCE.

Fig. 2 shows how a set of parallel rays from an infinitely distant, extra-axial point Q_1 are brought to a focus at Q'_1. The aerial image formed by the objective is inverted,

and since the image formed by the ocular is not reinverted,
the image seen by the eye is inverted.

An astronomical telescope is illustrated in Figure 1. Define the magnifying power of a telescope and determine its
value for the telescope shown in Figure 1.

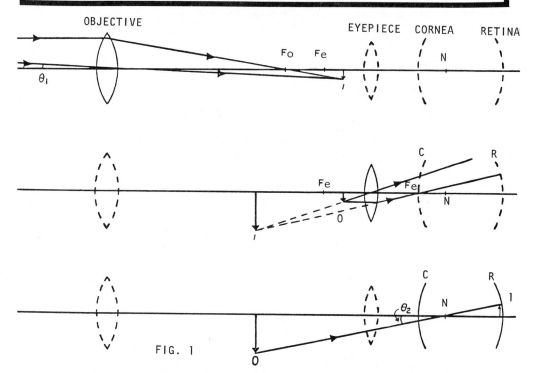

FIG. 1

Solution: A telescope is an optical system designed to
increase the apparent magnification of distant objects.
Schematically, two lenses are employed. The objective,
the first lens, forms a small image of the distant object.
A strong magnifying glass, the second lens, is then used
to look at the image formed by the objective. The final
apparent magnification of a telescope depends on the magnification produced by the objective and the apparent
magnification by the ocular. For the astronomical telescope shown in Figure 1, the image of an object at infinity
is formed at the focal point (F) of lens 1. Lens 2, the
eyepiece, is placed so that its focal point is also at F.
Thus rays from the image will be parallel as they leave the
eyepiece and enter the eye.

The angular magnification γ of a telescope is defined
as the ratio of the tangent of the angle subtended at the
eye by the final image I', to the tangent of the angle subtended at the (unaided) eye by the object. This is equivalent to defining γ as the ratio of retinal image size with
the telescope divided by retinal image size without the
telescope. With distant objects, for which a telescope is
used, the retinal image size is proportional to the angle

428

subtended by the object at the eye since when θ is very
small, tan θ ∼̃ θ. Therefore, the magnifying power is the
ratio of the apparent angle of an object at the eye with
the telescope to the apparent angle without the telescope.
The angles are illustrated in Figure 1. The magnifying
power is given by

$$\gamma \text{ (also denoted by M.P.) } \widetilde{\sim} \frac{\theta_2}{\theta_1} .$$

Since the image is at the focal points of each lens, it
can be shown that the ratio of the angles is equal to the
ratio of the focal length of the objective to that of the
eyepiece, that is,

$$\text{M.P. } \widetilde{\sim} \theta_2/\theta_1 = f_1/f_2$$

Inspection of Figure 1 indicates that the astronomical
telescope results in the formation of an inverted image.
Furthermore, the image of the objective has not been located
at the precise focal point of the ocular. The figure was
prepared in this manner to permit illustration of the image
formed by the ocular.

● **PROBLEM** 15-14

Explain the differences between an astronomical telescope,
a terrestrial telescope, and a prism binocular.

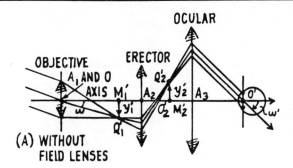

(A) **WITHOUT
FIELD LENSES**

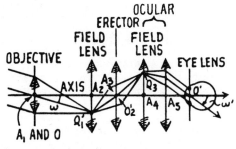

(B) **WITH FIELD LENSES**

FIG. I TERRESTRIAL
TELESCOPE. THE
OBJECT POINT Q LIES
OFF THE AXIS AT AN
INFINITE DISTANCE.

Solution: The terrestrial telescope (see Fig. 1) differs
from the astronomical telescope in that it includes an
erecting unit between the secondary focal plane of the objective and the primary focal plane of the ocular. This

429

unit, which may consist of two single convex lenses used in successive conjunction or a simple double convex lens, reinverts the image formed by the objective. The image viewed through the terrestrial telescope is therefore upright.

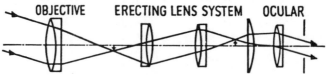

FIG. 2   A TERRESTRIAL TELESCOPE.

It has the disadvantage of requiring an unduly long tube, since four times the focal length of the erecting lens must be added to the sum of focal lengths of objective and ocular.

The long draw tube of the terrestrial telescope is avoided in the prism binocular, of which Fig. 3 is a cut-away view. A pair of 45°-45°-90° totally reflecting prisms are inserted between objective and ocular. The image formed by the objective serves as a virtual object for the pair of prisms. The process by which the image is inverted as a

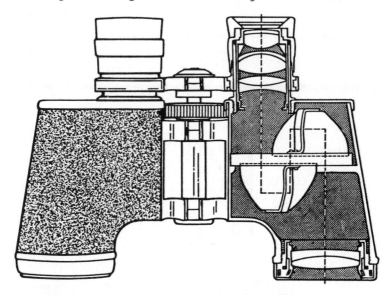

FIG. 3   THE PRISM BINOCULAR.

result of four reflections is illustrated in Fig. 4, where for simplicity a real object oabc is shown, and where one of the prisms has been omitted from the diagram to avoid confusion.

The first (virtual) image formed by reflection at the upper inclined face of the prism is at o'a'b'c'. The plane of the lower inclined face of the prism is extended by light lines, and o''a''b''c'' is the virtual image of o'a'b'c' formed by this face. Comparison of o''a''b''c'' with the object oabc shows that the second image is inverted. The orientation of the image in space is not the same as that of an inverted image formed by a lens but it must be remem-

430

bered that in the present case the direction of travel of
light has been reversed.

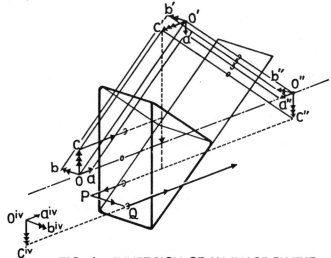

**FIG. 4   INVERSION OF AN IMAGE BY THE
PRISM SYSTEM OF A PRISM BINOCULAR.**

The path of a single ray from the head of arrow oc has
been traced through the system. This ray is initially
horizontal, is reflected down at the first inclined prism
face, then back horizontally. The second prism (not shown
in the figure) is mounted with its hypotenuse against that
of the first prism but with its triangular faces horizontal
instead of vertical. The ray from the head of arrow oc
enters the second prism through its hypotenuse, strikes one
of the shorter faces at point P at an angle of 45°, is
reflected across horizontally to point Q where it strikes
the other face, and then emerges from the hypotenuse
horizontally.

The final image $o^{iv}a^{iv}b^{iv}c^{iv}$ is shown in its correct
orientation but, to save space, not in its actual position,
which would be much farther to the left. If oabc represents
the once inverted image formed by the objective, the image
$o^{iv}a^{iv}b^{iv}c^{iv}$ is erect relative to the object being viewed.
Finally, since the ocular produces an erect (virtual) image,
the image seen by the eye is erect also.

● **PROBLEM** 15-15

List the essential features of the Herschel, Newton, Gregory, and Cassegrain telescopes.

Solution: Four types of reflecting telescopes are shown
in the Figure. In each case, a large concave mirror forms
an image of a distant object; the mirror corresponds to
the objective in a refracting telescope. The four types
differ in the arrangement made for observing the image with
an eyepiece.

In the Herschel telescope, the mirror is tilted so that the axis after reflection is not parallel to the axis before reflection. Therefore, it is not a centered optical system. A real image which can be viewed directly with an eyepiece is formed outside the path of the incoming beam.

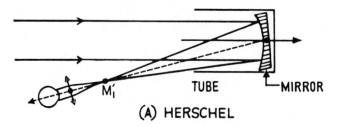

(A) HERSCHEL

In the Newton telescope, the beam is redirected by the reflecting prism that blocks the central portion of the incoming beam. After reflection, the axis of the beam is perpendicular to the main axis of the instrument.

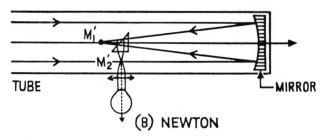

(B) NEWTON

In the Gregory telescope, a second concave mirror is centered on the axis to reinvert the image before it is viewed with an eyepiece through a hole in the center of the first mirror.

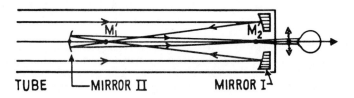

(C) GREGORY

The Cassegrain telescope is similar to the Gregory telescope, except that the second mirror is convex instead of concave, and the intermediate image is eliminated.

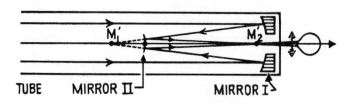

(D) CASSEGRAIN

432

As shown in Figure 2, when using a telescope to look at more than one object in the field of view, the eye is positioned so that the sighting intersect falls at the exit-pupil of the instrument. Explain why this is more desirable than placing the center of the entrance-pupil of the eye at the center of the exit-pupil of the telescope. (Note: the sighting intersect is a point on the eye which is fixed with respect to the head and through which the primary line of sight always passes, regardless of the direction in which it is pointing.)

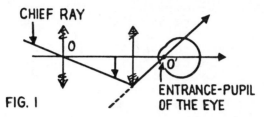

FIG. I

Solution: If the telescope is used for viewing a single object such as a star and the axis of the telescope is pointed toward the star, it is perfectly satisfactory to place the center of the entrance-pupil of the eye at the center of the exit-pupil of the telescope (see Fig. 1) and to let the primary line of sight of the eye coincide with the axis of the telescope. However, it is often desirable to keep the telescope immobile and to permit the eye to look at different objects in the field of view. In this case, it is more desirable to position the eye so that the sighting inter-sect falls at the exit-pupil of the instrument, as shown in

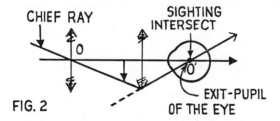

FIG. 2

Figure 2. Then the eye can be turned to look at any part of the image visible through the instrument. In this case, the primary line of sight of the eye always coincides with a chief ray through 0 and 0'. It is particularly important to have the primary line of sight coincide with a chief ray through the center of the exit-pupil of the telescope when the exit-pupil is smaller than the entrance-pupil of the eye. This is true because the part of the entrance-pupil of the eye penetrated by a narrow bundle of rays parallel to the primary line of sight determines the extent to which the foveal image is affected by chromatic dispersion of the eye and the Stiles-Crawford effect. The Stiles-Crawford effect refers to the fact that a beam of light entering the eye through the center of the pupil is more efficient in producing a brightness sensation than a similar beam passing through the edge of the pupil.

Since the rays from each object point emerge from an astronomical telescope as a set of parallel rays, the visual angle subtended by a pair of image points is independent of the position of the eye. As long as the rays from each object point emerge parallel and as long as the eye can converge a set of these parallel rays to form an image on the retina, the size of the image formed on the retina will not be affected by rotation of the eye or movement of it in a fore and aft direction.

In practice, the ocular of a telescope can be adjusted in a fore and aft direction to make the rays from a given object point convergent or divergent in order to compensate for the myopia or hyperopia of the eye. To focus an eyepiece, the device should be moved first toward the eye until the image appears blurred and then forward until it clears up. With this method, the eye is forced to keep its accommodation relaxed, so that when the final adjustment is made, a minimal amount of accommodation is required to use the telescope. If a person is 52 years old or older, he no longer can accommodate, and there is no problem. There is only one setting of the ocular which can be used for his fixed-focus eye.

The same type of "coupling-up" operation between the eye and the ocular is necessary for various other types of optical instruments.

● **PROBLEM** 15-17

Explain the meaning of the term "telecentric system" and how a telescope with a measuring scale in the primary focal plane of the eyepiece can be made telecentric.

Solution: A telecentric system is one in which the aperture-stop is placed so that the chief rays entering or leaving the system are parallel. In some telecentric systems both the entering chief rays and the emerging chief rays are parallel. A system is also called telecentric if the chief rays between any two components of the system are parallel.

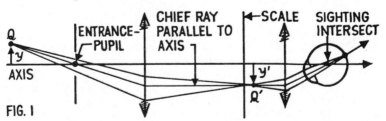

FIG. 1

An instrument such as a telescope (Fig. 1) with a measuring scale in the primary focal plane of the eyepiece can be made telecentric by the placement of an aperture-stop at the primary focal plane of the objective. The chief ray from Q is parallel to the axis at Q', and after refraction at the ocular, passes through the sighting intersect of the eye. No error is made in reading the scale, even though the instrument is not properly focused to put the image formed by the objective in the plane of the scale.

MICROSCOPES

Explain what advantage the compound microscope (or simply, microscope) has over the simple magnifier. Also determine the overall magnification of the compound microscope.

Solution: When an angular magnification higher than that attainable with a simple magnifier is desired, it is necessary to use a compound microscope, usually called merely a microscope. The essential elements of a microscope are

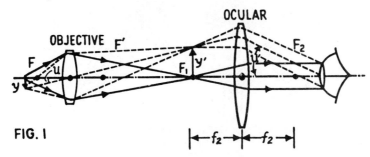

FIG. I

illustrated in Fig. 1. The object to be examined is placed just beyond the first focal point F of the objective lens, which forms a real and enlarged image in the first focal plane of the ocular. The latter then forms a virtual image of this image at infinity. While both the objective and ocular of an actual microscope are highly corrected compound lenses, they are shown as simple thin lenses for simplicity.

The overall magnification, M, of a compound microscope, like the angular magnification of a simple microscope, is defined as the ratio of the tangent of the angle u' subtended at the eye by the final image, to the tangent of the angle u that would be subtended at the unaided eye by the object at a distance of 25 cm. Let y represent the height of the object and y' the height of its image formed by the objective. Then

$$\tan u = \frac{y}{25} \ ,$$

and

$$\tan u' = \frac{y'}{f_2} \ ,$$

where f_2 is the focal length of the ocular. Hence

$$M = \frac{\tan u'}{\tan u} = \frac{y'/f_2}{y/25}$$

$$= \frac{y'}{y} \ \times \ \frac{25}{f_2} \ .$$

But y'/y is the lateral magnification m produced by the objective, and $25/f_2$ is the angular magnification γ produced by the ocular. The overall magnification M is

therefore the product of the lateral magnification of the
objective, and the angular magnification of the ocular.
Thus, the above equation becomes

$$M = m\gamma.$$

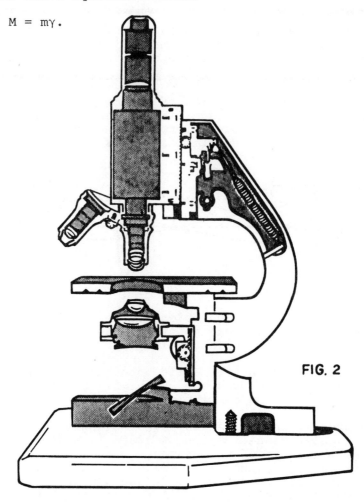

FIG. 2

Fig. 2 is a cut-away view of a modern microscope. The
instrument is provided with a rotating nosepiece to which
are permanently attached three objectives of different
focal lengths. This construction makes possible a rapid
and convenient exchange of one objective for another.

● **PROBLEM** 15-19

Describe the similarities and differences of the microscope
and the telescope.

<u>Solution</u>: A microscope is similar to a telescope in that
it consists of two parts, an initial lens (called an objective) and the second lens (called either an eyepiece
or an ocular). However, the microscope differs from the
telescope in that it is used to view small near objects,
whereas the telescope is employed for distant large objects.
This immediately changes the relations of the object to the

optics as illustrated in the figure. The microscope
objective usually has a very short focal length and the
object of regard is located near its focal point. The
image of the objective is therefore located at some distance from it. This image is viewed with an ocular which
acts as a simple magnifier. It is of interest to note that
the objective of the microscope contributes significant
magnification to the overall magnifying power of the system.
The large image formed by the objective is enlarged even
further by the ocular.

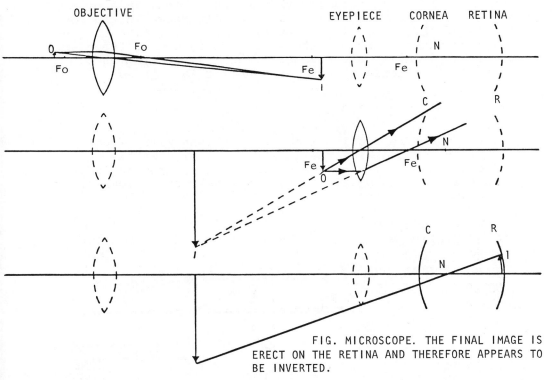

FIG. MICROSCOPE. THE FINAL IMAGE IS
ERECT ON THE RETINA AND THEREFORE APPEARS TO
BE INVERTED.

The magnifying power of a microscope is calculated in
principle as follows. The image size/object size ratio is
equal to the ratio of image distance/object distance. This
ratio is multiplied by the magnifying power of the eyepiece.

However, in practice, microscope objectives are marked
with their magnification (for example, 40x or 100x) and
eyepieces are also marked with their magnifying power (for
example 5x, 10x, or 15x). The total magnifying power is
then simply the product of the objective magnification and
the eyepiece magnifying power.

SPHERICAL ABERRATION AND ASTIGMATISM

● **PROBLEM** 15-20

Give a definition for spherical aberration and describe
two methods frequently used to reduce its effects.

437

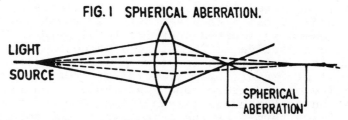

FIG. I SPHERICAL ABERRATION.

LIGHT
SOURCE

SPHERICAL
ABERRATION

<u>Solution</u>: Spherical aberration occurs in monochromatic light when the object is located on the optical axis of a lens (Fig. 1), and is defined as the difference in the locations of the images formed by peripheral relative to central rays passing through the lens. It is due to the spherical surfaces of the lens. Spherical aberration can be readily predicted by applying Snell's law

$$\frac{\sin \theta}{\sin \phi} = n$$

(where n = the refractive index of the lens with respect to the refractive index of the incident medium, θ = the angle of incidence of light upon the lens, and ϕ = the angle by which the light is refracted by the lens), to various points on the surface of the lens.

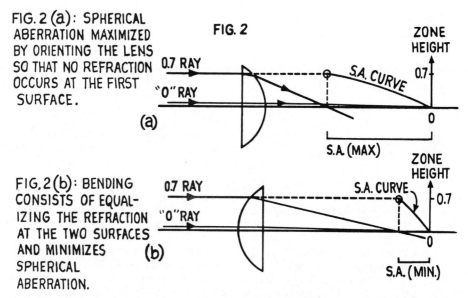

FIG. 2 (a): SPHERICAL ABERRATION MAXIMIZED BY ORIENTING THE LENS SO THAT NO REFRACTION OCCURS AT THE FIRST SURFACE.

FIG. 2

0.7 RAY

"0" RAY

(a)

ZONE HEIGHT

0.7

S.A. CURVE

0

S.A. (MAX)

FIG. 2 (b): BENDING CONSISTS OF EQUAL- IZING THE REFRACTION AT THE TWO SURFACES AND MINIMIZES SPHERICAL ABERRATION.

0.7 RAY

"0" RAY

(b)

ZONE HEIGHT

S.A. CURVE

0.7

0

S.A. (MIN.)

Two techniques are frequently employed by designers to correct spherical aberration. The simplest procedure is called bending (Fig. 2). The condition for minimum spherical aberration is equal refraction at the two surfaces of the lens. For an object at infinity, the best shape for a lens is very nearly convex-plano. For other distances the optimum shape (radii of the two surfaces) will be dependent on the range of distances of the object from the lens.

The second technique of reducing spherical aberration is to employ a doublet. This consists of cementing a somewhat weaker lens of different index of refraction to the principal lens; the weaker lens will be of opposite power,

and because it too has spherical aberration, it will reduce
the power of the peripheral rays more than the central (Fig.
3). The optical designer attempts to superimpose the central rays on the rays passing through the lens 70% of the
distance from the axis to the periphery. This is called the
70% zone. Not infrequently, the doublet is so calculated
as to correct both spherical aberrations and chromatic
aberration.

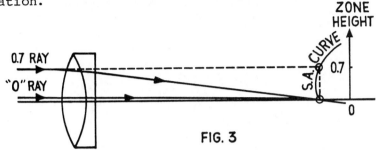

FIG. 3

• **PROBLEM** 15-21

(a)   Define spherical aberration at a spherical surface as
      well as a plane surface (the definitions are equiva-
      lent).

(b)   List one nonspherical surface for which no spherical
      aberration exists for two points relative to the mir-
      ror and determine where the points are located in re-
      lation to the mirror.

Solution: (a)   If rays from M are traced through a number
of points on the surface at different distances from the
axis, a diagram such as shown in Fig. 1 or 2 is obtained.

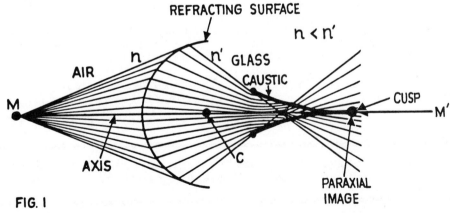

FIG. I

The rays which penetrate the surface close to the axis will
cross the axis at the point designated as the paraxial
image. Those which penetrate points further away from the
axis cross the axis at various other points. The refracted
rays are tangent to a surface known as the caustic surface,
which has its cusp at the paraxial image. The failure of
all of the rays to cross the axis at the paraxial image
constitutes spherical aberration.

(b) Spherical aberration cannot, of course, be eliminated from a spherical mirror. However, it is always possible to find a surface of revolution of nonspherical or
aspherical form, such that all rays diverging from any given
axial point are imaged at a second axial point. It does not
follow that rays from some other axial point will be sharply
imaged also. In other words, by the proper choice of an
aspherical surface, spherical aberration can be eliminated
from a mirror for any one pair of conjugate points.

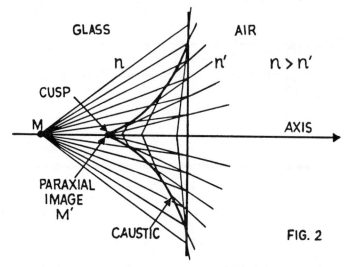

FIG. 2

It is a property of a paraboloid of revolution (that
is, the surface formed by the revolution of a parabola about
its axis) that rays from an object at infinity are all imaged at the same point on its axis. Conversely, rays from
a point source at this point are all reflected parallel to
the mirror axis. The conjugate points for which spherical
aberration is eliminated are then a point at infinity and
the focal point of the mirror.

The reflecting mirrors used in astronomical telescopes,
where all of the objects to be imaged are at extremely large
distances from the mirror, are paraboloidal surfaces.

Paraboloidal mirrors are also used in searchlights,
where a beam as nearly parallel as possible is desired.

● **PROBLEM** 15-22

Describe the cause of astigmatism and define the terms interval of Sturm and circle of least confusion.

Solution: Astigmatism is illustrated in Figure 1. Astigmatism occurs in an image when the object is located a significant distance off the optical axis. It is characterized
by two images located at unequal distances from the lens.
If the object is a point of light, the images are mutually
perpendicular lines. Astigmatism is characteristic of
spherical surfaces, and the astigmatic images may be predicted with precision by the application of Snell's law for

each ray at the surface of the lens. Approximately midway
between the horizontal and vertical images is an area of
maximum image quality, the circle of least confusion. The
distance between the horizontal and vertical images is known
as the interval of Sturm.

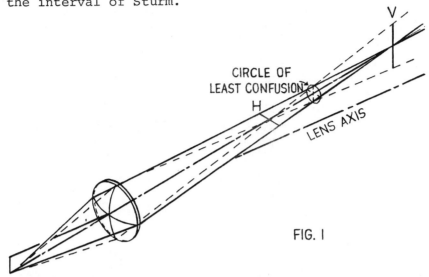

CIRCLE OF
LEAST CONFUSION

LENS AXIS

FIG. I

OPTICAL INSTRUMENTS

● **PROBLEM** 15-23

Describe the function of the Schmidt corrector and explain
why the Maksutov corrector is an improvement upon it.

<u>Solution</u>: A spherical mirror can be corrected for spheri-
cal aberration by inserting a lens in the path of the light
rays, either before or after reflection from the mirror.
The function of the lens is not primarily to alter the focal length or magnification of the system, but to offset
by its own spherical aberration the spherical aberration
of the mirror. Fig. 1 illustrates the system devised by
Schmidt in 1932. The spherical mirror M might be that of

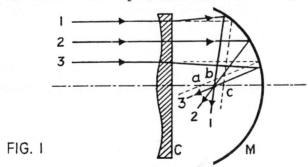

FIG. I

THE SCHMIDT CORRECTOR FOR MINIMIZING
SPHERICAL ABERRATION OF A MIRROR.

a reflecting telescope. In the absence of a correcting
lens, rays 1, 2, and 3, proceeding from a distant object,

441

would be reflected so as to cross the axis at points a, b, and c, as shown by the dotted lines. The correcting lens (or plate, as it is often called) is shown at C. It is plane on one surface. The other surface is convex in the central region and concave in the outer portion. The outer portion thus functions as a diverging lens and the central portion as a converging lens. The corrected paths of rays 1, 2, and 3 are shown by full lines.

Because the curved surfaces of the Schmidt corrector are aspherical, they cannot be produced by machine grinding and polishing.

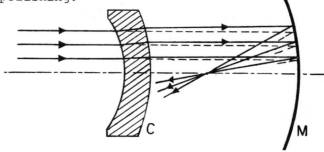

FIG. 2 THE MAKSUTOV CORRECTOR

The complicated aspherical surfaces of the Schmidt corrector can be avoided and excellent correction can still be retained in the system invented by D. D. Maksutov, of the State Optical Institute of the U.S.S.R., in 1941. As shown in Fig. 2, a thick meniscus lens having spherical surfaces of approximately equal radii of curvature is placed in front of the mirror. All rays originally parallel to the axis are deviated outward by the lens, but the deviation of the outer rays is greater than that of the paraxial rays and, as indicated by the full lines, spherical aberration is minimized. Since the spherical surfaces of the meniscus lens can be ground and polished by machine methods, these lenses are simple and cheap to manufacture.

Any type of correcting lens necessarily introduces some chromatic abberation. This results from the dependence of the index of refraction of the correcting lens on wavelength; rays of different wavelengths transmitted along a given path toward the correcting lens from a direction oblique to the surface will therefore be refracted different amounts by the lens. This effect, however, is not serious in either of the above systems.

● **PROBLEM** 15-24

For a projection lantern, such as the one shown in the Figure, explain the function of the condensing lens. Also state how long the focal length of the condensing lens has to be so that the area of the projecting lens is fully utilized.

Solution: The function of the condensing lens is to deviate the light from the source inward, so that it can pass through the projecting lens. If the condensing lens were omitted, light passing through the outer portions of the slide would not strike the projecting lens and only a small portion of the slide near its center would be imaged on the screen.

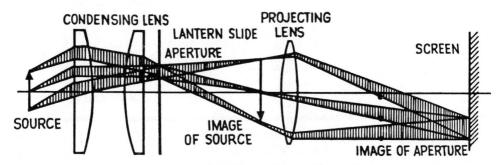

FIGURE: THE PROJECTION LANTERN.

A study of the figure will show that (a) for the three selected points of the source, only those rays within the shaded pencils can pass through the aperture, all others striking the condensing lens being intercepted by the opaque portions of the slide, and (b) similar pencils of rays could be drawn from every other point of the source.

Each of these pencils converges, after passing through the aperture, to form an image of its point of origin just to the left of the projecting lens. In practice, this image would be formed at the projecting lens, but for clarity in the diagram the image and the lens have been displaced slightly. The focal length of the condensing lens should be such that the image of the source just fills the projecting lens. If the image of the source is larger than the projecting lens, some of the light passing through the slide is wasted. If it is smaller, the area of the projecting lens is not being fully utilized. Thus in the diagram, the outer portions of the projecting lens serve no useful purpose. Money could be saved by buying a projecting lens of smaller diameter or, with the one illustrated available, the brightness of the image on the screen could have been increased by using a condenser of shorter focal length to produce a larger image of the source.

Three rays tangent to the upper edge of the aperture have been emphasized in the figure. These rays originate at different points of the source. Hence, although they intersect at the edge of the aperture, this point of intersection does not constitute an image of any point of the source. But these three rays diverge from a common point of the lantern slide, and therefore this point of the slide is imaged as shown on the screen. Similarly, rays tangent to any point of the edge of the aperture are imaged at a conjugate point on the screen. Thus, if the aperture is circular, a circular spot of light appears on the screen.

Notice that light from all points of the source illuminates every point of the image of the aperture, and would do the same were the aperture at any other point of the slide.

The preceding discussion has explained the conditions
that determine the focal length of the condensing lens and
the diameter of the projecting lens (the image of the
source formed by the condensing lens should just fill the
projecting lens). The diameter of the condensing lens
must evidently be at least as great as the diagonal of the
largest slide to be projected, while the focal length of
the projecting lens is detetermined by the magnification
desired between the slide and its image, and the distance
of the lantern from the screen.

● **PROBLEM** 15-25

Sketch typical object and image positions, indicating
suitable rays, for (a) a camera, (b) a slide projector,
and (c) a burning glass.

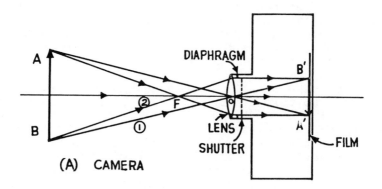

(A) CAMERA

Solution: (a) Camera. Ray 1 passing through the optical
center of the lens goes undeviated. Ray 2 passing through
the focal point enters the lens and proceeds parallel to
the optical axis.

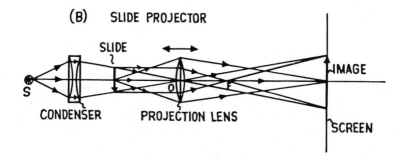

(B) SLIDE PROJECTOR

(b) Slide Projector. All rays emanating from the
slide pass through the projection lens and are imaged on
the screen. Rays parallel to the optical axis, after passing through the lens, go through the focal point, F. Rays
passing through the optical center pass through the lens
undeviated.

(c) Burning glass. All rays parallel to the axis are focused at one point where the burning takes place.

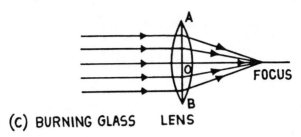

(C) BURNING GLASS   LENS

● **PROBLEM** 15-26

Describe the structural features of the Ramsden eye-piece, the one in common use in telescopes. Also state the reason why the Ramsden eyepiece is used.

Solution: The Ramsden eyepiece is an example of an achromatic ocular. It is designed to satisfy the condition that the refracting power of the ocular is the same for all wavelengths.

The Ramsden eyepiece consists of a combination of two converging lenses, of equal focal length, separated by a distance equal to two-thirds their common focal length. The lens nearest the eye shall be called the eye lens; that nearest the object, the field lens. While this eyepiece functions in exactly the same way as the single eye lens, it is an improvement on it because the defects are much less marked. To begin with, the eye ring is now much nearer the eye lens. In locating its position we shall assume that the instrument is adjusted, so that parallel bundles of rays leave the telescope. We must first of all, therefore, find where the eyepiece should be placed with reference to the image P'Q' formed by the objective, so that parallel bundles of rays emerge.

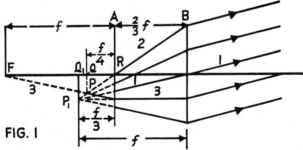

FIG. I

This is a problem that may be solved by either two methods.

(a) If p = distance of an object from lens A, Fig. 1, where A and B represent the two lenses of a Ramsden eye-piece from which parallel rays emerge,

$$p = -\frac{f}{4} \, .$$

445

The real image P'Q', therefore, should be placed at this distance from the field lens of the eyepiece.

(b) It is more instructive, however, to solve the problem graphically. Suppose that a bundle of parallel rays leaves the lens B (Fig. 1). We may locate the exact position of P_1 by taking on the central ray 1 the point which is distant f cm from the lens B. Once P_1 is located the direction of the complete bundle incident on B may then be drawn as shown in the figure. Now lens A is present and the position of P_1 enables us, as yet, to draw the actual rays only in between the lenses. Since, however, we know that the principal ray 2 emerges from A through its center unchanged in direction, and that the principal ray 3 emerging from A parallel to the axis (and apparently from P_1) must have been incident on A in a direction passing through F (a point f cm from R), P, the point of intersection of these two rays, gives us the original point from which the parallel rays must have come. If such a diagram is made to scale, the student will find by actual measurement that the distance QR = f/4.

OPTICAL SYSTEMS

● PROBLEM 15-27

Given the optical system shown in Figure 1, with focal distances F and F' (relative to principal planes H and H', respectively), having conjugate points V and V' and also W and W', and with object point Q; find the location of image point Q'.

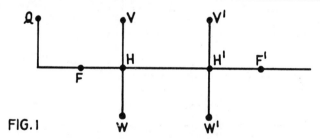

FIG. I

Solution: Having established the principal and focal points of a system, one can use these points to trace rays through the system from an extra-axial object point to locate the conjugate image point, or vice versa. The focal points and principal points are included in the list of points called the cardinal points of an optical system. The cardinal planes are normal to the axis at the cardinal points.

As shown in Fig. 2, a horizontal line is drawn parallel to the axis from the object point Q to the secondary principal plane. Since the two points V and V' are conjugate foci, an incident ray directed through V must emerge from the system along a path through V' and F'. A second ray may be

traced from Q along a path through F, to the primary principal plane at W, and then parallel to the axis. W and W'
are conjugate points having unit magnification, and thus a
ray directed toward W must emerge from the system through
W'.   The two rays cross at the image point Q', which is
conjugate to Q.   M' on the axis which lies in the same image plane as Q' is conjugate to M, which lies in the same
object plane as Q.

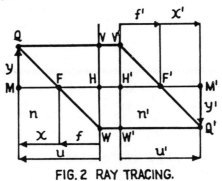

FIG. 2 RAY TRACING.

● **PROBLEM** 15-28

Using the methods of vergence and ray tracing, find the
image of an object O after the light rays from the object
have passed through the optical system of Fig.1.

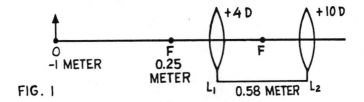

FIG. I

Solution: The application of the methods of vergence and
ray tracing to this problem is illustrated in Figure 2.
After an image has been formed by a given lens in an optical system, that image serves as an object for the next
lens or mirror in the system.

THE IMAGE IS REAL, ERECT, AND REDUCED IN SIZE.

FIG. 2 (a)

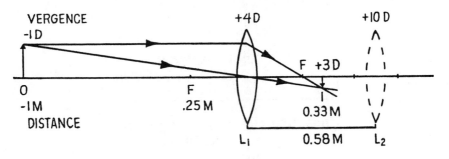

447

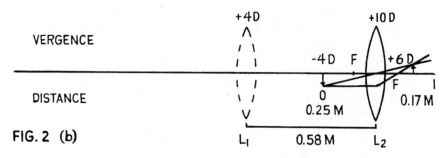

VERGENCE

+4D

+10D

-4D F +6D

F

I

DISTANCE

0
0.25 M

0.17 M

FIG. 2 (b)

L₁   0.58 M   L₂

● **PROBLEM** 15-29

In each of figures 1 through 7, find the distance
from the lens (as in figures 1, 2, and 3) or the mirror (as
in figures 4, 5, 6, and 7) of the image of an object O
using the method of vergence.

   Verify your results by determining the location of the
image by the method of ray tracing.

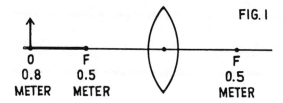

FIG. I

0   F   F
0.8   0.5   0.5
METER   METER   METER

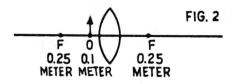

FIG. 2

F   O   F
0.25 0.1   0.25
METER METER   METER

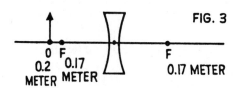

FIG. 3

O F   F
0.2 0.17   0.17 METER
METER METER

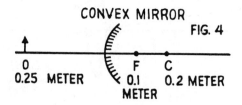

CONVEX MIRROR

FIG. 4

0   F   C
0.25 METER   0.1   0.2 METER
                    METER

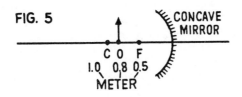

FIG. 5

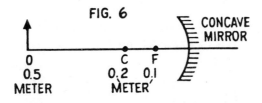

FIG. 6

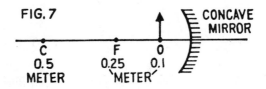

FIG. 7

Solution: Vergence is one of the three methods employed in geometrical optics to determine image characteristics. In ophthalmic practice, it is a technique of calculation to be used with the two ray trace procedure. Calculations of vergence are simple and provide a method of determining precisely the image size and location.

In most problems, the solution should be achieved through both the two ray trace procedure and vergence. The application of vergence requires the use of five simple rules. The rules of vergence are as follows:

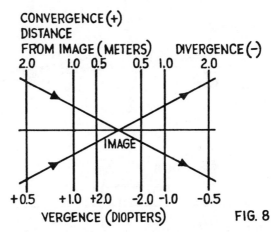

FIG. 8

1. The distances of the image and the object have diopteral value. The thin lens law states that

$$\frac{1}{O} + \frac{1}{I} = \frac{1}{F}$$

where O is the object distance, I is the image distance, and F is the focal distance. This law can be used to

find the strength or power of a lens, $\frac{1}{F}$. If F is expressed in meters, then the power (lens strength) is expressed in diopters.

2. Beams of light which diverge are designated by a minus
    sign   (Fig. 8).

3. Convergent beams have plus power (Fig. 8).

FIG. 9 THE VERGENCE OF OPTICAL SURFACES.
POWER IS EXPRESSED IN DIOPTERS (D).

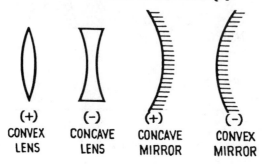

(+)	(–)	(+)	(–)
CONVEX	CONCAVE	CONCAVE	CONVEX
LENS	LENS	MIRROR	MIRROR

4. The power of each optical element,both lenses and mir-
    rors, is expressed in diopters. Positive or convex
    lenses and concave mirrors are plus and negative or con-
    cave lenses and convex mirrors are minus. The algebraic
    values of the four optical surfaces are illustrated in
    Figure 9.

5. The beam, mirror, and lens powers are added algebraically,
    for example,

        + 2 diopters + (–5) diopters = – 3 diopters

(a)
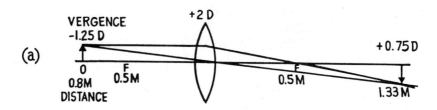

(b)
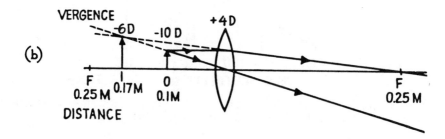

Figures A through G illustrate the application of the
two ray trace procedure and vergence to the optical systems
which were given in the problem. Figures A-G are the solu-

450

tions to the problems posed by figures 1-7, respectively. By convention, the diopteral powers are expressed above the optical axis and the distances, in meters, are indicated below the axis.

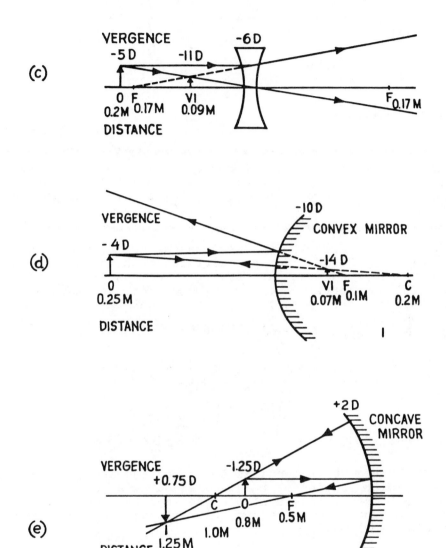

(c)

VERGENCE
-5D   -11D   -6D

O F   VI
0.2M 0.17M   0.09M

DISTANCE

F
0.17M

(d)

VERGENCE

-4D

0
0.25M

DISTANCE

-10D
CONVEX MIRROR
-14D

VI F   C
0.07M 0.1M   0.2M

(e)

+2D
CONCAVE
MIRROR

VERGENCE   -1.25D
+0.75D

C   O   F
0.8M 0.5M

1.0M

DISTANCE 1.25M

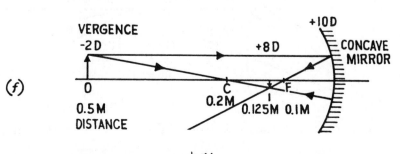

(f)

VERGENCE
-2D   +8D   +10D
                                    CONCAVE
                                    MIRROR

0   C   F
                      0.2M
0.5M   0.125M 0.1M
DISTANCE

451

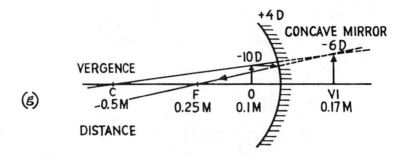

RAY BUNDLES

● **PROBLEM** 15-30

State the meanings of the terms chief ray, parachief rays, marginal rays, meridian section, and sagittal section, all with respect to a bundle of rays. Also give a definition of coma.

Solution: In Fig. 1, the chief ray of the bundle originating at Q is the one that passes through the center of the aperture-stop. Parachief rays are the rays from Q that pass through the aperture-stop near the center, and marginal rays are the ones that pass through at or near the margin.

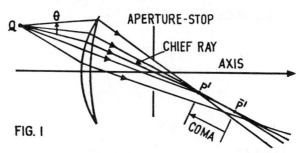

FIG. 1

The plane which contains the chief ray and the axis is the meridian section of the bundle and is also a meridian section of the entire system. The sagittal section of the emerging bundle contains the chief ray and is normal to the meridian section.

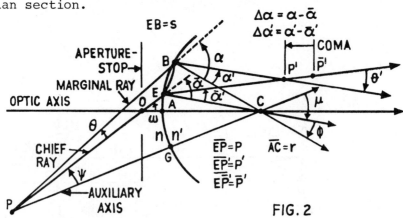

FIG. 2

In Fig. 2, the marginal rays as well as the parachief

rays verge at the point P in object space, but after refraction they fail to verge at a common point. The parachief rays converge at $\overline{P}'$, but the marginal rays in this meridian cross the chief ray at points other than $\overline{P}'$, some in front of $\overline{P}'$ and some behind. Let us consider the general case in which a given marginal ray crosses the chief ray at P' after refraction. The displacement of P' from $\overline{P}'$ represents the coma or aberration of the ray in question:

$$\text{Coma} = \overline{\overline{P}'P'} \; .$$

CHAPTER 16

PLANE MIRRORS

SPECULAR, SPREAD, AND DIFFUSE REFLECTION

● **PROBLEM** 16-1

Explain the different types of reflection: specular, spread, and diffuse.

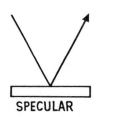 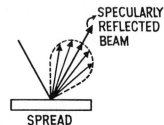 

SPECULAR · · · SPREAD · · · DIFFUSE

Solution: The difference between the different types of reflection is a matter of surface roughness. Specular reflection occurs on smooth, mirror-like surfaces, where a reflected beam of light is not significantly scattered. If the average depth of the surface irregularities of the reflector is substantially less than the wavelength of the incident light, a reflected beam will be formed. Diffuse reflection occurs on a rough surface such as a piece of paper, a ground piece of glass, or skin, where the depth of the irregularities on the surface is greater than the wavelength of the incident light. When reflected light is concentrated in the region around the specularly reflected beam, spread reflection occurs.

FERMAT'S PRINCIPLE

● **PROBLEM** 16-2

Prove that when light goes from one point to another via a plane mirror, the path chosen is the one which takes the least time (Fermat's principle).

Solution: Let the points be A and B, and let C be any general point on the mirror. Orient the diagram so that the x
and y-axes are as shown. Draw the normals to the mirror
surface passing through A, B and C. Now in specular reflection, the reflected ray lies in the plane determined by the
incident ray and the normal to the mirror at the point of
reflection. Hence A, B and C must be in the same plane.

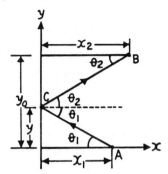

The coordinates of the three points are $A\left(x_1,\ 0\right)$;
$B\left(x_2,\ Y_0\right)$; $C\left(0,\ y\right)$.

The length of the path ACB is, by the Pythagorean
theorem,

$$P = \sqrt{x_1^2 + y^2} + \sqrt{x_2^2 + (y_0 - y)^2}$$

But the time of travel of light by this path, the
velocity of light being c, is $t = p/c$. For the path to be
traveled in minimum time, we must have $dt/dy = 0$, where y
is the variable which changes with path. Thus

$$t = \frac{1}{c}\left[\left(x_1^2 + y^2\right)^{1/2} + \left(x_2^2 + \left(y_0 - y\right)^2\right)^{1/2}\right]$$

$$\frac{dt}{dy} = \frac{1}{c}\left[1/2\left(x_1^2 + y^2\right)^{-1/2}(2y) + 1/2\left(x_2^2 + (y_0 - y)^2\right)^{-1/2}\right.$$

$$\left. \times\ 2(y_0 - y)(-1)\right].$$

$$\frac{dt}{dy} = \frac{1}{c}\left[\frac{y}{\sqrt{x_1^2 + y^2}} - \frac{(y_0 - y)}{\sqrt{x_2^2 + (y_0 - y)^2}}\right]$$

To find the values of y which make t a minimum, we
set $dt/dy = 0$. Hence,

$$0 = \frac{1}{c}\left[\frac{y}{\sqrt{x_1^2 + y^2}} - \frac{y_0 - y}{\sqrt{x_2^2 + (y_0 - y)^2}}\right]$$

But since $c \neq \infty$, the quantity in the braces must be
zero. Therefore,

$$\frac{y}{\sqrt{x_1^2 + y^2}} = \frac{y_0 - y}{\sqrt{x_2^2 + (y_0 - y)^2}} \tag{1}$$

From the figure,

$$\sin \theta_1 = \frac{y}{\sqrt{x_1^2 + y^2}} \quad \text{and} \quad \sin \theta_2 = \frac{y_0 - y}{\sqrt{x_2^2 + (y_0 - y)^2}}$$

Hence, (1) becomes

$$\sin \theta_1 = \sin \theta_2$$

and consulting the diagram we see that,

$$\theta_1 = \theta_2 \; ,$$

which is the law of reflection. Since light reflected specularly always satisfies this condition, the light ray follows the path which takes the least time.

LOCATIONS OF IMAGES FORMED BY PLANE MIRRORS

● PROBLEM 16-3

A 5-cm plane mirror is just large enough to show the whole image of a tree when held 30 cm from the eye of an observer whose distance from the tree is 100 m. What is the height of the tree?

Solution: Since the object is 100 m away from the mirror and the image is seen by the eye 0.30 m away, the magnification of the mirror is

$$m = \frac{0.30 \text{ m}}{100 \text{ m}} = 0.003 \; .$$

Thus if the image magnified by a factor of 0.003 is 0.05 m, the actual height of the tree must be $\frac{0.05 \text{ m}}{0.003 \text{ m}} = 16.67$ m.

● PROBLEM 16-4

Two parallel-plane mirrors face each other separated by a distance 4d. An object is placed between them and at a distance d from one of them. At what distances from the two mirror surfaces do successive images of the object occur?

Solution: The figure describes the given situation. The two mirrors, M_1 and M_2, are separated by a distance 4d.

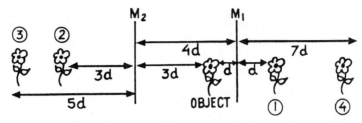

The object is located at a distance d from M_1. The images of the object are then at a distance d behind M_1 (image 1 in the figure) and at a distance 3d behind M_2 (image 2). Image 1 then becomes an object for reflection at M_2, and its image is at a distance (d + 4d) = 5d behind M_2 (image 3). This image, in turn, becomes an object for reflection at M_1 and its image is at a distance (5d + 4d) = 9d behind M_1. Similarly, image 2 had an image at a distance (3d + 4d) = 7d behind M_1 (image 4), and so on. Thus it may be seen that successive images will occur at d, 3d, 5d, 7d, 9d, 11d, 13d ...... etc. The nth image occurs at a distance $s_n = (2n - 1)d$ where n = 1,2,3 ..... etc.

● **PROBLEM 16-5**

Show that all the images of a luminous object placed between two plane mirrors lie on a circle.

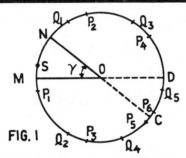

FIG. I

Solution: In Figure 1, a luminous object S is placed between two plane mirrors, OM and ON, inclined at an angle γ relative to one another. The images are formed by successive reflections from the two mirrors. There are two sets of images depending on whether the rays from the luminous point S fall first on mirror OM or on mirror ON. The rays which fall first on mirror OM will be reflected as though they came from the image P_1 of the luminous point in this mirror. Some of these rays falling on mirror ON will again be reflected as though they came from the point P_2, which is the image of P_1 in mirror ON. Thus, a series of images P_1, P_2, P_3,..... etc. will be formed by the rays which fall first on mirror OM.

Similarly, the rays which fall first on mirror ON produce a series of images Q_1, Q_2, ... etc., which can be
called the Q-series. Each of these series terminates with
an image which lies behind both mirrors in the dihedral
angle COD opposite the angle MON. Since OM is the perpendicular bisector of SP_1, S and P_1 are equidistant from every
point on the straight line OM. Similarly, since P_2 is the
image of P_1 on ON, P_2 and P_1 are equidistant from every
point on the straight line ON. Thus, S, P_1 and P_2 are
all equidistant from point 0 where OM and ON intersect.
It follows that the images of both series are arranged on
the circumference of a circle whose center is 0 and whose
radius is OS.

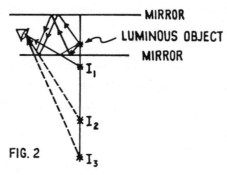

FIG. 2

If, however, the two mirrors are parallel to one another, as indicated in Figure 2 , then the images, formed
by successive reflections from the two mirrors, lie along
a straight line, as indicated. This situation is really a
special case of the situation of Figure 1, except that angle
γ in Figure 2 is zero. If one of the two mirrors in Figure 2
is tilted so that the angle γ ≠ 0, then the images no longer
lie along a straight line, but along the arc of a circle whose
radius decreases as angle γ increases.

DETERMINATION OF THE LENGTH OF A MIRROR

● **PROBLEM** 16-6

What is the minimum length L of a wall mirror so that a
person of height h can view herself from head to shoes?

Solution: This is not easily solved by a diagram. We sup-
pose that the person stands a distance x from the wall and
that her eyes (E) are a distance y from the top of her head
(H). To look at her toes (F) she looks at point A which
is the point of reflection of a light ray from her foot.
A must be at a height halfway between her eyes and feet (so
that the angle of incidence equals the angle of reflection).
Similarly to look at the top of her head she looks at point
B. If OP = h and BP = y/2, then the length of the mirror is
AB = PO - BP - OA = h - y/2 - 1/2(h - y) = h/2. Thus the

minimum length of the mirror is h/2, and this does not depend on the distance x that the person is standing away from the mirror.

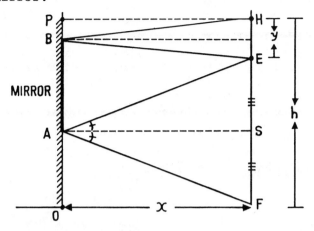

● **PROBLEM** 16-7

A man is 6 feet tall. How long should a mirror be, when placed 4 feet in front of him, in order to provide him with a full-length view of his reflected image? Diagram the rays.

Solution: A mirror offers no magnification. Thus for a 6 foot person to see his feet in a mirror, the point he must focus on is 3 feet above the ground, so the mirror need only be 3 feet long.

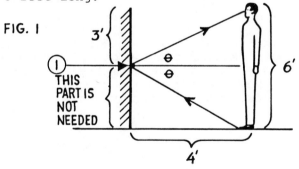

FIG. I

3'

① THIS PART IS NOT NEEDED

θ θ

6'

4'

This result can be shown geometrically by examining figure 2.

$\Delta I \cong \Delta II$

thus

$\overline{AB} \cong \overline{BC}$

AB + BC =

2AB = 6

AB = 3'

FIG. 2

I

II

θ

θ

A

B

C

6

REFLECTION OF LIGHT BY
TWO INCLINED MIRRORS

Two plane mirrors are inclined toward each other.
A ray of light is parallel to one of the mirrors, and
after four reflections it exactly retraces its path. What
angle do the mirrors subtend?

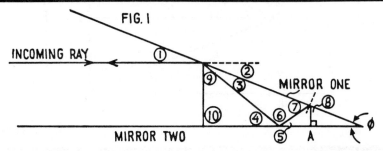

FIG. 1

INCOMING RAY

MIRROR ONE

MIRROR TWO

A

Solution: The situation is shown in Figure 1. At each
point of reflection the angle of reflection must equal the
angle of incidence, and at the fourth point of reflection
(point A in Figure 1) the ray must strike the mirror at
normal incidence so that it will be reflected back along
its incoming path. To determine the angle ϕ requires a
consideration of the geometry in Figure 1. Since the incoming ray is parallel to mirror two, angle 1 is clearly
just ϕ. Then, according to geometry, angle 2 must be ϕ,
and the law of reflection says that angle 3 must be ϕ;
since the sum of angles 2 + 3 equals 2ϕ, so must angles
4 (geometry) and 5 (the law of reflection). Now the sum
of angles 4, 5, and 6 equals 180°, so angle 6 must be
180° - 4ϕ; the sum of angles 3, 6 and 7 equals 180°; hence
angle 7 is 3ϕ. Again, the law of reflection says that
angle 8 is equal to 3ϕ, but geometry says in addition
that it must be true that angle 8 equals 90° - ϕ. Thus,
equating the two expressions for angle 8 results in:

$$3\phi = 90° - \phi$$

or:

$$\phi = \frac{90°}{4} = 22.5°$$

MIRROR ROTATION

A ray of light is reflected at a plane mirror. Show that
if the mirror is turned through an angle θ, the reflected
ray will be turned through an angle 2θ.

Solution: Figure 1 shows a mirror M and a beam of light
incident at an angle ψ. M' is the same mirror after ro-

tation through an angle θ.

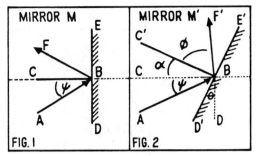

FIG. I   FIG. 2

According to the law of reflection, ∢ABC = ∢FBC and ∢ABC' = ∢F'BC'. The mirror, being rotated through an angle θ = ∢DBD', in effect also had its normal rotated through some angle α, where α is as shown in Figure 2. Since the normal is perpendicular to the mirror, ∢D'BC' = 90° and ∢DBC = 90°. From Figure 2 it can also be seen that ∢DBC = ∢DBD' + ∢D'BA + ∢ABC or 90° = θ + ∢D'BA + ψ and solving for θ yields

$$\theta = 90° - \psi - ∢D'BA \qquad (1)$$

Again from Figure 2, it can be seen that

$$∢D'BC' = ∢D'BA + ∢ABC + ∢CBC'$$

or

$$90° = ∢D'BA + \psi + \alpha$$

and solving for α yields

$$\alpha = 90° - \psi - ∢D'BA \qquad (2)$$

But from equation (1), that is precisely what θ equaled; therefore θ = α.

The incident beam makes an angle with M''s normal of α + ψ = θ + ψ. The reflected beam must also make this angle with the M' normal by the law of reflection. Thus this angle (φ in Figure 2) equals θ + ψ. With respect to M's normal, the reflected beam is at an angle of α + φ = θ + θ + ψ = 2θ + ψ. So by rotating the mirror through an angle θ, the reflected beam is rotated through an angle 2θ.

DEVIATION OF A RAY

• **PROBLEM** 16-10

Show that the deviation of a ray reflected once at each of two plane mirrors is equal to twice the angle between the mirrors.

Solution: In the figure, the 2 mirrors (M_1 and M_2) make an

461

angle θ with each other. The incoming beam makes an angle ψ with M_1.

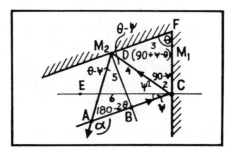

It is necessary to find ∢α (shown in the figure), the deviation. All quantities on the diagram with a number adjacent to them may now be found, and the numbers represent the sequence in which they may be found.

1) By the law of reflection, ∢ECD = ψ.

2) Since ∢ECF = 90°, ∢DCF = 90° - ψ.

3) In ΔCDF the sum of the angles = 180°; therefore
∢FDC = 180° - (θ + 90° - ψ) = 180° - θ - 90° + ψ = 90° + ψ - θ.

4) ∢FDB = 90°; therefore ∢BDC = 90° - ∢FDC or ∢BDC = 90° - (90 + ψ - θ) = θ - ψ

5) By the law of reflection, ∢BDA = ∢BDC = (θ - ψ)

6) In ΔADC the sum of the angles = 180°, so

$$(θ - ψ) + (θ - ψ) + ψ + ψ + ∢DAC = 180°$$

$$2θ - 2ψ + 2ψ + ∢DAC = 180°$$

$$180° - 2θ = ∢DAC$$

7) Finally, α and ∢DAC are supplementary, so

$$α + (180° - 2θ) = 180°$$

and so, α = 2θ.

NUMBER OF IMAGES OF A LUMINOUS POINT PLACED BETWEEN TWO PLANE MIRRORS

● **PROBLEM** 16-11

Two plane mirrors are inclined at an angle of 50°. Show that there will be 7 or 8 images of a luminous point placed between them, depending on whether its angular distance from the nearest mirror is less than 20°.

Solution: The images formed between two inclined mirrors

all lie on a circle of radius OS, as shown in the figure.

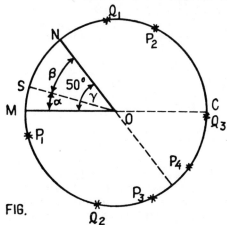

FIG.

The images marked with P's form a sequence starting with P_1 formed by mirror OM. The Q series starts with Q_1 from mirror ON. Both series terminate when the images enter the angle COD opposite the dihedreal angle MON.

Let ∢MON = 50° = γ   ∢MOS = α

and ∢SON = β, so that   α + β = γ. From the figure it can be seen that

$$∢P_1OS = 2α \tag{1}$$

$$∢P_1ON = β + 2α;$$

$$∢NOP_2 = β + 2α;$$

hence, $∢SOP_2 = 2(α + β) = 2γ.$ (2)

Now $∢MOP_2 = 2γ + α;$

$$∢MOP_3 = 2γ + α;$$

hence, $∢SOP_3 = 2γ + 2α.$ (3)

Following the same sequence,

$$∢SOP_4 = 2(α + β) + 2γ = 4γ \tag{4}$$

Thus $∢SOP_{2K} = 2Kγ$ and

$$∢SOP_{2K+1} = 2Kγ + 2α, \text{ K an integer.}$$

Similarly, $∢SOQ_{2K} = 2Kγ$ and

$$∢SOQ_{2K+1} = 2Kγ + 2β.$$

463

The first image in the P-series which will fall into ∢COD is that for which $2K\gamma > 180° - \beta$ on the OC side; and on the OD side, $2K\gamma + 2\alpha > 180° - \gamma + \alpha$, or $2K\gamma + 2\alpha > 180° - \beta$. The smallest integer is derived from the second equation, solving for K:

$$2K\gamma + \alpha + (\alpha + \beta) > 180°$$

$$(2K + 1)\gamma > 180° - \alpha$$

$$2K + 1 > \frac{180° - \alpha}{\gamma} .$$

That is, the total number of images of the P-series is given by the integer next higher than $(180 - \alpha)/\gamma$. Similarly, the total number of images of the Q-series will be given by the integer next higher than $(180 - \beta)/\gamma$.

Here, $\gamma = 50°$ and if $\alpha = \beta = 25°$,

$$\frac{180° - \alpha}{\gamma} = \frac{180° - \beta}{\gamma} , \text{ which is a number between 3 and 4.}$$

Thus, the total number of images is 4 + 4 (4 images of the P-series and 4 images of the Q-series) = 8.

If $\alpha = 10°$, $\beta = 40°$,

then $\left(\dfrac{180° - 10°}{50°}\right)$ lies between 3 and 4, but

$\left(\dfrac{180° - 40°}{50°}\right)$ lies between 2 and 3.

Thus, the total number of images = 7.

Note that $\left(\dfrac{180° - 30°}{50°}\right) = 3.$ That is, if α (or β) is $\leq 20°$, the number of images is 7.

If neither α nor $\beta \leq 20°$ (i.e., each lies between 20° and 30°) the number of images is 8.

CHAPTER 17

CURVED MIRRORS

CONCAVE MIRRORS

A gas-flame is 8 ft. from a wall, and it is required to throw on the wall a real image of the flame magnified three times. Determine the position of the object with respect to a concave mirror which would give the required image. In addition, find the focal length of the mirror.

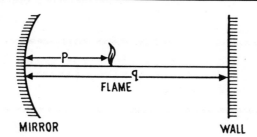

MIRROR   WALL

Solution: In this problem, the concave mirror and the wall must be on opposite sides of the flame, as shown in the figure. Since the distance between the wall and the flame is given to be 8 ft.,

$$q - p = 8 \qquad (1)$$

In addition, since the image is magnified three times,

$$3 = \frac{q}{p} \qquad (2)$$

From equation (1), q = p + 8 and substituting this value for q into equation (2) gives

$$p = \frac{q}{3} = \frac{p + 8}{3}$$

Thus,

$$p + 8 = 3p,$$

$$2p = 8$$

465

and so,

    p = 4 ft.

Thus, the flame is located at a distance of 4 ft. from the concave mirror.

From equation (1), q = p + 8 = 12 ft.

The focal length of the mirror can be found from the mirror equation, which is as follows:

$$\frac{1}{q} + \frac{1}{p} = \frac{1}{f}$$

where f is the focal length of the mirror. Substituting the values computed for p and q into this equation gives

$$\frac{1}{12 \text{ ft.}} + \frac{1}{4 \text{ ft.}} = \frac{1}{f} \; ;$$

hence,

$$\frac{1}{f} = \frac{4}{12 \text{ ft.}} = \frac{1}{3 \text{ ft.}}$$

and so, the focal length of the concave mirror = 3 ft.

● **PROBLEM** 17-2

Find the location and describe the first three real images of the object located between a plane mirror and a concave mirror, as shown in figure 1.

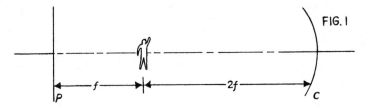

FIG. I

Solution: Image 1: With respect to mirror C, as shown in figure 1, the object distance p = 2f, where f represents the focal length of mirror C. Then, substituting p = 2f into the mirror equation,

$$\frac{1}{p} + \frac{1}{q} = \frac{1}{f} \; ,$$

where q is the image distance from mirror C, gives

$$\frac{1}{q} = \frac{1}{f} - \frac{1}{2f} = \frac{1}{2f} \; .$$

Thus,

    q = 2f.

466

That is, this image, due to mirror C, lands right on top of the object. It is not magnified, but it is inverted.

Image 2: Upon striking the plane mirror P, a virtual image will be formed a distance f (the focal length of mirror C) behind it, and erect. This acts as a real object for mirror C with $p_2 = 4f$. Thus,

$$\frac{1}{q_2} = \frac{1}{f} - \frac{1}{p_2} = \frac{1}{f} - \frac{1}{4f} = \frac{3}{4f}$$

Hence,

$$q_2 = (4/3) \ f$$

Thus, this image is closer to C than is the first, is one-third the size of the original, and is inverted. Image 2 is accompanied by another real image, at the same place and of the same size, but inverted. This comes from image 1, as reflected by P and then by C. All subsequent images will have such companions.

Image 3: Image 2 is also reflected by P. Since the image distance with respect to mirror C is $\frac{4}{3}$ f, the object distance with respect to mirror P $= \left(3 - \frac{4}{3}\right)f = \frac{5}{3}$ f. Thus, a virtual image is formed at a distance of $-(5/3)f$ from P, which is a real object for C with object distance $p_3 = \left(3 + \frac{5}{3}\right)f = \frac{14}{3}f.$

Thus,

$$\frac{1}{q_3} = \frac{1}{f} - \frac{3}{14f} = \frac{11}{14f} \text{ and so, } q_3 = \frac{14}{11} \ f.$$

This means that the image is real and magnified by

$$-\left(\frac{\frac{14}{11}}{\frac{14}{3}}\right) \quad \text{or} \quad \frac{-3}{11} \ .$$

This inverts the previous orientation, leaving this image erect with respect to the original and one-eleventh the size of the original object.

All subsequent real images are progressively smaller and progressively closer to the focal point of the curved mirror. This is just what we should have expected, since successive reflections in the plane mirror appear to be farther away.

● **PROBLEM 17-3**

A concave spherical mirror has a radius of curvature of 50 cm. (a) Find two positions of an object for which the image is four times as large as the object. (b) What is the position of the image in each case? (c) Are the images real or virtual?

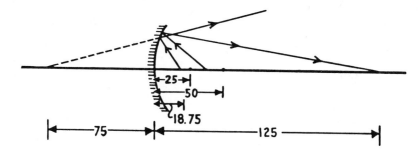

Solution: Given the radius of curvature of a mirror, R, its focal length, f, can be found since

$$f = \frac{R}{2} \; ;$$

thus, the focal length is always half the radius of curvature. In this problem, since the radius of curvature of the mirror is 50 cm., the focal length of the mirror is 25 cm.

Now, using the equation

$$\frac{1}{p} + \frac{1}{q} = \frac{1}{f} = \frac{1}{25 \text{ cm}} \tag{1}$$

where p and q represent the object and image distances, respectively, and using the fact that the magnification m = 4, take the first case when the image is erect. Thus,

$$m = -\frac{q}{p} = +4$$

so the image distance is

$$q = -4p \tag{2}$$

Substituting for q in equation (1) gives

$$\frac{1}{p} - \frac{1}{4p} = \frac{1}{25 \text{ cm}}$$

Thus,

$$\frac{3}{4p} = \frac{1}{25 \text{ cm}}$$

and so, the object distance

$$p = \frac{75}{4} \text{ cm} = 18.75 \text{ cm.}$$

Now from equation (2), the image distance q = -75 cm. Hence, when the object is 18.75 cm from the mirror, a virtual image is produced 75 cm in back of the mirror.

Now, the second case occurs when the image is inverted. Then,

$$m = -\frac{q}{p} = -4,$$

so

$$q = 4p \qquad \qquad (3)$$

and substituting into equation (1) gives

$$\frac{1}{p} + \frac{1}{4p} = \frac{1}{25 \text{ cm}} \; .$$

Then,

$$\frac{5}{4p} = \frac{1}{25 \text{ cm}}$$

and so,

$$p = \left(\frac{5}{4}\right) \; (25 \text{ cm}) = 31.25 \text{ cm},$$

and, substituting into equation (3) gives the image distance

$$q = 125 \text{ cm}.$$

Therefore, when the object is a distance of 31.25 cm from the mirror, a real and inverted image is formed at a distance of 125 cm in front of the mirror.

● **PROBLEM 17-4**

An object is 4 in. to the left of the vertex of a concave mirror of radius of curvature 12 in. Find the position and magnification of the image.

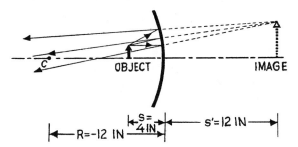

Solution: Using the mirror equation, $\frac{1}{s} + \frac{1}{s'} = \frac{2}{R}$, where s and s' are the object and image distances, respectively, and R is the radius of curvature of the mirror, and noting that

$$s = 4 \text{ in, and } R = 12 \text{ in,}$$

we have

$$\frac{1}{4 \text{ in}} + \frac{1}{s'} = \frac{2}{12 \text{ in}} \; ;$$

hence,

$$\frac{1}{s'} = \frac{1}{6 \text{ in}} - \frac{1}{4 \text{ in}} = \frac{2 - 3}{12 \text{ in}} = - \frac{1}{12 \text{ in}} \; .$$

469

Thus,

$$s' = -12 \text{ in.}$$

The magnification of the image, m, is given by the following equation:

$$m = \frac{-s'}{s}$$

Substituting the given value for s and the computed value for s' into this equation gives

$$m = - \left(\frac{-12 \text{ in}}{4 \text{ in}} \right) = +3.$$

Therefore, the image is 12 in. to the right of the vertex and is virtual (since s' is negative), erect (m is positive), and 3 times the height of the object. See the figure.

● **PROBLEM** 17-5

A dentist holds a concave mirror with radius of curvature 4 cm at a distance of 1.5 cm from a filling in a tooth. What is the magnification of the image of the filling?

Solution: Given the radius of curvature R of the mirror, and the object distance p, the image distance q can be found using the mirror equation,

$$\frac{1}{p} + \frac{1}{q} = \frac{2}{R} , \tag{1}$$

Thus, since in this problem R and p are given to be 4 cm and 1.5 cm, respectively, equation (1) gives

$$\frac{1}{q} = \frac{2}{4 \text{ cm}} - \frac{1}{1.5 \text{ cm}} = \frac{1}{2 \text{ cm}} - \frac{2}{3 \text{ cm}} = \frac{3 - 4}{6 \text{ cm}} = \frac{-1}{6 \text{ cm}} .$$

Thus, the image distance

$$q = -6 \text{ cm.}$$

The minus sign indicates that the image is virtual, and it is located at a distance of 6 cm behind the mirror. The magnification m can be found using the following equation:

$$m = - \frac{q}{p} \tag{2}$$

Substituting the known value for p and the computed value for q into equation (2) gives

$$m = - \left(\frac{-6 \text{ cm}}{1.5 \text{ cm}} \right) = 4.$$

Thus, the image is 4 times the size of the object.

Suppose an individual wants to view his face as reflected from an ordinary hand magnifying (concave) mirror. Let the mirror be 20 cm from the individual's face. He wishes to have an image 40 cm from the mirror. What should be the radius of curvature and the focal length of the mirror? What is the magnification of the image?

Solution: The image formed by a concave mirror must be virtual.   Thus, the image and object distances, denoted by q and p, respectively, are -40 cm (the minus sign being due to the fact that the image is virtual) and 20 cm. The mirror formula,

$$\frac{1}{p} + \frac{1}{q} = \frac{2}{R} \text{ ,}$$

where R is the radius of curvature of the mirror, gives

$$\frac{1}{20 \text{ cm}} - \frac{1}{40 \text{ cm}} = \frac{2}{R}$$

Hence,

$$\frac{2}{R} = \frac{2 - 1}{40 \text{ cm}} = \frac{1}{40 \text{ cm}} \text{ ,}$$

and so,

$$R = 80 \text{ cm.}$$

In addition, $f = \frac{R}{2}$, where f represents the focal length of the mirror.   Thus,

$$f = 40 \text{ cm.}$$

The magnification of the image, m, can be found by using the equation $m = \frac{-q}{p}$.

Substituting the given values for q and p into this equation gives

$$m = -\left(\frac{-40 \text{ cm}}{20 \text{ cm}}\right) = 2.$$

Thus, the image is erect and twice the size of the object.

● **PROBLEM** 17-7

At what distance must an object be placed from a concave mirror of focal length |f| to produce a magnification of m, where m is (a) negative, and (b) positive? In each case, state whether the image is real or virtual.

Solution: (a) If u and v represent the object and image distances to the mirror, respectively, and r = 2|f| is the radius of curvature of the mirror, the mirror equation states:

$$\frac{2}{r} = \frac{1}{u} + \frac{1}{v} = \frac{1}{|f|} = \frac{1}{u}\left(1 + \frac{u}{v}\right).$$

m, the magnification is defined as follows:

$$m = -\frac{v}{u}$$

Hence,

$$\frac{2}{r} = \frac{1}{u}\left(1 - \frac{1}{m}\right).$$

Therefore,

$$u = \frac{r}{2}\left(1 - \frac{1}{m}\right) = |f|\left(1 - \frac{1}{m}\right),$$

when m is negative. The image is real because since v = -mu and m is negative (while u is assumed positive), v is positive.

(b) as previously noted, $m = \frac{-v}{u}$. Thus, since u is positive, if m is also positive, v must be negative. This indicates that the image formed by the concave mirror is virtual. Therefore,

$$\frac{1}{f} = \frac{1}{u}\left(1 + \frac{u}{v}\right) = \frac{1}{u}\left[1 - \left(-\frac{u}{v}\right)\right] = \frac{1}{u}\left(1 - \frac{1}{m}\right)$$

and u = |f| [1 - (1/m)], when m is positive.

● **PROBLEM 17-8**

An object is placed 1 foot from a concave mirror of radius 4 feet. If the object is moved 1 inch nearer to the mirror, what will be the corresponding displacement of the image?

Solution: The relationship between the image and object distances with respect to a mirror with radius of curvature R is given by the following equation (known as the mirror equation):

$$\frac{1}{0} + \frac{1}{i} = \frac{2}{R} \tag{1}$$

where 0 is the object distance and i is the image distance.

Since the mirror is concave and the radius of curvature is 4 feet, then R = +48 in (the radius of curvature of a concave mirror is positive while for a convex mirror, it is negative). It is given that the object is initially 1 ft or 12 in from the vertex of the concave mirror;

thus,

$$0 = 12 \text{ in ,}$$

and so, substituting for R and 0 in equation (1) gives

$$\frac{1}{i} = \frac{1}{24 \text{ in}} - \frac{1}{12 \text{ in}} = \frac{-1}{24} \text{ in.}$$

Thus,

$$i = -24 \text{ in,}$$

and the image is located at a distance of 24 in from the mirror and is virtual. When the object is moved 1 inch nearer to the mirror, 0 = 11 in and reapplying equation (1) gives

$$\frac{1}{i} = \frac{1}{24 \text{ in}} - \frac{1}{11 \text{ in}} = \frac{(11 - 24)}{(11)(24) \text{ in}} = \frac{-13}{264 \text{ in}}$$

and so,

$$i = \frac{-264}{13} \text{ in} = -20.3 \text{ in}$$

Therefore, when the object in front of a concave mirror with radius of curvature 48 in is moved from a distance of 12 in away from the mirror to 11 in away from the mirror, the virtual image moves from a distance of 24 in to a distance of 20.3 in, with respect to the mirror.

Therefore, the image is displaced a distance of (24 - 20.3) in = 3.7 in closer to the mirror.

● **PROBLEM 17-9**

An image is produced by an object 1 m in front of a concave mirror whose radius of curvature is 30 cm. It is required to move the image 15 cm farther away from the mirror. How far and in which direction should the object be moved in order to accomplish this?

Solution: In this problem, the image distance can be found by making use of the following equation:

$$\frac{1}{p} + \frac{1}{q} = \frac{2}{R} \tag{1}$$

where the object distance p = 100 cm, the radius of curvature R = 30 cm, and the image distance is represented by q. Thus, equation (1) becomes

$$\frac{1}{100 \text{ cm}} + \frac{1}{q} = \frac{2}{30 \text{ cm}}$$

Thus, the image distance $q = \frac{(30 \text{ cm})(100 \text{ cm})}{(200 - 30) \text{ cm}} \cong 17.65 \text{ cm.}$

If the image is to be moved a distance of 15 cm further
away from the mirror, the image distance would be 32.65 cm.
Applying equation (1), using the new image distance
q' = 32.65 cm, and the same radius of curvature, gives

$$\frac{1}{p'} + \frac{1}{32.65 \text{ cm}} = \frac{2}{30 \text{ cm}}$$

where p' is the new object distance. Solving for p' gives

$$p' = \frac{(32.65 \text{ cm})(30 \text{ cm})}{(65.30 - 30) \text{ cm}} \cong 27.75 \text{ cm}.$$

Thus, the object is to be moved from a distance of 100 cm
away from the mirror to a distance of 27.75 cm away; hence,
it is moved 72.25 cm closer to the mirror.

● **PROBLEM** 17-10

A certain person can see distinctly objects which are
between 20 and 60 cm from his eye. Within what limits
of distance from his eye must a concave mirror of focal
length 15 cm be placed in order that he can focus sharply
the image of his eye as seen in the mirror?

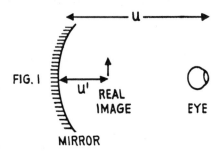

Solution: In this problem we need to find the range of the
mirror which will result in images located between 20 cm
and 60 cm from the eye.

We want then to investigate the use of the mirror
equation

$$\frac{1}{u} + \frac{1}{u'} = \frac{1}{f} \tag{1}$$

where u' is the image distance; u is the object distance
and f is the focal length of the mirror. Two possibilities

474

must be considered; first, that the mirror produces a
real image as in figure 1 and second, that the mirror
produces a virtual image as in figure 2. We want to find
the limits when the distance of the image is at the two
limits 20 cm and 60 cm for each case.

In figure (1) $u - u' = 20$ cm or $u - u' = 60$ cm.

In figure (2) $u + u' = 20$ cm or $u + u' = 60$ cm.

and using equation (1) for each condition,

$$\frac{1}{u_1} + \frac{1}{u_1 - 20} = \frac{1}{15} \tag{2}$$

$$\frac{1}{u_2} + \frac{1}{u_2 - 60} = \frac{1}{15} \tag{3}$$

$$\frac{1}{u_3} - \frac{1}{20 - u_3} = \frac{1}{15} \tag{4}$$

$$\frac{1}{u_4} - \frac{1}{60 - u_4} = \frac{1}{15} \tag{5}$$

Notice that equations 2 and 4 & 3 and 5 are equivalent and
each will yield a quadratic equation to be solved. So we
expect that both solutions of each of the two quadratic
equations will yield the answers. From equation (2),

$$\frac{1}{u_1} + \frac{1}{u_1 - 20} = \frac{1}{15}$$

$$\frac{u_1 - 20 + u_1}{u_1(u_1 - 20)} = \frac{1}{15}$$

$$(u_1 - 20 + u_1)15 = u_1(u_1 - 20)$$

$$30u_1 - 300 = u_1^2 - 20u_1$$

$$u_1^2 - 50u_1 + 300 = 0$$

$$u_1 = \frac{50 \pm \sqrt{50^2 - 4 \times 300}}{2} = \frac{50 \pm \sqrt{1300}}{2} = \frac{50 \pm 36.05}{2}$$

$$u_1 = 6.97 \text{ cm and } 43.03 \text{ cm.}$$

6.97 cm will be used for the virtual image case (fig 2) because this distance is less than the focal length (15 cm).

Similarly, from equation (3),

$$(u_2 - 60 + u_2)\ 15 = u_2(u_2 - 60)$$

$$30\ u_2 - 900 = u_2^2 - 60\ u_2$$

$$u_2^2 - 90u_2 + 900 = 0$$

$$u_2 = \frac{90 \pm \sqrt{90^2 - 4 \times 900}}{2} = \frac{90 \pm \sqrt{4500}}{2} = \frac{90 \pm 67.08}{2}$$

u_2 = 11.46 cm and 78.54 cm.

Again 11.46 cm is less than the focal length of the mirror, so it will be related to the virtual image of figure 2.

Thus, the person can see the real image of his eye if the mirror is between 43.03 and 78.54 cm from his eye. He will see the virtual image of his eye if the mirror is between 6.97 and 11.46 cm from his eye.

● **PROBLEM** 17-11

Show that a plane mirror in contact with a converging lens of focal length f is equivalent to a concave spherical mirror with radius of curvature f.

Solution: For this problem, the optical system can be treated by means of the thin lens/mirror equation each time rays of light go through an element of the system, and the initial object distance can be compared with the final image distance.

The thin lens/mirror equation is

$$\frac{1}{u} + \frac{1}{u'} = \frac{1}{f} \qquad (1)$$

where u is the object distance, u' is the image distance and f is the focal length of the optical system. Letting subscripts 1, 2 and 3 represent the elements of the optical system (notice that rays go through the lens, then through the mirror and through the lens again in the reverse direction) gives

$$\frac{1}{u_1} + \frac{1}{u_1'} = \frac{1}{f_1} \qquad (2)$$

$$\frac{1}{u_2} + \frac{1}{u_2'} = \frac{1}{f_2} \qquad (3)$$

$$\frac{1}{u_3} + \frac{1}{u_3'} = \frac{1}{f_3} \qquad (4)$$

Since the mirror is in contact with the lens, the following identities are valid:

$$u_2 = -u_1'; \ u_3 = -u_2'; \ f_1 = f_3 = f.$$

Also, the radius of curvature of the plane mirror is infinite. Thus, $1/f_2 = 2/r = 0$. Then equations (2), (3) and (4) can be rewritten as follows:

$$\frac{1}{u_1} + \frac{1}{u_1'} = \frac{1}{f}$$

$$-\frac{1}{u_1'} + \frac{1}{u_2'} = 0$$

$$\frac{-1}{u_2'} + \frac{1}{u_3'} = \frac{1}{f}$$

These three equations can be added to one another, yielding the following result:

$$\frac{1}{u_1} + \frac{1}{u_3'} = \frac{2}{f}$$

However, the focal length of a mirror is just $r/2$, so this optical system is equivalent to a concave mirror of radius f. It is concave because its focal length is positive.

CONVEX MIRRORS

● **PROBLEM** 17-12

A spherical light bulb 2 inches in diameter is imaged by a steel ball bearing located 20 inches away from the bulb. If the ball bearing is 1 inch in diameter, where is the image of the light bulb and what is its diameter?

Solution: In this problem, the steel ball bearing acts as a convex mirror with a radius of curvature of -1 inches. The light bulb acts as the object to be imaged by the steel ball. The following equation can be used:

$$\frac{1}{p} + \frac{1}{q} = \frac{2}{R} \quad , \tag{1}$$

where p is the distance the light is from the ball, R is the radius of curvature for the ball, and q is the distance from the image to the surface of the steel ball. Substituting the given values R = -1 inch and p = 20 inches, equation (1) becomes

$$\frac{1}{20 \text{ in}} + \frac{1}{q} = \frac{2}{-1 \text{ in}}$$

Hence,

$$\frac{1}{q} = \frac{-2}{\text{in}} - \frac{1}{20 \text{ in}} = \frac{-41}{20 \text{ in}}$$

Therefore, the image distance

$$q = \frac{-20 \text{ in}}{41} \cong -0.49 \text{ in.}$$

The magnification, m, is equal to $-\frac{q}{p}$ so, substituting the given value for p along with the computed value for q gives

$$m = \frac{0.49}{20} = 0.0245.$$

So the image of the light bulb is (0.0245)(2 inches) $\cong$ 0.05 inches in diameter, is erect, and is located at a distance of 0.49 in. beneath the surface of the ball bearing.

A man holds, halfway between his eye and a convex mirror 3 feet from his eye, two fine parallel wires, so that they are seen directly and also by reflection in the mirror. Show that if the apparent distance between the wires as seen directly is 5 times that as seen by reflection, the radius of the mirror is 3 feet.

Solution: The mirror equation can be stated as follows:

$$\frac{1}{u} + \frac{1}{u'} = \frac{1}{f} \tag{1}$$

where u is the object distance and u' the image distance with respect to the mirror, and f is the focal length of the mirror. The magnification of the mirror, m, is given by the following equation:

$$m = \frac{I}{0} = \frac{u'}{u} \tag{2}$$

where I is the image size and 0 is the object size. It is given that $\frac{0}{I} = 5$; in addition, u is given to be 1.5 ft. Hence, from equation (2),

$$\frac{\frac{0}{1.5}}{\frac{I}{3 + u'}} = 5$$

or

$$\frac{3 + u'}{1.5 \times 5} = \frac{I}{0} = \frac{u'}{u} = \frac{u'}{1.5}$$

Cross-multiplying gives

$$4.5 + 1.5u' = 7.5u'$$

$$6u' = 4.5$$

$$u' = 3/4 \text{ feet}$$

From equation (1),

$$\frac{1}{1.5} + \frac{1}{-0.75} = \frac{1}{f}$$

$$\frac{2}{3} - \frac{4}{3} = \frac{1}{f}$$

$$f = \frac{3}{2} \text{ feet}$$

but for a mirror R = 2f so the radius of curvature of the mirror is then 3 feet.

CONVEX AND CONCAVE MIRRORS

A concave and a convex mirror, each with a radius of 10 cm, face each other at a distance of 20 cm apart from one another. Halfway between them is an object 3 cm high. Find the position and the size of the final image formed by reflection, first at the convex mirror and then at the concave mirror.

Solution: The image formed by the first (convex) mirror can be found by using the following equation:

$$\frac{1}{p} + \frac{1}{q} = \frac{2}{R} . \tag{1}$$

It is given that the object distance, p, is 10 cm and the radius of curvature, R, is -10 cm (The radius of curvature of a convex mirror is always negative.), so, from equation (1),

$$q = \frac{pR}{2p - R} = \frac{(10 \text{ cm}) (-10 \text{ cm})}{20 \text{ cm} + 10 \text{ cm}} = -3.33 \text{ cm}$$

Thus, the image is 3.33 cm behind the convex mirror or 23.33 cm in front of the second (concave) mirror.

Now, using equation (1) for the second (concave) mirror gives the result

$$\frac{1}{23.33 \text{ cm}} + \frac{1}{q} = \frac{2}{10 \text{ cm}} .$$

Hence, the image produced by the second mirror is

$$q = \frac{(10 \text{ cm}) (23.33 \text{cm})}{2 (23.3 \text{ cm}) - 10 \text{ cm}} \cong 6.37 \text{ cm}$$

in front of the mirror. The magnification, m, of the final image is found by using the formula

$$m = -\frac{q}{p} \tag{2}$$

where q is the image distance and p is the object distance, each with respect to the second mirror. Thus,

$$m = -\frac{6.37 \text{ cm}}{23.33 \text{ cm}} = -0.273 .$$

Therefore the image is inverted and 0.273 times the original size of the first image. The size of the first image, with respect to the original object, can be found by using equation (2). Substituting q = -3.33 cm and p = 10 cm gives

$$m = -\frac{-3.33 \text{ cm}}{10 \text{ cm}} = \frac{1}{3} .$$

The first image is erect and is $\frac{1}{3}$ the size of the object. Thus, the size of the second image is

$$\frac{1}{3} \times (-.273) = -0.091$$

or about $\frac{1}{11}$ of the size of the original object.

An object is placed 60 cm in front of a spherical mirror. The mirror forms a virtual image at a distance of 15.0 cm from it. Find the radius of curvature, the type of mirror (concave or convex), and the magnification.

Solution: In this problem, both object distance p and the image distance q are given. Thus the radius of curvature of the mirror, R, can be found using the following equation:

$$\frac{1}{p} + \frac{1}{q} = \frac{2}{R} .$$

Substituting p = 60 cm and q = -15 cm (the negative sign is due to the fact that the image is virtual) into this equation gives

$$\frac{1}{60 \text{ cm}} - \frac{1}{15 \text{ cm}} = \frac{2}{R} ;$$

hence,

$$\frac{2}{R} = \frac{-3}{60 \text{ cm}} ,$$

and so,

$$R = \frac{(2)(60 \text{ cm})}{-3} = -40 \text{ cm}$$

Since the radius of curvature is negative, the mirror must be convex.

To get the magnification m, the following formula can be used:

$$m = - \frac{q}{p}$$

Substituting the given values for q and p into this equation gives

$$m = \frac{15 \text{ cm}}{60 \text{ cm}} = \frac{1}{4} .$$

(a) What type of mirror is required to form an image, on a wall 3 m from the mirror, of the filament of a headlight lamp 10 cm in front of the mirror? (b) What is the height of the image, if the height of the object is 5 mm?

Solution: (a) It is given that the object distance p = 10 cm and the image distance, q = 3 m = 300 cm. So, using the mirror equation,

$$\frac{1}{p} + \frac{1}{q} = \frac{2}{R} ,$$

gives $\frac{1}{10 \text{ cm}} + \frac{1}{300 \text{ cm}} = \frac{2}{R} ,$

Hence, $\frac{2}{R} = \frac{31}{300 \text{ cm}}$

and so,

$$R = \frac{600 \text{ cm}}{31} \cong 19.4 \text{ cm}.$$

Thus, the type of mirror that is required for the conditions described is a concave mirror (since the radius of curvature is positive), whose radius of curvature is 19.4 cm.

(b) The magnification m is given by the following equation:

$$m = -\frac{q}{p} .$$

Substituting the given values for q and p into this equation gives

$$m = \frac{-300 \text{ cm}}{10 \text{ cm}} = -30 .$$

Hence, the image is inverted because m is negative and is 30 times the height of the object. Thus, the height of the image = (5 mm)(30) or 150 mm.

● PROBLEM 17-17

A concave mirror A of focal length 10 cm and a convex mirror B of focal length 25 cm are coaxial and face each other with vertices 20 cm apart. An object of height 4 cm is placed at right angles to the axis and at a distance of 15 cm from A. Find the position, size, and nature of the image formed by reflection first at the surface of A and then at the surface of B. Repeat for rays reflected first at B and then at A.

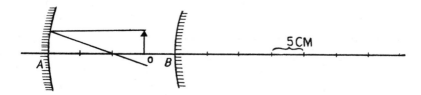

Solution: The position of the image produced by mirror A can be found using the following equation:

$$\frac{1}{p} + \frac{1}{q} = \frac{1}{f} \qquad (1)$$

where the object distance p, and the focal length f are given to be 15 cm and 10 cm, respectively.

Solving equation (1) for q gives

$$q = \frac{pf}{p - f} = \frac{150 \text{ cm}^2}{5 \text{ cm}} = 30 \text{ cm}.$$

The magnification, m, of mirror A is

$$m = - \frac{q}{p} = - \frac{30 \text{ cm}}{15 \text{ cm}} = - 2 \;.$$

The image is inverted and is twice the size of the object, or 8 cm high.

Now, take the image produced by mirror A and let it be the virtual object for mirror B. So, the object distance p = - 10 cm and the focal length of mirror B is 25 cm. From equation (1),

$$\frac{1}{-10 \text{ cm}} + \frac{1}{q} = \frac{1}{25 \text{ cm}} \;;$$

hence, the image distance q can be determined from the above equation to be

$$q = \frac{(25 \text{ cm}) (10 \text{ cm})}{(10 + 25) \text{ cm}} \cong 7.14 \text{ cm}$$

from mirror B. The magnification, m, is

$$m = - \frac{q}{p} = - \frac{7.14 \text{ cm}}{-10 \text{ cm}} = 0.714 ;$$

Thus, the size of the final image is 8 cm x 0.714 = 5.7 cm and it is still inverted, as before.

Following the same procedure, starting with mirror B instead of mirror A, the object distance is 5 cm (and the focal distance of mirror B is -25 cm (the minus sign is due to the fact that mirror B is convex). Thus, by equation (1),

$$\frac{1}{5 \text{ cm}} + \frac{1}{q} = \frac{1}{-25 \text{ cm}}$$

and so,

$$\frac{1}{q} = \frac{-1}{25 \text{ cm}} - \frac{1}{5 \text{ cm}} = \frac{-6}{25 \text{ cm}}$$

Then $q = -\frac{25}{6} \text{ cm} \cong -4.17 \text{ cm}$

and so, the first image is 4.17 cm to the right of mirror B; The magnification m of mirror B is

$$m = \frac{-q}{p} = \frac{4.17 \text{ cm}}{5} \cong .83$$

and so, the height of the image is $(.83)(4) \cong 3.32$ cm, and it is erect.

Since a virtual image of mirror B is a real object for mirror A, the object distance

$$p = (20 + 4.17) \text{ cm} = 24.17 \text{ cm}$$

and the focal length of mirror A, f, = 10 cm. From equation (1),

$$\frac{1}{24.17 \text{ cm}} + \frac{1}{q} = \frac{1}{10 \text{ cm}}$$

so,

$$q = \frac{(24.17)(10 \text{ cm})}{24.17 - 10 \text{ cm}} = 17.1 \text{ cm}$$

and the magnification, m, is

$$m = -\frac{q}{p} = -\frac{17.1 \text{ cm}}{24.17 \text{ cm}} = -0.707 \ .$$

Hence, the image will be $(0.707 \times 3.32 \text{ cm}) = 2.35$ cm high and inverted.

In the first part of the problem, the final image appeared 7.14 cm from mirror B and its size was 5.7 cm. However, in the second part, the final image appeared at a distance of (20 - 17.1) cm or 2.9 cm from mirror B and its size was 2.35 cm. Therefore, the final image is dependent on which mirror the rays of light struck first.

● **PROBLEM 17-18**

Derive the mirror formula for rays incident on a mirror of radius of curvature R, if each of the rays makes a small angle with the mirror's axis.

<u>Solution</u>: This proof will be totally geometrical (see

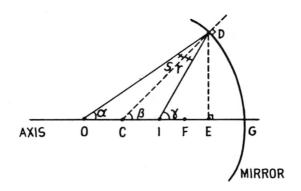

figure).   Ray OD is incident on mirror DG, at an angle s
with the normal to the mirror, CD.   (C is the center of
curvature of the arc forming the mirror.)   It is reflected at an angle r, and intersects the mirror axis at
point I.   By the law of reflection, the angle of incidence
is equal to the angle of reflection.   Hence,

$$s = r \tag{1}$$

Furthermore,

$$\beta = \frac{DG}{CG} \tag{2}$$

(β is measured in radians)

But, CG is the mirror radius R, so

$$\beta = \frac{DG}{R}$$

Also,

$$\tan \alpha = \frac{DE}{OE}$$

and $\tag{3}$

$$\tan \gamma = \frac{DE}{IE}$$

However, if α, β and r are small angles (that is, if
ray OD is close to the mirror axis), the approximations

$$\tan \alpha \simeq \alpha$$

and $\tag{4}$

$$\tan \gamma \simeq \gamma$$

may be used.

Furthermore,

$$DE \simeq DG \tag{5}$$

Substituting from relations (4) and (5) into relations

(3) gives

$$\alpha \simeq \frac{DG}{OE}$$

and   (6)

$$\gamma \simeq \frac{DG}{IE}$$

Also, note that, since γ is an exterior angle of triangle ICD,

$$\gamma = \beta + r \tag{7}$$

Similarly,

$$\beta = \alpha + s \tag{8}$$

Substituting $s = r$ (from equation (1)) into equation (7) gives

$$\gamma = \beta + s \tag{9}$$

and

$$\beta = \alpha + s \tag{10}$$

Eliminating s in equations (9) and (10) gives

$$\gamma - \beta = s = \beta - \alpha$$

or

$$2\beta - \gamma - \alpha = 0 \tag{11}$$

Substituting for α, β, and γ the expressions given in equations (6) and (2) into equation (11) gives

$$\frac{2DG}{R} - \frac{DG}{IE} - \frac{DG}{OE} = 0$$

and, dividing through by $-DG$,

$$\frac{1}{IE} + \frac{1}{OE} = \frac{2}{R} \tag{12}$$

However, if α, β and γ are small,

$$IE \simeq IG = i$$
                                                                             (13)
$$OE \simeq OG = 0$$

where i and 0 are the distances of the image from the mirror (image distance) and the object from the mirror (object distance), respectively. Hence, substituting from equation (13) into equation (12) gives the mirror formula,

$$\frac{1}{i} + \frac{1}{0} = \frac{2}{R}$$

Assuming that the eye is placed on the axis of a spherical
mirror, and that the rays are paraxial, explain how the
field of view is determined. Draw accurate diagrams for
concave and convex mirrors.

Solution: The eye will be the exit pupil for the optical
system. A chief ray is any ray that passes through the
center of the entrance pupil and by refraction or reflection
will also pass through the center of the exit pupil. So,
consider that particular chief ray which passes through the
center of the exit pupil and also intersects the perimeter
of the mirror. On reflection by the mirror, this chief ray
will then define the maximum field of view for the object
field. The entrance pupil will be the image of the exit
pupil in the mirror, so the entrance pupil can be located,
and from the chief ray that has been chosen the object field
of view can be determined.

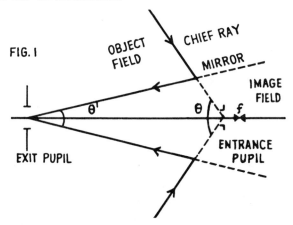

FIG. I

For a convex mirror, remember that all images formed
by a convex mirror are virtual. So, the entrance pupil will
be behind the convex mirror and at a distance of less than
the focal length of the mirror. In addition, it should be
remembered that the focal length of a mirror is just half
the radius of curvature of the mirror. A chief ray passing
through the perimeter of the mirror and the center of the
entrance pupil, as shown in figure 1, will then define the
object field of view. A light ray coincident with this
chief ray will then be reflected through the center of the
exit pupil. The angle θ in figure 1 will determine the object field of view.

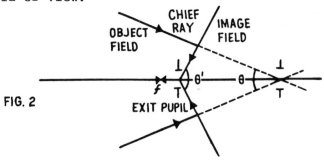

FIG. 2

For a concave mirror, there are two cases, one in which the eye (exit pupil) is outside the focal length of the mirror and the second in which the eye is inside the focal length of the mirror. For the latter case, the entrance pupil will be virtual and outside the focal length of the mirror as shown in figure 2. We proceed to draw rays as in the convex mirror case and again, the angle θ will determine the field of view in object space.

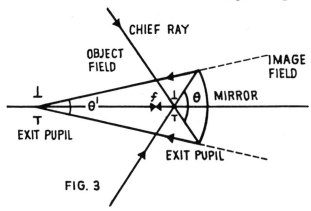

FIG. 3

If the eye is outside the focal length of the concave mirror, the entrance pupil will be inverted and real and inside the focal point. Again the chief rays are drawn as described above. This gives a cone of the field of view, as shown in figure 3.

● **PROBLEM** 17-20

Describe two common types of retrodirective reflectors.

Solution: A beam of light which strikes a retrodirective reflector will be reflected directly back toward its source, whether or not the source is directly in front of the reflector. Because of this feature, retrodirective reflectors are used as warning signals at dangerous spots on highways, where they reflect headlight beams back to the driver.

FIG. I

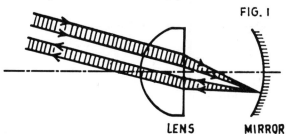

LENS   MIRROR

The so-called "reflector button," shown in figure 1, consists of a short-focusing converging thick lens combined with a concave mirror conforming to the second focal surface of the lens. A parallel incident beam, whether it is parallel to the lens axis or not, is converged to a point on the mirror and returned by the mirror to the lens as a beam diverging from the point at which reflection occurred. Since this point is in the second focal surface,

the lens renders the emergent beam parallel to the lens
axis, with its direction of travel just the reverse of the
direction of the incident beam.

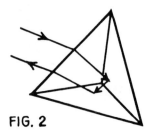

FIG. 2

Another common type of retrodirective reflector is
a metal cup several inches in diameter. Beginning about an
inch from the mouth, the sides flatten to form three mutually perpendicular reflecting surfaces which meet in a blunt
point at the bottom of the cup. The mouth of the cup is
sealed with a red cover glass. The three reflecting surfaces inside the cup have a property such that any light
ray which has been reflected in succession by all three
surfaces is exactly reversed in direction, as shown in figure 2.

FERMAT'S PRINCIPLE

● **PROBLEM** 17-21

Show that reflections from the inside of a prolate or
enlarged ellipsoid of revolution have the property that
light from a source at one focus of the ellipsoid is focused at the other focus.

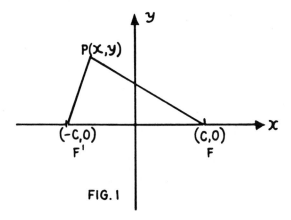

FIG. 1

Solution: An ellipse is the locus of a point such that the
sum of its distance from two fixed points is constant, and
equal to 2a, where a is a constant. If two fixed points
are chosen with coordinates (-C,O) and (C,O) (see figure 1),
then

$$\overline{F}'p + \overline{F}p = 2a,$$

where point p has coordinates (X,Y), as shown in figure 1

or

$$\sqrt{(X + C)^2 + Y^2} + \sqrt{(X - C)^2 + Y^2} = 2a$$

Subtracting $\sqrt{(X - C)^2 + Y^2}$ from both sides and squaring both sides of this equation gives

$$(X + C)^2 + Y^2 = 4a^2 + (X - C)^2 + Y^2$$

$$- 4a \sqrt{(X - C)^2 + Y^2}$$

Expanding both sides of this equation gives

$$X^2 + 2CX + C^2 + Y^2 = 4a^2 + X^2 - 2CX + C^2$$

$$+ Y^2 - 4a \sqrt{(X - C)^2 + Y^2}$$

or $\quad 2CX = 4a^2 - 2CX - 4a \sqrt{(X - C)^2 + Y^2}$.

Adding $2CX - 4a^2$ to both sides of this equation gives

$$4CX - 4a^2 = -4a \sqrt{(X - C)^2 + Y^2}$$

Dividing both sides by -4 gives

$$a^2 - CX = a \sqrt{(X - C)^2 + Y^2}$$

Dividing both sides by a gives

$$a - \frac{CX}{a} = \sqrt{(X - C)^2 + Y^2}$$

Squaring both sides gives

$$a^2 - 2CX + \frac{C^2}{a^2} X^2 = X^2 - 2CX + C^2 + Y^2$$

or rearranging,

$$a^2 - C^2 = X^2 \left(\frac{a^2 - C^2}{a^2} \right) + Y^2$$

and dividing both sides of this equation by $a^2 - C^2$ gives

$$1 = \frac{X^2}{a^2} + \frac{Y^2}{a^2 - C^2}$$

Since a is greater than C, let

$$b^2 = a^2 - C^2$$

489

Then,

$$1 = X^2/a^2 + Y^2/b^2 \ ,$$

which is the equation of an ellipse.

Now from Fermat's principle of least action, rays of light will travel the shortest optical path possible. Thus, all rays consistent with Fermat's principle will travel a distance of 2a from F to F'. So, light from one focus of an ellipse is focused at the other focus of the ellipse.

CHAPTER 18

LENSES

THIN LENSES

The distance between a real object and its real image in an infinitely thin lens is 32 inches. If the image is 3 times as large as the object find the position and focal length of the lens.

Solution: If we represent the object's distance from the lens as o, and the image's distance from the lens as i, then, from the given statement that the distance between the object and its image is 32 inches, we have

$$|o| + |i| = 32 \tag{1}$$

It is also given that the image is 3 times as large as the object, so

$$3 = \frac{-i}{o} \tag{2}$$

Solving (1) and (2) simultaneously gives

o = 8 inches and i = 24 inches.

Now applying the Gaussian lens formula, $\frac{1}{o} + \frac{1}{i} = \frac{1}{f}$, to the data above, we get f = 6 inches. So the focal length of the lens is 6 inches, the object is 8 inches away from the lens, and its image is 24 inches away from the lens.

An object 5 cm in diameter is 33.3 cm from a converging lens of 8 diopters. Calculate the position of the image from the lens and its size.

Solution: Using the Gaussian lens equation and the equation

for the power of a lens we have

$$\text{power} = \frac{1}{i} + \frac{1}{o}.$$

If the power is given as 8 diopters and the object distance is 0.333, m then the image can be found by

$$8\ m^{-1} = \frac{1}{i} + \frac{1}{0.333m}$$

$$i = 0.2\ m = 20\ cm.$$

Applying the equation for magnification, $m = \frac{-i}{o}$, we have

$$m = \frac{-20}{-33.3}$$

$$m = 3/5.$$

When substituting for o in the equation for magnification, we used -33.3 because it is on the opposite side of the image.

If the original object is 5 cm in diameter and it is magnified by a factor of 3/5, then the image is 3 cm in diameter.

● **PROBLEM** 18-3

A thin lens has focal length 50 mm. What is the magnification for the following object conjugates: 20 mm, -100 mm, +100 mm?

Solution: When given the focal length and the distance at which the object is from the lens, it is most convenient to use the Newtonian form to find the magnification, which is $M = \frac{-f}{o - f}$ where f is the focal length and o is the object distance.

Applying the given data to the Newtonian formula, we get

$M = 5/3$ for o = 20 mm,

$M = 1/3$ for o = -100 mm,

$M = -1$ for o = 100 mm.

● **PROBLEM** 18-4

An object is located 30 cm to the left of a thin lens of focal length 20 cm, as in the figure. Find the position and lateral magnification of its image, using both the Gaussian and Newtonian forms of the lens equation.

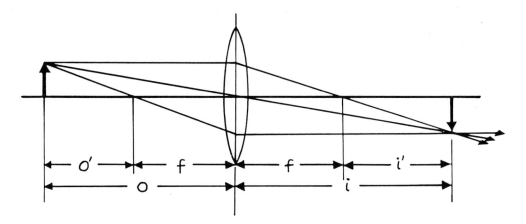

Solution: From the Gaussian lens equation,

$$\frac{1}{o} + \frac{1}{i} = \frac{1}{f},$$

we have $\frac{1}{30} + \frac{1}{i} = \frac{1}{20}$

so $i = 60$ cm.

The image is real (i is positive) and it lies 60 cm to the right of the center of the lens.

The lateral magnification, M, or the size of the image is found by applying the formula

$$M = -\frac{i}{o} = -\frac{60 \text{ cm}}{30 \text{ cm}} = -2.$$

The image is inverted (M is negative) and is twice the original size.

The Newtonian lens equation is

$o' \cdot i' = f^2$, where $o' = o - f$ and $i' = i - f$.

which gives us $(10 \text{ cm}) \cdot i' = (20 \text{ cm})^2$.

Solving we have

$i' = 40$ cm

which also puts the image $i' + f$ or 60 cm to the right of the center of the lens.

The lateral magnification, in Newtonian form, is

$$M = -\frac{i'}{f} = -\frac{40 \text{ cm}}{20 \text{ cm}} = -2$$

which is identical to the Gaussian solution.

An object 4 cm in diameter is placed 167 mm from a converging lens of 5 diopters. Calculate the position of the image from the lens and its size. Is the image real or virtual?

Solution: The power of a lens is measured in diopters when the focal length is in meters. The power is simply the reciprocal of the focal length; so the Gaussian lens formula becomes $\frac{1}{o} + \frac{1}{i} = P$, where o is the object distance, i is the image distance, and P is the power of the lens in diopters when the focal length is expressed in meters. Letting o = 0.167 m, P = 5 diopters, and solving for i in the equation above we have the image distance, i = -1.012 m.

Since i = -1.012 m, the image is a virtual one that is 1012 mm from the lens.

The magnification, m, of the image is found by applying

$$m = - \frac{i}{o}$$

so $\quad m = - \frac{-1.012}{0.167} = 6.06.$

If the original object that is 4 cm in diameter is magnified 6.06 times, then the image produced is 24.2 cm in diameter and is not inverted.

● **PROBLEM** 18-6

An object 5 cm in diameter is 33.3 cm from a diverging lens of 8 diopters. Calculate the position of the image from the lens and its size. Is this image real or virtual?

Solution: In general, given the power of a lens, we can write the thin lens equation as follows:

$$\frac{1}{o} + \frac{1}{i} = P \tag{1}$$

where o is the object distance and i is the image distance (note that these must be measured in meters, since the unit of power is diopters). For a diverging lens the power is negative, so for the given case, equation (1) becomes

$$\frac{1}{o} + \frac{1}{i} = -8 \tag{2}$$

Substituting o = 0.333 m in equation (2) we have the image distance, i, = -0.091 m. Thus the image produced is a virtual one that is 9.1 cm from the lens.

The magnification, m, of the image is found by applying

$$m = -\frac{i}{o} ;$$

hence, $m = -\dfrac{-0.091}{0.333} = 0.27$. So when an object that is 5 cm in diameter is magnified by a factor of 0.27, the final image is 1.35 cm in diameter. It is not inverted because the magnification is positive.

• **PROBLEM** 18-7

A thin biconvex glass lens is supported with its axis vertical on the surface of a pond. Its lower surface, of radius of curvature 20 cm, is in contact with the water, while its upper surface, of radius of curvature 50 cm, is exposed to the air. The refractive indices of the glass and the water are 1.5 and 1.33, respectively. An insect hovering above the lens and a fish below it see one another, each receiving sets of parallel rays from the other. What are the distances of the insect and the fish above and below the lens? What would be the effect, if any, of reversing the lens?

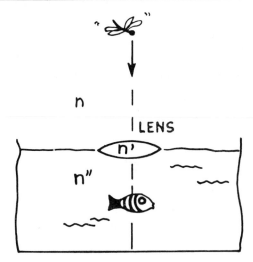

Solution: For a thin lens with different media on either side,

$$\frac{n}{f} = \frac{n' - n}{r_1} + \frac{n'' - n'}{r_2} = \frac{n''}{f''} \quad (1)$$

where f is the primary focal length of the lens and f" is the secondary focal length of the lens.

Hence, substituting n, n', n", r_1, and r_2 into equation (1) we get

$$\frac{1}{f} = \frac{1.5 - 1}{50 \text{ cm}} + \frac{1.33 - 1.50}{-20 \text{ cm}} = \frac{1.33}{f''}$$

or

$$\frac{1}{f} = \left(\frac{0.5}{50} + \frac{.17}{20}\right)\frac{1}{\text{cm}}$$

$$= \frac{37}{2000} \text{ cm}^{-1}$$

495

Thus,

$$f = \frac{2000}{37} \text{ cm}$$

$$= 54 \text{ cm}$$

and

$$f'' = f \times \frac{1.33}{1} \quad \text{(equation (1))}$$

$$= (54 \times 1.33) \text{ cm}$$

$$= 71.8 \text{ cm}.$$

Hence for the insect and fish to receive parallel rays from the other, each must be at the focal point of the lens.

Hence, the insect must be at a distance $f = 54$ cm above the lens and the fish must be at a distance 71.9 cm below the lens.

If the lens is reversed, then $r_1 = 20$ cm and $r_2 = -50$ cm.

Hence the primary focal length becomes

$$\frac{1}{f} = \frac{n' - n}{r_1} + \frac{n'' - n'}{r_2}$$

$$= \left(\frac{1.5 - 1}{20} + \frac{1.33 - 1.5}{-50}\right) \frac{1}{\text{cm}}$$

$$= \left(\frac{2.84}{100}\right) \frac{1}{\text{cm}} \quad .$$

Therefore,

$$f = \frac{100}{2.84} \text{ cm}$$

$$= 35.2 \text{ cm}$$

and

$$\frac{n''}{f''} = \frac{1}{f}$$

or

$$f'' = n''f$$

$$= 1.33 \times 35.2 \text{ cm}$$

$$= 46.8 \text{ cm} \quad .$$

When the lens is reversed, the insect must be 35.2 cm above the lens and the fish must be 46.8 cm below the lens for each to receive parallel rays.

Use both the Gaussian and Newtonian forms of the lens equation to compute the distance X from the focal length of the lens, at which an object O must be placed in the diagram below to be imaged at I.

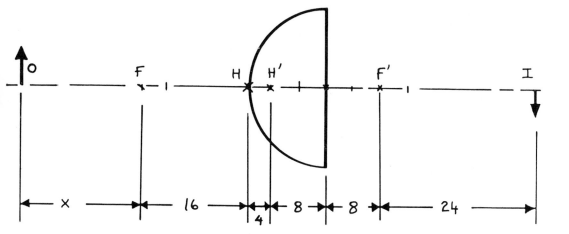

Solution: We will first use the Gaussian form of the lens equation, which is

$$\frac{1}{O} + \frac{1}{I} = \frac{1}{f}$$

where O is the object distance $\overline{HO}$, i is the image distance $\overline{H'I}$ = 40, and f is the focal length, which is 16. Hence,

$$\frac{1}{16+X} + \frac{1}{40} = \frac{1}{16}$$

from which X=10.67.

According to Newton, the object distance can be found by applying the equation

$$(X_i)(X_o) = f^2$$

where X_o is represented by $\overline{OF}$ in the diagram, X_i is represented by $\overline{F'I}$, and f is the focal length of the lens. Letting X_o = X, f = 16, and X_i = 24 we have

$$24X = (16)^2;$$

thus X = 10.67.

Therefore, the Gaussian and Newtonian lens equations predict that the object must be placed 10.67 units to the left of the first focal point of the lens shown in the figure to produce an image 24 units to the right of the second focal point.

For a converging lens, show that, in the case of real images,

$$p + q \geq 4f \quad ,$$

where p and q represent the object and image distances, respectively, from the lens and f denotes the focal length of the lens.

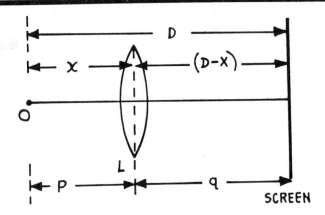

Solution: Let us suppose that an object and a screen, on which an image is formed by a lens, are located a distance D apart from one another. The lens, which forms the image of the object 'O' on the screen, is located at a distance x from the object.

Then $p = x$

and $q = D - x$.

Using lens formula we get

$$\frac{1}{p} + \frac{1}{q} = \frac{1}{f}$$

or

$$\frac{1}{x} + \frac{1}{D - x} = \frac{1}{f} \quad .$$

Then, placing $\frac{1}{x}$ and $\frac{1}{D - x}$ over a common denominator,

$$\frac{D - x + x}{x(D - x)} = \frac{D}{x(D - x)} = \frac{1}{f}$$

cross multiplying gives the result

$$x(D - x) = Df \quad .$$

Then,

$$x^2 - xD + Df = 0 \quad .$$

Using the quadratic equation,

$$x = \frac{D \pm \sqrt{D^2 - 4Df}}{2} \, .$$

Factoring D out from under the radical,

$$x = \frac{D}{2}\left[1 \pm \sqrt{1 - \frac{4f}{D}}\right] \, .$$

For x to be real, so that there is a position of the lens where the image is formed, we need

$$1 - \frac{4f}{D} \geq 0$$

or

$$1 \geq \frac{4f}{D}$$

or $D \geq 4f$.

This is the same as $p + q \geq 4f$.

• **PROBLEM** 18-10

Find the focal length of a plano-convex thin lens with a radius of curvature, R = 30, mm and an index of 1.50.

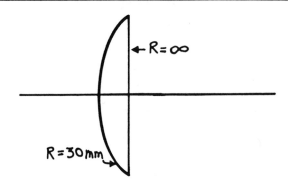

Solution: We will first find the focal length, f, of the thin lens when the convex surface faces the light. Using

$$\frac{1}{f} = (n_L - 1)\left[\frac{1}{R_1} - \frac{1}{R_2}\right] \tag{1}$$

where n_L is the index of the lens, R_1 the radius of curvature of one surface, and R_2 is the radius of curvature of the other surface. Letting $n_L = 1.50$, $R_1 = -30$ mm, and $R_2 = \infty$ yields

$$\frac{1}{f} = (1.50 - 1) \cdot \left[\frac{1}{-30\text{mm}} - \frac{1}{\infty}\right] ;$$

$f = -60$ mm.

Therefore, when the convex surface of the lens faces the light, the focal length, f, is 60 mm.

Now we will find the focal length of the lens when the plane surface faces the light. Using equation (1) again, but letting $R_1 = \infty$ and $R_2 = 30$ mm yields

$$\frac{1}{f} = (1.50 - 1) \cdot \left[\frac{1}{\infty} - \frac{1}{30 \text{ mm}}\right] ;$$

$$f = -60 \text{ mm}.$$

Again the focal length is 60 mm (the sign is irrelevant); so we can conclude that the focal length is independent of the surface of the lens facing the light.

● **PROBLEM** 18-11

A difference of 8 mm prevails between the positions of an image when the object is at infinity and when it is 0.2 m from the object-side of a convex lens. What is the focal length of the lens?

Solution: Applying the Gaussian lens formula, $\frac{1}{o} + \frac{1}{i} = \frac{1}{f}$ where o is the object distance, i is the image distance, and f is the focal length, to both situations, we have:

$$\frac{1}{\infty} + \frac{1}{i} = \frac{1}{f} \tag{1}$$

and

$$\frac{1}{0.2m} + \frac{1}{i'} = \frac{1}{f} . \tag{2}$$

Solving for i and i' in (1) and (2) and using the fact that the images are 0.008 m apart, we have:

$$i' - i = 0.008 \text{ m} = \left(\frac{1}{\frac{1}{f} - \frac{1}{0.2m}}\right) - f \tag{3}$$

Solving equation (3) yields

$$f = 0.0362 \text{ m}$$

which is equal to 36.2 mm.

● **PROBLEM** 18-12

A thin lens of focal length 10 inches in air and refractive index 1.53 is immersed in water (n = 1.33). What is its focal length in water?

Solution: The focal length, f, of a thin lens immersed in a given medium can be found by applying the equation

$$\frac{1}{f} = (n_L - 1) \cdot \left[\frac{1}{R_1} - \frac{1}{R_2}\right] \tag{1}$$

where n_L is the ratio of the index of the lens to the index of the medium. Since we are working with the same lens for both mediums we can represent $\left[\dfrac{1}{R_1} - \dfrac{1}{R_2}\right]$ in equation (1) by X, so equation (1) becomes

$$\frac{1}{f} = (n_L - 1)X. \tag{2}$$

If the focal length of the thin lens is 10 inches in air, then equation (2) becomes

$$\frac{1}{10 \text{ in}} = \left(\frac{1.53}{1.00} - 1\right)X \tag{3}$$

and if the same lens is immersed in water, equation (2) now becomes

$$\frac{1}{f} = \left(\frac{1.53}{1.33} - 1\right)X. \tag{4}$$

We now have two equations and two unknowns. To obtain the value of f, solve for X in the first equation and substitute this value into the second. From (3) we have

$$X = \frac{1}{10\left(\dfrac{1.53}{1.00} - 1\right)} = \frac{1}{5.3}$$

Substituting this into (4) gives us

$$\frac{1}{f} = \left(\frac{1.53}{1.33} - 1\right)\left(\frac{1}{5.3}\right) ;$$

hence,

$$f = 35.2 \text{ in} \quad .$$

Thus, if a lens of focal length 10 in. in air is immersed in water, the focal length increases to about 35.2 inches.

● **PROBLEM** 18-13

Find the ratio of the focal lengths of a glass lens in water and in air. The refractive indices of the glass and water are 1.5 and 1.33 respectively.

Solution: The focal length of a thin lens in a given medium can be found by applying the lensmaker's equation and the Gaussian lens formula to get

$$\frac{1}{f} = (n_L - 1) \cdot \left[\frac{1}{R_1} - \frac{1}{R_2}\right] \tag{1}$$

where R_1 and R_2 are the radii of curvature for each side of the lens and n_L is the ratio of the refractive index of the lens to the refractive index of the medium that the lens is in. In most problems, n_L would only be the index of the lens because the lens is in the air, which has an index of refraction of 1.00.

The focal length of the lens in water, f_w, can be found by applying

$$\frac{1}{f_w} = \left[\frac{1.50}{1.33} - 1\right]\left[\frac{1}{R_1} - \frac{1}{R_2}\right] \qquad (2)$$

and the focal length of the lens in air, f_A, is found by applying

$$\frac{1}{f_A} = \left[\frac{1.50}{1.00} - 1\right]\left[\frac{1}{R_1} - \frac{1}{R_2}\right] . \qquad (3)$$

Therefore, the ratio of the focal lengths of a glass lens in water to air, f_w/f_A, using equations (2) and (3), is

$$\frac{f_w}{f_A} = \frac{\left[\frac{1.50}{1.00} - 1\right]\left[\frac{1}{R_1} - \frac{1}{R_2}\right]}{\left[\frac{1.50}{1.33} - 1\right]\left[\frac{1}{R_1} - \frac{1}{R_2}\right]} = 3.91.$$

● **PROBLEM** 18-14

A thin lens with index of refraction n and radii of curvature R_1 and R_2 is located at the interface between two media with indices of refraction n_1 and n_2. If S_1 and S_2 are the object and image distances, respectively, and f_1 and f_2 the respective focal lengths, show that

$$(f_1/S_1) + (f_2/S_2) = 1 .$$

Solution: If S_1 is the object distance for the first lens surface, then the object distance for the second lens surface is $-S_1'$, where S_1' is given by Snell's law at small angles:

$$\frac{n_1}{S_1} + \frac{n}{S_1'} = \frac{n - n_1}{R_1}. \qquad (1)$$

Also,

$$\frac{-n}{S_1'} + \frac{n_2}{S_2} = \frac{n_2 - n}{R_2} \qquad (2)$$

Adding these two equations gives

$$\frac{n_1}{S_1} + \frac{n_2}{S_2} = \frac{n - n_1}{R_1} + \frac{n_2 - n}{R_2} \qquad (3)$$

The focal length f_1 is found by setting $S_2 = \infty$ in equation (3). Then

$$S_1 = f_1 = \frac{n_1}{(n - n_1)/R_1 + (n_2 - n)/R_2}$$

Similarly, f_2 is found by setting $S_1 = \infty$ in (3).

502

$$f_2 = \frac{n_2}{(n - n_1)/R_1 + (n_2 - n)/R_2}$$

Then

$$\frac{f_1}{S_1} + \frac{f_2}{S_2} = \frac{1}{(n - n_1)/R_1 + (n_2 - n)/R_2} \left[\frac{n_1}{S_1} + \frac{n_2}{S_2} \right]$$

By equation (3),

$$\frac{f_1}{S_1} + \frac{f_2}{S_2} = \frac{1}{(n - n_1)/R_1 + (n_2 - n)/R_2} \left[\frac{n - n_1}{R_1} + \frac{n_2 - n}{R_2} \right]$$

$$= 1 .$$

● **PROBLEM** 18-15

The usual definition of the focal length of a thin lens,

$$\frac{1}{f} = \frac{(n - n_o)}{n_o} \left(\frac{1}{R_1} - \frac{1}{R_2} \right)$$

(where n is the relative index of refraction of the lens material and the medium it is in, n_o is the relative index of refraction of the surrounding material, and R_1 and R_2 represent the radii of curvature of the lens), assumes a definite plane from which to measure the distance to the first principal focus. Obviously this does not apply for thick or compound lenses. A more general definition states that the focal length is the size of the image divided by the angle subtended at the lens by an infinitely distant object.

(a) Show that this new definition is in agreement with the formula given above for the thin lens.

(b) What is the focal length for the compound lens consisting of a thin front lens (closest to object) of focal length −3f and a rear lens of focal length f, coaxial and separated by a distance f/4. Check your result with the usual compound lens formula.

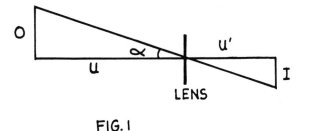

FIG. 1

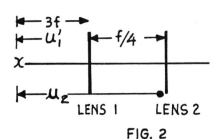

FIG. 2

503

Solution: There are many ways in which a person can man-
ipulate the geometry of optics for ease of handling problems. For example, for thin lenses one can use either the
Gaussian or Newtonian formulation. In this problem we are
asked to determine a different method of expressing the
focal length. Let us look at figure 1, where we look at
the ray that is not deviated by the lens and passes through
the axis at the lens. Then by geometry,

$$\frac{o}{u} = \tan \alpha = \frac{I}{u'} \qquad (1)$$

$$u' = \frac{I}{o/u} \qquad (2)$$

If u is reasonably large then α is small, so the approximation $\tan \alpha \sim \alpha$ can be made and so $u' = I/\alpha$. Now if
u is allowed to go to infinity then u' is just the focal
length or

$$f = I/\alpha , \qquad (3)$$

so that for a thin lens we need to a) measure for the lens
the two radii of curvature and the index of refraction of
glass and use the lensmaker's formula given in the question, b) measure the image size and the angular size of the
object, and use equation (3), or c) if the lens is a converging lens we can find the focal length experimentally.
So, we see that equation (3) gives us a method of determining the focal length of a lens with less complication than
other methods.

We can then write for the focal length of a combination of thin lenses,

$$f_{comb} = \frac{I_{final}}{\alpha_{initial}} = \frac{I_1 \times \text{magnification of lens 2}}{\alpha \text{ initial}} =$$

$$= \frac{I_1 \ u_2'/u_2}{\alpha_{initial}} = f_1 (u_2'/u_2)$$

where I's represent image size, u_2 represents the object
distance from the second lens, u_2' is the final image distance from the second lens and f_1 is the focal length of
the first lens of the combination. Now if the object is
at infinity, the image formed by the first lens will be at
a distance of -3f from the first lens. From figure 2, the
distance of this image from the second lens of the combination will be

$$u_2 = 3f + f/4 = \frac{13f}{4}$$

and from the thin lens equation,

$$\frac{1}{u_2} + \frac{1}{u_2'} = 1/f_2$$

Substituting the value for u_2 determined in the preceding step,

$$\frac{4}{13f} + \frac{1}{u_2'} = \frac{1}{f} \quad .$$

Solving for $\frac{1}{u_2'}$,

$$u_2' = \frac{13f}{9} \quad .$$

Then

$$f_{comb} = f_1(u_2'/u_2) = -3f \left(\frac{13f}{9}\right) \Big/ \left(\frac{13f}{4}\right) = \frac{-4f}{3} \quad .$$

Now for a lens combination we have from a standard optics text

$$\frac{1}{f_{comb}} = \frac{1}{f_1} + \frac{1}{f_2} - \frac{d}{f_1 f_2} \quad , \text{ where d is the distance between}$$

the lenses.

Substituting,

$$\frac{1}{f_{comb}} = \frac{1}{-3f} + \frac{1}{f} - \frac{f/4}{(-3f)(f)}$$

By algebra,

$$\frac{1}{f_{comb}} = \frac{2}{3f} + \frac{1}{12f} = \frac{3}{4f} \quad .$$

Therefore, $f_{comb} = \frac{4f}{3}$, and so, the two results agree with one another.

● **PROBLEM** 18-16

A lens with the designation +3.00 diopters is placed 2 m from an object (Fig. 1) so that it separates air (to the left of the lens) from water (to the right of the lens). Find the image distance using the vergence method.

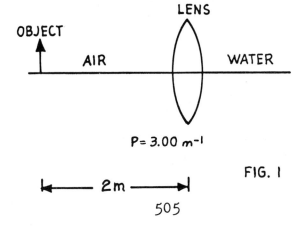

LENS

OBJECT

AIR

WATER

$P = 3.00 \ m^{-1}$

FIG. I

|← 2m →|

Solution: The vergence equation in general form is

$$V = \frac{n}{s} \tag{1}$$

where n is the index of refraction and s is the distance from the lens to the object or image. Since n = 1.00 for air, and considering distances to the left of the lens to be negative, the object vergence is just

$$V_o = - \frac{1.00}{2 \text{ m}} = -0.50 \text{ m}^{-1}$$

Now the image vergence is the sum of the object vergence and the lens designation:

$$V_i = V_o + P = (-0.50\text{m}^{-1}) + (+3.00 \text{ m}^{-1}) = 2.50 \text{ m}^{-1}$$

Rearranging equation (1) to solve for the image distance and remembering that the index of refraction for water is 1.33 gives:

$$s_i = \frac{n}{V_i} = \frac{1.33}{+2.50 \text{ m}^{-1}} = 0.532 \text{ m} = 53.2 \text{ cm}$$

● **PROBLEM** 18-17

Two converging lenses, with focal lengths 20 cm and 30 cm are placed coaxially 10 cm apart. Find the position of the image of an object placed 60 cm from the first lens.

Solution: Problems dealing with the passage of light through two or more coaxial lenses may easily be solved if we take one lens at a time. We will use the Gaussian form of the lens formula:

$$\frac{1}{s_o} + \frac{1}{s_i} = \frac{1}{f} \; . \tag{1}$$

For the first lens we have s_o = 60 cm, f = 20 cm;

$$\frac{1}{60 \text{ cm}} + \frac{1}{s_i} = \frac{1}{20 \text{ cm}}$$

$$s_i = 30 \text{ cm}$$

This means that each ray of light emerging from the first lens is incident on the second lens in such a way that they will meet at a point 20 cm beyond the second lens, had this lens had no effect upon the image.

Then, looking at the second lens, s_o = -20 cm and f = 30 cm.

Again using equation (1),

$$\frac{1}{S_i} + \frac{1}{-20} = \frac{1}{30}$$

$$S_i = 12 \text{ cm} .$$

Thus the image is 12 cm beyond the second lens. It can be readily seen that this method may be applied to the case of any number of lenses placed coaxially. The image due to one becomes the object for the next. Care must be exercised, however, to give all distances their proper signs.

An alternate method of solution would be to view the two lenses as one optical system and use the formula for the combination of lenses. The effective focal length, f, of a system of lenses of focal lengths f_1 and f_2 separated by a distance d is given by

$$\frac{1}{f} = \frac{1}{f_1} + \frac{1}{f_2} - \frac{d}{f_1 f_2} . \qquad (2)$$

So we have

$$\frac{1}{f} = \frac{1}{20} + \frac{1}{30} - \frac{10}{20(30)}$$

$$f = 15 \text{ cm}$$

The system now behaves as a thick lens. Equation (1) still holds, provided that the object and image distances are measured from the principal points H_1 and H_2 , shown in the figure.

The distance from H_1 to the first lens is given by

$$S_{H_1} = \frac{fd}{f_2} ; \text{ hence,}$$

$$S_{H_1} = \frac{(15)(10)}{30} = 5 \text{ cm} .$$

Similarly, the distance from H_2 to the second lens is given by

$$S_{H_2} = - \frac{fd}{f_1} = - \frac{(15)(10)}{20} = -7.5 \text{ cm.}$$

According to the sign convention, the negative sign indicates that H_2 is to the left of its vertex.

So we now have the following situation:

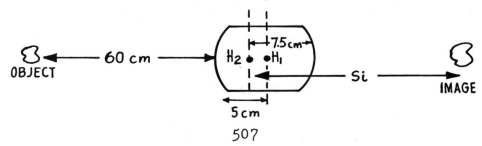

Then

$$S_o = 65 \text{ cm}$$

$$f = 15 \text{ cm}$$

$$\frac{1}{65} + \frac{1}{S_i} = \frac{1}{15}$$

$$S_i = 19.5 \text{ cm}$$

So the object is $S_i - SH_2 = 12$ cm from the second lens, as predicted.

● **PROBLEM** 18-18

Three lenses with focal lengths of +10 cm, -10 cm, and +10 cm, respectively, are placed one behind the other, 2 cm apart. If parallel light is incident on the first lens, how far behind the third lens will the light come to a focus?

Solution: The solution of this problem involves three successive applications of the thin lens equation,

$$\frac{1}{\theta} + \frac{1}{i} = \frac{1}{f} . \tag{1}$$

For the first lens, substitution of $\theta = \infty$ (parallel incident light) and $f = +10$ cm gives $i = +10$ cm; this places the image beyond the second lens, i.e., the light appears to converge to a point 8 cm beyond the second lens. Setting $\theta = -8$ cm and $f = -10$ cm, equation (1) gives $i = +40$ cm for the second lens. The rays thus again converge, this time to a point 38 cm beyond the third lens. Setting $\theta = -38$ cm and $f = +10$ cm, equation (1) yields $i = +7.91$ cm for the third lens.

● **PROBLEM** 18-19

The compound lens in the figure consists of a thin positive lens of focal length +20 cm, separated by a distance of 10 cm from a thin negative lens of focal length -20 cm. Find the focal length of the compound lens, and the positions of its focal points.

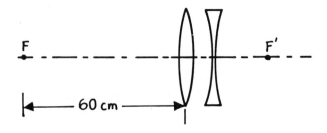

<u>Solution:</u>   We use $\dfrac{1}{o_1} + \dfrac{1}{i_1} = \dfrac{1}{f_1}$ $\hspace{3cm}$ (1)

where o_1 is the object distance, i_1 is the image distance, and f_1 is the focal length, with respect to the positive lens. Assuming that parallel light rays enter the lenses from the left side, we have

$$\dfrac{1}{\infty} + \dfrac{1}{i_1} = \dfrac{1}{20 \ cm} .$$

Hence, i_1 = +20 cm. Now, taking the position of the first image, i_1, and applying equation (1) with respect to the second lens, we have

$$\dfrac{1}{-10cm} + \dfrac{1}{i} = \dfrac{1}{-20cm} .$$

Thus i = +20cm. We used -10 cm as the object distance for the second lens because it is a virtual object that is 10cm to the right of the negative lens. One focal point is therefore 20 cm to the right of the negative lens.

To find the focal point on the left side of the compound lens, we let parallel light enter the lenses from the right side. Using equation (1) on the negative lens first yields

$$\dfrac{1}{\infty} + \dfrac{1}{i_2} = \dfrac{1}{-20cm}$$

so i_2 = -20 cm. Now taking that virtual image as a real object that is 30 cm to the right of the positive lens yields

$$\dfrac{1}{30cm} + \dfrac{1}{i} = \dfrac{1}{20cm} ; \ \text{hence,}$$

i = 60 cm. The other focal point is 60 cm to the left of the positive lens.

We can find the focal length of the compound lens by applying the equation,

$$\dfrac{1}{f} = \dfrac{1}{f_1} + \dfrac{1}{f_2} - \dfrac{d}{f_1 f_2} \hspace{3cm} (2)$$

where f_1 and f_2 represent the focal lengths of the individual lenses, d is the distance between the lenses, and f is the focal length of the compound lens.

Applying equation (2) where f_1 = +20 cm, f_2 = -20 cm, and d = 10 cm we have

$$\dfrac{1}{f} = \dfrac{1}{20cm} + \dfrac{1}{-20cm} - \dfrac{10 \ cm}{(20cm)(-20cm)} .$$

Hence the focal length of the compound lens, f, is 40 cm.

A point light source is on the axis of a convergent lens, and an image is formed 25 cm from the lens on the other side. When a second lens is placed in contact with the first, the image is formed 40 cm from the combination on the side opposite the source. What is the focal length of the second lens?

Solution: If the first lens focuses the light at a point 25 cm away from it on the opposite side of the source, then the second lens must take the image of the first lens and refocus it at a point 40 cm away from the lens (also on the opposite side of the source). Use the Gaussian lens formula, $\frac{1}{o} + \frac{1}{i} = \frac{1}{f}$, where o is the object distance, i is the image distance, and f is the focal length of the second lens.

Take the object distance as -25 cm for the second lens because it is a virtual object.

$$\frac{1}{-25\,cm} + \frac{1}{40\,cm} = \frac{1}{f}$$

$$f = -66.67 \text{ cm.}$$

In general, problems dealing with the passage of light through two or more coaxial lenses may be easily solved if one lens is taken at a time.

Two thin lenses of focal lengths $f_1 = -50$ mm and $f_2 = +100$ mm, respectively, are separated by 50 mm. What is the focal length of the combination? Where are the principal points of the combination?

Solution: When the focal lengths of two lenses and the distance between the lenses are known, the focal length of the combined lenses, F, can be found by applying the equation

$$\frac{1}{F} = \frac{1}{f_1} + \frac{1}{f_2} - \frac{d}{f_1 f_2} \tag{1}$$

where d is the distance between the two lenses and f_1 and f_2 are their individual focal lengths. When $f_1 = -50$ mm, $f_2 = 100$ mm, and d = 50 mm, equation (1) becomes

$$\frac{1}{F} = \frac{1}{-50} + \frac{1}{100} - \frac{50}{(-50)(100)},$$

$$\frac{1}{F} = 0,$$

therefore the focal length of the combination of the lenses is infinite. If the focal length of any lens is infinite then the position of any of the principal points cannot be determined.

Two thin lenses whose focal lengths are f_1 and f_2 are placed in contact with each other. Prove that the focal length of the combination, F , satisfies the relationship

$$\frac{1}{F} = \frac{1}{f_1} + \frac{1}{f_2} .$$

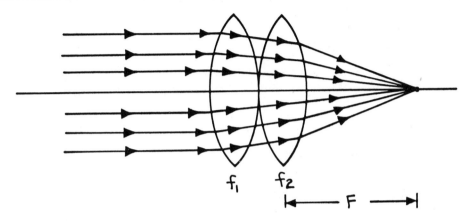

Solution: If the two lenses in the figure are placed in contact with each other at their vertices and if their individual focal lengths are f_1 and f_2 then the focal length of the combination of these two lenses is represented by F. When parallel rays of light, from a source an infinite distance away, strike the lenses from the left side these rays will converge at the focal point on the right side of the lens. Using the Gaussian lens formula,

$$\frac{1}{o_1} + \frac{1}{i_1} = \frac{1}{f_1}$$

for the first lens, where $o_1 = \infty$ we have

$$\frac{1}{\infty} + \frac{1}{i_1} = \frac{1}{f_1} ;$$

hence the image is produced at a distance f_1 away. Now taking that real image of the first lens and letting it be the object for the second lens, $o_2 = -f_1$, and using the Gaussian lens formula, we have

$$-\frac{1}{f_1} + \frac{1}{i_2} = \frac{1}{f_2},$$

$$\frac{1}{i_2} = \frac{1}{f_2} + \frac{1}{f_1}.$$

Since i_2 is the image distance after it passes the second lens, it is represented by F in the figure. Hence, we have

$$\frac{1}{F} = \frac{1}{f_1} + \frac{1}{f_2}.$$

What is the focal length of a combination of two thin convex lenses, each of focal length f, placed apart at a distance of 2f/3 ?

Solution: When two lenses with known focal lengths, f_1 and f_2, are combined, then the focal length of the combined lenses, F, is found by applying the equation

$$\frac{1}{F} = \frac{1}{f_1} + \frac{1}{f_2} - \frac{d}{f_1 f_2} \qquad (1)$$

where d is the distance between the two lenses. If the two lenses touch each other at their vertices, then equation (1) becomes

$$\frac{1}{F} = \frac{1}{f_1} + \frac{1}{f_2} .$$

In this problem, f_1 and f_2 are equal to f and the distance between the two lenses, d, is $\frac{2f}{3}$. Substituting this data into equation (1), we have

$$\frac{1}{F} = \frac{1}{f} + \frac{1}{f} - \frac{2f}{3ff}$$

from which the focal length of the combined lenses, $F, = \frac{3f}{4}$.

● **PROBLEM** 18-24

Two thin convex lenses of focal lengths f_1 and f_2 are separated by a distance equal to $2f_2$. If $f_1 = 3f_2$, what is the focal length of the combination?

Solution: When two lenses with known focal lengths are combined the new focal length of the combination of the lenses, F, is found by applying the equation,

$$\frac{1}{F} = \frac{1}{f_1} + \frac{1}{f_2} . \qquad (1)$$

When the two lenses are separated by a distance d, equation (1) becomes

$$\frac{1}{F} = \frac{1}{f_1} + \frac{1}{f_2} - \frac{d}{f_1 f_2} . \qquad (2)$$

If $f_1 = 3f_2$ and the distance between the lenses, $d, = 2f_2$ then equation (2) becomes

$$\frac{1}{F} = \frac{1}{3f_2} + \frac{1}{f_2} - \frac{2f_2}{3f_2 f_2}$$

from which the focal length of the combined lenses, $F, = \frac{3f_2}{2}$.

What single lens is equivalent to a thin converging lens of focal length 6 cm in contact with a thin diverging lens of 10 cm focal length?

Solution: When two or more thin lenses are combined together to form one lens, the focal length of their combination is given by

$$\frac{1}{f} = \frac{1}{f_1} + \frac{1}{f_2} + \frac{1}{f_3} + \ldots + \frac{1}{f_n} \qquad (1)$$

where f_i , $i = 1,2,\ldots,n$, is the focal length of each lens. In this problem, the two focal lengths are +6 cm (converging lens) and -10 cm (diverging lens). Applying this to equation (1), we have

$$\frac{1}{f} = \frac{1}{6cm} - \frac{1}{10cm}$$

hence, the focal length, f, is 15 cm and it is a converging lens.

If two thin lenses are placed on the same axis with their second focal points in coincidence, show that the second focal point of the combination is midway between the common focal point and the second lens, and that the deviation produced by the second lens is twice that produced by the first lens (assuming that the angles are small).

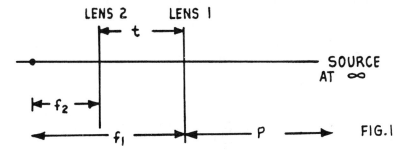

Solution: Figure (1) shows the optical arrangement. To find the focal point of the combination, we will start with the source distance, p, = infinity and successively apply the thin lens formula to each of the lenses. The final image point will be the second focal point of the combination. The thin lens equation is

$$\frac{1}{p} + \frac{1}{q} = \frac{1}{f}$$

where p is the object distance, q is the image distance and f is the focal length of the lens. So for the first lens

$$\frac{1}{\infty} + \frac{1}{q_1} = 1/f_1$$

$$q_1 = f_1 \quad ,$$

which puts the image formed by the first lens a distance f_1 to the left of the lens. Now the image of the first lens becomes an object for the second lens.

Now from figure (1) we determine that

$$p_2 = t - f_1 = -f_2$$

and

$$\frac{1}{-f_2} + \frac{1}{q_2} = 1/f_2$$

$$\frac{1}{q_2} = 2/f_2$$

$$q_2 = f_2/2$$

as required. The object distance, here, had to be negative because, by convention, a positive object distance represents an object to the right of the lens (in this problem).

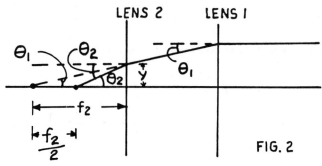

FIG. 2

To find the deviation of the rays we need to examine figure (2) which shows how a ray is deviated as it proceeds through the lens system. θ_1 is the deviation of the incoming ray at the first lens and θ_2 is the deviation of the ray at the second lens. By trigonometry we deduce that

$$\tan \theta_2 = \frac{y}{f_2/2} \; ; \; \tan \theta_1 = \frac{y}{f_2}$$

or

$$\frac{1}{2} \tan \theta_2 = \tan \theta_1 \; .$$

For small angles, we can make the approximation that

$$\tan \theta \sim \sin \theta \sim \theta$$

so

$$\theta_2 = 2\theta_1 \ .$$

Show that any thin lens which is thicker in the middle than out towards the edges is convergent, providing the lens medium is more highly refracting than the surrounding medium.

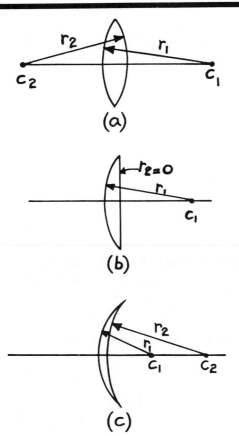

(a)

(b)

(c)

Solution: The general formula for a thin lens connecting the focal length f, radii of curvature of the two surfaces r_1 and r_2, and the refracting indices of the surrounding medium, n_m, and that of the lens, n_ℓ, is

$$\frac{1}{f} = \left(\frac{n_\ell - n_m}{n_m} \right)\left(\frac{1}{r_1} - \frac{1}{r_2} \right) \ .$$

Let us consider the case where the object beam impinges on the convex surface of radius r_1 . Then r_1 is considered positive because its center of curvature lies on the side where the refracting rays are going. Now since the lens is thick at the center and thin at the edges, this means that either

    (a) r_2 is negative (double convex)

515

or   (b) $r_2 = \infty$ (plano convex)

or   (c) r_2 is positive but $|r_2| > r_1$.

In these cases, the term $\frac{1}{r_1} - \frac{1}{r_2}$ is positive.

Hence, the sign of f depends on the sign of

$$\left(\frac{n_\ell - n_m}{n_m}\right)$$

The lens medium is more highly refracting than the surrounding medium, so

$$n_\ell > n_m .$$

Therefore

$$\left(\frac{n_\ell - n_m}{n_m}\right)$$

is positive and f must also be positive. A lens with a positive f is convergent.

● **PROBLEM** 18-28

Given a lens surface with f = + 10 in the object space and f' = + 8 in the image space, find the coordinates of the image (x',y') produced by an object located at x = - 12, y = + 6.

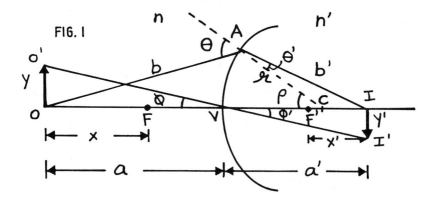

FIG. I

Solution: In figure 1 is shown an element of a single refracting surface. The object space of refractive index n is on the left and the image space of refractive index n' is on the right. The distances are positive from O toward V in object space and from I toward V in the image space. The ray from O is refracted at A, obeying Snell's law, and proceeds to I. Similarly, the ray from O' is refracted at V and proceeds to I' in the image space. From the figure using "triangles" OAC

516

and CAI, we have

$$\frac{\sin \phi}{\sin \rho} = \frac{a + r}{b} \tag{1}$$

and $\dfrac{\sin \phi'}{\sin \rho} = \dfrac{a' - r}{b'}$ (2) (2)

where r is the radius of curvature of the surface. Assuming A is not far from the axis we approximate b' = a' and b = a then using equations (1) and (2)

$$\frac{\sin \phi}{\sin \phi'} = \frac{a + r}{a' - r} \cdot \frac{a'}{a} = \frac{n'}{n} \tag{3}$$

where we have used Snell's law,

$$n \sin \phi = n' \sin \phi' \quad . \tag{4}$$

From equation (3),

$$n(a + r) a' = n'(a' - r)a \quad .$$

dividing throughout by aa'r,

$$\frac{n}{r} + \frac{n}{a} = \frac{n'}{r'} - \frac{n'}{a'}$$

$$\frac{n}{a} + \frac{n'}{a'} = \frac{n' - n}{r} \quad . \tag{5}$$

The principal focal point is defined as the position of the image in the image space when the object is at infinity.

$$f' = \frac{rn'}{n' - n} \tag{6}$$

from equation (5) .

Similarly, the principal focal point in the object space is the position of the object which produces an image at infinity.

$$f = \frac{rn}{n' - n} \tag{7}$$

Hence if we measure the distances from the principal focal points, we have

$$a = f - x \tag{8}$$

$$a' = f' - x' \tag{9}$$

Also from equations (6) and (7) we have

$$\frac{f}{a} = \frac{rn}{a(n' - n)}$$

$$\frac{f'}{a'} = \frac{rn'}{a'(n' - n)}$$

517

adding: $\dfrac{f}{a} + \dfrac{f'}{a'} = \dfrac{r}{n' - n}\left(\dfrac{n}{a} + \dfrac{n'}{a'}\right) = 1$ from equation (5)

using equations (8) and (9),

$$\dfrac{f}{f - x} + \dfrac{f'}{f' - x'} = 1 \tag{10}$$

$$ff' = xx' \tag{11}$$

From the figure, now considering $\triangle$'s OO'V and VII' formed by the ray O'VI', we have

$$\dfrac{\tan \phi}{\tan \phi'} = \dfrac{-y(f' - x')}{y'(f - x)} \approx \dfrac{\sin \phi}{\sin \phi'} = \dfrac{n'}{n}$$

But $\dfrac{n'}{n} = \dfrac{f'}{f}$ from equations (6) and (7) .

Hence

$$\dfrac{-y(f' - x')}{y'(f - x)} = \dfrac{f'}{f}$$

or $\dfrac{y'}{y} = \dfrac{-f(f' - x')}{f'(f - x)}$

But from equation (10)

$$\dfrac{f}{f - x} = 1 - \dfrac{f'}{f' - x'} = -\dfrac{x'}{f' - x'} \;;$$

hence,

$$\dfrac{y'}{y} = \dfrac{+(f' - x')}{f'} \cdot \dfrac{x'}{f' - x'} = \dfrac{x'}{f'}$$

Also $\dfrac{f'}{f' - x'} = 1 - \dfrac{f}{f - x} = \dfrac{-x}{f - x}$ from (10) ;

hence, $\dfrac{y'}{y} = \dfrac{f}{f - x} \cdot \dfrac{f - x}{x} = f/x$

Thus we have

$$ff' = xx' \tag{12}$$
$$\left(\dfrac{y'}{y} = \dfrac{x'}{f'} = f/x\right)$$

These equations are called collinear equations relating any point in the object space to another point in the image space.

With $f = +10$ and $f' = +8$, and $x = -12$ and $y = +6$

we have

$$xx' = ff'$$
$$x' = -\dfrac{80}{12} = -6.67$$

518

$$\frac{y'}{y} = f/x$$

$$y' = -\frac{6 \times 10}{12} = -5.0$$

An axial point object is located 25 cm to the left of a
thin lens of focal length +10.00 cm. A ray of light coming from the object subtends an angle of 10° with the
axis. At what angle does this ray, after refraction, intersect the axis?

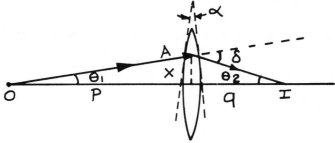

Solution: This problem can be solved by treating the lens
as a prism of very small refracting angle α.

The refractive index of a prism is given by the following relation:

$$n = \frac{\sin\left(\frac{\alpha + \delta}{2}\right)}{\sin\left(\frac{\alpha}{2}\right)}$$

where n is the refractive index, α is the refracting angle
of the prism and δ is the angle of minimum deviation.

If both α and δ are very small, then the sine of either
angle can be replaced by the angle itself and so,

$$n = \frac{\frac{\alpha + \delta}{2}}{\frac{\alpha}{2}}$$

Simplifying yields

$$n = \left(1 + \frac{\delta}{\alpha}\right).$$

Solving for δ,

$$(n - 1)\alpha = \delta .$$

Here the angle of deviation δ is dependent only on α,
which is dependent on the distance x measured from the
center of the lens to the point of incidence.

519

From the triangle OAI, we can write

$$\delta = \theta_1 + \theta_2$$

because the exterior angle of a triangle, δ, is equal to the sum of the two opposite interior angles.

If θ_1 and θ_2 are small, then

$$\tan \theta_1 = \frac{x}{p} \approx \theta_1$$

$$\tan \theta_2 = \frac{x}{q} \approx \theta_2$$

where p and q are the object and image distances, respectively.

Now the lens formula tells us that

$$\frac{1}{p} + \frac{1}{q} = \frac{1}{f}$$

where f is the focal length of the lens. Multiplying this equation by x gives

$$\frac{x}{p} + \frac{x}{q} = \frac{x}{f} \ .$$

Substituting θ_1 and θ_2 for $\frac{x}{p}$ and $\frac{x}{q}$ respectively,

$$\theta_1 + \theta_2 = \frac{x}{f} = \delta \tag{1}$$

Now

$$\theta_1 = 10° = 10 \times \frac{\pi}{180} = \frac{\pi}{18} \text{ rad.}$$

and p = 25 cm. Also f = 10 cm.

$$\frac{x}{p} = \theta_1 = \frac{\pi}{18}$$

Solving for x yields

$$x = p \frac{\pi}{18} = \frac{25\pi}{18} \text{ cm.}$$

Substituting values for f and x in equation (1),

$$\delta = \frac{x}{f} = \frac{25\pi/18}{10} = \frac{5\pi}{36} \text{ rad.}$$

Solving equation (1) for θ_2,

$$\theta_2 = \delta - \theta_1$$

Substituting values,

$$\theta_2 = \frac{5\pi}{36} - \frac{\pi}{18} = \frac{3\pi}{36} = \frac{3}{36} \pi \times \frac{180}{\pi} = 15^\circ \quad .$$

Hence the refracted ray makes an angle of 15° with the axis.

● PROBLEM 18-30

A lens is required to form a virtual image with a magnification of 5 at a distance of 25 cm from the lens. If the glass selected for its construction has a refractive index of 1.60 for the frequency of the light to be used, and one surface is to be plane, what must be the radius of curvature of the other surface of the lens?

Solution: The magnification of a lens is found by making use of the equation

$$m = \frac{-i}{0}$$

where i is the distance of the image from the lens and 0 is the distance of the object from the lens. Substituting the given values m = 5 and i = 25 cm into the above equation gives the result that 0 = -5 cm (negative because it's on the same side of the lens as the image).

Combining the Gaussian lens formula and the thin lens equation, we have

$$\frac{1}{0} + \frac{1}{i} = (n - 1) \left(\frac{1}{R_1} - \frac{1}{R_2} \right) \tag{1}$$

where n is the index of refraction of the lens, and R_1 and R_2 are the radii of curvature of the lens.

If one surface of the lens is to be plane, then $R_1 = \infty$ so $\frac{1}{R_1} = 0$. Equation (1) now becomes

$$\frac{1}{-5} + \frac{1}{25} = (1.6 - 1) \left(-\frac{1}{R_2} \right)$$

from which $R_2 = 3.75$ cm. Since the image formed was virtual, the lens must be concave with a radius of curvature of 3.75 cm on one side and the other side a plane.

● PROBLEM 18-31

A thin lens made of flint glass of n = 1.7 is to have a focal length of +5 cm. For parallel incident light, determine the Coddington position factor; for the lens to have minimum spherical aberration, determine the shape factor and the two radii of curvature necessary.

521

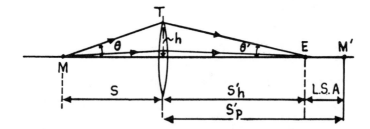

Solution: For a thin lens, the third-order theory of aberration gives

$$L_s = \frac{h^2}{8f^3 n(n-1)} \left[\frac{n+2}{n-1} q^2 + 4(n+1)pq + \right.$$

$$\left. (3n+2)(n-1)p^2 + \frac{n^3}{n-1} \right] \quad (1)$$

where

$$L_s = \frac{1}{S_h'} - \frac{1}{S_p'} \quad .$$

S_h' is the image distance for an oblique ray traversing the lens at a vertical distance h from the axis, S_p' is the image distance for paraxial rays, f is the focal length for paraxial rays. The constant p is called the Coddington position factor, and q is the shape factor, defined as

$$q = (r_2 + r_1)/(r_2 - r_1) \quad (2a)$$

$$p = \frac{s' - s}{s' + s} \quad (2b)$$

where s' is the image distance and s is the object distance. The lens equation states that

$$\frac{1}{f} = \frac{1}{s} + \frac{1}{s'} \quad \text{or} \quad f = \frac{ss'}{s' + s} \quad (3)$$

Adding and subtracting 1 from p as defined in equation (2b) gives the result

$$p = \frac{s' - s}{s' + s} + 1 - 1$$

$$= \frac{s' - s + s' + s}{s' + s} - 1$$

$$= \frac{2s'}{s' + s} - 1$$

Since $\dfrac{s'}{s + s'} = \dfrac{f}{s}$ equation (3),

$$p = \frac{2f}{s} - 1 \quad (4)$$

or p also $= \dfrac{s' - s - s' - s}{s' + s} + 1 = 1 - \dfrac{2s}{s' + s}$. From equation (3),

$$p = 1 - \dfrac{2f}{s'} \qquad\qquad (5)$$

Longitudinal spherical aberration is, LSA $= S'_p - S'_h$.

Equations useful in determining lens parameters for minimum spherical aberration are obtained by finding the shape factor that will make L_s, defined in equation (1), a minimum.

This is done by differentiating with respect to the shape factor and equating to zero:

$$\dfrac{dLs}{dq} = \dfrac{h^2}{8f^3}\left[\dfrac{2(n+2)q + 4(n-1)(n+1)p}{n(n-1)^2}\right] = 0$$

This gives

$$2(n+2)q + 4(n-1)(n+1)p = 0$$

Therefore,

$$q = \dfrac{-4(n-1)(n+1)p}{2(n+2)}$$

or

$$q = \dfrac{-2(n^2-1)p}{(n+2)} \ , \qquad\qquad (6)$$

the required relation between the shape and position factors to produce minimum spherical aberration.

In order to determine the radii that will correspond to such a calculated shape factor and still yield the proper focal length, one can use the lens maker's formula,

$$\dfrac{1}{s} + \dfrac{1}{s'} = (n-1)\left(\dfrac{1}{r_1} - \dfrac{1}{r_2}\right) = \dfrac{1}{f} \qquad\qquad (7)$$

Solving equation (2a) for r_1 gives the result

$$(r_1 + r_2) = q(r_2 - r_1)$$

or $\quad r_1(1+q) = r_2(q-1)$

or $\qquad\qquad r_1 = \dfrac{r_2(q-1)}{1+q} \qquad\qquad (8)$

Substituting for r_1 into equation (7) yields

$$\dfrac{1}{r_1} - \dfrac{1}{r_2} = \dfrac{1+q}{r_2(q-1)} - \dfrac{1}{r_2} = \dfrac{1}{f(n-1)}$$

or, $\qquad\qquad \dfrac{1}{r_2}\left[\dfrac{1+q}{q-1} - 1\right] = \dfrac{1}{f(n-1)}$

523

or,
$$\frac{1}{r_2}\left[\frac{1 + \cancel{q} - \cancel{q} + 1}{q - 1}\right] = \frac{1}{f(n - 1)}$$

Therefore,

$$r_2 = \frac{2f(n - 1)}{(q - 1)} \tag{9}$$

Similarly, substituting for r_2 in equation (8) gives

$$r_1 = \frac{2f(n - 1)}{q + 1} \tag{10}$$

Dividing equation (10) by equation (9), we get

$$\frac{r_1}{r_2} = \frac{q - 1}{q + 1} \tag{11}$$

Equations (2b), (6), (9), and (10) give us all we need in determining the parameters of a lens for minimum spherical aberration.

For the given lens,

$n = 1.7$

$f = 5$ cm

$s = \infty$

$s' = f = 5$ cm

The Coddington position factor is

$$p = \frac{s' - s}{s' + s} = \frac{5 - \infty}{5 + \infty} = -1$$

The shape factor, q, is given by equation (6):

$$q = -\frac{2(n^2 - 1)p}{n + 2}$$

$$= -\frac{2(1.7^2 - 1)(-1)}{(1.7 + 2)}$$

$$= 1.02$$

Using equations (9) and (10), we find that

$$r_2 = \frac{2f(n - 1)}{q - 1}$$

$$= \frac{2 \times 5(1.7 - 1)}{(1.02 - 1)} = 350 \text{ cm}$$

$$r_1 = \frac{2f(n - 1)}{q + 1}$$

$$= \frac{2 \times 5(1.7 - 1)}{(1.02 + 1)}$$

$$= 3.47 \text{ cm}$$

Assume that a plano-convex lens has a refractive index n = 1.5 and a center thickness of 6 mm. The convex surface has a radius of 2.5 cm and is facing the incident light. Derive the system matrix.

$R_1 = +2.5$ cm

$R_2 = \infty$

$d = 0.6$ cm

$n_1 = 1.0$

$n_2 = 1.5$

Solution: The front surface power is given by

$$P_1 = \frac{n_2 - n_1}{R_1} ,$$

where n_2 is the index of the lens, n_1 the index of the air, and R_1 is the radius of curvature of the front surface of the lens. So,

$$P_1 = \frac{1.5 - 1.0}{2.5 \text{ cm}} = 0.2 \text{ cm}^{-1}$$

and the back surface power is $P_2 = \frac{n_2 - n_1}{R_2}$, where R_2 is the curvature of the back surface of the lens.

$$P_2 = \frac{0.5}{\infty} = 0$$

The general system matrix is

$$S = R_2 T R_1 = \begin{bmatrix} 1 & -P_2 \\ 0 & 1 \end{bmatrix} \begin{bmatrix} 1 & 0 \\ \dfrac{d}{n_2} & 1 \end{bmatrix} \begin{bmatrix} 1 & -P_1 \\ 0 & 1 \end{bmatrix} ,$$

where T is known as the transfer matrix and d represents the center thickness of the lens.

Some of the elements in a matrix, for instance 1 and 1 in any of the three matrices shown, have no units. The units of the other elements depend on the physical parameters measured and, clearly, they have to be consistent. In this example, the powers, P_1 and P_2, have units of cm^{-1} and 0 has units of centimeters. We insert the numerical values:

$$S = \begin{bmatrix} 1 & 0 \\ 0 & 1 \end{bmatrix} \begin{bmatrix} 1 & 0 \\ \dfrac{0.6}{1.5} & 1 \end{bmatrix} \begin{bmatrix} 1 & -0.2 \\ 0 & 1 \end{bmatrix}$$

Then, multiplying the two right-hand matrices first gives

$$\begin{bmatrix} 1 + 0 & -0.2 & +0 \\ \dfrac{0.6}{1.5} + 0 & -\dfrac{0.12}{1.5} & +1 \end{bmatrix} = \begin{bmatrix} 1 & -0.2 \\ 0.4 & 0.92 \end{bmatrix}$$

In order to check the result, we calculate the determinant of the matrix, multiplying the absolute values of the matrix elements crosswise and adding the products: $0.92 + 0.08 = 1.00$. Since the result is unity, our computation, so far, is correct.

Further multiplication then leads to

$$S = \begin{bmatrix} 1 & 0 \\ 0 & 1 \end{bmatrix} \begin{bmatrix} 1 & -0.2 \\ 0.4 & 0.92 \end{bmatrix} = \begin{bmatrix} 1 & -0.2 \\ 0.4 & 0.92 \end{bmatrix}$$

Again, the determinant is unity. We note that the second refraction matrix has not changed the result. Indeed, the second surface is plane and its refraction matrix is a unit matrix.

● **PROBLEM** 18-33

Determine the system matrix for the lens shown.

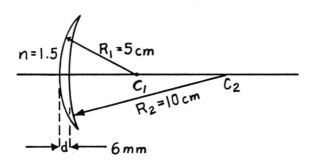

Solution: The system matrix for the above lens is given by

$$A = (R_2)[(F_{21})(R_1)]$$

where R_2 is the refraction matrix for the second surface given by

$$R_2 = \begin{pmatrix} 1 & -D_2 \\ 0 & 1 \end{pmatrix},$$

F_{21} is the transfer matrix for the lens given by

$$F_{21} = \begin{pmatrix} 1 & 0 \\ \dfrac{d}{n} & 1 \end{pmatrix}$$

and R_1 is the refraction matrix for the first surface

526

given by

$$R_1 = \begin{pmatrix} 1 & -D_1 \\ 0 & 1 \end{pmatrix} .$$

D_1 and D_2 represent the first and second surface powers, respectively.

The multiplication must be done in order, i.e., F_{21} must first be multiplied by R_1 on its right side and then

$$[(F_{21})(R_1)]$$

must be multiplied by R_2 on its left side.

R_1 is the radius of curvature of the first surface; R_2 is that of the second surface; n is the refractive index of the material of the lens (assuming that the lens is placed in a vacuum); d is the thickness of the lens.

Now the given values are:

$$R_1 = 5 \text{ cm}$$

$$R_2 = 10 \text{ cm}$$

$$n = 1.5$$

$$d = 0.6 \text{ cm}$$

$$D_1 = \frac{n - 1}{R_1}$$

$$D_2 = - \frac{(n - 1)}{R_2}$$

Hence

$$A = \begin{pmatrix} 1 & \frac{n-1}{R_2} \\ 0 & 1 \end{pmatrix} \left[\begin{pmatrix} 1 & 0 \\ \frac{d}{n} & 1 \end{pmatrix} \begin{pmatrix} 1 & -\frac{n-1}{R_1} \\ 0 & 1 \end{pmatrix} \right]$$

$$= \begin{pmatrix} 1 & \frac{1.5-1}{10} \\ 0 & 1 \end{pmatrix} \left[\begin{pmatrix} 1 & 0 \\ \frac{0.6}{1.5} & 1 \end{pmatrix} \begin{pmatrix} 1 & -\frac{1.5-1}{5} \\ 0 & 1 \end{pmatrix} \right]$$

$$= \begin{pmatrix} 1 & 0.05 \\ 0 & 1 \end{pmatrix} \left[\begin{pmatrix} 1 & 0 \\ 0.4 & 1 \end{pmatrix} \begin{pmatrix} 1 & -0.1 \\ 0 & 1 \end{pmatrix} \right]$$

$$= \begin{pmatrix} 1 & 0.05 \\ 0 & 1 \end{pmatrix} \begin{pmatrix} 1 & -0.1 \\ 0.4 & 0.96 \end{pmatrix}$$

$$= \begin{pmatrix} 1.02 & -0.052 \\ 0.4 & 0.96 \end{pmatrix}$$

THICK LENSES

A thick lens, which has principal points at $\alpha = 1.2$ cm and $\beta = -0.8$ cm, forms an image of a distant object 19.2 cm from the second surface of the lens. Find the position of the image of an object placed 38.8 cm from the first face. The sign convention used is that distances are positive if measured in the direction of light propagation and negative if measured in the opposite direction; α is measured from the first surface of the lens and β from the second.

Solution: Thick lenses may be treated using the thin lens equation,

$$\frac{1}{i} + \frac{1}{\theta} = \frac{1}{f} ,$$

if i and θ are measured from the principal points α and β, respectively. In this problem if $\theta = -\infty$, i = (19.2 + 0.8) cm = +20 cm. Substitution yields f = +20 cm. Now if θ is set equal to -(38.8 + 1.2) cm = -40 cm, substitution yields i = +40 cm; thus the image lies (40 - 0.8) cm = 39.2 cm from the second face of the lens.

Determine the focal length f of a glass lens of index 1.5 surrounded by air for which $r_1 = +10$, $r_2 = +9$ a) when the lens thickness is zero,   b) when the thickness is +1.

Solution: Using the lens maker's equation for thick lenses, we have:

$$\frac{1}{f} = (n - 1) \cdot \left[\frac{1}{r_1} - \frac{1}{r_2} + \frac{(n-1) \cdot d}{n \cdot r_1 \cdot r_2} \right] ,$$

where n is the index of refraction of the lens, d is the thickness of the lens, f is its focal length, and r_1 and r_2 are the radii of curvature for each side of the lens.

In the first part, if r_1 and r_2 are 10 and 9 respectively, the thickness is zero, and n = 1.5; then we have

$$\frac{1}{f} = (1.5-1) \cdot \left[\frac{1}{10} - \frac{1}{9} \right]$$

so f = -180 units.

In the second part, if the thickness is changed to 1 (assuming that the units are the same as for r and f), we have :

$$\frac{1}{f} = (1.5-1) \cdot \left[\frac{1}{10} - \frac{1}{9} + \frac{(1.5-1) \cdot (1)}{(1.5)(10)(9)} \right]$$

so f = -270 units.

● **PROBLEM** 18-36

What is the focal length of a bubble of air suspended in glycerin (n = 1.48) if the bubble has a diameter of 2 mm?

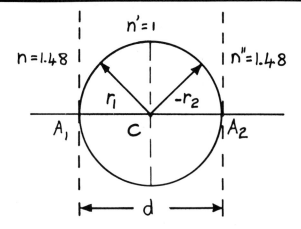

Solution: The general formula for the focal length of a thick lens of refractive index n', surrounded by a medium of index n on the left and another medium of index n" on the right, is given by

$$\frac{n}{f} = \frac{n'}{f'_1} + \frac{n''}{f''_2} - \frac{dn''}{f'_1 f''_2} \qquad (1)$$

where f'_1 is the focal length of the first surface of radius r_1, f''_2 is the focal length of the second surface of radius r_2, and d is the thickness of the lens.

In our case

$$n' = 1.00$$

$$n = 1.48$$

$$n'' = 1.48$$

$$r_1 = 1 \text{ mm}$$

$$r_2 = -1 \text{ mm}$$

$$d = 2 \text{ mm}$$

Hence, for the first surface,

$$\frac{n}{f_1} = \frac{n'}{f_1'} = \frac{n' - n}{r_1}$$

or

$$\frac{1.48}{f_1} = \frac{1}{f_1'} = \frac{1 - 1.48}{1}$$

Therefore,

$$f_1 = \frac{1.48}{-.48} = -3.083 \text{ mm}$$

and

$$f_1' = \frac{1}{-.48} = -2.083 \text{ mm} .$$

For the second surface,

$$\frac{n'}{f_2'} = \frac{n''}{f_2''} = \frac{n'' - n'}{r_2}$$

or

$$\frac{1}{f_2'} = \frac{1.48}{f_2''} = \frac{1.48 - 1}{-1}$$

Therefore,

$$f_2' = - \frac{1}{.48} = -2.083 \text{ mm}$$

and

$$f_2'' = \frac{1.48}{-.48} = -3.083 \text{ mm}$$

Substituting f_1' , and f_2'' in equation (1), we get

$$\frac{n}{f} = \frac{1}{-2.083} + \frac{1.48}{-3.083} - \frac{2(1.48)}{(-2.083)(-3.083)}$$

$$= -1.42 \text{ (mm)}^{-1}$$

Therefore,

$$f = \frac{1.48}{-1.42} = -1.04 \text{ mm} .$$

● PROBLEM 18-37

Find the focal length, the positions of the focal points,
and the principal points of the simple thick lens in the
figure. The index of the lens, n, = 1.5; its axial thickness,
t, = 25 mm; the radius of its first surface is 22 mm, and
that of its second surface is 16 mm.

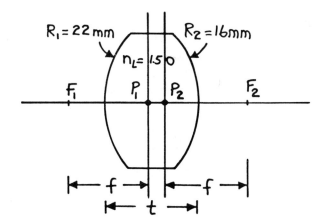

Solution: The best way to approach a problem like this is to analyze each surface of the lens separately. To find the focal point on the right side of the lens, allow parallel light rays, from a source an infinite distance away, to strike the thick lens from the left side. The light rays will converge at the focal point on the right side of the lens. We will use the equation

$$\frac{n_L}{i} + \frac{n_A}{o} = \frac{n_L - n_A}{R} \qquad (1)$$

where i is the image distance, o is the object distance, n is the index of refraction, and R is the radius of curvature of the surface. For the first surface of the lens, we have the radius of curvature, R_1, = -22 mm and the object distance, o, = ∞; so from equation (1) we have

$$\frac{1.50}{i} + \frac{1.00}{\infty} = \frac{1.50-1.00}{-22 \text{ mm}} \;;$$

hence the image distance, i, = -66 mm, which means that the first image is 66 mm to the right of the first surface.

Now we take the real image that was produced by the first lens and let it be a virtual object 41 mm to the right of the second surface. For the second surface, o = -41 mm and R = -16 mm, and applying the equation

$$\frac{n_L}{o} + \frac{n_A}{i} = \frac{n_A - n_L}{R}$$

we have

$$\frac{1.50}{-41 \text{ mm}} + \frac{1.00}{i} = \frac{1.00 - 1.50}{-16 \text{ mm}}$$

and i = 14.7 mm. Therefore, one focal point of the lens, F_2, is 14.7 mm to the right of the lens.

If parallel light rays strike the lens (normal to it) from the right side, then they will converge at the focal point; that is to the left of the lens, F_1. Following the same procedure as before, the first image is 48 mm to the left of the second surface (R_2 = 16 mm). The image produced by the first surface, taking the image of the second surface as its object, is 11.4 mm to the left of the first surface (R_1 = 22 mm); therefore, another focal point, F_1, is 11.4 mm to the left of the lens.

The focal length, f, of a thick lens is found by applying

$$\frac{1}{f} = (n_L - 1) \cdot \left[\frac{1}{R_1} - \frac{1}{R_2} + \frac{(n_L - 1) t}{n_L R_1 R_2} \right] \qquad (2)$$

where n_L is the index of the lens, R_1 is the radius of curvature of the first surface, R_2 the curvature of the second surface, and t is the thickness of the lens. Letting n_L = 1.50, R_1 = 22 mm, R_2 = -16 mm, and t = 25 mm, yields

$$\frac{1}{f} = (1.50 - 1) \cdot \left[\frac{1}{22 \text{ mm}} + \frac{1}{16 \text{ mm}} - \frac{(1.50 - 1)(25 \text{ mm})}{(1.50)(22 \text{ mm})(16 \text{ mm})} \right]$$

hence $\frac{1}{f}$ = 0.04214 mm^{-1} and the focal length, f = 23.7 mm.

The principal points of this lens, P_1 and P_2 can now be easily found because the focal length is the same on both sides of the lens. So, the principal point P_1 lies (23.7 mm -14.7 mm) = 9.0 mm to the right of the vertex of the first surface (R_1 = 22 mm) and the principal point P_2 lies (23.7 mm -11.4 mm) = 12.3 mm to the left of the vertex of the second surface of the lens (R_2 = 16 mm).

Another method of solving this problem is to find the focal length, using equation (2), and then find the distance between the vertices and its principal point. The distance, x_1, between the left vertex and P_1 is found by applying the equation

$$x_1 = \frac{f(n_L - 1) t}{R_2 \cdot n_L} \qquad (3)$$

Similarly, the distance, x_2, between the right vertex and P_2 is found by applying the equation

$$x_2 = \frac{f(n_L - 1) t}{R_1 \cdot n_L} \qquad (4)$$

Once the focal length, f, and the distances x_1 and x_2, are known, the position of the focal points F_1 and F_2 can be found by subtraction. Substituting the data into equations (3) and (4), we have

$$x_1 = 12.3 \text{ mm}$$

and $$x_2 = 9.0 \text{ mm}.$$

So F_1 and F_2 are, respectively, (23.7 - 12.3) mm = 11.4 mm and (23.7 - 9.0) mm = 14.7 mm away from the vertices of the lens, which agrees with the previous answers.

The curved surface of a plano-convex condensing lens has a radius of curvature of 10 cm, and the lens is 3 cm thick. With its plane side toward the light, how far must the lens be placed from a point source to produce a parallel beam of light?

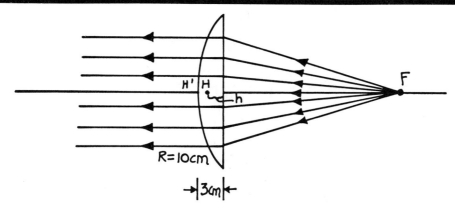

Solution: Note that the problem is really asking for the position of the focal point of the thick lens. When a beam of parallel rays is incident perpendicularly to the surface of a lens, the rays will converge at its focal point: In addition, we know that we can always reverse the direction of travel of the rays and still have a true situation; thus a point source placed at the focal point of the lens will produce a parallel beam of light.

Thus, the equation for the focal length, f, of a thick lens is

$$\frac{1}{f} = (n_L - 1) \cdot \left[\frac{1}{R_1} - \frac{1}{R_2} + \frac{(n_L - 1)d}{n_L \cdot R_1 \cdot R_2} \right]$$

where $n_L = 1.50$, $R_1 = 10$ cm, $R_2 = \infty$, and $d = 3$ cm. Using these values we find the focal length, $f, = 20$ cm. Therefore, the focal point is 20 cm from the principal point H. The distance, h, from the principal point H to the plane side of the lens is found by applying

$$h = \frac{f(n_L - 1)d}{R \cdot n_L}$$

where f is the focal length of the lens, n_L is its index of refraction, d is the thickness and R is the radius of curvature of the opposite surface of the lens. Applying the known data, we have

$$h = \frac{(20\ cm)(1.50 - 1)(3\ cm)}{(10\ cm)(1.50)} \quad ,$$

$$h = 2\ cm.$$

Hence, the point source of light must be 18 cm from the plane surface of the lens to produce a parallel beam of light.

If the two principal points of a lens surrounded by the same medium on both sides coincide with each other at a point midway between the two vertices, what is the form of the lens?

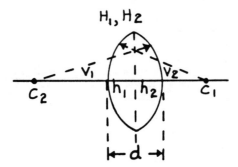

H_1, H_2

Solution: For a thick lens of thickness d, and refractive index n_ℓ, having radii of curvature R_1 and R_2 of the front and back surfaces, respectively, we can write the expression for the distance of the principal planes from the vertices of the lens, V_1 and V_2 (as depicted in the figure) as follows:

$$h_1 = \frac{-f(n_\ell - 1)d}{R_2 \, n_\ell} \qquad (1)$$

where the lens is assumed to be placed in a medium of refractive index 1 and h_1 is measured positive to the right of V_1 .

Similarly

$$h_2 = \frac{-f(n_\ell - 1)d}{R_1 \, n_\ell} \qquad (2)$$

where f is the focal length of the lens.

Since the two principal points coincide with one another at a point midway between the two vertices,

$$h_1 = -h_2$$

or $\quad |h_1| = |h_2| = \dfrac{d}{2}$

or $\quad |h_1| + |h_2| = d$

Then, from equations (1) and (2),

$$\frac{-f(n_\ell - 1)d}{R_2 \, n_\ell} = \frac{f(n_\ell - 1)d}{R_1 \, n_\ell} \, ,$$

534

or

$$R_1 = -R_2$$

Therefore, the lens must be a solid sphere so that the center of curvature of the two surfaces lies at a common point with R positive for one surface and negative for the other surface.

● **PROBLEM** 18-40

Discuss some of the major classifications of lenses.

FIG. I

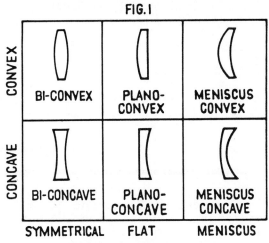

LENSES OF DIFFERENT FORM.

Solution: A lens having two surfaces of the same curvature but opposite in sign is called a symmetric lens. It may be either biconvex or biconcave (Fig. 1).

A lens having one plane surface and one curved surface is called a plano-convex or plano-concave lens (Fig. 1).

A lens which has two surfaces of different curvature but of the same sign is called a meniscus convex or meniscus concave, depending on whether the refracting power is positive or negative (Fig. 1).

Biconvex, plano-convex, and meniscus convex lenses are all referred to as convex lenses and have plus power. Biconcave, plano-concave, and meniscus concave lenses are all referred to as concave lenses and have minus power.

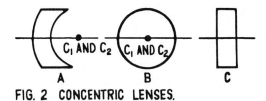

FIG. 2 CONCENTRIC LENSES.

A lens is called concentric if the two surfaces have a

535

common center of curvature. Such a lens has no unique optic
axis, because any ray normal to one surface is also normal
to the other (Fig. 2.).

A lens having two parallel flat surfaces is called a
plate. It is a special kind of concentric lens (Fig 2.c).

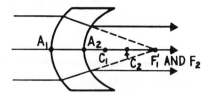

FIG. 3 LENS OF ZERO TRUE POWER.
THE RAYS WHICH ENTER PARALLEL
LEAVE PARALLEL.

A lens of zero true power (Fig. 3.) is one in which

$$F_1 + F_2 - \frac{F_1 F_2 t}{n_2} = 0$$

The rays enter parallel and leave parallel. Such a lens is
called an afocal lens. A lens of zero true power also has
zero vertex power.

● **PROBLEM** 18-41

An object is placed 60 cm from a thick double convex lens,
with faces of radii of curvature 20 cm and 30 cm, with
thickness = 2 cm, and index of refraction 1.5. Find the
position of the image.

Solution: Using the lens maker's equation,

$$\frac{1}{f} = (n-1) \cdot \left[\frac{1}{r'} - \frac{1}{r''} \right]$$

and the Gaussian lens formula,

$$\frac{1}{f} = \frac{1}{o} + \frac{1}{i} \; ,$$

we have $\frac{1}{o} + \frac{1}{i} = (n-1) \cdot \left[\frac{1}{r'} - \frac{1}{r''} \right]$ where o is the distance
the object is from the lens, i is the distance the image is
from the lens, n is the index of refraction, r' is the
radius of curvature of the face of the lens nearest the
object and r" is the radius of curvature of the other face
of the lens.
Substituting the given data into our equation, we have

$$-\frac{1}{60} + \frac{1}{i} = (1.5-1) \left[\frac{1}{-20} - \frac{1}{30} \right]$$

We have r' = -20 cm because the center of curvature of
the first surface is on the side opposite from the object.

Solving for i in the previous equation we, get i = -40 cm

536

which puts the image 40 cm away from the lens and on the opposite side of the object. Note that the position of the image is independent of the thickness of the lens.

● PROBLEM 18-42

You are given a thick double convex lens, whose faces have radii of curvature of 24 cm and 36 cm; the lens thickness is 2 cm, and it is made of material with an index of refraction equal to 1.524. (a) Locate the principal points. (b) If an object is placed 40 cm from the nearer face of the lens, find, by calculation, the position of the image. (c) Find the image location graphically. (d) Treating the lens as thin, and measuring distances from its center, calculate the position of the image. Note the error involved.

Solution: (a) For a thick lens the positions α and β of the principal points are determined by the expressions

$$\alpha = \frac{-f_1 t}{n(f_2 - f_1) - t} \tag{1}$$

and

$$\beta = \frac{-f_2 t}{n(f_2 - f_1) - t} \quad \left(= \frac{f_2}{f_1^2} \alpha \right), \tag{2}$$

where t represents the lens thickness, n the index of refraction, and f_1 and f_2 the focal lengths of the two refracting surfaces if they were acting independently; f_1 and f_2 are found from the expressions

$$f_1 = \frac{-r_1}{(n-1)} \tag{3}$$

and

$$f_2 = \frac{-r_2}{(n-1)}. \tag{4}$$

The sign convention used is that distances measured from the lens surface in the direction in which light is traveling are positive, and distances measured in the opposite direction are negative; α is measured from the first lens surface, β from the second. Substitution of $r_1 = +24$ cm, $r_2 = -36$ cm, and n = 1.524 into equations (3) and (4), and substituting the results into equations (1) and (2), give $\alpha = +0.53$ cm, $\beta = -0.80$ cm.

(b) Thick lenses may be treated may be treated by the thin lens equation,

$$\frac{1}{i} + \frac{1}{\theta} = \frac{1}{f}, \tag{5}$$

if i (image distance) is measured from the principal point β, θ (object distance) from α, and f is determined from the expression

$$f = \frac{-n f_1 f_2}{n(f_2 - f_1) - t}. \tag{6}$$

537

Substitution of the given values yields f = +27.8 cm; using
θ = (40 + 0.53) cm gives i = +88.5 cm.   Then from the <u>sur-
face</u> of the lens the image lies at a distance d = i - $\overline{0.80}$;
i.e., d = (88.5 - 0.80) cm, or

    d = +87.7 cm.

    (c) Images may be located graphically in a thick lens
if for the incident light the construction is treated as
though the lens were in the first principal plane, and for
the emergent light as though the lens were in the second
principal plane.

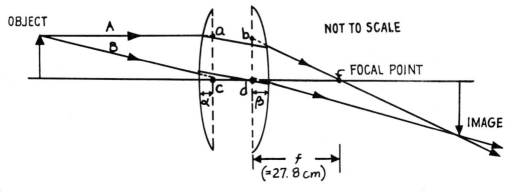

OBJECT

A

B

NOT TO SCALE

FOCAL POINT

IMAGE

f
(=27.8 cm)

    Thus: Ray A leaves the object, strikes the first
principal plane at a and leaves the second principal plane
at b, where $\overline{ac}$ = $\overline{bd}$, and finally passes through the focal
point.

    Ray B leaves the object in such a direction as to pass
through point c, and leaves the lens in a parallel direction
which passes through point d; the image is formed where the
two rays cross. Of course, a carefully drawn diagram, with
all distances scaled equally, is necessary to get acceptable
results.

    (d) For a thin lens, f is found from the radii of
curvature by the expression

$$\frac{1}{f} = (n - 1) \left(\frac{1}{r_1} - \frac{1}{r_2} \right); \tag{7}$$

substitution of the given values yields f = +27.48 cm. Setting θ = +(40+1) cm (measuring θ from the lens center) in
equation (5) and solving for i, i = +83.3 cm; the image
thus lies (83.3-1) cm = 82.3 cm from the second surface of
the lens (a difference of 5.4 cm from the answer to part
(b)).

● **PROBLEM** 18-43

A glass double convex lens, each of whose faces has a radius
of curvature of 30 cm, is surronded by air on one side, by
water on the other. If plane waves are incident on the air
side, find (by the method of change of curvature of wave-
front) to what point the waves are focused (n_{glass} = 1.56,
n_{water} = 1.33).

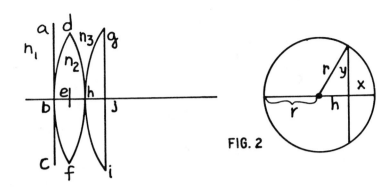

FIG. I   **FIG. 2**

Solution: Figure 1 shows the plane wave-front abc in air
$(n_1 = 1)$ incident on the lens $(n_2 = 1.56)$; the method of
change of curvature of wave-front relies on the geometrical
relations which apply to a circle, shown in figure 2.

We observe $x = r - h$ and $y^2 = r^2 - h^2$.

Hence $\dfrac{x}{y^2} = \dfrac{r - h}{(r+h)(r-h)} = \dfrac{1}{r + h}$.

Now if $x/r \ll 1$, $h \approx r$ so

$$\frac{1}{r} = \frac{2x}{y^2} . \tag{1}$$

In Fig. 1, the central ray behj travels from b to h in the
time required for the ray at the upper edge of the lens to
travel from a to g, so (using optical path length equals
actual distance multiplied by index of refraction)

$$n_1 \overline{ad} + n_3 \overline{dg} = n_2 \overline{bh}, \tag{2}$$

which implies (refer to Fig.1) that

$$n_1 \overline{be} + n_3 \overline{ej} = n_2 \overline{be} + n_2 \overline{eh} \tag{3}$$

and therefore

$$n_1 \overline{be} + n_3 \overline{eh} + n_3 \overline{hj} = n_2 \overline{be} + n_2 \overline{eh} \tag{4}$$

or

$$n_3 \overline{hj} = n_2 (\overline{be} + \overline{eh}) - n_1 \overline{be} - n_3 \overline{eh}. \tag{5}$$

But from equation (1),

$$\overline{hj} \propto \frac{1}{f} \text{ (the curvature of ghi)},$$

$$\overline{be} \propto \frac{1}{r_1}$$

$$\overline{eh} \propto \frac{1}{r_2}$$

with the same proportionality constant $2/y^2$, $y = \overline{ab} = \overline{ed} = \overline{jg}$ in each case.

539

So, equation (5) becomes

$$\frac{n_3}{f} = n_2\left(\frac{1}{r_1} + \frac{1}{r_2}\right) - \frac{n_1}{r_1} - \frac{n_3}{r_2} \quad . \tag{6}$$

Substitution of $n_1 = 1$, $n_2 = 1.56$, $n_3 = 1.33$ and $r_1 = r_2$ = 30 cm and solving for f gives

$$f = +50.5 \text{ cm}.$$

LENS POWER

● **PROBLEM** 18-44

A circular object 4 cm in diameter and 40 cm from a lens has an image 2 cm in diameter. What is the distance of the image from the lens, and what is the power of the lens?

<u>Solution:</u> Using the equation for magnification, $m = \frac{-i}{o}$, we have

$$\frac{1}{2} = \frac{-i}{0.4m}$$

so $i = -0.2$ m which is 20 cm away from the lens on the opposite side.

The power of the lens can be found by using the Gaussian lens equation, $\frac{1}{o} + \frac{1}{i} = \frac{1}{f}$, and since the power of the lens is

$\frac{1}{f}$ then

$$\text{power} = \frac{1}{o} + \frac{1}{i}$$

$$\text{power} = \frac{1}{0.4m} + \frac{1}{0.2m}$$

$$\text{power} = 7.5 \text{ diopters}.$$

● **PROBLEM** 18-45

It is found that the image of a distant scene, limited by the light passing through a window, can be focused sharply on a white card held 40 cm from a lens. What is the power of the lens?

<u>Solution:</u> The power of a lens is the reciprocal of its focal length. Power has units of diopters or meters^{-1} when the focal length is expressed in meters. The problem states that a distant object (assumed to be at ∞) is focused 40 cm from a lens, and since we know that rays of light from a source infinitely far from a lens will converge at its focal point, the focal length here is 40 cm or .4 m. Therefore the power of this lens is $\frac{1 \text{ m}^{-1}}{0.4}$ or 2.5 diopters.

540

A convex lens produces on a screen an image which is three times as large as the object. If the screen is 14.4 cm from the lens, find the refracting power of the lens.

Solution: We know that the power of a lens in diopters is given by $\frac{1}{f}$ where f is the focal length expressed in meters.

In this problem we are given the image distance i and the magnification m of the lens, so we must obtain an expression for f, or, more specifically, for $\frac{1}{f}$, in terms of these quantities.

The focal length is given by

$$\frac{1}{f} = \frac{1}{o} + \frac{1}{i}, \text{ where o is the object distance.} \qquad (1)$$

From the formula for magnification we have

$$m = \frac{i}{o} \qquad (2)$$

or

$$\frac{1}{o} = \frac{m}{i} \qquad (3)$$

Inserting equation (3) into equation (1) yields

$$\frac{1}{f} = \frac{m}{i} + \frac{1}{i} \qquad (4)$$

$$\frac{1}{f} = \frac{m+1}{i} \qquad (5)$$

Therefore the power of the lens, which is equal to $\frac{1}{f}$, is given by $\frac{m+1}{i}$.

$$\text{Power} = \frac{m+1}{i}$$

$$\text{Power} = \frac{3+1}{.144m} = 27.78m^{-1} = 27.78 \text{ diopters.}$$

A plano-convex lens in air has a power of 5 diopters. What is the power of the lens in water? The index of refraction of the glass in the lens is 1.60.

Solution: The lens maker's formula for thin lenses is

$$\frac{1}{f} = (N - 1)\left(\frac{1}{r_1} - \frac{1}{r_2}\right) = D \qquad (1)$$

where f is the focal length in meters; D is the power in

diopters; r_1 and r_2 the radii of curvature of the first
and second surface, respectively, with care taken concern-
ing sign convention;   and N the relative index of refraction
of the lens to the surrounding medium.   In this problem

$$D = 5; \quad \text{when } N = 1.6 = \frac{n_{glass}}{n_{air}} = \frac{1.6}{1.0} \; .$$

We need to find D when

$$N = \frac{n_{glass}}{n_{water}} = \frac{1.6}{1.33} = 1.2$$

so from (1)

$$\frac{D}{5} = \frac{(1.2-1)}{(1.6-1)}$$

$$D = \frac{0.2}{0.6} \times 5 = 1.67 \text{ diopters.}$$

● **PROBLEM** 18-48

The refractive power of a single refractive surface is -5.00
diopters.   If the medium on one side of the surface is air
and the other side has an index of 1.60, what is the radius
of curvature?

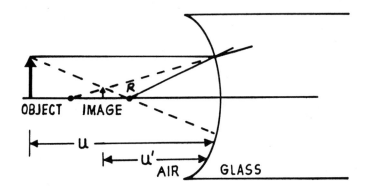

FIG. I

Solution: We can use the paraxial Gaussian equation,

$$\frac{n}{u} + \frac{n'}{u'} = \frac{n'-n}{R} \qquad (1)$$

where u' = image distance in a medium with index n'.
      u = object distance in a medium with index n.
      R = radius of curvature.

Since this problem gives us the refractive power of
the single simple surface and Power in this instance is the
reciprocal of the effective focal length, we then have

$$\frac{n'-n}{R} = D = -5 \qquad (2)$$

and with n' = 1.6; n = 1.0,

$$R = \frac{1.6-1.0}{-5} = -0.12 \text{ meters.}$$

or from the sign convention, the surface will appear as in
the figure.

● **PROBLEM** 18-49

A -10.00 diopter biconcave lens has 12 cm radii of curvature
for either surface. What is the refractive index of the
glass?

Solution: For this problem, we combine the definition for
the power of a lens, which is the reciprocal of its focal
length, and the lens maker's equation:

$$\text{Power} = \frac{1}{f} = (n - 1) \cdot \left[\frac{1}{r'} - \frac{1}{r''}\right],$$

where f is the focal length, n is the index of refraction of
the lens, and r' and r'' are the radii of curvature for each
side of the lens.

If the power is given as -10 diopters, then we must convert the given radii of curvature, 12 cm, to 0.12 m because
a diopter is the equivalent of m^{-1}. Substituting the given
data into our equation, we have:

$$-10.00 \text{ m}^{-1} = (n - 1)\left[\frac{1}{-0.12m} - \frac{1}{0.12 \text{ m}}\right]$$

Solving this, we conclude that the index of refraction of the
glass lens is 1.6. Note that r' is negative because its
curvature is opposite to that of r''.

● **PROBLEM** 18-50

(a) A negative meniscus has radii of curvature R_1 = 50 cm
and R_2 = -25 cm (Fig. 1). The refractive index of the
glass is n = 1.50. What is the refractive power of the
meniscus if it is considered a thin lens?

(b) The same meniscus is now mounted to have air on the
left and oil of n_3 = 1.8 on the right. If the object
distance is 83.3 cm what is the image vergence?

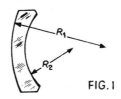

FIG. I

Solution: (a) The lens-makers formula:

$$P = \Delta n \left(\frac{1}{R_1} + \frac{1}{R_2} \right) ,$$

where P is the refractive power of the meniscus, Δn the change in refractive index from glass to air, and R_1 and R_2 are the radii of curvature of the meniscus. Substituting the values for R_1 and R_2 as well as $\Delta n = 1.50 - 1.00 = 0.50$ into the above equation gives the result

$$P = 0.50 \left(\frac{1}{0.50} + \frac{1}{-0.25} \right) m^{-1} =$$

$$0.5(2 - 4) = -1.00 \ m^{-1} .$$

(b) Both surfaces are now convex and have positive radii of curvature. For the first surface, the refractive power is

$$P_1 = \frac{\Delta n}{R_1} = \frac{1.50 - 1.00}{+0.50 \ m} = \frac{0.50}{+0.50 \ m} + 1.00 \ m^{-1}$$

For the second surface, the refractive power is

$$P_2 = \frac{\Delta n}{R_2} = \frac{1.80 - 1.50}{+0.25 \ m} = \frac{0.30}{+0.25 \ m}$$

$$= +1.20 \ m^{-1}$$

Thus, the total (nominal) power is

$$P = P_1 + P_2 = +2.20 \ m^{-1}$$

Then the object vergence

$$V_o = \frac{1.00}{-0.833 \ m} = -1.20 \ m^{-1} ,$$

and the image vergence

$$V_i = V_o + P = (-1.20 \ m^{-1}) + (+2.20 \ m^{-1}) = +1.00 \ m^{-1} .$$

A +5.00 diopter thin lens is placed 12.5 mm in front of a +8.00 diopter thin lens.

   a)   What is the true power of the combination?

   b)   What is the true focal length?

   c)   Calculate the position of the two principal points.

   d)   What is the distance of the posterior focal point from the second lens?   Of the anterior focal point from the first lens?

   e)   An object is placed 40 cm in front of the first lens.   How far is the image from the second lens?

Solution: (a)   The power of a lens in diopters is equal to the inverse-focal length in meters;   thus, a 5 diopter lens has a focal length of 20 cm and an 8 diopter lens has a focal length of 12.5 cm.   The combination separated by 1.25 cm has a focal length

$$\frac{1}{f} = \frac{1}{f_1} + \frac{1}{f_2} - \frac{d}{f_1 f_2}$$

$$\frac{1}{f} = 5 + 8 - (.0125) 5 \cdot 8$$

$$\frac{1}{f} = 12.5 \text{ diopters,}$$

(b) $f = 8$ cm.

(c)   The principal points are given by

$$\alpha = \frac{f_1 d}{f_1 + f_2 - d} = \frac{20 \times 1.25}{20 + 12.5 - 1.25} \text{ cm} = 8 \text{ mm}$$

$$\beta = -\frac{f_2 d}{f_1 + f_2 - d} = \frac{-12.5 \times 1.25}{20 + 12.5 - 1.25} \text{ cm} = -5 \text{ mm}$$

(d)   The distance of the posterior focal point from the second lens is:

$$f_p = \frac{f_2 (f_1 - d)}{(f_1 + f_2) - d} = 7.5 \text{ cm}$$

The anterior focal point from the first lens is

$$f_a = \frac{f_1 (f_2 - d)}{f_1 + f_2 - d} = \frac{20 (12.5 - 1.25)}{20 + 12.5 - 1.25} \text{ cm} = 7.2 \text{ cm.}$$

(e)   If S_{O_1} is the object distance, then the image distance from the second lens is given by:

$$S_{i_2} = \frac{f_2 d - f_2 S_{O_1} f_1 / (S_{O_1} - f_1)}{d - f_2 - S_{O_1} f_1 / (S_{O_1} - f_1)}$$

$$= 9.45 \text{ cm}$$

What will be the focal length of a cylindrical lens formed by bending a sheet of glass into a cylinder, if the thickness of glass is 2 cm, the index of refraction is 1.5, and the radius of the cylinder is 5 m?

Solution: The change P_i in the power of a series of refracting surfaces produced by the i th surface in the series is given by the Woodworth recursion relation,

$$P_i = P_{i-1} + \frac{h_i}{r_i}(n_i - n_{i-1}) \tag{1}$$

where r_i is the radius of the i th surface, n_i is the index of refraction of the medium to the right of that surface, and h_i is given by

$$h_i = h_{i-1} - \frac{tP_{i-1}}{n} \; ; \tag{2}$$

in equation (2), t is the distance between surfaces i-1 and i, occupied by medium of index n. For parallel light incident on such a series of surfaces, $P_O = 0$ and h_1 is taken to be 1. Direct substitution for two interfaces (assuming that one side of the cylinder is used) yields

$$P_1 = 0 + \frac{1}{r_1} (n-1)$$

since $n_o = n_{air} = 1$ and $n_1 = n_{glass} = n.$

Then

$$h_2 = 1 - t\frac{\left(\frac{n-1}{r_1}\right)}{n}$$

and

$$P_2 = \frac{(n-1)}{r_1} + \left(1 - \frac{\frac{t(n-1)}{nr_1}}{r_2}\right)(1-n)$$

$\left(\text{now} \quad n_2 = \text{air} = 1\right).$

Thus P_2, the final power, is

$$P_2 = (n-1)\left[\frac{1}{r_1} - \frac{1}{r_2} + \frac{t(n-1)}{nr_1r_2}\right] = \frac{1}{f} .$$

Using $r_1 \simeq r_2 \simeq +500$ cm, t = 2 cm, and n = 1.5,

$$f = 750,000 \text{ cm.}$$

CHAPTER 19

OPTICAL INSTRUMENTS

MAGNIFICATION

● **PROBLEM** 19-1

How is the size of an image related to the size of its object? Discuss other properties of magnification.

Solution: Magnification is a physical term referring only to the relation between the image size and the object size. It may be defined as follows:

$$M = I/O,$$

where I is the size of the image and O is the size of the object.

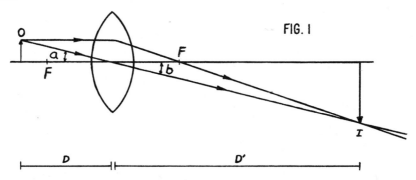

FIG. I

On inspection of the diagram in Figure 1, it is apparent that angles a and b are equal. Thus,

$$\tan a = \frac{O}{D} = \tan b = \frac{I}{D'}.$$

Then $\frac{I}{O} = \frac{D'}{D}$ and so,

magnification may also be defined in terms of image and object distances as follows:

$$M = \frac{\text{image distance}}{\text{object distance}} = \frac{D'}{D}.$$

547

In an experimental situation, magnification may be calculated by first measuring the size of the object with a ruler and then also the size of the image on a screen. Dividing object size into image size will provide the magnification.

Magnification is simply a geometrical relationship. In these definitions, there is no statement referable to the eye.

Magnifying power is also called angular magnification or apparent magnification. Magnifying power is concerned with the eye. It may be defined as the size of the retinal image when an object is viewed through an optical system compared to the size of the retinal image without an optical system. This may be expressed algebraically as follows:

$$M.P. = \frac{\text{size of the retinal image with an optical instrument}}{\text{size of the retinal image without an optical instrument}}.$$

● **PROBLEM** 19-2

A convergent lens of refractive power +15.00 diopters is to be used as a simple microscopic lens. What is the angular magnification produced compared to print at the usual reading distance of 40 cm?

Solution: The magnification of a single lens placed in front of the eye such that the image of the lens is at the distance of most distinct vision is found in any optics text to be

$$M = d/f \ ,$$

where d is the distance from the eye at which the image is located and f is the focal length of the lens. In addition, a diopter is defined to be the unit which the reciprocal of the focal length is expressed in when the focal length is measured in meters. In this problem, $d = 0.4$ m and $1/f = 15$ m, so

$$M = 0.4 \times 15 = 6.0$$

● **PROBLEM** 19-3

The frame in a home movie must be magnified 143 times before the picture formed on a screen 12 ft from the projection lens is large enough to please the family watching. What distance must the film be from the lens and what is the focal length of the lens?

Solution: The magnification produced by the lens is given by

$$m = -\frac{s'}{s} = -\frac{12 \text{ ft}}{s} = -143,$$

where s' and s are the image and object distance, respectively. (The image must be inverted; that is, the magnification is negative, since s must be positive (see figure).

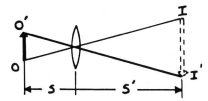

Thus the film-to-lens distance is

$$s = \frac{12}{143} \text{ ft} = \frac{144}{143} \text{ in.} = 1.007 \text{ in.}$$

Applying the lens formula $\frac{1}{s} + \frac{1}{s'} = \frac{1}{f}$,

we can obtain the focal length as follows:

$$\frac{1}{f} = \frac{143}{12 \text{ ft}} + \frac{1}{12 \text{ ft}} = \frac{144}{12 \text{ ft}}$$

$$f = \frac{12}{144} \text{ ft} = 1 \text{ in.}$$

● **PROBLEM** 19-4

A projector with a lens of 40 cm focal length illuminates an object slide 4.0 cm long and throws an image upon a screen 20 m from the lens. What is the size of the projected image?

<u>Solution</u>: We use the lens formula $\frac{1}{p} = \frac{1}{f} - \frac{1}{q}$ where p is the object distance, f is the focal length of the lens, and q is the image distance. Upon substitution of the given values in the formula, we have

$$\frac{1}{p} = \frac{1}{40 \text{ cm}} - \frac{1}{20 \text{ m}}$$

In order to do the subtraction, we must change 20 m to centimeters. Since $1 \text{ m} = 10^2 \text{ cm}$, $20 \text{ m} = 2000 \text{ cm}$ and

$$\frac{1}{p} = \frac{1}{40 \text{ cm}} - \frac{1}{2000 \text{ cm}}$$

$$\frac{1}{p} = \frac{2000 \text{ cm} - 40 \text{ cm}}{80000 \text{ cm}^2} = \frac{1960}{80000 \text{ cm}}$$

$$p = \frac{80000 \text{ cm}}{1960} = 40.8 \text{ cm}$$

This is the object distance.

The magnification M of the lens is defined as

$$M = \frac{q}{p} = \frac{2000 \text{ cm}}{40.8 \text{ cm}} = 49.$$

Therefore, given an object 4 cm long, the size of its projected image is

Image length = M x object length

$$= 49 \text{ x } 4 \text{ cm} = 196 \text{ cm}.$$

Hence, the size of the projected image is 196 cm.

● **PROBLEM** 19-5

A microscope has an objective lens of 10.0 mm focal length and an eyepiece of 25.0 mm focal length. What is the distance between the lenses, and what is the magnification if the object is in sharp focus when it is 10.5 mm from the objective?

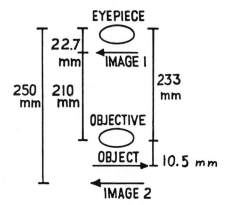

Solution: This is a compound microscope which uses converging lenses to produce large magnification. A short-focus lens, the objective, is placed near the object. It produces a real, inverted and magnified image. The eyepiece further magnifies this inverted image and produces a virtual image 250 mm from the eyepiece. This is the distance of most distinct vision.

Considering the image produced by the objective, we use the lens formula

$$\frac{1}{p} + \frac{1}{q} = \frac{1}{f} ,$$

where p represents the distance of the object from the objective lens, q the distance of image 1 from the lens, and f is the focal length. Substituting the given values for p and f into the above equation,

$$\frac{1}{10.5 \text{ mm}} + \frac{1}{q} = \frac{1}{10.0 \text{ mm}} , \text{ and solving for q gives}$$

the result   q = 210 mm

Therefore image 1 is 210 mm from the objective lens, and is real.

The eyepiece magnifies image 1 and produces a second virtual image 250 mm from the lens so as to provide most distinct vision. Since image 2 is virtual, on the same side of the lens as image 1, the distance q' of image 2 from the eyepiece is negative. Using the lens formula again,

$$\frac{1}{p'} + \frac{1}{q'} = \frac{1}{f'}$$

$$\frac{1}{p'} + \frac{1}{-250 \text{ mm}} = \frac{1}{25.0 \text{ mm}}$$

$$p' = 22.7 \text{ mm}$$

Therefore the eyepiece is 22.7 mm from image 1. The distance between the lenses is

$$q + p' = 210 \text{ mm} + 22.7 \text{ mm} = 233 \text{ mm} = 23.3 \text{ cm}$$

To find the magnification, first find the magnification produced by each lens using the equation

$$M = \frac{q}{p}$$

Magnification by objective:

$$M_0 = \frac{210 \text{ mm}}{10.5 \text{ mm}} = 20.0$$

Magnification by eyepiece:

$$M_e = \frac{-250 \text{ mm}}{22.7 \text{ mm}} = -11.0$$

Total magnification:

$$M = M_e M_0 = -11.0 \times 20.0 = -220$$

MICROSCOPES

● **PROBLEM 19-6**

A microscope has an optical tube length (distance between back focal plane and position of intermediary image) of 15 cm. If the objective lens has a focal length of 20 mm and the eyepiece has an angular magnification of 12.5, what is the total magnification that can be achieved? If the numerical aperture is 0.1, is this magnification within the reasonable limit?

Solution: The total magnification of a microscope is obtained by multiplying the linear magnification m_1 of the objective by the angular magnification m_2 of the eyepiece (in this problem, 12.5). The magnification m_1 can easily be found from the thin lens equations,

$$|m_1| = |i/\theta| \quad \text{and} \tag{1}$$

$$\frac{1}{\theta} + \frac{1}{i} = \frac{1}{f}, \tag{2}$$

where θ represents object distance, i image distance, and f lens focal length. Solving equation (2) for θ,

$$\theta = \frac{if}{i-f} ; \text{ substitution into equation (1) gives}$$

$$|m_1| = \left|\frac{i-f}{f}\right| . \tag{3}$$

For the microscope given, i (image distance from lens) is (150 mm + 20 mm) = 170 mm, and f = 20 mm. Substituting these values for i and f into equation (3) gives the result

$$m_1 = \frac{170 - 20}{20} = 7.5$$

Then the total magnification M is given by

$$M = m_1 m_2 = (7.5)(12.5) = 94.$$

The useful magnification of a microscope is taken to be about 1000 times the numerical aperture, in this case (1000) (.1) = 100; thus a magnification of 94x is within the reasonable limit.

● **PROBLEM 19-7**

The focal length of the ocular of a certain microscope is 2.5 cm. The focal length of the objective is 16 mm. The distance between objective and ocular is 22.1 cm. The final image formed by the ocular is at infinity. (a) What should be the distance from the objective to the object viewed? (b) What is the lateral magnification produced by the objective? (c) What is the overall magnification of the microscope?

Solution: (a) We will use the thin lens equation to find, u_1, the distance between the microscope objective and the original object. We will apply this equation twice, working backwards from the final image. The thin lens equation is

$$\frac{1}{u} + \frac{1}{u'} = 1/f \tag{1}$$

with $u_2' = - \infty$; $f_2 = 2.5$ cm

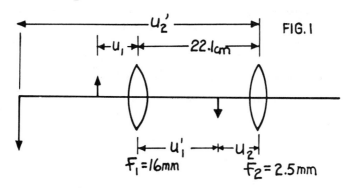

FIG. 1

$$\frac{1}{u_2} + \frac{1}{\infty} = \frac{1}{2.5} \qquad\qquad (2)$$

$$u_2 = 2.5 \text{ cm}$$

Then $\quad u_1' = d - u_2 = 22.1 - 2.5 = 19.6 \text{ cm}$

and

$$\frac{1}{u_1} + \frac{1}{19.6 \text{ cm}} = \frac{1}{1.6 \text{ cm}}$$

$$\frac{1}{u_1} = \frac{1}{1.6} - \frac{1}{19.6} = 0.625 - 0.051 = 0.574$$

$$u_1 = 1.74 \text{ cm}$$

The objective lens should be placed 1.74 cm from the object.

(b)   From u_1 and u_1' , the lateral magnification of the objective is

$$M_{obj} = - \frac{u_1'}{u_1} = \frac{-19.6}{1.74} = - 11.25 .$$

(c)   The overall magnification is the product of the magnification of the objective and eyepiece.   It can be shown that when the eyepiece is used to form an image at infinity the magnifying power of the eyepiece is $\frac{25}{f}$ where f is the effective focal length of the eyepiece,

$$f = \frac{3}{4} f_{eye} .$$

Hence

$$OM = (- 11.25) \left(\frac{25}{(3/4) 2.5} \right)$$

$$OM = - 150 \text{ x}$$

553

A compound microscope has an objective that produces a
lateral magnification of 10x. What focal length ocular
will produce an overall magnification of 100x?

Solution: In a compound microscope, the object is placed
near the focal point of the objective lens and its image
is formed within the body of the microscope. The eye piece
operates in a similar fashion. Thus, we can treat the
object lens and the eye lens separately to find the magnifying power of each of them. The overall magnification will
be the product of the two magnifying powers. For a single
optical element we place the object near the focal point
and have the image at about 25 cm from the eye (distance of
most distinct vision). So since the magnification in a
single optical element is

$$M = u'/u$$

where u' is the image distance and u is the object distance,

$$M_{obj} = \frac{25}{f_{obj}} \quad ; \quad M_{eye} = 25/f_{eye}$$

and the overall magnification is

$$O.M. = M_{obj} \times M_{eye} = \frac{25}{f_{obj}} \times 25/f_{eye}$$

or for this problem

$$100 = 10 \times 25/f_{eye}$$

or $\qquad f_{eye} = 2.5$ cm

A compound microscope of overall length 30 cm consists of
two lenses of focal lengths 1 cm and 5 cm. What is the
magnifying power of this microscope for a person whose
least distance for distinct vision is 25 cm? How far from
the objective is the object viewed?

Solution: First we must discuss what occurs in a compound
microscope. A compound microscope is composed in practice
of two lenses, an objective lens near the small object
which we wish to enlarge and an eyepiece lens which is near
the eye. We want to get the largest image possible so that
we can study the detail of the small object. Since the eye,
in this case, has a "least distance of distinct vision" of
25 cm., the final image of the microscope will be a virtual
image 25 centimeters from the eye lens. To get the largest
magnification, the small object will be just outside the

focal length of the objective lens and the small object will form a real image between the focal length of the eyepiece and the eyepiece. Since we also want to have the object as close to the microscope as possible, we then choose the objective lens to have a focal length of 1 cm and the eyepiece to have a focal length of 5 cm, and both lenses are converging lenses.

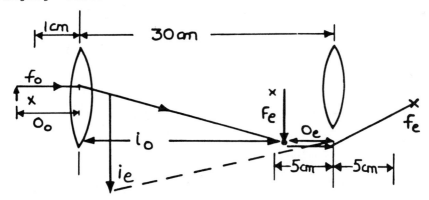

We are now ready to use the thin lens equations:

$$1/0 + 1/i = 1/f \tag{1}$$

and

$$M = -\,i/0 \tag{2}$$

to locate all the object and image positions and also their sizes. Here 0 is the object distance, i is the image distance, f the focal length and M the magnification.

We can do this by treating each lens separately. Since we know the final image position in the microscope is 25 cm, using (1) we have

$$\frac{1}{0_e} + \frac{1}{-25} = 1/5 \tag{3}$$

or the object distance for the eyepiece is located

$$\frac{1}{0_e} = 1/5 + 1/25 = 5/25 + 1/25 = 6/25 \text{ cm}^{-1} \tag{4}$$

$$0_e = 25/6 \text{ cm} \tag{5}$$

from the eyepiece. Since the overall length of the microscope is 30 cm, the image distance for the objective lens is

$$\left(30 - \frac{25}{6}\right)\text{cm} = \left(\frac{180 - 25}{6}\right)\text{cm} = 155/6 \text{ cm} \tag{6}$$

or applying equation (1) again,

$$\frac{1}{0_o} + \frac{6}{155} = 1 \tag{7}$$

555

or the object distance for the objective lens is

$$\frac{1}{0_o} = 1 - 6/155 = \frac{155}{155} - 6/155 = 149/155 \text{ cm} \qquad (8)$$

$$0_o = 155/149 = 1.04 \text{ cm}. \qquad (9)$$

Now using equation (2), the magnification of the objective lens is

$$M_0 = - \frac{155/6}{155/149} = - \frac{149}{6} \qquad (10)$$

and the magnification of the eye lens is

$$M_e = - \frac{-25}{25/6} = + 6 \qquad (11)$$

Now, since the overall magnification is the product of the magnification of each lens,

$$M_{overall} = M_o M_e = - \frac{149}{6} \times 6 = - 149 \qquad (12)$$

and we have an inverted, virtual final image of the small object.

The figure shows the arrangement of the lenses and various object-images, the subscript o being used for the objective lens and the subscript e being used for the eyepiece.

● **PROBLEM** 19-10

A compound microscope has an objective of 3 mm focal length. The objective forms an (intermediary) image 160 mm beyond the second focal plane of the objective. If the eyepiece alone gives 20x magnification (for the eye focused at infinity), what is the total magnification provided by the microscope?

Solution: The total magnification of a microscope is obtained by multiplying the linear magnification m_1 of the objective by the angular magnification m_2 of the eyepiece. Using the thin lens equation for the objective,

$$\left| m_1 \right| = \left| \frac{i}{\theta} \right| \qquad (1)$$

and

$$\frac{1}{\theta} + \frac{1}{i} = \frac{1}{f} , \qquad (2)$$

where θ represents object distance, i image distance (both measured from the lens), and f the focal length. Solving equation (2) for θ gives

$$\theta = \frac{if}{i-f} \ .$$ Therefore, substituting for θ in equation (1) gives

$$\left| m_1 \right| = \left| \frac{i-f}{f} \right| \ . \tag{3}$$

Using f = 3 mm and i = (160 + 3) mm,

$$m_1 = 53 \frac{1}{3} \ ,$$ and then the total magnification M of the microscope is

$$M = m_1 m_2 = \left(53 \frac{1}{3} \right) (20) \cong 1066.$$

TELESCOPES

● **PROBLEM** 19-11

What is the meaning of the number found on telescopes and binoculars?

Solution: Let us consider the number "7 x 50", for example. The 7 refers to the overall magnifying power of the optical system, and the 50 refers to the diameter in millimeters of the entrance pupil. In practical terms, the entrance pupil is usually the diameter of the objective (or eyepiece). The diameter of the beam of rays emerging from the ocular, and therefore entering the eye, may be calculated by dividing the magnifying power into the diameter of the entrance pupil: in the example, 7 into 50. In this case, the diameter of the exit beam is 7 mm. It is of interest to contrast binoculars specified as 7 x 50 with those indicated as 7 x 35. In both instruments, the magnifying power is 7x. However, the physical bulk of the 7 x 50 binoculars would be substantially greater than the 7 x 35, because of the larger objective. The advantage of the 7 x 50 binoculars is the large diameter of the bundle of rays emerging from the eyepiece, 7 mm, whereas in the 7 x 35 it measures 5 mm. The 7 x 50 glasses are known as night glasses because under conditions of reduced illumination the pupil of the eye dilates. Accordingly, the greater light-gathering power of the larger objective is utilized to fill the more dilated pupil. During daylight illumination with a smaller pupil in the observer's eye, much of the 7-mm beam in the night glasses would illuminate the iris and would not contribute to any brightness of the image on the retina.

● **PROBLEM** 19-12

A telescope is made from two lenses, having focal lengths of 5 and 1 cm.

557

a) What should be the distance between lenses if the initial object and the final virtual image are both very far away?

b) What is the magnification under these circumstances?

Solution: a) A telescope is made from two lenses with positive focal lengths placed a distance L apart with the lens having the shorter focal length nearest the eye. We are told that the initial object is very far away from the telescope; therefore, the real image formed by the objective lens will be 5 centimeters from the objective lens. We are also told that the final virtual image is very far away, so that the real image formed by the objective lens must be at the focal point of the eye lens or 1 centimeter from the eye lens. Therefore the distance between the lenses must be the sum of the focal lengths or 1 + 5 = 6 cm.

One can check the positions of the various images and objects formed by using successively the thin lens equation

$$\frac{1}{u} + \frac{1}{u'} = 1/f$$

where u is the object distance, u' is the image distance and f is the focal length of the lens. Here u for the objective lens is infinite and u' for the eye lens is infinite.

b) To find the magnification we recall that for a telescope the magnification is given as

$$M = f_o/f_e$$

where f_o is the focal length of the objective lens and f_e is the focal length of the eye lens

Thus, $M = f_o/f_e = 5/1 = 5$ times

Now if we turn the telescope around then the eye lens becomes the objective lens and the magnification becomes 1/5.

● **PROBLEM** 19-13

A telescope gives 3x angular magnification and has an objective of 50 cm focal length. What is the refractive power of the eyepiece and what is the distance between the lenses if the telescope is a) of the astronomical type and b) of the Gallilean type?

Solution: The refractive power is measured in diopters and is the reciprocal of the focal length when the focal length is measured in meters. For a telescope, the magnification M is given by

$$M = F/f$$

where F is the focal length of the objective and f is the focal length of the eyepiece.

An astronomical telescope consists of two lenses with positive focal lengths and a Gallilean telescope has an eye piece with negative focal length and forms an erect image of the object.

For the astronomical telescope,

$$3 = 0.5m/f.$$

The refractive power $\quad \frac{1}{f} = 3 \times 2 = 6$ diopters

and $\quad\quad\quad\quad\quad\quad\quad\quad f = 0.166$ m.

Since the telescope is adjusted so that the final image is an infinite distance away from the lens, the distance between the lenses is just the sum of the focal lengths, or d = 50 + 16.6 = 66.6 cm.

For the Gallilean telescope, the refractive power 1/f = - 6 diopters and f = - 0.166 m and again the distance between the lenses will be the sum of the focal lengths or d = 50 + (- 16.6) = 33.4 cm.

● **PROBLEM 19-14**

A distant object is observed through a telescope consisting of an objective lens of focal length 30 cm and a single eyepiece lens of focal length 5 cm. The telescope is adjusted so that the final image observed by the eye is 40 cm from the eye lens.   a) Find the distance between the two lenses.   b) Make a careful diagram tracing a ray bundle from a lateral point on the object to the retina.   c) Calculate the magnifying power of this arrangement.

Solution: (a) A distant object is viewed through the telescope. Hence, the object distance for the objective is ∞. Let S_{oi} be the image distance for the objective. Then $S_{oi} = f_o$ where f_o is the focal length of the objective (30 cm). Let x be the distance between the objective and the eyepiece The object distance for the eyepiece then is $S_{eo} = x - f_o =$ x - 30 cm. Also given is the image distance from the eyepiece. The image formed is virtual and hence

$S_{ei} = - 40$ cm, using the regular sign convention.

Using the thin lens equation, we have

$$\frac{1}{S_{eo}} + \frac{1}{S_{ei}} = \frac{1}{f_e}$$

where f_e is the focal length of the eyepiece (5 cm),

Then

$$\frac{1}{x - 30} - \frac{1}{40} = \frac{1}{5}$$

$$x - 30 = \frac{200}{45}$$

$$x = 34.44 \text{ cm.}$$

Therefore, the distance between the two lenses is 34.44 cm.

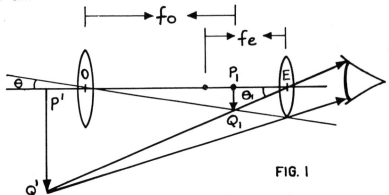

FIG. I

b) The diagram tracing a ray bundle is shown in figure 1. The image P_1Q_1 formed by the objective is at a distance f_o from the objective. If the image P_1Q_1 is also at a distance from the eyepiece equal to the focal length of the eyepiece, then the virtual image would be formed at ∞. However, since the image formed is at a distance of 40 cm from the eyepiece, P_1Q_1 is at a distance of 4.44 cm.

c) The magnifying power is

$$M = \frac{\tan \theta_1}{\tan \theta} ,$$

where θ_1 and θ are as shown in Figure 1. From Figure 1, we see that M =

$$\frac{P_1Q_1}{EP_1} \Big/ \frac{P_1Q_1}{f_o}$$

where EP_1 is the distance between the eyepiece and the image P_1Q_1.

$$M = \frac{f_o}{EP_1} = \frac{30}{4.44} = 6.75$$

● **PROBLEM** 19-15

When focused on a star, the distance of the eye lens of a simple telescope from the objective lens is 82 cm. The focal length of the eye lens is 2.0 cm. To see a certain tree

560

(with the same eye accommodation), the eye lens must be drawn out 1.0 cm. Find the distance of the tree from the telescope.

Solution: When an object is very distant, it can be said to be at ∞, and the image formed by the objective will be at the emergent principal focus. For best vision, this point should also be the incident principal focus of the eyepiece so that the image is formed at ∞, for the eye.

The focal length of the eyepiece is f_2 = 2.0 cm, and this is also the object distance for the eyepiece. The focal length of the objective, f_1, is given by $d - f_2$ where d is the distance between the two lenses.

$$f_1 = d - f_2 = 82 \text{ cm} - 2.0 \text{ cm} = 80 \text{ cm.}$$

When viewing the tree, the eyepiece is drawn out 1 cm. Hence the image distance ℓ' for the objective is 81 cm, so that the image is still formed on the principal focus of the eyepiece. If ℓ is the distance of the tree from the objective, then using the lens formula,

$$\frac{1}{\ell} + \frac{1}{\ell'} = \frac{1}{f_1}$$

$$\ell = \frac{\ell' f_1}{\ell' - f_1} = \frac{81 \text{ cm} \times 80 \text{ cm}}{1 \text{ cm}}$$

$$= 64.8 \text{ meters}$$

● **PROBLEM** 19-16

An astronomical telescope is pointed towards the sun, and a real image of the sun is obtained on a screen placed beyond the eye-lens at a distance d from it. If the diameter of this image is denoted by 2b, and if the apparent diameter of the sun is denoted by 2θ, show that the magnifying power of the telescope is $M = b \cot \theta / d$.

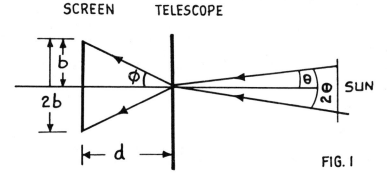

FIG. I

Solution: Figure 1 shows a diagram of a set of rays represented by this problem. The magnifying power of an

561

optical instrument is defined as M = ϕ/θ, where ϕ and θ are shown in the figure.

We can also write M = $\dfrac{\tan \phi}{\tan \theta}$ because if the angles ϕ and θ are very small, we can make the approximations $\phi \approx \tan \phi$ and $\theta = \tan \theta$. From the figure, $\tan \phi = b/d$, so

$$M = \frac{b}{d} \frac{1}{\tan \theta} = \frac{b \cot \theta}{d}.$$

• **PROBLEM** 19-17

An astronomical telescope, consisting of an objective lens of +40 cm focal length and an eyepiece of +2.5 cm focal length, is focused for visual observation at the distance of most distinct vision, on a scale 3 m away.

1) What is the length of the telescope (distance between the lenses)?

2) What is the total linear lateral magnification?

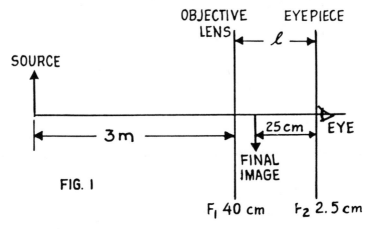

FIG. I

Solution: 1) Figure 1 shows the geometrical arrangement. To find the length of the telescope we observe that "the dis-tance of most distinct vision" is a final image distance from the eyepiece of -25 cm; in other words the eye is most comfortable when the object it is observing is 25 cm in front of it (The sign convention that distances to the right of the eyepiece are positive and those to the left negative has been assumed). Then applying the thin lens equation

$$\frac{1}{p} + \frac{1}{q} = 1/f$$

where p is the object distance, q is the image distance and f is the focal length of the eyepiece. We can locate the source point for the eyepiece as follows:

$$\frac{1}{P_2} + \frac{1}{-25 \text{ cm}} = \frac{1}{2.5 \text{ cm}}$$

562

$$\frac{1}{P_2} = \frac{1}{2.5} \left(1 + \frac{1}{10}\right) \ cm^{-1}$$

$$P_2 = \left(\frac{25}{11}\right) \ cm = 2.27 \ cm,$$

assuming that there is no gap between the eyepiece of the telescope and the eye.

Treating the initial object, we can also find the image distance in the objective lens as follows:

$$\frac{1}{300 \ cm} \cdot \frac{1}{q_1} = \frac{1}{40 \ cm}$$

$$\frac{1}{q_1} = \frac{1}{40 \ cm} - \frac{1}{300 \ cm} = \frac{260}{40 \ x \ 300} \ cm^{-1}$$

$$q_1 = 46.15 \ cm$$

and since q_1 and P_2 must coincide, the length of the tele-scope, $\ell = q_1 + P_2 = 46.15 + 2.27 = 48.42 \ cm$.

2) The total linear lateral magnification is just the product of the magnification of each lens or

$$TLLM = M_1 \ x \ M_2 = \frac{q_1}{P_1} \ x \ \frac{q_2}{P_2} = \frac{46.15}{300} \ x \ \frac{25}{2.27} = 1.7.$$

● **PROBLEM** 19-18

A beam of parallel rays, parallel to the axis, falls on the objective of a telescope equipped with a Ramsden eyepiece and adjusted so that the final image is at infinity. If the focal length of the objective is 30.00 cm and the common focal length of each of the lenses of the eyepiece is 6.0 cm, find the diameter of the beam of light emerging from the telescope. (Diameter of objective is 3.0 cm.)

Solution: A Ramsden eyepiece consists of two plano-convex lenses with equal focal length f separated by a distance $t = \frac{2}{3} f$. Given f = 6 cm, the effective focal length f_{eff} is given by

$$\frac{1}{f_{eff}} = \frac{1}{f} + \frac{1}{f_2} - \frac{t}{f_1 f_2}$$

In this problem, $f_1 = f_2 = f$, so

$$\frac{1}{f_{eff}} = \frac{1}{f} + \frac{1}{f} - \frac{2}{3} \frac{f}{f^2} = \frac{4}{3f}$$

563

$$f_{eff} = \frac{3}{4} f = \left(\frac{3}{4}\right) (6.0 \text{ cm.}) = 4.5 \text{ cm.}$$

All of the light that enters the objective and is refracted by the eyepiece must pass through the image of the objective formed by the eyepiece. This is called the exit pupil of the telescope. The eye is usually placed at the exit pupil, also called the eye point. The object and the virtual image viewed by the eye are both at ∞. If the objective is considered as the object for the ocular, the distance from the focal point to the object is given by $x = f_o$ where f_o is the focal length of the objective. The lateral magnification is then,

$$m = \frac{f_e}{x} = \frac{f_e}{f_o}$$

where f_e is the focal length of the eyepiece. The lateral magnification is also given by

$$m = \frac{\text{diameter of the objective}}{\text{diameter of the exit pupil}}$$

Then

diameter of the exit pupil =

$$\frac{f_o \times \text{diameter of the objective}}{f_e}$$

$$= \frac{30 \times 3}{4.5} \text{ cm.} = 20 \text{ cm.}$$

This is the diameter of the beam emerging from the telescope.

● **PROBLEM** 19-19

The refractive powers of the front and back lenses of a Galilean-type telescope are +10.00 diopters and -12.50 diopters respectively. What must the separation of the two lenses be if the system is to be afocal? What is the angular magnification?

Solution: In this problem we must remember the definition of diopters. Since much of our work with optical instruments involves the use of the thin lens equation and we recognize the need for reciprocals of distances and focal lengths, the diopter, which is the unit which the reciprocal of the focal length of an optical element is expressed in when the focal length is expressed in meters, helps us perform the arithmetic of optics problems. We also need to remember the definition of afocal. For a telescope, afocal means that both the object and the final image are infinitely distant from the telescope.

As a result, the image of the original object is at the focal point of the objective lens and this image, which is the object for the eye lens, must lie at the focal point of the eye lens.

In addition, the magnifying power of this type telescope is

$$MP = \frac{f_{obj}}{f_{eye}}$$

where f_{obj} is the focal length of the objective lens and f_{eye} is the focal length of the eye lens. With

$$D_{obj} = \frac{1}{f_{obj}} \; ; \; and \; D_{eye} = 1/f_{eye}$$

we have $\quad MP = \dfrac{D_{eye}}{D_{obj}}$.

Since D_{obj} and D_{eye} are given to be +10.00 diopters and -12.50 diopters, respectively,

$$f_{obj} = \frac{1}{10} \; m \; ; \; f_{eye} = -\frac{1}{12.5} = -0.08 \; m$$

and since the separation of the lenses will be the sum of the focal lengths,

$$S = f_{obj} + f_{eye} = (0.1 - 0.08)m = 0.02m = 2cm.$$

The angular magnification is

$$MP = \frac{-12.5}{10} = -1.25 \; .$$

The minus sign indicates that the final image is inverted.

● **PROBLEM** 19-20

A telescope has a focal length of 25 ft. What must be the focal length of an eyepiece which will magnify a planetary object by 300 diameters?

Solution: From a standard textbook derivation, we know that the magnifying power of a telescope is:

$$MP = \frac{f_{obj}}{f_{eye}}$$

where f_{obj} is the focal length of the objective lens and f_{eye} is the focal length of the eye lens.

Substituting MP = 300 and f_{obj} = 25 feet into the above equation,

$$300 = \frac{25 \text{ ft}}{f_{eye}}$$

or

$$f_{eye} = \frac{25 \text{ ft}}{300} = \frac{1}{12} \text{ ft} = 1 \text{ inch.}$$

● **PROBLEM** 19-21

An astronomical telescope consists of two lenses separated by a distance of 1 m. If the angular magnification, focusing at infinity, is 5x, what are the refractive powers of the two components?

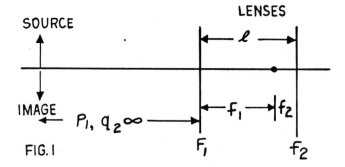

FIG. 1

Solution: Figure 1 shows the arrangement of the lenses. For an astronomical telescope, the object distance is infinite and the problem says the distance between the lenses is adjusted so that the final image is an infinite distance from the second lens. Therefore, the infinitely distant object has an image at a distance f_1 to the right of the first lens. This is the object for the second lens, and since it forms an image an infinite distance from the second lens it must be located a distance f_2 to the left of the second lens. Therefore

$$f_1 + f_2 = \ell,$$

where ℓ = the distance between the lenses.

For a telescope focused in this manner, the magnification is

$$M = f_1/f_2$$

and the refractive power in diopters is the reciprocal of the focal length, when the focal length is measured in meters. So since ℓ = 1 m

$$f_1 + f_2 = 1 \text{ m}$$

$$5 = f_1/f_2$$

$$5f_2 + f_2 = 1 \text{ m}$$

$$\frac{1}{f_2} = 6 \text{ m}^{-1} = 6 \text{ diopters}$$

$$\frac{1}{f_1} = \frac{1}{5f_2} = \frac{6}{5} \text{ m}^{-1} = 1.2 \text{ diopters}$$

Therefore, the refractive powers of lenses 1 and 2 are 1.2 diopters and 6 diopters, respectively.

● **PROBLEM 19-22**

A telescope is sighted on the image of a scale formed by reflection in a mirror. Both the telescope objective and the scale are 1 m from the mirror (see fig). What is the lateral magnification of the image of the scale formed by the objective, if the objective has a focal length of 50 cm? What should the angular magnification of the ocular be if the scale is to be read as easily through the telescope as it would be by the unaided eye with the scale 25 cm away?

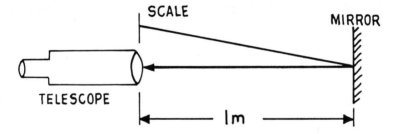

Solution: To find the lateral magnification of the scale in the objective lens we can use the relation

$$M = \frac{\text{image distance}}{\text{object distance}} \tag{1}$$

We are given that the object distance u is 2 meters (twice the distance of the objective lens to the mirror), and we can find the image distance u' from the thin lens equation

$$\frac{1}{u} + \frac{1}{u'} = 1/f \tag{2}$$

$$\frac{1}{2m} + \frac{1}{u'} = \frac{1}{.5 \text{ m}} \tag{3}$$

$$\frac{1}{u'} = (2 - 1/2)\,\text{m}^{-1} = 3/2 \text{ m}^{-1} \tag{4}$$

567

$$u' = 2/3 \text{ m} \tag{5}$$

Thus the total lateral magnification is

$$M_{obj} = \frac{2/3}{2} = 1/3 . \tag{6}$$

We will choose the eyepiece magnification of the telescope so that the image formed by the ocular (eyepiece) will be at a distance of 25 cm with an overall magnification of 1. This will provide an image equivalent to actually viewing the scale from 25 cm. Now the overall magnification of a telescope is

$$OM = M_{ocular} M_{obj} \tag{7}$$

or

$$1 = M_{ocular} \times \frac{1}{3} \tag{8}$$

so

$$M_{ocular} = 3 \tag{9}$$

● **PROBLEM** 19-23

Under what condition is it correct to state that the magnifying power of a telescope is equal to

$$\frac{\text{diameter of objective}}{\text{diameter of exit pupil}} ?$$

Solution: The angular magnification M is defined as the ratio of the angle θ' subtended by the image to the angle θ subtended by the object at the eye.

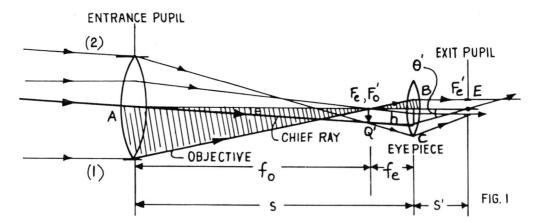

In figure 1, two rays are drawn, one parallel to the axis and another, chief ray from a distant off-axis object point.

The object (not shown in the figure) subtends an angle θ at the objective and would subtend approximately the same angle to the unaided eye. The angle subtended at the eye by the final image is the angle θ'.

Therefore, $M = \dfrac{\theta'}{\theta}$

From the right triangles ABC and EBC, we can write

$$\tan \theta = \frac{h}{s} \quad \text{and} \quad \tan \theta' = \frac{h}{s'} \, .$$

Since $\dfrac{1}{s} + \dfrac{1}{s'} = \dfrac{1}{f_e}$

(where f_e = the focal length of the eyepiece)

$$\frac{1}{s'} = \frac{1}{f_e} - \frac{1}{s}$$

We know that $s = f_o + f_e$ (f_o = the focal length of the objective). Hence,

$$\frac{1}{s'} = \frac{1}{f_e} - \frac{1}{(f_o + f_e)} = \frac{f_o + f_e - f_e'}{f_e (f_o + f_e)}$$

$$\frac{1}{s'} = \frac{f_o}{f_e (f_o + f_e)}$$

Thus,

$$\tan \theta = \frac{h}{(f_o + f_e)}$$

and

$$\tan \theta' = \frac{h f_o}{(f_o + f_e) f_e} \, .$$

For small angles θ and θ',

$$\tan \theta \approx \theta$$
$$\tan \theta' \approx \theta'$$

Therefore

$$M = \frac{\theta'}{\theta} = \frac{\left(\dfrac{h f_o}{f_e (f_o + f_e)} \right)}{\left(\dfrac{h}{(f_o + f_e)} \right)} = \frac{f_o}{f_e} \, .$$

If D and d represent the diameters of the objective and exit pupil, respectively, and considering the marginal rays 1 and 2 passing through f_o' and f_e in figure 1, we see that this gives two similar right triangles, from which we can write the ratio of corresponding sides;

$$\frac{f_o}{f_e} = \frac{D}{d} \, .$$

Therefore, $\qquad M = \dfrac{D}{d} \, .$

This is only true if the exit pupil is the image of the entrance pupil as formed by the eyepiece.

● PROBLEM 19-24

The objective lens of a telescope is 20 mm in diameter. Its focal length is 250 mm, and the eyepiece of the telescope is 2 mm in diameter. (a) What is the normal magnification of the telescope? (b) What focal length ocular should be used? (c) Find the position of the exit pupil. (d) What would be the diameter of the exit pupil if an ocular were used which gave a magnification 50% in excess of normal? (e) What would be the diameter of the exit pupil if the magnification were 50% of normal? Assume all lenses to be thin.

Solution: (a) The normal magnification γ is defined as follows: $\gamma = \dfrac{D}{D'}$, where D is the diameter of the objective and D' is the diameter of the eyepiece. Therefore,

$$\gamma = \frac{20}{2} = 10x$$

(b) γ is also defined as follows:

$$\gamma = \frac{f_1}{f_2} ,$$

where f_1 and f_2 represent the focal lengths of the objective and the ocular (or eyepiece), respectively. Then,

$$f_2 = \frac{f_1}{\gamma} = \frac{250 \text{ mm}}{10} = 25 \text{ mm}.$$

(c) The position of the exit pupil, x', is given by the equation

$$x' = \frac{f_2^{\,2}}{x} ,$$

where x represents the position of the entrance pupil.

In this problem, $x = f_1$ and so,

$$x' = \frac{f_2^{\,2}}{f_1} = \frac{f_2}{\gamma} = \frac{25 \text{ mm}}{10} = 2.5 \text{ mm}.$$

That is, the exit pupil is 2.5 mm to the right of the second focal point of the ocular, or 27.5 mm to the right of the ocular itself.

(d) If an ocular were used which gave a magnification 50% in excess of normal, γ would equal (150%)(10) = (1.50)(10) = 15. Then solving the equation

$$\gamma = \frac{D}{D'} \text{ for } D', \quad D' = \frac{D}{\gamma} = \frac{20 \text{ mm}}{15} = 1.33 \text{ mm}.$$

570

(e) If the magnification were 50% of normal, γ would equal (50%)(10) = (.50)(10) = 5.

Then $D' = \dfrac{D}{\gamma} = \dfrac{20 \text{ mm}}{5} = 4 \text{ mm}.$

A crude telescope is constructed of two spectacle lenses of focal lengths 100 cm and 20 cm respectively. a) Find its angular magnification. b) Find the height of the image formed by the objective of a building 200 ft high and one mile distant.

Solution: a) From our knowledge of telescopes, we recall that the objective lens should have a long focal length, the ocular should have a short focal length and the separation should be approximately equal to the sum of the focal lengths.

The magnification of a telescope is given by

$$M = \frac{f_{obj}}{f_{eye}} = \frac{100}{20} = 5 \tag{1}$$

b) The ratio of the size of the image formed by the objective lens to the size of the original object is the ratio of the image distance u' to the original object distance u;

$$\frac{\text{size image}}{\text{size object}} = \frac{u'}{u} \tag{2}$$

The problem states that the object size is 200 feet and the object distance is 1 mile, or 1.6×10^3 meters. We can find the image distance from the thin lens equations as follows:

$$\frac{1}{u} + \frac{1}{u'} = \frac{1}{f} \tag{3}$$

$$\frac{1}{1.6 \times 10^3} + \frac{1}{u_1'} = \frac{1}{1.0} \tag{4}$$

$$\frac{1}{u_1'} = 1 - \frac{10^{-3}}{1.6} \approx 1 \tag{5}$$

$$u_1' = 1.0 \text{ meter} \tag{6}$$

From equation (2)

$$\text{size image} = 200 \times \frac{1}{1.6 \times 10^3} \text{ feet} = 6.25 \times 10^{-4} \times 200 \text{ feet}$$

$$= 0.125 \text{ ft} = 1.5 \text{ inches.}$$

The diameter of the objective lens of a telescope is 30 mm and the angular magnification of the instrument is 5x. If the diameter of the pupil of the observer's eye is 5 mm, what fraction of the area of the objective is actually utilized?

Solution: When an object is viewed through a telescope, all the light which passes through the objective and is refracted by the eyepiece must pass through the image of the objective formed by the eyepiece. This image is called the exit pupil of the telescope. When the magnification is normal, the radius of the exit pupil is equal to the radius of the eye. When the radius of the exit pupil is increased by increasing the diameter of the objective, the eye cannot admit the wider beam, and only a portion of the objective is effectively used. If D is the diameter

of the objective and D' the diameter of the image, then by definition the lateral magnification is

$$m = \frac{D'}{D} .$$

Since the objective is placed at a distance equal to its focal length, f_1, from the first focal point of the ocular (eyepiece), the lateral magnification is also equal to

$$m = \left| \frac{-f_2}{f_1} \right|$$

where f_2 is the focal length of the eyepiece.

Then $\quad \dfrac{D}{D'} = \dfrac{f_1}{f_2} = \gamma$

where the angular magnification is $\gamma = \dfrac{f_1}{f_2}$. For normal

magnification, the exit pupil diameter D' must be equal to the diameter of the pupil of the observer's eye. With an angular magnification of 5, the diameter of the objective must be

$$D = \gamma D' = 5 \times 5 \text{ mm} = 25 \text{ mm}$$
$$\text{Area} = \pi \left(\frac{D}{2} \right)^2 = \pi (12.5)^2 \text{ mm}^2$$

However, the actual area of the objective used is

$$\pi \left(\frac{30}{2} \right)^2 \text{ mm}^2 = \pi (15)^2 \text{ mm}^2 .$$

Hence, the ratio of the area effectively used is

$$\frac{\pi (12.5)^2 \text{ mm}^2}{\pi (15)^2 \text{ mm}^2} = 0.694$$

which is approximately 70% or $\dfrac{7}{10}$.

CAMERA LENSES

If the f-number of the eye is 4.3 when the pupil diameter
is 4 mm, what is the f-number when the pupil diameter is
8 mm? How does the f-number compare with those for a
camera lens?

Solution: It can be shown that the flux density of light at
the image plane is proportional to $(D/f)^2$, where D is the
diameter of the lens and f is the focal length of the lens.
The flux density of light on a photographic film will determine the time necessary to get a good exposure or, flux
density at the image plane is proportional to the reciprocal of the exposure time. The "f-number" is the ratio of
f/D so that the flux density is proportional to the $1/(f\text{-}\\ number)^2$. In other words,

$$\left(\frac{D}{f}\right)^2 = \text{flux density} \propto \frac{1}{\text{exposure time}}$$

$$\text{f-number} = \frac{f}{D} \propto \frac{1}{(\text{flux density})^{1/2}}$$

thus, f-number $\propto$ exposure time

This "f-number" is then a useful concept in photography as
it yields an indication of the relative time needed for
taking a photograph. (The smaller the "f-number", the
shorter the exposure for constant light intensity.)

In this problem it is given that the "f-number", is
4.3 when the pupil (i.e., the diameter of the eye lens
exposed to light) is 4 mm. The focal length of the eye
lens is not known. So we can write

$$\text{f-number} = f/D \tag{1}$$

or,
$$4.3 = f/4 \ . \tag{2}$$

Now, when the pupil diameter is changed to 8 mm, assuming that the eye is focused for the same distance, which
means that the focal length of the eye is the same,

$$\text{f-number} = f/8 \tag{3}$$

dividing equation (3) by equation (2) yields

$$\frac{\text{f-number}}{4.3} = \frac{f/8}{f/4} \tag{4}$$

or, f-number $= 4.3 \times 4/8 = 2.15$. $\tag{5}$

In a camera, the lens markings of the diaphragm are
typically (from small to large) f-numbers of 16, 11, 8,

5.6, 4, 2.8, 2.0, and 1.4. An inexpensive camera lens very
likely has a minimum f-number of 2.8 and an expensive
camera very likely has an f-number of 1.4. As you
close the diaphragm from an f-number of 2.8 to an f-number
of 4 for the same light intensity, it is necessary to
double the exposure time. Therefore, the f-number found in
equation (5) is equal to that of a moderately priced camera.

● **PROBLEM** 19-28

A camera has a thin lens with an aperture of 8 mm and a
focal length of 10 cm. What is the f/number of the system
if a stop 7 mm in diameter is mounted 5 mm in front of the
lens? If it is mounted 5 mm behind the lens?

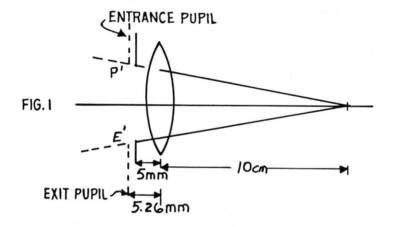

FIG. I

ENTRANCE PUPIL

EXIT PUPIL

5mm

10cm

5.26mm

P'

E'

Solution: (a) The image of the stop (entrance pupil) is
the exit pupil of the system. That is, rays passing through
the lens will behave as if they had come from points

p' and E' in the exit pupil. The position of the exit pupil
is determined from the equation

$$\frac{1}{0} + \frac{1}{i} = \frac{1}{f} ,$$

where 0 and i represent the object and image distance,
respectively, and f denotes the focal length of the lens.
In this problem, f = 100 mm and 0 = 5 mm.

Therefore, $i = \frac{0f}{0-f} = -5.26$ mm.

The f/number of the system is given by

$$\frac{f - i}{\text{diameter of stop}} = \frac{105.26}{7} \cong 15$$

i.e., f/15

(b) Here the stop itself is the exit pupil. We
obtain the f/number through the equation

$$\frac{f - 5}{7} = \frac{100 - 5}{7} = 13.5$$

i.e., f/13.5 .

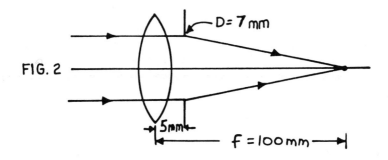

FIG. 2

D = 7 mm

5mm

f = 100mm

A lens found in 35 mm cameras has a focal length of 50 mm
and a diameter of 25 mm, corresponding to a maximum aperture of f/2. The resolution of a lens is commonly expressed
as the maximum number of lines per millimeter in the image
that can be resolved. If the resolution of the lens is
diffraction-limited, approximately what is the resolution
in lines per mm? (Good quality 35 mm camera lenses
typically have a resolution of the order of 100 lines/mm,
determined by surface precision rather than diffraction.)

Solution: From the diffraction formula two points (or
lines) can be resolved if their angle of separation is at
least θ, where θ is determined by

$$\theta = 1.22 \frac{\lambda}{a} \tag{1}$$

where λ is the wavelength of the light and a is the diameter
of the aperture. From the geometry of the situation we
know that,

$$\sin \theta = \frac{s}{f} .$$

where s is the distance between lines and f is the focal
length. Sin θ is small, so the approximation $\sin \theta = \theta$
is valid. Substituting $\theta = \frac{s}{f}$ into equation (1),

$$\frac{s}{f} = 1.22\frac{\lambda}{a} .$$

Solving for s,

$$s = 1.22 \frac{\lambda f}{a} \tag{2}$$

Substituting f = 50 mm, a = 25 mm, and $\lambda = 555 \cdot 10^{-6}$ mm
(the wavelength the eye is the most sensitive to) into
equation (2) gives the result

$$s = 1.22 \left(\frac{555 \cdot 10^{-6} \cdot 50}{25} \right) mm = 1.35 \times 10^{-3} mm.$$

The inverse, $\frac{1}{s} = 741$, is the number of lines per mm.

Camera lenses usually contain an aperture of variable
diameter to control exposure. Consider a lens of focal
length 50 mm and diameter 25 mm, with a resolution of 200
lines/mm. How far can this lens be stopped down before
diffraction effects begin to limit the image quality?

Solution: For light passing through an aperture, two point
sources may just be resolved if their images are separated
by an angle θ equal to the angular separation of the central
diffraction maximum and the adjacent minimum; for a circu-
lar aperture of diameter d, $\theta = 1.22 \lambda/d$, where λ is the
wavelength of light. This implies that the angular separa-
tion of the sources (measured from the aperture) must also
be at least $1.22 \lambda/d$. The given lens can resolve objects
(lines) separated by 1/200 mm when the lines lie a distance
of 50 mm from the lens (aperture); hence the angular separation ϕ of the lines is given by

$$\phi \simeq \tan \phi \quad \text{(this approximation can be made for}$$
$$\text{small } \theta) \simeq \frac{(1/200)\,\text{mm}}{50\,\text{mm}} = 10^{-4};$$

setting $\phi = \theta (=1.22 \lambda/d)$ and using $\lambda = 5 \times 10^{-4}$ mm
(roughly the center of the visible spectrum),

$$10^{-4} = \frac{1.22 \left(5 \times 10^{-4}\,\text{mm}\right)}{d}, \quad \text{or}$$

$$d = 6 \text{ mm.}$$

Therefore, the lens can be stopped down to a diameter of
6 mm before diffraction effects begin to limit the image
quality.

An enlarging camera has a maximum extension of 4 ft. between the negative and the paper. The focal length of the
lens is 10 inches and the separation of its principal
points, which are crossed, is 0.5 inch. What is the maximum enlargement that can be made with this equipment?
What is the minimum reduction?

Solution: In the problem stated, the total distance between
object and image is 48", i.e.,

$$x + 2f - (.5") + x' = 48" , \tag{1}$$

where x, x', and f are shown in the figure.

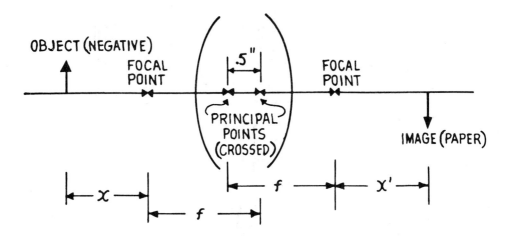

Using the Newtonian form of the lens equation,

$$xx' = f^2 \text{ , so } x' = f^2/x \qquad (2)$$

Eliminating x' from equation (1), a quadratic expression for x is obtained:

$$x^2 + (2f - 48.5")x + f^2 = 0 ; \qquad (3)$$

using f = 10" and solving for x by using the quadratic equation,

$$x = \frac{-b \pm \sqrt{b^2 - 4ac}}{2a} ,$$

with a = 1, b = 2f - 48.5" and c = f^2,

$$x = 24.4", \text{ and } 4.1".$$

Substituting these values of x into the Newtonian expression for the transverse magnification m,

$$m = \frac{f}{x} \left(= \frac{x'}{f} \right) \qquad (4)$$

gives,

$$m = 0.41, \text{ and } 2.4, \text{ respectively.}$$

Thus, placing the negative 24.4" from the first focal point of the lens would result in an image reduced by a factor of 0.41, and placing the negative 4.1" from the first focal point would produce an image enlarged by a factor of 2.4.

● **PROBLEM** 19-32

The lens of a camera has a focal length of 6 cm and the camera is focused for very distant objects. Through what distance must the lens be moved, and in what direction, when the focus is readjusted for an object 2 m from the lens?

Solution: This problem makes use of the thin lens formula

577

of optics,

$$1/p + 1/q = 1/f \qquad (1)$$

where p is the object distance, q is the image distance (lens to film distance), and f is the focal length of the camera lens. Since we want to have light energy interact with the photographic film we need a positive focal length for the camera lens so that we will get a real image. (Negative focal length lenses always yield a virtual image.)

First we need to find the image distance for the film when the object is very distant. Very distant is equivalent to an infinite distance and the reciprocal of an infinite distance is zero.

Therefore, 1/p is equal to zero and equation (1) reduces to

$$1/q_\infty = 1/f \qquad (2)$$

$$q_\infty = f = 6.0 \text{ cm.} \qquad (3)$$

Now, for an object 2 meters from the lens, substituting in (1), we get

$$\frac{1}{2m} + \frac{1}{q_2} = \frac{1}{0.06m} \qquad (4)$$

$$\frac{1}{q_2} = \frac{1}{0.06m} - \frac{1}{2m} = (16.6 - 0.5)m^{-1} = 16.1 \text{ m}^{-1} \qquad (5)$$

$$q_2 = 0.062 \text{ m} = 6.2 \text{ cm .} \qquad (6)$$

Therefore, it is necessary to move the lens 0.2 centimeters away from the film when changing from a very distant object to an object which is 2 meters from the camera.

MISCELLANEOUS
LENS COMBINATIONS

● PROBLEM 19-33

A magnifying glass with focal length 6 cm is used to view an object by a person whose smallest distance of distinct vision is 25 cm. If he holds the glass close to the eye, what is the best position of the object?

Solution: The eye by itself forms a real image of an object on the retina of the eye. This person's eye has a variable focal length lens which will transform an object at a distance of 25 centimeters from the eye to a real image on the retina. In order to improve the observation of detail we are going to place a single +6 centimeter focal length lens at the eye which will give us an enlarged image of the object; this image will then be the object at which the eye looks. `It will be a virtual image for the magnifying glass and a real object for the eye. So now we can use the thin lens equation:

$$\frac{1}{u} + \frac{1}{u'} = 1/f$$

where u is the object distance, to be determined, u' is the image distance = -25 cm, and f is the focal length = 6 cm.

So, substituting the value for u' and f into the above equation,

$$\frac{1}{u} + \frac{1}{-25} = \frac{1}{6}$$

Solving for u gives the result,

u = 4.84 cm,

and since u is positive, the object is in front of the eye and the magnifying glass.

● **PROBLEM** 19-34

The objective of a field glass, which utilizes prisms to give an erect final image, has a focal length of 24 cm. When it is used to view an object 2 m away the magnification is 3.5 . What is the focal length of the ocular? What will the magnification be for an object far away?

Solution: In the field glass, since prisms are used to invert the image, both the objective and eye lenses are converging lenses. We will choose the focusing distance such that the eye is most relaxed, which means that the final image is an infinite distance away from the field glass. This means that the object distance for the eye lens is just the focal length of the eye lens. Now the magnification of the field glass is,

$$M = \frac{\alpha_{eye}}{\alpha_{obj}} = \frac{\tan \alpha_{eye}}{\tan \alpha_{obj}} \qquad (1)$$

where the α's represent the angles respectively of final image seen by the eye through the field glass and the initial object seen by the eye without the field glass. (See the figures.) Since the angles are likely to be small we can use the approximation,

$$\tan \alpha = \alpha$$

when α is small, yielding equation (1).

From the figures,

$$\tan \alpha_{obj} = \frac{0}{u_{obj} + d} \; ; \; \tan \alpha_{eye} = I/f_{eye}$$

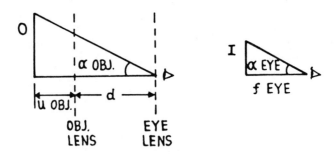

In addition,

$$\frac{I}{0} = \frac{u'_{obj}}{u_{obj}} \; ; \quad I = 0 \; \frac{u'_{obj}}{u_{obj}}$$

Then, substituting for tan α_{eye} and tan α_{obj} in (1), yields the result,

$$M = \frac{I}{0} \frac{\left(u_{obj} + d\right)}{f_{eye}}$$

and substituting for I/0,

$$M = \frac{\left(u_{obj} + d\right) u'_{obj}}{u_{obj} \, f_{eye}}$$

If $d << u_{obj} = 2$ m

then $M = \dfrac{u'_{obj}}{f_{eye}}$

$f_{eye} = u'_{obj}/M$.

Now we can use the thin lens equation to find u'_{obj} .

$$\frac{1}{u_{obj}} + \frac{1}{u'_{obj}} = 1/f_{obj}$$

$$\frac{1}{2m} + \frac{1}{u'_{obj}} = \frac{1}{.24 \text{ m}}$$

$$\frac{1}{u'_{obj}} = \left(\frac{1}{.24} - \frac{1}{2}\right) m^{-1} = (4.16 - 0.5)m^{-1} = 3.66 \text{ m}^{-1}$$

$$u'_{obj} = 0.272 \text{ m} \quad \text{and}$$

$$f_{eye} = \frac{u'_{obj}}{M} = \frac{0.272}{3.5} = 0.077 \text{ m} = 7.7 \text{ cm.}$$

For an object a large distance away,

$$M_\infty = \frac{f_{obj}}{f_{eye}} = \frac{24}{7.7} = 3.12$$

A converging lens of focal length 6 cm is used as a simple magnifier. Over what range of distances can an object be viewed and in all cases the image be seen clearly without undue eyestrain?

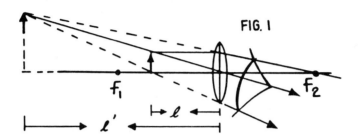

FIG. I

Solution: The apparent size of an object is determined by the size of its retinal image, which in turn depends on the angle subtended by the object at the eye. When we wish to see a small object, the object is brought close to the eye to increase the angle subtended and the retinal image. However, the eye cannot focus sharply on objects closer than the near point which is about 25 cm for an adult. Hence the eye can see an object without undue strain if it is anywhere between 25 cm and ∞.

When a converging lens is used as a magnifier, the eye looks at the virtual image formed by the magnifier, as shown in Figure 1. Assuming the eye is placed close to the magnifier, this virtual image can be viewed without undue strain if it is anywhere between 25 cm and ∞ from the magnifier. If the object is placed in the focal plane (6 cm from the lens), then the virtual image is formed at ∞. To form the virtual image at 25 cm from the lens, the object must be placed at a distance ℓ from the magnifier given by the lens formula

$$\frac{1}{\ell} + \frac{1}{\ell'} = \frac{1}{f}$$

Since ℓ' describes a virtual image and, hence, is negative, proper use of the sign convention yields,

$$\frac{1}{\ell} = \frac{1}{f} + \frac{1}{\ell'}$$

$$\ell = \frac{\ell' f}{\ell' + f} = \frac{25 \text{ cm} \times 6 \text{ cm}}{(25 + 6) \text{ cm}} = 4.84 \text{ cm}$$

Thus, an object can be viewed without undue strain if it is between 4.84 cm and 6 cm from the magnifier.

A Ramsden compound eyepiece consists of two converging lenses of the same focal length $|f|$ spaced apart a distance d, where $d = \frac{2}{3}|f|$. Show that, for relaxed-eye viewing, the object viewed (formed by the microscope or telescope objective) should be 3/8 d from the first lens.

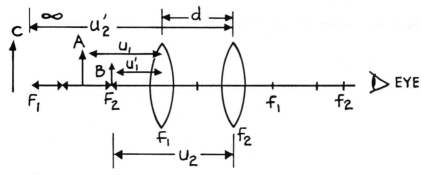

Solution: Here we shall use the principle that we can follow object-image formation successively through each optical element of an optical instrument. In the Ramsden compound eyepiece, we see from the figure that the object at A likely forms an image at B in the first lens, which is then the object for the second lens whose image will be an infinite distance from the second lens and will be a virtual image. Our eye is most relaxed when it is observing objects that are a long distance from the eye, so the "relaxed-eye viewing" tells us that the image in the second lens is an infinite distance away from the second lens.

For this problem we will start from the final image and work back to the original object using the thin lens equation,

$$\frac{1}{u} + \frac{1}{u'} = 1/f \tag{1}$$

where u is the object distance, u' is the image distance and f is the focal length of the optical element.

In the second lens,

$$\frac{1}{u_2} + \frac{1}{-\infty} = 1/f_2$$

$$u_2 = f_2 = |f|$$

From the figure we see that B should then lie to the left of the first lens and at distance f from the second lens. We see that the image formed by the first lens will then be virtual and at a distance u_1' given by

$$d - u_1' = u_2$$

$$u_1' = d - u_2 = \frac{2}{3}|f| - |f| = -|f|/3$$

from the first lens. So now we substitute in the lens equation again:

$$\frac{1}{u_1} + \left(-3/|f|\right) = 1/|f|$$

$$\frac{1}{u_1} = 4/|f| \quad ; \quad u_1 = |f|/4$$

and since
$$|f| = \frac{3d}{2} \quad ,$$

we get
$$u_1 = \frac{3d}{8} \quad .$$

An eyepiece is made of two thin lenses, each of 20 mm focal length, separated by a distance of 16 mm. Find:

(a) the equivalent focal length of the eyepiece,

(b) the distance of the focal plane from the nearer lens, and

(c) the angular magnification provided.

Solution: (a) To obtain the focal length of such a system of lenses, we note that the total transverse magnification M is given by

$$M = \frac{i_1}{\theta_1} \cdot \frac{i_2}{\theta_2} \quad ; \tag{1}$$

where the i's and θ's represent the image and object distances, respectively, and the subscripts 1 and 2 refer to the first and second lenses, respectively.

For a single equivalent lens we would have

$$M = i/\theta \quad , \tag{2}$$

where i and θ are related by the lens equation,

$$\frac{1}{\theta} + \frac{1}{i} = \frac{1}{f} \quad . \tag{3}$$

The focal length f would then be found by setting $\theta = \infty$ in equation (3) and solving for i; since this would give i = f (if $\theta = \infty$), equation (2) becomes,

$$f = \theta M \qquad (\theta \to \infty) \tag{4}$$

which, when combined with equation (1), yields,

583

$$f = \theta \, \frac{i_1}{\theta_1} \cdot \frac{i_2}{\theta_2} \qquad (\theta \to \infty) \qquad\qquad (5)$$

For incident parallel rays $(\theta \to \infty)$, θ, the object distance of the combination, and θ_1, the object distance of the first lens, are virtually equal so,

$$\frac{\theta}{\theta_1} = \mathop{\mathrm{Lim}}_{\theta \to \infty} \frac{\theta}{\theta_1} = 1$$

and thus, equation (5) can be simplified to

$$f = i_1 \, \frac{i_2}{\theta_2} \qquad (\theta, \theta_1 \to \infty) \ . \qquad\qquad (6)$$

However, if $\theta_1 = \infty$, $i_1 = f_1$, and

$$f = f_1 \, \frac{i_2}{\theta_2} \ , \qquad\qquad (7)$$

i_2 and θ_2 are related through the thin lens formula

$$\frac{1}{\theta_2} + \frac{1}{i_2} = \frac{1}{f_2} \ . \qquad (\theta_2 \text{ is virtual})$$

$$i_2 = \frac{\theta_2 \, f_2}{\theta_2 + f_2} \ ; \qquad\qquad (8)$$

θ_2 can be found since the object for the second lens is the image formed by the first lens, i.e., using $i_1 = f_1$, the object for the second lens is formed a distance f_1 from the first lens, or

$$\theta_2 = - \left(d - f_1 \right) . \qquad\qquad (9)$$

Substitution of equation (8) into equation (7) gives the following result:

$$f = \frac{f_1 \, \theta_2 \, f_2}{\theta_2 \left(\theta_2 + f_2 \right)} = \frac{f_1 \, f_2}{\theta_2 + f_2} \ .$$

Using equation (9) to eliminate θ_2 gives

$$f = \frac{f_1 f_2}{f_1 + f_2 - d} \qquad\qquad (10)$$

(Note that this is identical to the expression

$$\frac{1}{f} = \frac{1}{f_1} + \frac{1}{f_2} - \frac{d}{f_1 f_2} \qquad , \text{ which}$$

584

we have used previously to solve similar problems. The method used above is a good derivation of this relationship.)

Using $f_1 = f_2 = +20$ mm and d = 16 mm,

$$f = +16.67 \text{ mm} .$$

(b) The distance of the focal plane from the nearer (second) lens can be found from two successive applications of the general thin lens equation (3); for the first lens, setting $\theta_1 = \infty$ gives,

$$i_1 = f_1 = +20 \text{ mm} ;$$

since this image is 4 mm beyond the second lens, the object for the second lens is virtual, i.e., $\theta_2 = -4$ mm; substituting into equation (3), using $f_2 = +20$ mm ,

$$i_2 = 3.33 \text{ mm}.$$

(c) The angular magnification, or magnifying power (M.P.), of an eyepiece is given by

$$\text{M.P.} = \frac{25}{\text{equivalent focal length (in cm.)}} \qquad (11)$$

hence ,

$$\text{M.P.} = \frac{25}{1.67} = 15 .$$

● **PROBLEM** 19-38

A slide projector designed for 35-mm slides projects a picture on a screen 40 in by 60 in, 10 ft away.

What is the focal length of the lens?

Solution: A 35 mm slide is made from film which is 35 mm wide with holes in the edge so that the film will move in the camera. The final picture size resulting is approximately 23 mm by 35 mm. Therefore in this problem the 23 mm object size relates to the 40 inch image size and the 35 mm object size relates to the 60 inch image size.

Now we can use our formula for magnification

$$M = \frac{I}{0} = \frac{u'}{u} \qquad (1)$$

where I is the image size, 0 is the object size, u' is the image distance, and u is the object distance. The thin lens equation states:

$$\frac{1}{u} + \frac{1}{u'} = 1/f \qquad (2)$$

where f is the focal length of the lens.

Convert 35 mm to inches and 10 ft to inches:

(35 mm) $\left(\dfrac{1 \text{ in}}{25.4 \text{ mm}}\right) = 1.38$ inches ;

(10 ft) $\left(\dfrac{12 \text{ in}}{\text{ft}}\right) = 120$ inches.

Substituting for I and 0 in equation (1),

$$M = \dfrac{60}{1.38} = 43.54 \quad .$$

Solving equation (1) for u and substituting in values for M and u',

$$u = \dfrac{120}{43.54} = 2.75 \quad .$$

Substituting for u and u' in equation (2),

$$\dfrac{1}{2.75} + \dfrac{1}{120} = \dfrac{1}{f} \quad .$$

Solving for f,

$$f = 2.69 \text{ inches.}$$

● **PROBLEM 19-39**

A lens is used to project the image of a lantern slide on a screen located 160 ft from the projector. In this position the image on the screen is 100 times larger than the slide. If the screen is moved 100 inches closer, how far must the lantern slide be moved (relative to the lens) to keep the image on the screen in sharp focus?

Solution: The image on the screen is 100 times as large as the slide, so the magnification M = 100. The formula for magnification states

$$M = \dfrac{u'}{u}$$

where u' is the image distance and u is the object distance.

Solving for u,

$$u = \dfrac{u'}{M}$$

Substituting values with u' = 160 ft = 1920 inches

$$u = \dfrac{1920}{100} \text{ inches} = 19.20 \text{ inches.}$$

Using the thin lens equation,

$$\frac{1}{u} + \frac{1}{u'} = \frac{1}{f}$$

substituting for u and u' ,

$$\frac{1}{19.20} + \frac{1}{1920} = \frac{1}{f} \quad .$$

Solving for f gives the result that

f = 19.01 inches .

The screen is moved 100" so u' = (1920 - 100) in. = 1820 in

Using the thin lens formula again with f = 19.01 in and u' = 1820 in,

$$\frac{1}{u} + \frac{1}{1820 \text{ in.}} = \frac{1}{19.01 \text{ in.}}$$

Solving we obtain u = 19.21 in.

The slide should be moved (19.21 - 19.20) inches or, 0.01 inches further away from the lens in order to retain a sharp focus.

● **PROBLEM** 19-40

A projector for 1 inch x 1 inch lantern slides uses a projector lamp with a circular filament 0.25 inch in diameter. The condensing lens, of focal length 1 inch, forms an image of the filament which just fills a projection lens 1.25 inches in diameter. (a) Find the focal length of the projection lens. (b) How large an image of the slide will the projector produce on a screen located 25.5 ft from the slide? (c) What would be the effect on the image on the screen if half of the projection lens were covered by an opaque card?

Solution: (a) The image of the condensing lens will form the object for the projection lens; since the projection lens then uses this object to produce parallel rays, the focal length can be found from the thin lens equation,

$$\frac{1}{\theta} + \frac{1}{i} = \frac{1}{f} \quad , \tag{1}$$

if i is set equal to infinity and θ is the distance between the slide (or, equivalently, the condensing lens) and the projection lens. This distance θ can be found by applying equation (1) and the equation for transverse magnification,

$$m = \frac{-u'}{u} \quad , \tag{2}$$

where u and u' denote the object and image sizes, respectively.

$$m = -\frac{1.25}{.25} = -5, \text{ so } u' = 5u.$$

Since $\frac{u'}{u} = \frac{i}{\theta}$, $i = 5\theta$ and

substitution into equation (1), using $f = +1$ inch, gives

$$\frac{1}{\theta} + \frac{1}{5\theta} = \frac{1}{1} , \text{ or } \theta = 1.2",$$

and then $i = 6"$. Since the lantern slide is placed adjacent to the condensing lens, the object distance for the projection lens is also 6"; equation (1) applied to the projection lens then becomes

$$\frac{1}{6} + \frac{1}{\infty} = \frac{1}{f} , \text{ or } f = +6" .$$

(b) In part (a), it was determined that the object distance for the projection lens is 6 inches = 0.5 foot, hence, if the screen is 25.5 feet from the slide, it is 25 feet from the projection lens. Thus, for the projection lens $\theta = 0.5$ foot, $i = 25$ feet, and equation (2) yields

$$|m| = 50; \text{ the image of}$$

a slide 1 inch x 1 inch would be 50 inches x 50 inches.

(c) The lens diameters are chosen to fully utilize the light leaving the filament; covering half of the projection lens would reduce the intensity by one-half, but would not affect any calculations of θ, i and f made using the thin lens equation. Thus a complete image, half as bright, would be seen.

● **PROBLEM** 19-41

A small cube is placed on the axis of a symmetrical optical instrument with one pair of its faces perpendicular to the axis. Find the two places where the image of the cube will also be a cube.

Solution: In order for the image of the cube to also be a cube the transverse magnification must be equal to the longitudinal magnification. Now we have that the transverse magnification is

$$M_T = -\frac{u'}{u} \tag{1}$$

where u' is the image distance and u is the object distance. Also we have the thin lens equation

$$\frac{1}{u} + \frac{1}{u'} = 1/f \tag{2}$$

where u and u' are as above and f is the focal length of the lens system. For the front face of the cube we can write

588

$$\frac{1}{u_1} + \frac{1}{u_1'} = 1/f \tag{3}$$

and for the rear face of the cube,

$$\frac{1}{u_2} + \frac{1}{u_2'} = 1/f \tag{4}$$

By combining these two equations and with appropriate mathematical manipulations,

$$\frac{1}{u_1'} = \frac{1}{f} - \frac{1}{u_1} \tag{5}$$

$$\frac{1}{u_2'} = \frac{1}{f} - \frac{1}{u_2} \tag{6}$$

Subtracting equation (6) from equation (5),

$$\frac{1}{u_1'} - \frac{1}{u_2'} = - \frac{1}{u_1} + \frac{1}{u_2} \tag{7}$$

Combining fractions,

$$\frac{u_2' - u_1'}{u_1' u_2'} = - \frac{u_2 - u_1}{u_1 u_2} \tag{8}$$

$$\frac{u_2' - u_1'}{u_2 - u_1} = - \frac{u_1'}{u_1} \times \frac{u_2'}{u_2} = - M_{T_1} M_{T_2} = M_L \tag{9}$$

where M_L is the longitudinal magnification. If $u_2 - u_1$ is small, as the problem states, then $u_1 \cong u_2$; $u_1' \cong u_2'$; $M_{T_1} = M_{T_2}$ and

$$M_L = - M_T^2 \tag{10}$$

Therefore for a cube to remain a cube, the transverse magnification must be ±1.

● **PROBLEM** 19-42

Describe a sextant, how it functions, and explain its use.

Solution: Figure (1) shows the basic construction of a sextant. The point A contains a flat mirror and is rigidly

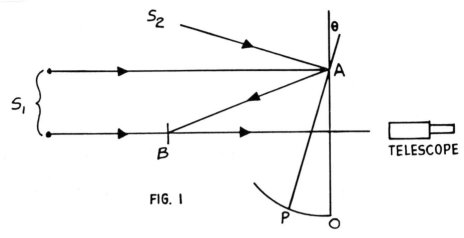

FIG. 1

attached to the arm AP which can rotate about the point A.
The arc OP is graduated in degrees such that the number appearing at 0 will be zero degrees and the number appearing
at P will be twice θ where θ is the angle which AP makes
with the vertical axis, as shown in Figure 1. The reason
for this factor of two will be explained shortly. At B is
a second flat mirror whose bottom half is silvered and whose
top half is transparent. When the arm AP is rotated so that
it coincides with AO, the flat surfaces of A and B are parallel. With AP coincident with AO, one holds the sextant
in a vertical plane and looks through the telescope at a
source S_1 on the horizon. Figure (2) shows the optical ar-

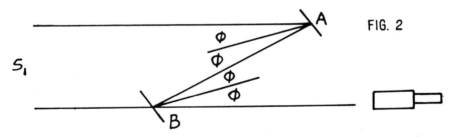

FIG. 2

rangement in this configuration. With the upper ray im-

pinging on mirror A at an angle ϕ with respect to its normal,
it is reflected at the same angle ϕ, and with mirror B parallel to mirror A, its incident angle with respect to the
normal is also ϕ so its reflected angle is ϕ and the top
ray is parallel and coincides with the bottom ray from S_1.

Since one half of mirror B is silvered and one half is

transparent, both the top and bottom rays are superimposed
in the telescope. So by this procedure, we can establish a
zero angle of θ for the horizon.

Now we change the angle θ until a second source is made
to superimpose its image by reflection in the A-B
mirror combination with the horizon image through the
transparent part of B. Figure 3 shows the optical arrangement in this configuration. We have now rotated mirror A
through an angle θ. We still want mirror B to have an incident and reflected angle ϕ, so that we will have superposition of images in the telescope. Since the normal to the

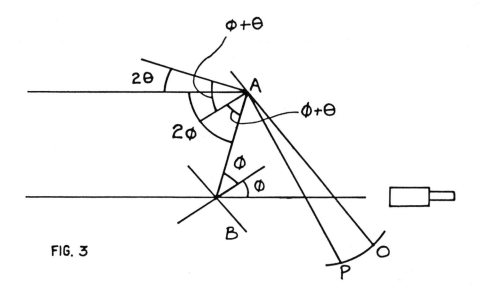

FIG. 3

mirror at A has been turned through an angle θ, the reflected angle at A with respect to the normal must now be φ + θ, if the incident angle at B is to remain φ. The incident angle at A must by laws of reflection also be φ + θ or the angle between the new source S_2 and the original source S_1 reflected in A must be 2θ. This explains why we mark the scale on the arc OP in units of 2.

Now that the operating characteristics of a sextant have been explained, what can it be used for? Suppose you are in a rowboat in the middle of a large ocean and for some reason you wish to paddle to the nearest shore. Since all you can see is ocean, there is no scientific method you can devise that will immediately tell you which way to paddle. However, by observing the positions in the sky where the sun rises and sets, it is possible to determine which direction is west and which is east. It is also possible to determine which direction is north and which is south by locating the north star in the night sky. At night, we observe the north horizon and the angle for the north star and so can determine the latitude at which we are located (south of the equator we use the southern cross). During the day, we can "shoot" the sun with our sextant at sunrise, noon and sunset and determine our longitude. With these measurements we can establish where we are. We can now paddle to the nearest land safely, using our sextant to make sure we are always heading in the proper direction.

In practice, since about 1730 when the sextant was invented, naval navigation has used sextants and star-solar tables to permit accurate determination of position and progress. With recent technological developments, including radar, satellites, electronics, inertial guidance, etc., modern navigation has become extremely sophisticated. However, sextants are probably still present on many vessels, even though they are not used to the extent they were in the past.

Find and describe the image in the following lens combinations:

(a) Simple magnifier:

Y_{obj} = 1 mm, p = 5 cm, f = 6 cm,

where Y_{obj} = the size of the object, p = the object distance, and f = the focal length of the lens.

(b) Compound microscope:

Y_{obj} = 0.01 mm, p_1 = 1.1 cm, f_1 = 1 cm, f_2 = 10 cm,
L = 18 cm, where f_1 and f_2 represent the focal lengths of
the objective and the ocular, respectively, and L denotes
the length of the microscope.

(c) Astronomical telescope:

Y_{obj} = 2.5 thousand miles, p_1 = 0.25 million miles,
f_1 = 10X miles, f_2 = X miles, 10X <<< 0.25 million miles.

(d) Opera glass (Gallilean telescope):

Y_{obj} = 2 m, p_1 = 50 m, f_1 = 0.10 m, f_2 = -0.05 m,
L = 0.05 m.

Does the image appear bigger or smaller?

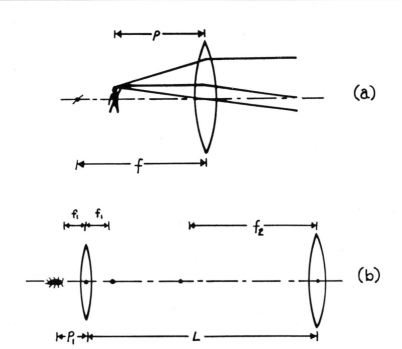

(a)

(b)

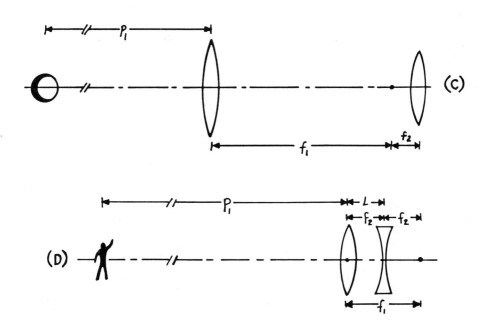

(c)

(D)

Solution: (a) For the simple magnifier, using the Gaussian lens formula

$$\frac{1}{p} + \frac{1}{q} = \frac{1}{f}$$

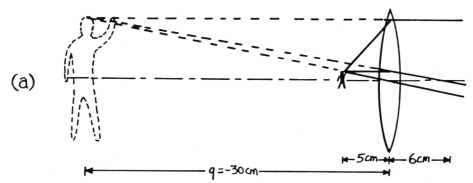

(a)

(p and q represent the object and image distances, respectively, and f represents the focal length of the lens) yields

$$\frac{1}{5 \text{ cm}} + \frac{1}{q} = \frac{1}{6 \text{ cm}}$$

So q = -30 cm. The negative solution implies that the image is virtual.

$$Y_{im} = -\left(\frac{q}{p}\right) Y_{obj} = -\left(\frac{-30}{5}\right) (1 \text{ mm}) = +6 \text{ mm (erect)}.$$

So the image is 30 cm away from the lens (on the same side as the object) and is six times as large as the original object.

(b) For the compound microscope, solving for the image distance in the Gaussian lens formula for the first lens yields

593

$$\frac{1}{q_1} = \frac{1}{f_1} - \frac{1}{p_1} = \frac{p_1 - f_1}{f_1 p_1} .$$

Therefore,

$$q_1 = \frac{f_1 \, p_1}{p_1 - f_1} = \left(\frac{1.1}{0.1}\right) \text{ cm} = +11\text{cm} \text{ (real).}$$

The size of the first image is

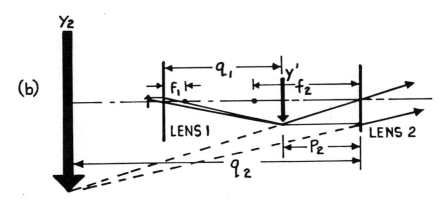

(b)

$$Y' = -\frac{11}{1.1} \,(0.01) \text{ mm} = -0.1 \text{ mm (inverted).}$$

For the second lens:

$$p_2 = L - q_1 = (18 - 11) \text{ cm} = +7 \text{ cm (real),}$$

$$q_2 = \frac{f_2 p_2}{p_2 - f_2} = \frac{-70}{3} \text{ cm} = -23.3 \text{ cm (virtual),}$$

and

$$Y_2 = -\left(\frac{-23.3}{7}\right) (-0.1 \text{ mm}) = -\frac{1}{3} \text{ mm} \quad \text{(inverted).}$$

So the final image is 23.3 cm to the left of the second lens and its size is $\frac{1}{3}$ mm, which is more than 33 times the original size of the object.

(c) For the astronomical telescope:

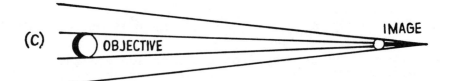

IMAGE

OBJECTIVE

$$q_1 = \frac{p_1 f_1}{p_1 - f_1} = \frac{2.5 \times 10^5 \times 10X}{2.5 \times 10^5 - 10X} = \frac{2.5 \times 10^5 \cdot X}{2.5 \times 10^4 - X}$$

594

$$= 10X \left(\frac{2.5 \times 10^4}{2.5 \times 10^4 - X} \right) = 10X \left(1 - \frac{10X}{.25 \times 10^6} \right)^{-1}$$

Using the binomial theorem,

$$(1 + x)^n = 1 + nx + \frac{n(n - 1) \, x^2}{2!} + \ldots$$

$$\cong 1 + nx \text{ for small } x \, ;$$

it is evident that $\left(1 - \dfrac{10X}{.25 \times 10^6} \right)^{-1}$

$$\cong 1 + \frac{10X}{.25 \times 10^6} \, .$$

Therefore, $q_1 \cong 10X \left(1 + \dfrac{10X}{.25 \times 10^6} \right) \, .$

Thus the first image q_1 is real.

The size, Y_1 , of the first image is

$$Y_1 = - \frac{q_1}{p_1} \cdot Y_{obj} = - \frac{2.5 \times 10^6 \cdot x \left(2.5 \times 10^3 \right)}{\left(2.5 \times 10^5 - 10X \right) \left(2.5 \times 10^5 \right)} =$$

$$\frac{- \, 2.5 \times 10^4 \, X}{\left(2.5 \times 10^5 - 10X \right)}$$

Dividing both numerator and denominator by 2.5×10^4 gives the result,

$$Y_1 = \frac{-X}{10 - \dfrac{10}{2.5 \times 10^4} X} =$$

$$\frac{-X}{10} \left(1 - \frac{X}{2.5 \times 10^4} \right)^{-1} \text{miles} \cong \frac{-X}{10} \left(1 + \frac{X}{2.5 \times 10^4} \right) \text{miles,}$$

by the binomial theorem.

Since 10X is given as being much much smaller than 2.5×10^5 miles, the term

$$\frac{X}{2.5 \times 10^4}$$

is negligible and hence, $Y_1 \cong \dfrac{-X}{10}$ miles.

Thus the first image is inverted.

The object for the second lens, $p_2 = f_2 - \left(q_1 - f_1 \right)$

595

because the image of the first lens is just inside f_2.

Therefore,

$$P_2 = \left(X - \left(10X + \frac{100X^2}{.25 \times 10^6} - 10X\right)\right) \text{ miles } =$$

$$\left(X - \frac{100X^2}{.25 \times 10^6}\right) \text{ miles}$$

The image produced by the second lens, q_2, is

$$q_2 = \frac{P_2 \cdot f_2}{P_2 - f_2} = \frac{\left(X - \frac{100X^2}{.25 \times 10^6}\right) X \text{ miles}}{X - \frac{100X^2}{.25 \times 10^6} - X} =$$

$$\left(X - .25 \times 10^4\right) \text{ miles } \cong - .25 \times 10^4 \text{ miles.}$$

Thus the image is virtual. The size of the final image, Y_{im} , is

$$Y_{im} = \frac{-q_2}{P_2} \cdot Y_1 =$$

$$- \left[\frac{- .25 \times 10^4}{X - \frac{100X^2}{.25 \times 10^6}}\right] \cdot \left(\frac{-X}{10} \text{ miles}\right)$$

$$= \frac{- .25 \times 10^3 \text{ miles}}{1 - \frac{100X}{.25 \times 10^6}}$$

$$= \left(- .25 \times 10^3\right)\left(1 - \frac{100X}{.25 \times 10^6}\right)^{-1} \text{ miles}$$

$$\cong \left(- .25 \times 10^3\right)\left(1 + \frac{100X}{.25 \times 10^6}\right) \text{ miles}$$

$$\cong - .25 \times 10^3 \text{ miles } = - 2.5 \times 10^2 \text{ miles .}$$

(d) For the opera glass: The first image, q_1 , is

$$q_1 = \frac{P_1 f_1}{P_1 - f_1} = \frac{50 (0.1)}{50 - 0.1} \text{ m } = 0.1 \left(\frac{1}{1 - \frac{0.1}{50}}\right) \text{m } \cong$$

$0.1 \left(1 + \frac{0.1}{50}\right)$ by the binomial theorem.

Then $q_1 = (0.1 + 0.0002)$ m (real),

then, the size of the first image, Y', is

$$Y' = -\frac{0.1}{50} \cdot 2 \text{ m} = -0.004 \text{ m (inverted)}.$$

Thus, the object for the second lens is at,

$$P_2 = q_1 - L = (0.05 + 0.0002) \text{ m} \left(\text{virtual, so } P_2 = -\left|P_2\right|\right);$$

the final image, q_2, is at

$$q_2 = \frac{P_2 f_2}{P_2 - f_2} = \frac{(-0.05-0.0002)(-0.05)}{(-0.05-0.0002)-(-0.05)} \text{ m} = \frac{0.0025}{-0.0002} \text{ m} = -12.5 \text{ m}$$

(virtual),

and the size of the final image, Y_{im}, is

$$Y_{im} = -\frac{-12.5}{-0.05} \cdot \frac{(-0.1)}{50} \cdot 2m = +\left(\frac{0.1}{0.1}\right) \text{ m} = 1 \text{ m (erect)}.$$

The image, 1 m high at 12.5 m distance, subtends an angle eight times as big as the object, which is 2 m high at 50 m distance. So the angular magnification is +8 and the image appears bigger.

FOURIER SPECTROSCOPY

● **PROBLEM** 19-44

Assume that the minimum illuminance in a series of square-wave targets is 40 lux throughout. If the maximum illuminance in different targets increases in steps of 20%, (i.e., 48 lux, 57.6 lux, etc.), how does the contrast increase? Calculate the contrast increase for 10 steps and plot the result. What conclusions do you draw?

Solution: Contrast is defined as

$$C = \frac{I_{max} - I_{min}}{I_{max} + I_{min}}$$

where I_{max} is the illuminance at a maximum in the interference-diffraction pattern and I_{min} is the illuminance at a minimum. In this problem, the minimum illuminance is 40 lux and the maximum illuminance increases in steps of 20%. So, for the first target,

FIG. 1

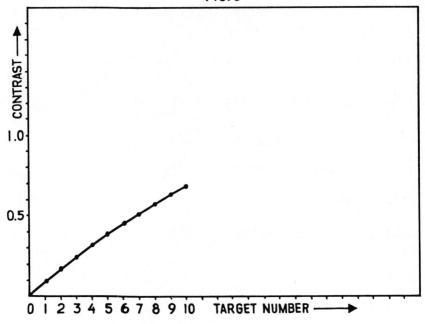

$$C_1 = \frac{48 - 40}{48 + 40} = \frac{8}{86} = 0.091$$

and for the second target,

$$C_2 = \frac{48 \times 1.2 - 40}{48 \times 1.2 + 40} = \frac{57.6 - 40}{57.6 + 40} = \frac{17.6}{97.6} = 0.18$$

and so, the following chart can be built giving I_{max} and C as functions of the target number:

target #	I_{max}	C
1	48	0.091
2	57.6	0.18
3	69.12	0.267
4	82.9	0.35
5	99.5	0.427
6	119.4	0.498
7	143.3	0.563
8	172.0	0.622
9	206.4	0.675
10	247.7	0.722

Figure 1 shows a plot of the contrast versus the number of steps.

Conclusions: (1) To get the best results, one should use the highest contrast possible.   (2) However, the curve is saturating as the target number (larger illuminance) increases.   Thus, the increase in contrast decreases as target number increases.

● **PROBLEM** 19-45

For light of 620 nm wavelength, determine (a) the linear wave number and (b) the band width, in units of wavelength, for a Fourier spectrometer which gives a resolution of $R = 0.4$ cm^{-1}.

Solution: The resolution of the spectrometer, R, is given by the following relation:

$$R = \frac{\Delta\lambda}{\lambda^2} \tag{1}$$

where $\Delta\lambda$ is the band width of the light and λ is the mean wavelength of the light. Wave number is defined as the reciprocal of the wavelength.   Hence,

$$\text{wave number} = \frac{1}{\lambda} = \frac{1}{620 \times 10^{-9} \text{ meter}} = 1.61 \times 10^6 \text{ per meter}$$

and since R is given to be 0.4 cm^{-1} = 40 m^{-1}, from equation (1),

$$\Delta\lambda = R\lambda^2 = 40\left(620 \times 10^{-9}\right)^2 \text{ m} = 1.53 \times 10^{-11} \text{ m}$$

$$= 0.153 \text{ Å} = 0.0153 \text{ nm}.$$

● **PROBLEM** 19-46

A Michelson type Fourier spectrometer is used for the analysis of yellow sodium light (λ = 589 nm).

What is the velocity of the moving mirror necessary to modulate the resulting photocurrent at a frequency of 5 kHz, and what is the modulation frequency?

Solution: A Michelson type Fourier spectrometer is shown in figure 1.   S is the source, and (1), (2) and (3) are flat mirrors.   Mirror (3) is half silvered so that the light beam is split into two equal intensity light beams, one of which proceeds to mirror (1), is reflected, and becomes beam B after transmission at mirror (3).   The remaining split beam proceeds to mirror (2), is reflected, and upon returning to mirror (3) is reflected as beam A.   D is a detector, l_1 is the optical path length from mirror (3) to mirror (1), and l_2 is the optical path length from mirror (3) to mirror (2).   At detector D, an intensity pattern dependent on the

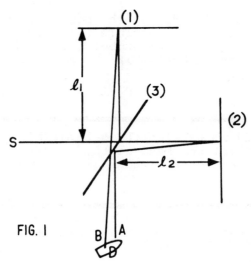

FIG. 1

difference in optical path length $2\, l_2 - 2\, l_1$ will be observed. When this difference is an integer multiple of the
source wavelength there will be a maximum and when the difference is an odd integer multiple of half a wavelength there
will be a minimum. Now mirror (2) is permitted to move with
a constant velocity parallel to the source-mirror (3)-
mirror (2) direction. Thus, the detector will have a varying
intensity pattern proportional to the velocity of mirror (2).

If Δs is chosen to represent the displacement of mirror
(2), then when $\Delta s = \lambda/2$ there will be a signal change in the
detector from one maximum to another. Consequently, the
velocity V can be written as follows:

$$V = \frac{\Delta s}{\Delta t} = \Delta s f = \frac{\lambda}{2}\, f$$

where f is the frequency of variation of the detector. Then,
substituting the given values for λ and f into the above
equation gives

$$V = \left[\frac{589 \times 10^{-9}}{2} \times 5 \times 10^{3}\right] \frac{m}{\text{sec}} = 1.47 \times 10^{-3} \text{ m/s}$$

$$= 1.47 \text{ mm/s} \ .$$

Now, since yellow sodium light is really a doublet line
with components 589 nm and 589.6 nm, there will be modulation of the basic 5 kHz signal. This modulation will be at
a much lower frequency than the 5 kHz. The modulation frequency is given by the following relation:

$$m_1 f = \frac{5 \text{ kHz}}{\sigma_1 - \sigma_2} = 5 \times 10^{3} \times 5.78 \times 10^{-4}$$

$$= 2.9 \text{ Hz}$$

The σ's are the wave numbers of the sodium doublet.

What should be the widest and the least spacing of a set
of single slits in the image plane, suitable for testing,
by transfer function, of a telescope of 10x angular magnification, aimed at a target 5 km away, consisting of bars
varying in width from 6 cm to 10 cm? Assume image distance
of 10 cm and the wavelength of light used is 5000 Å.

Solution: In Fourier Spectroscopy, we treat an object as a
"spread function". This represents the intensity pattern
over the object, the lens system as a "transfer parameter"
and the image as a "spread function" which represents the
intensity pattern over the image. Then both the convolution
theorem and fourier transforms can be used to get the relationships between each of the parts. In testing a lens
system, such as a telescope, we have access to the object
and so can specify the spread function for the object. We
also have access to the image and so can specify the spread
function for the image. The spread function of the image,
i(x), is given as follows:

$$i(x) = R \, o(x)$$

where o(x) represents the spread function for the object,
and R represents the transfer parameter which contains the
properties of the lens system.

In this problem, we have a set of bars 6 to 10 cm in
width, 5 km from a telescope of magnification 10x. Given
a perfect optical telescope, we can determine how the object
should transform to the image. Assuming that the telescope
is diffraction limited, the transfer parameter can be determined and what the ideal image will be can be indicated.
Thus, the type of slit structure which should be placed in
the image plane to extract the imperfections of the telescope can be determined.

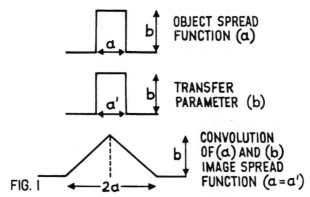

OBJECT SPREAD
FUNCTION (a)

TRANSFER
PARAMETER (b)

CONVOLUTION
OF (a) AND (b)
IMAGE SPREAD
FUNCTION (a=a')

FIG. I

Look at a simple example where the object is a spread
function, as shown in figure 1. A square object spread function convolutes with an identical transfer function (a=a')
parameter to yield a triangular image spread function. If
the transfer parameter has a width a' which is less than the
object spread function, the image spread function will appear

601

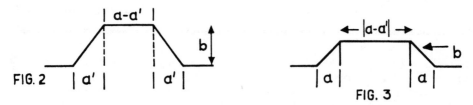

FIG. 2

FIG. 3

as in figure 2 and if a' is larger than a, it will be as in figure 3.

Since it is unlikely that a=a', it can be seen that by sampling the image spread function with a slit, the properties of the lens system can be determined. For figure 2 a range of slits (a-a') to a' is desired.

The widths of the bars on the image plane and the exit pupil of the telescope must be determined and for figure 3 a range of slits (a-a') to a is desired.

The widths of the bars on the image plane and the exit pupil of the telescope must be determined.

For a set of bars 6 to 10 cm in width, the bars of widths 10 cm will yield the smallest diffraction pattern. Thus, the width of the 10 cm bar on the image plane must be determined. The angle subtended by the 10 cm bar at the telescope will be (since θ is small, the approximation $\tan \theta \cong \theta$ is valid)

$$\tan \theta \sim \theta \cong \left(\frac{10 \text{ cm}}{5 \text{ km}}\right)\left(\frac{1 \text{ m}}{10^2 \text{ cm}}\right)\left(\frac{1 \text{ km}}{10^3 \text{ m}}\right) = \frac{10}{5 \times 10^5}$$

$$= 2 \times 10^{-5} \text{ radians.}$$

The telescope has magnification 10x, so the image angle is $10 \times 2 \times 10^{-5} = 2 \times 10^{-4}$ radians. Since the image distance is 10 cm, the width of the 10 cm bar in the image plane will be $10 \times 2 \times 10^{-4} = 2 \times 10^{-3}$ cm = 0.02 mm.

Now, consider the telescope exit pupil. Since it should be diffraction limited, the entrance pupil must correspond to the first minimum of the diffraction pattern. Hence,

$$\lambda = a \sin \theta = a \, y/R$$

where λ is the wavelength of light used, a is the width of the bar, y is the entrance aperture and R is the distance of the telescope from the bar. Therefore, the necessary entrance aperture is

$$y = \frac{\lambda R}{a} = \left(\frac{500 \times 10^{-9} \times 5 \times 10^3}{0.1}\right) \text{ m} = 25 \times 10^{-3} \text{ m}$$

$$= 2.5 \text{ cm.}$$

Now from geometric optics, the magnification can be expressed as the ratio of the diameter of the entrance

pupil to the diameter of the exit pupil.
Hence,

$$M = \frac{D_{\text{objective lens}}}{d_{\text{exit pupil}}}$$

where $D_{\text{objective}}$ is the diameter of the objective lens; M is the magnification and $d_{\text{exit pupil}}$ is the diameter of the exit pupil. Therefore,

$$d_{\text{exit pupil}} = \frac{D_{\text{obj lens}}}{M} = \frac{2 \times 2.5}{10} \text{ cm} = 5 \text{ mm} \ .$$

So, from the above discussion, there will be a convolution of a square spread function of 0.02 mm with a square transfer parameter of 5 mm.

Therefore, a slit system with spacing ranging from 0.02 mm to 5 mm is necessary.

● **PROBLEM** 19-48

Fourier spectroscopy using a Michelson interferometer is applied to (1) a source which emits monochromatic radiation, (2) a source which emits a doublet, and (3) a source whose spectrum has a gaussian profile.

In each case, describe the interferogram obtained, assuming unlimited movement of the mirror.

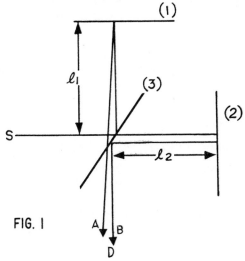

FIG. I

Solution: A Michelson type Fourier spectrometer is as shown in Figure 1, where S is the source and (1), (2) and (3) are flat mirrors. Mirror (3) is half-silvered so that the light beam is spilt into two beams of equal intensity, one of which proceeds to mirror (1), is reflected and becomes beam A after transmission at mirror (3). The remaining split beam proceeds to mirror (2), is reflected, and upon returning to mirror (3) is reflected as beam B. D is a detector, l_1 is

603

the optical path length from mirror (3) to mirror (1) and l_2 is the optical path length from mirror (3) to mirror (2). Then, at detector D an intensity pattern will be observed, dependent on the difference in optical path length, $2 l_2 - 2 l_1$. When this difference is an integer multiple of the source wavelength, there will be maximum intensity at the detector, and when the optical path difference is an odd multiple of half a wavelength, there will be a minimum. Now, permit mirror (2) to move with a constant velocity parallel to the source-mirror (3)-mirror (2) direction. Thus, the detector will then detect a varying intensity proportional to the velocity of mirror (2).

Using the Fourier Integral Theorem,

$$F(x) = \int_{-\infty}^{\infty} A(y) \, e^{-2\pi i x y} \, dy \equiv \mathcal{F}^{-1} \, (A(y)) \qquad (1)$$

$$A(y) = \int_{-\infty}^{\infty} F(x) \, e^{2\pi i x y} \, dx = \mathcal{F} \, (F(x)) \qquad (2)$$

where A and F are functions of variables x and y, respectively, $\mathcal{F}$ is the Fourier transform of F and $\mathcal{F}^{-1}$ is the inverse Fourier transform of A. The Fourier theorem is written with various multiplicative constants for normalization but for the purposes of this problem these are not important. In this problem, x will represent the wave number asssociated with the source, so that F(x) will be the intensity pattern of the source as a function of wave number. y will represent the optical path difference and A(y) will be the pattern as seen at the detector as the optical path difference $2l_2 - 2 l_1$ is varied.

(1) For a source of monochromatic radiation we can represent F(x) by the sum of two delta functions,

$$F(x) = \frac{1}{2} \left[\delta \left(x + x_o \right) + \delta \left(x - x_o \right) \right] \qquad (3)$$

where x_o is the wave number of the monochromatic radiation and x is the wave number of radiation of resonance. The delta function is defined as follows:

$$\delta(x) = \begin{cases} 0, & x \neq 0 \\ \infty, & x = 0 \end{cases} \qquad (4)$$

and

$$\int_{-\infty}^{\infty} \delta(x) \, dx = 1$$

$\delta(x)$ can also be defined as follows:

$$\delta(x) = \frac{1}{2\pi} \int_{-\infty}^{\infty} e^{-iyx} \, dy = \frac{1}{2\pi} \int_{-\infty}^{\infty} e^{iyx} \, dy \qquad (5)$$

604

From this the delta function can be considered to be the
Fourier transform of unity.

The interferogram can then be determined by using equations (2) and (3). Substituting the expression for F(x) given by
equation (3) into equation (2) yields:

$$A(y) = \frac{1}{2} \int_{-\infty}^{\infty} \left[\delta\left(x + x_o\right) + \delta\left(x - x_o\right)\right] \exp\left(i2\pi xy\right) dx$$

$$= \frac{1}{2} \left[\exp\left(i2\pi x_o y\right) + \exp\left(- i2\pi x_o y\right)\right] .$$

Using Euler's equations,

$$\exp(iz) = \cos z + i \sin z$$

and

$$\exp(-iz) = \cos z - i \sin z,$$

$$A(y) = \frac{1}{2} \left[\cos\left(2\pi x_o y\right) + i \sin\left(2\pi x_o y\right) + \right.$$

$$\left. \cos\left(2\pi x_o y\right) - i \sin\left(2\pi x_o y\right)\right] = \cos\left(2\pi x_o y\right).$$

(2) Here, a doublet will be represented as a sum of
two monochromatic sources, one with intensity α_1 and the
other with intensity α_2 . Hence,

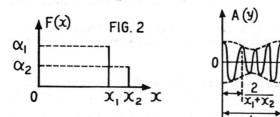

FIG. 2

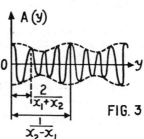

FIG. 3

$$F(x) = \frac{1}{2} \alpha_1 \left[\delta\left(x-x_1\right) + \delta\left(x+x_1\right)\right] + \frac{1}{2} \alpha_2 \left[\delta\left(x-x_2\right) + \delta\left(x+x_2\right)\right]$$

and substituting for F(x) in equation (2) gives,

$$A(y) = \frac{1}{2} \int_{-\infty}^{\infty} \left\{ \alpha_1 \left[\delta\left(x-x_1\right) + \delta\left(x+x_1\right)\right] + \alpha_2 \left[\delta\left(x-x_2\right) + \delta\left(x+x_2\right)\right]\right\}$$

$$\left[\exp\left(i2\pi xy\right) dx\right]$$

$$= \frac{\alpha_1}{2} \left[\exp\left(i2\pi x_1 y\right) + \exp\left(-i2\pi x_1 y\right)\right] + \frac{\alpha_2}{2} \left[\exp\left(i2\pi x_2 y\right) + \right.$$

$$\left. \exp\left(-i2\pi x_2 y\right)\right]$$

605

By Euler's equations,

$$A(y) = \alpha_1 \cos 2\pi x_1 y + \alpha_2 \cos 2\pi x_2 y \; .$$

Figure 2 shows the source spectrum and figure 3 shows the interferogram.

(3) A gaussian profile will have the following source pattern:

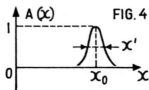

FIG. 4

$$F(x) = \exp\left[-\pi \left(\frac{x - x_o}{x'} \right)^2 \right]$$

making use of the delta function,

$$F(x) = \delta(x - x_o) \; \otimes \; \exp\left[-\pi \left(\frac{x}{x'} \right)^2 \right]$$

where x_o is the wave number at the peak of the source inten- sity, x' is the width of the intensity as shown in figure 4 and $\otimes$ represents the convolution of the two functions.

Now from the convolution theorem, the Fourier transform of $F(x)$ will be the product of the Fourier transforms of the two convoluted functions.

As has been shown in parts (1) and (2), the Fourier trans- form of the delta function yields $\cos 2\pi x_o y$. Thus, all that must be done is to find the Fourier transform of the gaussian.

$$\int_{-\infty}^{\infty} \exp\left[-\pi \left(\frac{x}{x'} \right)^2 \right] \exp(i2\pi xy)\,dx$$

Since, $e^A e^B = e^{A + B}$, this integral is equivalent to the following:

$$\int_{-\infty}^{\infty} \exp\left[\frac{-\pi}{x'^2} \left(x^2 - i2yx'^2 x \right) \right] dx$$

Completing the square of the expression $x^2 - i2yx'^2 x$, gives the result

$$x^2 - i2yx'^2 x - y^2 x'^4 + y^2 x'^4$$

or

$$\left(x - iyx'^2 \right)^2 + y^2 x'^4 \; .$$

606

Hence, the integral becomes,

$$\int_{-\infty}^{\infty} \exp\left\{\frac{-\pi}{x'^2}\left[\left(x - iyx'^2\right)^2 + y^2x'^4\right]\right\} dx$$

$$= \exp\left(-\pi y^2 x'^2\right)\int_{-\infty}^{\infty} \exp\left[\frac{-\pi}{x'^2}\left(x - iyx'^2\right)^2\right] dx \quad .$$

Now let $z^2 = \frac{\pi}{x'^2}\left(x - iyx'^2\right)^2$.

Then $z = \frac{\sqrt{\pi}}{x'}\left(x - iyx'^2\right)$

and $dz = \frac{\sqrt{\pi}}{x'} dx$.

Substituting z and dz for x and dx, the integral becomes,

$$\exp\left(-\pi y^2 x'^2\right)\int_{-\infty}^{\infty} \exp\left(-z^2\right)\frac{x'}{\sqrt{\pi}} dz$$

$$= \frac{x'}{\sqrt{\pi}}\exp\left(-\pi y^2 x'^2\right)\int_{-\infty}^{\infty} e^{-z^2} dz$$

From a table of integrals, it is found that

$$\int_{-\infty}^{\infty} e^{-z^2} dz = \sqrt{\pi} \quad .$$

Thus, the Fourier transform of the gaussian =

$$x' \exp\left(-\pi y^2 x'^2\right)$$

and hence, $A(y) = x' \cos\left(2\pi x_o y\right)\exp\left(-\pi y^2 x'^2\right)$.

Since x' is a constant, the functional relationship of the interferogram is

$$A(y) \propto \cos\left(2\pi x_o y\right)\exp\left(-\pi y^2 x'^2\right)$$

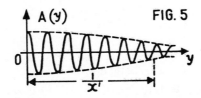

FIG. 5

This relationship is shown graphically in figure 5.

CHAPTER 20

APERTURE & FIELD OF OPTICAL INSTRUMENTS

THE ENTRANCE AND EXIT PUPILS

A point source is placed at a point on the axis 4.5 cm from a convex lens of focal length 5 cm and aperture 2 cm. Find through what distance an eye (considered as a point) may be moved in a direction at right angles to the axis, at a distance 2 cm from the lens, and in all positions see the image.

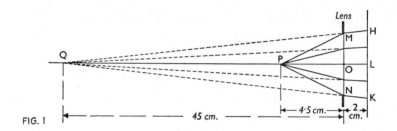

FIG. I

Solution: The position of the image may at once be calculated from the equation

$$\frac{1}{q} + \frac{1}{p} = \frac{1}{f} \, ,$$

where p and q are the object and image distances from the lens and f is the focal length of the lens. Solving this equation for $\frac{1}{q}$ and substituting in the given values p = 4.5 cm and f = 5 cm gives the result

$$\frac{1}{q} = \frac{1}{f} - \frac{1}{p} = \frac{1}{5 \text{ cm}} - \frac{1}{4.5 \text{ cm}}$$

$$= \frac{4.5 - 5}{(5)(4.5)} \text{ cm} = \frac{-.5}{22.5 \text{ cm}}$$

Hence,

$$q = \frac{-22.5}{.5} \text{ cm} = -45 \text{ cm}.$$

In Fig. 1 therefore, PO = 4.5, QO = 45, MN = 2, and the incident cone of rays leaves the lens as if coming from Q. An eye moved along the line HLK evidently can see the image Q only when between the points H and K.

Moreover, since triangles QOM and QLH are similar,

$$\frac{HL}{QL} = \frac{OM}{QO}$$

or, since QL = 45 cm + 2 cm = 47 cm,

$$OM = \frac{1}{2} \text{ (2 cm)} = 1 \text{ cm, and QO} = 45 \text{ cm,}$$

$$\frac{HL}{47} = \frac{1}{45}$$

and so,

$$HL = \frac{47}{45} \cong 1.04.$$

Hence,

HK = 2HL = 2.08 cm.

● **PROBLEM** 20-2

The diameter of a thin convex lens is 1 inch, and its focal length is 10 inches. The lens is placed midway between the eye and a plane object which is 10 inches from the eye. How much of the object is visible through the lens?

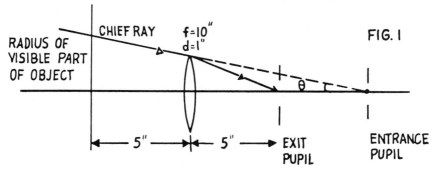

Solution: Any ray in object space that passes through the center of the entrance pupil is called a chief ray. After refraction, the chief ray also passes through the center of the exit pupil. With a single lens and the eye (also a lens), the eye will be the exit pupil. To see a large object through a small lens it is expected that it will be necessary to place the eye near the lens. Therefore, the distance from the lens to the exit pupil (the eye) will be

less than the focal length of the lens. The entrance pupil
will be the image of the exit pupil in the lens and will be
virtual. Therefore, a ray (in object space) from the extremity of the plane object, passing through the perimeter
of the lens and through the center of the entrance pupil,
as shown in figure 1, can be used as a chief ray. Now the
location of the entrance pupil can be found by making use
of the following thin lens equation:

$$\frac{1}{u} + \frac{1}{u'} = \frac{1}{f} \; ,$$

where u is the object distance, u' is the image distance
and f is the focal length of the lens.

Substituting the given values u = 5 in and f = 10 in into
this equation gives

$$\frac{1}{5} + \frac{1}{u'} = \frac{1}{10}$$

$$\frac{1}{u'} = \frac{1}{10} - \frac{1}{5} = -\frac{1}{10}$$

$$u' = -10 \text{ inches}$$

Using a chief ray from the entrance pupil to the perimeter
of the lens, it can be seen from figure 1 that

$$\tan \theta = \frac{1/2"}{10"} = \frac{1}{20}$$

However, from figure 1, it can also be seen that

$$\tan \theta = \frac{r}{15} = \frac{1}{20}$$

Thus equating the two expressions for tan θ gives

$$\frac{r}{15} = \frac{1}{20}$$

and so,

$$r = \left(\frac{1}{20}\right) (15 \text{ inches}) = \frac{3}{4} \text{ inch.}$$

Thus, the diameter of the object seen through the lens is

$$2 \left(\frac{3}{4} \text{ inches}\right) = 1.5 \text{ inches}$$

A thin convex lens of focal length 10 cm and diameter 4 cm is used as a magnifying glass. If an eye adapted for parallel rays is placed at a distance of 5 cm from the lens, what will be the diameter of the portion of the object on which the eye is focused that can be seen directly?

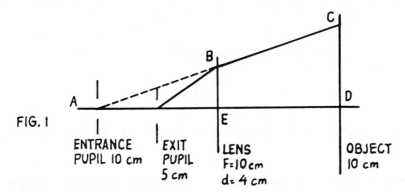

FIG. 1

ENTRANCE PUPIL 10 cm   EXIT PUPIL 5 cm   LENS F=10cm d= 4 cm   OBJECT 10 cm

Solution: If the eye is adapted for parallel rays, the object on which it is focused is at the focal point of the magnifying glass and on the side of the lens opposite to the eye.

In addition, any ray passing through the center of the entrance pupil will be refracted in such a way that it will also pass through the center of the exit pupil. In this problem, the exit pupil is the eye, so to find the location of the entrance pupil, it is necessary to find the image of the exit pupil in the lens. To accomplish this, the thin lens equation,

$$\frac{1}{u} + \frac{1}{u'} = \frac{1}{f} ,$$

where u is the object distance, u' is the image distance and f is the focal length of the lens, is used.

Substituting the given values u = 5 cm and f = 10 cm into this equation gives

$$\frac{1}{5} + \frac{1}{u'} = \frac{1}{10}$$

or

$$\frac{1}{u'} = - \frac{1}{10}$$

Hence,

u' = -10 cm.

Thus, the entrance pupil is on the same side of the lens as the eye and is 10 cm from the lens.

If a chief ray from the center of the entrance pupil to the periphery of the lens is chosen, the field of view which the eye can see will have been defined, since this chief ray will proceed after refraction by the lens from the periphery of the lens to the center of the exit pupil (the eye) (see figure 1).

It follows from the fact that the triangles ABE and ACD are similar that

$$\frac{BE}{AE} = \frac{CD}{AD}$$

BE = 4 cm, AE = 10 cm, and AD = 20 cm.   Therefore,

$$CD = \left(\frac{4}{10}\right) (20) \text{ cm} = 8 \text{ cm}.$$

Hence, the diameter of the object that can be seen directly = 8 cm.

● **PROBLEM** 20-4

A thin lens of diameter 3 cm and focal length 6 cm is used as a magnifying glass. If the lens is held 5 cm from a plane object, how far from the lens must the eye be placed if the entire area of an object 8 cm in diameter is to be seen?

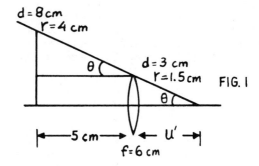

FIG. 1

Solution: Any ray in object space that passes through the center of the entrance pupil is called a chief ray. After refraction, the chief ray also passes through the center of the exit pupil. With a single lens and the eye (also a lens), the eye will be the exit pupil. To see a large object, 8 cm in diameter, through a small lens, 3 cm in diameter, with a focal length of 6 cm, it will be necessary to place the eye near the lens. Therefore, the distance between the exit pupil (the eye) and the lens will be less than the focal length of the lens. The entrance pupil will be the image of the exit pupil in the lens and will be virtual. So, a chief ray (in object space) from the extremity of the plane object, passing through the perimeter of the lens and through the center of the entrance pupil, as shown in figure 1, can be used.

From figure 1, it can be seen that

612

$$\tan \theta = \frac{4 - 1.5}{5} = 1/2$$

From figure 1, it can also be seen that

$$\tan \theta = \frac{1.5}{u'} = 1/2$$

Hence,

$$u' = 3 \text{ cm},$$

so to see all of the 8 cm diameter plane object, the entrance pupil must be 3 cm from the lens. Since this is the image in the lens of the exit pupil (the eye), the thin lens equation can be used to find the appropriate position of the eye as follows:

$$\frac{1}{u} + \frac{1}{u'} = \frac{1}{f}$$

$$\frac{1}{u} + \frac{1}{-3} = \frac{1}{6}$$

$$\frac{1}{u} = 1/2$$

$$u = 2 \text{ cm}.$$

Thus, the eye must be 2 cm or less from the lens.

● **PROBLEM** 20-5

A circular aperture 1 cm in diameter acts as an entrance pupil. The aperture is placed halfway between an extended light source and a lens of 10 cm focal length which projects an image of the light source onto a screen 14 cm away from the lens. What is the diameter of the exit pupil?

Solution: The diameter and position of the exit pupil will be the image of the entrance pupil formed by the lens. First, the thin lens equation can be used to locate the position of the exit pupil. Since the screen is a distance of 14 cm away from the lens and the lens has a focal length of 10 cm, the source location can be found. The lens equation is as follows:

$$\frac{1}{u} + \frac{1}{u'} = \frac{1}{f} \tag{1}$$

Substituting $u' = 14$ cm and $f = 10$ cm into equation (1) gives

$$\frac{1}{u} + \frac{1}{14} = \frac{1}{10}$$

$$\frac{1}{u} = \frac{1}{10} - \frac{1}{14} = \frac{1}{35}$$

$$u = 35 \text{ cm.}$$

The entrance pupil is located halfway between the source and the lens. Thus, the object distance (where the object is the entrance pupil) = 1/2 (35 cm) = 17.5 cm, and so, from equation (1),

$$\frac{1}{17.5} + \frac{1}{u'} = \frac{1}{10}$$

$$\frac{1}{u'} = \frac{1}{10} - \frac{1}{17.5} = \frac{7.5}{175}$$

$$u' = 23.33 \text{ cm.}$$

Now the size of the exit pupil can be found by equating the expressions for the magnification, m, as follows:

$$m = \frac{I}{O} = \frac{u'}{u} \tag{2}$$

where I is the image size and O is the object size.

Thus,

$$I = O \frac{u'}{u} = 1 \times \frac{23.33}{17.5} \cong 1.33 \text{ cm}$$

and so, the diameter of the exit pupil $= 1.33$ cm.

● **PROBLEM** 20-6

A cylindrical tube, 2 cm in diameter and 10 cm long, is closed at one end by a thin convex lens of focal length 4 cm. (1) If this end of the tube is pointed towards a distant object, what will be the position and diameter of the entrance pupil? (2) Where must the object be so that the lens itself might act as entrance pupil?

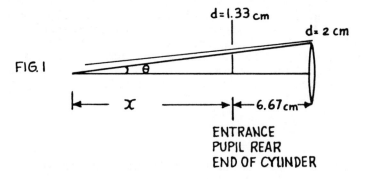

FIG. 1

d=1.33 cm

d= 2 cm

x

6.67 cm

ENTRANCE
PUPIL REAR
END OF CYLINDER

Solution: (1) The limiting aperture will be the open end of the cylinder. The entrance pupil can be found by making use of the thin lens equation,

$$\frac{1}{u} + \frac{1}{u'} = 1/f \tag{1}$$

where u is the object distance, u' is the image distance and f is the focal length of the lens.

Substituting the given values u = 10 cm and f = 4 cm into equation (1) gives

$$\frac{1}{10} + \frac{1}{u'} = \frac{1}{4}$$

$$\frac{1}{u'} = \frac{1}{4} - \frac{1}{10} = \frac{6}{40}$$

$$u' \cong 6.67 \text{ cm}.$$

Thus, the entrance pupil is located at a distance of approximately 6.7 cm in front of the lens. In addition, the magnification m of the lens can be expressed as follows:

$$m = \frac{I}{O} = u'/u \tag{2}$$

where I is the image size and O is the object size.

Given that the diameter of the object, O, is 2 cm, and that u = 10 cm, and since u' has been calculated to be 6.67 cm, equation (2) becomes

$$\frac{I}{2} = \frac{6.67}{10}$$

Solving for I gives

$$I \cong 1.33 \text{ cm}.$$

Thus, the diameter of the entrance pupil is 1.33 cm.

(2) From figure 1 it can be seen that

$$\tan \theta = \frac{1.33/2}{x} = \frac{1}{x + 6.67}$$

or cross-multiplying,

$$1.33 \ (x + 6.67) = 2x$$

$$0.67x = (1.33)(6.67)$$

$$x \cong 13.2 \text{ cm}.$$

or for the lens to act as the entrance pupil, the object must be located from a maximum distance of (13.2 + 6.7) cm = 19.9 cm down to a minimum distance of 4 cm (the focal length of the lens) from the lens. At an object distance of 4 cm, the image formed becomes virtual.

In a simple telescope, it is given that F, the focal
length of the objective, = 24 cm; f, the focal length of
the eyepiece, = 4 cm; the aperture of the objective is
equal to 2 cm; and the aperture of the eye lens is equal
to 1 cm. Find:

(a) where the eye (treated as a point) must be placed to
    see the greatest extent of a distant object;

(b) the diameter of the eye ring;

(c) the angular size of the largest object which can be
    seen, given that the eye is treated as a point and is
    located at the eye point.

Solve part (c) using (i) magnifying power, and (ii) without
using magnifying power.

Solution: (a) In this problem, it is necessary to make use
of the thin lens equation;

$$\frac{1}{u} + \frac{1}{u'} = 1/f \tag{1}$$

where u is the object distance, u' is the image distance
and f is the focal length of the lens being considered.
The magnification m is given by the following relation;

$$m = \frac{I}{O} = \frac{u'}{u} \tag{2}$$

where O and I are the object and image sizes, respectively.

      First it is necessary to find the image of the objec-
tive lens in the eyepiece. The distance from the object,
in this case the objective, to the eyepiece is equal to the
sum of the focal lengths, or 28 cm. Then substituting the
values u = 28 cm and f = 4 cm into equation (1) gives the
result

$$\frac{1}{28} + \frac{1}{u'} = \frac{1}{4}$$

$$\frac{1}{u'} = \frac{1}{4} - \frac{1}{28} = \frac{24}{4 \times 28} = \frac{3}{14} .$$

Thus,

$$u' = \frac{14}{3} \text{ cm} \cong 4.67 \text{ cm},$$

and so, in order to see the greatest extent of a distant
object, the eye should be placed at a distance of 4.67 cm
behind the eyepiece of the telescope.

(b) Solving equation (2) for I gives the result

$$I = O \left(\frac{u'}{u}\right) = (2 \text{ cm}) \left(\frac{\frac{14}{3}}{28}\right) = \frac{1}{3} \text{ cm}.$$

Thus, the diameter of the eye ring (also known as the exit pupil) is equal to 1/3 cm.

(c) (i) The entrance pupil will be located at the objective lens. Now, the limiting size can be found by examining the chief ray, which passes through the center of the entrance pupil, through the periphery of the eye lens, and thence through the center of the exit pupil. The magnification m is given by the following relation:

$$m = F/f = \frac{\tan \theta'}{\tan \theta} \tag{3}$$

where F is the focal length of the objective, f is the focal length of the eyepiece, θ is the object field angle and θ' is the image field angle. In this problem, substituting the given values F = 24 cm and f = 4 cm into equation (3) gives

$$m = F/f = 24/4 = 6$$

and since

$$\tan \theta' = \frac{\text{eyepiece diameter}}{\text{distance of eyepiece from exit pupil}}$$

$$= \frac{1 \text{ cm}}{\frac{14}{3} \text{ cm}} = \frac{3}{14},$$

from equation (3),

$$\tan \theta = \frac{\tan \theta'}{m} = \frac{3/14}{6} = \frac{1}{28}$$

or

$$\theta = \tan^{-1}\left(\frac{1}{28}\right) \cong 2.04°$$

(ii) The angular size of the largest object which can be seen is also given by the relation

$$\tan \theta_\ell = \frac{\text{eyepiece diameter}}{\text{separation of the lenses}}$$

$$= \frac{1}{28}$$

and so,

$$\theta_\ell = \tan^{-1}\left(\frac{1}{28}\right) = 2.04°,$$

as computed in part (i).

617

A camera objective of 50 mm focal length is set at aperture stop f/4. If the camera is then focused at an object 20 cm away what will the effective f-number be?

Solution: The f-number is defined as follows:

$$f\# = f/a \tag{1}$$

where f is the focal length of the lens and a is the diameter of the lens. The f-number is a measure of the intensity of light passing through the optical system and is therefore a measure of the solid angle subtended at the image. Since the aperture stop is given to be f/4, the diameter of the aperture is then

$$a = \frac{f}{f\#} = \frac{50 \text{ mm}}{4} = \frac{5 \text{ cm}}{4} = 1.25 \text{ cm}$$

Given an object distance of 20 cm, it is necessary to find the image distance. The following equation, known as the lens equation, can be used:

$$\frac{1}{u} + \frac{1}{u'} = \frac{1}{f} \tag{2}$$

where u is the object distance, u' is the image distance and f is the focal length of the lens. Substituting the given values u = 20 cm and f = 5 cm into equation (2) gives

$$\frac{1}{20} + \frac{1}{u'} = \frac{1}{5}$$

$$\frac{1}{u'} = \frac{1}{5} - \frac{1}{20} = \frac{20 - 5}{100} = \frac{15}{100} = \frac{3}{20} \; .$$

Hence, u' = 20/3 and from equation (1), the effective f number is

$$f\# = \frac{20/3}{1.25} = \frac{20/3}{5/4} = \frac{16}{3} = 5.33$$

● **PROBLEM** 20-9

The objective lens of an astronomical telescope has a focal length of 40 cm and an f-number of f/5. For parallel rays the exit pupil has a diameter of 2 cm. Find the angular magnification of the telescope and the focal length of the eyepiece.

Solution: The magnification of a telescope, M, is given by the following relation:

$$M = F/f \tag{1}$$

where F is the focal length of the objective and f is the focal length of the eyepiece. In addition, the f-number is defined as follows:

$$f\text{-number} = f/a \qquad (2)$$

where f is the focal length of the lens and a is the diameter of its aperture.

Now for the eyepiece, the exit pupil defines the aperture. Thus, substituting the given values for the f-number and for a into equation (2) gives

$$f\text{-number} = 5 = f/2 \text{ cm}$$

and so, the focal length of the eyepiece = 10 cm.

Since F is given to be 40 cm, equation (1) becomes

$$M = F/f = \frac{40}{10} = 4x$$

● **PROBLEM** 20-10

A thin lens of 50 mm focal length has a diameter of 4 cm. A stop with a circular opening of 2 cm is placed 3 cm to the left of the lens, and an axial point object is located 20 cm to the left of the stop.

1) Which of the two, the aperture stop or the lens aperture, limits the light passing through the system?

2) What is the effective f-number of the system?

3) At what distance from the lens is the exit pupil located?

Solution: To find which of the two apertures limits the light passing through the optical system it is necessary to find the tangent of the angle subtended by the aperture at the source, θ. For the aperture stop,

$$\tan \theta = \frac{2}{20} = \frac{1}{10} = 0.100.$$

For the lens,

$$\tan \theta = \frac{4}{20 + 3} = \frac{4}{23} = 0.174.$$

Therefore, since $\tan^{-1} (0.100)$ is smaller than $\tan^{-1} (0.174)$, the aperture stop will limit the light entering the optical system more than the lens aperture will.

To determine the location and size of the exit pupil, it is necessary to find the image of the aperture stop in the lens. The thin lens equation is as follows:

$$\frac{1}{u} + \frac{1}{u'} = \frac{1}{f} \qquad (1)$$

619

where u is the object distance, u' is the image distance and f is the focal length of the lens, and the expressions for the magnification m, are as follows:

$$m = \frac{I}{O} = \frac{u'}{u} \tag{2}$$

where I is the image size and O is the object size. Substituting the given values u = 3 cm and f = 50 mm = 5 cm into equation (1) gives

$$\frac{1}{3} + \frac{1}{u'} = 1/5$$

$$\frac{1}{u'} = \frac{1}{5} - \frac{1}{3} = -\frac{2}{15}$$

$$u' = -7.5 \text{ cm}$$

$$I = O\frac{u'}{u} = 2 \times \left(\frac{-7.5}{3}\right) = -5 \text{ cm.}$$

Hence, the exit pupil is 7.5 cm from the lens on the side of the aperture stop, and has a diameter of 5 cm.

The f-number is a measure of the total intensity of light arriving at the image point and therefore is a measure of the solid angle which the exit pupil subtends about the image point. Now, the diameter of the exit pupil is known, and it is necessary to find the distance of the exit pupil from the image. Substituting the given values u = 23 cm and f = 5 cm into equation (1) gives

$$\frac{1}{23} + \frac{1}{u'} = 1/5$$

$$\frac{1}{u'} = \frac{1}{5} - \frac{1}{23}$$

$$u' = 6.39 \text{ cm}$$

or then the image is located at a distance of (7.5 + 6.39) cm = 13.89 cm away from the exit pupil. The f number is defined as

$$f\# = f/a \; ,$$

where a and f denote the distance of the image from the exit pupil and the diameter of the exit pupil, respectively.

Thus, the effective f-number, f#, is given by

$$f\# = \frac{13.89}{5} \cong 2.78.$$

NUMERICAL APERTURE

An oil-immersion microscope will resolve a set of 112,000 test lines per inch, using blue light of wavelength 4500 $\overset{\circ}{A}$. Find the numerical aperture.

Solution: The numerical aperture is defined as n sin i, where n is the index of refraction of the oil-immersion microscope and i is the angle of incidence which light rays make with the apparatus. The book "Fundamentals of Optics," by Jenkins and White, states that Abbe investigated the resolving power of a microscope and determined the following relation:

$$S = \frac{\lambda}{2n \sin i} \tag{1}$$

which, using the above definition of numerical aperture, reduces to

$$S = \frac{\lambda}{2 \text{ N.A.}} \tag{2}$$

where S is the distance of resolution of the object, and λ is the wavelength of light used.

Since it is given that the microscope used in this problem can distinguish test lines of 112,000 per inch,

$$S = \frac{2.54 \times 10^{-2} \frac{\text{meter}}{\text{inch}}}{112,000 \text{ inch}^{-1}} \cong 2.27 \times 10^{-7} \text{ m,}$$

and so solving equation (2) for N.A. and substituting in the values for λ and S gives

$$\text{N.A.} = \frac{\lambda}{2S} = \frac{450 \times 10^{-9} \text{ m}}{2 \times 2.27 \times 10^{-7} \text{ m}} \cong 0.991.$$

Ultraviolet light of wavelength 2750 $\overset{\circ}{A}$, has been used in photomicrography, using quartz lenses. Assuming a numerical aperture of 0.85, what is the smallest possible distance between two points on a slide which will still enable the points to be resolved?

Solution: The linear distance Z between two just resolvable

points is given by the following relation:

$$Z = \frac{0.61 \, \lambda_o}{n \sin u} \tag{1}$$

In this equation, n is the index of refraction of the quartz lens, in object space, u is the angle which the margin of the first lens makes with the axis, and λ is the wavelength of the light used. In addition, the numerical aperture (N.A.) is defined as n sin u. Thus, equation (1) becomes

$$Z = \frac{0.61 \, \lambda_o}{N.A.} \tag{2}$$

and since λ_o and N.A. are given to be 275×10^{-9} meter and 0.85, respectively, equation (2) becomes

$$Z = \frac{0.61 \times 275 \times 10^{-9} \, m}{0.85} \cong 1.97 \times 10^{-7} \, m \, .$$

APERTURE STOP

● **PROBLEM** 20-13

Define the aperture stop of an optical system and state its location for the following optical instruments: astronomical telescope, spotting telescope, prism binocular, rifle telescope, compound microscope, Galilean telescope, magnifier, lensometer, ophthalmoscope, binocular indirect ophthalmoscope, slit lamp, and box camera.

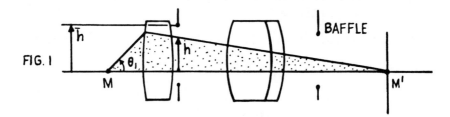

FIG. I

Solution: The aperture-stop of an optical system limits the size of the bundle of rays from a given specified point M on the optical axis. In order to determine which of the various stops constitutes the aperture stop, a single ray can be traced from M at any given slope angle θ_1 through the system. At each stop, the displacement of the ray from the axis, h, can be compared with the radius of the stop, $\bar{h}$. The stop which has the minimum ratio, $\bar{h}/h$, is the aperture stop. (See figure 1.)

Figure 2 indicates the locations of the aperture stops for
the astronomical telescope, the Galilean telescope, and
the box camera.

(a) ASTRONOMICAL TELESCOPE

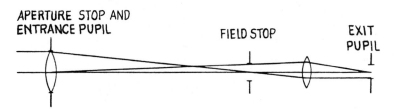

APERTURE STOP AND
ENTRANCE PUPIL   FIELD STOP   EXIT
                                                         PUPIL

(b) GALILEAN TELESCOPE

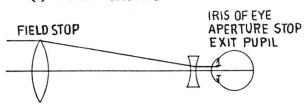

                                          IRIS OF EYE
        FIELD STOP   APERTURE STOP
                                          EXIT PUPIL

(c) BOX CAMERA

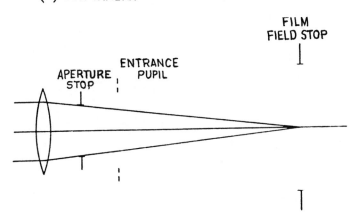

                                                 FILM
                                            FIELD STOP

                        ENTRANCE
        APERTURE   PUPIL
          STOP

FIG. 2   STOPS OF THREE COMMON INSTRUMENTS

The following table lists the location of the aperture
stop for each of the optical instruments given in this
problem.

Instrument	Location of Aperture Stop
Astronomical telescope	Objective lens or mirror
Spotting telescope	Objective lens
Prism binocular	Objective lens or observer's eye

Instrument	Location of Aperture Stop
Rifle telescope	Observer's eye
Compound microscope	Objective lens
Galilean telescope (Binocular loupe, opera glass)	Observer's eye
Magnifier	Observer's eye
Lensometer	Nosepiece aperture
Ophthalmoscope	Image of illuminating Lamp filament
Binocular indirect ophthalmoscope	Observer's eye
Slit lamp	Microscope objective
Box camera	Iris near objective

CHAPTER 21

ABERRATION

SPHERICAL ABERRATION

The radii of curvature of both faces of a thin convergent lens are equal. Show that for an object placed a distance h, equal to twice the focal length, the longitudinal spherical aberration is given by

$$\frac{h^2 \, n^2}{2f(n-1)^2} \text{ , where } h \text{ is the distance off}$$

axis and n is the index of refraction of the lens.

Solution:
$$L_s = \frac{h^2}{8f^3} \frac{1}{n(n-1)} \left[\frac{n+2}{n-1} q^2 + 4(n+1)qp + (3n+2)(n-1)P^2 + \frac{n^3}{n-1} \right] \quad (1)$$

where

$$L_s = \frac{1}{u'_h} - \frac{1}{u'_p} \quad (2)$$

$$q = \frac{r_2 + r_1}{r_2 - r_1} \text{ ; shape factor} \quad (3)$$

$$P = \frac{u' - u}{u' + u} \text{ ; position factor} \quad (4)$$

and longitudinal spherical aberration (LSA) is $u'_p - u'_h$. From (2) we have

$$L_s = \frac{u'_p - u'_h}{u'_p u'_h} = \frac{\text{LSA}}{u'_p u'_h} \quad (5)$$

$$\text{LSA} = L_s u'_p u'_h \quad (6)$$

where u'_p is the image distance from the lens of a paraxial ray; u'_h is the image distance from the lens of a marginal ray intersecting the lens at a distance h from the optical axis; f is the focal length of the thin lens; n is the index of refraction of the lens; r_2, r_1 are the radii of curvature of the lens (be careful about sign convention!); u',u are the paraxial image and object distances.

In this problem

$$r_2 = -r_1 = r$$

$$u = 2f = u'$$

as can be seen from

$$\frac{1}{2f} + \frac{1}{u'} = \frac{1}{f}$$

$$\frac{1}{u'} = \frac{1}{2f} \quad \text{or} \quad u' = 2f$$

so $q = 0$, $p = 0$ which then allows us to find

$$L_s = \frac{h^2}{8f^3} \frac{1}{n(n-1)} \left(\frac{n}{n-1}\right)^3$$

and with the approximation

$$u'_h \approx u'_p \approx 2f \quad ,$$

$$\text{LSA} = L_s u'_p u'_h = \frac{h^2 (2f)^2 n^2}{(2f)^3 (n-1)^2} = \frac{h^2 n^2}{2f(n-1)^2} \quad .$$

● **PROBLEM** 21-2

A single spherical surface of radius +10 cm. separates two media of index $n_1 = 1.0$ and $n_2 = 1.5$, respectively. Calculate   a) the longitudinal and   b) the lateral spherical aberration for parallel incident light through a zone at height $h = 2$ cm.

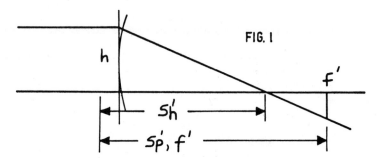

FIG. I

Solution: From a standard optics text such as "Fundamentals of Optics" by Jenkins and White, for parallel incident light we find the equation for the image distance $s_{h'}$ of a parallel incident ray of height h from the optical axis as

$$\frac{n'}{s'_h} = \frac{n'}{f'} + \frac{h^2 n^2}{2f' r^2 n'} \tag{1}$$

where n' is the index of refraction in the refracting medium, n is the index of refraction outside the refracting surface, r is the radius of the refracting surface and $1/f' = (n' - n)/n'r$. The longitudinal spherical aberration will be the difference between the value s'_h found from equation (1) and that found from a paraxial ray, s'_p which in this case will be just f' .

First let us determine f'

$$\frac{1}{f'} = \frac{n' - n}{n'r} = \frac{1.5 - 1.0}{1.5 \times 10} = \frac{.5}{15} = \frac{1}{30}$$

$$f' = 30 \text{ cm}$$

626

and then
$$s'_p = f' = 30 \text{ cm.}$$

Now let us find s'_h .

From equation (1),
$$\frac{1.5}{s'_h} = \frac{1.5}{30} + \frac{2^2(1.0)^2}{2 \times 30 \times 10^2 \times 1.5}$$

$$\frac{1}{s'_h} = \frac{1}{30} \left(1 + \frac{2^2}{2 \times 10^2 \times 1.5^2}\right)$$

$$\frac{1}{s'_h} = \frac{1}{30} \left(1 + 8.88 \times 10^{-3}\right)$$

$$s'_h = \frac{30}{1.0088} = 29.738 \text{ cm.}$$

or the longitudinal spherical aberration $s'_p - s'_h = (30 - 29.738) \text{cm} = $
.262 cm = 2.62 mm.

The lateral spherical aberration can be found from a set of similar triangles as seen in Figure 1 .

$$\frac{h}{s'_h} = \frac{\text{Lat sA}}{f' - s'_h}$$

$$\text{Lat sA} = \frac{f' - s'_h}{s'_h} h$$

$$= \text{Long sA} \frac{h}{s'_h}$$

$$= 0.262 \times 2/29.74 = 0.0176 \text{ cm} = 0.176 \text{ mm.}$$

● **PROBLEM** 21-3

The words of a road sign at a distance of 25 meters are just barely legible when viewed by a person with normal vision. If the depth of focus for letters of this size in the discrimination by the average eye at this distance is 1.20 diopters, how much uncorrected myopia could a person have and still be able to read the sign at this distance?

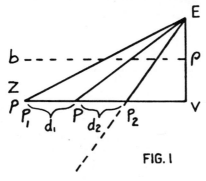

FIG. I

Solution: Let us first look at figure 1. Because of spherical aberration a point source object will not form a point image but will form a circular image with a radius of least confusion. Assuming that there is a point source at P, and due to the effects of both resolving power (proportional to aperture) and spherical aberration (proportional to aperture squared), it appears as an object with radius of least confusion z, then the points P_1 and P_2 considered also as point sources each will have a radius of z at the object point P.

In triangle P_1VE,

$$\frac{P_1 - P}{z} = \frac{P_1}{\rho}$$

with

$$d_1 = P_1 - P \quad .$$

Hence,

$$P_1 = d_1 + P$$

and so,

$$\frac{d_1}{z} = \frac{d_1 + P}{\rho} \quad . \tag{1}$$

In triangle PVE

$$\frac{P - P_2}{z} = \frac{P_2}{\rho}$$

with

$$d_2 = P - P_2 \quad .$$

$$P_2 = P - d_2$$

$$\frac{d_2}{z} = \frac{P - d_2}{\rho} \quad . \tag{2}$$

d, the "depth of focus", is given by

$$d = d_1 + d_2 = zP\left(\frac{1}{\rho - z} + \frac{1}{\rho + z}\right)$$

$$= zP\left(\frac{\rho + z + \rho - z}{\rho^2 - z^2}\right)$$

$$= 2zP\rho/(\rho^2 - z^2) \quad . \tag{3}$$

Now in optics, because many of the equations use reciprocals, we define power as the reciprocal of length, and when the length is in meters we use the unit diopters. So we can define a power of depth of focus and radius of confusion as,

$$P_d = 1/d \quad \text{and} \quad P_z = 1/z \quad .$$

Equation (3) becomes

$$P_d = \frac{P_z}{2} \frac{\rho^2 - z^2}{P\rho} \simeq \frac{P_z}{2} \rho/P \tag{4}$$

since $\rho \gg z$.

Now our road sign has in essence a set of letters whose width is equivalent to the z we have used so far and the problem states that the discrimination depth of focus for the average eye at 25 meters is 1.20 diopters. This means in our terminology the $P_z = 1.2$. Since ρ and P are the same for a set of eyes reading the road sign

$$P_d = P_z\Big/2 = 1.2/2 = 0.6 \text{ diopters}.$$

Also the road sign is 25 meters away, so it has an equivalent power of 0.04 diopters. So if the myoptic eye can provide an accomodation of 0.6 + 0.04 diopters it should just resolve the letters on the sign.

● **PROBLEM** 21-4

A thin lens of index 1.60 has radii $R_1 = +15$ cm and $R_2 = -30$ cm.

a) Determine the Coddington shape factor.
b) Determine the position factor for an object 1.2 m away.

Solution: The spherical aberration is best discussed in terms of two parameters called the Coddington Shape and Position factors. This is accomplished by expressing the reciprocal values of object and image distances in terms of shape and position factors designated by σ and π.

$$\sigma = -\frac{R_2 + R_1}{R_2 - R_1} \tag{1}$$

and

$$\pi = \frac{s' - s}{s' + s} \tag{2}$$

where s is the object distance and s' is the image distance. R_1 and R_2 are the radii of curvature of the lens. The lens equation,

$$\frac{1}{s} + \frac{1}{s'} = (n-1)\left(\frac{1}{R_1} - \frac{1}{R_2}\right) = \frac{1}{f} \tag{3}$$

where f is the focal length relates the reciprocals to the Position and Shape Factors: From equation (2),

$$\pi + 1 = \frac{s' - s + s' + s}{s' + s} = \frac{2s'}{s' + s}$$

$$\frac{\pi + 1}{2} = \frac{1}{1 + s/s'} = \frac{1}{1 + s\left(\frac{1}{f} - \frac{1}{s}\right)}$$

$$= \frac{1}{s/f}$$

$$1/s = \frac{\pi + 1}{2f}. \tag{4}$$

Substituting the values for R_1 and R_2 into equation (1), we find that

$$\sigma = -15/45 = -1/3$$

from equation (3),

$$(1.6 - 1)\left(\frac{1}{15} - \frac{1}{30}\right) = \frac{1}{f}$$

$$f = 50 \text{ cm}.$$

From equation (4)

$$\pi = \frac{2(50)}{120} - 1 = -0.167.$$

σ is a dimensionless quantity which describes the shape of the lens. The quantity π is also a dimensionless quantity and characterizes the degree to which the rays are convergent or divergent. In the first order theory, the image position is unchanged if R_1 and R_2 are changed, keeping the focal length the same. However, in higher orders even though the focal length is the same, the lenses are different depending on R_1 and R_2. The shape factor σ, n, and f then define a lens uniquely. The values of σ and π range from $-\infty$ to ∞. By varying σ and π in the design of the lens it is possible to reduce the spherical aberration to zero.

● **PROBLEM** 21-5

Explain and illustrate how a thick spherical lens can be designed to have no spherical aberration by causing the object to be virtual.

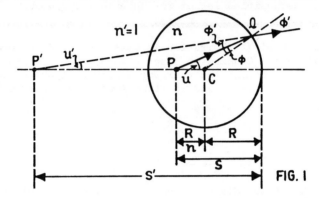

FIG. I

Solution: As a general rule, spherical aberration will be minimized if a lens is designed or used in such a way that the deviation is equally divided between the two surfaces. Spherical aberration can never be entirely eliminated from a lens having spherical surfaces, if both object and image are real. However, if the object or image is virtual, it is possible to design a (thick) lens of zero spherical aberration, for one particular pair of object and image points.

Consider a ray which originates at P, in figure 1, within a transparent sphere of radius R and index n. If the distance PC = R/n, all rays originating at P will, after refraction, appear to diverge from a point P', independent of the slope angle u of the ray. We may apply the general formulas for ray tracing. The object distance s in Fig. 1 is

$$s = - \left(R + \frac{R}{n} \right),$$

where the negative sign is introduced, since R is negative. Then

$$\frac{R + s}{R} = - \frac{1}{n},$$

and it follows that

$$\sin \phi = - \frac{1}{n} \sin u. \qquad (1)$$

In Fig. 1, n' = 1, so

$$\sin \phi' = n \sin \phi \qquad (2)$$

From Eqs. (1) and (2),

$$\sin \phi' = -\sin u,$$

$$\phi' = - u. \qquad (3)$$

then

$$u' = -\phi.$$

Therefore

$$\sin u' = -\sin \phi,$$

630

and from Eq. (1),

$$\sin u' = - \frac{1}{n} \sin \phi' .$$

Finally,

$$s' = R - R \ \frac{\sin \phi'}{- \frac{1}{n} \sin \phi'} = R + nR .$$

Since R is negative, the image lies a distance R + nR to the left of the vertex V, and is virtual. Furthermore, since the final expression for s' does not contain the angle u, all rays from P which are refracted by the surface appear to originate at P'.

A lens of this sort is frequently used as the front lens of a high-power microscope objective. Of course a real object cannot be embedded within a solid spherical lens, but it can be embedded optically by grinding away a portion of the lens and placing a drop of oil having the same index as the lens between the lens surface and the object to be examined. An objective used in this way is called an "oil immersion" objective.

● **PROBLEM** 21-6

Define and describe the different kinds of aberrations.

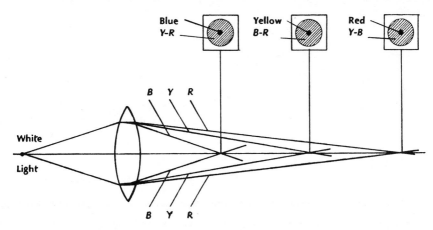

Solution: The behavior of light rays and the characteristics of optical images have been determined by the ray trace procedure and by the principle of vergence. These two procedures assume that the optical system is perfect. A perfect optical system may be defined more completely at this point as follows:

1. Every ray of a pencil of rays proceeding from a single point of the object must, after passing through the optical system, converge to or diverge from a single point of the image. This has been one of the basic assumptions preliminary to the ray trace technique.

2. If the object is a plane surface perpendicular to the axis of the optical system, the image of any point on the object must also lie in a plane perpendicular to the axis. This means that flat surfaces must be imaged as flat surfaces and, if the object is a curved surface, the curvature should be similar in the image.

3. An image must be similar to the object whether its linear dimensions are altered or not. This means that irregular magnification or minification should not occur in various parts of the image relative to the object. The image should be a symmetrical likeness of the object.

The ray trace procedure and vergence are precisely true for mono-

chromatic light, if the object and image are located on the optical axis
and the light rays are only paraxial. This means that light rays do not
fill the lens but are confined only to the area immediately adjacent to
the optical axis. Under these circumstances, the ray trace procedure
and vergence provide really satisfactory information on image characteristics and are perfectly adequate for ophthalmic application.

Lens aberrations may be defined as alterations in an image as a con-
sequence of light rays not obeying precisely the three rules describing
a perfect optical system. In other words, the image is not that predicted by the ray trace procedure and vergence and the departure of the
true image from the predicted image results from aberrations.

Aberrations result from two principal factors. The first is the
multiple wavelength nature of light. The index of refraction varies
with wavelength and therefore the power of an optical element is dependent on the wavelength, as shown in the figure. Greater refraction occurs for shorter wavelengths and therefore the focal length of the lens
is less for blue than for red light. The images obtained at different
distances from the lens on the optical axis are illustrated by the figure.
The second cause of aberrations is the spherical contour of lens surfaces.
The lens surfaces are spherical for reasons of facility in manufacture.
Precise application of Snell's law at each point on the surface of a
spherical lens followed by a large-scale precise drawing will result in
a true representation of the image. A wide variety of image abnormal-
ities will be apparent, and they may be subjected to a logical classifi-
cation as follows:

1. Aberration resulting from the multiple-wavelength nature of light:
      chromatic aberration
2. Monochromatic aberrations:
   a. Aberration occurring on the optical axis:
      spherical aberration
   b. Aberrations occurring off the optical axis:
      astigmatism   distortion
      coma   curvature of field

APLANATIC POINTS

● **PROBLEM** 21-7

Locate the conjugate aplanatic points of a spherical glass refracting
surface of radius +5 cm, if the index is 1.57.

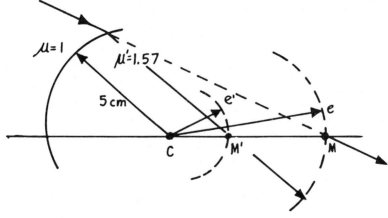

Solution: The aplanatic points of a single surface are located where

632

the two construction circles cross the axis in the figure. All rays initially travelling toward M will pass through M', and similarly all rays diverging from M' will after refraction appear to originate at M.

With C as the center and with radii $\rho' = \frac{\mu r}{\mu'}$ and $\rho = \frac{\mu' r}{\mu}$ (where $\frac{\mu'}{\mu}$ is the relative index of refraction of the refracting surface) the broken circular arcs are drawn. The aplanatic points are M and M'.

$$\rho' = \frac{5}{1.57} = 3.18$$

$$\rho = \frac{1.57(5)}{1} = 7.85$$

Hence,

$$M = r + \rho = (5 + 7.85)\text{cm} = 12.85 \text{ cm} \quad \text{along axis from vertex.}$$

and

$$M' = r + \rho' = (5 + 3.18)\text{cm} = 8.18 \text{ cm} \quad \text{along axis from vertex.}$$

● **PROBLEM** 21-8

a. Consider an aplanatic pair of points P_1, P_1' . Draw a sphere of radius S about P_1 and one of radius S' about P_1' where S and S' are the Gaussian object and image distances measured from the principal points H and H'. The ray P_1Q comes out as the ray $Q'P_1'$. Show that h' = h.

b. It is tempting to say that the principal planes are now the spheres HQ and H'Q'. But the spheres are not conjugate to each other for large θ; that is, Q' is not an approximate image of Q. Consider the expression

$$\Delta = \left[\text{O.P.L.}\left(P_2QQ'P_2'\right) - \text{O.P.L.}\left(P_2Q\right) - \text{O.P.L.}\left(Q'P_2'\right) \right]$$
$$- \left[\text{O.P.L}\left(P_1QQ'P_1'\right) - \text{O.P.L.}\left(P_1Q\right) - \text{O.P.L.}\left(Q'P_1'\right) \right]$$

which is the optical path length from Q to Q' of the virtual path $P_2QQ'P_2'$ minus the path length of the true ray $P_1QQ'P_1'$. A measure of the angular deviation of the two paths is provided by the distance x. Δ would have to be at least third order in x for Q' to be an approximate image of Q. Show that the leading term in Δ is

$$\frac{nx^2}{2S} \left[\sin^2\theta - \sin^2\theta' \right] .$$

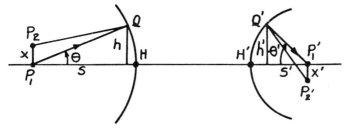

Solution: a) An aplanatic pair of points is free of spherical aberration and also coma. Now for spherical aberration we can write with

633

s the object distance, s' the image distance, and f the focal length of the lens system, the following equation:

$$\frac{1}{s} + \frac{1}{s'} = \frac{1}{f} + A$$

where A is a term correction for spherical aberration. Since there is to be no spherical aberration, we then have A = 0. So that for all angles θ and θ', the paraxial equation

$$\frac{1}{s} + \frac{1}{s'} = \frac{1}{f}$$

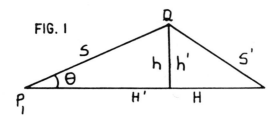

FIG. I

with s and s' now being measured from the principal points H and H' respectively. If we rearrange the distance between the principal point HH' such that the diagram is as in Figure 1, then certainly Q' must fall on Q so h must equal h', since in optical calculations one can determine the positions of H and H' numerically and measure the object distance s and the image distance s' from H and H' in all cases for an aplanatic system h = h'.

b) By the law of cosines we can write $(\overline{P_2 Q})^2$ as

$$\left(\overline{P_2 Q}\right)^2 = x^2 + s^2 - 2xs \cos(90 - \theta) = x^2 + s^2 - 2xs \sin \theta$$

and

$$\left(\overline{P_2' Q'}\right)^2 = x'^2 + s'^2 - 2x's' \cos(90 + (-\theta'))$$

$$= x'^2 + s'^2 - 2x's' \sin \theta'$$

and

$$\Delta = \left(\text{OPL}\left(P_2 QQ'P_2'\right) - \text{OPL}\left(P_1 QQ'P_1'\right) \right) - n\left(x^2 + s^2 - 2xs \sin \theta\right)^{1/2}$$

$$- n\left(x'^2 + s'^2 - 2x's' \sin \theta'\right)^{1/2} + ns + ns'$$

and factoring out s and s' we can write

$$\Delta = \left(\text{OPL}\left(P_2 QQ'P_2'\right) - \text{OPL}\left(P_1 QQ'P_1'\right) \right) - ns\left(1 + \frac{x^2}{s^2} - \frac{2x}{s} \sin \theta\right)^{1/2}$$

$$- ns'\left(1 + \frac{x'^2}{s'^2} - \frac{2x'}{s'} \sin \theta'\right)^{1/2} + ns + ns'$$

and now make use of the approximation $(1 + x)^{1/2} = 1 + \frac{1}{2} x + \dots$

to yield

$$\Delta = \left(\text{OPL}\left(P_2 QQ'P_2'\right) - \text{OPL}\left(P_1 QQ'P_1'\right) \right) - ns\left(1 + \frac{1}{2}\frac{x^2}{s^2} - \frac{x}{s} \sin \theta\right)$$

$$- ns'\left(1 + \frac{1}{2}\frac{x'^2}{s'^2} - \frac{x'}{s'} \sin \theta'\right) + ns + ns'$$

or

$$\Delta = \left(\text{OPL}\left(P_2 QQ'P_1'\right) - \text{OPL}\left(P_1 QQ'P_1'\right) \right) - \frac{nx^2}{2s} - \frac{nx'^2}{2s'} + nx \sin \theta + nx' \sin \theta'.$$

634

Now we can invoke the absence of coma which yields the Abbe sine theorem, $nx \sin \theta = nx' \sin \theta'$, but, since x' is negative the last two terms cancel and we have left

$$\Delta = \left(\text{OPL}\left(P_2 QQ'P_2'\right) - \text{OPL}\left(P_1 QQ'P_1'\right)\right) - \frac{nx^2}{2s}\left(1 + \frac{x'^2 s}{x^2 s'}\right)$$

but from the figure $h = h' = s \sin \theta = s' \sin(-\theta') = -s' \sin \theta'$ so the last term is then

$$\frac{nx^2}{2s}\left(1 - \frac{x'^2 \sin \theta'}{x^2 \sin \theta}\right)$$

and using the Abbe sine theorem again

$$\Delta = \left(\text{OPL}\left(P_2 QQ'P_2'\right) - \text{OPL}\left(P_1 QQ'P_1'\right)\right) - \frac{nx^2}{2s}\left(1 - \frac{\sin \theta}{\sin \theta'}\right) .$$

● **PROBLEM** 21-9

A given optical system has at most one pair of aplanatic points. In fact, the system gives perfect image formation only for the aplanatic pair of points and for points displaced laterally a small distance x. It will not give perfect image formation for points displaced axially a small distance z. Show that the condition for perfect image formation of P_1 onto P_1' and of P_2 onto P_2' gives this expression to first order in z:

$$n''z' \sin^2 \frac{1}{2} \theta' = nz \sin^2 \frac{1}{2} \theta$$

(Hint. Use the rays shown.)
    Except for a plane mirror, it is incompatible with the sine condition. Why?

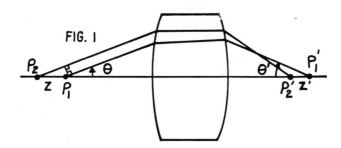

FIG. I

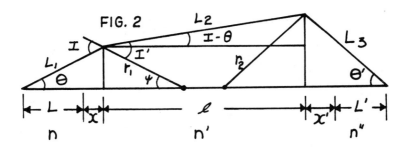

FIG. 2

Solution: From Figure 2 we can get the following relations,

$$\cos \theta = \frac{L + x}{L_1} \tag{1}$$

$$L_2 == \frac{\ell}{\cos(I - \theta)} \tag{2}$$

$$\cos \theta' = \frac{L' + x'}{L_3} \tag{3}$$

so that for P_1' to be an image of P_1, the optical path along the axis must be the same as the optical paths $L_1 + L_2 + L_3$ or

$$nL + n'x + n'\ell + n'x' + n''L' = nL_1 + n'L_2 + n''L_3$$

$$= \frac{n(L+x)}{\cos \theta} + n'\left[\frac{\ell}{\cos(I-\theta)}\right] + n''\frac{(L'+x')}{\cos \theta'} \tag{4}$$

For P_2' to be an image of P_2 we can also write

$$n(L+z) + n'x_1 + n'\ell_1 + n'x_1' + n''(L'-z) = \frac{n(L+z+x_1)}{\cos \theta} + \frac{n'\ell_1}{\cos(I_1-\theta)}$$

$$+ \frac{n''(L'-z'+x_1')}{\cos(\theta'+\psi)} \tag{5}$$

where the subscripts (1) are used for equivalent measure in Figure 2 (i.e., now $L_1 = L + z$, $L_1' = L' - z$, etc). If both P_2' and P_1' are to be image points we can investigate the conditions for this to occur by subtracting equation(4) from equation(5) which yields

$$nz - n''z' = \frac{n}{\cos \theta}(z+x_1-x) + n'\left[\frac{\ell_1}{\cos(I_1-\theta)} - \frac{\ell}{\cos(I-\theta)}\right]$$

$$+ n''\left[-\frac{L'+x'}{\cos \theta'} + \frac{(L'-z'+x_1')}{\cos(\theta'+\psi)}\right]$$

and rearranging,

$$nz\left(1 - \frac{1}{\cos \theta}\right) = n''z'\left(1 - \frac{1}{\cos(\theta'+\psi)}\right) + \frac{n}{\cos \theta}(x_1-x)$$

$$+ n'\left[\frac{\ell_1}{\cos(I_1-\theta)} - \frac{\ell}{\cos(I-\theta)}\right] - n''\left(\frac{L'+x'}{\cos \theta'} - \frac{L'+x_1'}{\cos(\theta'+\psi)}\right)$$

and some more manipulation yields

$$\frac{nz}{\cos \theta}(\cos \theta-1) = \frac{n''z'}{\cos(\theta'+\psi)}(\cos(\theta'+\psi)-1) + \frac{n}{\cos \theta}(x_1-x)$$

$$+ \frac{n'}{\cos(I_1-\theta)\cos(I-\theta)}(\ell_1\cos(I-\theta) - \ell\cos(I_1-\theta))$$

$$- \frac{n''}{\cos \theta' \cos(\theta'+\psi)}((L'+x')\cos(\theta'+\psi) - (L'+x_1')\cos \theta') .$$

Now the following approximations may be made: a) $x_1 \sim x$ second term on right goes to zero; b) $\ell_1 \cos(I - \theta) \sim \ell\cos(I_1 - \theta)$ third term on right goes to zero; c) $\psi \sim 0$; $x_1' \sim x'$ fourth term on right goes to zero leaving,

$$\frac{nz}{\cos \theta}(\cos \theta - 1) = \frac{n''z'}{\cos \theta'}(\cos \theta' - 1)$$

and by the trigonometric identity

$$\cos \theta - 1 = -2 \sin^2 \theta/2$$

$$\frac{nz \sin^2 \theta/2}{\cos \theta} = \frac{n''z' \sin^2 \theta'/2}{\cos \theta'}$$

and with a final approximation

$$\theta \sim \theta' \sim 0; \cos \theta = \cos \theta' = 1$$

$$nz \sin^2 \theta/2 = n''z' \sin^2 \theta'/2$$

Since the two pairs of points P_1, P_1' and P_2, P_2' are not both conjugate points there will be aberration including coma. The sine condition is only applicable in the absence of coma. Hence, this expression is incompatible with the sine condition.

ASTIGMATISM

Find the lengths and positions of the astigmatic line images formed by a concave mirror whose diameter is 10 cm. and whose radius of curvature is 50 cm. if the source is a point 75 cm. from the axis on a plane 125 cm. from the vertex of the mirror. Find also the astigmatic difference.

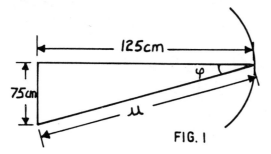

FIG. I

Solution: From an optics text, such as G.S. Monk, "Light, Principles and Experiments", we can find a derivation for astigmatic aberration which yields the equations for a mirror:

$$\frac{1}{u} + \frac{1}{u_t'} = \frac{1}{f \cos \varphi} = \frac{2}{R \cos \varphi} \tag{1}$$

$$\frac{1}{u} + \frac{1}{u_s'} = \frac{\cos \varphi}{f} = \frac{2 \cos \varphi}{R} \tag{2}$$

where u is the distance measured along a principal ray from the object to the mirror surface, u_t' is the image distance measured along the principal ray for tangential focus, u_s' is the sagittal image distance measured along the ray, φ is the angle of inclination of the principal ray and R is the radius of curvature of the mirror.

637

First observe from figure 1 that

$$u = \sqrt{75^2 + 125^2} = 145.77$$

and

$$\cos \varphi = \frac{125}{u} = \frac{125}{145.77} = 0.857493$$

$$R = 50 \text{ cm.}$$

Now solve for u'_t and u'_s:

$$\frac{1}{145.77} + \frac{1}{u'_s} = \frac{(2 \times 0.857493)}{50}$$

$$\frac{1}{u'_s} = 0.034299 - 0.0068599$$

$$\frac{1}{u'_s} = 0.027439 \qquad u'_s = 36.44 \text{ cm.}$$

$$\frac{1}{145.77} + \frac{1}{u'_t} = \frac{2}{50 \times 0.857493}$$

$$\frac{1}{u'_t} = 0.046647 - 0.0068599 = 0.03978$$

$$u'_t = 25.13 \text{ cm,}$$

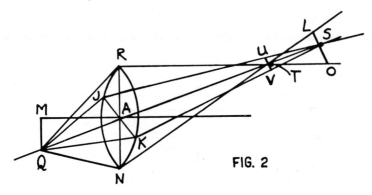

FIG. 2

and the astigmatic difference is $u'_s - u'_t = 11.31$ cm.

To find the lengths of the images formed we must do some geometric calculations based on Figure 2, where RAN is the tangential plane and JAK is the sagittal plane. In the similar triangles RTN and LTO

$$\frac{RAN}{AT} = \frac{LO}{ST}$$

or

$$\frac{10}{25.13} = \frac{LO}{11.31}$$

LO (the length of the secondary image) = 4.5 cm,

and in similar triangles JSK and USV

$$\frac{JAK}{AS} = \frac{UV}{ST} \text{ ,}$$

$$\frac{10}{36.44} = \frac{UV}{11.3}$$

UV = 3.10 cm, the length of the primary image.

● **PROBLEM** 21-11

The refracting powers of a thin astigmatic lens in its two principal sections are +3 and +5 dptr. The lens is made of glass of index 1.5. Find the radii of the two surfaces for each of the following forms: (a) Cross-cylinder (b) Sphero-cylinder (c) Plano-toric.

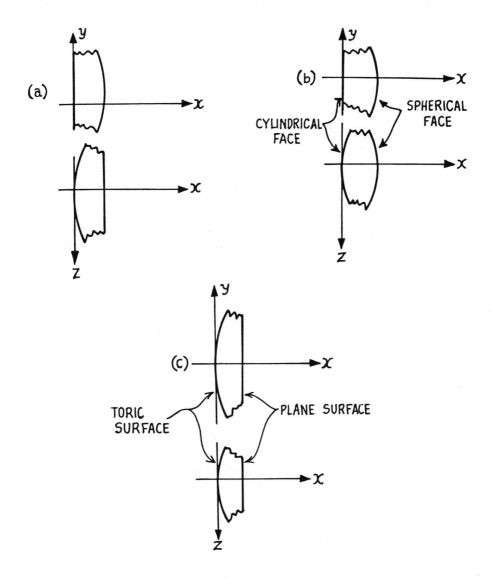

Solution: The refracting power of a spherical surface, P can be expressed as $P = \frac{\Delta\mu}{r}$, where P is expressed in diopters, $\Delta\mu = \mu'-\mu$ is the difference between the indices of refraction on opposite sides

639

of the surface, and r is the radius of curvature (in meters). $P_{y,1}$, $P_{y,2}$, and $P_{z,1}$, $P_{z,2}$ denote the refracting powers of the two surfaces of an astigmatic lens in the xy-plane and xz-plane, respectively. The total refracting power P of a thin lens is equal to the sum, P_1 and P_2 of the powers of the two surfaces of the lens, so that the refracting power in the two principal sections of an astigmatic lens is $P_y = P_{y,1} + P_{y,2}$, $P_z = P_{z,1} + P_{z,2}$.

(a)   In a cross-cylinder lens let y and z be parallel to the cylinder axes. If the cylindrical axis of the first surface of the lens is parallel to the y-axis, we have

$$P_{y,1} = P_{z,2} = 0$$

$$P_y = P_{y,2} = -(\Delta\mu)\frac{1}{r_2} \quad \text{and} \quad \Delta\mu = 0.5$$

$$P_y = 5$$

Then
$$r_2 = 10 \text{ cm.}$$

$$P_z = P_{z,1} = (\Delta\mu)\frac{1}{r_1} = 3$$

$$\frac{1}{r_1} = 6 \qquad r_1 = 16\frac{2}{3} \text{ cm}$$

(b) Sphero-cylinder: Assume that the axis of the cylindrical surface is parallel to the y-axis, and that this surface is also the first surface of the lens.   Then

$$P_{y,1} = 0 \qquad P_{y,2} = P_{z,2} = P_z$$

$$P_y = P_{y,2} = -\Delta\mu\left(\frac{1}{r_2}\right)$$

$$P_z = P_{z,1} + P_y = \Delta\mu\left(\frac{1}{r_1} - \frac{1}{r_2}\right).$$

Then,
$$P_y = -(0.5)\frac{1}{r_2} = 3$$

or
$$r_2 = 16 \ 2/3 \text{ cm,}$$

and
$$5 = \Delta\mu\left(\frac{1}{r_1} - (-6)\right) = 0.5\left(\frac{1}{r_1} + 6\right)$$

or
$$r_1 = 25 \text{ cm.}$$

(c)   We assume the 2nd face to be plane, so that

$$P_y = P_{y,1} \qquad P_{y,2} = 0$$

$$P_z = P_{z,1} \qquad P_{z,2} = 0$$

and
$$P_y = \Delta\mu\left(\frac{1}{r_1}\right) = 5$$

$$r_1 = 10 \text{ cm.}$$

$$P_z = \Delta\mu \left(\frac{1}{r_2}\right) = 3$$

$$r_2 = 16 \ 2/3 \text{ cm.}$$

● **PROBLEM** 21-12

The figure below shows the field of view of a stigmatic lens with the point in the center identifying the optic axis. Prepare two similar drawings, one for the tangential focus, the other for the radial focus and indicate how the images change at these foci in the case of extreme astigmatism .

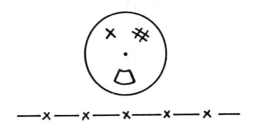

FIG.1   TANGENTIAL FOCUS

FIG.2   RADIAL FOCUS

Solution: Figure 1 shows the field of view of the astigmatic lens in the tangential focus. In this case, all object points off axis give rise to a horizontal line image, perpendicular to the tangential plane. Hence all lines running tangentially would give sharp line images, and all other lines would be blurred.

In Figure 2, we present the field of view of an astigmatic lens in the radial focus. Here all points off axis are imaged as vertical lines or radial lines. Hence, all radial lines in the object would lie sharply in focus in the radial focus and the others would be blurred. Hence, the rim and all lines parallel to it would be out of focus while radial lines would be in focus.

A large stigmatic lens has a tangential focal length of 22.4 cm. and a radial focal length of 23.2 cm. To what diameter must an iris diaphragm close to the lens be stopped down in order to produce a circle of least confusion 1 mm in diameter?

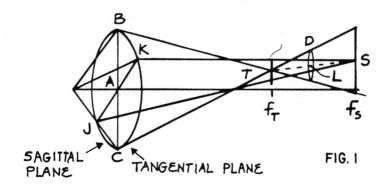

f_T f_S

SAGITTAL PLANE   C   TANGENTIAL PLANE   FIG. I

Solution: Figure 1 shows a picture of what happens in astigmatism. The tangential limiting rays will focus at T a distance f_T from the lens and the sagittal limiting rays will focus at S a distance f_S from the lens. At the tangential focus the sagittal rays will form a line and at the sagittal focus the tangential rays will form a line and at L we will have a circle of least confusion.

Now triangles BTA and DTL are similar so

$$\frac{R}{f_T} = \frac{\overline{DL}}{\overline{LT}}$$

where R is the aperture radius. Likewise triangles KAS and SDL are similar so

$$\frac{R}{f_S} = \frac{\overline{DL}}{\overline{LS}}$$

solving both for $\overline{LT}$ and $\overline{LS}$ we have

$$\overline{LT} = \frac{\overline{DL}}{R} f_T$$

$$\overline{LS} = \frac{\overline{DL}}{R} f_S$$

From the figure, it can be seen that

$$\overline{LS} + \overline{LT} = f_S - f_T$$

so

$$\overline{LS} + \overline{LT} = f_S - f_T = \frac{\overline{DL}}{R}\left(f_S + f_T\right)$$

or

$$R = \overline{DL} \ \frac{f_S + f_T}{f_S - f_T}$$

or

$$R = 1 \text{ mm} \times \frac{22.4 + 23.2}{23.2 - 22.4} = 57 \text{ mm}.$$

Hence, the diameter to which the iris diaphragm must be stopped down is

$$(2)(57 \text{ mm}) = 114 \text{ mm.}$$

● **PROBLEM** 21-14

A lens 70 mm in diameter may have a tangential focal length of 16.7 cm, and a radial focal length of 18.5 cm. Find the position of the circle of least confusion.

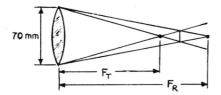

Solution: The circle of least confusion, which is also known as the interval of Sturm, is located at the "dioptric midpoint" of the tangental and radial focal lengths. To find its position we must first change the focal lengths into refractive powers,

$$P_T = \frac{1}{f_T} = \frac{1}{16.7 \text{ cm}} = \frac{1}{0.167 \text{ m}} = 6.0 \text{ m}^{-1}$$

$$P_R = \frac{1}{f_R} = \frac{1}{18.5 \text{ cm}} = \frac{1}{0.185 \text{ m}} = 5.4 \text{ m}^{-1} .$$

The "dioptric midpoint" is found by taking the reciprocal of the average of the refractive powers, which is as follows:

$$\frac{1}{\frac{1}{2}(P_T + P_R)} = \frac{1}{\frac{1}{2}(6.0\text{m}^{-1} + 5.4\text{m}^{-1})} = 0.175 \text{ m} = 17.5 \text{ cm.}$$

So, the circle of least confusion is located 17.5 cm to the right of the lens, which is slightly closer to the tangential focal point.
The diameter d, of the circle of least confusion can be found by using similar triangles:

$$\frac{70 \text{ mm}}{16.7} = \frac{d}{17.5-16.7} ,$$

$$d = 3.35 \text{ mm.}$$

● **PROBLEM** 21-15

(a) The radii and thickness of a meniscus lens made of glass of index 1.51 and surrounded by air are: $r_1 = -10$, $r_2 = -8.4$, d = +1. The lens is provided with a front stop with its center at a distance equal to 1 from the vertex of the surface. The chief ray coming from an infinitely distant point drosses the axis at an angle of 35°.
Find the astigmatic difference along this ray.

(b) Now, suppose the thickness of the lens is changed to d = +1.5 everything else remaining the same as before. Find the astigmatic difference now.

(c) Working with the original data of part (**a**), suppose the stop is
5 times as far away, everything else remaining the same as before.
What is the astigmatic difference now?

(d) Now, once again starting with the original data, suppose the index
of the glass is changed to 1.61, everything else remaining the same as
before. What is the astigmatic difference now?

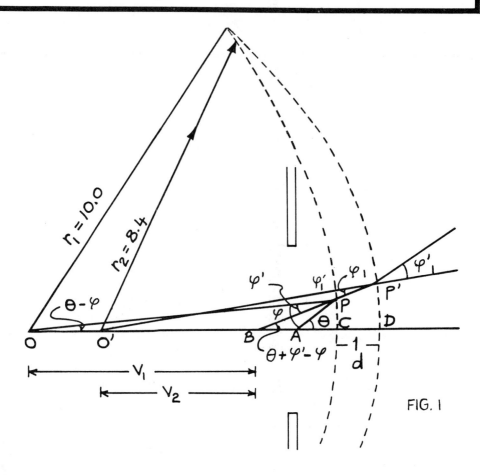

FIG. I

Solution: The solutions to parts (a), (b), (c),and (d) of this problem
will be presented together, as the background derivations for each of
them are the same. Problems in aberration are not generally amenable to
algebraic-geometric manipulations which result in a concise resultant
equation but are best completed by a long laborious string of calculations. With current access to a computer or a small calculator with
high accuracy sine and cosine tables, much better optical designs are
now possible than in "olden times" when logarithmic tables and adding
machines were the only help available to the designer.

     So let us look at the geometry of figure 1. A ray at an angle θ to
the optical axis and crossing the optical axis at A, the location of
the front stop, proceeds to P, the intersection of the first surface
of the lens. Here it is refracted and proceeds to P', the intersection
with the second surface of the lens, and is further refracted.

     We wish to first consider the triangle OPA, where O is the center
of curvature of the first surface. Side OP has magnitude of length
r_1 (r_1 is the radius of curvature of the first surface); side OA
has magnitude of length $(r_1 - \ell_1)$ (ℓ_1 is the distance of the stop from

644

the vertex of the first surface). Angle OPA is the angle of incidence (φ) at the first surface; angle $OAP = 180 - \theta$, θ is the angle of inclination of the incoming ray to the optical axis; and angle POA is $\theta - \varphi$.

By the law of sines,

$$\frac{\sin(\theta - \varphi)}{\overline{AP}} = \frac{\sin \varphi}{r_1 - \ell_1} = \frac{\sin(180 - \theta)}{r_1} = \frac{\sin \theta}{r_1} \tag{1}$$

By Snell's law of refraction the angle of refraction, φ', at the first surface can be found

$$\sin \varphi' = 1/n' \sin \varphi \tag{2}$$

Now we shift to the triangle OPB, where the angle OPB is the refraction angle, φ', the angle PBA is $\theta + \varphi' - \varphi$. Again by the law of sines

$$\frac{\sin(\theta - \varphi)}{\overline{PB}} = \frac{\sin \varphi'}{v_1} = \frac{\sin(\theta + \varphi' - \varphi)}{r_1} \tag{3}$$

or

$$v_1 = \frac{r_1 \sin \varphi'}{\sin(\theta + \varphi' - \varphi)} \tag{4}$$

Now we shift to the triangle O'P'B, where angle O'P'B is the incident angle, φ_1, at the second surface, v_2 is the length O'B and the radius of curvature of the second surface is r_2 and its center is at O'. Again the law of sines yields

$$\frac{\sin \varphi_1}{v_2} \quad \frac{\sin(\theta + \varphi' - \varphi)}{r_2} \tag{5}$$

and by Snell's law, with φ_1' being the angle of refraction at the second surface we obtain

$$\sin \varphi_1' = n' \sin \varphi_1 \tag{6}$$

In a derivation, related to astigmatism (Monk Light: Principles and Experiments or Jenkins and White) the following two equations can be found for a single spherical surface:

$$\frac{n_0}{s_0} + \frac{n'}{s_{is}} = \frac{n'\cos \varphi' - n \cos \varphi}{r} \tag{7}$$

and

$$\frac{n}{s_0} + \frac{n' \cos^2 \varphi'}{s_{it}} = \frac{n'\cos \varphi' - n \cos \varphi}{r} \tag{8}$$

where s_0 is the object distance along the ray; s_{is} is the image distance along the ray for the sagittal focus; s_{it} is the image distance along the ray for the tangential focus; n is the index of refraction in object space, n' is the index of refraction in image space; φ is the angle of incidence at the surface, φ' is the angle of refraction; and r is the radius of curvature of the spherical surface.

So our plan is to determine from equations (1), (2), (4), (5) and (6) the angles needed in equations (7) and (8) twice, once for each of the surfaces.

a. s_0 for the first surface is infinite, so $1/s_0 = 0$.

b. n is in air, so n = 1.0.

c. s_0 for the second surface differs from s_i for the first
surface by d, the thickness of the lens.

We will now build a table for our calculations, from which hopefully
from what has been said so far, you will be able to follow the progress
of the calculations. The numbers inserted in the table have been
rounded off to four places, for convenience in the table, and are the
results obtained from a computer calculation and agree with those
numbers obtained from a hand held calculator.

	(a)	(b)	(c)	(d)
θ	35°	35°	35°	35°
r_1	-10	-10	-10	-10
r_2	-8.4	-8.4	-8.4	-8.4
ℓ_1	1	1	5	1
n'	1.51	1.51	1.51	1.61
d	1	1.5	1	1
$\sin\varphi = \dfrac{r_1 - \ell_1}{r_1}\sin\theta$	0.5162	0.5162	.2868	.5162
φ	31.08°	31.08°	16.67°	31.08°
$\sin\varphi' = \dfrac{1}{n'}\sin\varphi$	0.3419	0.3419	.1899	0.3206
φ'	19.99°	19.99°	10.95°	18.70°
$\theta' = \theta + \varphi' - \varphi$	23.91°	23.91°	29.28°	22.62°
$\sin\theta'$	0.4053	0.4053	0.4891	0.3847
$v_1 = \dfrac{\sin\varphi'}{\sin\theta'}, r_1$	8.434	8.434	3.883	8.336
$\ell_2 = 00'$	2.6	3.1	2.6	2.6
$v_2 = v_1 - \ell_2$	5.834	5.334	1.283	5.736
$\sin\varphi_1 = \dfrac{v_2 \sin\theta'}{r_2}$	0.2815	0.2574	0.07471	0.2626
φ_1	16.35°	14.92°	4.284°	15.23°
$\sin\varphi_1' = n'\sin\varphi_1$	0.4251	0.3886	0.1128	0.4228
φ_1'	25.16°	22.87°	6.477°	25.02°
$\cos\varphi$	0.8565	0.8565	0.9580	0.8565
$\cos\varphi'$	0.9397	0.9397	0.9818	0.9472
$\cos\varphi_1$	0.9596	0.9663	0.9972	0.9649

	(a)	(b)	(c)	(d)
$\cos\varphi_1'$	0.9051	0.9214	0.9936	0.9062
$\dfrac{n'\cos\varphi'-\cos\varphi}{r_1}$	-0.5626×10^{-1}	-0.5626×10^{-1}	-0.5245×10^{-1}	-0.6685×10^{-1}
$n'\cos^2\varphi'$	1.334	1.334	1.456	1.444
$s_{1_t}' = \dfrac{n'\cos^2\varphi'}{\frac{n'\cos\varphi'-\cos\varphi}{r_1}}$	-23.70	-23.70	-27.75	-21.61
$s_{1_s}' = \dfrac{n'r_1}{n'\cos\varphi'-\cos\varphi}$	-26.84	-26.84	-28.79	-24.08
$s_{2t} = -s_{1t}'+d$	24.70	25.20	28.75	22.61
$s_{2s} = -s_{1s}' + d$	27.84	28.34	29.79	25.08
$n'\cos^2\varphi_1/s_{2t}$	0.5628×10^{-1}	0.5594×10^{-1}	0.5223×10^{-1}	0.6631×10^{-1}
n'/s_{2s}	0.5424×10^{-1}	0.5328×10^{-1}	0.5069×10^{-1}	0.6419×10^{-1}
$(\cos\varphi_1'-n'\cos\varphi)/r_2$	0.6474×10^{-1}	0.6402×10^{-1}	0.6097×10^{-1}	0.7706×10^{-1}
$\left\{ \dfrac{(\cos\varphi_1'-n'\cos\varphi)/r_2}{} - \dfrac{n'\cos^2\varphi'}{s_{2t}} = \Delta_t \right.$	0.8457×10^{-2}	0.8076×10^{-2}	0.8743×10^{-2}	0.1075×10^{-1}
$\left\{ \dfrac{(\cos^2\varphi_1'-n'\cos\varphi)/r_2}{} - n'/s_{2s} = \Delta_s \right.$	0.1050×10^{-1}	0.1074×10^{-1}	0.1028×10^{-1}	0.1287×10^{-1}
$s_{2t}' = \cos^2\varphi_1'/\Delta_t$	96.87	105.1	112.9	76.38
$s_{2s}' = 1/\Delta_s$	95.24	93.13	97.27	77.71
Astigmatic difference $= s_{2s}'-s_{2t}'$	-1.634	-11.99	-15.65	+1.331

n	AD	Angle	AD
stop at 0.9704			
1.31	-24.77	34.9	-1.576
1.41	-7.926	35.0	-1.635
1.51	-1.306	35.1	-1.694
1.56	0.4256		
1.61	1.591		

The computer calculates following set of astigmatic differences vs. various changes in parameters. You may want to incorporate this with the solutions as that really is what this problem was trying to demonstrate.

As you can see, a change in location of the stop by 3% changes AD by about 30%. A change of angle by 3% changes AD by about 6 parts/163.

Location of stop	AD	stop	AD
.84	+.1708	5.2	-14.90
.85	$+.562 \times 10^{-1}$	5.3	-14.49
.86	$-.582 \times 10^{-1}$	5.4	-14.05
.87	-.1723		
.88	-.2866		
.89	-.4004		
.90	-.5139		
.95	-1.078		
.96	-1.189		
.97	-1.301		
.9704	-1.306		
.98	-1.412		
.99	-1.523		
1.0	-1.635		
1.1	-2.727		
1.2	-3.790		
1.3	-4.823		
1.4	-5.822		
4.5	-17.10		

648

Location of stop	AD	stop	AD
4.6	-16.87		
4.7	-16.61		
4.8	-16.31		
4.9	-16.00		
5.0	-15.65		
5.1	-15.29		

REFRACTION BY A CURVED SURFACE

● **PROBLEM** 21-16

Using the refractive indices listed below consider a plano-convex lens made of flint glass and having a radius of curvature of +20 cm. Find the focal lengths of the lens for blue and red light.

Fraunhofer line	Color	Wavelength (nm)	Refractive Index Crown	Flint
F	Blue	486.1	1.52225	1.71748
D	Yellow	589.6	1.51666	1.70100
C	Red	656.3	1.51418	1.69427

Solution: When the index of refraction and the radius of curvature for each surface of a lens is known, the focal length of the lens can be found by applying the equation,

$$\frac{1}{f} = \left(n_L - 1\right)\cdot\left[\frac{1}{R_1} - \frac{1}{R_2}\right]$$ (1)

where n_L is the index of refraction of the lens, R_1 is the radius of curvature of one surface, and R_2 is the radius of curvature of the other surface.

For the lens described in this problem, $R_1 = 20$ cm. and $R_2 = \infty$. For the blue light, the index is 1.71748 and equation (1) becomes,

$$\frac{1}{f} = (1.71748 - 1)\cdot\left[\frac{1}{20 \text{ cm}} - \frac{1}{\infty}\right]$$

from which the focal length, f = 27.9 cm. For red light, the index is 1.69427 and we have,

$$\frac{1}{f} = (1.69427 - 1)\cdot\left[\frac{1}{20 \text{ cm}} - \frac{1}{\infty}\right]$$

from which f = 28.8 cm. Therefore, the focal lengths of the lens for blue and red light are 27.9 cm and 28.8 cm, respectively.

The principal refracting powers of a thin lens are +4 and -5 dptr. If the refracting power in an oblique normal section is +2 dptr, what will be its refracting power in a normal section at right angle to the first? What is the angle of inclination of the +2 section to the +4 section?

Solution: There is a geometric relationship between the curvature of any normal section of a curved refracting surface and the curvatures of the principal sections of the surface at this point. This relationship is $R_\theta = R_y \cos^2\theta + R_z \sin^2\theta$ where $R = 1/r$, and where θ denotes the angle which the normal section makes with the xy plane. The principal curvatures are R_y and R_z respectively. In a normal section at right angles to the first,

$$R_{\theta + 90°} = R_y \cos^2(\theta + 90°) + R_z \sin^2(\theta + 90°)$$

$$= R_y \sin^2\theta + R_z \cos^2\theta$$

Thus,

$$R_\theta + R_{\theta+90°} = R_y + R_z .$$

But $P_y = (\Delta\mu) R_y$ and $P_z = (\Delta\mu) R_z$ and $P_\theta = (\Delta\mu) R_\theta$

From which $P_\theta + P_{\theta+90°} = P_y + P_z$

Given that $P_\theta = 2$, $P_y = 4$, $P_z = -5$ dptrs.

Then, $P_{\theta+90°} = (4 - 5 - 2) = -3$ dptrs.

$$P_\theta = P_y \cos^2\theta + P_z \sin^2\theta$$

$$2 = 4 \cos^2\theta + (-5)(1 - \cos^2\theta)$$

$$7 = 9 \cos^2\theta , \qquad \theta = 28.1255°$$

or $\theta = 28°\ 7'\ 32''.$

A curved refracting surface separates air and glass (relative index 1.5), and the radii of greatest and least curvature at a point A on the surface are $r_y = +10$ cm and $r_z = +5$ cm. Find the interval between the two principal image points corresponding to an object point lying on the normal to the surface at A in front of the surface and at a distance of 30 cm from it.

Solution: Gauss' formula for refraction at a refracting surface states that

$$\frac{\mu_1}{0} + \frac{\mu_2}{i} = \frac{\mu_2 - \mu_1}{R}$$

Here, μ_1 (the index of refraction of air) = 1.0

μ_2 (the index of refraction of glass) $= 1.5$

O (the object distance) $= 30$ cm

$\quad r_y = 10$ cm, and $r_z = 5$ cm.

$$\frac{1}{30} + \frac{1.5}{i_y} = \frac{0.5}{10} \; ; \; i_y = \frac{1.5 \text{ cm}}{\frac{0.5}{10} - \frac{1}{30}} = \frac{1.5 \text{ cm}}{\frac{1}{60}} = (60)(1.5) \text{ cm} = 90 \text{ cm}, \quad \text{and}$$

$$\frac{1}{30} + \frac{1.5}{i_z} = \frac{0.5}{5} \; ; \; i_z = \frac{1.5 \text{ cm}}{\frac{0.5}{5} - \frac{1}{30}} = \frac{(1.5)(30)\text{cm}}{2} = 22.5 \text{ cm}.$$

Hence, the desired result is

$$i_y - i_z = 67.5 \text{ cm}.$$

CHAPTER 22

THE PRISM

THE ANGLE OF MINIMUM DEVIATION

● PROBLEM 22-1

Prove that the deflection angle δ of a prism is a minimum
for symmetrical ray paths.

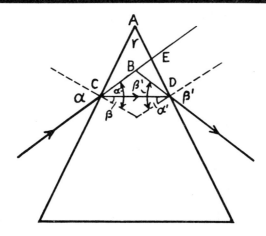

Solution: Applied to the front and rear surfaces of the
prism shown in the figure, the law of refraction requires
that

$$\frac{\sin \alpha}{\sin \beta} = n \quad \text{and} \quad \frac{\sin \alpha'}{\sin \beta'} = n' \tag{1}$$

where n and n' are the indices of refraction of the front
and rear surfaces of the prism, respectively, and where
n' = 1/n if both surfaces border on air. From the sum of
the angles in the triangle formed by the prism faces and
the interior ray, it follows that

$$\gamma = \beta + \alpha'. \tag{2}$$

The total deflection, δ, is found as follows: angle CBD =
180° - δ since a straight line is composed of 180 degrees.
Since the sum of the angles of a triangle = 180°, angle

652

BCD + angle CDB + 180° − δ = 180°. Angle BCD = α − β and angle CDB = β' − α'. Hence, α − β + β' − α' + 180° − δ = 180°, and so,

$$\delta = \alpha - \beta + \beta' - \alpha'. \tag{3}$$

Substituting for −β − α' from equation (2), equation (3) becomes

$$\delta = \alpha + \beta' - \gamma \tag{4}$$

Substituting in equation (1) for β (from equation (2)) and β' (from equation (4)) gives

$$\frac{\sin \alpha}{\sin (\gamma - \alpha')} = n \text{ and } \frac{\sin \alpha'}{\sin (\delta + \gamma - \alpha)} = n' = \frac{1}{n} \tag{5}.$$

By eliminating α', δ can be represented as a function of α. Differentiating equation (5) with respect to α (before eliminating α') gives the following conditions for the minimum deflection dδ = 0:

$$\cos \alpha \, d\alpha + n \cos (\gamma - \alpha') \, d\alpha' = 0. \tag{6}$$

$$n \cos \alpha' \, d\alpha' + \cos (\delta + \gamma - \alpha) \, d\alpha = 0. \tag{7}$$

dα = dα'; hence, equations (6) and (7) become

$$\cos \alpha + n \cos (\gamma - \alpha') = 0. \tag{8}$$

and $n \cos \alpha' + \cos (\delta + \gamma - \alpha) = 0.$ (9)

Subtracting equation (9) from equation (8) gives

$$\cos \alpha - n \cos \alpha' + n \cos (\gamma - \alpha')$$
$$- \cos (\delta + \gamma - \alpha) = 0 \tag{10}$$

Equation (10) is satisfied when

$$n \cos (\gamma - \alpha') = n \cos \alpha' \tag{11}$$

and $\cos \alpha = \cos (\delta + \gamma - \alpha).$ (12)

Solving equations (11) and (12) gives

$$\alpha' = \gamma - \alpha' \text{ or } \alpha' = \frac{\gamma}{2}$$

and α = δ + γ − α   or α = (δ + γ)/2.

Substituting for γ in equation (2) gives

$$\gamma = 2\alpha' = \beta + \alpha'; \text{ hence, } \alpha' = \beta.$$

From equation (4), δ + γ = α + β'.

Since α = (δ + γ)/2, δ + γ = 2α and so,

2α = α + β' or β' = α.

Hence, if the ray is symmetrical with respect to the bisector plane of the prism angle, one obtains by substitution into the first of the equations (1) the following equation, which is used in the determination of n:

$$n = \sin\left[\frac{1}{2}(\delta + \gamma)\right] \Big/ \sin\left[\frac{1}{2}\gamma\right]$$

From equation (3), $\delta = \alpha - \beta + \beta' - \alpha' = 2\alpha - 2\alpha'$
Hence,

$$\frac{d\delta}{d\alpha} = 2\left(1 - \frac{d\alpha'}{d\alpha}\right).$$

Since $d\alpha' = d\alpha$, $\frac{d\delta}{d\alpha} = 0$ and so, δ is a minimum.

● **PROBLEM 22-2**

Show that the minimum deviation angle δ_m for a prism with index of refraction n_2 and apex angle γ, satisfies the equation

$$\frac{n_2}{n_1} = \frac{\sin\left[\frac{1}{2}(\gamma + \delta_m)\right]}{\sin\left(\frac{\gamma}{2}\right)}$$

where n_1 is the index of refraction of the surrounding medium. Also find δ_m for $\gamma = 60°$ and $n_2/n_1 = 1.69$.

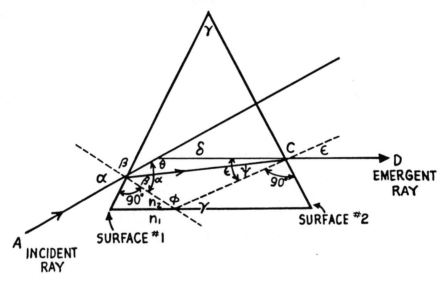

SURFACE #1

SURFACE #2

EMERGENT RAY

INCIDENT RAY

Solution: The magnitude of the angle of deviation, δ, will depend upon the angle of incidence, α, shown in the figure. It can be determined experimentally by rotating the prism that there is one and only one position of the prism for which the deviation is a minimum. Since this is the case, the angles α and ε must be equal. This fact can be proven by the following reasoning: Suppose that when the prism is in the position of least deviation, $\alpha \neq \varepsilon$. Then, imagine the beam of light reversed in direction; that is, incident parallel to line segment $\overline{DC}$, and emergent parallel to line segment $\overline{BA}$. The deviation is not altered, still being equal to δ, and is therefore still a minimum. Therefore, under the assumption that $\alpha \neq \varepsilon$, minimum deviation exists for two angles of incidence, α and ε. However, by experiment this cannot be the case. Thus, the hypothesis is false, and in the position of minimum deviation, $\alpha = \varepsilon$.

From the figure,

$$\delta = 180° - \theta = 180° - (180° - [(\alpha - \beta) + (\varepsilon - \psi)])$$

$$= \alpha + \varepsilon - \beta - \psi \tag{1}$$

But

$$\gamma = 180° - \phi = 180° - [180° - (\beta + \psi)]$$

$$= \beta + \psi \tag{2}$$

So, equation (1) becomes

$$\delta = \alpha + \varepsilon - \gamma \tag{3}$$

Let $r = \alpha = \varepsilon$

Then

$$\delta_m = 2r - \gamma$$

(where δ_m denotes minimum deviation),

Thus,

$$r = \frac{\delta_m + \gamma}{2} \tag{4}$$

Now, applying Snell's law at surface 1 of the prism gives the result

$$n_1 \sin r = n_2 \sin \beta \tag{5}$$

At surface 2, applying Snell's law gives the result

$$n_2 \sin \psi = n_1 \sin r \tag{6}$$

Equating the expressions given for $n_1 \sin r$ in equations (5) and (6) gives $n_2 \sin \beta = n_2 \sin \psi$ or $\psi = \beta$. Then, from equation (2), $\beta = \psi = \gamma/2$. Thus, equation (5) becomes

$$n_1 \sin r = n_2 \sin \frac{\gamma}{2} \tag{7}$$

Finally, substituting the expression for r given in equation (4) into equation (7) yields the desired result:

$$n_1 \sin \frac{\delta_m + \gamma}{2} = n_2 \sin \frac{\gamma}{2}$$

or

$$\frac{n_2}{n_1} = \frac{\sin\left[\frac{1}{2}(\gamma + \delta_m)\right]}{\sin\left(\frac{1}{2}\gamma\right)} \qquad (8)$$

For $\gamma = 60°$, and $\frac{n_2}{n_1} = 1.69$,

$$\frac{n_2}{n_1} = \frac{\sin\left[\frac{1}{2}(\gamma + \delta_m)\right]}{\sin\left(\frac{1}{2} \cdot \gamma\right)}$$

$$1.69 = \frac{\sin \frac{1}{2}(60° + \delta_m)}{\sin\left(\frac{1}{2} \cdot 60\right)}$$

$$(1.69)(\sin 30°) = \sin \frac{1}{2}(60° + \delta_m)$$

$$.845 = \sin \frac{1}{2}(60° + \delta_m)$$

$$\text{arcsin } (.845) = \frac{1}{2}(60° + \delta_m)$$

$$57.7° = \frac{1}{2}(60° + \delta_m)$$

$$\frac{\delta_m}{2} = 57.7° - 30°$$

$$\delta_m = 55.4° \ .$$

● **PROBLEM** 22-3

What is the smallest refracting angle that a glass prism
(n = 1.5) can have so that no ray can be transmitted through
it?   What is this angle for a water prism (n = 1.33)?

Solution: In a prism, the minimum angle of deviation, δ,
of the emergent ray of light is found by making use of the
following equation:

$$n = \frac{\sin\left(\frac{\delta + \gamma}{2}\right)}{\sin\left(\frac{\gamma}{2}\right)} \qquad (1)$$

where n is the index of refraction of the prism and γ is
the refracting angle of the prism.   Rearranging equation
(1) gives

$$n \sin\left(\frac{\gamma}{2}\right) = \sin\left(\frac{\delta + \gamma}{2}\right).$$

656

By the trigonometric identity for the sine of the sum of two angles,

$$n \sin\left(\frac{\gamma}{2}\right) = \sin\left(\frac{\delta}{2}\right) \cos\left(\frac{\gamma}{2}\right) + \cos\left(\frac{\delta}{2}\right) \sin\left(\frac{\gamma}{2}\right).$$

Dividing both sides by $\cos\left(\frac{\gamma}{2}\right)$ gives

$$n \tan\left(\frac{\gamma}{2}\right) = \sin\left(\frac{\delta}{2}\right) + \cos\left(\frac{\delta}{2}\right) \tan\left(\frac{\gamma}{2}\right).$$

Then,

$$\tan\left(\frac{\gamma}{2}\right) = \frac{\sin\left(\frac{\delta}{2}\right)}{n - \cos\left(\frac{\delta}{2}\right)}$$

and so,

$$\gamma = 2 \cdot \tan^{-1}\left[\frac{\sin\left(\frac{\delta}{2}\right)}{n - \cos\left(\frac{\delta}{2}\right)}\right] \tag{2}$$

When no ray of light may be transmitted through a prism, then the angle of deviation of the prism is greater than 90°. Thus, the minimum angle for total internal reflection, δ, = 90°. Substituting δ = 90° and n = 1.5 into equation (2) gives

$$\gamma = 2 \cdot \tan^{-1}\left[\frac{\sin\left(\frac{90°}{2}\right)}{(1.5) - \cos\left(\frac{90°}{2}\right)}\right]$$

$$\gamma = 83°27'13".$$

Similarly, for a water prism with an index of 1.33, the smallest refracting angle is calculated to be 97°14'46".

● **PROBLEM 22-4**

The minimum deviation for a prism of refracting angle 40° is found to be 32°40'. Find the value of the index of refraction.

Solution: The angle of minimum deviation for a prism, δ_{min}, can be found by applying the equation

$$n = \frac{\sin\left(\frac{\delta_{min} + \gamma}{2}\right)}{\sin\left(\frac{\gamma}{2}\right)} \tag{1}$$

where n is the index of the prism and γ is the refracting angle, also known as the dihedral angle. Given δ_{min} = 32°40' and γ = 40°,

657

equation (1) becomes

$$n = \frac{\sin \left(\frac{32°40' + 40°}{2} \right)}{\sin (20°)}$$

or the index of refraction of the prism = 1.7323.

● **PROBLEM 22-5**

A prism of apex angle 72° and refractive index 1.66 is immersed in water, which has an index of refraction of 1.33. Find the angle of minimum deviation.

Solution: The apex angle of a prism is identical to the refracting angle of a prism; it is also referred to as the dihedral angle between two refracting surfaces. Solving the known equation

$$n = \frac{\sin \left(\frac{\delta_{min} + \gamma}{2} \right)}{\sin \left(\frac{\gamma}{2} \right)} \tag{1}$$

for δ_{min} gives the result

$$\delta_{min} = 2 \sin^{-1}\left[n \sin \left(\frac{\gamma}{2} \right) \right] - \gamma,, \tag{2}$$

where n is the relative index of refraction of the prism, δ_{min} is the angle of minimum deviation and γ is the refracting angle of the prism or the apex angle.

n is the relative index of refraction, the ratio of the index of refraction of the prism to that of the surrounding medium, in this case, water.

Thus,

$$n = \frac{n_{prism}}{n_{water}} = \frac{1.66}{1.33}$$

Then, substituting the given value for γ and the value just computed for n into equation (2) gives

$$\delta_{min} = 2 \cdot \sin^{-1} \left[\left(\frac{1.66}{1.33} \right) \cdot \sin\left(\frac{72°}{2} \right) \right] - 72°$$

$$\delta_{min} = 22.4° .$$

658

What is the angle of minimum deviation of an equiangular prism whose index of refraction is 2? Illustrate with a diagram the path of a ray passing through the prism at this angle.

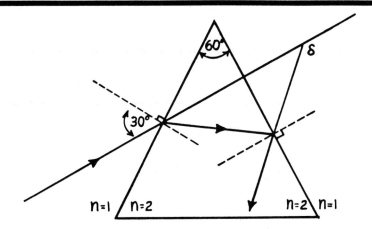

Solution: The angle of minimum deviation for a prism is found by applying the following equation:

$$n = \frac{\sin \frac{1}{2}\left(\delta_{min} + \gamma\right)}{\sin \frac{1}{2}\left(\gamma\right)} \tag{1}$$

where n is the index of refraction of the prism, γ is the apex angle, more commonly known as the refracting angle, and δ_{min} is the angle of minimum deviation. From equation (1),

$$\sin \left[\frac{1}{2}\left(\delta_{min} + \gamma\right)\right] = n \sin \left[\frac{1}{2}\left(\gamma\right)\right].$$

Taking the inverse sine of both sides gives

$$\frac{1}{2}\left(\delta_{min} + \gamma\right) = \sin^{-1}\left[n \sin \left(\frac{1}{2}\gamma\right)\right]$$

and so, solving for δ_{min} in equation (1), we obtain

$$\delta_{min} = 2 \cdot \sin^{-1}\left[n \cdot \sin \frac{1}{2}\left(\gamma\right)\right] - \gamma \tag{2}$$

Substituting the given values n = 2 and γ = 60° into equation (2) gives

$$\delta_{min} = 2 \sin^{-1}[2 \sin (30°)] - 60° =$$

$$2 \sin^{-1}[1] - 60° = 2(90°) - 60° = 120° .$$

It can be shown that if the angle of deviation is

greater than 90°, there is total internal reflection at
the second surface, as in this case.   The path of a ray
of light which has the angle of minimum deviation for this
prism is illustrated in the figure.

    It should be noted that a light ray which has an angle
of incidence greater than 30°, from a medium of index 2 to
a medium of index 1, will always be internally reflected.

● **PROBLEM** 22-7

Find the angle of minimum deviation for a glass prism
(n = 1.54) of refracting angle 60°.

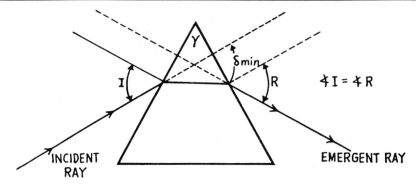

INCIDENT   EMERGENT RAY
RAY

Solution: The minimum deviation of a prism refers to the
least total deviation, which is the angle between the extended incident ray (beyond the prism) and the emergent
ray.   The condition exists when the angle   of incidence of
the ray on the front surface and the angle of refraction
on the back surface are equal.   The angle of minimum deviation can be found by applying the equation

$$ n = \frac{\sin \left(\frac{\delta_{min} + \gamma}{2} \right)}{\sin \left(\frac{\gamma}{2} \right)} \tag{1} $$

where n is the index of refraction of the prism, γ is the
refracting angle, and δ_{min} is the angle of minimum deviation.   Solving equation (1) for δ_{min} gives

$$ n \sin \frac{\gamma}{2} = \sin \frac{\delta_{min} + \gamma}{2} $$

$$ \arcsin \left(n \sin \frac{\gamma}{2} \right) = \frac{\delta_{min} + \gamma}{2} $$

$$ \delta_{min} = 2 \arcsin \left(n \sin \frac{\gamma}{2} \right) - \gamma $$

Substituting the given data, n = 1.54 and γ = 60°,

660

into the above equation gives

$$\delta_{min} = 2 \text{ arcsin } (1.54 \sin 30°) - 60°$$

or $\quad \delta_{min} = 40°41'28''$

Show that a prism with small refracting angle γ deviates light rays through an angle $(n - 1)\gamma$, where n is the refractive index of the prism.

Solution: The equation for the deviation associated with a prism is the following:

$$n = \sin \left(\frac{\gamma + \delta_{min}}{2} \right) \Big/ \sin \left(\gamma/2 \right) \tag{1}$$

γ is given to be a small angle; so,

the following approximations may be used:

$$\sin \gamma = \gamma \tag{2}$$

$$\cos \gamma = 1 \tag{3}$$

Equation (1) can be rewritten as follows:

$$n \sin \left(\frac{\gamma}{2} \right) = \sin \left(\frac{\gamma}{2} + \frac{\delta_{min}}{2} \right) \tag{4}$$

Using the trigonometric identity for the sine of the sum of two angles, equation (4) becomes

$$n \sin \left(\frac{\gamma}{2} \right) = \sin \left(\frac{\gamma}{2} \right) \cos \left(\frac{\delta_{min}}{2} \right) + \sin \left(\frac{\delta_{min}}{2} \right) \cos \left(\frac{\gamma}{2} \right) \tag{5}$$

Using the approximations given in relations (2) and (3), equation (5) becomes

$$n \frac{\gamma}{2} = \frac{\gamma}{2} + \frac{\delta_{min}}{2}$$

and so,

$$n\gamma = \gamma + \delta_{min} \quad .$$

Therefore,

$$\delta_{min} = (n - 1)\gamma \quad .$$

Thus, for a prism with small refracting angle γ, the light rays will be deviated through an angle of $(n - 1)\gamma$.

For small prism angles and small angles of incidence, calculate the deflection δ due to a double prism composed of two different glasses with refractive indices n_1 and n_2 and prism angles γ_1 and γ_2, respectively.

Prism 1 is upright and prism 2 is upside down so that its edge is adjacent to the base surface of prism 1. Determine the ratio γ_2/γ_1 for (a) $\delta = 0$ (direct vision prism) and (b) for $d\delta/d\lambda = 0$ (achromatic prism; λ refers to the wavelength of light).

Solution: When the prism angle, γ, is small, the angle of minimum deviation, δ, is given by

$$\delta = (n - 1)\gamma ,$$

where n is the index of refraction of the prism.

In order to be able to apply this result directly to the twin prisms, it is convenient to imagine prisms 1 and 2 as separated by a narrow air space. Thus, taking into account the opposite positions of the two prism edges, one obtains for the total deflection

$$\delta = \delta_1 - \delta_2 ,$$

where

$$\delta_1 = (n_1 - 1)\gamma_1$$

and

$$\delta_2 = (n_2 - 1)\gamma_2 .$$

Thus,

$$\delta = (n_1 - 1)\gamma_1 - (n_2 - 1)\gamma_2 . \tag{1}$$

(a) For a direct vision prism it is to be required that

$\delta = 0$, and so equation (1) becomes

$$(n_1 - 1)\gamma_1 - (n_2 - 1)\gamma_2 = 0;$$

hence,

$$\frac{\gamma_2}{\gamma_1} = \frac{n_1 - 1}{n_2 - 1} . \tag{2}$$

Since n_1 and n_2 depend on the wavelength, this condition can only be satisfied for some average wavelength such as $\lambda = 0.590 \mu$.

(b) For an achromatic prism, it is required that

$$\frac{d\delta}{d\lambda} = 0.$$

Differentiating equation (1) with respect to λ gives

$$\frac{dn_1}{d\lambda} \gamma_1 - \frac{dn_2}{d\lambda} \gamma_2 = 0 ;$$

hence,

$$\frac{\gamma_2}{\gamma_1} = \frac{dn_1/d\lambda}{dn_2/d\lambda} \qquad\qquad (3)$$

From the table below, the ratio $\dfrac{\gamma_2}{\gamma_1}$ for a direct vision prism is found to be $\dfrac{1.5103 - 1}{1.7562 - 1} = 0.675$ for $\lambda = 0.590 \mu$. For an achromatic prism,

$$\frac{\gamma_2}{\gamma_1} \simeq \frac{\Delta n_1/\Delta\lambda}{\Delta n_2/\Delta\lambda} = \frac{\Delta n_1}{\Delta n_2} = \frac{n_{1b} - n_{1a}}{n_{2b} - n_{1a}}$$

for the same difference in wavelength (from $\lambda = 0.590 \mu$ to $\lambda = 0.656 \mu$).

$$\text{Thus, } \frac{\gamma_2}{\gamma_1} = \frac{1.5103 - 1.5076}{1.7562 - 1.7473} = 0.303$$

is an approximation of the ratio at $\lambda = 0.590 \mu$.

Dispersion of crown glass (n_1) and of flint glass (n_2):

$\lambda (\mu)$	n_1	n_2
0.761	1.5050	1.7390
0.656	1.5076	1.7473
0.590	1.5103	1.7562
0.486	1.5156	1.7792
0.397	1.5245	1.8403

POWER

● PROBLEM 22-10

What is the power and meridian angle of a single prism that gives a prismatic deviation of 5 prism diopters base-in and 2 prism diopters base-down before the right eye?

Solution: For prisms having a small refracting angle of

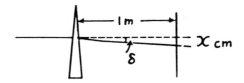

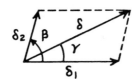

only a few degrees, the angle of minimum deviation, δ, is given by the relation

$$\delta = (n - 1)\alpha$$

when the prism is surrounded by air. n is the refractive index of the prism and α is its refracting angle.

The unit which is used in describing the power of a prism is the prism diopter. It is measured by the deflection of the ray in centimeters at a distance from the prism of 1 m.

For small values of δ, the power (in prism diopters) is essentially the angle of deviation δ, measured in units of .01 radians.

To determine the power and direction of deviation of a combination of two prisms, use the fact that the deviations add vectorially. If two prisms of powers δ_1 and δ_2, making an angle of β with respect to one another, are added together, the resultant deviation δ will be given by the following expression, which comes from the law of cosines:

$$\delta = \sqrt{\delta_1{}^2 + \delta_2{}^2 - 2\delta_1\delta_2 \cos \beta} \qquad (1)$$

and its direction with respect to prism 1 alone is given by the angle γ, where

$$\tan \gamma = \frac{\delta_2 \sin \beta}{\delta_1 + \delta_2 \cos \beta} \qquad (2)$$

In this problem, the following values are given:

$$\delta_1 = .05 \text{ rad.}$$

$$\delta_2 = .02 \text{ rad.}$$

and $\beta = -90°$ since this is the angle between the position of the prism base-in and the position of the prism base-down. Hence, substituting these values into equation (1) gives

$$\delta = \sqrt{(.05)^2 + (.02)^2 - 2(.05)(.02)\cos(-90°)}$$

or

$$\delta = 5.4 \times 10^{-2} \text{ rad.}$$

$$= .054 \text{ prism diopters.}$$

$$\tan \gamma = \frac{\delta_2 \sin \beta}{\delta_1 + \delta_2 \cos \beta}$$

$$= \frac{.02 \sin (-90°)}{.05 + .02 \cos(-90°)}$$

$$= \frac{-.02}{.05}$$

$$= -0.4$$

Hence, $\gamma = \tan^{-1}(-0.4)$

or $\gamma = -21.8°$.

Hence the meridian angle of the prism is

$$(-21.8° + 180°) = 158.2°.$$

[The meridian angle which gives the position of the prism is 180° opposite to the deviation.]

● **PROBLEM** 22-11

A prism with power equal to 5 prism diopters is placed with base-appex meridian at an angle of 30° with respect to the horizontal. What are the horizontal and vertical prismatic effects?

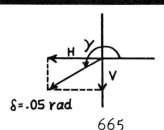

$\delta = .05$ rad

Solution: The power of a prism is given by the relation
$\overline{P = 100}$ tan δ, where δ represents the angle of deviation
of the prism. In this problem, P is given to be 5 prism-
diopters. Thus,

$$\delta = \tan^{-1}\left(\frac{P}{100}\right) = \tan^{-1}\left(\frac{5}{100}\right) = \tan^{-1}(.05) \cong 2.86°$$

Converting δ into units of radians,

$$\delta = (2.86 \text{ degrees})\left(\frac{\pi \text{ radians}}{180 \text{ degrees}}\right) \cong .05 \text{ rad.}$$

The angle γ made by the deviation is $(30 + 180)° = 210°$,
as shown in the figure.

The horizontal and vertical deviations are given as follows:

$$H = \delta \cos \gamma$$

$$= .05 \cos(180° + 30°).$$

Since $\cos(180° + \theta) = - \cos\theta$,

$$H = - .05 \cos 30° \cong - .043 \text{ radians}$$

$$= - 4.3 \text{ prism diopters.}$$

$$V = \delta \sin \gamma$$

$$= .05 \sin(180° + 30°)$$

$\sin(180° + \theta) = - \sin \theta$; hence,

$$V = - .05 \sin 30° = - .025 \text{ radians} = - 2.5 \text{ prism}$$
diopters.

● **PROBLEM 22-12**

A prism of refracting angle 1°25' bends a beam of light
through an angle of 1°15'. Calculate the index of refraction and the power of the prism in prism-diopters.

Solution: When a beam of light is refracted through a
$\overline{\text{prism, it}}$ is bent through an angle called the angle of
deviation, δ. The index of refraction of a prism, n,
the refracting angle, γ, and the angle of deviation, δ,
are related by the equation

$$n = \frac{\sin\left(\frac{\delta + \gamma}{2}\right)}{\sin\left(\frac{\gamma}{2}\right)} \tag{1}$$

Given that $\gamma = 1°25' = 1.42°$ and $\delta = 1°15' = 1.25°$,
from equation (1), the index of refraction of the prism is

$$n = \frac{\sin\left(\frac{1.25° + 1.42°}{2}\right)}{\sin\left(\frac{1.42°}{2}\right)} \cong 1.880.$$

The power of a prism is given by the relation

$$P = 100 \tan \delta . \qquad (2)$$

When δ is in degrees, the power P is given in prism-diopters. If the angle of deviation is 1.25°, then the power of the prism is found to be approximately 2.18 prism-diopters.

● **PROBLEM** 22-13

A glass prism of index 1.5 has a refracting angle of 2°. What is the power of the prism in prism-diopters?

Solution: The power of a prism, P, is found by the relation

$$P = 100 \tan \delta \qquad (1)$$

where δ is the angle of deviation for the prism. P can be found by using the angle of minimum deviation δ_{min}, which is found by applying the equation

$$n = \frac{\sin\left(\frac{\delta_{min} + \gamma}{2}\right)}{\sin\left(\frac{\gamma}{2}\right)} . \qquad (2)$$

Rearranging equation (2) gives

$$\sin\left(\frac{\delta_{min} + \gamma}{2}\right) = n \sin\left(\frac{\gamma}{2}\right) .$$

Taking the arcsin of both sides of this equation gives

$$\frac{\delta_{min} + \gamma}{2} = \sin^{-1}\left[n \sin\left(\frac{\gamma}{2}\right)\right] \quad \text{and so,}$$

$$\delta_{min} = 2 \cdot \sin^{-1}\left[n \cdot \sin\left(\frac{\gamma}{2}\right)\right] - \gamma . \qquad (3)$$

Substituting the given values $n = 1.5$ and $\gamma = 2°$ into equation (3) gives

$$\delta_{min} = 2 \sin^{-1}((1.5 \sin(1°)) - 2° \cong 1.00°.$$

Now substituting this value for δ_{min} into equation (1) gives

$$P = 100 \tan 1°$$

from which $P = 1.746$ prism-diopters.

The power of a prism can also be specified in terms of the number of centrads of prism power, which is given by

$$P = 100\delta$$

where δ is expressed in radians. One centrad equals a hundredth of a radian. Thus,

$$P = (100)(1 \text{ degree})\left(\frac{\pi \text{ radians}}{180 \text{ degrees}}\right)\left(\frac{100 \text{ centrads}}{\text{radian}}\right)$$

$$= 175 \text{ centrads}$$

THE REFRACTING ANGLE

● **PROBLEM** 22-14

Find the refracting angle of a glass prism (n = 1.52) for which the minimum deviation is 15°.

Solution: The refracting angle of a prism, γ, the index of refraction, n, and the angle of minimum deviation, δ_{min}, are related by the following equation:

$$n = \frac{\sin\left(\frac{\delta_{min} + \gamma}{2}\right)}{\sin\left(\frac{\gamma}{2}\right)} \tag{1}$$

By the trigonometric identity for the sine of the sum of two angles,

$$\sin(\alpha + \beta) = \sin\alpha \cdot \cos\beta + \cos\alpha \cdot \sin\beta .$$

Therefore,

$$\sin\left(\frac{\delta_{min} + \gamma}{2}\right) = \sin\left(\frac{\delta_{min}}{2}\right) \cdot \cos\left(\frac{\gamma}{2}\right)$$

$$+ \cos\left(\frac{\delta_{min}}{2}\right) \cdot \sin\left(\frac{\gamma}{2}\right) .$$

Thus, equation (1) becomes

$$n = \frac{\sin\left(\frac{\delta_{min}}{2}\right) \cdot \cos\left(\frac{\gamma}{2}\right)}{\sin\left(\frac{\gamma}{2}\right)} + \cos\left(\frac{\delta_{min}}{2}\right) \tag{2}$$

and so,

$$n = \frac{\sin\left(\frac{\delta_{min}}{2}\right)}{\tan\left(\frac{\gamma}{2}\right)} + \cos\left(\frac{\delta_{min}}{2}\right) \tag{3}$$

Now, solving for γ gives

$$n - \cos\left(\frac{\delta_{min}}{2}\right) = \frac{\sin\left(\frac{\delta_{min}}{2}\right)}{\tan\left(\frac{\gamma}{2}\right)}$$

$$\tan\left(\frac{\gamma}{2}\right) = \frac{\sin\left(\frac{\delta_{min}}{2}\right)}{n - \cos\left(\frac{\delta_{min}}{2}\right)}$$

Thus,

$$\gamma = 2 \tan^{-1}\left[\frac{\sin\left(\frac{\delta_{min}}{2}\right)}{n - \cos\left(\frac{\delta_{min}}{2}\right)}\right] \qquad (4)$$

Substituting the given data, $n = 1.52$ and $\delta_{min} = 15°$, into equation (4) gives

$$\gamma = 2 \tan^{-1}\left[\frac{\sin\left(\frac{15}{2}\right)}{1.52 - \cos\left(\frac{15}{2}\right)}\right]$$

$$= 27°44'36" \ .$$

● **PROBLEM** 22-15

The refracting angle of a prism is 60° and the index of refraction is $\sqrt{7/3}$. What is the limiting angle of incidence of a ray that will be transmitted through the prism?

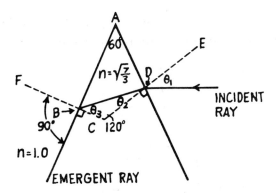

Solution: In this problem, the limiting angle of incidence occurs when the emergent ray is refracted along (parallel to) the second surface of the prism. This occurs when θ_3, shown in the figure, is the critical angle of the second surface. θ_3 can be determined by applying the law of refraction:

$$n_p \cdot \sin \theta_3 = n_A \cdot \sin 90°$$

where n_p is the index of the prism and n_A is the index of the air. Given that

$$n_p = \sqrt{\frac{7}{3}}$$

and assuming $N_A = 1.00$, $\sin \theta_3 = \sqrt{\frac{3}{7}}$ or $\theta_3 = 40.9°$.

Then $\theta_2 = 180 - (120 + 40.9) = 19.1°$ because the sum of the angles of a triangle $= 180°$.

Applying the law of refraction at point D, where the incident ray strikes the first surface,

$$n_A \cdot \sin \theta_1 = n_p \cdot \sin 19.1°$$

$$\sin \theta_1 = \sqrt{\frac{7}{3}} \cdot \sin 19.1°$$

from which $\theta_1 = 30°$

● **PROBLEM** 22-16

A ray "grazes" the first face of a prism and emerges at the second face in a direction perpendicular to the first face. Show that the refracting angle α satisfies the relation

$$\cot \alpha = \sqrt{n^2 - 1} - 1$$

where n is the index of refraction of the prism material.

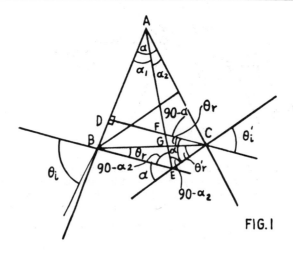

FIG. 1

<u>Solution:</u> Snell's law of refraction states:

$$n = \frac{\sin \theta_i}{\sin \theta_r} \qquad (1)$$

where n is the index of refraction, θ_i is the incident angle measured with respect to the normal, and θ_r is the refracted angle. From the figure, it can be seen that angle DCA = $90 - \alpha$. This follows from the fact that the sum of the angles of a triangle must equal 180 degrees. Thus, since angle ECA is a right angle, $90° - \alpha +$ angle ECF = $90°$; hence, angle ECF = α. Then, $\alpha =$ angle GCF + angle ECG = $\theta_r + \theta_r'$. In addition, it is given that $\theta_i = 90°$.

Since $\alpha = \theta_r + \theta_r'$, $\alpha - \theta_r = \theta_r'$

and so,

$$\sin(\alpha - \theta_r) = \sin \theta_r' . \qquad (2)$$

In addition, substituting the value $\theta_i = 90°$ into equation (1) gives

$$\sin \theta_r = 1/n \qquad (3)$$

By the trigonometric identity for the sine of the difference of two angles, equation (2) becomes

$$\sin(\alpha - \theta_r) = \sin \alpha \cos \theta_r - \cos \alpha \sin \theta_r = \sin \theta_r' . \qquad (4)$$

From the figure, it can also be seen that

$$\theta_i' = \alpha .$$

Snell's law states that

$$\frac{\sin \theta_i'}{\sin \theta_r'} = \frac{\sin \alpha}{\sin \theta_r'} = n \qquad (5)$$

From the trigonometric identity

$$\sin^2 \theta_r + \cos^2 \theta_r = 1 ,$$

it follows that $\cos \theta_r = \sqrt{1 - \sin^2 \theta_r}$.

By equation (3), $\sin^2 \theta_r = \frac{1}{n^2}$ and so,

$$\cos \theta_r = \sqrt{1 - \frac{1}{n^2}} = \frac{\sqrt{n^2 - 1}}{n} . \qquad (6)$$

671

Substituting for $\cos \theta_r$ (from equation (6)), $\sin \theta_r$ (from equation (3)), and $\sin \theta_r'$ (from equation (5)), equation (4) becomes

$$\sin \alpha \frac{\sqrt{n^2 - 1}}{n} - \cos \alpha \frac{1}{n} = \frac{\sin \alpha}{n}.$$

Solving for $\cos \alpha$ gives

$$\cos \alpha = \sin \alpha \left(\sqrt{n^2 - 1} - 1\right)$$

and so,

$$\frac{\cos \alpha}{\sin \alpha} = \cot \alpha = \sqrt{n^2 - 1} - 1.$$

CHAPTER 23

DISPERSION

DISPERSIVE POWER

● PROBLEM 23-1

The indices of refraction of rock salt for the Fraunhofer lines C, D, and F are 1.5404, 1.5441, and 1.5531, respectively. Calculate the value of the reciprocal of the dispersive power.

Solution: The dispersive power of a material is defined as the ratio of $(n_F - n_C)$ to $(n_D - 1)$.

Thus,

$$\frac{1}{\text{Dispersive Power}} = \frac{1}{\left[\dfrac{n_F - n_C}{n_D - 1}\right]} \quad .$$

Substituting the given values for n_F, n_C, and n_D into this equation gives

$$\frac{1}{\text{Dispersive Power}} = \frac{1}{\left[\dfrac{1.5531 - 1.5404}{1.5441 - 1}\right]}$$

$$= 42.84.$$

SPECTRAL LENGTH

● PROBLEM 23-2

Make a complete diagram of the optical system of a spectrograph. Trace the path of bundles of rays corresponding to two different wavelengths, and use your diagram

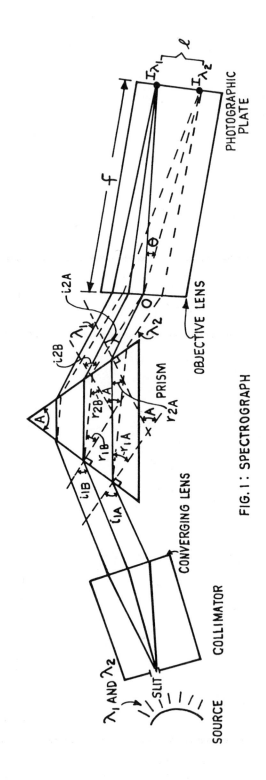

FIG. 1 : SPECTROGRAPH

674

to show how you could calculate the linear length of the spectrum included between these two wavelengths.

Solution: It is frequently desirable to have a permanent record of the spectrum of a source, in which case a spectrograph is used. A prism spectrograph is essentially a spectrometer with the eyepiece of the telescope removed and a photographic plate placed in the focal plane of the objective lens. Again, as in the case of the spectrometer, the prism is placed in the position of minimum deviation for one of the given wavelengths.

Figure 1 illustrates the spectrograph. The slit is illuminated by a source emitting various wavelengths (here we used λ_1 and λ_2). The collimator consists of the slit whose width and whose distance from the converging lens may be adjusted. Here the slit is placed so that parallel rays emerge from the collimator lens. The parallel rays then pass through the prism, which is set for minimum deviation for one of the wavelengths (λ_1). The deviated rays then pass through the objective lens of the telescope, which focuses the images of the slit on a photographic plate placed in its focal plane.

To calculate the linear length of the spectrum (ℓ) we first look at the angular separation (θ) of the two images. Since the prism is not quite in the position of minimum deviation for λ_2 , but is nearly so, the angle θ will, in practice, be a small angle. We can then say that, since θ is very small,

$$I_{\lambda_1} O = I_{\lambda_2} O = f_{objective\ lens} = f$$

Then $\tan \theta = \dfrac{\ell}{f}$

and $\ell = f \tan \theta$.

To find θ, we apply Snell's Law at the prism for both wavelengths. Assume the prism has a refractive index of n_1 for light of wavelength λ_1 and a refractive index of n_2 for light of wavelength λ_2. For wavelength λ_1 , the prism is in the position of minimum deviation. Referring to the indicated angles in figure 1, i denotes an angle of incidence and r an angle of refraction, the subscript 1 refers to the first surface and 2 to the second surface, and A refers to λ_1 while B refers to λ_2. For wavelength λ_1 , according to the rule for minimum deviation,

$$i_{1A} = i_{2A} \quad and \quad r_{1A} = r_{2A} = \frac{A}{2} \quad where\ A$$

is the angle of the prism. Then, applying Snell's Law at the first surface,

$$\sin i_{1A} = n_1 \sin r_{1A}$$

$$\sin i_{1A} = n_1 \sin \frac{A}{2} \tag{1}$$

$$i_{1A} = \sin^{-1}\left(n_1 \sin \frac{A}{2}\right)$$

and since $\quad i_{2A} = i_{1A}$,

$$i_{2A} = \sin^{-1}\left(n_1 \sin \frac{A}{2}\right). \tag{2}$$

For wavelength λ_2 , Snell's Law must be applied at both surfaces. At the first surface:

$$\sin i_{1B} = n_2 \sin r_{1B}$$

$i_{1B} = i_{1A}$ since the angle of incidence is equal for all incident wavelengths. Then (from equation (1))

$$\sin i_{1A} = \sin i_{1B} = n_1 \sin \frac{A}{2}$$

and $\quad n_1 \sin \frac{A}{2} = n_2 \sin r_{1B}$

$$r_{1B} = \sin^{-1}\left[\frac{n_1}{n_2} \sin \frac{A}{2}\right]$$

But, $\quad r_{1B} + r_{2B} = A \quad$ (see figure 1)

so $\quad r_{2B} = A - r_{1B}$

$$r_{2B} = A - \sin^{-1}\left[\frac{n_1}{n_2} \sin \frac{A}{2}\right]$$

Then applying Snell's Law at the second surface, we get

$$\sin i_{2B} = n_2 \sin r_{2B}$$

$$\sin i_{2B} = n_2 \sin\left[A - \sin^{-1}\left(\frac{n_1}{n_2} \sin \frac{A}{2}\right)\right]$$

$$i_{2B} = \sin^{-1}\left[n_2 \sin\left[A - \sin^{-1}\left(\frac{n_1}{n_2} \sin \frac{A}{2}\right)\right]\right] \tag{3}$$

Now θ, the angular separation of the two images, is given by

$$\theta = i_{2B} - i_{2A}$$

and from equations (2) and (3),

$$\theta = \sin^{-1}\left[n_2\sin\left[A - \sin^{-1}\left(\frac{n_1}{n_2}\sin\frac{A}{2}\right)\right]\right]$$

$$- \sin^{-1}\left(n_1\sin\frac{A}{2}\right).$$

Then, having found θ, the length of the spectrum is given as $\ell = f\tan\theta$ as derived before.

● **PROBLEM 23-3**

A 60° flint glass prism, having an index of refraction equal to 1.6222 for D light and equal to 1.6320 for F light, is set in the position of minimum deviation for D light.
(a) When the incident light consists of a beam of parallel rays, find the angular separation between the emergent D and F beams.
(b) If the emergent light is focused on a screen by an achromatic lens of focal length 60 cm, find the linear distance (or length of spectrum) between the D and the F images.

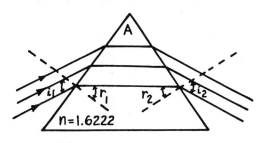

FIG.1: D LIGHT

Solution: (a) When a prism is set in a position of minimum deviation (see fig. 1), it is known that

$$i_1 = i_2$$

and $\quad r_1 = r_2 = \frac{A}{2}$

Then for a 60° prism, $r_1 = r_2 = 30°$. Applying this to the case of D light, where $n_{prism} = 1.6222$, we have from Snell's Law the following:

$$n_{air}\sin i_1 = n_{prism}\sin r_1$$

$$\sin i_1 = 1.6222\sin 30°$$

677

$$i_1 = 54.20°$$

Then, for D light, $i_2 = i_1 = 54.20°$.

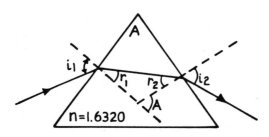

FIG.2 : F LIGHT

To find i_2 for F light it must be remembered that for this wavelength, the prism is not in the position of least deviation. We must then deal with refraction at each surface separately.

At the first surface, since the angle of incidence is the same for all wavelengths, $i_1 = 54.20°$. Then applying Snell's Law as follows,

$$\sin 54.20° = 1.6320 \sin r_1$$

$$r_1 = 29.80°.$$

But $r_1 + r_2 = A$ (see figure 2)

so $r_2 = 60° - 29.80°$

$$r_2 = 30.20°.$$

Then at the second surface, again applying Snell's Law,

$$1.6320 \sin 30.20° = \sin i_2$$

$$i_2 = 55.18°.$$

Therefore, the required angular separation between the F and D images is given by the following:

$$i_{2F} - i_{2D} = 55.18° - 54.20° = 54° + 1.18° - 54.20°$$

$$= .98° \quad \text{or} \quad 59'.$$

(b) Now referring to figure 3, we see that if D represents the D image of the slit and F the F image, then

$$\angle FOD = .98°$$

678

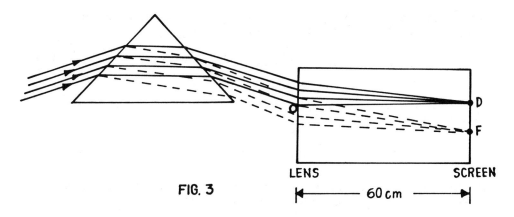

FIG. 3

The focal length of the lens is 60 cm. Since ∢FOD is a small angle, OF and OD are each approximately equal to 60 cm. Then,

$$FD = 60 \tan .98°$$

$$FD = 1.03 \text{ cm}.$$

Thus, the length of the spectrum = 1.03 cm.

MEAN DEVIATION AND DISPERSION

● **PROBLEM** 23-4

Compute the mean deviations and dispersions produced by a crown prism of apex angle 10° and a flint prism of apex angle 10°. Assume the indices of refraction for crown and flint glass to be approximately 1.508 and 1.620, respectively. The dispersive powers for crown and flint glass are .018 and .031, respectively.

Solution: For flint glass: The mean deviation δ_D, is defined by the following relation:

$$\delta_D = (n_D - 1)A \tag{1}$$

where n_D and A are the index of refraction of the prism and the apex angle of the prism, respectively. From the given values for n_D and A,

$$\delta_D = (1.620 - 1)10° = 6.20°.$$

The dispersion is defined by the following relation:

$$\text{Dispersion} = \omega\delta_D \tag{2}$$

where ω is the dispersive power.

Substituting in the given value for ω and the value just computed for δ_D gives the result

Dispersion = (.031)(6.20°) = 0.192°.

For crown glass: Substituting the given values for n_D and A into equation (1) gives

δ_D = (1.508 - 1)10° = 5.08°.

Substituting the given value for ω and the value just computed for δ_D into equation (2) gives

Dispersion = (.018)(5.08°) = 0.091°.

THE APEX ANGLE OF A PRISM

● PROBLEM 23-5

An achromatic prism combination is to be constructed of crown- and flint-glass components. For light of wave-lengths 6563 Å, 5893 Å, and 4861 Å, the crown glass has relative indices of refraction of 1.5146, 1.5171, and 1.5233, respectively and the relative indices of refraction of the flint glass are 1.6224, 1.6272, 1.6385, respectively. The wavelengths of 6563 Å, 5893 Å, and 4861 Å correspond to red, yellow, and blue light, respectively. The crown-glass prism to be used has an angle of 10°. What must be the angle of the flint-glass prism?

Solution: The dispersive power ω of a prism is given by

$$\omega = \frac{n_b - n_r}{n_y - 1}$$ (1)

n_b , n_r , and n_y are the indices of refraction of the prism when blue, red, and yellow light, respectively, pass   through it. The deviation, δ, for a prism of small refracting angle A, is given by

$$\delta = \left(n_y - 1\right)A$$ (2)

For a combination of two prisms of different materials to be achromatic, the dispersive powers of the two prisms must be equal and the two prisms must be opposed to cancel their respective deviation. In other words, the two conditions which must be fulfilled are:

$$\omega_{(1)} = \omega_{(2)} \quad \text{and} \quad \left|\delta_{(1)}\right| = \left|\delta_{(2)}\right|$$

where (1) and (2) refer to the crown-glass and the flint-glass prisms, respectively.

Hence, from equations (1) and (2) we see the following:

$$\omega_{(1)} = \frac{n_b^{(1)} - n_r^{(1)}}{n_y^{(1)} - 1} \tag{3}$$

$$\delta_{(1)} = \left[n_y^{(1)} - 1 \right] A_1 \tag{4}$$

$$\omega_{(2)} = \frac{n_b^{(2)} - n_r^{(2)}}{n_y^{(2)} - 1} \tag{5}$$

$$\delta_{(2)} = \left[n_y^{(2)} - 1 \right] A_2 \tag{6}$$

The condition $\omega_{(1)} = \omega_{(2)}$ gives:

$$\frac{n_b^{(1)} - n_r^{(1)}}{n_y^{(1)} - 1} = \frac{n_b^{(2)} - n_r^{(2)}}{n_y^{(2)} - 1} \tag{7}$$

From equations (4) and (6) respectively,

$$n_y^{(1)} = \frac{\delta_{(1)}}{A_1} + 1 \quad \text{and} \quad n_y^{(2)} = \frac{\delta_{(2)}}{A_2} + 1.$$

Substituting these expressions for $n_y^{(1)}$ and $n_y^{(2)}$ into equation (7) gives the result

$$\frac{n_b^{(1)} - n_r^{(1)}}{\dfrac{\delta_{(1)}}{A_1}} = \frac{n_b^{(2)} - n_r^{(2)}}{\dfrac{\delta_{(2)}}{A_2}} \tag{8}$$

Since $\delta_{(1)} = \delta_{(2)}$ (by the second condition which must be satisfied for the prism combination to be achromatic), equation (8) becomes

$$A_1 \left[n_b^{(1)} - n_r^{(1)} \right] = A_2 \left[n_b^{(2)} - n_r^{(2)} \right] \tag{9}$$

or
$$A_2 = \frac{A_1\left[n_b^{(1)} - n_r^{(1)}\right]}{\left[n_b^{(2)} - n_r^{(2)}\right]}$$
(10)

Substituting the given values for A_1, $n_b^{(1)}$, $n_r^{(1)}$, $n_b^{(2)}$, and $n_r^{(2)}$ into equation (10) gives

$$A_2 = \frac{10°\,[1.5233 - 1.5146]}{[1.6385 - 1.6224]} = 5.40°.$$

● **PROBLEM 23-6**

A silicate crown prism of apex angle 15° is to be combined with a prism of silicate flint so as to be achromatic for rays of wavelength 400 mμ and 700 mμ. For crown glass, $n_{400} = 1.522$, $n_{700} = 1.504$. For flint glass, $n_{400} = 1.662$, $n_{700} = 1.613$ (n denotes the index of refraction of the prism). Find the apex angle of the flint prism.

Solution: The refractive index n of a prism is given as

$$n(\lambda) = \frac{\sin\left(\dfrac{A + \delta(\lambda)}{2}\right)}{\sin\left(\dfrac{A}{2}\right)}$$
(1)

where λ is the wavelength, A is the apex angle of the prism and δ is the angle of minimum deviation for λ.

When A is small, δ is also small. For small angles A and δ, the approximations

$$\sin\left(\frac{A + \delta(\lambda)}{2}\right) = \frac{A + \delta(\lambda)}{2}$$

and $\sin\left(\dfrac{A}{2}\right) = \dfrac{A}{2}$ are valid. Thus, equation (1) becomes

$$n(\lambda) = \frac{\left(\dfrac{A + \delta(\lambda)}{2}\right)}{\left(\dfrac{A}{2}\right)} = \frac{A + \delta(\lambda)}{A} = 1 + \frac{\delta(\lambda)}{A}.$$

Hence,

$$\delta(\lambda) = A \cdot (n(\lambda) - 1)$$
(2)

Let A_1 represent the apex angle of the flint prism and $A_2 = 15°$ represent the apex angle of the crown prism. Then, from equation (2) we have the following:

682

$$\delta_1(400) = A_1\Big(n_1(400) - 1\Big)$$

$$\delta_2(400) = A_2\Big(n_2(400) - 1\Big)$$

$$\delta_1(700) = A_1\Big(n_1(700) - 1\Big)$$

$$\delta_2(700) = A_2\Big(n_2(700) - 1\Big).$$

Then
$$\Delta\delta_1 = \delta_1(700) - \delta_1(400) = A_1\Big(n_1(700) - n_1(400)\Big)$$

$$= A_1[1.613 - 1.662] = -0.049 \, A_1 \quad (3)$$

and
$$\Delta\delta_2 = \delta_2(700) - \delta_2(400) = A_2\Big(n_2(700) - n_2(400)\Big)$$

$$= A_2[1.504 - 1.522] = 15 \times (-.018) = -0.27. \quad (4)$$

Since the combination of the two prisms is achromatic,

$$\Delta\delta_1 + \Delta\delta_2 = 0 = -0.27 - 0.049 \, A_1 \, .$$

Thus,
$$A_1 = \frac{-0.27}{0.049} = -5.5° \quad (5)$$

Hence, the flint prism must have an apex angle of 5.5°. The negative sign implies that it must be used with its apex opposite to the crown prism so that its dispersion is in the opposite direction to that of the crown prism.

● **PROBLEM 23-7**

Using flint-glass and crown-glass prisms with dispersive powers .031 and .018, respectively, a direct-vision prism is to be designed such that $\delta_D = \delta_D{}'$, where δ_D and $\delta_D{}'$ represent the mean angles of deviation of the crown-glass and flint-glass prisms, respectively.
(a) If the apex angle of the flint-glass prism, A', is 10.0°, find the apex angle of the crown-glass prism, A.
(b) Find the net dispersion of the direct-vision prism. (The indices of refraction of the crown-glass and flint-glass prisms are 1.508 and 1.620, respectively.)

Solution: (a) The mean angles of deviation of the crown-glass and flint-glass prisms, denoted by δ_D and $\delta_D{}'$, respectively, are given by the following relations:

$$\delta_D = (n_D - 1)A \quad (1)$$

$$\delta_D' = (n_D' - 1)A' \qquad (2)$$

n_D and n_D' represent the indices of refraction of the crown-glass and flint-glass prisms, respectively. If the two prisms are combined apex to base and the angles A and A' are chosen so that $\delta_D = \delta_D'$, the mean deviation of the first prism is offset by that of the second. Hence, the expressions on the right-hand sides of equations (1) and (2) can be equated and so,

$$\frac{A}{A'} = \frac{n_D' - 1}{n_D - 1} \qquad (3)$$

Thus, $A = A'\left(\dfrac{n_D' - 1}{n_D - 1}\right)$ and substituting in the given

values for A', n_D', and n_D into this equation gives

$$A = 10°\left(\frac{1.620 - 1}{1.508 - 1}\right) = 12.2°.$$

(b) The dispersion produced by the flint-glass prism is given as follows:

$$\text{Dispersion} = \omega'\delta_D' \qquad (4)$$

and that produced by the crown-glass prism is given as follows:

$$\text{Dispersion} = \omega\delta_D \qquad (5)$$

ω and ω' denote the dispersive powers of the crown-glass and flint-glass prisms, respectively. Then, the net dispersion is given as follows:

$$\text{Net Dispersion} = \text{Dispersion}_{(flint)} - \text{Dispersion}_{(crown)}$$

$$= \omega'\delta_D' - \omega\delta_D$$

(from equations (4) and (5), respectively).

Since $\delta_D = \delta_D' = (n_D - 1)A$,

$$\text{Net Dispersion} = (n_D - 1)A\,(\omega' - \omega). \qquad (6)$$

Substituting the given values for n_D, ω', and ω, and the value for A determined in part (a), into equation (6) gives:

$$\text{Net Dispersion} = (1.508-1)(12.2°)(.031-.018)$$

$$= 0.081°.$$

684

ANOMALOUS DISPERSION

Show the relative positions of the various visible
spectral colors in the spectrum formed by a prism of a
substance showing anomalous dispersion with the center of
its band at $\lambda = 5000$ Å.   Compare with the normal order of
the colors in the spectrum formed by a glass prism.

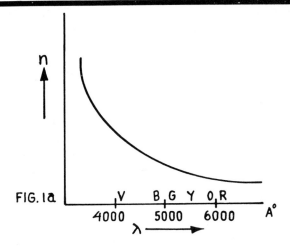

FIG. 1a

Solution: The normal dispersion from a glass prism produces a spectrum in which the long wavelengths are
deviated the least and the short wavelengths are deviated
the most.   The index of refraction is inversely proportional to the wavelength of light (see fig. 1a).   Hence,
from the expression for angular dispersion,

$$\frac{d\theta}{d\lambda} = \left(\frac{d\theta}{dn}\right)\frac{dn}{d\lambda}$$

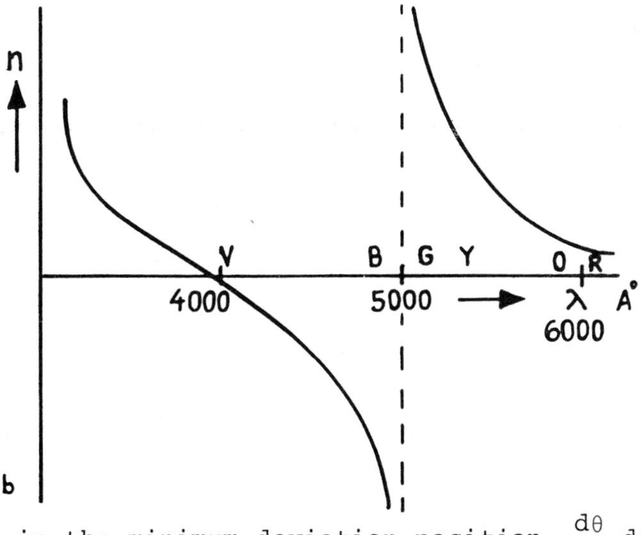

FIG. 1b

For a prism in the minimum deviation position, $\dfrac{d\theta}{dn}$ depends
upon geometrical factors, and n is the index of refraction

of the prism. Hence given the prism, $\frac{d\theta}{d\lambda}$ is directly
proportional to $\frac{dn}{d\lambda}$ and hence, the order of colors away
from the undeviated beam is red, orange, yellow, green,
blue, and violet (from the longest to the shortest wavelength, in order).

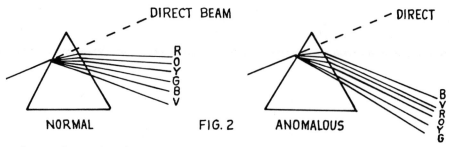

For the prism showing anomalous dispersion, the refractive index, n, shows an abrupt change at a given wavelength. This occurs in this case at 5000 Å and is shown
in the figure lb. It is clearly shown in this figure
that n is smallest for wavelengths just shorter than
5000 Å and then increases as wavelength approaches the
violet end of the spectrum. n is small at the red part
of the spectrum and increases as the wavelength of light
approaches 5000 Å. Hence, the spectrum as observed away
from the direct beam position will appear as blue, violet,
red, orange, yellow, and green. Figure 2 shows the normal
and anomalous spectrum from a prism.

RESOLUTION OF A GRATING

• PROBLEM 23-9

(a) What is the resolution of a grating with 600 lines
per mm and 15 cm wide?
(b) How far apart must two green lines be for such a
grating to resolve them?
(c) How wide would a glass prism have to be to give the
same resolution as the grating?

Solution: (a) Resolution is generally defined as R =
$\frac{\lambda}{\Delta\lambda}$, and in the case of a diffraction grating, as

$$R = \frac{\lambda}{\Delta\lambda} = Nm \qquad (1)$$

where m is the order of the interference fringe, N is the
total number of lines on which light falls, and λ and $\Delta\lambda$
are the mean wavelength of two spectrum lines that can
barely be recognized as separate and the wavelength distance between them, respectively. Thus, the resolution is

$$R = Nm = (15cm)(600 \text{ lines/mm})\left(10\frac{mm}{cm}\right)(1)$$

$$= 90,000.$$

(b) Green light has wavelength λ equal to approximately 5500 Å, so from equation (1),

$$\Delta\lambda = \frac{\lambda}{Nm} = \frac{5500 \text{ Å}}{90,000} = 0.06 \text{ Å}.$$

So, any two green lines must be at least 0.06 Å apart for the diffraction grating of part (a) to be able to resolve them.

(c) For a prism, resolution is given by the following relation:

$$R = \frac{\lambda}{\Delta\lambda} = B \frac{dn}{d\lambda} \tag{2}$$

where B is the base width of the prism and $\frac{dn}{d\lambda}$, the change in index of refraction of the prism with respect to wavelength, for green light through glass, is given in tables as $12 \times 10^4 \text{ m}^{-1}$. So, solving equation (2) for B gives

$$B = \frac{\lambda/\Delta\lambda}{dn/d\lambda} = \frac{R}{dn/d\lambda} = \frac{90,000}{12 \times 10^4 \text{m}^{-1}} = .75 \text{ m} = 75 \text{ cm}.$$

Thus, a prism would have to be 75 cm wide to give the same resolution as the grating.

PHASE AND GROUP VELOCITIES

● **PROBLEM** 23-10

The group velocity of light in a certain substance is found to vary inversely with wavelength. How does the index of refraction vary with wavelength?

Solution: The group velocity v_g, and the wave velocity, v, are related to each other according to the following relation:

$$v_g = v - \lambda \frac{dv}{d\lambda} \tag{1}$$

where $\quad v = f\lambda = \frac{c}{n} \tag{2}$

(f is the frequency of the wave, n is the refractive index of the medium, c is the velocity of light in a vacuum, and λ is the wavelength of light, evaluated in the medium.)

Substituting for v from equation (2) in equation (1) gives

$$v_g = f\lambda - \lambda \frac{d}{d\lambda}\left(\frac{c}{n}\right)$$

$$\frac{d}{d\lambda}\left(\frac{c}{n}\right) = c \frac{d}{d\lambda}\left(\frac{1}{n}\right)$$

$$\frac{d}{d\lambda}\left(\frac{1}{n}\right) = \frac{d\left(\frac{1}{n}\right)}{dn} \cdot \frac{dn}{d\lambda} = \frac{-1}{n^2}\frac{dn}{d\lambda} \ .$$

Thus,
$$\frac{d}{d\lambda}\left(\frac{c}{n}\right) = \frac{-c}{n^2}\frac{dn}{d\lambda}$$

and so,
$$v_g = f\lambda + \frac{\lambda c}{n^2}\left(\frac{dn}{d\lambda}\right) = b'\lambda + \frac{c\lambda}{n^2}\left(\frac{dn}{d\lambda}\right) \tag{3}$$

where $f = b'$ (a constant).

But
$$v_g \propto \frac{1}{\lambda} = \frac{a'}{\lambda} \tag{4}$$

where a' is a constant.

Equating the expressions on the right-hand side of equations (3) and (4),

$$b'\lambda + \frac{c\lambda}{n^2}\left(\frac{dn}{d\lambda}\right) = \frac{a'}{\lambda}$$

Rearranging this equation,

$$c\frac{\lambda}{n^2}\left(\frac{dn}{d\lambda}\right) = \left(\frac{a'}{\lambda} - b'\lambda\right).$$

Multiplying both sides of this equation by $\frac{d\lambda}{\lambda}$ gives

$$c\frac{dn}{n^2} = \left(\frac{a'}{\lambda^2} - b'\right)d\lambda.$$

Integrating both sides,

$$\int \frac{c}{n^2}\,dn = \int\left(\frac{a'}{\lambda^2} - b'\right)d\lambda$$

or
$$-\frac{c}{n} = -\frac{a'}{\lambda} - b'\lambda$$

Hence,
$$\frac{c}{n} = \frac{a'}{\lambda} + b'\lambda = \frac{a' + b'\lambda^2}{\lambda}$$

688

Thus, $\dfrac{n}{c} = \dfrac{\lambda}{a' + b'\lambda^2}$

or $\quad n = c\,\dfrac{\lambda}{\left(a' + b'\lambda^2\right)} = \dfrac{\lambda}{\left(\dfrac{a'}{c} + \dfrac{b'}{c}\,\lambda^2\right)}$

$$= \dfrac{\lambda}{\left(a + b\lambda^2\right)}$$

where $\quad a = \dfrac{a'}{c} \quad$ and $b = \dfrac{b'}{c}$.

Hence, $\quad n = \dfrac{\lambda}{a + b\lambda^2}$, where a and b are constants.

• PROBLEM 23-11

The dispersion curve of glass can be represented approximately by Cauchy's empirical equation

$$n = A + B\lambda^{-2}$$

(n represents the index of refraction of the glass, λ represents the vacuum wavelength of light used, and A and B are constants). Find the phase and group velocities at $\lambda = 5000\ \text{Å}$ for a particular glass for which $A = 1.40$ and $B = 2.5 \times 10^6\,(\text{Å})^2$.

Solution: Let c denote the velocity of light in a vacuum. The phase velocity v_p and the group velocity v_g are given by

$$v_p = \dfrac{c}{n} \tag{1}$$

and $\quad v_g = v_p - \lambda_m \dfrac{dv_p}{d\lambda_m} \tag{2}$

where λ_m is the wavelength in the medium.

Now $\quad n = A + \dfrac{B}{\lambda^2}$.

Substituting the given values for A, B, and λ into the above equation gives

$$n = 1.4 + \dfrac{2.5 \times 10^6}{(5000)^2}$$

$$n = 1.5$$

689

Substituting for n in equation (1) gives

$$v_p = \frac{c}{1.5} \tag{3}$$

To find v_g divide equation (2) by c, the velocity of light in a vacuum, and take the reciprocal. Then

$$\frac{c}{v_g} = \frac{c}{v_p - \lambda_m \frac{dv_p}{d\lambda_m}} = \frac{1}{\frac{v_p}{c} - \frac{\lambda_m}{c} \cdot \frac{dv_p}{d\lambda_m}}$$

Since $\frac{c}{v_p} = n$, and since $c = f\lambda$ and $v_p = f\lambda_m$ (f denotes the frequency of the light used),

$$n = \frac{f\lambda}{f\lambda_m} \qquad \text{or} \qquad \frac{\lambda_m}{\lambda} = \frac{1}{n} .$$

Thus, substituting $\frac{v_p}{c} = \frac{1}{n}$ and $\frac{\lambda_m}{c} = \frac{\lambda}{nc}$ into the above

equation gives,

$$\frac{c}{v_g} = \frac{1}{\left(\frac{1}{n}\right) - \frac{\lambda}{nc} \frac{dv_p}{d\lambda_m}} .$$

Since $dv_p = d\left(\frac{c}{n}\right) = cd\left(\frac{1}{n}\right)$,

$$\frac{c}{v_g} = \frac{1}{\left(\frac{1}{n}\right) - \frac{\lambda}{n} \frac{d\left(\frac{1}{n}\right)}{d\left(\frac{\lambda}{n}\right)}} = \frac{n}{1 - \lambda \frac{\left[-\frac{1}{n^2} dn\right]}{\left[\frac{d\lambda}{n} - \frac{\lambda dn}{n^2}\right]}}$$

$$= \frac{n\left[\frac{d\lambda}{n} - \lambda \frac{dn}{n^2}\right]}{\frac{d\lambda}{n} - \lambda \frac{dn}{n^2} + \frac{\lambda}{n^2} dn} = \frac{n^2}{d\lambda}\left[\frac{d\lambda}{n} - \lambda \frac{dn}{n^2}\right]$$

$$= n - \lambda \frac{dn}{d\lambda} \tag{4}$$

Now $\quad \dfrac{dn}{d\lambda} = \dfrac{d}{d\lambda}\left[A + \dfrac{B}{\lambda^2}\right] = \dfrac{-2B}{\lambda^3} .$

690

Thus, $\lambda \dfrac{dn}{d\lambda} = -2 \dfrac{B}{\lambda^2}$ (5)

Substituting for $\lambda \dfrac{dn}{d\lambda}$ from equation (5) into equation (4) gives

$$\frac{c}{v_g} = n + 2 \frac{B}{\lambda^2} = 1.5 + \frac{2 \times 2.5 \times 10^6}{(5000)^2}$$

$$= 1.5 + 0.2 = 1.7$$

Thus, $v_g = \dfrac{c}{1.7}$

IMAGE SEPARATION

● **PROBLEM** 23-12

A narrow bundle of light is incident at an angle of 45°
on a plane-parallel plate 1 cm thick. If the refractive
indices for blue and red light are 1.653 and 1.614,
respectively, what is the sideways separation of the two
colors after leaving the plate?

<u>Solution:</u> In figure 1, let θ be the angle of
refraction for blue light and let θ' be the angle of
refraction for red light. The sideways separation is
represented by x. It must be noted that the separation
between the blue and red light rays is greatly exaggerated
for reasons of clarity.

According to Snell's Law, sin i = n sin r, where i and r
are the angles of incidence and refraction, respectively,
and n is the index of refraction of the plate. Then,

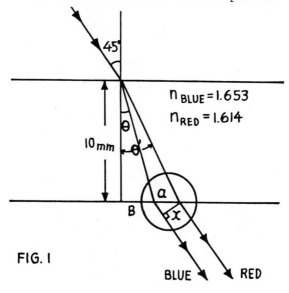

FIG. I

691

$$\sin 45° = 1.653(\sin \theta)$$

and $\quad\sin 45° = 1.614(\sin \theta')$

from which,

$$\theta = \sin^{-1}\left(\frac{\sin 45°}{1.653}\right) \tag{1}$$

and $\quad\theta' = \sin^{-1}\left(\frac{\sin 45°}{1.614}\right)$. $\tag{2}$

From the definition of the tangent of an angle, for the blue light,

$$\tan \theta = \frac{b}{10\text{mm}} \text{ .}$$

Substituting for θ from equation (1) and solving for b, we have

$$b = (10\text{mm}) \cdot \tan\left[\sin^{-1}\left(\frac{\sin 45°}{1.653}\right)\right] \text{ .} \tag{3}$$

Similarly, for the red light,

$$\tan \theta' = \frac{a + b}{10 \text{ mm}}$$

Substituting for b from equation (3),

$$\tan\left[\sin^{-1}\left(\frac{\sin 45°}{1.614}\right)\right] = \frac{a + (10\text{mm}) \cdot \tan\left[\sin^{-1}\left(\frac{\sin 45°}{1.653}\right)\right]}{(10 \text{ mm})}$$

Solving for a gives the result

$$a = (10\text{mm}) \cdot \tan\left[\sin^{-1}\left(\frac{\sin 45°}{1.614}\right)\right]$$

$$- (10\text{mm}) \cdot \tan\left[\sin^{-1}\left(\frac{\sin 45°}{1.653}\right)\right]$$

$$= 0.1411 \text{ mm} \tag{4}$$

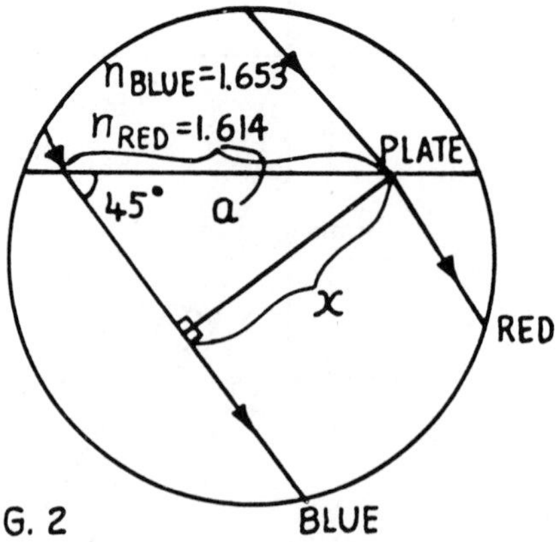

FIG. 2

The circled area in Figure 1 is enlarged in Figure 2 to

clarify the angles involved. The angle between the plate and the beam of blue light is 45° because it is parallel to the incident light beam. By trigonometry,

$$x = a \cdot \sin 45° ,$$

and from equation (4), the sideways separation of the two colors after leaving the plate is

$$x = (0.1411 \text{ mm}) \sin 45° \cong 0.100 \text{ mm}.$$

● **PROBLEM** 23-13

A lens is made of borate flint glass for which ν (the reciprocal of the dispersive power of the lens-medium) = 55.2. The focal length of the lens for sodium light is 30 inches. Find the distance between the red and blue images of the sun formed by the lens.

Solution: Two methods of solving this problem are shown.
Method 1:

The focal length of a lens, f, is given by the lens-maker's formula:

$$\frac{1}{f} = (n-1)\left(\frac{1}{r_1} - \frac{1}{r_2}\right) = (n-1)\rho_1 \tag{1}$$

where ρ_1 is the shape factor, n is the index of refraction of the lens, and r_1 and r_2 are the radii of curvature of the lens.

Solving for f,

$$f = \frac{1}{(n-1)\rho_1} \tag{2}$$

Now $$f_D = \frac{1}{(n_D-1)\rho_1} \quad \text{or} \quad \rho_1 = \frac{1}{f_D(n_D-1)} \tag{3}$$

$$f_F = \frac{1}{(n_F-1)\rho_1} \quad \text{or} \quad (n_F-1) = \frac{1}{f_F\rho_1} \tag{4}$$

$$f_C = \frac{1}{(n_C-1)\rho_1} \quad \text{or} \quad (n_C-1) = \frac{1}{f_C\rho_1} \tag{5}$$

Subtracting equation (5) from equation (4),

$$(n_F-1) - (n_C-1) = \frac{1}{f_F\rho_1} - \frac{1}{f_C\rho_1}$$

or $\qquad (n_F - n_C) = \dfrac{1}{\rho_1}\left[\dfrac{1}{f_F} - \dfrac{1}{f_C}\right]$

Hence,

$$\dfrac{1}{f_F} - \dfrac{1}{f_C} = \rho_1(n_F - n_C) = \dfrac{n_F - n_C}{f_D(n_D - 1)} \quad \text{(from Eq.(3))}$$

$$= \dfrac{1}{f_D \nu}$$

or $\qquad \dfrac{f_C - f_F}{f_F f_C} = \dfrac{1}{f_D \nu}$

or $\qquad \dfrac{\Delta f}{f_D^2} = \dfrac{1}{f_D \nu} \quad .$

Here it is assumed that the focal lengths for the red and blue colors are not much different from that for the yellow; thus, $f_F \approxeq f_C \approxeq f_D$ and $\Delta f = (f_C - f_F)$.

Thus, $\qquad \Delta f = \dfrac{f_D}{\nu} = \dfrac{30 \text{ inches}}{55.2} = 0.54 \text{ inches.}$

The sun is assumed to be at infinity. Thus, the image is formed at the focal point of the lens.

Method 2:

From the lens maker's formula for the focal length of a lens

$$\dfrac{1}{f} = (n-1)\left[\dfrac{1}{r_1} - \dfrac{1}{r_2}\right] = (n-1)\rho_1 \tag{6}$$

where ρ_1 is a constant for the given lens.

Taking logarithms of both sides,

$$\ln\left(\dfrac{1}{f}\right) = \ln\left[(n-1)\rho_1\right] . \tag{7}$$

Since $\ln (AB) = \ln A + \ln B$ and $\ln \dfrac{A}{B} = \ln A - \ln B$, equation (7) becomes

$$\ln 1 - \ln f = \ln(n-1) + \ln\rho_1 \tag{8}$$

Differentiating f with respect to n gives,

$$-\dfrac{df}{f} = \dfrac{dn}{(n-1)} . \tag{9}$$

Now the dispersive power $= \dfrac{dn}{(n-1)}$ (10)

Thus, $\dfrac{1}{\text{dispersive power}} = \nu = \dfrac{(n-1)}{dn}$ (11)

and substituting into equation (9) gives,

$$-\frac{df}{f} = \frac{1}{\nu} \ .$$

Thus, $|df| = \dfrac{f}{\nu} = \dfrac{30 \text{ in.}}{55.2} = 0.54 \text{ in.}$

Here, $|df|$ is the difference between the focal lengths for the red and blue images of the sun which is assumed to be at infinity.

DETERMINATION OF THE FOCAL LENGTH OF A LENS

● **PROBLEM** 23-14

A converging crown glass lens and a diverging flint glass lens form a converging achromatic lens of focal length 50 cm. Find the focal length of each lens for C, D, and F light, from the given data.

Light	Wavelength (Å)	Refractive Index for Crown Glass	Refractive Index for Flint Glass
C	6563	1.5145	1.6444
D	5893	1.5170	1.6499
F	4861	1.5230	1.6637

Solution: When two lenses are in contact, the effective focal length f of the combination is given by the equation

$$\frac{1}{f} = \frac{1}{f_1} + \frac{1}{f_2} \ ,$$ (1)

where f_1 and f_2 are the focal lengths of each lens separately. The individual focal lengths f_i can be calculated using the thin lens equation,

$$\frac{1}{f_i} = (n_i - 1) \cdot \left(\frac{1}{r_a} - \frac{1}{r_b} \right)$$ (2)

where n_i is the index of refraction of the lens for one particular wavelength and r_a, r_b are the radii of curvature of the lens.

695

Substituting the expression given in equation (2) for f_1 and f_2 in equation (1), using the indices of refraction given for C light and F light, we have

$$\frac{1}{50} = (1.5145 - 1)\left(\frac{1}{r_1} - \frac{1}{r_2}\right)$$

$$+ (1.6444 - 1)\left(\frac{1}{r_3} - \frac{1}{r_4}\right) \tag{3}$$

and

$$\frac{1}{50} = (1.5230 - 1)\left(\frac{1}{r_1} - \frac{1}{r_2}\right)$$

$$+ (1.6637 - 1)\left(\frac{1}{r_3} - \frac{1}{r_4}\right), \tag{4}$$

respectively, where r_1, r_2 are the radii of curvature of the faces of the crown lens and r_3, r_4 are the radii of curvature of the faces of the flint glass lens.

Letting $x = \left(\frac{1}{r_1} - \frac{1}{r_2}\right)$ and $y = \left(\frac{1}{r_3} - \frac{1}{r_4}\right)$ \tag{5}

equations (3) and (4) become

$$\frac{1}{50} = 0.5145x + 0.6444y \tag{6}$$

and

$$\frac{1}{50} = 0.5230x + 0.6637y \tag{7}$$

These equations can be solved simultaneously to yield

$$x = 0.08669 \quad \text{and} \quad y = -0.03818.$$

Now that the value of $\left(\frac{1}{r_a} - \frac{1}{r_b}\right)$ for each lens is known, the focal lengths for light of varying wavelengths can be computed.

Applying equation (2) for each wavelength of light through the crown glass lens, we have

$$\frac{1}{f_C} = (1.5145-1)(0.08669), \text{ from which } f_C = 22.42 \text{ cm}$$

$$\frac{1}{f_D} = (1.5170-1)(0.08669), \text{ from which } f_D = 22.31 \text{ cm}$$

$$\frac{1}{f_F} = (1.5230-1)(0.08669), \text{ from which } f_F = 22.06 \text{ cm}.$$

696

Similarly, for the flint glass lens, we have

$$\frac{1}{f_C} = (1.6444-1)(-0.03818), \text{ from which } f_C = -40.64 \text{ cm}$$

$$\frac{1}{f_D} = (1.6499-1)(-0.03818), \text{ from which } f_D = -40.30 \text{ cm}$$

$$\frac{1}{f_F} = (1.6637-1)(-0.03818), \text{ from which } f_F = -39.46 \text{ cm}.$$

● **PROBLEM** 23-15

A thin lens is made of crown glass for which $v_1 = 60.2$ (v = 1/dispersive power). Another thin lens is made of flint glass for which $v_2 = 36.2$. When the two lenses are placed in contact they form an achromatic combination with focal length 10 cm. Find the focal length of each lens.

Solution: Here we use the lens maker's formula for the focal length of a lens:

$$\frac{1}{f} = (n-1)\left(\frac{1}{r_1} - \frac{1}{r_2}\right) = (n-1)\rho \tag{1}$$

where ρ is the shape factor, r_1 and r_2 represent the radii of curvature of the lens, and n represents the index of refraction of the lens.

Also, $\quad v = \dfrac{1}{\text{dispersive power}} = \dfrac{1}{\left(\dfrac{dn}{n-1}\right)} = \dfrac{(n-1)}{dn} \tag{2}$

Now for the two lenses, we can write by differentiating f with respect to n, from equation (1),

$$-\frac{df_1}{f_1^2} = \rho_1 dn_1 \tag{3}$$

$$-\frac{df_2}{f_2^2} = \rho_2 dn_2 \tag{4}$$

Substituting for $\frac{1}{f}$ the expression given in equation (1) into equations (3) and (4), we get

$$-\frac{df_1}{f_1} \cdot (n_1-1)\rho_1 = (dn_1\rho_1)$$

697

or
$$-\frac{df_1}{f_1} = \frac{dn_1}{(n_1-1)}$$

Thus, $\quad -df_1 = f_1 \frac{dn_1}{(n_1-1)}$

Using equation (2), $-df_1 = f_1/v_1$, or

$$-df_1 = \frac{f_1}{60.2} \tag{5}$$

Similarly,

$$-\frac{df_2}{f_2} \cdot (n_2-1)\rho_2 = dn_2\rho_2$$

Then, $\quad -\frac{df_2}{f_2} = \frac{dn_2}{n_2-1}$

$$-df_2 = f_2 \frac{dn_2}{n_2-1} = \frac{f_2}{v_2}$$

or $\quad -df_2 = \frac{f_2}{36.2} \tag{6}$

Since the combination of two lenses is achromatic, $df_1 + df_2 = 0$.

Adding equations (5) and (6) gives

$$-(df_1+df_2) = \frac{f_1}{60.2} + \frac{f_2}{36.2} = 0. \tag{7}$$

Now $\quad \dfrac{1}{f_1} + \dfrac{1}{f_2} = \dfrac{1}{10cm} \qquad$ (given) $\tag{8}$

and $\quad \dfrac{f_1}{60.2} + \dfrac{f_2}{36.2} = 0. \tag{9}$

From equation (9),

$$f_1 = -60.2 \frac{f_2}{36.2}. \tag{10}$$

Substituting the expression for f_1 given by equation (10) into equation (8),

$$-\frac{36.2}{60.2f_2} + \frac{1}{f_2} = \frac{1}{10cm}$$

698

or $\quad \dfrac{1}{f_2} \cdot \left[-\dfrac{36.2}{60.2} + 1 \right] = \dfrac{1}{10} \text{ cm}$

Hence, $\quad f_2 = 10 \left[\dfrac{24}{60.2} \right] \text{ cm.} = 3.99 \text{ cm.}$

Substituting this value for f_2 into equation (10) gives

$$f_1 = -60.2 \ \dfrac{f_2}{36.2} = -60.2 \times \dfrac{3.99 \text{cm}}{36.2}$$

$$= -6.63 \text{ cm.}$$

● **PROBLEM** 23-16

A crystal quartz lens has a focal length of 20 cm for sodium light. Calculate its focal length for a wavelength of 51 μ. Draw to scale a diagram showing how the infrared light of this wavelength could be isolated from visible light by the method of focal isolation.

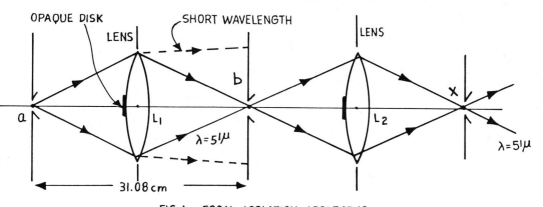

FIG. I   FOCAL ISOLATION APPARATUS

Solution: Using the lens maker's formula for the focal length of a lens, we can write

$$\dfrac{1}{f} = (n-1)\rho \qquad\qquad (1)$$

where f is the focal length, n is the refractive index, and ρ is the shape factor.

The refractive index of crystal quartz for sodium light is

n(sodium wavelength) = 1.5436

and the focal length f is given to be 20 cm.

Substituting for n and f in equation (1),

699

$$\frac{1}{20} = (1.5436 - 1)\rho$$

Hence, $\rho = \dfrac{1}{20 \text{ x } .5436} = \dfrac{1}{10.872}$

For 51μ radiation, the refractive index of quartz as measured by Rubens is 2.40. Thus, from equation (1),

$$\frac{1}{f} = (2.40 - 1) \ \frac{1}{10.872}$$

or $f = \dfrac{10.872}{1.40} = 7.77 \text{ cm.}$

Hence the focal length of crystal quartz at 51μ is 7.77 cm.

The method of focal isolation depends on the peculiar optical properties of quartz. The refractive index is approximately 1.5 for the visible part of the spectrum that is to be disposed of, while the index of refraction is greater than 2.0 for the desired long wavelength that is to be saved. The set up to accomplish this objective is shown in figure 1.

The light of short wavelength from the source passing through the entrance aperture 'a' either is obstructed by the opaque disk or is not converged so that it cannot go through the middle aperture 'b'. The long wavelengths, however, do go through 'b'. This combination of two lenses and the apertures a, b, and x with central obscurations thus isolates the longest wavelengths in the emission of the source.

CHAPTER 24

PHOTOMETRY

LENSES

Two lenses, A and B, have equal focal lengths but A has twice the diameter of B. (a) What is the ratio of energy collected by lens A to that collected by lens B? (b) What is the corresponding ratio of the areas of the diffraction patterns? (c) What is the ratio of the energy per unit area in the two patterns?

Solution: If A has twice the diameter of lens B, then lens A has four times the area of B, since area is proportional to the square of the diameter.

(a) The energy collected by a lens is proportional to the area of the lens; thus, the ratio of the energy collected by lens A to lens B is 4:1.

(b) The area of a diffraction pattern is proportional to the reciprocal of the area; thus, for the diffraction patterns of lenses A and B, the area is ¼:1 or 1:4.

(c) Since the energy absorbed is proportional to the square of the area, the ratio of the energy per unit area for lenses A and B is 16:1.

● PROBLEM 24-2

A simple lens having a diameter of 8 cm and a focal length of 25 cm is used to focus the light of the sun onto a white screen. What is the ratio of the image brightness to the screen brightness with no lens present?

Solution: Since the sun is very far away from the lens, the object distance O from the sun to the lens can be approximated as infinity. By using the lens equation $\frac{1}{O} + \frac{1}{i} = \frac{1}{f}$ (i = the image distance from the lens and f = the focal length of the lens), i is determined to be approximately equal to f, or i = 25 cm. Therefore, the

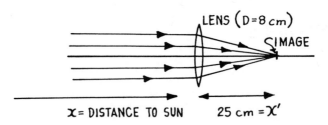

LENS $(D=8\,cm)$

ς IMAGE

$x=$ DISTANCE TO SUN   25 cm $=x'$

image of the sun formed by the lens is approximately 25 cm from the lens. The following constants will be used: x = distance from sun to earth = 1.50×10^{11} m; S = area of the sun as seen through the lens = πr^2, where r = 6.96×10^8 m = the mean solar radius.

The illumination E, at the lens (or screen, with no lens present), is given by $E = LS/x^2$, where L = the luminance of the sun. If we assume that the total transmission factor of the lens, $T \cong 1$, then the total luminous flux transmitted to the image is $\left(\dfrac{LS}{x^2}\right)\left(\dfrac{\pi D^2}{4}\right)$ where $\dfrac{\pi D^2}{4}$ is the lens area (D is the diameter of the lens). The image area is $S\left(\dfrac{x'}{x}\right)^2$, where x' is the image distance from the lens ($= i$). Therefore, the luminance of the image, L_I = $\left(\dfrac{LS}{x^2}\dfrac{\pi D^2}{4}\right)\left(\dfrac{x^2}{S(x')^2}\right)$ or $L_I = \dfrac{L\pi D^2}{4(x')^2}$.

Then $\dfrac{\text{image brightness}}{\text{screen brightness (no lens)}} = \dfrac{L_I}{E} = \dfrac{(L\pi D^2)/[4(x')^2]}{(L\pi r^2)/(x^2)} =$

$\dfrac{D^2 x^2}{4(x')^2 r^2}$ or substituting for D, x, x', and r,

$\dfrac{L_I}{E} = \dfrac{(64)\,[1.50 \times 10^{11}]^2}{4\,(25)^2\,(6.96 \times 10^8)^2} \cong 1189.$

THE LAMBERTIAN EMITTER

● **PROBLEM** 24-3

What is the radiant intensity of a Lambertian emitter which projects 50 mW into a hemisphere?

Solution: A Lambertian emitter projects 50 mW of flux. There are 4π steradians in a sphere. Thus there are 2π steradians in a hemisphere.

We know that the following equation is true:

I = F/A

where I is the intensity, F is the flux and A is the area.

Substituting the values for F and A into this equation gives

$$I = \frac{50 \cdot 10^{-3}}{2\pi} = .00795 \text{ W/sr}$$

LUMINOUS FLUX AND RADIANT FLUX

● PROBLEM 24-4

A sample of radiant flux consists of 20 watts of mono-chromatic light of wavelength 500 mµ and 10 watts of monochromatic light of wavelength 600 mµ. (a) What is the radiant flux in the sample? (b) What is the luminous flux in the sample? (c) What is the luminous efficiency of the sample?

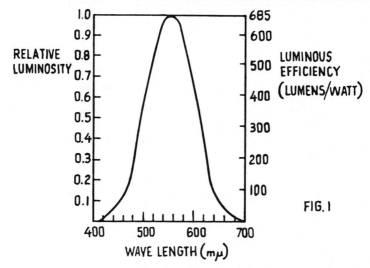

FIG. I

Solution:

(a) Radiant flux is defined as the power emitted by a source of radiation. Since our two sources have radiant flux of 20 and 10 watts respectively, the total power radiation will be 30 watts or the total radiant flux is 30 watts.

(b) Radiant flux, evaluated with respect to its capacity to evoke the sensation of brightness, is called luminous flux. Illumination engineers have established a standard for which light at 555 nm and radiant flux 1 watt will produce 685 lumens of luminous flux. Since the luminous flux is related to how the eye perceives brightness we need to have an eye response curve such as shown in Figure 1. This curve allows us to determine that at 500 nm, the luminous flux is 249 lumens per watt and at 600 nm, the luminous flux is 411 lumens per watt. Therefore the total luminous flux is

$$\left(249 \times 20\right) + \left(411 \times 10\right) = 9090 \text{ lumens}$$

(c) The luminous efficiency of a source is the ratio of the luminous flux to the power (radiant flux) applied to the source. So

$$\text{luminous efficiency} = \frac{9090}{30} = 303 \text{ lumens/watt}$$

● **PROBLEM** 24-5

The output of a helium-neon laser, which emits at a wavelength of approximately 633 nm, is 0.5 mW. What is the luminous flux?

TABLE OF RELATIVE LUMINOSITY VALUES
Based on $V_\lambda = 1.000$ at 0.555 micron

Wave-length, microns	V_λ	Wave-length, microns	V_λ	Wave-length, microns	V_λ
0.400	0.00120	0.520	0.710	0.640	0.175
0.420	0.00400	0.530	0.862	0.650	0.107
0.430	0.0116	0.540	0.954	0.660	0.0610
0.440	0.0230	0.550	0.995	0.670	0.0320
0.450	0.0380	0.560	0.995	0.680	0.0170
0.460	0.0600	0.570	0.952	0.690	0.00820
0.470	0.0910	0.580	0.870	0.700	0.00410
0.480	0.139	0.590	0.757	0.710	0.00210
0.490	0.208	0.600	0.631	0.720	0.00105
0.500	0.323	0.610	0.503	0.730	0.000520
0.510	0.503	0.620	0.381	0.740	0.000250
		0.630	0.265	0.750	0.000120

TABLE. I

Solution: The radiant energy which a source emits per unit time is called the 'radiant flux' and represents the time rate of flow of energy. When a sample of radiant flux is evaluated with respect to its ability to produce a visual sensation, it is called 'luminous flux.' If equal quantities of different colors produced the same brightness to the eye, then the radiant flux would provide a measure of the luminous flux. However, the human eye is most sensitive to a wavelength of 555 mμ and least sensitive to wavelengths of 400 mμ and 650 mμ. To express this difference quantitatively, an arbitrary unit of luminous flux is chosen so that the relative visibility of the radiation is included in this definition. This unit is called the 'lumen' and is defined as the luminous flux of a sample of radiant flux of wavelength 555 mμ and of amount 1.46 milliwatts. In other words, a radiant flux of 1 watt at 555 mμ is equivalent to 685 lumens. If the radiant flux in a sample at another wavelength λ is 1 watt, then the luminous flux is 685 V_λ lumens, where V_λ is the relative luminosity at the wavelength λ. The relative luminosity values are given in Table 1. If the light source contains many wavelengths, then the luminous flux is

$685 \times \int_0^\infty V_\lambda P_\lambda d\lambda$ where P_λ is the power corresponding to the wavelength λ.

Corresponding to the He-Ne laser wavelength 633 mμ, the relative luminosity from the table is approximately 0.265. Hence the luminous flux is given by 685 × 0.265 × .5 × 10^{-3} lumens = 0.09 lumens.

LUMINANCE

● **PROBLEM** 24-6

A lamp filament in the form of a flat ribbon of area 10 mm^2 radiates 10 W of light. (a) What is its luminance, and (b) how much power is collected by a lens of diameter 30 mm which is 100 mm from the filament?

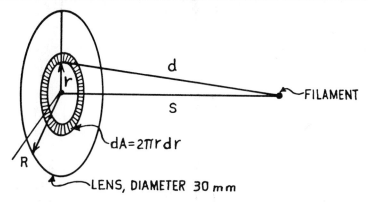

Solution: (a) Luminance is equivalent to the luminous flux per unit area per solid angle. Here, light is radiated at all angles, so the solid angle is equal to 4π steradians. Applying the definition of luminance

$$L = \frac{F}{A4\pi} ,$$

where F = the power radiated and A = the area of the filament. Substituting for F and A,

$$L = \frac{10}{10 \cdot 4\pi} = \frac{1}{4\pi} \text{ W mm}^{-2} \text{ sr}^{-1}$$

(b) If the ribbon is circular, its radius, r, can be determined by solving the equation $\pi r^2 = 10$ mm^2 for r. Solving for r gives the result r = 1.78 mm and since this is small compared to the distance between the ribbon and the lens, the ribbon can be treated as a point source.

   dP = power collected by area dA of lens

$$dP = LA_f \frac{dA}{d^2} \tag{1}$$

where

   P = the power collected by the lens ,

705

$$L = \text{Luminance} = \frac{1}{4\pi} \; W \; mm^{-2} \; sr^{-1} \; , \quad \text{and}$$

$$A_f = \text{Area of filament}$$

$$= 10 \; mm^2 \; .$$

Integrating equation (1),

$$P = \int dP = \int LA_f \frac{dA}{d^2} = LA_f \int_0^R \frac{2\pi r dr}{(s+r)^2}$$

where $s = 100$ mm and $r = 15$ mm.

Let $r + s = u$. Then $r = u - s$ and $dr = du$. Hence,

$$P = 2\pi LA_f \int \frac{(u-s)\,du}{u^2} = 2\pi LA_f \left[\int \frac{du}{u} - \int \frac{s\,du}{u^2} \right] = 2\pi LA_f \left[\ell n u + \frac{s}{u} \right].$$

Then $P = 2\pi LA_f \left[\frac{s}{r+s} + \ell n(r+s) \right]_0^R =$

$$2\pi LA_f \left[\frac{s}{R+s} + \ell n(R+s) - 1 - \ell ns \right] =$$

$$2\pi LA_f \left[\frac{s-R-s}{R+s} + \ell n\left(\frac{R+s}{s} \right) \right] = 2\pi LA_f \left[\ell n\left(1 + \frac{R}{s} \right) - \frac{R}{R+s} \right].$$

Substituting for L, A_f, R, and s,

$$P = (\frac{1}{4\pi}) \, 10 \, (2\pi) \, (.00933)$$

$$= 0.047 \text{ watts.}$$

Note: We have assumed that the plane of the lamp filament is parallel to that of the lens, so that the lens views the whole 10 mm^2 area of the light source. Any other assumption will reduce the power collected by the lens.

ILLUMINATION

• PROBLEM 24-7

A relay is to be controlled by a vacuum photocell, actuated by the light passing through an aperture measuring 15 mm by 40 mm. At least 0.2 lumen must strike the photocell to operate the relay. What is the maximum permissible distance from the aperture to a uniform point source of intensity 50 candles, if the light from the source is to trigger the relay?

Solution: The illumination is measured as the light energy per unit area per unit time falling on a surface or, if we use candlepower as our measure of emitted light source energy per unit time, the illumination in lumens per square millimeters is given by

$$E_{1umens/mm^2} = \frac{I_{cp}\cos\theta}{r^2} \tag{1}$$

where I is the source intensity, θ is the angle between the source rays and the unit vector normal to the surface being illuminated and r is the distance in millimeters from the source to the surface being illuminated. Also,

$$E = F/A \tag{2}$$

where F is the number of lumens of energy striking the photocell and A is the area being illuminated. In this problem, F = 0.2 lumen; A = 15 × 40 square millimeters, so

$$E = \frac{.2\ 1umen}{(15)(40)mm^2} = 3.3 \times 10^{-4}\ 1umens\ per\ square\ millimeter$$

which will activate the photocell. From equation (1), since we have $\theta = 0$,

$$3.3 \times 10^{-4} = \frac{50}{r^2}$$

$$r^2 = 1.5 \times 10^5\ mm^2$$

$$r = 387\ mm = 38.7\ cm.$$

● **PROBLEM 24-8**

A room is 16 ft high, 30 ft long, and 20 ft wide. Four sources of intensity 200 candles each are suspended from the ceiling on cords 4 ft long. Each cord is 5 ft from both side walls in its respective corner. Compute the direct illumination of a table top in the center of the room, 30 inches above the floor.

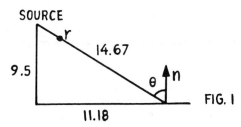

SOURCE

FIG. I

Solution: The illumination is measured as the light energy per unit area per unit time falling on a surface or, if we measure emitted source energy per unit time in candle powers, then the illumination in lumens per square foot is given by

$$E_{1umens/ft^2} = \frac{I_{cp}\cos\theta}{r^2_{ft}} \tag{1}$$

where I is the source intensity, θ is the angle between the source rays and the unit vector normal to the surface being illuminated, and r is the distance in feet from the source to the surface illuminated.

Here we see that each of the four light sources are equidistant from the table top to be illuminated, so the total illumination will be four times the illumination of a single source of intensity 200 cp. Looking at the location of the light sources and the table top, we see that the light sources are suspended 4 ft from a ceiling 16 ft high. Therefore, the light sources are 12 ft or 144 inches above the floor. Then the light sources are (144 - 30) inches = 114 inches or 9.5 feet above the table top. Also, we see that the horizontal distances between the center of the table top and the light source are 30/2 - 5 = 10 ft and 20/2 - 5 = 5 ft or by the Pythagorean theorem in three dimensions,

$$r^2 = x^2 + y^2 + z^2 = 9.5^2 + 10^2 + 5^2 = 215.25$$

$$r = 14.67 \text{ ft}$$

The horizontal distance is computed as follows:

$$h^2 = y^2 + z^2 = 10^2 + 5^2 = 125$$

$$h = 11.18 \text{ ft}$$

Thus, in two dimensions we have the picture as shown in Figure 1. So

$$E_1 = \frac{200 \times 9.5/14.67}{215.25} = 0.602$$

$$E_{total} = 4E_1 = 2.407 \text{ lumens/ft}^2$$

● **PROBLEM** 24-9

Two extended light sources, one emitting 25 W and the other 100 W, are 1 m apart from each other. Where must the screen of a Bunsen grease spot photometer be located in order to have equal illuminance on either side?

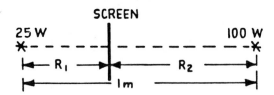

Solution: The illumination, E, of a surface placed at a distance R from the source of intensity, I, is given by the following equation:

$$E = \frac{I}{R^2} \qquad (1)$$

provided the light rays are perpendicular to the surface.

For two sources of intensities I_1 and I_2, placed at distances R_1 and R_2, respectively, from a screen placed normally to the light beam and producing equal illumination,

$$E_1 = E_2$$

and so, from equation (1),

$$\frac{I_1}{R_1^2} = \frac{I_2}{R_2^2} \qquad (2)$$

In our case, we have

$$I_1 = 25 \text{ W}$$

$$I_2 = 100 \text{ W}$$

It is also given that

$$R_1 + R_2 = 1 \text{ m}$$

Hence,

$$R_2 = (1 - R_1) \ .$$

Substituting for I_1, I_2, and R_2 in (2) gives the following result:

$$\frac{25}{R_1^2} = \frac{100}{(1 - R_1)^2}$$

or

$$(1 - R_1)^2 = 4R_1^2 \ .$$

Expanding this equation,

$$1 - 2R_1 + R_1^2 = 4R_1^2$$

or

$$3R_1^2 + 2R_1 - 1 = 0 \ .$$

Solving for R_1 by the quadratic equation gives

$$R_1 = \frac{-2 \pm \sqrt{4 + 12}}{6}$$

$$= -1, \frac{1}{3}$$

Hence, the 25 W lamp must be $\frac{1}{3}$ m from the screen.

A "point-source" unshaded electric lamp of luminous intensity 100 candles is 4.0 ft above the top of a table. Find the illuminance of the table (a) at a point directly below the lamp and (b) at a point 3.0 ft from the point directly below the lamp.

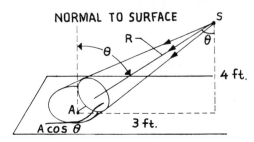

NORMAL TO SURFACE

ILLUMINANCE OF A SURFACE BY A POINT SOURCE

Solution:

(a)   Illuminance E is defined as the luminous flux F incident per unit area A.   Then

$$E = \frac{F}{A}$$

Also

$$F = I\omega$$

and

$$\omega = \frac{A}{R^2}$$

If the area A is perpendicular to the path of radiation from the point source, the illuminance can also be expressed as

$$E = \frac{F}{A} = \frac{I\omega}{A} = \frac{I(A/R^2)}{A} = \frac{I}{R^2}$$

which is the equation needed, since the luminous intensity I and the distance R from the point source are given in the statement of the problem.   Furthermore, we know that the area is perpendicular to the radiation being emitted by the lamp.   Therefore,

$$E = \frac{I}{R^2} = \frac{100 \text{ candles}}{(4.0 \text{ ft})^2} = 6.25 \text{ lu/ft}^2$$

(b)   For this second point, the area illuminated is a distance

$$R = \sqrt{(4.0 \text{ ft})^2 + (3.0 \text{ ft})^2} = 5.0 \text{ ft}$$

from the lamp, which was found by using the trigonometric relation for a right triangle. The illuminance is

$$E = \frac{F}{A}$$

where

$$F = I\omega.$$

The solid angle ω is defined as the ratio of the area upon which the source radiates at a radius R to this distance R. The area upon which the source radiates for this case can be seen from the figure to be A cos θ. Therefore,

$$\omega = \frac{A \cos \theta}{R^2}$$

and

$$E = \frac{F}{A} = \frac{I\omega}{A} = \frac{I(A \cos \theta/R^2)}{A} = \frac{I \cos \theta}{R^2}$$

Using trigonometry, cos θ is found to be

$$\cos \theta = \frac{4.0 \text{ ft}}{5.0 \text{ ft}} = 0.80$$

Then the illuminance on the area A is

$$E = \frac{I \cos \theta}{R^2} = \frac{(100 \text{ candles})(0.80)}{(5.0 \text{ ft})^2} = 3.2 \text{ lu/ft}^2$$

● **PROBLEM** 24-11

At what height above the center of a circular table of radius R should a point light source be suspended, to produce the maximum illumination at the edges of the table?

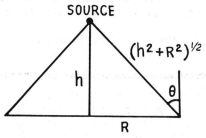

SOURCE

$(h^2+R^2)^{1/2}$

h

θ

R

Solution: Our equation for illumination is

$$E = \frac{I \cos \theta}{r^2} \tag{1}$$

where r represents the distance from the source to an edge

711

of the table, and θ is shown in the figure. We want to get the maximum illumination at the edge of a circular table. Then, from the figure, we see that for any h,

$$r^2 = h^2 + R^2 \text{ (by the Pythagorean theorem) and}$$

$$\cos \theta = h/(h^2 + R^2)^{\frac{1}{2}}$$

and so,

$$E = \frac{I}{h^2 + R^2} \times \frac{h}{\sqrt{h^2 + R^2}} = \frac{Ih}{(h^2 + R^2)^{3/2}} \qquad (2)$$

Now to find the maximum illumination we must differentiate E with respect to h and set

$$\frac{dE}{dh} = 0 \qquad (3)$$

Differentiating equation (2) with respect to h and equating it to zero gives the result

$$\frac{dE}{dh} = \frac{I}{(h^2 + R^2)^{3/2}} - \frac{Ih(3/2)(2h)}{(h^2 + R^2)^{5/2}} = 0 \qquad (4)$$

or

$$\frac{I[h^2 + R^2 - 3h^2]}{(h^2 + R^2)^{5/2}} = 0 \qquad (5)$$

or

$$R^2 = 2h^2 \qquad (6)$$

$$R = \sqrt{2}\, h \qquad (7)$$

Therefore, $h = \dfrac{R}{\sqrt{2}} = \dfrac{\sqrt{2}\,R}{2}$, and so,

to produce maximum illumination at the edges of the table, the source should be suspended at a height of $\dfrac{\sqrt{2}}{2}$ R above the center of the table.

● **PROBLEM** 24-12

Find two points on the straight line joining two sources at which the illumination from both sources is the same. The sources have intensities of 20 candlepower and 30 candlepower, respectively, and are 300 cm apart.

Solution: Since we are trying to find two points at which the illumination from both light sources is the same, one of the points must be between the two light

712

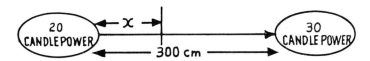

sources and the other point must be outside of the two sources (on the same side as the less intense source). We will first try to locate the point between the two sources.

Since the illumination E of a point is given by $E = \dfrac{I}{b^2}$, where I is the intensity of the source and b is the distance between the point and the source, we can set up the equation

$$\frac{20 \text{ candlepower}}{x^2} = \frac{30 \text{ candlepower}}{(300 \text{ cm} - x)^2} \qquad (1)$$

where x is the distance from the 20 candlepower source to the point, and 300 cm - x is the distance from the 30 candlepower source to the point, as shown in the figure. Cross-multiplying equation (1) gives:

$$(300 \text{ cm} - x)^2 (20) = 30x^2$$

Expanding this equation,

$$(9 \times 10^4 \text{cm}^2 - 600x \text{ cm} + x^2)(20) = 30x^2$$

or

$$2x^2 - 1200x \text{ cm} + 18 \times 10^4 \text{cm}^2 = 3x^2$$

This is equivalent to the following:

$$x^2 + 1200x \text{ cm} - 18 \times 10^4 \text{cm}^2 = 0$$

Solving for x by using the quadratic equation yields:

$$x = \frac{-1200 \text{ cm} \pm \sqrt{144 \times 10^4 \text{cm}^2 + 72 \times 10^4 \text{cm}^2}}{2}$$

$$= \frac{-1200 \text{ cm} \pm \sqrt{216 \times 10^4 \text{cm}^2}}{2}$$

$$\cong 135 \text{ cm}$$

Now, we will try to locate the point that is to the left of the 20 candlepower source, in the figure, by the equation

$$\frac{20}{x^2} = \frac{30}{(300 + x)^2} \qquad (2)$$

Solving equation (2) by the same methods used to solve

equation (1), we get x = - 135 cm and x = 1335 cm.
x = - 135 cm is the same result as that obtained from
equation (1). Therefore, the two points at which the
illumination is the same are at distances of 135 cm to
the right, and 1335 cm to the left, of the 20 candlepower
source.

● **PROBLEM** 24-13

Compute the illumination, on a screen parallel to the
surface, due to a partly diffuse surface of infinite extent
whose luminance is B candles/m^2.

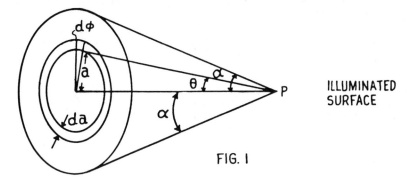

ILLUMINATED
SURFACE

FIG. I

Solution: Illumination, E, is defined as the luminous
flux per unit area and can be expressed as follows:

$$E = \frac{dF}{dA} = \frac{I \cos \theta}{r^2} \tag{1}$$

where I is the intensity of the source, r is the distance
of the surface illuminated from the source, and θ is the
angle between the normal to the surface illuminated and the
direction of r to the source. For an extended source, we
need to add the contributions of each part of the source to
the illumination of the surface or, differentiating E with
respect to I,

$$dE = \frac{dI \cos \theta}{r^2} \tag{2}$$

If we assume constant intensity per unit area of the
source we can write

$$dI = BdA \cos \theta \tag{3}$$

where B is the luminance of the source, dA is the element
or area of the source, and θ is the angle between a normal
to the source surface and the direction of r to the illuminated surface.

From Figure 1, we have:

$$dI = Ba(da)(d\phi) \cos \theta \tag{4}$$

$$r = R/\cos \theta \tag{5}$$

$$a = R \tan \theta \qquad\qquad (6)$$

Equation (6) can also be expressed as follows:

$$a = R \frac{\sin \theta}{\cos \theta} \; .$$

Differentiating a with respect to θ gives:

$$da = R\left[\frac{\cos^2\theta + \sin^2\theta}{\cos^2\theta} \right] d\theta$$

or

$$da = \frac{Rd\theta}{\cos^2\theta} \qquad\qquad (7)$$

Substituting the expression for dI given in equation (4) into equation (2) yields

$$dE = \frac{[Ba(da)(d\phi)\cos \theta] \cos \theta}{r^2}$$

and substituting the expression for r given in equation (5),

$$dE = \frac{[Ba(da)(d\phi)\cos \theta] \cos \theta}{R^2/\cos^2\theta} \qquad\qquad (8)$$

Now, substituting for a and da the expressions given in equations (6) and (7), respectively, we find that

$$dE = \frac{BR \tan \theta \, (R/\cos^2\theta)(d\theta)(d\phi) \cos \theta \cos \theta}{R^2/\cos^2\theta} \qquad\qquad (9)$$

$$= B \sin \theta \cos \theta \, d\theta d\phi \qquad\qquad (10)$$

$$E = \iint B \sin \theta \cos \theta \, d\theta d\phi$$

$$= \int_0^{2\pi} \int_0^{\alpha} B \sin \theta \, d(\sin \theta) d\phi = \frac{2\pi \, B \, \sin^2\alpha}{2} =$$

$$= \pi B \sin^2\alpha$$

For a surface of infinite extent, $\alpha = 90°$ so

$$E = \pi B \sin^2 90° = \pi B \; \text{lum/m}^2$$

The full moon is capable of producing an illuminance of
0.2 lumen/m^2 on the surface of the earth. Assuming the
full moon to be optically equivalent to a uniform circular
disk 2200 miles in diameter and at a distance of 250,000
miles from earth, compute the luminance of the moon.
Neglect any atmospheric effects.

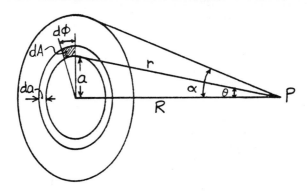

Solution: As derived in the preceding problem,
$E = \pi B \sin^2 \alpha$, where E is the illumination, B is the
luminance of the source, and α is as shown in the figure.

   In this problem, E is given to be 0.2 lumen/m^2. For
small α, the approximation $\sin \alpha \cong \tan \alpha$ is valid and so,

$$\sin \alpha \cong \tan \alpha = \frac{\text{radius of moon}}{\text{distance of moon from earth}} = \frac{1100}{250000}.$$

Solving the above equation for B and substituting the
values for E and sin α,

$$B = \frac{.2}{\pi} \left(\frac{250000}{1100} \right)^2 = 3.3 \times 10^3 \text{ candles/m}^2$$

● PROBLEM 24-15

A lamp whose intensity is known to be 20 candles is set up
at one end of a photometer bar 3 meters long, with an
unknown lamp at the other end. (a) The photometer head
indicates a balance when at a distance of 2 meters from
the standard lamp. What is the intensity of the unknown
lamp, in the direction of the photometer? (b) The unknown
lamp is placed in a box, in one side of which is a circular
hole 10 cm in diameter covered with diffusely transmitting
opal glass. The photometer now balances when it is 180 cm
away from the glass. What is the luminance of the glass?
(c) What is the intensity of the glass disk, considering
it to be a point source, in a direction at 45° with the
normal to its surface? (d) If the disk transmits 60% of
the light incident on it, what is the illuminance at its
inner surface?

(a)   The illuminance of the photometer by the standard lamp is given by the formula

$$E = \frac{I}{b^2} \qquad (1)$$

where E is the illuminance, I is the intensity of the lamp, and b is the distance between the photometer and lamp. Letting I = 20 candles and b = 2 m, we have

$$E = \frac{20 \text{ candles}}{(2 \text{ m})^2} = 5 \text{ candles/m}^2 \ .$$

If the photometer indicates a balance, then

$$\frac{I_2}{(1 \text{ m})^2} = 5 \text{ candles/m}^2 \ ,$$

where I_2 is the intensity of the unknown lamp.   Solving for I_2, we have I_2 = 5 candles.

(b)   For this part, equate I to BA in equation (1) to get

$$E = \frac{BA}{b^2}$$

where B is the luminance of the source of light and A is the area of the glass.   Now our standard lamp is (3 - 1.8)m = 1.2 m or 120 cm away from the photometer, so it has an illuminance of

$$E = \frac{20 \text{ candles}}{(120 \text{ cm})^2} = 1.39 \times 10^{-3} \text{ candles/cm}^2$$

on the photometer.   The photometer being balanced, we have

$$1.39 \times 10^{-3} \text{ candles/cm}^2 = \frac{BA}{(180 \text{ cm})^2}$$

where the area A is = πr^2 (r = the radius of the hole = 5 cm) = $\pi (5 \text{ cm})^2$.   Solving for the luminance B, we have

$$B = 0.573 \text{ candles/cm}^2$$

for the glass lens.

(c)   The intensity of the disk in a direction θ with the normal to its surface is given by

$$I_\theta = I \cos \theta \qquad (2)$$

where I_θ is the intensity of the disk at an angle of θ and

I is the intensity of the disk normal to the surface.   The
intensity normal to the surface is equal to the product of
the luminance B and the area of the glass A.   So we have

$$I_\theta = B \cdot A \cdot \cos \theta,$$

$$I_\theta = (0.573 \text{ candles/cm}^2) \cdot (25\pi \text{ cm}^2) \cdot \cos 45° ,$$

so

$$I_\theta \simeq 32 \text{ candles} .$$

(d)   The luminance of the outer surface equals the
illuminance on the inner surface multiplied by the fraction
of light transmitted, so

$$0.573 \quad \frac{\text{candles}}{\text{cm}^2} = E \times 0.6$$

$$E = 0.955 \text{ candles/cm}^2 .$$

If the luminance is 1 candle per unit area then the
luminous emittance or illuminance is π lumens per unit
area.   Hence, the illuminance at the inner surface of the
glass disk is 0.955π lumens/cm^2 or 3 lumens/cm^2.

It can also be noted that 1 lambert = 1 lumen/m^2.
Therefore, the illuminance can also be expressed as

$$\left(\frac{3 \text{ lumens}}{\text{cm}^2} \right) \left(\frac{10^4 \text{cm}^2}{\text{m}^2} \right) = 3 \times 10^4 \text{ lamberts}$$

CHAPTER 25

COLOR, ILLUMINANCE, AND ALPHANUMERIC DISPLAYS

COLOR

● PROBLEM 25-1

Two pieces of colored glass, represented by A and B, respectively, have spectral transmittance curves as shown in figures 1 and 2 . Sketch the transmittance curve for the two filters used together.

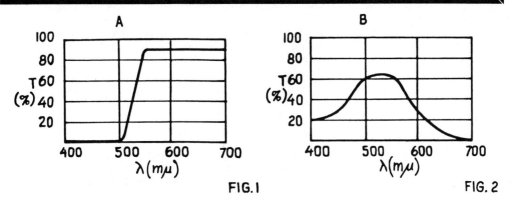

FIG.1

FIG. 2

Solution: The transmittance curves shown in figures 1 and 2 show the fraction of the incident light transmitted by the two colored glass pieces for wavelengths from 400mμ to 700mμ .

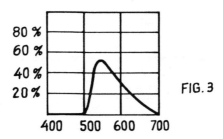

FIG. 3

At each wavelength, figure 1 gives the fraction of the incident light transmitted by the first piece of glass. If the second piece of glass, obeying the transmittance curve shown in figure 2, is placed next to it, figure 3 gives the fraction of the fraction of incident light transmitted by the first piece of glass which is also transmitted by the second piece of glass. For example, at a wavelength of 600mμ , the first piece of glass transmits 90% of the incident light and the second piece of glass transmits 30% of the light incident upon it. Thus, the combination transmits $(.9)(.3) \times 100 = 27\%$ of the light incident upon it. In this manner, the transmittance curve for both filters used together can be found by multiplying the values for the transmittance of filters A and B for various values of the wavelength. The resulting curve is shown in figure 3.

● **PROBLEM** 25-2

Find the relationship between the chromaticity coordinates of two sets of primary colors, represented by $\vec{R}$, $\vec{G}$, $\vec{B}$, and $\vec{R}'$, $\vec{G}'$, and $\vec{B}'$ (these are vectors, each of which represents a unit amount of each color).

Solution: The tristimulus values of a color are defined to be the amounts of the three primary colors required to give, by additive mixture with one another, a match with a color under consideration. The chromaticity coordinates of a color are the ratios of each tristimulus value of the color to the sum of its tristimulus values. In this problem, assume that the tristimulus values of a color $\vec{Q}$ with respect to the set of primary colors $\vec{R}$, $\vec{G}$, and $\vec{B}$ are R, G, and B, respectively. In addition, with respect to the set of primaries $\vec{R}'$, $\vec{G}'$, and $\vec{B}'$, the tristimulus values of $\vec{Q}$ are R', G', and B', respectively.

Each member of one set of primaries can be matched with an additive combination of another set of primaries; hence, the following set of linear equations hold:

$$R' = a_{11}R + a_{12}G + a_{13}B$$
$$G' = a_{21}R + a_{22}G + a_{23}B \tag{1}$$
$$B' = a_{31}R + a_{32}G + a_{33}B \, ,$$

where the terms a_{Ki} (K,i = 1,2,3) are constants.

By the definition of the term chromaticity coefficients, the chromaticity coordinates associated with R, G, B; denoted by r, g, and b, respectively, are defined by the following equations:

$$r = \frac{R}{R + G + B}$$

$$g = \frac{G}{R + G + B} \tag{2}$$

$$b = \frac{B}{R + G + B}$$

(r', g', and b', the chromaticity coordinates associated with the tristimulus values R', G', and B', are defined analogously.) Hence,

$$r' = \frac{R'}{R' + G' + B'} \, ,$$

and substituting for R', G', and B' the expressions indicated in equations (1) gives the result that

$$r' = \frac{a_{11}R + a_{12}G + a_{13}B}{(a_{11}+a_{21}+a_{31})R + (a_{12}+a_{22}+a_{32})G + (a_{13}+a_{23}+a_{33})B} \tag{3}$$

From equations (2), it follows that $R = r(R + G + B)$, $G = g(R + G + B)$ and $B = b(R + G + B)$. Substituting these expressions into equation

720

(3) gives the result that

$$r' = \frac{a_{11}r(R+G+B) + a_{12}g(R+G+B) + a_{13}b(R+G+B)}{(R+G+B)\left[(a_{11}+a_{21}+a_{31})r + (a_{12}+a_{22}+a_{32})g + (a_{13}+a_{23}+a_{33})b\right]}$$

$$= \frac{a_{11}r + a_{12}g + a_{13}b}{(a_{11}+a_{21}+a_{31})r + (a_{12}+a_{22}+a_{32})g + (a_{13}+a_{23}+a_{33})b}$$

Similarly, the equations giving b' and g' in terms of r, g, and b
are

$$g' = \frac{a_{21}r + a_{22}g + a_{23}b}{(a_{11}+a_{21}+a_{31})r + (a_{12}+a_{22}+a_{32})g + (a_{13}+a_{23}+a_{33})b}$$

and
$$b' = \frac{a_{31}r + a_{32}g + a_{33}b}{(a_{11}+a_{21}+a_{31})r + (a_{12}+a_{22}+a_{32})g + (a_{13}+a_{23}+a_{33})b}$$

● **PROBLEM** 25-3

Describe the properties possessed by protanomalous and deuter-
anomalous trichromats and compare the color-matching properties
of trichromats with those of dichromats.

Solution: A trichromat is an observer who requires mixtures of three
fixed and independent primaries to color-match (match the brightness,
hue, and/or saturation of two samples of light) all color stimuli.
A trichromat is classified as normal if the quantitative properties
of his color-matches are sufficiently close to the average for the
entire population.
   In testing for color-normality, it is convenient to first consider
the observer's color-matching functions (which are the tristimulus
values, with respect to three given primary colors, of monochromatic
lights of equal radiant energy, regarded as functions of wavelength
$\bar{r}_\lambda$, $\bar{g}_\lambda$, and $\bar{b}_\lambda$). These color-matching functions refer to a set of
monochromatic primaries located in the red, green and blue segments
of the visible spectrum, respectively, and the corresponding wavelengths are designated as λ_R, λ_G, and λ_B, respectively. The
ratios

$$W_1 = \left(\frac{\bar{r}_\lambda}{\bar{g}_\lambda}\right)_{\lambda_y} \qquad \text{and} \qquad W_2 = \left(\frac{\bar{b}_\lambda}{\bar{g}_\lambda}\right)_{\lambda_{BG}}$$

where the subscripts λ_y and λ_{BG} indicate that the ratios W_1 and
W_2 are evaluated at wavelengths in the yellow and blue-green portions
of the visible spectrum, respectively, provide the means necessary to
determine whether a given observer is a normal or an anomalous trichromat. The two groups of anomalous trichromats are the protanomalous
trichromats, whose values of W_1 are abnormally high, and the deuter-
anomalous trichromats, whose values of W_1 are abnormally low. The
red-green ratio is measured on an instrument known as an anomaloscope.
Dichromats are observers who require only two independent primaries
to make color-matches, rather than the three which are required for
trichromats. They are classified as color defectives.
   For a dichromat who will accept any full color-match made by a

particular trichromat, the dichromat's two color-matching functions, denoted by $\bar{h}_\lambda$ and $\bar{j}_\lambda$, must be independent linear combinations of the color-matching functions of the trichromat, denoted by $\bar{r}_\lambda$, $\bar{g}_\lambda$, and $\bar{b}_\lambda$. Hence, the following must hold true:

$$\bar{h}_\lambda = P_{11}\bar{r}_\lambda + P_{12}\bar{g}_\lambda + P_{13}\bar{b}_\lambda$$

and

$$\bar{j}_\lambda = P_{21}\bar{r}_\lambda + P_{22}\bar{g}_\lambda + P_{23}\bar{b}_\lambda \,,$$

where the P_{iK} (i = 1,2; K = 1,2,3) are constants. However, if a dichromat can accept any trichromatic match only after he has adjusted the luminance (the luminous flux per unit solid angle per unit area of emitting surface) of one of the stimuli being compared, then his color-matching functions will not necessarily be expressible as linear combinations of those of the trichromat.

● **PROBLEM** 25-4

State the difference between the terms "metameric colors" and "isomeric colors". In addition, describe what it means for two colors to possess isomeric and metameric differences.

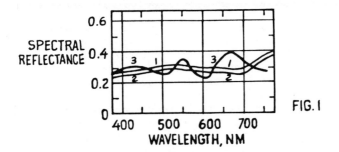

FIG. 1

Solution: Metameric colors are defined to be color stimuli of identical tristimulus values (the amounts of each of three primary colors which are required to give by additive mixture a match with the color under consideration) but different spectral energy distributions. On the other hand, isomeric colors are color stimuli with the same spectral energy distributions and hence, identical tristimulus values.

To duplicate the color of a given specimen, two principal procedures are followed. First it may be possible to use the same colors and combine them in the same proportions as those used originally to produce the specimen. The chances are good that an exact duplicate of the original both in color and in spectral reflectance over the entire spectrum will be obtained; the duplicate and its original will then be in isomeric match with one another under any incident flux. However, in a first trial the spectral reflectance curve of the duplicate may have approximately the same shape as that of the original but show some small displacements from it. In general, the spectral reflectance curves of the original specimen and the duplicate will not intersect but instead will be parallel to one another. The specimens that fail to be isomeric, are then said to exhibit an isomeric difference. The isomeric difference will most frequently be noticed as a difference in lightness of the two specimens, hue and saturation (which is the attribute of a color perception which determines the degree of its dif-

ference from the achromatic color perception most resembling it)
remaining about the same.

In the second procedure colors which are different from those used
for the original specimen may be compounded to produce the same color
(tristimulus values) for a given incident flux and observer. A metameric match is attempted, but, again, the first trial will not generally
produce the desired result, and then duplicate and original exhibit
what is called a metameric difference. The spectral reflectance curve
of the duplicate specimen will usually intersect the curve of the original
at three or more wavelengths and deviate widely from it at other wavelengths of the visible spectrum. The metameric difference is generally
noticed as a difference involving lightness, hue, and saturation.
As shown in figure 1, the curves which are labeled as 1 and 2
represent an isomeric difference while those labeled as 1 and 3
represent a metameric difference.

● **PROBLEM** 25-5

As shown in figure 1, the point C with coordinates (X_W, Y_W)
represents an achromatic color. Find the dominant wavelengths
of the colors S_1 and S_2, which are also shown in the chromaticity
diagram (figure 1).

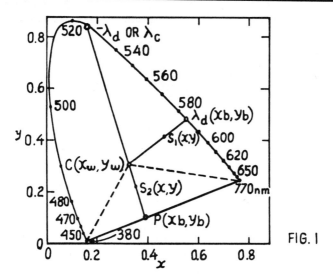

FIG. 1

Solution: The dominant wavelength of a color is defined to be the
wavelength of the spectrum band, which when mixed with an achromatic
color, matches the given color.

Figure 1 is the 1931 CIE(International Commission on Illumination)
chromaticity diagram with respect to the CIE standard source C. The
variables X and Y represent chromaticity coordinates, and in
terms of wavelength, the visible spectrum extends from 380 nm to
770 nm.

In order to determine the dominant wavelength of the point S_1, a
straight line is drawn through the point representing the achromatic
color (in this case source C) and the point S_1 representing the
color to be evaluated in the direction from C to S_1, intersecting
the spectrum locus. The wavelength of the intersection is the re-

quired dominant wavelength of the given color. For S_1 this inter-section falls at approximately 583 nm.

For colors such as $S_2(x,y)$ in the triangular region of the chromaticity diagram defined by the corners (C), (380 nm), (770 nm), sometimes described as the region of the purple colors, there is no dominant wavelength. This is due to the fact that the straight line drawn from C to S_2 does not intersect the spectrum locus. How-ever, the line drawn from S_2 to C meets the spectrum locus at a point defining the complementary wavelength, which is the wavelength of the spectrum band which when mixed with the given color, matches the specified achromatic color. To distinguish the complementary from the dominant wavelength, the former is assigned a negative sign or a "C" is placed after it. Thus, as shown in figure 1, S_2 has a complementary wavelength of -530 nm or 530 C nm.

● **PROBLEM 25-6**

Describe the usefulness of the single monochromator and explain how it differs from the double monochromator. In addition, if two spectral lines of wavelengths 4000A° and 5000A° are just resolved by a monochromator, find the monochromator's resolving power.

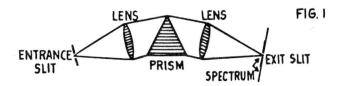

Solution: A monochromator is an apparatus designed to disperse the incident radiant flux into its spectrum from which any desired narrow band of wavelengths can be isolated with a slit aperture. In its simplest form a monochromator comprises a dispersion prism, two imaging lenses, and an entrance and exit slit, as shown in figure 1. A diffraction grating may be used instead of the prism, with lenses replaced by concave mirrors. The radiant flux passing through the entrance slit is collimated by the first lens (or mirror) and then dispersed by the prism (or grating) into its spectrum which is brought to a focus in the plane of the exit slit by means of the second lens (or mirror). The exit slit may be placed at any position within the spectrum so that the emergent radiant flux contains, in principle, only the desired narrow band of wavelengths. In fact, there will be mixed with it some flux of all wavelengths entering the monochromator. This additional flux, usually referred to as stray energy or stray light, arises from inter-reflections between components and scattering by dust, scratches, and other imperfec-tions in the dispersing element and imaging components of the monochromator. An effective way of reducing stray energy is to combine two monochromators in series in such a way that the exit slit of the first becomes the entrance slit of the second. Such an ap-paratus is called a double monochromator (see figure 2), in contrast to a single monochromator with just one dispersing system.

There are two ways of combining the two dispersive systems in a double monochromator. The two systems can be combined either to give subtractive or additive dispersion; that is, the dispersion

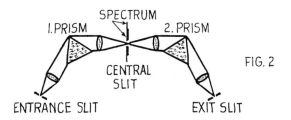

SPECTRUM

I. PRISM   2. PRISM

FIG. 2

CENTRAL
SLIT

ENTRANCE SLIT   EXIT SLIT

of each half of the double monochromator may either annul the other
or combine with it to give double dispersion. With subtractive
dispersion the losses experienced by rays in different parts of the
instrument field (by prism absorption, for example) are more nearly
identical.

The usable spectral range of a monochromator is limited by
absorption of the dispersing prisms and the lenses and is confined
to the visible and near infrared (0.38 to 2.0μ) when the optical
components are of glass. With quartz prisms and lenses the spectral
range is extended into the ultraviolet down to approximately 0.2μ .
In monochromators going beyond the visible the lenses are commonly
replaced by mirrors that have a high reflectance over a wide spectral
range and, in addition, do not introduce chromatic aberrations in the
optical imagery. Fluorite, rocksalt, and potassium bromide are used
as prism materials to extend the spectral range into the infrared.
Fluorite gives a usable range of approximately 0.5 to 9.0μ , rocksalt
of 0.5 to 16.0μ , and potassium bromide of 0.5 to 25.0μ . There are
other materials (potassium iodide, thallium bromide) which allow a
still further extension of the spectral range, but beyond 40 μ a
grating must be used as the dispersing element. The fundamental
quantities that characterize every monochromator are the resolving
power and the ratio of the radiant flux (in the selected wavelength
band) emerging from the exit slit to that received through the entrance
slit. The resolving power R of a monochromator is defined as the
ratio of the mean wavelength λ of two spectral lines of wavelengths
λ_1 and λ_2, that are just resolved, to their wavelength difference
$\delta\lambda$; that is,

$$R = \frac{\lambda}{\delta\lambda} \tag{1}$$

The mean wavelength of the two given spectral lines of wavelengths
$4000A°$ and $5000A°$ is $4500A°$ and the wavelength difference, $\delta\lambda$,
is equal to $1000A°$. Hence, from equation (1),

$$R = \frac{4500A°}{1000A°} = 4.5 .$$

For a prism the resolving power R_p can be expressed in terms of the
angular dispersion $d\theta/d\lambda$ or the material dispersion $dn/d\lambda$ of the
prism; thus

$$R_p = a_p \left(\frac{d\theta}{d\lambda}\right)_p$$

and

$$R_p = b \frac{dn}{d\lambda} .$$

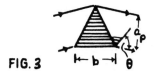

FIG. 3

The quantity a_p is the width of the rectangular beam leaving the
prism, and b is the base length of the prism, as shown in figure 3.

● **PROBLEM** 25-7

Describe the function of the spectrophotometer and explain how the
tristimulus values of a fluorescent material can be determined by means
of spectrophotometry.

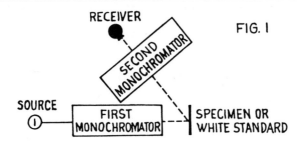

FIG. I

Solution: The spectrophotometer is an apparatus designed to measure
the spectral transmittance and the spectral reflectance of objects.
It accomplishes this by measuring at each wavelength the ratio of the
radiant flux leaving the object to that incident on it.
    To analyze a fluorescent material spectrophotometrically, a spectro-
photometer such as that shown in figure 1 must be used. The fluorescent
specimen is irradiated by radiant flux in a narrow band of wavelengths
coming through the exit slit of the first monochromator. Flux either
reflected from the specimen or emitted by the specimen as fluorescent
light is analyzed by the second monochromator and photoelectric
receiver. The measurements are usually made in arbitrary units against
a nonfluorescing white standard, such as a magnesium-oxide surface,
using a photoelectric receiver of known relative spectral sensitivity.
The wavelength range of the first monochromator needs to be from 300
to 770 nm, that of the second monochromator at least from 380 to 770 nm,
if colorimetric computations are to be made on the basis of the spectrophotometric measurements.

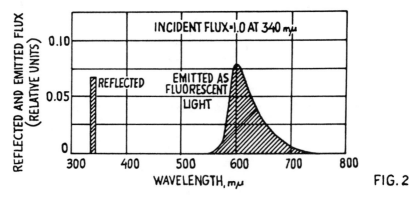

FIG. 2

An example of a spectrophotometric record obtained for a fluorescent
red ink on white paper is illustrated in figure 2. The incident flux
depicted in this example is of wavelength 340 nm. The reflected flux
at this wavelength is approximately 5.8 percent of the incident flux.
The fluorescent light appears in the wavelength band from 560 to 740 nm,
with a peak value of approximately 8 percent at 600 nm. Similar records
are obtained for incident flux of wavelengths ranging from 300 to about

580 nm. The amount of reflected flux varies somewhat from wavelength
to wavelength but not much; the spectral distribution of the fluorescent
flux retains its shape and location throughout but varies in height.
When the wavelength of the incident flux enters the fluorescent band
the generation of fluorescent light drops sharply and vanishes completely from about 600 nm upward. Only reflected flux is recorded
from then on. This is in accordance with Stokes's law; that is, the
wavelength of the fluorescent flux is longer than that of the incident
(exciting) flux. The tristimulus values (X,Y,Z) can be computed by
first arranging the spectrophotometric data in matrix form as follows:

Wavelength λ (nm) of Reflected and Emitted flux	Wavelength μ (nm) of Incident Flux						
	300	310	320	. . .	750	760	770
300	$r_{\lambda\mu}$	—	—	. . .	—	—	—
310	$r_{\lambda\mu}$	$r_{\lambda\mu}$	—	. . .	—	—	—
320	$r_{\lambda\mu}$	$r_{\lambda\mu}$	$r_{\lambda\mu}$	. . .	—	—	—
.	.	.	.	. . .	.	.	.
.	.	.	.	. . .	.	.	.
750	$r_{\lambda\mu}$	$r_{\lambda\mu}$	$r_{\lambda\mu}$	. . .	$r_{\lambda\mu}$	—	—
760	$r_{\lambda\mu}$	$r_{\lambda\mu}$	$r_{\lambda\mu}$	. . .	$r_{\lambda\mu}$	$r_{\lambda\mu}$	—
770	$r_{\lambda\mu}$	$r_{\lambda\mu}$	$r_{\lambda\mu}$	. . .	$r_{\lambda\mu}$	$r_{\lambda\mu}$	$r_{\lambda\mu}$

Here $r_{\lambda\mu}$ is radiant-flux reflected, or emitted by fluorescence, in
the wavelength interval $\Delta\lambda$ centered on λ, when the radiant flux
incident on the specimen is confined to the wavelength interval $\Delta\mu$,
centered on μ, and is of unit amount. The matrix is of triangular
form; that is, nonzero entries occur only below the diagonal, going
from the upper left-hand to the lower right-hand corner of the matrix.
This is because, in general, Stokes's law applies, and fluorescent
light has wavelengths not less than that of the incident light. For
a nonfluorescing specimen only reflected light of the same wavelength
as the incident light is present, and the matrix reduces to a diagonal
matrix. A fluorescing specimen will generally have diagonal elements
different from zero in addition to some below-diagonal elements that
occupy one or more definite groups of rows of λ, independent of the
exciting wavelength μ, and corresponding to one or more fluorescent
bands.

From this matrix the relative spectral distribution $\{R_\lambda \Delta\lambda\}$ of
the reflected and emitted radiant flux, when the incident flux has
the spectral distribution $\{H_\mu \Delta\mu\}$, is computed from the equation

$$R_\lambda \Delta\lambda = \left(\sum_{\mu=300}^{770} r_{\lambda\mu} H_\mu \Delta\mu \right) \Delta\lambda . \tag{1}$$

The tristimulus values X, Y, Z can then be obtained by making use
of the following equations:

$$X = \sum_\lambda \rho_\lambda H_\lambda \bar{x}_\lambda \Delta\lambda$$

$$Y = \sum_\lambda \rho_\lambda H_\lambda \bar{y}_\lambda \Delta\lambda \tag{2}$$

$$Z = \sum_\lambda \rho_\lambda H_\lambda \bar{z}_\lambda \Delta\lambda$$

where ρ_λ is the spectral reflectance of the object, $H_\lambda \Delta\lambda$ is the spectral distribution of the flux irradiating the object, and $\bar{x}_\lambda$, $\bar{y}_\lambda$ and $\bar{z}_\lambda$ are the color-matching functions of either the 1931 or the 1964 CIE standard observer.

In equations (2), $\rho_\lambda H_\lambda$ can be replaced by R_λ. Hence, the tristimulus values are, by equations (2), as follows:

$$X = \sum_\lambda R_\lambda \bar{x}_\lambda \Delta\lambda$$

$$Y = \sum_\lambda R_\lambda \bar{y}_\lambda \Delta\lambda \qquad (3)$$

$$Z = \sum_\lambda R_\lambda \bar{z}_\lambda \Delta\lambda ,$$

where $R_\lambda \Delta\lambda$ is given by equation (1).

In carrying out these computations it is assumed that the fluorescent light increases proportionally with the amount of radiant flux incident on the specimen and that the contributions of all wavelengths are additive.

● **PROBLEM** 25-8

Light falls nearly normally on a table top from two sources whose tristimulus values are $\bar{x} = 20$, $\bar{y} = 60$, $\bar{z} = 20$, and $\bar{x}' = 20$, $\bar{y}' = 10$, $\bar{z}' = 20$, respectively.
(a) What are the trichromatic coefficients (also known as chromaticity coordinates) of the two sources?
(b) If the distances of the two sources above the table are adjusted until the light illuminating the table is white, what must the ratio of these distances be?

Solution: (a) It has been found that a human eye has three types of receptors for determining the color of an object. Each of the receptors has a different spectral response. To codify this response, the international Commission on Illumination has developed a color mixture curve representing the response of three receptors such that the area under the individual spectral response curves are equal. By this codification a specific color can be specified by three tristimulus values, x, y, and z. These values include not only the spectral response but also the intensity of the light. As three values are necessary to specify a color, it appears that there is a need for a three dimensional representation to specify a particular color mixture. To avoid this, the tristimulus values are normalized as follows:

$$x = \frac{\bar{x}}{\bar{x}+\bar{y}+\bar{z}} \; ; \; y = \frac{\bar{y}}{\bar{x}+\bar{y}+\bar{z}} \; ; \; z = \frac{\bar{z}}{\bar{x}+\bar{y}+\bar{z}} \qquad (1)$$

where x, y, and z are called the trichromatic coefficients. Since by definition, $x + y + z = 1$, a two dimensional representation of these parameters is sufficient, as any one of the parameters is dependent upon the other two.

Since the tristimulus values indicate both flux and spectral response and the effect of several sources is additive, it can be seen that white light corresponds to the following values for x, y, and z: $x = y = z = 0.3333$.

The trichromatic coefficients can be calculated by making use of equation (1):

$$x = \frac{20}{20+60+20} = \frac{20}{100} = 0.2; \quad y = \frac{60}{100} = 0.6; \quad z = \frac{20}{100} = 0.2 \tag{2}$$

$$x' = \frac{20}{20+10+20} = \frac{20}{50} = 0.4; \quad y' = \frac{10}{50} = 0.2; \quad z' = \frac{20}{50} = 0.4 \tag{3}$$

(b) Note that $\bar{x} + \bar{y} + \bar{z} = 100$, while $\bar{x}' + \bar{y}' + \bar{z}' = 50$. Hence, the flux of the first source is twice that of the second. Also since
$$ax + bx' = x'' = ay + by' = y'' = az + bz' = z'' \tag{4}$$
where a and b are constants, it can be seen that $a = 1$ and $b = 2$ yields $x'' = y'' = z'' = 1$. Thus, the second source must provide twice the illumination on the surface that the first source provides. Since the intensity of the first source is initially twice that of the second source, the expression relating the illumination provided by the first source, E_1, to the illumination provided by the second source, E_2, must be as follows:

$$E_1 = \tfrac{1}{4} E_2 \tag{5}$$

or

$$\frac{E_2}{E_1} = 4 \tag{6}$$

The inverse square law is as follows:

$$E \propto \frac{I \cos \theta}{r^2} \tag{7}$$

where I is the intensity of the source, θ is the angle between a normal to the surface and a ray from the source to the surface and r is the source-surface distance. Substituting the ratio

$$\frac{\left(I_2 \cos \theta\right)/r_2^2}{I_1 \cos \theta / r_1^2}$$

for E_2/E_1 (from equation (7)) into equation (6) gives the following result:

$$\frac{\left(I_2 \cos \theta\right)/r_2^2}{\left(I_1 \cos \theta\right)/r_1^2} = 4 \tag{8}$$

Assuming that $I_1 = I_2$, equation (8) becomes

$$\frac{r_1^2}{r_2^2} = 4 \tag{9}$$

or

$$\frac{r_1}{r_2} = 2 \ .$$

Thus,

$$r_1 = 2r_2 \ ,$$

and so, the desired ratio is 2:1. For a further discussion of colorimetry, see Sears, "Optics" or Sears and Zemansky, "College Physics".

What is the wavelength of monochromatic light complementary to
(a) the red cadmium line at 644 mμ?
(b) the sodium D-line at 589 mμ?

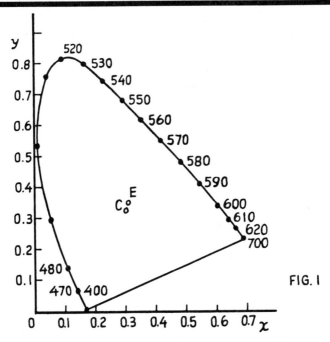

FIG. I

Solution: The human eye has three types of receptors for determining
the color of an object. Each of the receptors has a different spectral response. To codify this response the International Commission
on Illumination has developed a color mixture curve representing the
response of three receptors such that the areas under the spectral
responses of each receptor are equal. This means that a specific
spectrum color can be designated by three tristimulus values; $\bar{x}$,
$\bar{y}$, and $\bar{z}$. This indicates the necessity for a three dimensional
representation to specify a particular color mixture. To avoid this,
the three spectrum color values $\bar{x}$, $\bar{y}$ and $\bar{z}$ are normalized as
follows:

$$x = \frac{\bar{x}}{\bar{x}+\bar{y}+\bar{z}} \; ; \; y = \frac{\bar{y}}{\bar{x}+\bar{y}+\bar{z}} \; ; \; z = \frac{\bar{z}}{\bar{x}+\bar{y}+\bar{z}} \tag{1}$$

where x,y and z are called the trichromatic coefficients. Since by
definition x + y + z = 1, only a two dimensional plot of these parameters is necessary as the third parameter is dependent upon the other
two.
    Inherent in the concept of three receptors is the view that if each
receptor has equal illumination then all wavelengths will be represented
in the eye response and the eye will interpret this as white light.
    On the basis of the trichromatic coefficients, white light should
correspond to an eye illumination of

$$x = y = z = 0.3333 \tag{2}$$

Now suppose that there are two spectrum colors, one with x = 0.7222,
y = 0.2778, and z = 0.00002, which corresponds to Cadmium red (644nm)
and another spectrum color which when added to the Cadmium red will

730

yield white light. Clearly, the second spectrum color must have
x,y,z values and intensities such that the resultant light has the
following values for x,y, and z:

$$x = y = z = 0.3333 \ .$$

This second spectrum color is then called the complementary spectrum
color. Figure 1 shows the curve for the spectrum colors where C and
E are the "white points", E the equal energy point and C "average
sunlight". From this figure it can be seen that if a single monochromatic complement to the Cadmium red color is desired, it is
necessary to draw a straight line from Cadmium-red through the "white"
point to the spectrum color curve, which then appears to be in the
range of 490nm.

   To get an accurate determination, the American Institute of Physics
Handbook table for the standard observer can be used, where the trichromatic coefficient values are presented at 5 nm intervals. This
table yields the following data:

wavelength nm	x	y	z
645	.7230	.2770	.0000
640	.7190	.2809	.0001
590	.5752	.4242	.0006
585	.5448	.4544	.0008

By linear interpolation, the following set of data is obtained from
the preceding table:

644 nm	.7222	.2778	.00002
589 nm	.5691	.4302	.0006

   Now to find the wavelengths which are complementary to 644 mμ
and 589 mμ , it is necessary to draw straight lines from 644 nm and
589 nm, respectively, on figure 1 through the "white" point to the
intersection at the other spectrum color.

$$\text{slope } 644 = \frac{y_2 - y_1}{x_2 - x_1} = \frac{.2778 - .3333}{.7222 - .3333} = - 0.1427 \qquad (3)$$

$$\text{slope } 589 = \frac{y_2 - y_1}{x_2 - x_1} = \frac{.4302 - .3333}{.5691 - .3333} = + 0.4109 \qquad (4)$$

   The complementary color has coordinates (x_3, y_3). Hence, the
slopes of the two lines are expressed by the formula

$$\frac{y_2 - y_3}{x_2 - x_3} = m \ . \qquad (5)$$

   Solving equation (5) for y_3 gives

$$y_3 = y_2 - mx_2 + mx_3 \qquad (6)$$

Substituting $y_2 = 0.2778$, m = -0.1427 and $x_2 = 0.7222$ into
equation (6) gives the result that

$$y_{644comp} = 0.2778 + \left(0.1427\right) \left(0.7222\right) - 0.1427 \ x_{644comp} \qquad (7)$$

$$y_{644comp} = 0.3809 - 0.1427 \ x_{644comp} \qquad (8)$$

From figure 1 it can be seen that $x_{644comp} \sim 0.$ $x_{644comp} = 0$ is in the range of 490 nm. The American Institute of Physics Handbook table gives the following data for wavelengths near 490 nm:

wavelength nm	x	y	z
495	.0235	.4127	.5638
490	.0454	.2950	.6596
485	.0687	.2007	.7306

The slope of the straight line between $\lambda = 495$ nm and 490 nm (see figure 1) can be found as follows:

$$m = \frac{.4127 - .2950}{.0235 - .0454} \cong -5.37 \ .$$

Now, from equation (6),

$$y_{644comp} = 0.4127 + (5.37)(0.0235) - 5.37 x_{644comp}$$

or

$$y_{644comp} = 0.5389 - 5.37 x_{644comp} \qquad (9)$$

Equating the expressions determined for $y_{644comp}$ given in equations (8) and (9) gives

$$0.3809 - 0.1427 x_{644comp} = 0.5389 - 5.37 x_{644comp}$$

Solving for $x_{644comp}$ gives

$$x_{644comp} = \frac{0.5389 - 0.3809}{5.37 - 0.1427} \cong 0.030 \qquad (10)$$

From the table in the range 495 - 490 nm, the rate of change of x with respect to the wavelength λ can be found as follows:

$$\frac{\Delta x}{\Delta \lambda} = \frac{0.0235 - 0.0454}{-5 \ nm} = 4.38 \times 10^{-3}/nm \ . \qquad (11)$$

Thus, $\frac{0.0235 - 0.030}{\Delta \lambda} = 4.38 \times 10^{-3}/nm$ and so,

$$\Delta \lambda = \frac{0.0235 - 0.030}{4.38 \times 10^{-3}/nm} \cong - 1.48 \ nm \ .$$

Thus, $\lambda_{644comp} = 495 \ nm - 1.48 \ nm, = 493.52 \qquad (12)$

For $\lambda_{589comp}$, from the tables and from equation (4), equation (6) becomes $y_{589com} = 0.4302 - (0.4109)(0.5691) + 0.4109 x_{589com}$

$$= 0.1964 + 0.4109 x_{589comp} \qquad (13)$$

The slope m of the straight line between 490 nm and 485 nm can be computed from the table to be

$$m = \frac{.2950 - .2007}{.0454 - .0687} \cong -4.05$$

Equation (6) thus becomes

$$y_{589comp} = 0.2950 + (4.05)(0.0454) - 4.05 x_{589comp}$$

732

$$= 0.4789 - 4.05x_{589comp} \tag{14}$$

Now, equating the expressions determined for $y_{589comp}$ in equations (13) and (14) gives the result

$$0.1964 + 0.4109x_{589comp} = 0.4789 - 4.05x_{589comp}$$

or

$$x_{589comp} = \frac{0.2825}{4.4609} \cong 0.063 \tag{15}$$

From the data in the range from 490nm to 485 nm, the rate of change of x with respect to the wavelength λ can be found as follows:

$$\frac{\Delta x}{\Delta \lambda} = \frac{0.0454 - 0.0687}{-5} = 4.66 \times 10^{-3}/nm \ . \tag{16}$$

Utilizing the results of equation (15), equation (16) becomes

$$\frac{0.0454 - 0.063}{\Delta \lambda} = 4.66 \times 10^{-3}/nm \ .$$

Hence,

$$\Delta \lambda = \frac{0.0454 - 0.063}{4.66 \times 10^{-3}/nm} \cong -3.78 \ nm. \tag{17}$$

and so,

$$\lambda_{589comp} = (490 - 3.78)nm.$$
$$= 486.22 \ nm. \tag{18}$$

● **PROBLEM** 25-10

From the CIE diagram (figure 1) find the dominant hue, peak wavelength, and saturation of a colored panel given by the coordinates (0.30, 0.50) and seen in white light. If the same panel is seen in orange light of coordinates (0.45, 0.45), what would be its dominant hue, peak wavelength, and saturation?

Solution: The CIE diagram is developed by specifying three color response detectors, and measuring for an arbitrary color the response on each of the specified detectors. This yields a set of tristimulus values which are then normalized such that if X, Y, and Z are the tristimulus values, then the trichromatic coefficients (or chromaticity coordinates), x, y, and z, are:

$$x = \frac{X}{X+Y+Z} \ , \quad y = \frac{Y}{X+Y+Z} \ , \quad \text{and} \quad z = \frac{Z}{X+Y+Z}$$

Thus, if two of these trichromatic coefficients (i.e., x and y) are known, then z can be determined since z = 1 - x - y. A source giving illumination yields trichromatic coefficients x and y. For daylight sun, x = 0.3442 and y = 0.3534, hence, z = 1 - (0.3442 + 0.3534) = 0.3024 . Then a straight line can be drawn from the points with the source's trichromatic coefficients through the colored sample's trichromatic coefficients. The intersection of this line with the outer curve of the CIE diagram determines the dominant hue and the peak wavelength.

Thus, in white light (x = 0.3442 and y = 0.3534) the given sample (x = 0.30 and y = 0.50) yields a straight line (represented by 1)

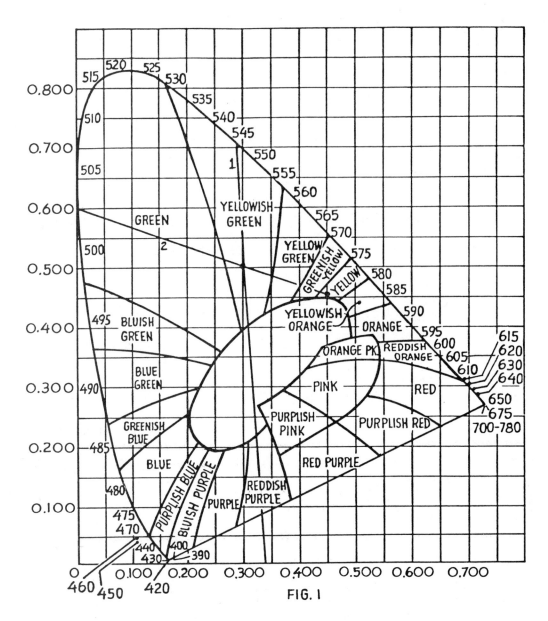

FIG. I

on figure 1, indicating that the dominant hue is yellowish-green and its peak wavelength is between 545 and 540 nm. To find the saturation, it is necessary to determine the ratio of the lengths of line 1 from the source point to the sample point and the length from the source point to the CIE diagram boundary. For white light, the first length as measured on the diagram is 16 in arbitrary units and the second length is 35 in arbitrary units, hence, the saturation is 16/35 = 45.7%.

For illumination by orange light the source has trichromatic co-efficients x = 0.45 and y = 0.45 and drawing a line through the points (0.45, 0.45) and (0.30, 0.50) gives line 2 on the diagram. This yields a dominant hue of green and a peak wavelength between 500 and 505 nm. The length between the points (0.45, 0.45) and (0.30,0.50) is 15 in arbitrary units and the length between the point (0.45,0.45) and the CIE diagram boundary is 44 arbitrary units and so the saturation value is 15/44 = 34%.

(a) A filter represented as filter #1 has a thickness of 2mm. In addition, its transmittance $\tau_{1\lambda}$ = 0.512 and its internal optical

density $\delta_{1\lambda}$ = 0.2518 . Compute the internal transmittance $v_{1\lambda}$ of

filter 1.
(b) Now consider filter #1', which is composed of the same glass as is filter #1, but which has a thickness of 5mm. If the internal transmittance $v_{1\lambda}'$ of filter #1' is 0.235, determine the values of the internal optical density $\delta_{1\lambda}'$ and the transmittance $\tau_{1\lambda}'$ of

filter #1'. In this problem, the computations are to be carried out for normal incidence of light, and with a constant relative refractive index between the filters and the surrounding media of n = 1.53.

Solution: (a) For normal incidence, the fraction ρ_λ of radiant-flux which is reflected from filters #1 and #1' is given by Fresnel's law of refraction, which is as follows:

$$\rho_\lambda = \left(\frac{n-1}{n+1}\right)^2 \tag{1}$$

where n is the relative refractive index. Since n is given as 1.53, it follows from equation (1) that

$$\rho_\lambda = \left(\frac{.53}{2.53}\right)^2 \cong 0.0439 .$$

The spectral transmittance of filter #1, $\tau_{1\lambda}$, and the internal spectral transmittance of filter #1, $v_{1\lambda}$ (which is defined as the ratio of the radiant flux reaching the back surface of the filter to the flux that enters the filter at its front surface), are related to one another by the following equation:

$$\tau_{1\lambda} = (1 - \rho_\lambda)^2 v_{1\lambda} . \tag{2}$$

Hence, substituting both the computed value for ρ_λ and the given value for $\tau_{1\lambda}$ into equation (2) and solving for $v_{1\lambda}$ gives the result that

$$v_{1\lambda} = \frac{0.512}{(1 - 0.0439)^2} \cong 0.560 .$$

(b) For homogeneous isotropic absorption filters such as filters #1 and #1', the internal spectral transmittance v_λ is related to the path length, d, of the beam of radiant flux in the filter medium and to m_λ , the spectral absorptivity of the medium, by the following equation, known as Bouguer's law:

$$v_\lambda = 10^{-dm_\lambda} \tag{3}$$

Now, if $d_{1\lambda}$ and $d_{1\lambda}'$ represent the original and new thicknesses, respectively (corresponding to filters #1 and #1', respectively) of an absorption filter which obeys Bouguer's law and if $v_{1\lambda}$ and $v_{1\lambda}'$ are the corresponding internal spectral transmittances, then the following relation known as Lambert's law, is valid:

$$v'_{1\lambda} = v_{1\lambda}^{q'_{1\lambda}/d_{1\lambda}} \tag{4}$$

The internal optical density $\delta_{1\lambda}$ is defined in terms of v_λ as follows:

$$\delta_{1\lambda} = -\log_{10} v_{1\lambda} = \log_{10} \frac{1}{v_{1\lambda}} \tag{5}$$

From equation (3), it can be seen that

$$\log_{10} \frac{1}{v_{1\lambda}} = \log_{10}(10^{d_{1\lambda}m_\lambda}) = d_{1\lambda}m_\lambda$$

and substituting back into equation (5) gives the result that

$$\delta_{1\lambda} = d_{1\lambda}m_\lambda \tag{6}$$

It then follows that $\delta'_{1\lambda} = d'_{1\lambda}m_\lambda$ \hfill (7)

where $\delta'_{1\lambda}$ is the internal optical density of the filter with thickness $d'_{1\lambda}$ and internal spectral transmittance $v'_{1\lambda}$. Hence, dividing equation (7) by equation (6) gives the result that

$$\frac{\delta'_{1\lambda}}{\delta_{1\lambda}} = \frac{d'_{1\lambda}}{d_{1\lambda}} \quad \text{or} \quad \delta'_{1\lambda} = \frac{d'_{1\lambda}}{d_{1\lambda}} \delta_{1\lambda} \ . \tag{8}$$

Substituting the given values $\delta_{1\lambda} = 0.2518$, $d_{1\lambda} = 2\text{mm.}$ and $d'_{1\lambda} = 5\text{mm.}$ into equation (8) gives

$$\delta'_{1\lambda} = \left(\frac{5\text{mm}}{2\text{mm}}\right)(0.2518)$$

$$= 0.6295.$$

The transmittance of filter #1', $\tau'_{1\lambda}$ can be found by reapplying equation (2). Hence,

$$\tau'_{1\lambda} = (1 - \rho_\lambda)^2 \, v'_{1\lambda} \tag{9}$$

and substituting the value computed in part (a) for ρ_λ and the given value for $v'_{1\lambda}$ into equation (9) gives the result that

$$\tau'_{1\lambda} = (1 - 0.0439)^2 (0.235)$$

$$\cong 0.215 \ .$$

ILLUMINATION

● **PROBLEM 25-12**

Define the following terms, and describe the relationships between them: luminous flux, intensity, illuminance, and luminance.

Solution: Luminous flux is the rate of flow of luminous energy and is measured in terms of lumens.

Intensity is the luminous flux emmitted by a point source of light per unit solid angle and is expressed in terms of candelas.

Illuminance is defined as being the quantity of luminous flux incident on a unit area of a surface and is expressed in terms of lumens/meter^2.

The intensity of a source, I, and the illuminance E on a surface at a distance D from the source are related by the equation $E = I/D^2$. In addition, illuminance is a nondirectional or scalar quantity, while intensity is a directional or vector quantity.

Luminance is the equivalent of intensity, applied to extended sources of light. It is defined as the luminous flux per unit solid angle per unit area of emitting surface and it is expressed in terms of candelas/meter^2 or nits. Hence, in any problem, it must be determined whether it is necessary to find the intensity or the luminance of the light source, based upon its size. However, there are some cases in which both parameters must be solved for. For example, a tail light on a car is a point source when located very far away from the observer and so, the intensity must be found. However, if the car is located a few feet in front of the observer, the tail light will be considered to be an extended source, and so luminance will be the desired parameter.

● **PROBLEM** 25-13

If a surface is illuminated by a source of intensity I, uniform in all directions, as shown in figure 1, find the illuminance at point P of the surface

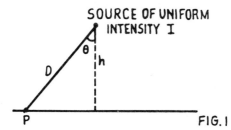

SOURCE OF UNIFORM
INTENSITY I

FIG.1

Solution: If a surface is normal to the direction of light propagation from a light source of intensity I and is located a distance D away from the source, then the illuminance, E, of the surface, is given by the equation
$$E = \frac{I}{D^2} .$$

However, if the surface is tilted at an angle of θ with respect to the normal, as in figure 1, then the expression for the illuminance becomes
$$E = \frac{I}{D^2} \cos \theta .$$

From figure 1, it can be seen that $\cos \theta = h/D$ or $D = h/\cos \theta$.

Then $D^2 = h^2/\cos^2\theta$ and thus,
$$E = \frac{I}{\frac{h^2}{\cos^2\theta}} \cos \theta = \frac{I}{h^2} \cos^3\theta .$$

● **PROBLEM** 25-14

Show that given that the object and image of an optical system lie in media of the same index of refraction, the luminance of the object cannot be increased by optical means.

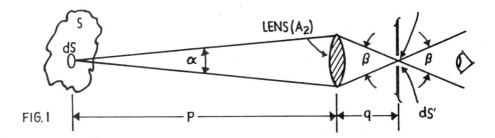

FIG. 1

Solution: Consider the optical system shown in figure 1. As shown, the object distance from the lens to dS, p, is much larger than the distance from the lens to the image of dS(dS'), q.   The area of the lens is denoted by A_2 .   Assuming no transmittance losses in the lens and that it is free of imperfections, the flux contained in solid angle α , originating in dS is the same as the flux contained in solid angle β on both sides of dS'. It can be seen from figure 1 that the following two relations are valid:

$$\alpha = \frac{A_2}{p^2} \tag{1}$$

and

$$\beta = \frac{A_2}{q^2} \tag{2}$$

The intensities emitted by dS and dS' are represented as I and I', respectively, and if the flux is represented as F, then I = F/α and I' = F/β and so, the ratio of intensities is I/I' = F/α/F/β = β/α . Substituting the expressions for α and β determined in equations (1) and (2) gives the result that

$$\frac{I}{I'} = \frac{A_2/q^2}{A_2/p^2} = \frac{p^2}{q^2} \tag{3}$$

The ratio of the diameters of dS and dS' (represented by d and d', respectively) is given by the relation d/d' = p/q .   Hence, the ratio of the areas of dS and dS' is given by

$$\frac{A_{dS}}{A_{dS'}} = \frac{\pi\left(\frac{d}{2}\right)^2}{\pi\left(\frac{d'}{2}\right)^2} = \frac{d^2}{d'^2} = \frac{p^2}{q^2} \tag{4}$$

Since luminance is equal to intensity per unit area, the ratio of the luminances of dS and dS' (L and L', respectively) can be solved for as follows:

$$\frac{L}{L'} = \frac{I/A_{dS}}{I'/A_{dS'}} = \frac{I}{I'}\frac{A_{dS'}}{A_{dS}} \tag{5}$$

Substituting for I/I' and $A_{dS'}/A_{dS}$ from equations (3) and (4), respectively, equation (5) becomes

$$\frac{L}{L'} = \left(\frac{p^2}{q^2}\right)\left(\frac{q^2}{p^2}\right) = 1$$

and so, the luminances of dS and dS' are equal.

738

Explain how visual processes differ when the eyes are fully dark adapted than when they are in a bright environment. In addition, describe
how it is possible to maintain a high degree of dark adaptation while
simultaneously retaining the capacity to see photopically.

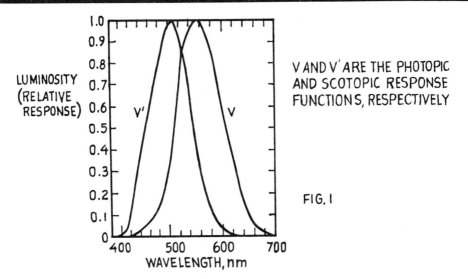

V AND V' ARE THE PHOTOPIC
AND SCOTOPIC RESPONSE
FUNCTIONS, RESPECTIVELY

FIG. I

Solution: Two types of retinal elements mediate vision, rods and cones.
In the fovea, where visual acuity is a maximum, vision is controlled
entirely by cones. Cones are distributed throughout the periphery of
the retina, but to a much lesser extent than within the fovea. At
high levels of illumination of the eye (called photopic vision),
peripheral vision is dominated by the cones within the retina. However, at low levels of illumination (called scotopic vision), vision
is mediated by the rods in the periphery of the retina.

   Thus, when the eyes are fully dark adapted, vision is mediated by
the retinal rods. Since no rods exist in the fovea, when the eyes are
fully dark adapted, detection of light is only possible in the periphery
of the retina. Figure 1 illustrates the photopic and scotopic luminosity
response functions.

   From observing figure 1, it can be deduced that the scotopic response
function is much lower at high wavelengths than is the photopic response
function. Thus, if a situation arises in which it is desirable to
maintain a high degree of dark adaptation and at the same time be able
to read a display(for example, a pilot flying at night who must be able
to see his instrument panel and at the same time see the outside
environment through which he is flying), the display light should be
confined to high wavelengths, preferably over 620 nm (see figure 1).
Since at such wavelengths, the photopic response function is relatively
high, the display can still be seen foveally. At the same time, the
peripheral rods are fairly insensitive to the display light and progress
toward dark adaptation as though the eye were in near darkness.

● **PROBLEM** 25-16

Describe the functions performed by both the Bunsen photometer and
the Lummer-Brodhun photometer.

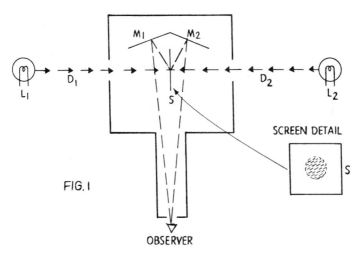

FIG. I

SCREEN DETAIL

S

OBSERVER

Solution: The major features of the Bunsen photometer are shown in Figure 1. The essential element of the Bunsen photometer is a paper screen, represented by S, with a translucent spot at its center, obtained by allowing some melted paraffin to penetrate it. M_1 and M_2 are mirrors and L_1 and L_2 are two light sources. The spot shown in Figure 1 disappears when the illuminances of both sides of S are equal. Since the illuminance, E, on a surface, is related to the intensity of the source, I, by the equation

$$E = \frac{I}{D^2} ,$$

where D represents the distance from the light source to the illuminated surface, the spot will disappear when

$$\frac{I_1}{D_1^2} = \frac{I_2}{D_2^2} ,$$

where I_1 and I_2 represent the intensities of lamps 1 and 2, respectively, and D_1 and D_2 are the distances from S to lamps 1 and 2, respectively. The spot can be made to disappear by adjusting D_1 and D_2. Hence if either I_1 or I_2 is known, the other intensity may be computed from the above equation.

The Lummer-Brodhun photometer head, shown in simple form in figure 2, is another photometric device which permits visual comparison of intensities, and is the essential element in most visual photometers currently in use.

The heart of the Lummer-Brodhun photometer is the double prism P_1-P_2. These are highly precise prisms in which the hypotenuse side of P_1 is ground or etched in such a way that its center portion is in optical contact with P_2, but the outer portion is separated from P_2. Where there is optical contact, light is transmitted so that light from the left side of the screen, S_1, as reflected in the mirror, M_1, is transmitted through the prisms and passes into the sighting telescope, T. Where there is no optical contact, complete internal reflection takes place in P_2. Light originating on the right side of S, and reflected in M_2, passes into P_2 where it is totally internally reflected (except for a small central area) and is then

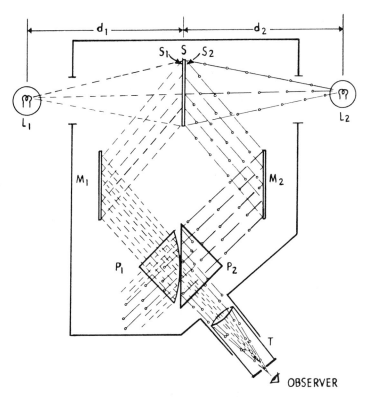

OBSERVER

passed into the sighting telescope. The telescope is focused on the interface between P_1 and P_2. The appearance of the field of view is similar to that shown in figure 1 except that the edge of the central spot is sharp and clear until the illuminances of both sides of the screen, S_1 and S_2, are equal, when it disappears.

Operation of the Lummer-Brodhun photometer is similar to that of the Bunsen photometer but it is capable of considerably greater sensitivity and precision.

● **PROBLEM** 25-17

Describe the basic features and usefullness of the Macbeth Illumino-meter and explain how it can be converted into an image - forming meter. Also state what types of measurements can best be made with a baffle tube luminance meter as opposed to an image-forming luminance meter.

Solution: The Macbeth Illuminometer is an example of a very well known commercial visual baffle-tube luminance meter which incorporates a number of features that make it versatile, convenient and fairly reliable. Its designation as an "illuminometer" is somewhat misleading since it is essentially a luminance meter which can be used for illuminance measurements, as can any other luminance meter, by use of an accessory Lambert diffuser test plate. The essential construction of the meter is shown in figure 1.

The visual comparison field is provided by a Lummer-Brodhun prism, L-B. The reference luminance field is provided by the opal glass, S, whose luminance is determined by the distance away from and the intensity of the lamp, L. The position of the lamp is adjusted by the operator with the rack and pinion mechanism, R. An auxiliary control box, not

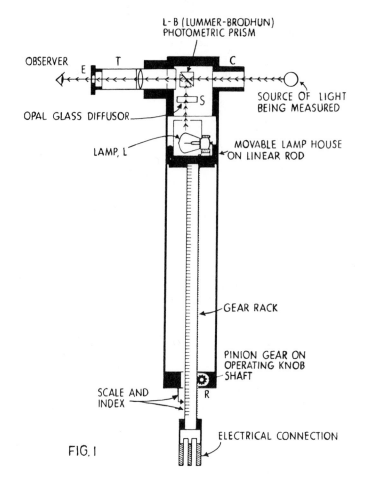

FIG. 1

shown, is equipped with necessary battery, meters, switches, and rheostats to enable the operator to set and monitor lamp operation at standardized values. The observer sights through the eyetube, T, with his eye at E, through the Lummer-Brodhun prism, and then through the baffle-tube C to the surface to be measured. The lens in the eyetube provides a magnified image of the Lummer-Brodhun comparison field on which the observer may focus by manipulation of the eyetube. The optical system is such that the comparison field is essentially in focus but the measured surface is out of focus.

The analysis of the visual test field is complicated by the fact that the limits of the field are defined by the optical system and by the geometry of the Lummer-Brodhun prism (or cube) and its pattern design. There is a central area which contributes fully to the luminance of the field, and there are outer penumbral areas that contribute partially. Thus, the test field size is not precisely definable. In the Macbeth illuminometer, it is approximately 2-3 degrees in angular extent.

The Macbeth Illuminometer can be converted into an image-forming meter by installing an objective lens on the baffle-tube, C, so that an image of a target surface is focused on the Lummer-Brodhun prism interface. The Luckiesh-Taylor luminance meter (no longer manufactured) is a very compact version of such an instrument.

Baffle tube luminance meters are most suited to measuring large areas of fairly uniform luminance, a few degrees or larger in subtense, while image-forming luminance meters are more suited to measuring smaller areas of luminance.

Describe the basic characteristics of the photocell.

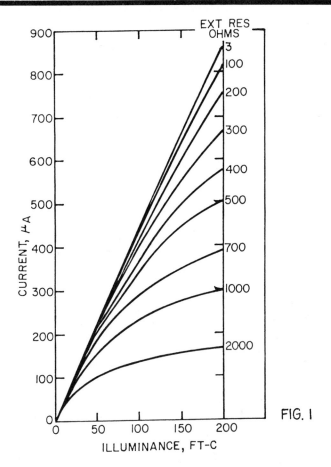

FIG. 1

Solution: Photovoltaic cells (or, in short, photocells) are light-sensitive devices which convert luminous energy into electrical energy without undergoing change themselves. In modern hermetically sealed versions, they are excellent sensors for use in photometry. They can be used in simple circuits with a high degree of stability, good linearity, and sensitivity, and can be corrected readily with built-in filters so that their spectral response characteristic is a fair approximation of the CIE (International Commission on Illumination) Standard Observer (or Standard Luminosity Function).

Photocells generate output current in the presence of light without the need for an external power supply. Thus, a photocell can be used as a photometer with only a micro-ammeter connected to it. It is, however, important that the microammeter have very low external resistance. The relationship between illuminance and the output current for a typical photocell with various values of external resistance is shown in figure 1.

It can be observed from figure 1 that the higher the maximum illuminance to be measured, the lower the external resistance must be in order to attain a given linearity. It is also found that variation of output with ambient temperature is generally less with very low external resistance.

Photocells are subject to a small fatigue effect, in which, on abrupt exposure to light, the output current tends to drift in time. Fatigue varies from cell to cell, with the illuminance and with the external resistance, and it may be positive or negative. It tends to be less with low external resistance. It seldom amounts to more than 1% or 2% at moderate illuminances and with low external resistance. Individual cells may have negligibly small amounts of it. For the most precise work, waiting for 1/2 to 1 minute will be sufficient to stabilize readings.

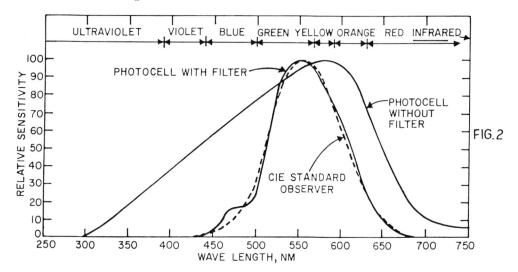

FIG. 2

Photocells are readily corrected for spectral response with eye-response-correcting filters that can be incorporated integrally in a hermetically sealed cell. Typical spectral response curves for a photocell, with and without a response-correcting filter, are shown in figure 2.

For most purposes, the degree of correction found in commercial corrected photocells will be adequate, but for highest accuracy, or for measurements of highly chromatic sources or materials, or sources with very irregular spectral distributions, these curves should not be considered applicable. The departures of the spectral sensitivity of a particular cell and filter from the Standard Observer may lead to significant error.

Photocells respond to the flux incident on their sensitive surfaces. If the flux is incident at near normal angles, this means that the cell responds to illuminance, since the area of any given cell is fixed. Beyond incident angles of 20-30 degrees an increasing fraction of the incident flux is lost, as far as the sensitive surface of the cell is concerned, because of increasing first surface reflection and increased absorption of the cover glass and filters, and because of shielding by the cell case. Photocells may be fitted with special diffusing covers or "lenses" of special geometric configurations designed to make them respond more or less accurately to illuminance, regardless of the direction of incidence. Hence, since a photocell responds to illuminance, it can be used to determine the intensity of a light source by making use of the following equation:

$$E = \frac{I}{D^2} \, ,$$

where E is the illuminance of the surface, I is the intensity of the light source, and D is the distance between the light source and the surface.

Explain how the Ulbricht integrating sphere serves as an aid in measuring the total luminous flux emitted by a light source.

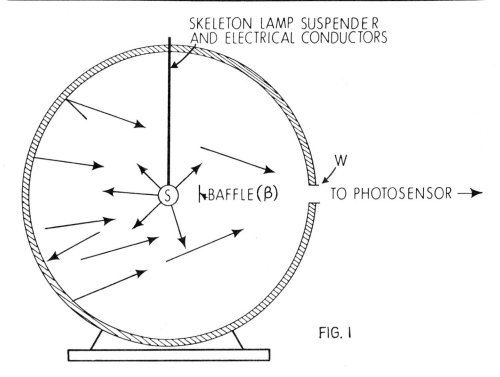

SKELETON LAMP SUSPENDER
AND ELECTRICAL CONDUCTORS

BAFFLE(β)

W
TO PHOTOSENSOR →

FIG. I

<u>Solution</u>: It is very often of interest to measure the total luminous flux emitted by light sources; that is, the summation of the flux emitted in all directions. In principle, this can be obtained by measuring the intensity (flux per unit solid angle) in all directions and then summing these intensities to obtain total flux. This is a laborious procedure and is complicated by the fact that practical goniometers (angle measuring devices on which light sources are mounted) provide angular settings that are not related to solid angle in a simple way, so that measurements must be weighted with "zone factors" to yield total flux summations.

   A convenient and very widely used photometric aid to the direct measurement of total luminous flux is the Ulbricht integrating sphere- into which a light source of interest is introduced. The inner surface of the sphere is constituted of a high-reflectance, highly diffusing coating composition. It can be shown that the illuminance on any portion of the sphere (if the coating composition is a nearly perfect diffuser) is a function of the total flux of a light source, regardless of the intensity distributions around it, if the light source itself and its mounting arrangements are very small compared to the radius of the sphere. With simple precautions (such as baffling the direct emission of the source from impinging on the portion of the sphere where the illuminance will be evaluated), it can further be shown that the sphere wall illuminance will be a sufficiently close approximation of total flux. The simplest form of the integrating sphere is shown in figure 1. In the figure, S is the light source whose total flux is to be measured, W is the window through which the sphere surface illuminance is measured,

and B is a baffle shielding the window from direct light from the
source. The window may in fact be a photovoltaic cell which, as was
shown in the preceding problem, measures illuminance. More commonly,
the window is a diffusing glass, the inner side of which is a near-
conforming part of the sphere surface and contiguous with it. In
this case, the luminance of the window, as viewed from the outside,
is proportional to the illuminance on the inside, and can be measured
with a luminance meter such as the Macbeth Illuminometer.

The required size of an integrating sphere is more or less proportional to the physical size of the light sources to be measured.
General service 50-100, etc., watt lamps may be measured in 1 1/2-
meter spheres while subminiature fractional candle power lamps may
be measured reliably in spheres of the order of 12 inches in diameter.

● **PROBLEM** 25-20

Describe the significance of the color-correction factor and show
that if the spectral energy distributions of the light being tested
and the standard used in calibrating the photometer are identical
to one another, no correction is required.

Solution: All electro-optical methods of directly measuring light
in photometric units contain the inherent problem that it is necessary
to shape the response function of the optics-photoreceptor system of
the photometer to closely match the 1931 CIE photopic luminosity
function. This CIE function has been universally adopted as descrip-
tive of human daylight (photopic) visual response. The matching of
CIE response, however, is never perfect. In the photometry of colored
signals in particular, there may be large differences in the results
obtained through the use of presumably duplicate instruments. Even
in the photometry of nominally "white" lights, large differences in
measurement may be encountered when "color temperature changing"
filters or lamp dyes are incorporated in the lamps or signal devices
and the resulting spectral energy distributions (SED's) depart
significantly from the SED of the tungsten lamp that was used to
establish the initial photometric calibration.

When dealing with telephotometers, the spectral response of the
complete photometer (not merely the built-in filter and photo-
multiplier combination) must first be determined. Should the overall response of a focused photometer prove to be virtually that of
the CIE luminosity function, then no "color corrections" would have
to be applied. Should the spectral response of the photometer system
have significant departures from the CIE curve, then valid corrections
would require computations based on radiometric analysis of the SED
of the colored light signal and of the light source used in the photometric calibration of the photometer.

If an electro-optical photometer could be designed to have a
spectral sensitivity exactly in the form of the CIE Standard Observer,
no "color-correction" factor would be needed. The photometer could
be calibrated against any standard of known luminance. Measurements
could then be made on any light or surface no matter how its SED
might differ from that of the luminance standard and the calibrated
photometer would yield correct results. Photometers generally do
not have spectral sensitivities that correspond precisely enough with
the CIE (photopic) Standard Observer. Even so, if the SED of the
light being tested corresponds exactly with the SED of the standard
used in calibrating the photometer, no correction is necessary. Thus,
there are two conditions, either one of which if met, permits correct

photometric measurements to be made without the necessity of applying corrections:

> (1) If the photometer response is precisely that of the CIE Standard Observer.
>
> (2) If the SED of the standard of luminance and that of the light being tested are precisely alike.

In general, neither condition is met, and a correction must be made which takes into account the difference between the photometer's response and the CIE Standard Observer, as well as the difference between the SED of the calibrating standard and the SED of the light under test.

The complete procedure calls for calibrating the photometer against a luminance standard having a known luminance, L_s. The calibration factor, F, of the photometer, is then given by the equation

$$F = \frac{L_s}{R_s} \; ,$$

where R_s is the reading of the photometer for the luminance L_s.

For those photometers that have an adjustable gain control, the reading, R_s, may be adjusted so that $F = 1$ or a decimal multiple of 1.

If no color-correction factor is required - that is, if either of the two conditions cited above is met - then a measurement, L, of luminance is obtained from a photometer reading, R, on a test object, by the equation

$$L = FR \; .$$

If a color-correction is required, then

$$L = CFR \; .$$

Hence, the luminance, L, represented by a reading, R, in the photometer, is equal to the product of the reading, the calibration factor, F, and the color-correction factor, C. An equation for C is

$$C = \frac{S_8}{S_6} \times \frac{S_7}{S_9} \tag{1}$$

where the four S terms are defined as follows:

$$S_6 = E_S = \text{eye response to standard lamp}$$

$$S_7 = E_T = \text{eye response to signal (test) lamp}$$

$$S_8 = P_S = \text{photometer response to standard lamp}$$

$$S_9 = P_T = \text{photometer response to signal (test) lamp.}$$

Hence, equation (1) may be written as follows:

$$C = \frac{P_S}{E_S} \times \frac{E_T}{P_T}$$

or, rearranging the terms,

$$C = \frac{P_S}{P_T} \times \frac{E_T}{E_S} \tag{2}$$

The two fractions on the right, P_S/P_T and E_T/E_S, have a special contributory significance to the overall color-correction. Equation (2) may be written as follows:

$$C = C_p \times C_E$$

where

$$C_p = \frac{P_S}{P_T}$$

and

$$C_E = \frac{E_T}{E_S}$$

C_p is a correction factor that takes into account the difference in response of the photometer to the standard and test light, and C_E accounts for the differences in response of the eye (CIE Standard Observer) to the two energy distributions.

C_p and C_E are independent of each other - that is, C_p is not affected by eye response, and C_E is a function of the two SED's and the eye response characteristic.

A hypothetical nonselective photoreceptor - that is, a radiation detector equally sensitive at all wavelengths - responds to radiant energy without regard to the SED. If the standard and the test luminances, although different in SED, happen to have equal radiances (the radiant energy analog of luminance), the nonselective receptor will measure them as equal and $C_p = 1$. In other words, the receptor could be calibrated with light of one SED and measure the light of the other SED without correction. (It should be emphasized again that eye response is not considered in C_p).

If, however, a selective photoreceptor is used, the response to different SED's may be quite different. If the photoreceptor, for example, responds twice as strongly to the test light as to the standard, for equal radiant energy content, the measurements on the test lamp should be reduced by 50%. Or, if the photoreceptor reading on the test lamp is one-third of the reading on the standard, for equal energy content, the test reading should be multiplied by three.

A similar analysis may be carried out to explain C_E. Here, C_E evaluates the different response of the eye to different SED's. C_p corrects the photoreceptor for the difference between its response to the radiant energy with which it is calibrated and that which is being measured. C_E takes into account the fact that the eye may respond quite differently to lights of equal radiant energy but different SED's. Hence, if the eye responds twice as strongly to the test light as to the standard, the photoreceptor test readings should be doubled, etc. Assuming that the spectral energy distributions of the light being tested and the standard used in calibrating the photometer are identical, $E_T = E_S$ and $P_T = P_S$.

Hence, from equation (2),

$$C = \frac{P_S}{P_T} \times \frac{E_T}{E_S} = 1 \ .$$

Therefore, no color-correction factor is necessary.

● PROBLEM 25-21

Suppose that a marking on a display has a luminance of $B_T = 200$ candelas/m^2 and the surround luminance is $B_0 = 100$ candelas/m^2. Determine the contrast. If a neutral filter with a transmittance of 20% is placed in front of the display, as shown in figure 1,

by what factor is the contrast increased over its initial value?
Assume that all of the surround luminance and none of the marking luminance is due to the ambient light.

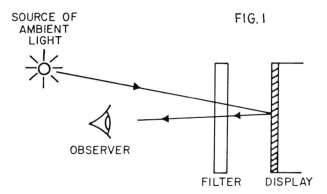

SOURCE OF
AMBIENT
LIGHT

FIG. I

OBSERVER

FILTER   DISPLAY

Solution: The contrast   C   can be computed from the equation

$$C = \frac{B_T - B_0}{B_0} \qquad (1)$$

where B_T is the luminance of the target (or marking) and B_0 is the surround luminance. Thus, substituting the given values for B_T and B_0 into equation (1) gives the result that initially,

$$C = \frac{200 - 100}{100} = 1 \ .$$

If a neutral filter is then placed in front of the display, and if the filter has a transmittance of 20%, the marking luminance, as viewed by the observer, is reduced to

$$(200 \ cd/m^2)(0.20) = 40 \ cd/m^2 \ .$$

In addition, the surround luminance is reduced by $0.20 \times 0.20 = 0.04$, since the ambient light is reduced to 20% in passing through the filter, and the resulting surround luminance is reduced to 20% again in passing back through the filter to the observer. The surround luminance, for the observer, is $100 \times 0.04 = 4 \ cd/m^2$. The contrast with the filter is then

$$C = \frac{40 - 4}{4} = \frac{36}{4} = 9 \ .$$

Even though the target luminance has been reduced to 1/5 of its initial value, the contrast has been increased by a factor of 9.

● **PROBLEM** 25-22

For a self-luminous display, initially the luminance of the target is 100 candelas/m^2 and the luminance of the background is 10 candelas/m^2. Then the ambient light is increased so that the luminances of both the display and the background are increased by 20 candelas/m^2. Find the corresponding reduction of contrast. Also, describe a situation in which contrast is not a useful concept.

Solution: The contrast, C, is defined as follows:

$$C = \frac{B_T - B_0}{B_0} \qquad (1)$$

where B_T is the luminance of the target and B_0 is the luminance of the background. Thus, initially $B_T = 100$ candelas/m^2 and $B_0 = 10$ candelas/m^2. Hence, by equation (1),

$$C = \frac{100 - 10}{10} = 9 .$$

If both B_T and B_0 are increased by 20 candelas/m^2, $B_T = 120$ candelas/m^2 and $B_0 = 30$ candelas/m^2. Thus, by equation (1),

$$C = \frac{120 - 30}{30} = 3$$

and so, the contrast is reduced by 3/9 or 1/3.

When a display, its lighting, and the ambient or surrounding light are such that the luminance of both the target and the background are significant, then the contrast is a very important concept. However, it is not particularly useful when dealing with self-luminous displays observed in a dark environment.

● **PROBLEM** 25-23

Consider the data given in table 1, where E_λ, V_λ and $V_\lambda{}'$ are the spectral energy distribution in a wavelength interval (in this case, 10 nm.), the photopic sensitivity function, and the scotopic sensitivity function, respectively, of a blackbody source at a temperature of 1600°K. Compute the cone-to-rod ratio (CRR) of the source.

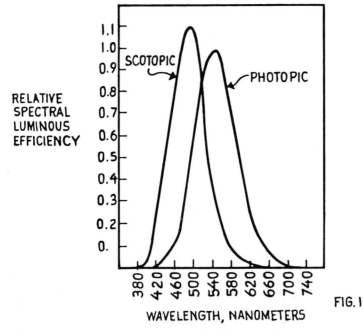

FIG. 1

WAVELENGTH, NANOMETERS

<u>Solution</u>: There are two basic types of receptor elements in the retina of the eye. Cones are distributed throughout the retina but are especially dense in the central portion or fovea where the image of a fixated object is formed. Visual acuity is highest in the fovea. Critical seeing tasks, such as reading instruments, are best carried out with fovea vision and relatively high illumination. The rods are distributed through all the retina except the fovea. At high levels

750

TABLE 1

E = Blackbody, 1600° K

40 ordinates - 380 to 770 nm

λ nm	1 $(EV)_\lambda$	2 $(EV')_\lambda$
380	0	0
390	0	0
400	0	1
10	0	5
20	1	21
30	3	64
40	10	151
450	22	296
60	49	510
70	101	827
80	207	1300
90	410	1959
500	830	2776
10	1665	3632
20	2992	4338
30	4577	4740
40	6315	4736
550	8132	4327
60	9950	3619
70	11548	2772
80	12696	1947
90	13188	1256
600	13028	754
10	12223	425
20	10825	230
30	8748	119
40	6673	65
650	4686	35
60	3052	15
70	1820	6
80	1094	6
90	594	0
700	333	0
10	190	0
20	101	0
30	56	0
40	37	0
750	14	0
60	15	0
70	0	0
	136185 cones	40932 rods

of light adaptation, vision is mediated by cones only. At low levels, the rods become functional, and at the very lowest levels when retinal images are below cone thresholds, only the extremely sensitive rods mediate vision. However, the high rod sensitivity is achieved only when the eye is dark adapted. After exposure to bright light, it may take as long as 30 to 45 minutes for the eye to become fully dark adapted and the rods to attain maximum sensitivity.

Therefore, a requirement for high ambient illumination for good

751

visual acuity and the requirement for prolonged dark adaptation for maximum sensitivity in the dark are in general contradictory to one another when both requirements must be met simultaneously or in rapid succession.

It has been found possible to achieve a satisfactory compromise in many important situations by taking advantage of the Purkinje effect: the fact that the spectral sensitivity distribution for the cones is quite different from that of the dark-adapted rods. The relative spectral luminous efficiency curves for scotopic (dark-adapted) rod vision and for photopic cone vision are shown in figure 1. The curves have been normalized by making the areas under the two curves equal. The cone-to-rod ratio relates the sensitivities of the cones and the rods of the eye to a given light source.

The luminous effectiveness (in suitable terms such as luminance, intensity, etc.) of light with a given spectral energy distribution (SED) is given by $\Sigma E_\lambda V_\lambda \Delta_\lambda$, where E_λ is the spectral energy in a wavelength interval $(\Delta\lambda)$, and V_λ is the luminous efficiency in that interval, as shown by the photopic curve of figure 1. If a similar computation is carried out with respect to the scotopic sensitivity function V'_λ, then the ratio of the two summations thus obtained is a measure of the relative photopic efficiency or cone-to-rod ratio. If the ratio is represented by "CRR", it may be written as follows:

$$CRR = \frac{\Sigma E_\lambda V_\lambda \Delta_\lambda}{\Sigma E_\lambda V'_\lambda \Delta_\lambda} = \frac{\Sigma E_\lambda V_\lambda}{\Sigma E_\lambda V'_\lambda} \tag{1}$$

In equation (1), the $\Delta\lambda$'s cancel out and may be dropped if $\Delta\lambda$ is a constant throughout the computations as is the case in this problem. It is necessary, of course, that the E_λ and $\Delta\lambda$ be the same in computing the cone function as in computing the rod function. As mentioned above, the two curves shown in figure 1 are normalized so that the areas enclosed by them are equal. This produces a CRR equal to one for a hypothetical equal-energy source (a source that emits equal amounts of energy at all wavelengths through the visible spectrum.)

The products of E_λ and V_λ (represented as $(EV)_\lambda$) and of E_λ and V'_λ (represented as $(EV')_\lambda$) are given in table 1 for wavelengths from 380 nm. to 770 nm., in intervals of 10 nm. The sums of the values of $(EV)_\lambda$ and $(EV')_\lambda$ for each wavelength indicated in table 1 are 136185 and 40932, respectively, as shown in table 1. Hence, by equation (1) the cone-to-rod ratio is

$$CRR = \frac{\Sigma E_\lambda V_\lambda}{\Sigma E_\lambda V'_\lambda} = \frac{136185}{40932} \cong 3.33 .$$

ALPHANUMERIC DISPLAYS

● **PROBLEM** 25-24

Describe the major features of an alphanumeric display terminal and explain what features it has which makes it more useful than either the typewriter or the teletypewriter.

Solution: An alphanumeric display terminal is typically a compact unit that resembles a small television set equipped with a keyboard.

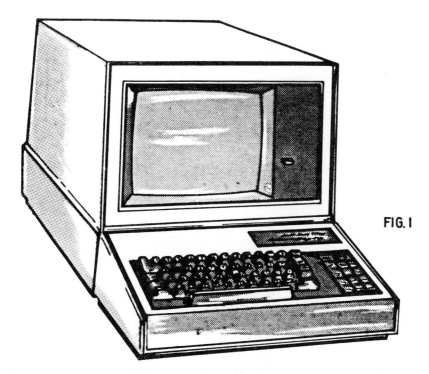

FIG. I

These terminals display data on the face of a cathode-ray tube. The
data can be entered from a keyboard or received from a computer.
Figure 1 illustrates a typical alphanumeric display unit.

Data displayed by an alphanumeric display terminal may be in the
form of alphabetic letters, numeric digits, punctuation marks, and
specialized symbols. Some units can display only a subset, such as
numeric digits, of the character set mentioned. In this text, any
displayed symbol is referred to as a character. Other, more sophisticated devices used to display graphs and other complex shapes are
commonly referred to as line-drawing units.

Most commercially available alphanumeric terminals can be connected
either directly to a computer input/output channel or remotely via an
appropriate controller or adapter at the computer site and a communi-
cations line.

The basic function of alphanumeric terminals is to provide rapid,
easy access to data stored in a computer system or to the computa-
tional facilities of the computer. The following two general types
of operation are well suited for alphanumeric display terminals:

1. Obtaining information on a particular account or subject,
such as credit, bank balance, inventory, or seating availability.
Data files maintained at the central computer site serve as the
source of information. These files can be quickly updated from the
remote display stations as events and transactions take place.

2. Providing convenient man-machine "conversations" that permit
the operator of the remote display station to base his inquiries upon
prior results calculated by the computer and displayed on the screen.
This type of application allows programmers, engineers, designers, and
others to create and execute programs in a step-by-step fashion while
being informed of programming errors and intermediate results at each
step. One major feature of alphanumeric display systems which is not
common to the typewriter or the teletypewriter is that alphanumeric
display systems enable data to be transmitted to a remote location
and read in an extremely short time. Graphic display systems generate

extremely complex graphs, line drawings, vector plots, and images that
can be magnified, reduced, or varied in perspective. These systems
can be either passive (closed to human communication during operation)
or interactive (responsive to communication introduced by such different methods as key punching, switch tripping, light-pen operation,
and teletypewriter messages). For passive, or noninteractive systems,
the display is simply an output device, and the information presented
on the screen is intended strictly for viewing by the user. In interactive systems the display operator becomes a part or component of the
system. He may call for the display of particular data, activate a
different program, ask for status information of the system, request
changes in the size or content of the display, and even change the
stored data by changing the image.

Thus, the alphanumeric display is an obvious threat to the typewriter and teletypewriter.

Display devices are used in many different data input and output
situations. The unique features of the device often dictate its
selection in a particular situation. Its speed, noiseless operation,
flexibility, appearance, and ability to substantially reduce human
errors are significant factors in the use of a display. However,
since a display is only part of a total system, it is usually evaluated
along with other terminal devices in relationship to the total system
environment.

● **PROBLEM** 25-25

Describe the operating features of the cathode-ray tube (CRT) and of
the charactron, video display and storage tube, three special kinds
of CRT's. In addition, describe the procedures by which the CRT
deflects electrons.

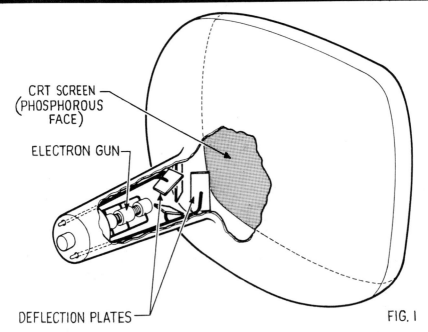

CRT SCREEN
(PHOSPHOROUS
FACE)

ELECTRON GUN

DEFLECTION PLATES   FIG. I

Solution: The CRT is common in today's world as the picture tube of
commercial television sets. All CRT's incorporate a basic set of
components: the tube enclosure, a cathode, an electron-gun assembly,
a processing structure, deflection electrodes or an external deflec-

tion assembly, and a phosphor coating on the viewing surface. Figure 1 illustrates the arrangement of basic components in a cathode-ray tube.

In the operation of the CRT, the cathode emits a stream of electrons that are accelerated and focused into a beam aimed at the tube center by the electron-gun assembly. The beam impacts on the phosphor-coated surface to form a spot of light. The specific location of impact at any time depends upon the amount of beam bending induced by deflection control settings. The beam is deflected along horizontal and vertical axes by deflection amplifier circuits, which receive analog signals that have been generated in accordance with the digital pulses provided by the computer. Intensity controls located outside the tube determine the energy of the beam.

Two basic methods of focus and deflection control are possible, namely, electromagnetic and electrostatic. An electromagnetic system consists of two pairs of yoke coils that rest on opposite sides of the tube and generate perpendicular magnetic fields in proportion to the current flow through the coils. Together, the magnetic fields exert both a horizontal and vertical deflection force on the electron beam. In the electrostatic system, two pairs of electrically charged plates interact with the beam to cause deflection in both the horizontal and vertical directions. Of the two methods, electromagnetic deflection is normally less expensive, but electrostatic action usually provides more accurate control.

Many graphic display systems use a tube that relies upon electro-magnetic deflection as the primary control but supplements with a minor electrostatic deflection control for the display of alphanumeric characters.

As the electrons fall upon the screen, they transfer their energy to the phosphor coating. The phosphor converts some of this energy into light upon impact and stores the remainder; this initial emission of light is called fluorescence. Once the beam has passed a particular section of phosphor, the phosphor continues to radiate through the conversion of its stored energy. This phenomenon is called phosphor-escence, and the period during which it lasts is called the persistence of the phosphor. The decay rate specifies the rate at which the stored energy decreases.

Changing the electrostatic and/or electromagnetic field between the deflection plates permits the use of one of two basic deflection schemes in alphanumeric display units:

1. Raster scan: The electron beam is moved in a regular pattern across the face of the CRT. It can be best described by picturing the electron beam as being positioned at the upper left-hand corner of the CRT. The beam is then moved rapidly in the horizontal direction. When it reaches the end of the screen it is reset to the left of the screen, displaced downward slightly, and moved again in the horizontal direction. This pattern is continued until the beam is in the lower right-hand corner. While the beam is going through this scanning process, it can be modulated in intensity to form an image- in this case, alphanumeric characters. This scan technique typically matches an ordinary TV scan, which consists of 525 horizontal scanning lines. The complete pattern is repeated 30 times a second.

2. Directed beam: The electron beam is moved across the face of the CRT while it is turned off. It can be moved simultaneously in the horizontal and vertical directions to arrive at a particular position on the face of the CRT, the major positioning. Once at this position, the beam may be turned on or modulated while it is repositioned or moved to write or stroke characters. In this manner an alphanumeric

character or symbol is "drawn" on the screen.

The type of phosphor used in a CRT determines the amount of energy that can be delivered to the phosphor without damage, the color of light emitted during fluorescence and phosphorescence, and the persistence of the phosphor. These factors in turn determine the brightness of the display and the rate at which the picture must be refreshed in order to remain stable.

The charactron is a special type of CRT; it is constructed as a regular CRT but includes a stencil in which the shapes of characters, and other symbols are etched. The electron beam is sent through a shaped-character aperture and assumes this shape when focused on the screen. Since no time is spent in deflecting the beam to form the character, this method is faster than techniques that require deflection.

A video display is another special kind of CRT. With this type of CRT, the beam systematically scans the entire face of the tube. The picture is generated by continuously varying the intensity of the beam in accordance with the video intelligence to be presented. Television is perhaps the best known example of a video display.

A storage tube is a video display device with a memory element that has the ability to control the beam intensity during the scan. Thus, a storage tube is a special type of CRT that combines the scanning function of a video display with a storage element. The advantages of the storage tube are its greater brightness and persistence. The latter reduces the memory requirements for refreshing the screen.

● **PROBLEM** 25-26

Describe the relationships between alphanumeric displays and the following products: televisions, indicators, graphic displays and large area displays.

Solution: The development of display devices was important to many related technologies, and products in a number of diversified areas utilize their capabilities.

Television is related to alphanumeric displays in a number of ways. First of all, the increased use of the Cathode Ray Tube (CRT) and related circuits owes a great deal to television. The low price of displays has been brought about, in part, by the mass production techniques developed for television sets. In addition, the TV raster scan, which also has been developed for mass production and is therefore inexpensive, may also be used for displays. The newer, smaller companies in the computer field use this technique more than any other. Some display companies use a commercial TV set for display. Furthermore, the most prevalent method of generating color displays is by using television techniques and the ordinary TV three-gun shadow-mask CRT. These displays simply color-code the characters that are used to generate the display. Red, green, blue, and yellow are generally the only colors used.

Indicators are alphanumeric character devices used for adding machines, equipment readout devices, stock quote board displays, and the like. Indicators are related to alphanumeric displays because some applications that require a limited set of alphanumeric and/or a few characters per display use either indicators or alphanumeric displays. In fact, the early stock quote terminals used indicators, and some are still in use today.

Graphic displays are similar to alphanumeric displays except that they are much larger, can provide extensive line drawings, and can display many more numeric characters at one time than can an alphanumeric display. Because of the complexity of graphic displays, they are almost always directly associated with a computer (usually a minicomputer), whose function specifically is to operate the graphic display. Much of the early work in the development of display technology was aimed at perfecting graphic displays.

One type of graphic display competes in some applications with alphanumeric displays. This is a display centered around the direct-view storage tube (DVST). The storage-tube display provides alphanumerics and graphics (i.e., complex line drawings) much more cheaply than the graphic displays previously described. Storage-tube displays are made by a number of new firms that specialize in this field, but because of their limitations, there are only certain applications where they can be used effectively. Where some graphics are required, but extensive interaction between the human operator and computer is not required, the storage-tube display can be very effective.

Large area displays, typically, are those used to show train and plane arrivals and departures in terminal buildings. In some cases, menu boards are used with closed-circuit TV, and monitors are placed around as enunciators for these applications. Other large area displays consist of very bright CRT tube displays, projected through special optics onto a screen. The circuits and other parts of such displays are similar to those used in alphanumeric displays.

CHAPTER 26

LASERS & HOLOGRAPHY

LASERS

A piece of ground glass of diameter D is illuminated uniformly by a laser beam, and a speckle pattern is formed on
a screen at a distance L. Show that the smallest detail in
the pattern is of order of size λL/D, where λ is the wavelength of the beam of light. If the screen is viewed from
a distance of 250 mm and if L = 2 m, how large must the
ground glass be to make the smallest detail unobservable
to the eye? (λ = 632.8 nm)

Solution: This problem is really a problem in interference-
diffraction. The eye has a minimum resolution of approximately 47 seconds of arc, so we can find the minimum size
on the screen that the eye can resolve as follows:

$$\tan (47 \text{ seconds}) = \frac{\text{radius of resolution}}{250 \text{ mm}}$$

or, the radius of resolution = tan (47 seconds)(250 mm) =
0.056 mm.

From diffraction, we have for the condition of the
first minimum,

$$\lambda = d \sin \theta_m = \frac{dD}{L}$$

where λ is the wavelength of the light used; d is the diameter of the first minimum at the image screen; D is the
diameter of the ground glass and L is the distance between
the ground glass and the image screen.

We will not have details smaller than the first minimum
of diffraction. Thus,

$$d = \frac{\lambda L}{D}$$

Solving for D,

$$D = \frac{\lambda L}{d}$$

Letting d be the diameter of resolution of the eye and substituting in the values

$L = 2$ m, $\lambda = 632.8$ nm $= 632.8 \times 10^{-9}$ m and d =

$$2 \times .056 \times 10^{-3}$$

$$D = \frac{(632.8 \times 10^{-9})(2)}{(2)(.056 \times 10^{-3})} \quad m = 11300 \times 10^{-6} \ m = 11.3 \ mm.$$

● **PROBLEM** 26-2

A helium-cadmium laser emits a beam of light 2 mm in diameter and containing the wavelengths 325 and 488 nm, respectively. At what distance from the laser, assuming diffraction-limited performance and propagation through free space, would these two components be separated by 1 cm?

Solution: In this problem, we have a source 2 mm in diameter of coherent light with two wavelengths, 325 nm, and 488 nm. If we place a screen some distance from the source, a diffraction pattern will appear. The radius of the first minimum is given by the standard equation for Fraunhofer diffraction of a circular aperture:

$$q_r = 1.22 \, \frac{R\lambda}{2a}$$

where q_r is the radius of the first minimum, R is the distance source to screen, λ is the wavelength of light used, and a is the radius of the aperture. The number 1.22 is a result of the numerical factors in the conditions of the minimum and the circular nature of the aperture (i.e., zeros of the Bessel function).

Since we have two wavelengths in our source, there will be two minima, q_1 and q_2. The problem requires a separation between the two wavelengths of 1 cm, or, substituting into the equation and solving for R gives the following result:

$$q_2 - q_1 = 1 \ cm = \frac{1.22 \ R}{2a} (\lambda_2 - \lambda_1)$$

$$R = \frac{q_2 - q_1}{\lambda_2 - \lambda_1} \, \frac{2a}{1.22}$$

$$R = \left(\frac{10^{-2} \times 2 \times 10^{-3}}{1.22(488 - 325) \times 10^{-9}} \right) m = 100 \ m$$

759

A ruby laser is aimed in free space at a target 10,000 Km
away. If the laser beam initially is 14 mm in diameter,
how large in diameter will the beam be when it hits the target?   (λ = 694.3 nm)

Solution: This problem consists of a circular aperture of
diameter 14 millimeters, irradiated with coherent parallel
light of wavelength 694.3 nm. A screen is then placed
10,000 kilometers from the circular aperture and we wish to
determine the diameter of the diffracted spot (to the first
diffraction minimum) at the screen. From any standard optics text, the Fraunhofer diffraction of a circular aperture is given by the following equation:

$$r = \frac{1.22 \ R\lambda}{D}$$

where r is the radius of the first minimum of the circular
aperture Fraunhofer diffraction, R is the distance between
the aperture and the screen, λ is the wavelength of the
light used, and D is the diameter of the aperture. Therefore the diameter of the spot on the screen to the first
minimum is

$$d = 2r = \left(\frac{2 \times 1.22 \times 10^7 \times 694.3 \times 10^{-9}}{14 \times 10^{-3}} \right) m = 1210 \ m$$

If a laser delivers 1 mW of power and has a beam diameter
of 2 mm, what is its power density, per mm^2, in a spot
1×10^{-3} mm in diameter, assuming a loss of 20% in the focusing system?

Solution: Here we are starting with 1 milliwatt of power
confined to a diameter of 2 mm. Hence, the power density
(P.D.) will be

$$P.D. = \frac{Power}{Area} = \frac{Power}{\frac{\pi d^2}{4}}$$

where d is the diameter of the beam. Therefore, substituting the given values for the power output of the laser and
the beam diameter, the initial power density will be

$$P.D. = \frac{1 \times 10^{-3}}{\frac{\pi (2 \times 10^{-3})^2}{4}} = 318 \ watts/m^2 \ .$$

Now we will use a lens system to reduce the area of the
beam to 1×10^{-3} mm diameter. In the process of focusing,
some of the energy will be lost by scattering, reflection

and absorption. It is given that the lens system will account for a loss in energy of 20%; thus, 80% of the energy
will remain after focusing. Therefore, the focused beam
will have a power output of 0.8 milliwatts or

$$P.D. = \frac{0.8 \times 10^{-3}}{\frac{\pi (10^{-6})^2}{4}} = 1 \times 10^9 \text{ watts/m}^2 = 1 \text{ Kw/mm}^2$$

● **PROBLEM** 26-5

In a helium-neon laser, transition from the 3s to the 2p
neon level gives laser emission of wavelength 632.8 nm.
If the 2p level has energy equal to 15.2×10^{-19} J, how
much pumping energy is required assuming no loss in the
helium-neon transition?

Solution: A laser is an optical device which produces a
highly coherent, highly monochromatic light source. It
depends on narrow energy levels in a gas, liquid, or crystal,
of which the upper state is a metastable state and has a
higher population density than the lower level to which it
decays. In atomic physics, the energy difference between
the levels of the atoms is equal to $h\nu$, where h is Planck's
constant and ν is the frequency of the photon emitted or absorbed as the atom changes energy levels. To leave an atom
in the metastable state which will permit lasing, it must
have sufficient energy to raise a ground state electron to
the metastable state. Therefore, the pumping energy must
be at least as great as the energy difference between the
ground state and the metastable state. In this problem, the
2p level is 15.2×10^{-19} joules above the ground state and
the wavelength of the He-Ne laser is 632.8 nm or, since

$$E_{3s} - E_{2p} = h\nu = \frac{hc}{\lambda} = \frac{6.6 \times 10^{-34} \times 3 \times 10^8}{632.8 \times 10^{-9}} = 3.12 \times 10^{-19} \text{ J}$$

the input energy (pumping energy) must be

$$\left(E_{2p} - E_{gnd}\right) + \left(E_{3s} - E_{2p}\right) = (15.2 + 3.12) \times 10^{-19} \text{ J}$$

$$= 18.32 \times 10^{-19} \text{ J}$$

● **PROBLEM** 26-6

The line width of a He-Ne laser is 10^3 Hz. The operating
wavelength is 6328Å and the power is 1 milliwatt. (a) How
many photons are emitted per second? (b) If the output beam
is 1 mm in diameter, at what temperature would a blackbody
have to be in order to emit the same number of photons from
an equal area and over the same frequency interval as the
laser?

<u>Solution</u>: (a) The energy in a photon is given by

$$E = hf = \frac{hc}{\lambda}$$

where h is Planck's constant, and f, λ, and c represent the frequency, wavelength, and speed, respectively, of light.

Substituting the given value for λ and the known values for h and c,

$$E = \frac{\left(6.6 \times 10^{-34}\right)\left(3 \times 10^{8}\right)}{632.8 \times 10^{-9}} \text{ joules} = 3.12 \times 10^{-19} \text{ joules}$$

Since the power in the beam is 1mW, the number of photons per second is

$$\# \text{ photons/sec} = \frac{10^{-3}}{3.12 \times 10^{-19}} = 3.2 \times 10^{15} \text{ photons/sec}$$

(b) The amount of energy $W_{B\lambda}$ in a wavelength interval $d\lambda$ is given by

$$W_{B\lambda} \, d\lambda = \frac{c_1}{\lambda^5} \left(e^{c_2/\lambda T} - 1\right)^{-1} d\lambda \qquad\qquad (1)$$

where T is in degrees Kelvin, $C_1 = 3.74 \times 10^{-16}$ watts m^2 and $c_2 = 1.4385 \times 10^{-2}$ m °K, and $W_{B\lambda}d\lambda$ is in watts/m^2 .

We need to compare the amount of energy in our laser beam with that produced by a blackbody at temperature T. So let us find $d\lambda$ for the laser beam. The line width is given as a frequency 10^3 Hertz. Now,

$$f\lambda = c$$

and

$$f = c/\lambda .$$

Differentiating f with respect to λ gives

$$\Delta f = \frac{c\Delta\lambda}{\lambda^2} \quad \text{(ignoring sign)}$$

$$\Delta\lambda = \frac{\Delta f \lambda^2}{c} .$$

Substituting the given values for Δf and λ along with the known value for c into the preceding equation gives the result

$$\Delta\lambda = \frac{10^3\left(632.8 \times 10^{-9}\right)^2}{3 \times 10^8} \text{ m}$$

$$= 1.33 \times 10^{-18} \text{ m}$$

Now, solving for the energy density in the laser beam,

$$W_{B\lambda} d\lambda = \frac{\text{power}}{\text{area of output beam}} = \frac{p}{\pi \left(\frac{d}{2}\right)^2}$$

where p represents the power output of the laser and d is the diameter of the output beam. Thus $W_{B\lambda} d\lambda =$

$$\frac{10^{-3} \text{ watts}}{\pi \left(\frac{10^{-3}}{2}\right)^2 m^2} = \frac{4}{\pi} \times 10^3 \text{ watts/m}^2 = 1.27 \times 10^3 \text{ watts/m}^2$$

so substituting into equation (1),
$$1.27 \times 10^3 =$$

$$= \frac{3.74 \times 10^{-16}}{\left(632.8 \times 10^{-9}\right)^5} \left(\left(e^{\frac{1.4385 \times 10^{-2}}{632.8 \times 10^{-9}T}}\right) - 1\right)^{-1} \times \left(1.33 \times 10^{-18}\right)$$

or

$$e^{\left(\frac{2.27 \times 10^4}{T}\right)} - 1 = 3.85 \times 10^{-6}$$

In this case, we can approximate $e^x \simeq 1 + x$ (from the Taylor series expansion for e^x).

Thus

$$\frac{2.27 \times 10^4}{T} = 3.85 \times 10^{-6}$$

$$T = \frac{2.27 \times 10^4}{3.85 \times 10^{-6}} = 5.9 \times 10^9 \text{ °K}.$$

● **PROBLEM 26-7**

Calculate the inversion density $n_j - n_i \frac{g_j}{g_i}$ for a helium-neon laser operating at a wavelength of 6328 Å. The gain constant is 2% per meter, and the temperature of the discharge is 100°C. The lifetime of the upper state against spontaneous emission to the lower state is 10^{-7} sec.

Solution: Let us first look at how a laser works. Consider an atomic system which has two atomic levels. If this system is in thermal equilibrium, the lower state will have a higher population density than the upper state such that the ratio of the population densities will be

$$e^{\frac{-h\nu}{KT}}$$

763

from the Maxwell-Boltzmann distribution where h is Planck's
constant, ν is the frequency of the transition between the
two states (i.e., $h\nu = E_j - E_i$; E_j being the upper state
energy and E_i being the lower state energy), K is the
Boltzmann constant, and T is the temperature of the discharge in degrees Kelvin. Now if we shine radiation of
frequency ν on this confined system, there will be transitions j to i and i to j. Because of the population density,
we expect more to go i to j than j to i. As a result, we
see that we need to get a population density inversion so
that there will be more j states than i states occupied.
With the external radiation of frequency ν, more transitions will occur j to i than i to j, and as a result, more
radiation out than the incident radiation. In going from i
to j the external radiation is absorbed (lost) while from
j to i we still have the incident photon plus the j to i
photon in our beam.

So, to keep our energy balance, the energy into the
atomic system must equal the sum of the i to j transitions
and losses of photons to the surroundings.

In practice, we use an atomic system that has more than
two energy levels, including the states i and j, and such
that in the chain of transitions, a metastable state exists
to promote the population density inversion. In addition,
we arrange our system so that most of the radiation is
trapped in the confined region with a relatively small
amount of the stimulated emission being able to escape from
the region. Then by a suitable technique, we pump energy
into the cavity to invert the population density and let
the spontaneous decays initiate the lasing action.

Now to solve our problem, we need to have some quantitative method of determining this population inversion. To
start from basic principles would require a prodigious effort so we refer you to a text describing quantitatively
these principles, such as "Laser Parameter Measurements
Handbook," H. G. Heard, J. Wiley and Son (1968) starting
with page 199. From this or other sources we find:

$$\left(n_j - n_i \frac{g_j}{g_i} \right) = 4\pi^2 \sqrt{\frac{2}{\pi}} \frac{\gamma \tau_{ji}}{\lambda^3} \sqrt{\frac{kT}{M}} \tag{1}$$

where the n's are the population densities of the upper (j)
and lower (i) states of the laser radiation, the g's are
the statistical weights of the states, γ is the gain constant, τ_{ji} is the lifetime of the transition j to i, λ is
the wavelength of the emitted laser radiation, K is the
Boltzmann constant, T is the temperature of the gas in
degrees Kelvin, and M is the atomic mass of the atom undergoing the transition. If all units are expressed in the
mks system, then the population density inversion will be
in units of per cubic meters.

So now we can substitute the given values for γ, τ_{ji},
λ, T = (273 + 100)°K = 373°K, and the known values for K

and M, into equation (1):

$$\left(n_j - n_i \frac{g_j}{g_i}\right) = 4\pi^2 \sqrt{\frac{2}{\pi}} \frac{0.02 \times 10^{-7}}{\left(632.8 \times 10^{-9}\right)^3} \sqrt{\frac{1.38 \times 10^{-23} \times 373}{20 \times 1.6 \times 10^{-37}}}$$

$$= 1 \times 10^{19} \text{ per m}^3.$$

HOLOGRAMS

● **PROBLEM** 26-8

In a hologram interference experiment with a helium-neon laser, the surface under test is illuminated and viewed at normal incidence. If the displacement to be determined is 2500 nm, by how many fringes will it be represented if (a) the displacement is normal to the surface, (b) it is 45° to the normal, and (c) it is in the plane of the surface?

Solution: In an interferometer if we move one of the mirrors by one fringe the distance moved will be one-half wavelength. Hence,

$$\Delta s = \frac{\lambda}{2} \text{ for one fringe,}$$

where Δs = the distance moved by the mirror and λ = the wavelength of light used.

$$2\Delta s_1 = n\lambda$$

for n fringes.

Thus, assuming that $\lambda \cong 632.8$ nm and substituting the given value for Δs_1 into the preceding equation,

(a) $n = \dfrac{2\Delta s_1}{\lambda} = \dfrac{2 \times 2500}{632.8} = 7.9$ fringes .

Now, if the displacement is at some angle θ to the normal, then,

$$n = \frac{2\Delta s}{\lambda} \cos \theta .$$

(b) For $\theta = 45°$

$$n_1 = 7.9 \cos 45° = 5.6 .$$

(c) If the displacement is in the plane of the surface, then $\theta = 90°$ and

$$n_2 = 7.9 \cos 90° = 0 .$$

● **PROBLEM** 26-9

In a holography experiment, the reference source and the object are both 1 m from the hologram plate, and they are

100 mm apart. Estimate the scale of detail in the hologram fringes if the wavelength is 632.8 nm.

Solution: In this problem, we have coherent light from two sources 100 mm apart each located 1 meter from the holographic plate. Therefore, this problem can be treated as an interference problem. The radius of the first minimum of the interference pattern must be determined. From interference, we have:

$$q_r \simeq \frac{\lambda D}{a}$$

where q_r is the radius of the interference pattern, λ is the wavelength of the light used, D is the distance from the object to the hologram plate, and a is the separation of the reference source and the object. Therefore, substituting the given values for λ, D, and a into the equation,

$$q_r = \left(\frac{632.8 \times 10^{-9} \times 1}{100 \times 10^{-3}} \right) m = 6.33 \times 10^{-6} m$$

● **PROBLEM** 26-10

Suppose a hologram is made with light of wavelength 600 nm (orange) and then viewed with light of wavelength 500 nm (green). How will the images differ from those that would be formed with the orange light?

Solution: It is possible to develop for holography a set of equations similar to geometric optics and lenses, which will relate the reference source distance and the object source distance to the reconstructed image distance.

There are two reconstructed images, the normal image, which will be represented with primes ('), and the conjugate image, which will be represented with double primes ("). For the normal image we can locate the image by making use of the following equation:

$$\frac{1}{p'} = \frac{\lambda'}{\lambda} \left(\frac{1}{p} - \frac{1}{\rho} \right) + \frac{1}{\rho'} \qquad (1)$$

$$\frac{1}{p''} = \frac{\lambda'}{\lambda} \left(-\frac{1}{p} - \frac{1}{\rho} \right) + \frac{1}{\rho'} \qquad (2)$$

where ρ represents reference source distance, p the object distance for the formation of the hologram and ρ', p', p'' the reference source distance and the image distance on reconstruction. λ is the wavelength of coherent light used in making the hologram and λ' is the wavelength of light used in reconstruction.

The magnification is found by the following relations:

$$M = \frac{\lambda'}{\lambda} \frac{p'}{p} \qquad (3)$$

For this problem, we need to make some assumptions regarding ρ and ρ'. It is reasonable to choose ρ and ρ' large with respect to p. Then $\frac{1}{\rho}$ and $\frac{1}{\rho'}$ will be negligible compared with $\frac{1}{p}$ and so, with this assumption, equations (1) and (2) become $\frac{1}{p'} = \frac{\lambda'}{\lambda} \frac{1}{p}$ and $\frac{1}{p''} = \frac{-\lambda'}{\lambda} \frac{1}{p}$, respectively. Hence,

$$\frac{1}{p'} = - \frac{1}{p''} = \frac{\lambda'}{\lambda} \frac{1}{p} \qquad (4)$$

Solving for p' in equation (4) yields:

$$p' = -p'' = \frac{\lambda p}{\lambda'} \quad .$$

Substituting the given values for λ and λ' into this equation gives:

$$p' = -p'' = \frac{6}{5} p \qquad (5)$$

Substituting for p' in equation (3),

$$M = \frac{\lambda'}{\lambda} \frac{\lambda p}{p\lambda'} \text{ or } M = 1.$$

Since the hologram photograph is an interference pattern between the reference source and the light from the object, and is formed with monochromatic coherent light of wavelength λ, when we use a different source wavelength λ' in reconstruction, there will result a modified reconstruction, which will also result in a color change for the reconstructed image. In addition, the reconstructed image distance = $\frac{6}{5}$ the object distance.

● **PROBLEM 26-11**

A plane diffraction grating is to be produced holographically using light of wavelength 632.8 nm. Sketch the arrangement to be used, and calculate the required angles if the grating is to have 1000 rulings per millimeter. What is the closest grating spacing which could be made this way?

Solution: A plane diffraction grating can be produced holographically by using two monochromatic plane waves interfering with each other. The arrangement is sketched in figure 1. The mirrors M_1 and M_2 are illuminated by a plane wave. The two mirrors are inclined with respect to each other so that two waves, represented as $A_1 e^{i\phi 1}$ and $A_2 e^{i\phi 2}$ incident on a distant photographic plate, form angles θ_1 and θ_2 with the plate. Here the phases are

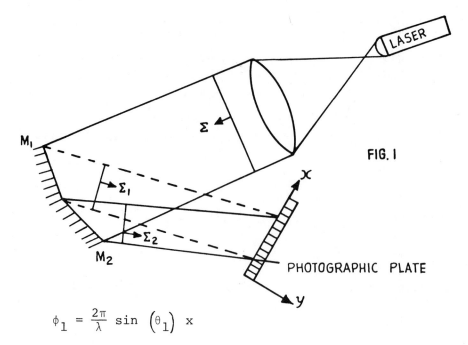

FIG. I

$$\phi_1 = \frac{2\pi}{\lambda} \sin \left(\theta_1\right) x$$

and

$$\phi_2 = \frac{2\pi}{\lambda} \sin \left(\theta_2\right) x \quad \text{where x is the length of the fringe.}$$

The resultant intensity is

$$A_1^2 + A_2^2 + 2|A_1| \, |A_2| \, \cos \left(\phi_1 - \phi_2\right)$$

There will be a bright fringe when $\cos \left(\phi_1 - \phi_2\right)$ is a maximum, i.e., when $\phi_1 - \phi_2 = 2m\pi$, m an integer. By the definitions of ϕ_1 and ϕ_2,

$$\sin \theta_1 = \frac{\lambda \phi_1}{2\pi x} \quad \text{and} \quad \sin \theta_2 = \frac{\lambda \phi_2}{2\pi x} .$$

Then $\sin \theta_1 - \sin \theta_2 = \frac{\lambda}{2\pi x} \left(\phi_1 - \phi_2\right)$

$$= \frac{\lambda}{2\pi x} \, (2m\pi) = \frac{m\lambda}{x} \quad \text{or}$$

$$x = \frac{m \, \lambda}{\sin \theta_1 - \sin \theta_2}$$

The fringe spacing is

$$\Delta x = \Delta m \, \frac{\lambda}{\sin \theta_1 - \sin \theta_2}$$

In case when the two beams are such that the recording plane bisects the angle formed by the two beams $\left(\theta_1 = - \theta_2\right)$, the spatial frequency is given by

768

$$v = \frac{2 \sin \phi/2}{\lambda}$$

where ϕ is the total angle between the two beams. Thus for $v = 1000$ rulings/mm,

$$\sin \frac{\phi}{2} = \frac{\lambda}{2} v$$

or the beams cross at

$$\phi = 2 \sin^{-1} \left(\frac{\lambda}{2} v\right) = 2 \sin^{-1} \left[\frac{\left(632.8 \times 10^{-6} mm\right)(1000/mm)}{2}\right] = 36.89$$

Hence, the beams cross at $\frac{\phi}{2} = 18.45$.

The maximum rulings are obtained when

$\sin (\phi/2) = 1$ or when

$$v = \frac{2}{\lambda} = 3160.6 \text{ per mm.}$$

● **PROBLEM 26-12**

If holograms are taken with light from a helium-neon laser ($\lambda \sim 633$ nm) in the first order, what is the limiting angle between the signal and reference beam if the space frequency in the hologram is not to exceed 200 mm^{-1}?

Solution: When a hologram is recorded in the first order (called the Fresnel hologram), usually the object is near the hologram plane. In this case, the plane wave approximation usually is valid and the reference wave and the object beam can both be represented by the plane waves $A_r e^{i\phi_r}$ and $A_o e^{i\phi_o}$ respectively where

$$\phi_r = \frac{2\pi}{\lambda} \sin \left(\theta_r\right) x$$

and

$$\phi_o = \frac{2\pi}{\lambda} \sin (\theta_o) x$$

Here xz is the plane of the hologram.

The resultant is given by

$$A_r^2 + A_o^2 + 2|A_r| |A_o| \cos \left(\phi_r - \phi_o\right)$$

Thus there will be a bright fringe when $\cos \left(\phi_r - \phi_o\right)$ is a maximum; i.e., when $\phi_r - \phi_o = 2m\pi$, m an integer.

By the definitions of ϕ_r and ϕ_o ,

$$\sin \theta_r = \frac{\lambda \phi_r}{2\pi x} \text{ and } \sin \theta_o = \frac{\lambda \phi_o}{2\pi x} .$$

Then $\sin \theta_r - \sin \theta_o = \dfrac{\lambda}{2\pi x}\left(\phi_r - \phi_o\right) =$

$$\dfrac{\lambda}{2\pi x}(2m\pi) = \dfrac{m\lambda}{x} \quad \text{or}$$

$$x = \dfrac{m\,\lambda}{\sin\theta_r - \sin\theta_o}$$

The fringe spacing is

$$\Delta x = \Delta m \dfrac{\lambda}{\sin\theta_r - \sin\theta_o}$$

when the reference beam and the object beam are such that the hologram bisects the angle formed by the two beams

$$\theta_r = -\theta_o$$

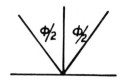

and the spatial frequency $\nu = 1/\Delta x$

$$= \dfrac{2\sin\phi/2}{\lambda}$$

where ϕ is the total angle between the two beams.

Given $\nu = 2000\ /\text{cm}$

solving for $\sin\phi/2$ gives

$$\sin\phi/2 = \dfrac{6.33 \times 10^{-5}\ \text{cm} \times 2000\ /\text{cm}}{2}$$

or $\qquad \phi = 7.259°$.

COHERENCE

• **PROBLEM** 26-13

The figure shows the phase $\phi(t)$ of a source that interferes with another source which has constant phase.

a) Will the eye detect interference?

b) Will a phototube of 1 nanosecond response time detect interference?

c) Are the two sources coherent?

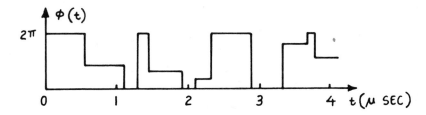

Solution: (a) The eye has a detection time of a few milli-
seconds; so it will not detect interference. The fringes
will shift position many times during the time necessary
for the eye to perceive them and thus they appear as a uniformly illuminated blur.

(b) The phototube has a response time of 1 nanosecond
or 10^{-3} μsecond, so it will register the fringe positions
before they change, thereby detecting interference.

(c) This depends on the observer. For visual observation, the answer is no; for the fast phototube, the answer
is yes.

● **PROBLEM** 26-14

A monochromator is used to obtain approximately monochromatic light from a white source. The linear dispersion of
the monochromator is $\dfrac{1 \text{ mm}}{20 \text{ Å}}$ and an exit slit of 0.2 mm is
used. What is the coherence time and coherence length of
the light from the monochromator when the mean wavelength is
5000 Å?

Solution: In order to determine the coherence time, Δt,
and coherence length, L, we must know the bandwidth of the
radiation, Δf. Since linear dispersion is defined as

$$\frac{dx}{d\lambda}$$

we know the reciprocal linear dispersion

$$\frac{d\lambda}{dx} = 20 \text{ Å}/mm = \frac{\Delta\lambda}{\Delta x}$$

where Δx is the width of the slit which is given to be
0.2 mm.

We have

$$\Delta\lambda = \Delta x \ (20) \text{Å}$$

$$= 0.2 \times 20$$

$$= 4\text{Å} = 4 \times 10^{-10} \text{ m} . \qquad (1)$$

Using the relationship between the frequency bandwidth
and the wavelength bandwidth,

771

$$\frac{\Delta f}{f} = \frac{\Delta \lambda}{\lambda} \qquad\qquad (2)$$

we find

$$\Delta f = f \frac{\Delta \lambda}{\lambda}$$

$$= \frac{c}{\lambda} \frac{\Delta \lambda}{\lambda}$$

$$= c \left(\frac{\Delta \lambda}{\lambda^2}\right)$$

$$= 3 \times 10^8 \frac{m}{sec} \left(\frac{4 \times 10^{-10} \, m}{\left(5 \times 10^{-7}\right)^2 m^2}\right)$$

$$= 4.8 \times 10^{11} \text{ Hz .} \qquad\qquad (3)$$

The coherence time $\Delta t = \dfrac{1}{\Delta f}$

$$= \frac{1}{4.8 \times 10^{11}}$$

$$= 2.1 \times 10^{-12} \text{ sec .}$$

The coherence length $L = c \, \Delta t$

$$= 3 \times 10^8 \times 2.1 \times 10^{-12}$$

$$= 6.3 \times 10^{-4} \text{ m .}$$

● **PROBLEM** 26-15

What is the lateral coherent width of sunlight? (Take the effective wavelength as 6000 Å.) The apparent angular diameter of the sun is 1/2 degree.

Solution: As we discuss interference and diffraction we always start by saying that we have perfectly monochromatic light and that each part of the light beam has a definite phase relation with respect to all other parts of the light beam. The definite phase relation is our definition of coherence. However, in practice the uncertainty principle will not allow us to have both perfectly monochromatic and perfectly coherent light. So we need to determine under what conditions of loss of perfect monochromatic and loss of perfect coherence, interference and diffraction will still occur.

Suppose we have a single quasi-monochromatic source S (figure 1). If we define E', E" and E''' to be the electric fields at the points P', P", and P''', respectively, then

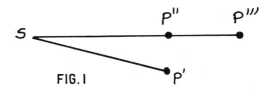

FIG.I

since P" and P''' are in the same direction from the source, E" and E''' measure the longitudinal spatial coherence of the field. Similarly, if P' and P" are the same distance from S, then E' and E" measure the lateral spatial coherence of the field.

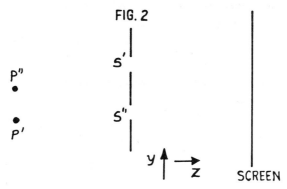

FIG. 2

Thus, for this problem we wish to determine how large the distance P'P" can be before we no longer will have interference and diffraction produced. If, now following the Huygen's construction, we treat P' and P" as two sources, and allow these two sources to illuminate a double slit as in figure 2, then P" will produce an interference pattern on the screen. P' will also produce an interference pattern on the screen with its maxima and minima shifted in y with respect to the y coordinate axis from P". Now if the maxima from P" are shifted by half a wavelength from P', the interference pattern of the two sources separately will be eliminated when both sources P' and P" are used to illuminate the slits S' and S". Therefore, lateral coherence has been lost.

The sun appears as a disk rather than a set of slits, so we need an equation that will measure lateral coherence of a disk. Such an equation is the following:

$$\ell w = \frac{1.22\lambda}{\theta} \qquad (1)$$

where ℓw is the lateral coherence width, λ is the wavelength of the light used and θ in radians is the angle subtended at the earth by the sun. Substituting the given values for λ and θ into equation (1),

$$\ell w = \left(\frac{1.22 \times 600 \times 10^{-9}}{\frac{\pi}{180} \times 1/2} \right) m$$

$$= 8.4 \times 10^{-5} \ m$$

$$= 8.4 \times 10^{-2} \text{ mm}$$

In other words, to get a two slit interference pattern from the sun, the two slits should be less than 8.4×10^{-2} mm apart.

BAND WIDTH AND FREQUENCY SPREAD

● **PROBLEM** 26-16

Red light, obtained from an incandescent lamp by means of a conventional absorptive filter, may have wavetrains only about 10 λ long. If λ = 650 nm, what is the spread in wavelength and in frequency?

Solution: If we look at the Fourier transform of a beam that has an extent in space of $\ell = c\tau$, then the uncertainty or spread in frequencies needed in the Fourier transform will be given by

$$\tau \, \Delta \, \nu \sim 1 \tag{1}$$

Now with a wave, we also have the following relationship between wavelength λ, frequency ν and velocity c.

$$\nu \, \lambda = c \tag{2}$$

or

$$\nu = c/\lambda \tag{3}$$

and differentiating with respect to λ gives

$$\Delta\nu = - \frac{c\Delta\lambda}{\lambda^2} \tag{4}$$

$$\ell = c\tau; \text{ thus, } \tau = \ell/c$$

Substituting into equation (1),

$$\frac{\ell}{c} \times c \, \frac{\Delta\lambda}{\lambda^2} \sim 1$$

$$\frac{\ell\Delta\lambda}{\lambda^2} \sim 1$$

$$\Delta\lambda \sim \frac{\lambda^2}{\ell} = \frac{\lambda^2}{10\lambda} = \frac{\lambda}{10} = 65 \text{ nm.}$$

Going back to equation (4) and substituting for c, $\Delta\lambda$ and λ gives

$$\Delta\nu = \frac{c\Delta\lambda}{\lambda^2} = \left(\frac{3 \times 10^8 \times 65 \times 10^{-9}}{\left(650 \times 10^{-9} \right)^2} \right) \text{ Hz}$$

$$= 4.62 \times 10^{13} \text{ Hz}$$

A narrow band of light centered around a mean wavelength of 520 nm is chopped by a shutter at a frequency of 40 MHz. Determine the bandwidth (in Å) of the resulting light.

Solution: If we look at the Fourier transform of a beam that has an extent in space $\ell = c\tau$, where τ is the period of the beam, then the uncertainty or spread in frequencies needed in the Fourier transform will be given by

$$\tau \ \Delta\nu \ \sim \ 1 \tag{1}$$

Now with a wave, we also have the following relationship between wavelength λ, frequency ν and velocity c:

$$\nu\lambda \ = \ c \tag{2}$$

or

$$\nu \ = \ c/\lambda \tag{3}$$

and differentiating equation (3) with respect to λ,

$$\Delta\nu \ = \ - \ \frac{c\Delta\lambda}{\lambda^2} \tag{4}$$

Rewriting equation (1) in terms of wavelength (ignoring the minus sign),

$$\frac{\tau c\Delta\lambda}{\lambda^2} \ \sim \ 1 \tag{5}$$

Then the spread in wavelength is

$$\Delta\lambda \ \sim \ \frac{\lambda^2}{c\tau}$$

Now if we chop a 520 nm light beam at a frequency of 40 MHz, then τ is of order $\dfrac{1}{40 \times 10^6}$ = 2.5 x 10^{-8} seconds or

$$\Delta\lambda \ \sim \ \frac{\left(520 \times 10^{-9}\right)^2}{3 \times 10^8 \times 2.5 \times 10^{-8}} \ m$$

$$= \ 3.6 \times 10^{-14} \ m$$

$$= \ 3.6 \times 10^{-5} \ nm$$

Therefore, a monochromatic light beam with wavelength 520 nm chopped by a shutter at a frequency of 40 MHz will produce a spread about 520 nm of order 4 x 10^{-5} nm.

LASER CAVITIES

Limiting apertures are placed at the mirrors of a confocal cavity in order to suppress the higher modes. If the cavity is one meter in length, what should the diameter of the apertures be in order that the loss for the TEM 0,1 mode be 1 percent? What is the corresponding loss for the TEM 0,0 mode (see figure)? The wavelength is 6238 Å.

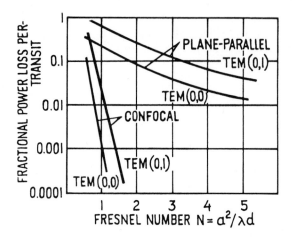

Solution: In the figure, the diffraction loss is plotted as a function of the Fresnel number,

$$N = \frac{a^2}{\lambda d} \, ,$$

where a is the mirror radius, λ is the wavelength of light used, and d is the separation between mirrors. For the loss to be 1% (a fractional loss of 0.01), corresponding to this value, the Fresnel number from the figure for the TEM (0,1) mode is 1. Hence,

$$a = \sqrt{N\lambda d}$$

$$= \sqrt{6.238 \times 10^{-5} \text{ cm} \times 100 \text{ cm}}$$

$$= 7.898 \times 10^{-2} \text{ cm}$$

Hence the diameter of the aperture is 2a = 0.158 cm. From the figure it is also clear that the fractional loss is less than 0.07% for the TEM (0,0) mode.

CHAPTER 27

ATOMIC SPECTRUM
AND THERMAL RADIATION

ATOMIC SPECTRA

Compute the longest and shortest wavelengths of light in the Lyman, Paschen, and Brackett series of atomic hydrogen.

Solution: For atomic hydrogen the Lyman Series is given by

$$\frac{1}{\lambda} = R_\infty \left(1 - \frac{1}{n^2} \right) \quad n = 2, 3 \ldots \ldots$$

where $R_\infty = 1.09678 \times 10^7 \text{ meters}^{-1}$

$$= (1.09678 \times 10^7 \text{ meters}^{-1}) (1 \text{ meter}/10^9 \text{ m}\mu)$$

$$= \frac{1.09678}{100 \text{ m}\mu}$$

Hence,

$$\lambda = \frac{100 \text{m}\mu}{1.09678 \left(1 - \frac{1}{n^2} \right)} ; \quad n = 2, 3 \ldots \ldots \ldots$$

The longest wavelength (λ_ℓ) is given by letting n = 2 and the shortest (λ_s) is given by letting n = ∞ :

$$\lambda_\ell = 121.57 \text{ m}\mu$$

$$\lambda_s = 91.18 \text{ m}\mu \quad .$$

The Paschen Series is given by

$$\frac{1}{\lambda} = R_\infty \left(\frac{1}{9} - \frac{1}{n^2} \right) \quad n = 4, 5 \ldots \ldots$$

and $\lambda = \dfrac{100}{1.09678} \dfrac{1}{\left(\frac{1}{9} - \frac{1}{n^2} \right)} \text{m}\mu.$

$$\lambda_\ell = 1875.62 \text{m}\mu \quad n = 4$$

$$\lambda_s = 820.58 \text{m}\mu \quad n = \infty \quad .$$

The Brackett Series is given by

$$\frac{1}{\lambda} = R_\infty \left(\frac{1}{16} - \frac{1}{n^2}\right) \quad n = 5, 6 \ldots\ldots$$

or

$$\lambda = \frac{100 \text{m}\mu}{1.09678 \left(\frac{1}{16} - \frac{1}{n^2}\right)}$$

Therefore

$$\lambda_\ell = 4052.27 \text{m}\mu \quad n = 5$$

and $\lambda_s = 1458.82$ mμ $n = \infty$

● **PROBLEM** 27-2

The atomic weight of hydrogen is 1.0082, and of deuterium 2.01445. Compute the separation in wave number and wavelength of the first two lines of the isotopes in the Balmer series.

Solution: The Bohr formula for the hydrogen spectrum is given by

$$\bar{\nu} = R_\infty \frac{1}{1 + \dfrac{m}{M_H}} \left(\frac{1}{K^2} - \frac{1}{n_2^2}\right)$$

where R_∞ is the Rydberg constant

$R_\infty = 109678 \text{ cm}^{-1}$, m is the mass of the electron and M_H is the mass of the hydrogen atom. The ratio m/M_H is approximately equal to $\frac{1}{1840}$. The Balmer series is given by $K = 2$ and $n = 3, 4 \ldots\ldots$

The first two lines H_α and H_β are

$$\bar{\nu}_{H_\alpha} = R_\infty \left(\frac{1}{1 + \dfrac{1}{1840}}\right)\left(\frac{1}{4} - \frac{1}{9}\right) = 15224.78 \text{ cm}^{-1}$$

$$\bar{\nu}_{H_\beta} = R_\infty \left(\frac{1}{1 + \dfrac{1}{1840}}\right)\left(\frac{1}{4} - \frac{1}{16}\right) = 20553.45 \text{ cm}^{-1}$$

778

On the other hand $\bar{\nu}_{H_\alpha}2$ and $\bar{\nu}_{H_\beta}2$ for a deuterium (H^2) spectrum is obtained by using

$$\frac{m}{M_{H^2}} = \frac{1}{3680}$$

$$\bar{\nu}_{H_\alpha}2 = R_\infty \left(\frac{1}{1 + \frac{1}{3680}} \right) \left(\frac{1}{4} - \frac{1}{9} \right) = 15228.92 \text{ cm}^{-1}$$

$$\bar{\nu}_{H_\beta}2 = R_\infty \left(\frac{1}{1 + \frac{1}{3680}} \right) \left(\frac{1}{4} - \frac{1}{16} \right) = 20559.04 \text{ cm}^{-1}$$

$$\Delta\bar{\nu}_\alpha = \bar{\nu}_{H_\alpha}2 - \bar{\nu}_{H_\alpha} = 4.14 \text{ cm}^{-1}$$

$$\Delta\bar{\nu}_\beta = \bar{\nu}_{H_\beta}2 - \bar{\nu}_{H_\beta} = 5.59 \text{ cm}^{-1}$$

Since $\lambda = \frac{1}{\nu}$, we have

$$\Delta\lambda_\alpha = 6568.24 \text{ Å} - 6566.45 \text{ Å} = 1.79 \text{ Å}$$

$$\Delta\lambda_\beta = 4865.36 \text{ Å} - 4864.04 \text{ Å} = 1.32 \text{ Å}$$

● **PROBLEM 27-3**

Using the Bohr formula, calculate the wave numbers of the first five members of the spectrum emitted by ionized helium.

Solution: According to Bohr's formula, the wave number $\bar{\nu}$ of the spectral line corresponding to the two energy levels (or orbits) with quantum numbers n_1 and n_2 is given by

$$\bar{\nu} = \frac{2\pi^2 \mu e^4 Z^2}{h^3 c} \left(\frac{1}{n_1^2} - \frac{1}{n_2^2} \right)$$

where μ is the reduced mass

$$\mu = \frac{m}{1 + \frac{m}{AM_h}}$$

A is the atomic number, m is the electron mass, e is the electron charge, Z is the nuclear charge, M_h is the mass of the hydrogen atom and h is Planck's Constant. For ionized helium A = 4, Z = 2 and hence

$$\bar{\nu} = \frac{2\pi^2 \left(9.1091 \times 10^{-28} \text{gms}\right) \left(4.803\right)^4 10^{-40} \left(\text{esu}\right)^4 \, 4 \left[\frac{1}{n_1^2} - \frac{1}{n_2^2} \right]}{\left(1 + \frac{1}{7344.4}\right) \left[(6.625)^3 \times 10^{-81} \text{ erg}^3 \text{ sec}^3\right] \left(2.998 \times 10^{10} \frac{\text{cm}}{\text{sec}}\right)}$$

$$\tilde{\nu} \approx 439002.7 \; \text{Cm}^{-1} \left(\frac{1}{n_1^2} - \frac{1}{n_2^2} \right)$$

Then the following table can be constructed, giving the wave-numbers of the first five members of the spectrum emitted by ionized helium:

n_1	n_2	$\bar{\nu} \; (\text{cm}^{-1})$
4	5	9877.56
4	6	15243.17
4	7	18478.43
4	8	20578.25
4	9	22017.88

● PROBLEM 27-4

1) What is the short-wave limit of the continuous x-ray spectrum produced by an x-ray tube operating at 30,000 volts?   2) What is the wavelength of the shortest x-rays that could be produced by a Van de Graaff generator developing 5,000,000 volts?

Solution: 1) The energy of an electron traveling through a potential difference of V Volts is

   eV joules

where e is the charge of the electron in coulombs and V is in volts.

   If all of this energy is converted into producing one x-ray photon, then the wavelength associated with this photon will be shortest.   Hence

$$h\nu = eV$$

or $h \dfrac{c}{\lambda} = eV \; ,$

where h is Planck's constant, c is the speed of light, ν is the highest frequency, and λ is the shortest wavelength.

   Solving for λ

$$\lambda = \frac{hc}{eV} \tag{1}$$

   Substituting the known values for h, c, e, and V into equation 1,

$$\lambda = \frac{6.626 \times 10^{-34} \times 3 \times 10^8}{1.602 \times 10^{-19} \times 30,000}$$

$$\lambda = 4.14 \times 10^{-11} \; m$$

$$\lambda = 0.414 \; A^\circ$$

(2)   For the Van de Graaff generator we use eq 1 with
$$V = 5 \cdot 10^6$$

$$\lambda = \frac{hc}{eV}$$

Substituting for h, c, e, and V,

$$\lambda = \frac{6.626 \times 10^{-34} \times 3 \times 10^{8}}{1.602 \times 10^{-19} \times 5 \times 10^{6}}$$

$$\lambda = 2.48 \times 10^{-13} \text{ m}$$

$$\lambda = 2.48 \times 10^{-3} \text{ A}° .$$

● **PROBLEM** 27-5

Will the normal longitudinal Zeeman effect, produced in a field of 10,000 gauss, be observable as a distinct separation of components with a spectrometer using a grating 7.5 cm long and having 6,000 rulings per centimeter? The perpendicular effect? Assume actual resolving power about 60% of theoretical, and specify the order used.

Solution: The resolving power of a grating can be expressed as

$$\frac{\Delta\lambda}{\lambda} = \frac{1}{mN} \tag{1}$$

where $\Delta\lambda$ is the difference in wavelengths of light resolved, λ is the wavelength of light used, N is the number of lines of the grating and m is the order of the spectrum produced. Now since the Zeeman effect equation (see any atomic spectra text) is given by

$$\Delta f = 1.4 \times 10^{6} \text{ H} \quad \text{per gauss-seconds} \tag{2}$$

where Δf is the shift in frequency of the Zeeman pattern and H is the magnetic field applied to the source, we want to convert equation (1) to frequency by using $f \lambda = c$; where c is the velocity of light or

$$f = c/\lambda \tag{3}$$

Differentiating f with respect to λ and ignoring the minus sign,

$$\Delta f = \frac{\Delta\lambda}{\lambda^2} c \tag{4}$$

Substituting for $\frac{\Delta\lambda}{\lambda}$ from equation (1),

$$\Delta f = \frac{c}{\lambda mN} \tag{5}$$

Now for our problem (including efficiency)

$$N = 0.6 \times 6000 \times 7.5 = 2.7 \times 10^{4}$$

effective lines on the grating, and H = 10000 gauss.

Solving equation (5) for $m\lambda$ and substituting the values

781

for N, H, and c

$$\left(= 3 \times 10^8 \ \frac{m}{sec} \right) \ ,$$

$$m\lambda = \frac{3 \times 10^8}{1.4 \times 10^6 \times 10^4 \times 2.7 \times 10^4} = 7.936 \times 10^{-7} \ \text{meters}$$

We will then be able to see both the longitudinal and the perpendicular Zeeman effect if the zero field wavelength is 793.6 nm in first order;

$$\frac{1}{2} \ (793.6) \ \text{nm}$$

or 396.8 nm in second order; and

$$\frac{1}{3} \ (793.6) \ \text{nm}$$

or 264.5 nm in third order, etc.

● **PROBLEM** 27-6

The first line of the principal series of sodium is the "D" line at 5890Å. This corresponds to a transition from the first excited state (3p) to the ground state (3s). What is the energy in eV of the first excited state?

Solution: The energy of the excited state is given by $\Delta E = h\nu = \frac{hc}{\lambda}$ where h is Planck's constant (6.626 $\times$ 10^{-27} erg. sec), c is the velocity of light (2.998 $\times$ 10^{10} cm/sec), ν is the frequency and λ is the wavelength of the sodium D line. Since 1.6021 $\times$ 10^{-12} ergs are equivalent to 1 ev we have

$$\Delta E = \frac{6.626 \times 10^{-27} \ \text{erg sec} \times 2.998 \times 10^{10} \ \text{cm/sec}}{5.89 \times 10^{-5} \ \text{cm} \times 1.6021 \times 10^{-12} \ \text{erg/ev}}$$

$$= 2.105 \ \text{ev}$$

● **PROBLEM** 27-7

Find the frequency of the radiation emitted by the pure rotational transition J = 1 → J = 0 in HCℓ where J represents the rotational quantum number. The distance between the H atom and the Cℓ atom is 1.3Å.

Solution: The rotational energy E_{rot} is the kinetic energy of rotation of the molecule as a whole. The quantization of the rotational energy is expressed in terms of the rotational quantum numbers. How many of these rotational quantum numbers are required to specify the rotational state depends on the geometry of the molecule. HCℓ is a linear molecule and only one quantum number is needed. The correct quantum mechanical treatment allows the angular momenta to be given

by $\sqrt{J(J + 1)} \dfrac{h}{2\pi}$ where J is the rotational quantum number and h represents Planck's constant. Thus the angular momentum is

$$I\omega = \sqrt{J(J + 1)} \; \frac{h}{2\pi} \tag{1}$$

where I is the moment of inertia of the molecule, and ω is the angular velocity of rotation of the molecule.

The rotational energy of the molecule is given by the expression

$$E_{rot} = \frac{1}{2} I\omega^2$$

squaring equation (1) and substituting for ω^2 in equation (2) gives the result

$$E_{rot} = \frac{h^2}{8\pi^2 I} J(J + 1) \tag{2}$$

Hence the radiation from two rotational levels is given by

$$\Delta\nu = \frac{E_2 - E_1}{h} = \frac{h}{8\pi^2 I} (J_2(J_2 + 1) - J_1(J_1 + 1)) \tag{3}$$

For the transition from J = 1 → J = 0,

$$\Delta\nu = \frac{2h}{8\pi^2 I} = \frac{h}{4\pi^2 I} \tag{4}$$

The moment of inertia for a diatomic linear molecule is given by

$$I = \frac{m_1 m_2}{(m_1 + m_2)} \gamma^2 \tag{5}$$

where m_1 and m_2 are the masses of the two atoms and γ is the distance between the two atoms.

For HCℓ,

$$I = \frac{35 \times 1}{36} \times 1.66 \times 10^{-24} \; \text{gm} \times (1.3 \times 10^{-8} \; \text{cm})^2$$

$$= 2.727 \times 10^{-40} \; \text{gm cm}^2$$

$$= 2.727 \times 10^{-40} \; \text{erg sec}^2$$

Substituting the known value for h and the value just com-

783

puted for I into equation (4),

$$\Delta v = \frac{6.6256 \times 10^{-27}}{4\pi^2 \ 2.727 \times 10^{-40}}$$

$$= 0.615 \times 10^{12} \text{ Hz.}$$

Calculate the frequency of the hydrogen transition n = 101 → n = 100, where n represents the principal quantum number.

Solution: The hydrogen transition between two levels of quantum numbers n_1 and n_2 can be derived using Bohr's pos-tulate that the angular momentum of an electron orbiting around the hydrogen nucleus is an integral multiple of the quantity h/2π, where h is Planck's Constant (= 6.6256 x 10^{-27} erg sec). An electron of mass m travelling with a velocity v in an orbit of radius r then has an angular momentum

$$mvr = \frac{nh}{2\pi} \quad (n = 1,2....) \tag{1}$$

where n is called the principal quantum number. The re-quirement that the electrostatic attraction on the electron by the nucleus is balanced by the centrifugal force gives the relation

$$\frac{e^2}{4\pi\varepsilon_o r^2} = \frac{mv^2}{r} \quad \text{(where } \varepsilon_o = 8.85 \times 10^{-12} \text{ farad/meter)}$$

or

$$r = \frac{e^2}{4\pi\varepsilon_o mv^2} \tag{2}$$

where e is the charge on the electron.

Squaring equation 1 and solving for v^2 yields the re-sult

$$v^2 = \frac{n^2 h^2}{4\pi^2 m^2 r^2} \quad .$$

Substituting the above expression for v^2 into equation (2),

$$r = \frac{e^2}{4\pi\varepsilon_o \dfrac{mn^2 h^2}{4\pi^2 m^2 r^2}}$$

or

$$r = \frac{\varepsilon_o h^2}{\pi m e^2} n^2$$

784

The total energy of the orbit is the sum of the potential and kinetic energies. Therefore,

$$E = \frac{1}{2} mv^2 - \frac{e^2}{4\pi\varepsilon_o r}$$

From equation (2), $v^2 = \frac{e^2}{4\pi\varepsilon_o mr}$

and hence,

$$E = \frac{e^2}{8\pi\varepsilon_o r} (1 - 2) = -\frac{e^2}{8\pi\varepsilon_o r}$$

$$= \frac{-me^4}{8\varepsilon_o^2 h^2 n^2} \qquad (3)$$

(determined by substituting the expression

$$\frac{\varepsilon_o h^2}{\pi me^2} n^2$$

for r in the above equation).

With Planck's relation $h\nu = \Delta E$, where ν denotes the frequency of the emitted (or absorbed) radiation, the transition between two levels with quantum numbers n_1 and n_2 is

$$\nu = \frac{\Delta E}{h} = \frac{me^4}{8\varepsilon_o^2 h^3} \left(\frac{1}{n_2^2} - \frac{1}{n_1^2} \right) \qquad (4)$$

With $n_1 > n_2$ the quantity

$$\frac{me^4}{8\varepsilon_o^2 h^2}$$

is called the Rydberg Constant (denoted by R), and

$$\frac{me^4}{8\varepsilon_o^2 h^3} = \frac{R}{h} = 3.288 \times 10^{15} \text{ Hz.}$$

Hence the transition from n = 101 → n = 100 has a frequency of

$$\nu = 3.288 \times 10^{15} \left(\frac{1}{100^2} - \frac{1}{101^2} \right) \text{ Hz}$$

$$= 6.5 \times 10^9 \text{ Hz.}$$

BLACKBODY RADIATION

● **PROBLEM** 27-9

A carbon filament, which may be considered a blackbody
radiator, is heated successively to 500°C, 1000°C, 1500°C,
and 2500°C. Find the corresponding wavelengths at which
the most energy is emitted at these temperatures.

Solution: Wien's law states that a blackbody at a temperature T emits maximum energy at a wavelength λ, which is
given by the equation

$$\lambda_{max} \, T = 2898\mu \ °K,$$

where λ_{max} is in microns and T is in °K.

   Converting T from °C to °K by using the relation
$(T)_{°K} = (T)_{°C} + 273$, and solving for λ_{max}, the following
set of results is obtained:

T°C	T°K	λ_{max}
500	773	3.75μ
1000	1273	2.28μ
1500	1773	1.63μ
2500	2773	1.05μ

● **PROBLEM** 27-10

At what wavelength is the spectral emittance of a blackbody a maximum, if its temperature is a) 500°K, b) 5000°K?
c) At what temperature does the maximum spectral emittance
lie at a wavelength of 555 mμ, where the eye is most sensitive?

Solution: The wavelength of maximum spectral emittance
is inversely proportional to the temperature in degrees
kelvin, therefore, as the temperature is increased, the
maximum shifts toward shorter wavelengths. This fact is
expressed by Wien's displacement law;

$$\lambda_{max} \, T = const = 2.8971 \times 10^{6} \ m\mu \ °K$$

Hence

$$\lambda_{max} = \frac{2.8971 \times 10^{6}}{T} \ m\mu$$

Therefore, by substituting in the values T = 500°K and
T = 5000 °K into the above equation, the following values

for λ_{max} can be determined:

	T	λ_{max}
(a)	500°K	5794 mμ
(b)	5000°K	579.4 mμ

$$T = \frac{2.8971 \times 10^6 \, °K}{\lambda_{max}} \quad ,$$

so for $\lambda_{max} = 555$ mμ,

(c) $\quad T = \frac{2.8971 \times 10^6}{555} \quad °K = 5220 \; °K$

● **PROBLEM** 27-11

A thermopile is placed near a furnace having a small circular opening. When the furnace is at 2000 °K, and its distance from the thermopile is such that the hole subtends the same solid angle as the sun's disk, the galvanometer deflection is found to be 1/80 of that when the thermopile is placed in full sunlight. Find the temperature of the sun.

Solution: The energy radiated by a blackbody is given by the Stefan-Boltzmann law

$$W = \sigma T^4$$

where W is the energy radiated per unit area, σ is a constant and T is the temperature in degrees Kelvin. In our problem, the area of the thermopile subtended by the two sources is the same and we can then form the ratio

$$\frac{W_1}{W_2} = \frac{T_1^4}{T_2^4} \quad .$$

Since the galvanometer deflection is proportional to the energy received, $W_1/W_2 = 80$ and $T_2 = 2000$ °K or

$$T_1^4 = \frac{W_1}{W_2} \, T_2^4 = 80 \times (2000)^4$$

$$T_1 = (80)^{1/4} \; 2000 = 5981 \; °K \quad .$$

787

The emissivity of tungsten is approximately 0.35. A tungsten sphere 1 cm in radius is suspended within a large evacuated enclosure whose walls are at a temperature of 300 °K. What power input is required to maintain the sphere at a temperature of 3000 °K, if heat conduction along the supports is neglected?

Solution: The Stefan-Boltzmann law states that for a body with emissivity e, the total energy W emitted by the surface of a body in watts per square meter is

$$W = e\sigma T^4$$

where T is the temperature in degrees Kelvin and σ is 5.672×10^{-8} watts meter^{-2} °K^{-4}. So the net energy lost by the hot surface (since the cold surface also emits energy) will be

$$W = e\sigma (T_{hot}^4 - T_{cold}^4) = 0.35 \times 5.672 \times 10^{-8}$$

$$\times (3000^4 - 300^4) \; 4\pi (10^{-2})^2 = 2020 \text{ watts}$$

or 2020 watts input is needed to maintain the hot temperature.

Two large closely spaced surfaces, both of which are ideal radiators, are maintained at temperatures of 200°K and 300°K respectively. The space between them is evacuated. a) What is the net rate of heat lost from the warmer surface, in watts per square meter?

Now a thin sheet of aluminum foil of emissivity 0.1 on both surfaces is placed between the two surfaces. Assume steady state has been established and that both faces of the foil are at the same temperature. b) Compute the temperature of the aluminum foil, c) the new net rate of loss of heat from the warmer surface.

Solution: For a body at a temperature T in degrees Kelvin, the amount of energy radiated per unit surface area, W, is given by the Stefan-Boltzmann law.

$$W = e\sigma T^4$$

where e is the emissivity and σ is a constant factor $(5.672 \times 10^{-8} \text{ watts/m}^2 \text{ °K}^4)$.

Since both surfaces are ideal radiators, e = 1, so the surface at temperature T_1 will lose energy at a rate $W_1 =$

$\sigma T_1{}^4$ but will gain energy from the other surface at a rate $W_2 = \sigma T_2{}^4$ so the net heat lost will be

$$W_1 - W_2 = \sigma(T_1{}^4 - T_2{}^4) = 5.672 \times 10^{-8} (300^4 - 200^4) =$$

$$368 \text{ watts/m}^2$$

Now by inserting an aluminum foil between the two surfaces with an emissivity of 0.1, which will have a reflectivity of 0.9, the aluminum surface at equilibrium will absorb from the surface T_1 as much energy as it rejects to surface T_2. Therefore,

$$e\sigma(T_1{}^4 - T_3{}^4) = e\sigma(T_3{}^4 - T_2{}^4)$$

or

$$2T_3{}^4 = T_2{}^4 + T_1{}^4$$

$$T_3{}^4 = \frac{1}{2}(300^4 + 200^4)$$

$$= \frac{1}{2}(81 + 16) \times 10^8$$

$$= 48.5 \times 10^8$$

$$T_3 = 264\,°K$$

and the amount of heat flow from hot to cold surface will be

$$e\sigma(T_1{}^4 - T_3{}^4) = 0.1 \times 5.672 \times 10^{-8}(300^4 - 264^4)$$

$$= 18.4 \text{ watts/m}^2$$

Just a thin aluminum film reduces energy flow by a factor of 18.4/368.

● **PROBLEM 27-14**

By what factor would the heat transfer by radiation between the walls of a thermos bottle be increased if the reflectance of each wall were reduced from 0.9 to 0.3?

Solution: From the Stefan-Boltzmann equation relating the radiated energy, W, emitted by a body at a temperature T in degrees Kelvin and emissivity e we have

$$W = e\sigma T^4$$

where σ is a constant. By consulting the textbook Sears,

Optics, Addision Wesley, 3rd edition, 1949, a derivation is given which relates the net heat transfer $(H_2 - H_1)$ between two closely spaced surfaces, one at temperature T_1 and emissivity e_1 and the other at temperature T_2 and emissivity e_2 as

$$H_2 - H_1 = \frac{\sigma\left(T_2^4 - T_1^4\right)}{\frac{1}{e_2} + \frac{1}{e_1} - 1} \quad ,$$

so we want to form the ratio

$$\frac{(H_2 - H_1)'}{(H_2 - H_1)} = \frac{\left(\frac{1}{e_2} + \frac{1}{e_1} - 1\right)}{\left(\frac{1}{e_2} + \frac{1}{e_1} - 1\right)'} = \frac{\frac{1}{e_2} + \frac{1}{e_1} - 1}{\frac{1}{e_2'} + \frac{1}{e_1'} - 1}$$

Now in our problem we are given the reflectance, r, but the emissivity, e, is related to the reflectance by

$$e = 1 - r$$

and since the two surfaces are similar,

$$e_2 = e_1 = 1 - r = 1 - 0.9 = 0.1$$

$$e_2' = e_1' = 1 - r = 1 - 0.3 = 0.7$$

and our ratio is then

$$\frac{(H_2 - H_1)'}{(H_2 - H_1)} = \frac{\left(\frac{1}{.1} + \frac{1}{.1} - 1\right)}{\left(\frac{1}{.7} + \frac{1}{.7} - 1\right)} = \frac{20 - 1}{2.86 - 1} = \frac{19}{1.86} = 10.2 \quad .$$

So, reducing the reflectance from 0.9 to 0.3 would increase the heat transfer by a factor of 10.2.

● **PROBLEM 27-15**

A 100-W tungsten lamp operates at a temperature of 1800°K. How many photons does it emit per second in the interval 5000Å to 5001Å, in the blackbody approximation?

Solution: Planck's law for the distribution of black body radiation is

$$E_\lambda d\lambda = \frac{c_1}{\lambda^5} (e^{c_2/\lambda T} - 1)^{-1} d\lambda \tag{1}$$

where $E_\lambda d\lambda$ is the energy per unit area emitted by radiation in the wavelength interval $d\lambda$; c_1 is a constant (3.7413×10^{-16} watt m^2); λ is the wavelength of the radiation; c_2

is a constant (1.4388×10^{-2} m deg K); T is the temperature of the black body in degrees Kelvin. This will yield the energy per unit wavelength interval. We also have the Stefan-Boltzmann law

$$E_T = \sigma T^4 \qquad (2)$$

where E_T is the total energy radiated per unit area of the source by a blackbody at temperature T (in degrees Kelvin) and σ is the constant 5.669×10^{-8} watts/(m^2 °K^4). By forming the ratio of equations (1) and (2), we can determine the fraction of the energy radiated in the wavelength interval $d\lambda$ to be

$$\frac{E_\lambda d\lambda}{E_T} \qquad (3)$$

or, substituting in equation (1) for c_1, c_2, λ, and $d\lambda$,

$$E_\lambda d\lambda = \frac{3.7413 \times 10^{-16}}{(500 \times 10^{-9})^5} \times \left(e^{\frac{1.4388 \times 10^{-2}}{500 \times 10^{-9} \times 1800}} - 1 \right)^{-1}$$

$$\cdot \; 0.1 \times 10^{-9} \; watts/m^2$$

$$= 1.19 \times 10^6 \; (e^{15.98} - 1)^{-1} \; watts/m^2$$

$$= 0.1366 \; watts/m^2$$

and substituting in equation (2),

$$E_T = 5.669 \times 10^{-8} \; (1800)^4 = 5.95 \times 10^5 \; watts/m^2$$

so the fractional part of the total energy radiated that lies in the interval 500 nm to 500.1 nm is

$$\frac{E_\lambda d\lambda}{E_T} = \frac{.1366}{5.95 \times 10^5} = 2.29 \times 10^{-7} \qquad (4)$$

Since our lamp is rated at 100 watts, we have $100 \times 2.29 \times 10^{-7} = 2.29 \times 10^{-5}$ watts of energy in the range 500 to 500.1 nm.

Now the energy of a photon is given by

$$E_{photon} = h\nu = \frac{hc}{\lambda} \qquad (5)$$

where h is Planck's constant; c is the velocity of light; ν the frequency and λ the wavelength of the photon.

Substituting the known values for h and c, and the given value for λ into equation (5),

791

$$E_{500\ nm} = \frac{6.63 \times 10^{-34} \times 3 \times 10^8}{500 \times 10^{-9}} = 3.978 \times 10^{-19} \text{ joules/photon}$$

or the number of photons emitted per second is

$$\frac{2.29 \times 10^{-5}}{3.978 \times 10^{-19}} = 5.8 \times 10^{13} \text{ photons/sec.}$$

THERMAL RADIATION

● **PROBLEM** 27-16

Calculate the total number of photons of all frequencies in a cavity of volume V at a temperature T.

Solution: According to Planck's hypothesis, a cavity of volume V at equilibrium with thermal radiation at a tempera-ture T has a density of photon modes D(w) given by

$$D(w) = \frac{V}{\pi^2 c^3} w^2 ,$$

where $w = 2\pi f$, (f represents the frequency of the radiation), and c = the speed of light.

The thermal average number of photons in each mode of frequency is

$$<n(w)> = \frac{1}{e^{\frac{hw}{2\pi KT}} - 1}$$

(h = Planck's constant and K = Boltzmann's constant.) Hence the total no. of photons at any frequency w is

$$N(w) = D(w) \quad <n(w)>$$

The total number of photons of all frequencies is

$$N = \int_o^\infty dw\ D(w) \quad <n(w)>$$

$$= \frac{V}{\pi^2 c^3} \int_0^\infty \frac{w^2\ dw}{e^{\frac{hw}{2\pi KT}} - 1}$$

Let $\quad x = \frac{hw}{2\pi KT} ,$

then $\quad w = \frac{2\pi x KT}{h}$

and $\quad dw = \frac{2\pi KT}{h}\ dx$

Substituting x and dx for w and dw, respectively, in the preceding equation, we get,

$$N = \frac{V}{\pi^2 c^3} \left(\frac{2\pi KT}{h}\right)^3 \int_0^\infty \frac{x^2 dx}{e^x - 1}$$

Multiplying both the numerator and denominator of the integrand by e^{-x} gives the result

$$N = \frac{V}{\pi^2 c^3} \left(\frac{2\pi KT}{h}\right)^3 \int_0^\infty \frac{x^2 e^{-x} dx}{1 - e^{-x}}$$

$$\sum_{p=0}^\infty x^p = \frac{1}{1 - x}$$

Therefore

$$\sum_{p=1}^\infty x^p = \sum_{p=0}^\infty x^p - 1 =$$

$$\frac{1}{1 - x} - 1 = \frac{1 - (1 - x)}{1 - x} = \frac{x}{1 - x} \quad .$$

Hence,

$$\frac{e^{-x}}{1 - e^{-x}} = \sum_{p=1}^\infty e^{-px} \quad ,$$

and so,

$$N = \frac{V}{\pi^2 c^3} \left(\frac{2\pi KT}{h}\right)^3 \int_0^\infty dx \, x^2 \sum_{p=1}^\infty e^{-px}$$

Let $px = y$

Then

$$N = \frac{V}{\pi^2 c^3} \left(\frac{2\pi KT}{h}\right)^3 \sum_{p=1}^\infty \frac{1}{p^3} \int_0^\infty dy \, y^2 e^{-y}$$

Now

$$\int_0^\infty dy \, e^{-y} y^2 = - \int_0^\infty de^{-y} y^2 \quad .$$

Set $u = y^2$ and $dV = de^{-y}$. Then

$du = 2ydy$ and $V = e^{-y}$.

Integrating by parts, $\int u dV = uV - \int V du$,

or

$$- \int_0^\infty de^{-y} y^2 = - y^2 e^{-y} \Big|_0^\infty + 2 \int_0^\infty y e^{-y} \, dy$$

$$= 2 \int_0^\infty y \, e^{-y} \, dy$$

$$= - 2 \int_0^\infty de^{-y} \, y$$

Let $de^{-y} = dV$ and $y = u$. Then $du = dy$ and $V = e^{-y}$; hence,

$$\int_0^\infty dy \, e^{-y} \, y^2 = - 2y \, e^{-y} \Big|_0^\infty + 2 \int_0^\infty e^{-y} \, dy .$$

$$= - 2 \, e^{-y} \Big|_0^\infty = -2 (0 - 1) = 2 .$$

The sum $\sum_{p=1}^\infty \frac{1}{p^3}$ can be easily evaluated numerically and is equal to 1.2 .

Therefore,

$$N = \frac{2.4 \, K^3}{\pi^2 c^3 \left(\frac{h}{2\pi}\right)^3} \, T^3 \, V$$

$$= 2 \times 10^7 \quad T^3 \, V \, / (°K \, m)^3$$

APPENDIX

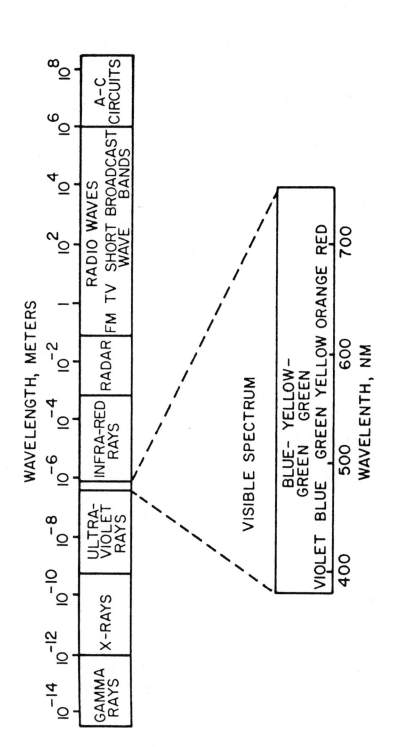

The Radiant Energy Spectrum

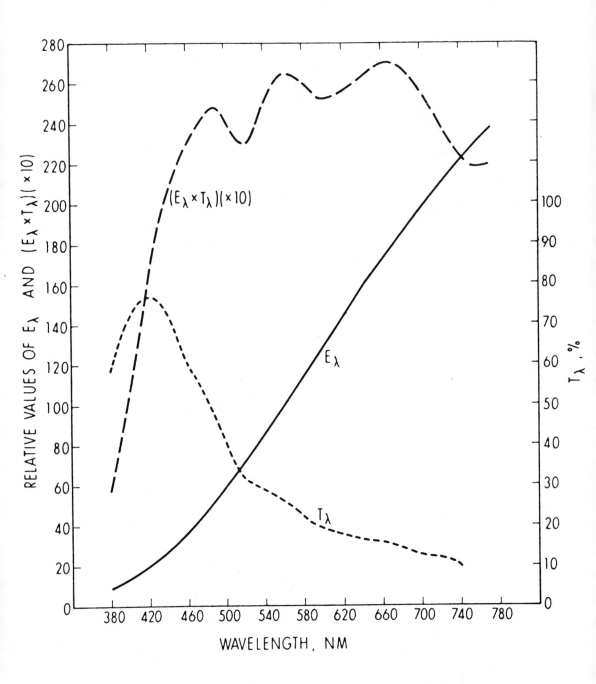

Example — Spectral Characteristics of Light Source Energy,
Filter Transmittance, and Transmitted Energy

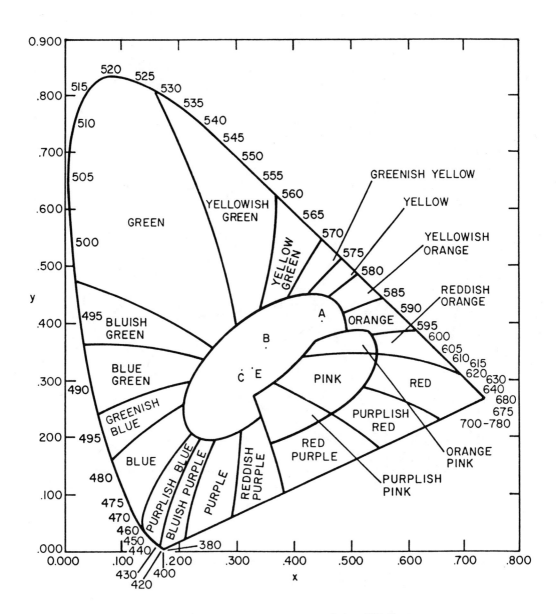

The (x, y) Chromaticity Diagram of the CIE System,
Showing Sources A, B, and C and Color Names of Areas

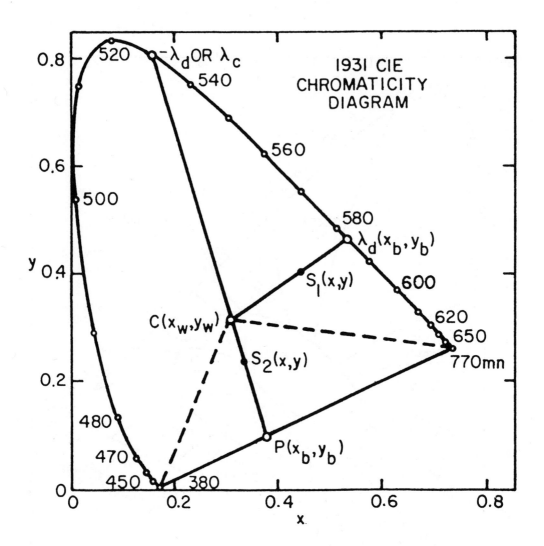

Graphical Determination of
Dominant Wavelength and Purity

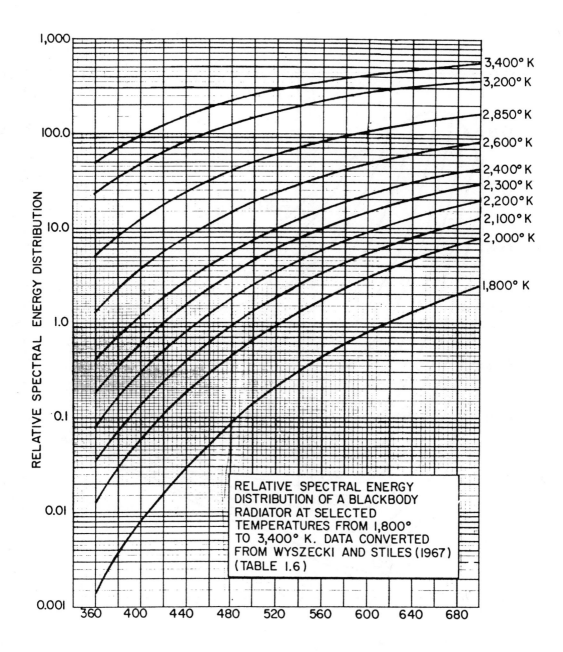

Spectral Energy Distributions of Planckian Radiators at Various
Practical Temperatures — Not Normalized

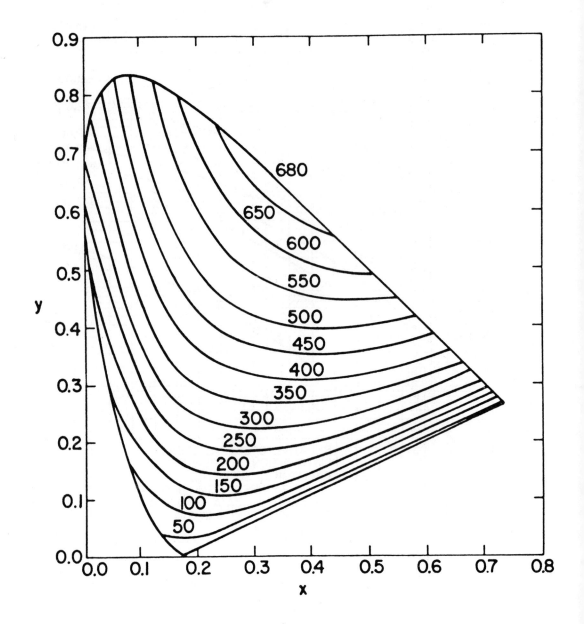

Curves of Maximum Luminous Efficacy (Lumens per Watt)
Plotted on CIE Chromaticity Diagram

CONVERSION TABLE – UNITS OF LUMINANCE

Unit	Definition	Nit	Stilb	Bougie Hectomètre Carré	Apostilb	Milli-apostilb	Micro-apostilb	Lambert	Milli-lambert	Micro-lambert	Foot-lambert	Candle Per Sq. ft.	Candle Per Sq. Inch
1 Nit (nt)	$1\ \text{Candela}/\text{m}^2$	1	10^{-4}	10^4	3.14	3.14×10^3	3.14×10^6	3.14×10^{-4}	3.14×10^{-1}	3.14×10^2	2.919×10^{-1}	9.29×10^{-2}	6.452×10^{-4}
1 Stilb (sb)	$1\ \text{Candela}/\text{cm}^2$	10^4	1	10^8	3.14×10^4	3.14×10^7	3.14×10^{10}	3.14	3.14×10^3	3.14×10^6	2.919×10^3	9.29×10^2	6.452
1 Bougie Hectomètre Carré	$1\ \text{Candela}/(100\text{m})^2$	10^{-4}	10^{-8}	1	3.14×10^{-4}	3.14×10^{-1}	3.14×10^2	3.14×10^{-8}	3.14×10^{-5}	3.14×10^{-2}	2.919×10^{-5}	9.29×10^{-6}	6.452×10^{-8}
1 Apostilb (asb)	$1\ \text{Candela}/(\pi\times\text{m}^2)$	3.183×10^{-1}	3.183×10^{-5}	3.183×10^3	1	10^3	10^6	10^{-4}	10^{-1}	10^2	9.29×10^{-2}	2.957×10^{-2}	2.054×10^{-4}
1 Milli-apostilb (masb)	$1\ \text{Candela}/(\pi\times1000\times\text{m}^2)$	3.183×10^{-4}	3.183×10^{-8}	3.183	10^{-3}	1	10^3	10^{-7}	10^{-4}	10^{-1}	9.29×10^{-5}	2.957×10^{-5}	2.054×10^{-7}
1 Micro-apostilb (μasb)	$1\ \text{Candela}/(\pi\times10^6\times\text{m}^2)$	3.183×10^{-7}	3.183×10^{-11}	3.183×10^{-3}	10^{-6}	10^{-3}	1	10^{-10}	10^{-7}	10^{-4}	9.29×10^{-8}	2.957×10^{-8}	2.054×10^{-10}
1 Lambert (L)	$1\ \text{Candela}/(\pi\times\text{cm}^2)$	3.183×10^3	3.183×10^{-1}	3.183×10^7	10^4	10^7	10^{10}	1	10^3	10^6	9.29×10^2	2.957×10^2	2.054
1 Milli-lambert (mL)	$1\ \text{Candela}/(\pi\times10^{-3}\times\text{cm}^2)$	3.183	3.183×10^{-4}	3.183×10^4	10	10^4	10^7	10^{-3}	1	10^3	9.29×10^{-1}	2.957×10^{-1}	2.054×10^{-3}
1 Micro-lambert (μL)	$1\ \text{Candela}/(\pi\times10^{-6}\times\text{cm}^2)$	3.183×10^{-3}	3.183×10^{-7}	3.183×10	10^{-2}	10	10^4	10^{-6}	10^{-3}	1	9.29×10^{-4}	2.957×10^{-4}	2.054×10^{-6}
1 Foot-lambert (ftL)	$1\ \text{Candela}/(\pi\times\text{ft}^2)$	3.426	3.426×10^{-4}	3.426×10^4	10.764	1.0764×10^4	1.0764×10^7	1.0764×10^{-3}	1.0764	1.0764×10^3	1	0.3183	2.21×10^{-3}
1 Candle Per Sq. ft.	$1\ \text{Candela}/\text{ft}^2$	1.0764×10	1.0764×10^{-3}	1.0764×10^5	3.382×10	3.382×10^4	3.382×10^7	3.382×10^{-3}	3.382	3.382×10^3	3.14	1	6.944×10^{-3}
1 Candle Per Sq. inch	$1\ \text{Candela}/\text{inch}^2$	1.55×10^3	1.55×10^{-1}	1.55×10^{-5}	4.869×10^3	4.869×10^6	4.869×10^9	4.869×10^{-1}	4.869×10^2	4.869×10^5	4.524×10^2	1.44×10^2	1

ILLUMINATION UNITS

	LUMEN/mm²	LUMEN/cm² = PHOT	LUMEN/in²	LUMEN/ft² = FOOT-CANDLE	MILLIPHOT	LUMEN/m² = METER-CANDLE = LUX	LUMEN/hm² = HECTOMETER-CANDLE	LUMEN/km² = KILOMETER-CANDLE	LUMEN/mi² = MILE-CANDLE	LUMEN/naut.mi² = SEA-MILE-CANDLE
LUMEN/mm²	1	10^{-2}	1.550×10^{-3}	1.076×10^{-5}	10^{-5}	10^{-6}	10^{-10}	10^{-12}	3.861×10^{-13}	2.912×10^{-13}
LUMEN/cm² = PHOT	10^2	1	.1550	1.076×10^{-3}	10^{-3}	10^{-4}	10^{-8}	10^{-10}	3.861×10^{-11}	2.912×10^{-11}
LUMEN/in²	6.452×10^2	6.452	1	6.944×10^{-3}	6.452×10^{-3}	6.452×10^{-4}	6.452×10^{-8}	6.452×10^{-10}	2.491×10^{-10}	1.878×10^{-10}
LUMEN/ft² = FOOT-CANDLE	9.290×10^4	9.290×10^2	144	1	.9290	9.290×10^{-2}	9.290×10^{-6}	9.290×10^{-8}	3.587×10^{-8}	2.705×10^{-8}
MILLIPHOT	10^5	10^3	1.550×10^2	1.076	1	10^{-1}	10^{-5}	10^{-7}	3.861×10^{-8}	2.912×10^{-8}
LUMEN/m² = METER-CANDLE = LUX	10^6	10^4	1.550×10^3	10.76	10	1	10^{-4}	10^{-6}	3.861×10^{-7}	2.912×10^{-7}
LUMEN/hm² HECTOMETER-CANDLE	10^{10}	10^8	1.550×10^7	1.076×10^5	10^5	10^4	1	10^{-2}	3.861×10^{-3}	2.912×10^{-3}
LUMEN/km² = KILOMETER-CANDLE	10^{12}	10^{10}	1.550×10^9	1.076×10^7	10^7	10^6	10^2	1	.3861	.2912
LUMEN/mi² = MILE-CANDLE	2.590×10^{12}	2.590×10^{10}	4.014×10^9	2.788×10^7	2.590×10^7	2.590×10^6	2.590×10^2	2.590	1	.7541
LUMEN/naut. mi² = SEA-MILE-CANDLE	3.435×10^{12}	3.435×10^{10}	5.324×10^9	3.697×10^7	3.435×10^7	3.435×10^6	3.435×10^2	3.435	1.326	1

ONE UNIT OF "A" IS SAME ILLUMINATION
AS "F" UNITS OF "B"

OPTICAL PROPERTIES OF SELECTED CLEAR MATERIALS

Type of Material	n_D	V	r_c Degrees	θ_B Degrees	R_o %
Glass					
Fluor Crown	1.466	66.3	43.0	55.7	3.57
Borosilicate Crown	1.498	67.0	41.9	56.3	3.97
Crown	1.524	59.5	41.0	56.7	4.31
Light Flint	1.575	41.4	39.4	57.6	4.99
Barium Flint	1.584	46.0	39.2	57.7	5.11
Lanthanum Flint	1.720	46.0	35.5	59.8	7.01
Silica (SiO$_2$)					
Fused Silica	1.458	67.6	43.3	55.3	3.47
Crystalline Quartz					
Extraordinary Ray	1.553	68.7	40.1		
Ordinary Ray	1.544	69.9	40.3		
Plastics					
Polymethyl Methacrylate (Acrylics)[1]	1.498	53.6	41.9	56.3	3.98
Polystyrene	1.591	30.8	39.0	57.8	5.20
Polycarbonate[2]	1.586	29.9	39.1	57.8	5.13
Miscellaneous					
Air	1.0003				
Water	1.333	55.5	48.6	53.1	2.04

[1] Trade names: "Plexiglas," "Lucite," "Acrylite."
[2] Trade name : "Lexan."

Notes:

1   n_D = n at 589.3 nm, index of refraction.
2   V   = V value = relative reciprocal dispersion

$$= \frac{n_D - 1}{n_F - n_c},$$

F = 486.1 nm
D = 589.3 nm
C = 656.3 nm

3   V_c = critical angle of refraction at an interface with air.

$$r_c = \sin^{-1} \frac{1}{n}$$

4   R_o = reflectance at an interface with air, normal incidence.

$$R_o = \left(\frac{n - 1}{n + 1}\right)^2$$

5   θ_B = Brewster's Angle = angle of incidence for minimum reflectance of light polarized in plane of incidence

$$\theta_B = \tan^{-1} n$$

	Color Name Designations			Numeral and/or Letter Color Designations		
Level of Fineness of Color Designation	Level 1 (least precise)	Level 2	Level 3	Level 4	Level 5	Level 6 (most precise)
Number of Divisions of Color Solid	13	29	267*	943-7056*	≃100,000	≃5,000,000
Type of Color Designation	Generic hue names and neutrals (See circled designations in diagram below)	All hue names and neutrals (See diagram below)	ISCC-NBS All hue names and neutrals with modifiers (NBS-C553)	Color-order Systems (Collections of color standards sampling the color solid systematically)	Visually inter-polated Munsell notation (From Munsell Book of Color)	CIE (x,y,Y) or Instrumentally Interpolated Munsell Nota-tion
Example of Color Designation	brown	yellowish brown	light yellow-ish brown (centroid #76)	Munsell 1548* 10YR 6/4**	9½ YR 6.4/4¼ **	x = 0.395 y = 0.382 Y = 35.6% or 9.6YR 6.4$_5$/4.3**
Alternate Color-Order Systems Usable at Given Levels			SCCA 216* (9th Std.) 70128 HCC 800* H407	M&P 7056* (1st Ed.) 12H6 Plochere 1248* 180 0 5-d Ridgway 1115* XXIX 13 "b CHM 943* (3rd Ed.) 3 gc		

General Applicability	⟶⟶⟶ Increased Fineness of Color Designation ⟶⟶⟶ ⟵⟵⟵ Statistical Expression of Color Trends (roll-up method) ⟵⟵⟵

* Figures indicate the number of color samples in each collection.
** The smallest unit used in the Hue, Value and Chroma parts of the Munsell notation in Levels 4 (1 Hue step, 1 Value step and 2 Chroma steps), 5 (½ Hue step, 0.1 Value step and ¼ Chroma step) and 6 (0.1 Hue step, 0.05 Value step and 0.1 Chroma step) indicates the accuracy to which the parts of the Munsell notation are specified in that Level.

Schematic Diagram Illustrating the Six Levels of The Universal Color Language.

INDEX

Numbers on this page refer to **PROBLEM NUMBERS,** not page numbers